www.wadsworth.com

wadsworth.com is the World Wide Web site for Wadsworth and is your direct source to dozens of online resources.

At wadsworth.com you can find out about supplements, demonstration software, and student resources. You can also send e-mail to many of our authors and preview new publications and exciting new technologies.

wadsworth.com
Changing the way the world learns®

FORENSIC PSYCHOLOGY

Second Edition

Lawrence S. Wrightsman
University of Kansas

Solomon M. Fulero
Sinclair College

THOMSON ™

WADSWORTH

Australia • Canada • Mexico • Singapore • Spain
United Kingdom • United States

THOMSON
WADSWORTH

Senior Acquisitions Editor, Psychology: Michele Sordi

Assistant Editor: Jennifer Keever

Technology Project Manager: Erik Fortier

Marketing Manager: Chris Caldeira

Marketing Assistant: Laurel Anderson

Advertising Project Manager: Tami Strang

Project Manager, Editorial Production: Jennie Redwitz

Print/Media Buyer: Judy Inouye

Permissions Editor: Sarah Harkrader

Production Service: Sheila McGill, Lachina Publishing Services

Copy Editor: Carolyn Crabtree

Cover Designer: Larry Didona

Cover Images: Books/gavel: SuperStock; hands: Comstock Images/Getty Images; puzzle piece left: © Corbis; puzzle piece right: © Helen King/Corbis

Compositor: Lachina Publishing Services

Text and Cover Printer: Quebecor World/Kingsport

For more information about our products, contact us at:

Thomson Learning Academic Resource Center
1-800-423-0563

For permission to use material from this text or product, submit a request online at

http://www.thomsonrights.com.

Any additional questions about permissions can be submitted by email to

thomsonrights@thomson.com.

Library of Congress Control Number: 2004107989

Student Edition: ISBN 0-534-63225-4

Thomson Wadsworth
10 Davis Drive
Belmont, CA 94002-3098
USA

Asia
Thomson Learning
5 Shenton Way #01-01
UIC Building
Singapore 068808

Australia/New Zealand
Thomson Learning
102 Dodds Street
Southbank, Victoria 3006
Australia

Canada
Nelson
1120 Birchmount Road
Toronto, Ontario M1K 5G4
Canada

Europe/Middle East/Africa
Thomson Learning
High Holborn House
50/51 Bedford Row
London WC1R 4LR
United Kingdom

Latin America
Thomson Learning
Seneca, 53
Colonia Polanco
11560 Mexico D.F.
Mexico

Spain/Portugal
Paraninfo
Calle Magallanes, 25
28015 Madrid, Spain

Brief Contents

Contents

CHAPTER 15   Death Penalty Trials and Appeals   325

Preface

The field of forensic psychology has gotten the attention of the public as we enter the 21st century. Prominent cases involving such topics as the insanity defense (see chapter 5), the use of jury consultants with psychological training (see chapter 12), the use of psychology in the profiling of criminal suspects (see chapter 4), eyewitness memory (see chapter 10), interrogations and confessions (see chapter 11), child custody (see chapter 9), and child sexual abuse (see chapter 8) have been featured in the press, television, and movies. Within the field of psychology itself, forensic psychology has become an important focus of clinical practice as well as scientific research and has become one of the most popular topics for both undergraduate and graduate students.

But what is forensic psychology? One definition has been proposed by Bartol and Bartol:

> It is both (a) the research endeavor that examines aspects of human behavior directly related to the legal process (e.g., eyewitness memory and testimony, jury decision-making, or criminal behavior), and (b) the professional practice of psychology within or in consultation with a legal system that encompasses both criminal and civil law and the numerous areas where they interact. Therefore, forensic psychology refers broadly to the *production* and *application* of psychological knowledge to the civil and criminal justice systems. (1999, p. 3, italics in original)

In this book, we have used a similarly broad conception of the field of forensic psychology: The application of psychological research, theory, and practice to the answering of legal questions. Consistent with our broad approach to forensic psychology, we believe that:

1. *Forensic psychology, as a field, encompasses and includes psychologists of all sorts of training and orientation.* For some, forensic activities derive from clinical training and roles; for others, an experimental, social, or developmental psychology background leads to involvement in forensic work when they testify as expert

witnesses in court or help to prepare amicus briefs for appellate review. Thus, the coverage in a book entitled *Forensic Psychology* should be broad and inclusive, rather than restricted to clinical issues involving assessment or treatment of criminal defendants or offenders. Indeed, a perusal of the table of contents will demonstrate that we intend to cover everything from jury selection to child custody, from competency assessment to the psychology of interrogations and confessions.

2. *Forensic psychology is a profession as well as a field of study.* This book focuses on the variety of roles that forensic psychologists can and do play in the legal system, and should fulfill the expectations of readers who are curious about just what forensic psychologists do. We try to show how forensic psychologists can be of use to the legal system by applying the knowledge, techniques, and instruments available to psychologists. Ethical considerations in these roles are also discussed.

3. *The forensic psychologist is a participant in the legal system and, as such, must be knowledgeable about the legal system's rules.* When psychologists move from the classroom, the lab, or the clinical office to enter the legal system as forensic psychologists, they enter a domain with different rules and expectations. Indeed, the expectations of judges, police officers, attorneys, jurors, and others may conflict with what psychologists can ethically or realistically provide. We attempt in this book to focus on the responsibilities and temptations that can and often do arise when psychologists enter the legal realm.

4. *Sources of information about forensic psychology topics are rich, varied, and extensive.* We attempt in this book to include not only empirical data but also descriptions of real cases that can provide graphic illustrations of the phenomena that we discuss. In that sense, we have tried to capture the vitality of this field,

which is constantly confronting new inquiries and issues. We include in each chapter some suggested readings that will help the interested reader to find out more about the material covered. The References section at the end of the book includes hundreds, even thousands, of references to psychological textbooks and scientific journals, court cases, law texts and law reviews, and popular periodicals. We have also included some relevant electronic references, including websites and discussion groups.

5. *A textbook about forensic psychology should be user friendly.* In addition to the extensive list of references and the suggested readings, each chapter of the book contains an introductory outline, a closing summary, and a list of key terms. Each of these terms is printed in bold-face type when introduced in the text. Boxes in each chapter provide further exploration of selected topics, case examples, and summaries of research findings.

FEATURES OF THE SECOND EDITION

There are several important changes in the second edition of this text apart from the addition of a second author. First, the total number of chapters has been reduced from 18 to 16 to reflect more closely the realities of the college schedule. Some chapters have been combined, and coverage of some topics has been reduced in scope (as coverage of others has increased) in order to accomplish this. Second, a new Chapter 6 on Risk Assessment has been added to reflect the legal system's increased interest in the use of psychological experts to provide opinions about such things as the risk of future criminality or the question of sexual predator status. Current references have been added that reflect changes in the field of forensic psychology since the first edition was published in 2001.

ACKNOWLEDGMENTS

No book is produced without the help of many people other than the authors. We are greatly indebted to Michele Sordi, our editor at Wadsworth Publishing Company, and her able assistant, Chelsea Junget. Michele arranged for manuscript reviews from the following experts in the field of forensic psychology: George Blau, University of Wyoming; Deborah Davis, University of Nevada, Reno; Margaret Bull Kovera, Florida International University; William McDaniel, Georgia College and State University; Lavita Nadkarni, University of Denver; and Lori Van Wallendael, University of North Carolina, Charlotte. The suggestions of our reviewers made for a better product, and any failings that remain are our responsibility. A capable team at Wadsworth also worked on the production of the book, from the cover to the photos, and we are grateful to them for their expert assistance. Finally, we want to dedicate this book to Bea Gray (LW), and to Joshua, Asher, and David Fulero (SF).

About the Authors

LAWRENCE S. WRIGHTSMAN (Ph.D., University of Minnesota, 1959) is a professor of psychology at the University of Kansas, Lawrence. Wrightsman is an author or editor of 10 other books relevant to the legal system, including *Psychology and the Legal System* (5th edition, coauthored with Edie Greene, Michael T. Nietzel, and William H. Fortune), *The American Jury on Trial*

(coauthored with Saul M. Kassin), and *Judicial Decision Making: Is Psychology Relevant?* He was invited to contribute the entry on the law and psychology for the recently published *Encyclopedia of Psychology* sponsored by the American Psychological Association and published by Oxford University Press. His research topics include jury selection procedures, reactions to police interrogations, and the impact of judicial instructions. He has also served as a trial consultant and testified as an expert witness. Wrightsman is a former president of both the Society for the Psychological Study of Social Issues and the Society of Personality and Social Psychology. In 1998, he was the recipient of a Distinguished Career Award from the American Psychology-Law Society.

SOLOMON FULERO is both a practicing attorney and a psychologist. Dr. Fulero received his Ph.D. in social psychology and his law degree from the University of Oregon in August 1979 and December 1979, respectively, and a respecialization certificate in clinical psychology from Wright State University in June 1988. He is professor and former chair of psychology at Sinclair College in Dayton, Ohio, and clinical professor of psychology and psychiatry at Wright State University in Dayton. Dr. Fulero maintains private practices in both psychology and law, and is a frequent expert witness on matters pertaining to legal psychology, in both social/experimental (eyewitness testimony, interrogations and confessions, pretrial publicity, etc.) and clinical (competency, sanity, sexual predator status, competency to waive *Miranda* rights, etc.)

areas. He is the author of the *Ohio Law and Psychology Handbook,* published in 1988, as well as numerous scholarly articles in both psychology journals and law reviews. He appeared on the "Eyewitness" episode of *48 Hours* on CBS and was a member of the National Institute of Justice Technical Working Group on Eyewitness Evidence. Dr. Fulero is a Fellow of the American Psychological Association. He has been on the Executive Committee of the American Psychology-Law Society (APLS), was the APLS representative to the governing Council of Representatives of the American Psychological Association in 1999–2002, and was president of APLS in 2003–2004.

1

Forensic Psychology: Promises and Problems

WHAT *IS* FORENSIC PSYCHOLOGY?

The term *forensic psychology* has taken a quantum leap in national awareness over the past few decades. However, in the minds of most members of the public, the term evokes a particular image: that of a clinical psychologist evaluating and testifying about a criminal defendant's sanity at the time of the offense. But what *is* forensic psychology? As a beginning definition, this book proposes that **forensic psychology** is broadly defined as, "*any application of psychological research, methods, theory, and practice to a task faced by the legal system*" (see also Bartol & Bartol, 1999, for a similarly broad definition). Thus, appropriate subjects for forensic psychology expertise can include such widely varying activities as clinical psychological evaluations in child custody or criminal cases, and social psychological consultation on jury selection or pretrial publicity effects (see Box 2-3 in chapter 2). Forensic psychologists can be found doing research, working with law enforcement officials, serving as expert witnesses, advising legislators on public policy, and in general doing things that people might not expect. Consider the following real-life examples:

- Gary Wells is a professor of psychology at Iowa State University. His training is in social psychology, and his specialty is the psychology of eyewitness identification (see chapter 10 of this text). Dr. Wells teaches classes and mentors graduate students. He has also published numerous articles in scholarly journals on the question of eyewitness identification and the factors that affect eyewitness accuracy. Apart from his basic teaching and research, Dr. Wells is frequently asked to be an expert witness in criminal cases. In addition, he is active in educating lawyers and judges about eyewitness issues and in attempting to change public policy on eyewitness identification (for example, by testifying in front of congressional committees with regard to legislative changes, or by

working with law enforcement officials to change eyewitness evidence collection techniques; see Wells et al., 2000).

- Ericka B. Gray, a psychologist and a mediator, has been employed by Endispute, Inc., of Boston, Massachusetts; as a **mediator,** her job is to attempt to resolve legal disputes before they go to trial. "Legal disputes" may include anything from personal injury cases to town zoning matters to claims of age discrimination. Frequently, Dr. Gray's work on a particular case begins when someone walks into her office carrying a court file and says, "The judge sent us, and told us we had to mediate this" (Gray, 1993, p. 220; see chapter 16 of this text).

- Joy Stapp was trained as a social psychologist; she currently is a partner and co-owner of a firm, Stapp Singleton, that specializes in trial consulting. The firm is hired by attorneys representing defendants in lawsuits—that is, in civil cases, not criminal trials. Her firm concentrates on cases dealing with trademark disputes, intellectual property conflicts, and other commercial litigation. Other trial consultants may assist in personal injury cases; for example, an electrician may have been injured on the job and is claiming that the manufacturer of a transformer was negligent in constructing the piece of equipment. **Trial consultants** attempt to assess the attitudes of people role-playing jurors in a trial in order to identify issues as seen by the actual trial jurors; they assemble attitude questions based on psychological concepts that may influence the mock jurors who have observed a rehearsal of the trial. Are the verdicts of the mock jurors related to attitudes they expressed prior to the trial? Could the selection of actual jurors for the trial be influenced by such attitudes? Trial consultants may also be asked to conduct surveys to determine the extent and nature of pretrial publicity in a case (see chapter 12 of this text).

- Margaret Coggins received her Ph.D. in counseling psychology; she currently is the chief of behavioral research at the U.S. Secret Service. Among other tasks, she supervises the design of research on the assessment and management of violent behaviors (Murray, 1998). National leaders are the recipients of an untold number of threats, but how can those that might lead to assassination attempts be distinguished from those that simply "let off steam" or are otherwise less serious? Can FBI agents and other law-enforcement officials identify those individuals whose threats are a function of mental illness? (See chapter 4 of this text.)

The foregoing examples reflect the variety of activities that may be subsumed under the label "forensic psychology." These examples were chosen for several reasons. First, note that the training and past experiences of these forensic psychologists differ, depending on their role. A forensic psychologist who does court-ordered child custody or criminally related evaluations, or who works in a prison or with law enforcement, will come from a background in clinical psychology and is likely to have had a more diversified clinical practice before he or she came to focus on forensic psychology. Other forensic psychologists, for example, those who specialize in eyewitness reliability and the factors that affect it, or trial consultants who work with attorneys on issues related to jury selection or pretrial publicity effects, may have been trained as experimental psychologists or social psychologists. In this book, chapters 3–9 will focus on clinically related applications of forensic psychology, while chapters 10–16 will focus on social, cognitive, and experimental applications of forensic psychology.

To assert that forensic psychology is "*any* application" of psychology to the legal system, as is done here, fails to acknowledge an ongoing controversy within the field as to just who *is* a forensic psychologist and how one should be trained to become a forensic psychologist. The development of doctoral training programs with "forensic psychology" in their title has acceler-

ated in the last five years and is still evolving (Melton, Huss, & Tomkins, 1999). Not all observers would agree that each of the four preceding examples reflects their definition of forensic psychology.

Even a recent president of the American Psychology-Law Society, in his presidential address, asked, "What is forensic psychology, anyway?" (Brigham, 1999). Brigham's (1999) thoughtful review examined the definitions of forensic psychology in the professional literature and separated them into broad and narrow types. The definition that began this chapter is, of course, a broad one; a more narrow definition would limit the focus of forensic psychology to clinical and professional practice issues, such as assessing insanity or mental competency, testifying about rape trauma or battered woman syndrome, conducting child custody evaluations, and other activities that rely upon professional training as a clinical or counseling psychologist. This type of definition would exclude the evaluation-research function as well as many specific activities, including those by the research psychologist who testifies as an expert witness or the trial consultant who conducts surveys about the effects of pretrial publicity. Those psychologists trained in experimental, social, or developmental psychology, but who lack clinical training, would not be eligible. Thus, it must be recognized that for many psychologists, "forensic psychology" is seen as a subspecialization of clinical psychology. As an illustration, the workshops offered by the American Academy of Forensic Psychology are primarily on clinical-psychology topics (Brigham, 1999); recent sessions covered child sex abuse allegations, the MMPI-2 and the Rorschach in court, assessing psychopathy, and the battered woman defense.

Thus, honest disagreement exists over how encompassing the definition should be. With a narrow definition, many psychologists would be left in, to use Brigham's term, a "definitional limbo." Consider Brigham's own situation: A social psychologist and a professor, he has not had training in clinical psychology. He carries out research on eyewitnesses' memory and sometimes provides expert testimony in criminal trials. If asked in court, "Are you a forensic psychologist?" he has said:

> My most accurate current response would seem to be, "Well, it depends. . . ." And, in my experience, judges *hate* responses of that sort, which they see as unnecessarily vague or evasive. (Brigham, 1999, p. 280, italics in original)

As more and more graduate students seek training in forensic psychology, the lack of an agreed-upon definition increases the magnitude of the problem. One manifestation of the issue is the question of whether the American Psychological Association (APA) should certify a "specialty" or "proficiency" in forensic psychology. (Recently, only three specializations in psychology had such a designation—clinical, counseling, and school psychology.) Although it is true that the purpose of a **"specialty" designation** is to evaluate specific graduate-school training programs and not to credential individuals, a concern exists that such labels in the future may be applied to individual psychologists. So should a training program that seeks a specialty designation as forensic psychological include only clinical-type training, or should it be broader? Or, should such a specialty designation even be sought? Arguments have been offered for each perspective (see Brigham, 1999; Heilbrun, 1998). After completing a survey of its membership and extensive discussion, the Executive Committee of the American Psychology-Law Society voted in August 1998 to support a narrow clinical definition of the specialty area of forensic psychology, with a request that the American Psychological Association (APA) designate this specialty as "clinical forensic." During 2000, the American Psychology-Law Society submitted an application for the forensic psychology specialty designation, and, in 2001, the APA approved it, but without the word *clinical* in the name.

Throughout the preceding discussion, the theme of "either-or" has reared its head—that

is, only training limited to clinical psychology or more than clinical training. Some forensic psychologists have suggested a richer, less adversarial conception of what training in forensic psychology should be. Kirk Heilbrun (described in Brigham, 1999) has offered a model that reflects three training areas and two approaches; this conceptualization is reprinted in Table 1-1. This approach is a comprehensive one, and the coverage of what is forensic psychology in this book is in keeping with Heilbrun's conceptualization. Note that among the training topics in his model are consultation in jury selection and in litigation strategy (the topics of chapter 12 of this book), policy and legislative consultation (described in chapter 16), and expert testimony on the state of the science on such topics as eyewitness reliability (chapter 10) or confessions (chapter 11), as well as such traditional topics as forensic assessments of various sorts (chapters 5–9).

HISTORY OF THE RELATIONSHIP BETWEEN PSYCHOLOGY AND THE LAW

We have seen the diversity of activities by contemporary forensic psychologists. But how did we get where we are today? What was the relationship of the two fields when they began to interrelate? How have matters changed?

The division between those contemporary psychologists who conduct research in search of scientific laws ("basic" psychology) and those psychologists who work toward the alleviation of detrimental behaviors in individuals ("applied" psychology) can be traced back to the beginnings of the 20th century (see the following sections), and the distinction is certainly of relevance to the origin of forensic psychology.

The Applied Side

On the one hand, the courts have been facing the applied challenge of dealing with those people, who, because of mental disturbance or per-

Table 1-1	Heilbrun's Conceptualization of Training in Forensic Psychology		
	Law and Psychology Interest Areas (with associated training)		
	Clinical (clinical, counseling, school psychology)	*Experimental* (social, developmental, cognitive, human experimental psychology)	*Legal* (law, some training in behavioral science)
Research/ Scholarship	1. Assessment tools 2. Intervention effectiveness 3. Epidemiology of relevant behavior (e.g., violence, sexual offending) and disorders	1. Memory 2. Perception 3. Child development 4. Group decision making	1. Mental health law 2. Other law relevant to health and science 3. Legal movements
Applied	1. Forensic assessment 2. Treatment in legal context 3. Integration of science into practice	1. Consultation re jury selection 2. Consultation re litigation strategy 3. Consultation re "state of science" 4. Expert testimony re "state of science"	1. Policy and legislative consultation 2. Model law development

Source: From "What Is Forensic Psychology, Anyway?" by J. C. Brigham, 1999, *Law and Human Behavior*, 23, p. 282, Table 3. Reprinted by permission of Kluwer Academic/Plenum Publishers.

haps a criminal tendency, cannot or will not conform their behavior to legal requirements. Cesare Lombroso, an Italian who lived from 1836 to 1909, is considered the father of modern criminology, because he sought to understand the causes of crime (see Lombroso, 1876), albeit from a biological perspective. In the United States, the development of separate juvenile courts, first done in Illinois in 1899, led William Healy, a physician, to initiate a program to study the causes of juvenile delinquency. His founding of the Juvenile Psychopathic Institute in 1909, with a staff that included psychologist Grace M. Fernald, led to increased emphasis on the foundations of criminal behavior. Dr. Fernald was one of the first psychologists to specialize in the diagnosis and treatment of juvenile delinquency. Also, during the late 1800s and early 1900s, Sigmund Freud was developing his theory of personality, and his writings about psychopathology influenced thinking about the causes of criminal behavior. In a speech in 1906 to a group of judges, Freud pro-

posed that psychology could be of practical use to their field (Horowitz & Willging, 1984).

The Academic Side: The Role of Hugo Münsterberg

But a second thrust came from academic psychology. Consider the following quotation from a prominent psychology-and-law researcher regarding his building facilities: "[V]isiting friends [would find], with surprise, twenty-seven rooms overspun with electric wires and filled with (equipment), and a mechanic busy at work" (Münsterberg, 1908, p. 3). Five pages later, this psychologist wrote: "Experimental psychology has reached a stage at which it seems natural and sound to give attention to its possible service for the practical needs of life" (p. 8).

A contemporary statement? No, it is from *On the Witness Stand* (1908), written by psychologist Hugo Münsterberg a century ago. It is an appropriate indication of the importance, longevity, and centrality of forensic psychology to note that one of the original founding members of the American Psychological Association in 1892, James McKeen Cattell, was an active researcher in eyewitness reliability (Fulero, 1999; see chapter 10 of this book). A few months later, five other psychologists were added to the membership list. One of these was none other than Hugo Münsterberg, who, in September 1892, had come from Germany to the United States, to establish—at William James's invitation—the psychological laboratory at Harvard University. At the APA's first annual meeting in December 1892 in Philadelphia, a dozen papers were presented. Münsterberg's was the final one; in it, he criticized his colleagues' work as "rich in decimals but poor in ideas" (see Cattell, 1894, 1895).

Although psycho-legal issues captured only a small portion of Münsterberg's professional time, his impact on the field was so prodigious that it is appropriate to call him the founder of forensic psychology. His choices of what to do are still implicitly reflected in research activities of psychologists interested in the legal system. For example, the chapter topics of Münsterberg's 1908 book—memory distortions, eyewitness accuracy, confessions, suggestibility, hypnosis, crime detection, and the prevention of crime—in varying degrees define what some psychologists think of as topics for contemporary forensic psychology.

Münsterberg was by no means the sole instigator of a movement. In some ways, he was a less-than-ideal symbol; he was arrogant and pugnacious, and he often engaged in self-important posturing. Even William James later described him as "vain and loquacious" (Lukas, 1997, p. 586). More importantly, there were other pioneers, too (see Ogloff, 2000). Even before Münsterberg published his book, Hermann Ebbinghaus (1885), using himself as a subject, demonstrated the rapid rate of early memory loss. In France, Alfred Binet, as early as 1900, was seeking to understand children's competence as eyewitnesses (Yarmey, 1984). In Germany, Louis William Stern began publishing eyewitness research as early as 1902; during the next year, he was admitted to German courts of law to testify as an expert witness on eyewitness identification. Stern (1903) established a periodical dealing with the psychology of testimony. While it is true that much of the early work published there was classificatory (for example, six types of questions that might be asked of an eyewitness), other contributions were empirical; for example, Stern compared the memory abilities of children and adults. Wells and Loftus observed: "Not surprisingly, the early empirical work was not of the quality and precision that exists in psychology today" (1984, p. 5). Yet the foundation was set.

Guy Montrose Whipple (1909, 1910, 1911, 1912), in a series of *Psychological Bulletin* articles, brought the *Aussage* (or eyewitness testimony) tradition into English terminology, introducing American audiences to classic experiments relating testimony and evidence to perception and memory. Even before World War I, "law was acknowledged as a fit concern for psychology and vice versa" (Tapp, 1976, pp. 360–361).

But Münsterberg was the psychologist "who pushed his reluctant American colleagues into the practical legal arena" (Bartol & Bartol, 1999, p. 7), and thus he had the greatest impact—for good or bad. Some of the topics first illuminated by Münsterberg and his contemporaries remain in the limelight. Especially with regard to the accuracy of eyewitness identification, the immense interest in recent times can be directly traced to Münsterberg's work (see Moskowitz, 1977).

Münsterberg's Goals for Psychology and the Law

Münsterberg's mission has been described as raising the psychological profession to a position of importance in public life (Kargon, 1986), and the legal system was one vehicle for doing so. Loftus (1979) has commented: "At the beginning of the century, Münsterberg was arguing for more interaction between the two fields, perhaps at times in a way that was insulting to the legal profession" (p. 194). "Insulting" is a strong description, but it is true that Münsterberg wrote things like this: "[I]t seems astonishing that the work of justice is carried out in the courts without ever consulting the psychologist and asking him for all the aid which the modern study of suggestion can offer" (1908, p. 194). At the beginning of the 20th century, chemists and physicists were routinely called as expert witnesses (Kargon, 1986). Why not psychologists? Münsterberg saw no difference between the physical sciences and his own.

Münsterberg's Values

Münsterberg's specific views toward the court system help us understand the actions he took. More importantly, they cause us to ask: How different are our values and beliefs from his?

The jury system rests on a positive assumption about human nature—that a collection of reasonable people are able to judge the world about them reasonably accurately. As Kalven and Zeisel put it, the justice system

> recruits a group of twelve lay [people], chosen at random from the widest population; it convenes them for the purpose of a particular trial; it entrusts them with great official powers of decision; it permits them to carry out deliberations in secret and report out their final judgment without giving reasons for it; and, after their momentary service to the state has been completed, it orders them to disband and return to private life. (1966, p. 3)

Furthermore, our society values the rights of the accused; it protects suspects against self incrimination and places the burden of proof on the state to show guilt beyond a reasonable doubt. As his biographer, Matthew Hale, Jr., saw it, Münsterberg took a very different view of society and the role of the psychologist as expert. "The central premise of his legal psychology . . . was that the individual could not accurately judge the real world that existed outside him, or for that matter the nature and processes of his own mind" (Hale, 1980, p. 121).

Thus, police investigations and courtroom procedures required the assistance of a psychologist.

Three Crucial Activities

Münsterberg reflected his desire to bring psychology into the courtroom by:

1. Demonstrating the fallibility of memory, including time overestimation, omission of significant information, and other errors.
2. Publishing *On the Witness Stand,* which was actually a compilation of highly successful magazine articles. As a result of these articles, he was, after William James, America's best-known psychologist (Lukas, 1997). His goal in these *McClure's Magazine* pieces was to show an audience of laypeople that "experimental psychology has reached a stage at which it seems natural and sound to give attention also to its possible service for the practical needs of life" (1908, p. 8).
3. Offering testimony as an expert witness in highly publicized trials. Perhaps most controversial was his intrusion in the 1907 Idaho trial of labor leader "Big Bill" Haywood (Hale, 1980; Holbrook, 1987). The IWW (International Workers of the World) leader was charged with conspiracy to murder Frank Steunenberg, a former governor of Idaho and a well-known opponent to organized labor. On December 30, 1905, in Caldwell, Idaho, Steunenberg had opened the gate to his modest home and was blown apart by a waiting bomb. The murder trial transformed Haywood into an international symbol of labor protest; Clarence Darrow offered his services as defense attorney, and people like Eugene V. Debs and Maxim Gorky rallied support (Hale, 1980).

The case against Haywood rested on the testimony of the mysterious Harry Orchard, a one-time IWW organizer who—after a four-day interrogation—confessed to committing the bombing (as well as many other crimes) at the behest of an "inner circle" of radicals, including Haywood.

Münsterberg firmly believed that one of psychology's strongest contributions was in distinguishing false memory from true; thus, he examined Orchard in his cell, during the trial, and conducted numerous tests on him over a period of seven hours, including some precursors of the polygraph; in Münsterberg's mind, the most important of these was the word association test. Upon returning to Cambridge, Münsterberg permitted an interview with the Boston *Herald* (July 3, 1907), which quoted him as saying, "Orchard's confession is, every word of it, true" (Lukas, 1997, p. 599). This disclosure, coming before a verdict had been delivered, threatened the impartiality of the trial, and Münsterberg was rebuked by newspapers from Boston to Boise. Still, the jury found Haywood not guilty, as the state did not produce any significant evidence corroborating Orchard's confession, as Idaho required. Two weeks later, Münsterberg amended his position by introducing the concept of "subjective truthfulness." His free association tests, he now concluded, revealed that Orchard genuinely believed he was telling the truth, but they couldn't discern the actual facts of the matter.

Despite the adverse publicity, Münsterberg maintained his inflated claims for his science. In a letter to the editor, he wrote: "To deny that the experimental psychologist has indeed possibilities of determining the 'truth-telling' process is just as absurd as to deny that the chemical expert can find out whether there is arsenic in a stomach or whether blood spots are human or animal origin" (quoted by Hale, 1980, p. 118). His claims took on exaggerated metaphors; he could "pierce the mind" and bring to light its deepest secrets.

In fairness, it should be noted that Münsterberg did not limit his advocacy to one side in criminal trials. In one case, he felt the defendant's confession was the result of a hypnotic induction and hence false, so Münsterberg offered to testify for the defense. In the Idaho case, his conclusions (which, if not derived from his political ideologies, were certainly in keeping with his antipathy to anarchy and union protest) supported the prosecution.

Münsterberg, like most true believers committed to their innovative theories, may have exaggerated claims in order to get attention and convince himself of the merits of his claims. His biographer, Matthew Hale (1980), has made a strong case that Münsterberg "deceived himself with alarming frequency, and his distortions in certain cases bordered on outright falsification" (1980, p. 119).

Reaction From the Legal Community

Not surprisingly, Münsterberg's advocacy generated withering abuse from the legal community. One attack, titled "Yellow Psychology" and written by Charles Moore, concluded that the laboratory had little to lend to the courtroom and expressed skepticism that Münsterberg had discovered a "Northwest Passage to the truth" (quoted in Hale, 1980, p. 115).

An article by John Henry Wigmore (1909), a law professor and a leading expert on evidence, cast in the form of a trial against Münsterberg during which lawyers cross-examined him for damaging assertions, was, in the words of Wallace Loh, "mercilessly satiric" (1981, p. 316); it suggested that experimental psychology, at the time, lacked enough knowledge to be practical (Davis, 1989). Furthermore, Wigmore argued that the jury system distrusted those outside interferences, such as Münsterberg's, that intruded upon their commonsense judgments. But Wigmore made a telling point in this article. As Loftus (1979) has reminded us, in Wigmore's courtroom drama, "Before the jurors left the courtroom to go home, the judge took a few moments to express his personal view. He said essentially this: In no other country in the civilized world had the legal profession taken so little interest in finding out what psychology and other sciences had to offer that might contribute to the nation's judicial system" (p. 203).

A Period of Inactivity

Perhaps for these reasons—exaggeration by Münsterberg and avoidance by legal authorities—

research by scientific psychology applicable to the courts languished from the First World War until the latter half of the 1970s (see Ogloff, 2000). There were contributions in the 1920s (Marston, 1924), 1930s (Stern, 1939), 1940s (Weld & Danzig, 1940), and into the 1960s (Toch, 1961), but they were infrequent. Historical treatments of the development of the field (for example, Bartol & Bartol, 1999; Davis, 1989; Foley, 1993; Kolasa, 1972) noted that a few works examined the legal system from the psychological perspective; those included such books as Burtt's *Legal Psychology* in 1931 and Robinson's *Law and the Lawyers* in 1935 and some speculative reviews in law journals (Hutchins & Slesinger, 1928a, b, c; Louisell, 1955, 1957). There were even books like McCarty's *Psychology for the Lawyer* in 1929 (McCarty, 1929). But until the 1960s, a good deal of the work on the social science of law was done by anthropologists, sociologists, and psychiatrists (Tapp, 1977; see, e.g., Kalven & Zeisel, 1966).

The relationship between eyewitness confidence and accuracy is an example of the gap in research activity. Münsterberg did perhaps the first empirical test of this relationship (Wells & Murray, 1984). In his test, children examined pictures for 15 seconds and then wrote a report of everything they could remember. Subsequently, he asked them to underline those parts of their report of which they were absolutely certain. Münsterberg reported that there were almost as many mistakes in the underlined sentences as in the rest. Other studies in the first years of this century, by Stern and by Borst, were reported by Whipple (1909). Paradoxically, no further empirical interest surfaced until almost 65 years later (Wells & Murray, 1984).

Explanations for the "lull" in empirical psychological research on legal issues came from Sporer (1981, cited by Wells & Loftus, 1984): "zealous overgeneralizations drawn from experimental studies that did not meet adequately the demands of complex courtroom reality" (quoted by Wells & Loftus, 1984, p. 6). Another reason is offered by Wells and Loftus: that "psychological research during that time was oriented primarily toward theoretical issues with little focus on practical problems" (1984, p. 6).

Resurgence in the 1970s

Interest in legal issues by experimental psychologists and social psychologists did not resume until the 1970s (Ogloff, 2000); with regard to one example, eyewitness identification, Wells and Loftus (1984) estimated that over 85% of the entire published literature surfaced between 1978 and the publication of their book in 1984.

Why the rise in the 1970s? One reason, according to Wells and Loftus (1984), was a renewed emphasis on the necessity to make observations in natural contexts in order to understand social behavior and memory. More generally, social psychology in the 1970s responded to a crisis about its relevance by extending its concepts to real-world topics, including health and the law (Davis, 1989). Nagel went so far as to claim: "The contemporary law and psychology movement has been the direct outgrowth of social psychologists' self reflection on the failure of their discipline to advance social policy: it was an explicit rejection of the academically effete nature of much social psychological curiosity and an attempt to become more 'action-oriented'" (1983, p. 17).

James H. Davis (1989) took a different approach:

It is tempting to draw a general parallel between the temporal sequence of the past: Münsterberg's proposals; reaction and critique of other scholars, disenchantment among social psychologists; and finally, abandonment of efforts at application of psychology to law. But something different happened "the next time around." The general disenchantment that was characteristic of the latter "crisis" period was not followed by an "abandonment phase." Rather, we have seen a continuous evolution and strengthening of some new developments during the succeeding years—a period in which *applied research in social psychology came to be recognized in its own right.* (p. 201, italics in original)

The Present

Where do we stand now? Psychologists do research on a number of topics relevant to the real world of the legal system; beyond the extensive work on jury decision making, psychologists have studied such diverse phenomena as sentencing decisions, the impact of the specific insanity definition, children's abilities as eyewitnesses, and the impact of the battered woman defense. Much of this work has been done in laboratories, with limitations to its applications to real-world decisions.

At the same time, judges, trial attorneys, police, and other representatives of the legal system are making real-world decisions—about the competency of a defendant, about which jurors to dismiss, about how to interrogate a suspect. Applied psychologists sometimes have an influence in such decisions as well as the thousands of others made daily in the legal system.

It is our position that it is time for psychologists to move beyond basic research and to focus on how their perspective can improve the decisions made in law offices and courtrooms. In doing so, we will need to face the obstacles alluded to earlier in this chapter. Each profession and each discipline has its own way of doing things, its own way of seeing the world and defining the experiences in it. Police operate out of shared assumptions about the nature of the world; the experience of going through law school socializes attorneys to emphasize certain qualities; judges learn certain values and emphasize them in their decisions. Forensic psychologists must recognize these values (as well as their own) as they attempt to have an impact.

CONFLICTS BETWEEN PSYCHOLOGY AND THE LAW

Disagreement within the field as to the extent and limits of forensic psychology is not the only problem we face. When psychology seeks to apply its findings to the legal system, it faces the task of working with another discipline, that of the law. Lawyers—including judges, trial lawyers, and law school professors—are trained to look at human behavior in a way different from the perspective of psychologists (Horowitz & Willging, 1984). Thus, we next examine the nature of these conflicts between the law and psychology (and other social sciences). Only after that exploration may we move to a more extensive description of the various roles of forensic psychologists, in chapter 2.

If forensic psychology can succeed in any systematic way, it must first confront the conflicts between the goals and values of the legal profession and those of psychology. The following paragraphs examine some of these conflicts in depth (see also Box 1-1).

Laws and Values

Laws are human creations that evolve out of the need to resolve disagreements. In that sense, laws reflect values, and values are basic psychological concepts (see Darley, Fulero, Haney, & Tyler, 2002; Finkel, Fulero, Haugaard, Levine, & Small, 2001). **Values** may be defined as standards for decision making, and thus laws are created, amended, or discarded because society has established standards for what is acceptable and unacceptable behavior. Society's values can change, leading to new laws and new interpretations of existing laws. For example, for many years society looked the other way when a married man forced his wife to have sexual relations against her will, but society has become increasingly aware of and concerned about what is called **spousal rape,** and now every state in the United States has laws that prohibit such actions.

Each discipline approaches the generation of knowledge and the standards for decision making in a different way. An attorney and a social scientist will often see the same event through different perspectives, because of their specialized training. Judges may use procedures and concepts different from those of psychology in forming their opinions. It is not that one approach is cor-

BOX 1-1

Tensions Between Law and Psychology

The tensions between law and psychology may be expressed as dichotomies (Haney, 1980). Nagel (1983, p. 3) and Haney (1980) list the following as the most frequently cited:

1. Psychology's emphasis on innovation and counterintuitive thinking versus law's *stare decisis* model and conservative stance, which resist innovation.
2. Psychology's empirical versus law's authoritarian epistemology, based on a hierarchy.
3. Psychology's experimental methodology versus law's adversarial process.
4. Psychology's descriptive versus law's prescriptive discourse.
5. Psychology's nomothetic versus law's ideographic focus.

6. Psychology's probabilistic and tentative conclusions versus law's emphasis on certainty, or at least the assumption that legal conclusions are irrevocable.
7. Psychology's academic and abstract orientation versus law's pragmatic and applied orientation.
8. Psychology's proactive orientation versus law's reactive orientation.

It should be noted that, though fundamental differences are agreed upon, some psychologists (cf. Laufer & Walt, 1992) argue that some of these differences may be more apparent than real. In particular, they believe that the influence of **precedent** on explanation in psychology has been underemphasized. For example, "normal science" imposes existing paradigms on interpretations and explanations of facts; these paradigms direct new research endeavors.

---

rect and that the other is wrong; rather, they are simply different.

Some lawyers rely on psychologists to help plan effective trial tactics, and many courts now accept psychologists as expert witnesses on a variety of topics. But obstacles stand in the way of full application, and many of these obstacles are at the most basic level—the level of values and goals. Conflicts between the values of psychology and the values of the legal system are a focus for this chapter, because they play a role in evaluating the topics covered in subsequent chapters, especially in the degree to which psychology is successful in influencing the decisions of the legal system.

Many ways exist to distinguish these contrasting goals and values; John Carroll (1980) put it as follows:

The goals of the law and the goals of social science are different and partially in conflict. The law deals in morality, social values, social control, and justifying the application of abstract principles to specific cases. In day-to-day operation, the system values efficiency and expediency. . . . In contrast, social science deals in knowledge, truth, and derives

abstract principles from specific instances. These are thought to be value free. In operation, the scientific method values reproducible phenomena and underlying concepts and causes rather than the specifics or form in which these appear. (1980, p. 363)

The response of the American Psychological Association after the verdict in John Hinckley's trial is an example of the expression of psychology's values. After Hinckley was found not guilty by reason of insanity, the insanity defense came under increased attack from both the public sector and various professional organizations; both the American Psychiatric Association and the American Bar Association called for more stringent standards. Some states adopted a "guilty but mentally ill" plea, while several states actually abolished the insanity defense (see chapter 5). The American Psychological Association (March 1984), in contrast, argued for an **empirical approach** "in which both existing standards and proposals for change would be carefully examined for their scientific merit" (Rogers, 1987, p. 841). A recent review done by psychologists of the changes proposed by those who call for changes in the insanity defense, or its actual abolition, has found them generally lacking in research support (Borum & Fulero, 1999; see also Fulero & Finkel, 1991, and Finkel & Fulero, 1992).

What Determines "Truth"?

The most fundamental conflict arises from the nature of truth, albeit also the most elusive and challenging quest. Suppose we ask a psychologist, a police officer, a trial attorney, and a judge the same question: How do you know that something is true? Each might say, "Look at the evidence," but for each the evidence is defined differently.

Psychologists are trained to answer a question about human behavior by collecting data. A conclusion about behavior is not accepted by psychologists until the observations are objectively measurable, they show **reliability** (they are consistent over time), and they possess **replicability** (different investigators can produce similar results). In contrast, lawyers are more willing to

rely on their own experience, their own views of life, and their intuition or "gut feelings." J. Alexander Tanford (1990), a professor of law, proposed that the Supreme Court tends "to approve legal rules based on intuitive assumptions about human behavior that research by psychologists has shown to be erroneous" (p. 138). For example, in the decision in *Schall v. Martin* (1984), the majority of the Supreme Court agreed that "judges *can* predict dangerous behavior, no matter what the relevant research says" (Melton, 1987, p. 489, italics in original).

Tanford's indictment of the Supreme Court is devastating:

> From 1970 to 1988, the United States Supreme Court decided 92 cases concerning the propriety of various rules of evidence and trial procedure. In most cases, relevant psychological literature on juror behavior was readily available in interdisciplinary journals, widely circulated books, law reviews, journals for practicing lawyers, law student

BOX 1-2
Inductive Versus Deductive Methods of Reasoning

Induction and deduction are two contrasting methods used to solve a problem. **Deduction** requires the *application* of rules or a theory, while **induction** requires the *generation* of rules or a theory. Usually, deduction goes from the general to the specific, while induction uses several specifics to generate a general rule.

In a creative analysis, Bruce Frey contrasted the ways that two popular fictional detectives solved crimes. Sherlock Holmes's investigative procedure was to examine a set of clues, develop a number of possible solutions, and eliminate them one by one. "When you have eliminated all the possibilities but one, that remaining one, no matter how improbable, must be the correct solution"—so goes his credo. (Further examples of Holmes's approach can be found in chapter 4). Frey (1994) labeled this the inductive process because it examined many possibilities and used observations to create a theory, to infer a conclusion.

In contrast, Miss Jane Marple, the heroine of many of Agatha Christie's mysteries, used quite different,

deductive skills. A polite, elderly woman who lived in the village of St. Mary Mead, she possessed an intimate knowledge of human interactions and behaviors among the inhabitants of her hometown. Her procedure when entering a problem-solving situation was to use the model of St. Mary Mead as a template and to apply that model to the facts. We know that both detectives were quite successful (their authors made sure of that!). And neither procedure has a clear superiority over the other. Do these approaches distinguish between the problem-solving styles of the psychologist and the lawyer? Psychology as a science relies on the deductive method: A general theory leads to specific hypotheses; the testing of these hypotheses leads to results that confirm, disconfirm, or revise the theory. With its emphasis on precedent and previous rulings, the law would seem, in a broad sense, to be inductive. But each discipline is multifaceted, and specific psychologists, legal scholars, and attorneys might follow either procedure.

textbooks, and even the popular press. In a number of instances, the Justices were provided with nonpartisan *amicus* briefs explaining in detail relevant jury behavior research. Yet, not a single Supreme Court majority opinion has relied even partly on the psychology of jury behavior to justify a decision about the proper way to conduct a trial. (1990, pp. 138–139)

Here is a pungent example: In *Holbrook v. Flynn* (1986), the Court unanimously ruled that the jury had not been biased by seeing the defendant surrounded by armed security guards; the judicial opinion admitted it was based on "[the Court's] own experience and common sense" and rejected an empirical study with contradictory findings.

For the police officer, personal observation is a strong determinant of the truth. Police take pride in their ability to detect deception and their interrogative skills as ways of separating truth-telling from falsification. Gisli Gudjonsson (1992), a psychologist and a former police officer, noted that many police interrogators have blind faith in the use of nonverbal signs of deception. Certainly they also rely on physical measures: Speeding is determined by the reading on the radar gun; alcohol level by the blood-alcohol test.

However, crime investigation may reflect either inductive or deductive methods of reasoning; see examples of this distinction, developed by Bruce Frey (1994), in Box 1-2.

As the preceding implies, a belief in the validity of intuition is a part of a police officer's evidence evaluation. Hays (1992), a 20-year veteran of the Los Angeles Police Department, wrote: "Most cops develop an instinct for distinguishing the legitimate child abuse complaints from the phony ones" (p. 30). Police are willing to use a broader number of methods to determine truth than are psychologists. For example, a substantial number of police departments are willing to use psychics to help them solve crimes, while most psychologists are appalled by the notion that psychics have any valid avenues toward knowledge. Box 1-3 provides an example.

What about attorneys and judges—what determines truth for them? Within the courtroom, for some attorneys, truth may be irrelevant. Probably for more judges and trial attorneys, the assumption is that the adversary system will produce truths or at least fairness. Courts have repeatedly stated that "a fair trial is one in which evidence [is] subject to adversarial testing" (*Strickland v. Washington*, 1984, p. 685, quoted by Tanford and Tanford, 1988, p. 765). The nature of the adversary system leads some trial attorneys

---

BOX 1-3
Police and the Use of Psychics in Crime Investigation

On April 24, 1983, a 28-year-old woman disappeared from Alton, Illinois. Three days later, her boyfriend, Stanley Holliday, Jr., was arrested in New Jersey and brought back to Illinois, where he was charged with murder. But the woman's body had not been found—even six months later—and in a last-ditch effort, the police called in a psychic named Greta Alexander.

Ms. Alexander ran her hand over the map and then drew a circle around a limited area where the police should concentrate their search. Furthermore, she told the police that the head and foot would be separated from the body, the letter *s* would be important in the discovery, and the man who would find the victim

would have a "bad hand." Despite having searched this area many times, the police tried again. They found the young woman's body on this search, and the skull was found 5 feet from the body, and the left foot was missing. Furthermore, the auxiliary police officer who found the body, named Steve Trew, had a deformed left hand (Lyons & Truzzi, 1991).

A lucky coincidence? A prearranged discovery? Most psychologists would reject the use of psychics in criminal investigation, but some police, at least in "last-resort" cases, will be amenable to any source of possible assistance.

to value conflict resolution over the elusive quest for the truth. Another conception sometimes offered (Pulaski, 1980) is that trials are conducted not to find out what happened—the police, the prosecutor, and the defense attorney all probably know what happened—but as a game to persuade the community that proof is strong enough to justify punishment.

Martha Deed (1991), a psychotherapist, quoted the view of Paul Ivan Birzon, the president of New York State's Academy of Matrimonial Lawyers:

> The law assumes that truth emerges from the clash of adversaries in the courtroom. The law assumes that: Uneven skills of counsel do not exist; bias doesn't influence the decision-maker; evidence can be clearly presented. . . . Right and morality are irrelevant. Personal convictions are irrelevant. Only "truth" produced through trial is relevant. "Truth" for the law is a legal construct which relates to facts as they emerge at trial. "Truth" does not necessarily coincide with reality. (quoted by Deed, 1991, p. 77)

But if trial attorneys and, especially, judges focus on the assessment of truth in a court-related context, evidence and the law are determinants. Legal authorities rely heavily on precedents in reaching decisions. The principle of *stare decisis* ("let the decision stand") has the weight, for judges, equivalent to the importance of the principle of experimentation for scientific psychologists.

As we have seen, appellate judges are not as bound as psychologists by empirical findings when they draw conclusions about the real world. In the case of *California v. Greenwood* (1988), which involved the police confiscating the garbage bags left by Bobby Greenwood at the street side for collection, the majority opinion of the U.S. Supreme Court stated that people have no **"subjective expectation of privacy"** when they put out their garbage for collection. No psychologist would make such a statement without obtaining confirmatory data first.

This is not to say that the courts always ignore social science research when that research can help clarify or resolve empirical issues that arise in litigation; in fact, Monahan and Walker (1991) concluded that "increasingly in recent decades the courts have sought out research data on their own when the parties have failed to provide them" (p. 571). Use of psychological research in the courtroom traces back to 1908 in the landmark case of *Muller v. Oregon*. Was social welfare legislation constitutional when it limited to 10 hours the workday of any female working in a factory or laundry? Louis Brandeis assembled medical and social science research that showed the debilitating effect of working long hours and then presented this material to the Supreme Court in a brief that defended Oregon's limits on work hours. (This brief became the model for what are now called **Brandeis briefs,** those that focus on empirical evidence and similar types of evidence rather than reviewing past cases and statutes.) Never before had a litigant explicitly relied on social science findings in a Supreme Court brief (Tomkins & Cecil, 1987). The majority opinion in *Muller v. Oregon* upheld the legislation, ruling that it was not a violation of the Fourteenth Amendment for a state to limit women's workdays, and referred to the social science evidence in a long footnote, stating that although they (social scientists) "may not be, technically speaking, authorities" (p. 420), they would receive "judicial cognizance" (p. 421).

Tomkins and Oursland (1991), among others, have observed that the historic tension between social science and the law "does not imply that social science has been excluded from the courts" (p. 103). Even Justice Frankfurter, who often noted the immaturity of social sciences, included in one of his opinions a "Brandeis brief" of several hundred pages that cited only eight legal cases among the extensive coverage of empirical data (Perkins, 1988). The *Brown v. Board of Education* (1954) decision regarding school desegregation, the most visible example of inclusion, is examined in detail in chapter 2.

The Nature of Reality

In the novel *Body of Evidence* (1991) by Patricia D. Cornwell (an expert on medical forensics), a character expresses the opinion that "everything depends on everything else" (p. 13); that is, you can't identify cause and effect, as variables interact with each other in undecipherable ways. To what extent do people give credence to such a view? Psychologists are trained to disabuse this notion; the experimental method emphasizes an analytic nature of the world. There are *independent* variables out there—each has a separate influence. Even if one variable's impact is influenced by the amount of another variable, we talk about an interaction; psychology assumes a view that influences can be separated and distinguished from each other. None of the other professions or disciplines holds adamantly to such a conception of the world.

While the psychological field assumes that the world is composed of separable variables that act independently of or interactively on other variables, it also is more tolerant of ambiguity than is the legal field. In fact, the focus of psychology can be labeled as probabilistic, for several reasons. We express our "truths" as "statistically significant" at, for example, the .05 level, meaning that we are saying it is likely—but not certain—that a real effect or difference exists.

Even more basic is psychology's assumption that people think in terms of probabilities and likelihoods. If you examine the instruments used by research psychologists, you find that they often will ask subjects "What is the likelihood that . . .?" or similar questions. In contrast, the courts, lawyers, and people in general may well think in yes-or-no, right-or-wrong categories.

Dawes (1988), Kahneman, Slovic, and Tversky (1982; Tversky & Kahneman, 1974, 1983), Koehler (1992, 2001; Kaye & Koehler, 1991), and Thompson (1989a) have provided numerous examples of the lay public's tendency to misunderstand probabilities and their difficulties in applying probabilistic reasoning; for example, the adherence to the "gambler's fallacy," ignorance

of regression-to-the-mean effects, and failure to pay attention to base rates.

In our legal system, proof is based "on showing direct cause and effect: action A caused (or at least in measurable ways contributed to) result B; Jones pulled the trigger and Smith died; Roe violated the contract and as a consequence Doe lost money" (Rappeport, 1993, p. 15). In contrast, psychologists are more concerned with the probability that A is related to B.

The Legal System's Criticisms of Psychology

If psychology wants to make a contribution to the functioning of the legal system, then it is incumbent on psychology to understand the criticisms of it and indicate what it can provide. Some of these criticisms are evaluated in the following paragraphs.

The Lack of Ecological Validity of Psychological Research

The oldest criticism, going back to Wigmore's response to Münsterberg's work, notes the dissimilarity between the procedures and subjects of psychological research studies and the procedures and participants in the actual legal system. Jury research has been a significant source of such criticism, both by lawyers and by some psychologists (Bornstein, 1999; Dillehay & Nietzel, 1980; Konecni & Ebbesen, 1981; Ogloff, 2000). It is erroneous to assume that simply because a manipulation has an effect in the laboratory, it will automatically have the same effect on jurors in the courtroom (Tanford & Tanford, 1988).

Perhaps the most detailed criticism of the validity of social science research is found in Chief Justice Rehnquist's majority opinion in *Lockhart v. McCree* (1986), involving the use of death-qualified jurors. (Chapter 2 examines this case in detail.) Most research psychologists (but not all; see Elliott, 1991a, 1991b) support the conclusion that death-qualified jurors are conviction-prone, and the American Psychological Association submitted an *amicus* brief reviewing the research leading to such a conclusion. But, in a five-page review, Justice Rehnquist attacked these studies and especially their methodology.

He presented six criticisms (summarized by Tanford, 1990):

1. "Only" six studies specifically demonstrated conviction-proneness, too small a number from which to draw reliable conclusions. Another eight studies that corroborated this conclusion were considered irrelevant because they assessed jurors' attitudes rather than verdicts.
2. Three of the six "relevant" studies had been presented to the Supreme Court in an earlier case (*Witherspoon v. Illinois*, 1968), at which time the justices considered them too tentative.
3. Three of the six studies used randomly selected individuals, instead of real jurors sworn to apply the law.
4. Two experiments that did use actual jurors did not include jury deliberations and, therefore, were, for Justice Rehnquist, of no value (*Lockhart v. McCree*, 1986, p. 171).
5. The studies did not say whether the outcome, considering all the evidence, would have been different if the jury were not death-qualified.
6. Only one study investigated the possibility of the independent "nullifier" phenomenon—that is, whether someone opposed to the death penalty would vote not guilty just to prevent a death sentence (Tanford, 1990, p. 146).

Justice Rehnquist, finally, contended that other serious methodological problems existed, but that he didn't have time to mention them (*Lockhart v. McCree*, 1986, p. 173). Given such a rejection, how should psychology proceed? Diamond (1989) noted that there are topics for which the courts believe that psychology has some answers—child custody or deceptive advertising—but sometimes the quality of the research offered the courts is not good. She quoted the reaction of an exasperated court in a trial in which the judge rejected surveys produced by both sides:

> It is difficult to believe that it was a mere coincidence that when each party retained a supposedly independent and objective survey organization, it ended up with survey questions which were virtually certain to produce the particular results it sought. This strongly suggests that those who drafted the survey questions were more likely knaves than fools. If they were indeed the former, they must have assumed that judges are the latter. (*American Home Products Corp. v. Johnson & Johnson*, 1987, quoted by Diamond, 1989, p. 250)

Going Beyond the Data to Make Moral Judgments

Former Judge David Bazelon (1982), who was one of the strongest supporters of psychology on the federal bench, has chastised psychologists for going beyond their data and venturing beyond their expertise to make moral judgments. Melton, Petrila, Poythress, and Slobogin (1997), in an introductory chapter for a handbook on psychological court evaluations, used this admonition as a springboard to examine what they call the "current ambivalence" about the relationship of mental health and the law.

For example, psychologists may be encouraged to testify in court over theories and findings that lack validity. These and other temptations are examined in detail in chapter 2. The quality of the scientific evidence supporting conclusions of forensic psychologists is, in truth, a prevailing theme throughout this book.

Intruding Upon the Legitimate Activities of the Legal System

Some attorneys, law professors, and social critics fear that the infusion of psychological knowledge into the legal system will somehow change it for the worse and will subvert its legitimacy. An example is the use of psychologists as trial consultants; Gold (1987) argued that their use has created a set of superlawyers who are able to control the decision making of juries. According to this view, the psychologists' knowledge of persuasion techniques and jury decision making will somehow increase the likelihood of extraneous influences affecting verdicts. For example, Gold fears that, armed with such knowledge, "lawyers can induce jurors to make judgments about the credibility of a speaker through manipulation of the 'powerfulness' of the speaker's language" (Gold, 1987, p. 484).

Gold's detailed critique reflects the fact that many lawyers "fundamentally misunderstand the psychology of jury behavior and the trial process" (Tanford & Tanford, 1988, p. 748). This is regrettable, but is once more an indication that forensic psychology must reach out and seek to correct such false assumptions. The actual contributions and effectiveness of psychologists as trial consultants are examined in chapter 12.

Two Illustrative Court Decisions

Two Supreme Court decisions in the 1980s neatly illustrate the conflict in values between the legal profession and scientific psychology. In one of these, the majority decision by the U. S. Supreme Court went against a massive pattern of statistical evidence; in the other, the Court's opinion was consistent with the position of the psychologist who testified as an expert witness, but the impact of the psychologist's testimony is not clear. These two cases are chosen as illustrative for several reasons: The research methods differ from one case to the other, the cases deal with differing but equally noteworthy contemporary examples of discrimination, and they reflect the difference of opinion both between disciplines and within each discipline. (The latter point is important because—just as few Supreme Court majority opinions reflect acceptance by all nine justices—psychologists are not always in agreement about the proper applications of research findings.)

A Criminal Case: *McCleskey v. Kemp* (1987)

Warren McCleskey was an African American man who participated in the armed robbery of an Atlanta furniture store in the late 1970s; he was convicted of killing a White police officer who responded to the alarm that a robbery was in progress. McCleskey was sentenced to death, but he challenged the constitutionality of this sentence on the grounds that the state of Georgia administered its death-sentencing laws in a racially discriminatory manner. But in 1987, the United States Supreme Court rejected his claim in a 5 to 4 vote, and McCleskey was later executed.

What was the basis for McCleskey's claim? And what was the rationale for the Supreme Court's decision? What can we learn from this case about the conflict in values between psychology and the legal system?

McCleskey's claim of racial bias used a statistical analysis, clearly a fundamental method employed by the field of psychology. The use of statistical analysis is central to the empirical approach; in this study, the procedures were clearly described and the data were quantifiable, so that other investigators could repeat the procedures and find the same results. A law professor at the University of Iowa, David Baldus, and his associates (Baldus, Woodworth, & Pulaski, 1990) carried out two studies of Georgia's use of the death penalty. The raw data for the larger of these consisted of the 2,484 homicide cases in Georgia between 1973 and 1979 that led to a conviction for murder or voluntary manslaughter. Of these, 1,620, or 65%, included facts that made the defendant eligible to be sentenced to death, under Georgia law. Of these, 128 defendants, or 8.7%, were actually sentenced to death.

Analysis of the results found that defendants whose victims were White encountered a substantially higher likelihood of receiving a death sentence than those with African American victims; when the victim was White, 11% of homicide defendants were sentenced to death, but with African American victims, between 1% and 2% of defendants were sentenced to death.

When all four possible combinations of race of defendant and race of victim were compared, the combination that led to a death sentence most often (in 21% of the cases) was a White victim and an African American defendant (the other combinations had the following percentages: White defendant and White victim, 8%; White defendant and African American victim, 3%; and African American defendant and African American victim, 1%).

But is it fair to conclude, based only on these percentages, that the race of the participants (especially the victim) is the determining factor leading to the choice of a death sentence? When a jury or judge considers whether to impose the sentence of death, many states provide a consideration of the presence of any **aggravating or mitigating factors.** For example, did the defendant have a history of having been abused? A woman who killed her husband might claim, as a mitigating factor, that he had battered, threatened, and tortured her for years. Baldus and his associates recognized that characteristics of some killings reflected aggravating factors, making them more susceptible to severe sentences—for example, if the victim was also raped or if torture was used, or if the defendant killed several people. It is possible that the victims in these most heinous of homicides were more often White than another race, thus contributing to the results in the first analysis. By evaluating the impact of these factors, Baldus and his colleagues were able to clarify and pinpoint the racial discrimination. For example, when the crime involved extremely aggravating factors, such as multiple stab wounds, an armed robbery, a child victim, or the defendant having a prior record, the race of the victim had little effect on the sentence given; severe sentences were given regardless of the race. But, with respect to those homicides that included a moderate level of aggravating factors, the race of the victim was quite influential, leading to a ratio of 3 to 1 (38% death-sentencing rate for murderers with White victims, versus 13% death-sentencing rate for murderers with African American victims).

Interestingly, in the analysis by Baldus and his colleagues, "the case of Warren McCleskey falls at 42 on the aggravation scale, squarely in the midrange of cases, where the race-of-the-victim effects are the strongest" (Baldus, Woodworth, &

Pulaski, 1992, p. 262). (In contrast, there is a "total absence" of a race-of-victim effect among the most-aggravated cases, those between 60 and 100 on the level-of-aggravation scale.) What is perplexing about this detailed analysis is Baldus's placement of McCleskey's crime in the midrange on the level-of-aggravation scale; McCleskey participated in an armed robbery (#29 in severity on a list of 41 case characteristics), and the victim was a police officer on duty (an oddly placed #18 on the 41-item severity list).

Let us consider McCleskey's appeal before the Supreme Court; specifically, his attorneys made two claims: the first was that "the persistent race-of-victim disparities, which [Baldus's] studies identified after adjusting for all plausible legitimate aggravating and mitigating circumstances, provided a sufficient basis for invalidating McCleskey's death sentence under the equal-protection clause of the 14th Amendment" (Baldus, Woodworth, & Pulaski, 1992, p. 262). The second claim derived from the Eighth Amendment's clause that protects defendants from cruel and unusual punishments.

The Supreme Court rejected both these claims. In the majority opinion, Justice Lewis Powell chose to focus on any *intent* to discriminate; he wrote that no equal-protection violation occurred because McCleskey's attorneys did not prove "that the decision-makers in *his* case acted with discriminatory purpose," that no evidence was presented "specific to his own case that would support an inference that racial considerations played a part in his sentence" (*McCleskey v. Kemp,* 1987, pp. 292–293, italics in original). Justice Powell went on to write that statistical evidence of classwide, purposeful discrimination was not even relevant to equal-protection claims of racial discrimination in death-sentencing cases (*McCleskey v. Kemp,* 1987, pp. 296–297, quoted by Baldus, Woodworth, & Pulaski, 1992, p. 263).

Furthermore, the Court held that any suggestion of discrimination in the sentence given McCleskey was overcome by the presence of two factors that, by Georgia state statute, were cited as aggravating ones—the previously mentioned armed robbery and the victim's being a police officer. For the Court, each of these provided a sufficient basis for imposing a death penalty.

As an aside, it should be noted that the courts, including the U.S. Supreme Court, have regularly inferred intent to discriminate on the basis of statistical evidence; furthermore, they have endorsed jury decisions and employment discrimination rulings brought under Title VII of the Civil Rights Act of 1964 that rely on such data. (Some of the latter will be reviewed in chapter 13 on discrimination and the legal system.) Here, for McCleskey, paradoxically, the Court imposed a more severe burden of proof. (As Justice Blackmun noted in his dissenting opinion, one would have expected the Court to impose a less stringent burden of proof because in death-sentence cases, society's ultimate sanction is involved; *McCleskey v. Kemp,* 1987, pp. 347–348.)

Clearly, we have a conflict here. What are we to make of this conflict? First, we need to note that the goals of the researchers and the judges are different. Psychologists derive the truth from empirical proof; the fact that in a large number of cases, a significant racial disparity was demonstrated justified McCleskey's claim of lack of due process. That is, in psychology, the standard procedure is to focus on trends emerging from a number of observations. The scientific method seeks general laws that can be applied to specific cases.

But for the courts, other considerations were more salient. Court decisions are case specific, and here the statistically demonstrated pattern of racial bias in sentencing in previous cases was ignored. Also, the courts have issues to consider beyond the determination of truth. Justice Powell's opinion acknowledged that if McCleskey had been granted relief, it would have threatened all the previously sentenced capital cases in Georgia and disrupted the American death-sentencing system (Baldus, Woodworth, & Pulaski, 1992). At the time of the *McCleskey* decision, more than 3,000 death sentences had been imposed since its reinstatement in 1976, but only 100 of these prisoners had actually been executed.

Both positions could be defended. As psychologists, we have been socialized to believe that empirical results define the truth, that data have power. In contrast, Justice Powell concentrated on the specific case and noted that Warren McCleskey had been convicted of murder, he had killed a police officer, and he had been participating in an armed robbery. In effect, the Court asked: In a state that permits the death penalty, is this not a heinous crime? If any crime justifies such a sentence, does not this one?

Justice Powell's majority opinion in the *McCleskey* case also noted that any inequity in sentencing on the basis of race was, in his view, *properly* rectified by legislative action rather than by judicial fiat. He threw down the gauntlet to the U.S. Congress and state legislatures to pass laws if they felt a correction was needed. In 1994, the U.S. House of Representatives did just that. It passed, by a narrow margin, a bill that would permit people sentenced to death to challenge their sentence by using statistics of past racial discrimination in executions to show that their sentence reflected racial bias (Seelye, 1994). They might show, for example, that in the case of certain types of crimes, such as killing a police officer, only African Americans had been executed, or that the death penalty was given only to defendants whose victims were White. But the U.S. Senate opposed this bill, so it was not adopted.

A Civil Case: *Price Waterhouse v. Hopkins* (1989)

The previous example reflected a decision in a criminal case by the U.S. Supreme Court that refused to acknowledge racial discrimination. In *Price Waterhouse v. Hopkins* (1989), the Court acknowledged the presence of sex discrimination in a civil suit, after reviewing the testimony of a psychologist about the nature of stereotyping. But how much difference did the testimony of the psychologist make?

Ann Hopkins, in 1982, was in her fourth year as a very successful salesperson at Price Waterhouse, one of the nation's leading accounting firms. She had brought in business worth $25,000,000; her clients raved about her, and she had more billable hours than any other person proposed for partner for that year (Fiske, Bersoff, Borgida, Deaux, & Heilman, 1991). No one at the firm disputed her professional competence. But she was not made a partner—not that year and not the next year. Price Waterhouse apparently rejected her because of her heavy-handed managerial style and her "interpersonal skills problems"; she was described as "macho," lacking "social grace," and needing "a course at charm school." A colleague didn't like her use of profanity; another reportedly advised her that she would improve her chances if she would "walk more femininely, talk more femininely, dress more femininely, wear makeup, have her hair styled, and wear jewelry" (*Hopkins v. Price Waterhouse,* 1985, p. 1117). She was caught in a double-bind: Women were censured for being aggressive even though aggressiveness was, in reality, one of the job qualifications (Chamallas, 1990).

So Ann Hopkins took the firm to court, claiming sex discrimination and a violation of Title VII of the Civil Rights Act of 1964. The preceding information, though disturbing, was not enough; she had to demonstrate that the stereotypic remarks accounted for discrimination in the decision rejecting her as a partner. Thus, social psychologist Susan Fiske, of the University of Massachusetts at Amherst, was asked to testify as an expert witness. She agreed, because she felt the case fit the scientific literature on **sex stereotyping** in organizations to a striking degree.

An account by Fiske and her colleagues describes the nature of her testimony in the trial (called *Hopkins v. Price Waterhouse*); it "drew on both laboratory and field research to describe antecedent conditions that encourage stereotyping, indicators that reveal stereotyping, consequences of stereotyping for out-groups, and feasible remedies to prevent the intrusion of stereotyping into decision making. Specifically, she testified first that stereotyping is most likely to intrude when the target is an isolated, one- or few-of-a-kind individual in an otherwise homogeneous

environment. The person's solo or near-solo status makes the unusual category more likely to be a salient factor in decision making" (Fiske et al., 1991, p. 1050). Of 88 candidates proposed for partner in 1982, Ann Hopkins was a token woman; of 662 partners at Price Waterhouse, only 7 were women.

Among many relevant matters, Professor Fiske also testified that subjective judgments of interpersonal skills and collegiality—apparently essential in the partnership decision—are quite vulnerable to stereotypic biases, and decision makers should be alert to the possibility of stereotyping when they employ subjective criteria. She concluded that sexual stereotyping played a major role in the firm's decision to deny Hopkins a partnership.

In Price Waterhouse's decisions on partners, the opinions of people with limited hearsay information were given the same weight as the opinions of those who had more extensive and relevant contact with Ann Hopkins (Fiske, Bersoff, Borgida, Deaux, & Heilman, 1991, 1993), and Price Waterhouse had no policy prohibiting sex discrimination. As Fiske and her colleagues observed, "Consistent with this failure to establish organizational norms emphasizing fairness, overt expressions of prejudice were not discouraged" (Fiske et al., 1991, p. 1051). Professor Fiske, in her testimony, noted that many of Price Waterhouse's practices could be remedied if the firm applied psychological concepts and findings.

At the original trial, the presiding judge, Gerhard Gesell, expressed some frustration over the psychologist's testimony. He seemed to have great difficulty understanding what the psychologist was saying, and "at times he undermined her position by changing the meaning of her statements and then challenging her to explain herself more clearly" (Chamallas, 1990, p. 110). Some of his trial statements and his written opinion cause one to wonder if he appreciated the substance of Dr. Fiske's testimony; for example, he misunderstood the concept of a stereotype and seemed to view it as some disease or malady; he wondered if the partner who advised

Hopkins to act more femininely had been bitten by what he called the "stereotype bug" (quoted by Chamallas, 1990, p. 113).

But after considering all the evidence, Judge Gesell ruled in favor of Ann Hopkins's claim, writing that an "employer that treats [a] woman with [an] assertive personality in a different manner than if she had been a man is guilty of sex discrimination" (*Hopkins v. Price Waterhouse,* 1985, p. 1119). Price Waterhouse—not surprisingly—appealed Judge Gesell's decision and, in doing so, argued that the social psychologist's testimony was "sheer speculation" of "no evidentiary value" (*Price Waterhouse v. Hopkins,* 1987, p. 467). After Judge Gesell's decision was upheld by a three-judge panel of the U.S. Circuit Court of Appeals for the District of Columbia, Price Waterhouse asked the U.S. Supreme Court to review the case, and because various appellate court decisions in *Hopkins* and other similar cases had been in conflict, the Court accepted the case for review. Indeed, the American Psychological Association was one of the groups that filed an *amicus* ("friend of the court") brief for the consideration of the Court.

On May 1, 1989, the Supreme Court handed down its decision, voting 6 to 3 to uphold a significant portion of Judge Gesell's decision.[1] Specifically, the majority ruled that in such cases as these, "it is not permissible for employers to use discriminatory criteria, and they (not the plaintiff) must bear the burden of persuading the trier of fact that their decision would have been the same if no impermissible discrimination had taken place" (quoted by Fiske et al., 1991, p. 1054). However, the Court also ruled that Judge Gesell had held Price Waterhouse to too high a standard of proof (i.e., clear and convincing evidence) and that he should review the facts in light of a less stringent (preponderance of the evidence) standard, to determine if Price Waterhouse was still liable.

Thus it would appear that the testimony of a research psychologist had a significant impact on the judge's decision in a landmark case—a case for which a major aspect of the ruling was upheld by the Supreme Court. But some of the justices were hostile to Professor Fiske's message; in his dissenting opinion, Justice Anthony Kennedy questioned her ability to be fair, implying that Fiske would have reached the same conclusion *whenever* a woman was denied a promotion. Even the majority opinion by Justice William Brennan downplayed the impact of the expert witness's testimony; the majority opinion stated:

> Indeed, we are tempted to say that Dr. Fiske's expert testimony was merely icing on Hopkins' cake. It takes no special training to discern sex stereotyping in a description of an aggressive female employee as requiring "a course at charm school." Nor . . . does it require expertise in psychology to know that, if an employee's flawed "interpersonal skills" can be corrected by a soft-hued suit or a new shade of lipstick, perhaps it is the employee's sex and not her interpersonal skills that has drawn criticism. (*Price Waterhouse v. Hopkins,* 1989, p. 1793)

Fiske and her colleagues had the following reaction to this comment:

> One can interpret this comment in various ways; as dismissive, saying that the social science testimony was all common sense; as merely taking the social psychological expertise for granted; or as suggesting that one does not necessarily require expert witnesses to identify stereotyping when the evidence is egregious. (Fiske et al., 1991, p. 1054)

Although any of these is a possibility, none is congruent with a claim that the social science evidence really made a difference in the Court's opinion.

Furthermore, not all psychologists have endorsed the application of Fiske's conclusions (Barrett & Morris, 1993). Not only do judges disagree with each other (recall that the votes in the two cases described here were 5 to 4 and 6

---

[1] The majority opinion was written by Justice Brennan; others in the majority were Justices Blackmun, Marshall, Stevens, White, and O'Connor. The minority included Justices Kennedy, Rehnquist, and Scalia.

to 3—hardly ringing endorsements) but psychologists do, too. In fact, the lack of uniform agreement within the field creates problems for the establishment of agreed-upon procedures for forensic psychologists. For example, is there sufficient scientific evidence to justify a psychologist's testifying that a murder defendant's behavior reflected the battered woman syndrome (see chapter 7)? Are the data extensive enough and reliable enough for the American Psychological Association to submit an *amicus* brief arguing that adolescent females are mature enough to decide whether to have an abortion (which, in fact, the APA did)? These are just two examples of the acceptability of applying psychological knowledge to the legal system.

THE FUTURE OF THE RELATIONSHIP BETWEEN PSYCHOLOGY AND THE LAW

Courts have sometimes been sympathetic to psychological research; sometimes they have not. Can we detect why? And can we predict the future of this relationship? Tanford (1990) reviewed two types of theories of the interaction between social science and the law. One type predicts that the obstacles to use of social science research in the courts can be overcome, and that science will eventually assume a prominent role in legal policy-making. This view notes that modern Western culture has elevated science to a prominent position. In contrast, the other approach predicts that social science will not have much impact on the law in the near future. This position is based on the current reluctance of the courts to rely on empirical research. Tanford (1990) offered six reasons for this reluctance:

1. Judges are conservative and perceive social scientists to be liberal.
2. Judges are self-confident and do not believe that they need any assistance from non-

lawyers. For example, Justice Frankfurter once said, "I do not care what any . . . professor in sociology tells me" (quoted by Tanford, 1990, p. 1953).
3. Judges are human, and it is human nature to be unscientific.
4. Judges are ignorant of, inexperienced with, or do not understand empirical social science. Samuel R. Gross (1980), a law professor who argued the *Hovey* death-qualified jury case before the California Supreme Court (*Hovey v. Superior Court,* 1980), has proposed that "much of the abuse that social science has suffered in the courts is a product of nothing more sinister than ignorance" (p. 10).
5. Judges perceive science as a threat to their power and prestige.
6. Law and social science are rival systems with competing logics (Tanford, 1990, p. 152).

Any of these reasons for reluctance to accept forensic psychology can surface in a specific case. Chapter 2 examines some of the roles for psychologists in the legal system and some of the ways that psychologists may abuse their opportunities, thus contributing to the conflict between the two disciplines.

SUMMARY

Forensic psychology may be broadly defined as any application of psychological knowledge or methods to a task faced by the legal system. This definition implies that forensic psychologists can come from many backgrounds in psychology—clinical, experimental, social, developmental—and play many roles: researcher and educator, consultant to law enforcement, trial consultant, evaluator and expert witness, and consultant to judges through the presentation of legal briefs. But other definitions of forensic psychology have tried to limit it to clinical applications of psychology to the legal system. Current training programs reflect these diverse definitions.

In their attempts to apply their knowledge to the legal system, forensic psychologists need to be aware of the history of the relationship and the conflicting values between the scientific and legal approaches. In the 100-year-old history of the relationship, influences can be traced from criminology and from experimental psychology. Hugo Münsterberg, a professor and director of the Psychological Laboratory at Harvard University in the first two decades of the 20th century, may be considered the founder of forensic psychology because of his research (on such contemporary topics as eyewitness accuracy and memory), his influential articles for the lay public, and his involvement in several prominent trials. But he was only one of a number of experimental psychologists who were active in applying their knowledge to the courts during the period from 1900 to 1920. For various reasons, the relationship between the two fields languished for 50 years, until the mid-1970s. Since that time, there has been an explosion of research and a similar expansion in the application of psychological concepts and findings to such diverse legal issues as the battered woman syndrome, the use of police interrogations to elicit confessions, and the selection of juries.

But psychology has not always had the effect it has sought. Two court decisions, in the cases of *McCleskey v. Kemp* and *Price Waterhouse v. Hopkins,* were described to illustrate the conflict between psychology and the law with regard to their bases for decision making. Some conflicts are fundamental, dealing with the nature of truth and reality. Furthermore, the legal system is sometimes uninformed about, and hence unsympathetic to, the methods used in psychology. It is the job of forensic psychology to see that this changes.

KEY TERMS

aggravating versus mitigating factors
amicus brief
Brandeis briefs
deduction
empirical approach
forensic psychology
induction
mediator
precedent
reliability
replicability
sex stereotyping
"specialty" designation
spousal rape
stare decisis
subjective expectation of privacy
trial consultant
values

INFOTRAC®
COLLEGE EDITION

InfoTrac College Edition is a FREE, powerful, online learning resource, consisting of full-text articles from thousands of journals and periodicals. With each new copy of *Forensic Psychology,* Second Edition, you receive four months of free access to the InfoTrac College Edition database. By doing a simple keyword search (try using the Key Terms from the list above), you can quickly generate a list of relevant articles from thousands of possibilities and can select articles to read, explore, and print for reference or further study. InfoTrac College Edition's continuously updated collection of articles can be useful for doing reading and writing assignments that reach beyond the pages of this text!

SUGGESTED READINGS

Bartol, C. R., & Bartol, A. M. (1999). History of forensic psychology. In A. K. Hess & I. B. Weiner (Eds.), *Handbook of forensic psychology* (2nd ed., pp. 3–23). New York: John Wiley.

A readable history of the field that reviews developments in five major topics: courtroom testimony, cognitive and personality assessment, correctional psychology, police psychology, and criminal psychology.

Hess, A. K., & Weiner, I. B. (Eds.). (1999). *Handbook of forensic psychology* (2nd ed.). New York: John Wiley.

An updated collection of comprehensive and detailed reviews of many of the topics explored in this book, including lie detection, hypnosis, testifying in court, assessing competency, and police consultation.

Lyons, A., & Truzzi, M. (1991). *The blue sense: Psychic detectives and crime.* New York: Mysterious Press.

An analysis of the use by police of psychics to help solve crimes. While the book exposes the tricks of charlatans, it is sympathetic to the use of paranormal techniques in crime investigation.

Melton, G. B., Huss, M. T., & Tomkins, A. J. (1999). Training in forensic psychology and the law. In A. K. Hess & I. B. Weiner (Eds.), *Handbook of forensic psychology* (2nd ed., pp. 700-720). New York: John Wiley.

A chapter of special value to those considering further training in forensic psychology. The following models for professional training are described and critiqued: joint Ph.D.–J.D. programs, Ph.D. specialty programs, a Ph.D. minor, and postdoctoral programs. Internship opportunities are also described.

Münsterberg, H. (1908). *On the witness stand.* Garden City, NY: Doubleday.

Worth extracting from stuffy library stacks, to determine just how prescient it is for the forensic psychology of the 21st century.

Nietzel, M. T., & Dillehay, R. C. (1986). *Psychological consultation in the courtroom.* New York: Pergamon Press.

Written by two forensic psychologists with extensive "hands-on" experience, this book not only illustrates a number of activities but also considers professional and ethical dilemmas.

2

Forensic Psychologists:
Roles and Responsibilities

THE MULTITUDE OF FORENSIC PSYCHOLOGY ROLES AND ACTIVITIES

Chapter 1 introduced four people whose activities qualify them to be called forensic psychologists, even though their day-to-day work dramatically differs. The activities of these four people by no means encompass the entire scope of forensic psychology. Consider the following two examples, both of which demonstrate that **evaluation** is a primary responsibility of many forensic psychologists with clinical psychology backgrounds, who act as evaluators and potential expert witnesses (discussed later in this chapter).

Neuropsychologists engage in forensic activities when they examine a criminal defendant to determine if he or she has damage to the right hemisphere of the brain, affecting judgment and impulse control (Dywan, Kaplan, & Pirozzolo, 1991; Pirozzolo, Funk, & Dywan, 1991). In their forensic capacity, neuropsychologists may carry out specific or comprehensive evaluation of brain functioning, and may testify as expert witnesses with regard to what they find. A number of tests have been developed to assess normal versus impaired brain functioning, and several handbooks and textbooks review these procedures, including those by Lezak (1995), Kolb and Whishaw (1990), Goldstein and Incagnoli (1997), and Adams, Parsons, and Culbertson (1996). (This last book includes a chapter by Adams and Rankin, 1996, specifically on forensic applications of neuropsychology.)

The assessment of other, non-neuropsychological characteristics of defendants is also a task for forensic psychology. As an example, it might be important to know the extent to which a criminal defendant could or should be classified as "psychopathic." This could have an impact on sentencing, as it might relate to the likelihood of the commission of future offenses. Although perhaps 1% of the general population may be classified as psychopaths, they comprise 15% to 25% of the prison population "and are responsible for a markedly disproportionate amount of

the serious crime, violence, and social distress in every society" (Hare, 1996, p. 26). **Psychopathy** reflects the following characteristics: impulsivity, a lack of guilt or remorse, pathological lying and manipulativeness, and a continual willingness to violate social norms. Forensic psychologists have sought to develop instruments to assess psychopathy; among the most prominent is the Hare Psychopathy Checklist—Revised (or PCL-R), developed by Robert Hare; it employs a 20-item rating scale, completed on the basis of a semistructured interview and on other information about the subject (Hare, 1991; Fulero, 1995; see chapter 6). Characteristics to be rated by the psychologist include lack of realistic long-term goals and callous lack of empathy; each item is rated on a 3-point scale, according to specific criteria.

In conjunction with all their roles, temptations exist for forensic psychologists to go beyond the limits of their expertise. We will discuss the ethical responsibilities of psychologists as they respond to the demands of the legal system. In doing so, we will also take a look at the five basic roles for forensic psychologists: researcher, law enforcement consultant, trial consultant, evaluator/expert witness, and consultant on *amicus* briefs presented to appellate courts.

SPECIFIC ROLES: RESEARCHER

Researchers in all fields of psychology share a common scientific method. Hypotheses are generated, tested empirically, interpreted statistically, and then shared with others in the scientific community through the process of peer review and publication (for an excellent review of the scientific method in the context of eyewitness identification, see Cutler and Penrod, 1995, chapter 4).

In forensic psychology research, ethical questions arise as they do in other areas of psychology. For example, most would agree that it would not be appropriate to commit actual crimes in front of test subjects. But what sort of scenarios can eyewitness researchers ethically create? Similarly, jury researchers interested in pretrial publicity effects may do survey research on actual members of a jury pool in a particular case. What should the researchers do to ensure that the identities of the participants in their research remain anonymous? Fortunately, there is guidance in answering these questions. Researchers in forensic psychology, just as in other areas of psychological research (assuming they are APA members), are subject to the American Psychological Association Code of Ethics (most recently revised in 2002 and published in the *American Psychologist,* July 2002). In addition, forensic psychology researchers will look to the Specialty Guidelines for Forensic Psychologists (Committee on Ethical Guidelines for Forensic Psychologists, 1991).

SPECIFIC ROLES: CONSULTANT TO LAW ENFORCEMENT

Another important role for forensic psychologists is assisting law enforcement (see chapter 3). Clearly, ethical issues may arise during such work. Foremost among these is the question of who the client is (see Brodsky, 1973, for a prescient and cogent discussion of ethical issues). For example, when a police officer is referred for psychological treatment or counseling, is the client the officer or the department (for purposes of confidentiality)? Ethical issues may also arise in the roles that forensic psychologists have with regard to personnel selection, promotion, and training.

SPECIFIC ROLES: THE TRIAL CONSULTANT

Increasingly, trial attorneys are relying on psychologists and other social scientists to aid them in preparing for and carrying out a trial. This role has variously been called a **trial consultant,** a litigation consultant, or a jury consultant (see Fulero & Penrod, 1990). Some trial consultants have doctoral degrees, some have master's degrees, and some have bachelor's degrees. But it is important to note that at present, not a single state licenses or certifies trial consultants, so it is actually possible for *anyone* with any level of training to hang up a shingle and proclaim himself or herself a "trial consultant." As Jeffrey Frederick, a long-time jury consultant, has noted, "All you need is a client" (quoted by Mandelbaum, 1989, p. 18).

What do trial consultants do? A firm of trial consultants (which might be a single consultant with a small support staff) is hired by a law firm to assist in identifying the major issues in a case, determine if there has been excessive pretrial publicity in the case (see Posey & Dahl, 2002), prepare witnesses for trial, and advise in jury selection. "We try to give the trial team the perspective of the jurors, and the things we find are often counterintuitive," stated Greg Mazares, president of Litigation Sciences, Inc. (quoted in Lawson, 1994, p. B14). For example, Litigation Sciences worked on the case of a child who fell from an electrical tower and was injured. His mother sued the power company for damages. In assisting the power company's defense team, the trial consultants found that, contrary to expectations, possible jurors who were parents "sympathized with the defendant company because they understood parental responsibility and what it takes to control a child" (Lawson, 1994, p. B14). Trial consultants also may participate in continuing education seminars offered frequently to improve lawyers' negotiation, jury selection, and trial presentation skills (Beisecker, 1992). At such sessions, they may try to disabuse trial attorneys of the belief that successful jury selection requires nothing but the application of intuition (see Fulero & Penrod, 1990).

Chapter 12 will describe the duties of trial consultants in detail. At this point, note that trial consultants are most often hired by law firms representing clients involved in large civil trials, so the types of cases they handle do not cover the spectrum. It used to be rare that a trial consultant would work in a criminal trial, simply because one side didn't have the resources and the other side didn't have the inclination to hire one. But the pattern is shifting; the trial of William Kennedy Smith for rape, the trial of the four Los Angeles police officers charged with beating Rodney King, and that of Damian Williams and Henry Watson for the attack on truck driver Reginald Denny all used consultants. In the latter trial, Los Angeles County approved the hiring of (and paying for) a $175-per-hour trial consultant to assist the defendants, because they were indigent (Cox, 1993).

One type of ethical problem emerges because trial consultants are not only social scientists; they may have to be entrepreneurs, too. Some (though not all) advertise and market what they have to offer. Larger firms distribute glossy brochures extolling their various services. These firms also have a number of fixed costs, including support staff salaries, office rental, and computer costs, that persist regardless of the number of clients they have (see Strier, 1999, for a thoughtful discussion of trial consulting in terms of both efficacy and ethical issues).

Conflicts may arise between trial consultants and their employer-attorneys. These can be divided into procedural and substantive conflicts. With regard to procedures, consultants must always remember that they are employed by the attorneys, and thus it is the attorneys who are ultimately responsible for making decisions involving the case. For example, a trial consultant may believe that questions about prospective jurors' reading habits or television-viewing preferences are diagnostic of the jurors' biases regardless of the issue at trial. The attorney, however, may feel such questions are inappropriate invasions of privacy (or, conversely, it may be the attorney who wants such questions while the trial consultant believes them to be inappropriate; see Posey and Dahl, 2002). Substantive conflicts can be generated over any topic: the appropriate "theory" of the case, how witnesses should present themselves, which prospective jurors should

be excused, which witnesses should be presented first (see chapter 12).

The dual occupational nature of the consultant—applied scientist plus businessperson—makes for challenging ethical responsibilities. As an applied researcher, the consultant must follow the standard guidelines for ethical research; these take the form of a list of moral imperatives:

1. Thou shalt not fake data.
2. Thou shalt not plagiarize.
3. Thou shalt not draw false conclusions from thy data.

Furthermore, the consultant has the moral responsibility not to break the law, even if the consultant's client wishes it. Trial consultant Hale Starr and attorney Kathleen Kauffman posed this question: What do you do if you know a witness is lying about important case facts, but the attorney wants you to help the witness appear as credible as possible? Starr's response included the following: "If we believe that the witness is lying, then we should inform the lawyer. . . . If they're saying, 'Is it okay to teach someone how to lie, credibly,' the answer to that is: that's not our job and that's not what we do" (Starr & Kauffman, 1993, p. 5).

The guidelines for professional standards of the American Society of Trial Consultants (American Society of Trial Consultants, 1998) urge consultants not to compile win-loss records. Consultants should not suggest that their services will inevitably help win a case for their client, because many events can intervene between preparation for the trial and the jury verdict (Mandelbaum, 1989). Despite such admonitions, the conflicting roles—scientist versus entrepreneur—may tempt the trial consultant to sound as if he or she is bragging; here is one example: "Because of our experience and our proprietary research procedures, Litigation Sciences has been associated with the winning side of the most prominent and highly publicized cases that have gone to trial. These have included assisting our clients to obtain defense verdicts in difficult product liability, antitrust, toxic tort, contract, securities, and wrongful termination cases. We have also been associated with the largest plaintiff verdicts ever returned in intellectual property, securities, and contract/tortious interference cases" (Litigation Sciences, 1988, p. 3).

A fundamental principle within the scientific community is the sharing of data and ideas. Researchers do not ordinarily maintain a proprietary interest in their findings or terminology; in contrast, Litigation Sciences, early in its brochure, notes "The terms 'Psychological Anchor, Polarization Profile, and Shadow Jury' are trademarks of Litigation Sciences" (1988, p. 2). According to Hale Starr, founder of another trial consulting organization (quoted by Mandelbaum, 1989, p. 18), Litigation Sciences sent out letters to various consultants and researchers telling them to cease using the term *shadow jury* because Litigation Sciences had trademarked it. Fulero and Penrod (1990) have noted that by and large, trial consultants have viewed their work as "proprietary" and thus have not made their data and methods available for scientific peer review, which is critical for scientific reliability and acceptance. Fulero and Penrod (1990) also called on trial consultants to make their data available for scientific scrutiny.

Confidentiality is a particular concern for trial consultants, who need to avoid unreasonable intrusion into the privacy of others, including members of focus groups or mock juries. It is essential that trial consultants recognize that all information about a particular case remains private and confidential. For example, in carrying out surveys, trial consultants must assure respondents of confidentiality, or many of them will not participate. Without such participation, trial consultants cannot obtain a representative sample. Promises of confidentiality also immunize the results against inaccuracies or bias in the information given. Yet there may be problems in keeping such information confidential, as lawyers for the other side seek to undermine the results of the survey (see Posey and Dahl, 2002, for a discussion of such issues).

Codes of several professional organizations that survey respondents carry caveats, such as the following: "Unless the respondent waives confidentiality for specified uses, we shall hold as privileged and confidential all information that might identify a respondent with his or her responses" (quoted by Hubbert, 1992, p. 3). For example, the National Jury Project, a trial-consulting organization, routinely removes and destroys all respondent-identifiable information from the questionnaires, telephone-listing sheets, and any other survey documents, after the survey is completed (Hubbert, 1992). A conflict arises when the results of the survey are presented at court and a judge wants the names of the interviewees and proof that subjects were in fact interviewed and that the results are accurate representations of responses. On such occasions, a reinterview may take place to determine whether the subjects had been interviewed before and whether they felt coerced in any way (Hubbert, 1992). A court-appointed witness or notary public may observe the reinterview. But it has been the experience of the National Jury Project that when its policy is fully explained in court, the results are never rejected.

SPECIFIC ROLES: FORENSIC EVALUATOR AND EXPERT WITNESS

Forensic psychologists may be called on to evaluate parties in criminal or civil cases and to provide expertise in court. Other than a doctoral degree and a license to practice, is there any way to tell who has a special interest in forensic psychology? The American Board of Professional Psychology (ABPP; see www.abfp.com, the board's website, for more information) offers a Diplomate in Forensic Psychology, indicating the recipient as being at the highest level of excellence in his or her field of forensic competence. The American Board of Forensic Psychology was established in 1978 to protect the consumer of forensic psychology; since 1985, it has operated as a specialty of the American Board of Professional Psychology, Inc. Other, so-called vanity licenses and diplomates should be considered very carefully, as they do not require the same levels of training and experience that the American Board of Professional Psychology demands (Golding, 1999). Regardless, different types of ethical issues may surface in the roles of evaluator and of expert witness.

Evaluation and Assessment

Forensic psychologists asked by attorneys or courts to do assessments specifically for purposes of criminal or civil cases must understand, and make sure that the parties understand, that such evaluations are not "therapy" and, as a result, anything said during such an assessment does not have the same confidentiality as nonforensic counseling or assessment. Indeed, when a person is evaluated for purposes of a legal case, anything that is said or done will be open to scrutiny in a forensic report or in expert testimony. Psychologists who work in forensic contexts are required

to inform the parties of this fact (see APA Code of Ethics, 2002, Section 4.02(a), and Specialty Guidelines for Forensic Psychologists, Section IV-E). Box 2-1 illustrates the difficult issue of confidentiality in another way, by focusing on a particular case, that of the Menendez brothers, who were accused of killing their parents. In that case, the confidentiality issue arose during the court case, but the therapy was instituted before any forensic purpose was contemplated.

Another ethical issue that arises in the context of assessment and testimony is the "dual relationship" problem. A psychologist who is evaluating a divorced couple for child custody accepts an invitation to have dinner with the wife. Another psychologist who is seeing a woman as a psychotherapy client attempts to initiate a romantic relationship with her. These are examples of **dual relationships** that can lead to ethical problems. A less explicit temptation occurs when the forensic psychologist is engaged in more than one type of professional activity with the same individuals, such as a business relationship along with therapy.

When a child reports having been sexually abused, the court may request a psychologist to

---

> ### BOX 2-1
> ## Confidentiality and Psychotherapists
>
> In most states, the psychotherapist-client privilege of confidentiality ends if the therapist believes the client is "dangerous to himself or to the person or property of another and that disclosure of the communication is necessary to prevent the threatened danger" (see Fulero, 1988; Reinhold, 1990, p. B9). But what of evidence of past crimes? Is confidentiality provided? Should it be? In the famous case of Lyle and Erik Menendez, police were informed by Ms. Judalon Smyth, a former "friend" (and patient) of the brothers' psychotherapist, Beverly Hills psychologist L. Jerome Oziel, that tapes existed on which the brothers had confessed to their parents' murders, and that at Dr. Oziel's request, she had made transcriptions of those tapes. So a further question arose: Can psychologist-client privilege be broken by the presence of a third party?
>
> In 1992, two years after the brothers' arrest, the California Supreme Court suppressed the tape from evidence as an invasion of psychologist-client privilege. But when the first trial began in late 1993, the brothers presented their mental state as an issue. The trial judge ruled that the privilege was waived and that the tape could be introduced as evidence. The judge acknowledged that his ruling had little precedent and that the issue was "a unique situation not addressed by any other case in any other court" (quoted by Associated Press, 1993, p. A7). Because of the disclosures made by the woman, Dr. Oziel was stripped of his license to practice psychology in California (CNN, January 3, 1997, http://www.cnn.com/US/9701/03/menendez.psychologist/). (The 1993 trial ended in a hung jury; the Menendez brothers were later retried and convicted of first-degree murder in 1996, and sentenced to life without parole.)

do an evaluation. If the psychologist has served as a psychotherapist for the child or someone in the child's family, it is inappropriate for the same psychologist to evaluate the claims of abuse. The forensic evaluator has to maintain a stance of absolute impartiality, while the therapist often serves as an advocate for his or her clients (Greenberg & Shuman, 1997; Lawlor, 1998). A similar temptation to fill two competing roles may occur in child custody decisions (see chapter 9), or in situations in which a psychologist both treats individual clients in sex offender therapy at the local jail and evaluates their status as continued sexual predators.

Evaluators must also guard against the strong temptation to skew their evaluation results to what they know the referral source would like to hear, and instead must "call them as they see them." (see Diamond, 1959, for an early and provocative discussion of this issue). Box 2-2 illustrates this issue nicely, by showing an actual letter from an attorney to a forensic psychologist.

Expert Witnessing

During a trial, each side may ask the judge to permit expert witnesses to testify, as part of its presentation of the evidence. In contrast to other witnesses (called **fact witnesses**), who can only testify about what they have observed or what they know as fact, expert witnesses may express opinions, for they are presumed to possess special knowledge about a topic, knowledge that the average juror does not have. The judge must be convinced that the testimony that any expert will present reflects the requisite knowledge, skill, or experience and that the testimony will aid in resolving the dispute and leading jurors toward the truth.

It has been estimated that more than 20% of the cases before the federal courts have a strong scientific or technological component (Slind-Flor, 1994). The topics for which a psychologist may be called as an expert witness are extensive; Box 2-3, reprinted from Nietzel and Dillehay

BOX 2-2
Letter Sent to a Psychologist by an Attorney

A forensic psychologist recently gave us a letter that he received from an attorney. The psychologist, whose background is clinical psychology, often did forensic assessments upon referral from attorneys who represented clients seeking eligibility for Social Security Disability payment. What follows is the edited and sanitized text of the letter, sent in 2001:

Dear Dr. _____:

I wanted to write you a note to tell you that there have been some developments occur during psychological evaluations. It has always been difficult for me to convince clients to come to _____ to see you because of the distance.

The past few reports from you have not been good. I'm not being critical but I have sent the same people who I sent to you to other psychologists with different results.

In other words I understand that you have to call things as you see them and I'm not criticizing you for that but I also have a duty to my clients to try to win their cases if I can. Most of the people who I represent are destitute and have nowhere else to turn. While I don't expect any of my medical providers to break the

law for me I do expect them to bend the rules to some extent or to at least state things as favorably as possible. I know that you know what I'm trying to say.

We have recently started using Bill _____. Bill _____ does not have your credentials and he is not as good as you are but I am getting good reports from him. Also, he comes to _____ and sees clients here so that the client is not inconvenienced by the travel. Mr. _____ has probably seen somewhere between seven and ten people for me over the past six months and every report has been favorable. You may read into that what you will but you can see what position that puts me in.

When you consider everything it doesn't look good right now. I wanted to write you a note to explain what was going on. If you have any ideas on correcting the situation I would be happy to listen. We continue to want you to see our clients but again we have to give the client an option. Your report is the most desirable but it's also the most difficult to obtain. Hopefully we will be able to send some more folks down your way in the near future.

Sincerely yours,

(1986), describes several. Some topics reflect forms of clinical expertise, and some reflect forms of social, experimental, cognitive, or developmental psychology expertise.

In the past, an expert witness primarily served the court rather than the litigants (Lands-man, 1995). Today, most expert witnesses are recruited by trial attorneys and only rarely by the judge, even though Federal Rule of Evidence 706 explicitly allows the court to use its own expert ("The court may on its own motion or on the motion of any party enter an

---

BOX 2-3
Examples of Topics for Psychologists as Expert Witnesses

Insanity defense	What is the relationship between the defendant's mental condition at the time of the alleged offense and the defendant's responsibility for the crime with which the defendant is charged?
Competence to stand trial	Does the defendant have an adequate understanding of the legal proceedings? Is he or she able to work with his or her attorney?
Sentencing	What is the appropriate disposition? What is the risk of reoffense?
Eyewitness identification	What are the factors that affect the accuracy of eyewitnesses?
Trial procedure	What effects do pretrial and/or trial procedures have?
Civil commitment	Does a mentally ill person present an immediate danger or threat to self or others that requires treatment in a hospital setting?
Psychological damages in civil cases	What psychological consequences has an individual suffered as a result of tortious conduct? How treatable are these consequences? To what extent are the psychological problems attributable to a preexisting condition?
Psychological autopsies	In equivocal cases, do the personality and circumstances under which a person died indicate a likely mode of death?
Negligence and product liability	How do environmental factors and human perceptual abilities affect an individual's use of a product or his or her ability to take certain precautions in its use?
Trademark litigation	Is a certain product name or trademark confusingly similar to a competitor's? Are advertising claims likely to mislead consumers?
Class action suits	What psychological evidence is there that effective treatment is being denied or that certain testing procedures are discriminatory against minorities in the schools or in the workplace?
Guardianship and conservatorship	Does an individual possess the necessary mental ability to make decisions about living conditions, financial matters, health, etc.?
Child custody	What psychological factors will affect the best interests of the child whose custody is in dispute? What consequences are these factors likely to have on the family?
Adoption and termination of parental rights	What psychological factors will affect the best interests of the child whose custody or visitation schedule is in dispute?
Professional malpractice	Did defendant's professional conduct fail to meet the standard of care owed to plaintiffs?
Social issues in litigation	What are the effects of pornography, violence, spouse abuse, etc., on the behavior of a defendant who claims that his or her misconduct was caused by one of these influences?

Source: From *Psychological Consultation in the Courtroom,* by M. T. Nietzel and R. C. Dillehay, 1986, pp. 100–101. Published by Allyn and Bacon, Boston, MA. Copyright © 1986 by Pearson Education. Reprinted by permission of the publisher.

order to show cause why expert witnesses should not be appointed, and may request the parties to submit nominations. The court may appoint any expert witnesses agreed upon by the parties, and may appoint expert witnesses of its own selection"). Regardless of who proffers the expert, it is the judge who must determine the expert witness's acceptability. The criteria used by the attorneys and by the judge are not in direct opposition, but are quite different from each other. And, sometimes psychologists may be tempted to "sell themselves" to each, if they want to serve as experts.

As far as the presiding judge is concerned, the expert witness at trial "is cast in the role of a witness, not as one of the advocates and not as a decision maker" (Saks, 1992, p. 191). As with other witnesses, experts must promise to "tell the truth, the whole truth, and nothing but the truth." At the same time, however, judges are dubious about what experts have to say (Saks & Van Duizend, 1983, cited in Saks, 1992). One decision by a court of appeals is typical: "Hired experts, who generally are highly compensated—and by the party on whose behalf they are testifying—are not notably disinterested" (*Tagatz v. Marquette University*, 1988, p. 1042, quoted by Saks, 1992, p. 194).

And, at least sometimes, judges' concerns are warranted. Every issue of legal periodicals, such as the *National Law Journal*, carries classified advertisements offering services by expert witnesses, and some seem to reflect sympathy with one side. For example, an advertisement by a neurologist reflected his ability to "quantify subtle brain damage not seen in MRI and CT" ("Closed head injuries," 1994).

As noted in Box 2-4, not only judges are critical of expert witnesses. Several advocates of tort reform, including former Vice President Dan Quayle (1992) and especially Peter Huber in his book *Galileo's Revenge* (1991), have claimed that **"junk science"** in the form of scientific "experts" hired by "unscrupulous plaintiffs' attorneys [are] responsible for the awarding of millions of dollars each year against blameless corporations" (Landsman, 1995, p. 131). It should be

noted that Huber has not been without his critics (see Chesebro, 1993, and Faigman, Porter, & Saks, 1994); chapter 12 reviews some of Huber's claims about the biases of jurors in civil trials.

Conflict is inevitable when expert witnesses are invited into the courtroom. As Saks (1992) observed, in the courtroom, experts "control" the knowledge of their fields; they determine how to conceptualize and organize the material and what to emphasize. But judges and lawyers control the case, including just what part of the expert's store of information they consider to be relevant. Thus, "the paradigms of the legal process and virtually any field of knowledge are almost assured to be in conflict with each other" (Saks, 1992, p. 185). If a trial attorney concludes that his or her preliminary choice for an expert witness is unsatisfactory, that expert can be dismissed prior to trial and another one selected. Furthermore, expert witnesses often learn the "facts" of the case from the attorneys who hired them, teachers who have a very particular agenda (Saks, 1992).

A second conflict concerns the role of the expert witness. We saw in chapter 1 that Hugo Münsterberg did not hesitate to take sides; he played the role of advocate. In contrast, contemporary psychologists have been trained to be impartial scientists. Which role is appropriate? Elizabeth Loftus (Loftus & Ketcham, 1991) posed it this way:

> Should a psychologist in a court of law act as an advocate for the defense or an impartial educator? My answer to that question, if I am completely honest, is *both*. If I believe in his innocence with all my heart and soul, then I probably can't help but become an advocate of sorts. (p. 238, italics in original)

As John Brigham responded, "Loftus's implication that one will become an advocate could prove destructive in the creative hands of an aggressive attorney who is seeking to destroy an impartial expert witness's credibility" (1992, p. 529). Furthermore, in surveys by Kassin, Ellsworth, and Smith (1989) and Kassin, Tubb, Hosch, and Memon (2001), eyewitness experts said that they

BOX 2-4
Are Psychologists "Whores of the Court?"

With its bright yellow jacket and its provocative title—*Whores of the Court*—splashed across the entire cover, Margaret Hagen's book was bound to attract attention. But it is the book's contents that have generated the strongest reaction. For Dr. Hagen, an experimental psychologist on the faculty of Boston University, the whores are those forensic psychologists, psychiatrists, and social workers who mislead judges and juries about child sexual abuse, insanity, psychological disability, and a variety of other topics, leading to the book's subtitle, *The Fraud of Psychiatric Testimony and the Rape of American Justice*.

Those concerned with the powerful temptations of forensic psychology will find much to applaud in the book. Hagen reflected the caution that should be the basis of forensic applications when she questioned whether mental health professionals can distinguish between real victims of post-traumatic stress disorder and those who fake symptoms. She described on page 262 how a professional staff member at a trauma clinic testified that no one could fake traumatic memories or fool psychiatric tests. She has been justifiably critical of psychologists who serve as hired guns in child custody disputes.

But many believe that Hagen weakened her case by overreaction, exaggeration, and stereotyping. Saul Kassin (1998a), in a thoughtful review, summarized:

> Underlying much of Hagen's attack are three underlying themes, or stereotypic portraits, of forensic clinical psychologists. One is that they are simply not competent on the basis of science (not to mention their lack of education in such areas as neuroscience, learning, memory, development, and behavior in social groups) to testify as they do. Second is that many clinical psychologists are driven by missionary liberal motives . . . The third theme is that

forensic clinical psychologists are economically motivated by the almighty dollar . . . This last motive is what gives rise to the image of psychologists as "whores" of the court. (p. 322)

Some of Hagen's statements are wildly divergent from our experiences as expert witnesses; for example, she wrote:

> For the whole clinical psychological profession in whatever guise, the increase in power and prestige in the civil litigation arena has been dizzying. Just think of it. Judges genuflecting before your sagacious testimony, and changing the law to fit your word. . . . It is a compelling picture of a powerful profession flexing its muscles as never before. (1997, p. 255)

We cannot recall a judge "genuflecting"—to the contrary, our experience is that other, less complimentary types of judicial nonverbal behavior have been sharply pointed in our direction. Finally, another review of Hagen's book (Fulero, 1997), noted that she committed precisely the same mistakes that she attributed to forensic psychologists:

> I agree here that while Hagen's essential point is well-taken—that is, a number of psychological experts are offered in courts to testify about shaky theories, questionable ideas, and conclusions without solid empirical evidence—the manner in which this point is presented "throws out the baby with the bathwater," obscuring valid comments about the proper types and uses of psychological expert testimony with anecdotes, errors, flaming over-generalizations, and inflammatory charges. Further, the presentation of the essential point in such a manner will actually make it more difficult to rein in the very excesses Hagen deplores. (p. 10)

were as willing to testify for the prosecution as for the defense, if asked (see chapter 10 for more on this subject).

In 1986, a psychic testified in court that a CAT scan had caused her to lose her psychic powers, and a physician—testifying as an expert witness—backed her claim. The jury awarded her $1 million in damages. (The award was later overturned.) The expert witness in a trial has a great opportunity to influence that is only

accentuated by the fact that "it is virtually impossible to prosecute an expert witness for perjury" (*Sears v. Rutishauser*, 1984, p. 212). Michael Saks concluded that an expert witness who manages to overlook contrary findings or who commits errors "still is likely to remain safe from any formal penalty" (1992, p. 193). This includes protection from civil liability. Testimony given in court is privileged; "a witness may say whatever he or she likes under oath, and no private remedies are available to persons who may be harmed as a result" (Saks, 1992, p. 193). Saks has described an incredible case (reflected in three court decisions: *In re Imbler*, 1963; *Imbler v. Craven*, 1969; and *Imbler v. Pachtman*, 1976): An object was offered as evidence linking the defendant to a crime. This object had three different fingerprints on it, but the fingerprint expert testifying for the prosecution reported only the two that were the defendant's. (The defendant was convicted and sentenced to death; the third print was only revealed later.) Was the expert deliberately deceitful or only incompetent? Unless evidence for dishonesty exists, the court must conclude that the defendant was "only" incompetent.

Suppose that an expert witness, at the end of extended testimony, looks at the jury intently and says:

"I guess you noticed that I withheld some information from the court, stretched other information, and offered an opinion that sounded more certain than our field's knowledge really permits. I did that because I am committed to making the world a better place, and I think it will be better if the court reaches the outcome I want to see in the case." (Saks, 1992, pp. 187–188)

Such actions do happen, even if they are not acknowledged by the experts, who may disregard contradictory evidence or exaggerate their own credentials. Every expert witness must consider this question: Do I tell the court things that will undercut my own seemingly authoritative knowledge (Saks, 1992)? And, as is considered in detail later in this chapter, every expert must make a personal decision about what the standard should be for reporting on a particular finding or the validity of a specific diagnostic tool.

Every expert witness must decide how to resolve the central dilemma of "relating his or her field's knowledge to the cause at stake in the litigation" (Saks, 1992, p. 190). Is one loyal to one's field of expertise or to the outcome of the case? Saks (1992) identified three ways to resolve this conflict:

1. The mere conduit-educator: As a **conduit-educator,** the expert regards his or her own field as the first priority; the thinking might go like this:

"My first duty is to share the most faithful picture of my field's knowledge with those who have been assigned the responsibility to make the decisions. To do this may be to be a mere technocrat, rather than a complete human being concerned with the moral implications of what I say and with the greatest good of society. The central difficulty of this role is whether it is all right for me to contribute hard-won knowledge to causes I would just as soon see lose." (Saks, 1992, p. 189)

2. The philosopher-ruler/advocate: If the expert witness views himself or herself as a kind of **philosopher-ruler/advocate,** the oath of telling "the whole truth" is of less concern. Hans described it as follows:

Some experts chose a legal-adversary stance, in which they volunteered only research evidence that supported their side, de-emphasized or omitted the flaws in the data, or refrained from discussing opposing evidence. In the words of one expert: "I understand the partisan nature of the courtroom and I realized that I would be on the stand arguing for a position without also presenting evidence that might be contrary to my . . . side. But, you see, that didn't bother me, because I knew that the other side was also doing that." (Hans, 1989, p. 312)

3. The "hired gun": Although somewhat similar to the second role, **hired guns** work in the service of their employer's values rather than trying to advance their own (Saks, 1992). The motivation is to help the person who hired the expert. The American Psychological Association's ethical guidelines (APA, 2002) are clear on this point: "Psychologists seek to promote accuracy, honesty, and truthfulness in the science, teaching, and practice of psychology. In these activities psychologists do not steal, cheat, or engage in fraud,

subterfuge, or intentional misrepresentation of fact." (2002, Ethical Principle C).

The guidelines of the American Academy of Forensic Sciences are equally explicit:

The forensic scientist should render technically correct statements in all written or oral reports, testimony, public addresses, or publications, and should avoid any misleading or inaccurate claims. The forensic scientist should act in an impartial manner and do nothing which would imply partisanship or any interest in a case except the proof of facts and their correct interpretation. (quoted by Saks, 1992, p. 191)

Saks, perhaps only half tongue-in-cheek, has suggested one "test" of how well the expert has assumed the honest educator's role. He suggests that the opposing attorney ask the witness to "please tell the court everything you know about this case that the party who called you to the witness stand hopes does not come out during your cross-examination" (1992, p. 191).

The courts have, of course, established some standards for admissibility of proposed experts. For 70 years, the **Frye test** (*Frye v. United States,* 1923) served as one criterion for some courts in the United States; it stated that the well-recognized standards regarding principles or evidence for a particular field should determine the admissibility of expert testimony. But that rule, which is still the operative criterion in some states, such as New York, has been strongly criticized (see Imwinkelreid, 1992). Additional guidelines were established in 1975 with the adoption of the Federal Rules of Evidence, which specified in Rule 702 that qualified experts can testify "if scientific, technical, or other specialized knowledge will assist the trier of fact to understand the evidence or to determine a fact in issue" (quoted by Bottoms & Davis, 1993, p. 14).

Thus, the Federal Rules of Evidence acknowledged the importance of general acceptance but did not limit admissibility on that basis, emphasizing whatever is relevant and "helpful." The United States Supreme Court, in the case of *Daubert v. Merrell Dow Pharmaceuticals, Inc.* (1993), sought to clarify the distinction between the Federal Rules of Evidence and the more restrictive Frye test, because the Federal Rules of Evidence applied only in federal courts, and most state courts in the United States were still using the Frye rule.

Hence, we have a central issue in the conflict between science and the law: "To what extent should judges be gatekeepers, screening out what has come to be known as junk science from naive jurors who might otherwise be misled, overly awed, or moved by compassion for plaintiffs? Conversely, to what extent should juries be permitted to serve their traditional role as fact finders?" (Greenhouse, 1992, p. A9).

In this so-called junk science case (Huber, 1991), Joyce Daubert had borne a child with a deformed limb after taking Merrell Dow's morning-sickness drug Bendectin (the only drug developed in the United States for the nausea resulting from pregnancy). Jason Daubert, of San Diego, born in 1974 and thus 19 years old when the case went to the Supreme Court, was missing three fingers and a major bone in his right arm.

Despite its approval by the FDA, Bendectin was removed from the market in 1983; Merrell Dow cited the costs of litigation and insurance as the reason. (More than 2,000 lawsuits against Bendectin were filed in the 1980s, according to Rebello, 1993.) When the cases went to trial, juries ruled for the plaintiff at least half the time, but invariably these verdicts were tossed out on appeal.) One example is a Texas case in October 1991. A Nueces County jury ordered Merrell Dow to pay more than $33 million to Kelly Havner, after concluding that her birth defects were caused by her mother's use of Bendectin during pregnancy. The award included $30 million in punitive damages, but the judge reduced the award, cutting the punitive damages in half while retaining the $3.75 million award for actual damages. Merrell Dow appealed the award, and in March 1994, the Court of Appeals for the state of Texas found no scientific evidence to support the jury's decision (*Merrell Dow Pharmaceuticals, Inc. v. Havner,* 1994). The

Chief Justice wrote, "All the primary researchers who have studied Bendectin have reached but one conclusion, and it does not support the theory postulated by the Havners' experts" (quoted by Fisk, 1994, p. A16). The court found the testimony of the five expert witnesses for the plaintiff to be deficient; because they were unable to cite a single epidemiological study that reflected a statistically significant relationship between Bendectin and birth defects, several of these experts "sought to rely on scientific data concerning test tube analysis and chemical composition analogies" (Birnbaum & Jackson, 1994, p. B7).

The decision by Merrell Dow reflects one of the underlying issues in these cases. Product manufacturers claim that the litigation over product liability has run amok; they claim that in such junk science cases, an expert may be hired to testify that virtually anything caused a particular aberration (Birnbaum & Crawford, 1993). The manufacturers want to maintain the procedure of **summary judgment,** by which a judge's ruling avoids an expensive trial. They contend that "if all cases involving disputes between scientific experts must go to trial, manufacturers may be forced to remove other products from the market and will be disinclined to create and market new products" (Birnbaum & Crawford, 1993, p. 18).

Attorneys for persons claiming defects, such as Ms. Daubert, argued that allowing judges to rule on the substance of innovative scientific testimony would generate a "scientific orthodoxy" discouraging the development of science; this was the basis for questioning "whether the Federal Rules of Evidence require courts to measure the foundation of expert scientific testimony before submitting that testimony to the jury and, if so, by what standard" (Birnbaum & Crawford, 1993, p. 18). Thus the Dauberts argued for a lenient standard or judicial restraint, leaving to the jury those decisions about the acceptability of scientific methodology. They further accused the appeals court of a "blatant abuse of judicial power" in "trampling over" the goal of making the courts more open to scientific evidence (quoted in Greenhouse, 1992, p. A9).

(This refers to Congress's action in 1975; when it enacted the Federal Rules of Evidence, it told judges to admit all evidence they considered relevant.)

In contrast, Merrell Dow strongly argued that it was up to the judge to determine if a foundation existed for an expert's testimony that was grounded in agreed-upon standards set by the scientific community. In the *Daubert* suit, Merrell Dow had "moved for a summary judgment, arguing that in light of the consensus in the scientific community, the Dauberts could not establish that Bendectin caused their infant's birth defects" (Birnbaum & Crawford, 1993, p. 18). The company argued that a high standard for admissibility of scientific evidence was necessary to protect jurors "from scientific shamans who, in the guise of their purported expertise, are willing to testify to virtually any conclusion to suit the needs of the litigant with resources sufficient to pay their retainer" (quoted in Greenhouse, 1992, p. A9).

Bendectin litigation began in the 1970s, when individual cases surfaced noting that pregnant women had taken the drug and then produced children with birth defects (Green, 1992; Sanders, 1992, 1993). More than 30 epidemiological studies were done; Merrell Dow claimed that none of these showed any association between Bendectin and birth defects (Birnbaum & Crawford, 1993). In 1980, the Food and Drug Administration reached the same conclusion.

In their suit against the pharmaceutical company, Ms. Daubert's lawyers used eight expert witnesses who relied upon chemical, in vitro, and in vivo animal studies; most importantly, they also cited an unpublished statistical "reanalysis" of data from the 30 previously published studies that had, in contrast, found no detrimental effects from taking Bendectin. This reanalysis was carried out by statistician Shanna Helen Swan, of the California Department of Health Sciences (Begley, 1993). One of the experts gave the opinion that Bendectin was *the* cause of the child's deformities. But the expert's "reanalysis" did not use the conventional .05 level of significance to test the association. Nevertheless, the plaintiff's experts concluded that Bendectin is a teratogen—that is, it causes limb reduction (Frazier, 1993).

In the original suit, the trial court granted Merrell Dow's motion for summary judgment, holding that the animal and pharmacological studies, plus the epidemiological reanalysis, were insufficient to show causation; hence, no justification existed for a jury trial. The trial court relied on the Federal Rules of Evidence (specifically Rules 702 and 403); the Ninth U.S. Circuit Court of Appeals, in upholding the summary judgment, relied on standards from the *Frye* decision.

Both the state court and the appeals court (the latter in 1991) ruled the experts' testimony inadmissible because the "reanalysis" was unpublished and had not been evaluated by other scientists (or subjected to **peer review**); that is, in the court's view, the evidence was not generally accepted by the appropriate scientific community. Thus, in appealing to the U.S. Supreme Court, attorneys for Ms. Daubert challenged the lower court's interpretation of what "general expectation" meant, and specifically the use of the Frye test rather than the Federal Rules of Evidence.

In a Supreme Court decision announced in June 1993, the majority opinion (reflecting a 7 to 2 vote) held that the Frye criterion was unnecessarily restrictive and was superseded (at least in federal courts) by the Federal Rules of Evidence. The latter's Rule 702 was interpreted in Justice Harry Blackmun's majority opinion to be adequate in limiting admissibility to that testimony grounded in relevant and reliable evidence, with those considerations to be decided by the presiding judge (Bottoms & Davis, 1993). Justice Blackmun was explicit: federal judges were obligated to "ensure that any or all scientific testimony or evidence admitted is not only relevant, but reliable" (quoted by Sherman, 1993, p. 28). (Note that what judges call "reliable," psychologists call "valid"; when psychologists say something is "reliable," they mean it is consistent, but not necessarily accurate.) Several criteria were considered appropriate for judges to use in determining the scientific validity of research; these included (1) whether the research

had been peer-reviewed (favorably, we assume, as the Court didn't say); (2) how testable it was (or how it stacked up on "falsifiability" or "refutability"); (3) if it had a recognized rate of error, and (4) if it adhered to professional standards in using the technique in question (Bersoff, 1993). Thus, the Supreme Court remanded the case to the San Diego court, saying the contested evidence had to be reevaluated on the basis of the Federal Rules of Evidence. The judge would have to decide if the proposed evidence by the plaintiff was both relevant and reliable; thus, in the words of one observer, "By adopting an evidentiary standard of scientific validity, the High Court replaced a test that was deferential to outsiders with one that requires judges themselves to make the necessary determination" (Faigman, 1995, pp. 960–961).

The minority opinion, written by Chief Justice Rehnquist, shed no tears over the abandonment of the Frye standard; one of its major differences with the majority opinion was its belief that U.S. federal judges now had the "obligation or the authority to become amateur scientists in order to perform that role." Justice Rehnquist expressed the view that such matters were "far afield from the expertise of judges" (quoted by Bottoms & Davis, 1993, p. 14). During the oral arguments for the case, Justice Rehnquist had expressed a great deal of skepticism that judges, who lacked doctorates in science, could determine whether scientific testimony was valid (Bersoff, 1993).

Now, several years later, attorneys, judges, and psychologists are all trying to understand the effect of the *Daubert* decision (Dyk & Castanias, 1993; Ebert, 1993; Erard & Seltzer, 1994; McGough, 1998; Sanders, 1994; Symposium, 1994; Tomkins, 1995). Even an occasional judge has expressed his concerns in public (Gless, 1995). Does it open the doors for the admissibility of junk science or do just the opposite?

E. Wayne Taff, one of the attorneys who prepared an *amicus* brief in the *Daubert* appeal, says: "Take *Daubert* itself. The court could have said the evidence here was valid or not, but they didn't. What are we going to do when the 9th

Circuit says we don't believe animal studies are valid and another circuit says the contrary. We're going to have divergent opinions all over until the Supreme Court takes another case. I see another decade of disputes" (quoted by Coyle, 1993, p. 12).

Some observers at first thought that the ruling would be applied only to novel or unconventionally tested scientific evidence, but federal court decisions that were rendered within three months of the Supreme Court's decision showed that nearly all expert testimony might be evaluated according to the *Daubert* criteria (Sherman, 1993). Within a few months, experts so scrutinized included an accountant, a product liability expert, a clinical physician, several economists, and an accidentologist. One example was a case from the Virgin Islands (described by Birnbaum & Jackson, 1994) in which the plaintiff claimed that her use of nonprescription asthma medications during her pregnancy caused her daughter's birth defects. The trial judge conducted a hearing that lasted seven days and evaluated the testimony of five expert witnesses for the plaintiff and four for the defense. The judge then decided that the plaintiff's expert testimony was inadmissible and granted a summary judgment for the defendant.

As Melton (1993) has asked, will the decision apply to the testimony of clinical psychologists expressing opinions on specific issues? Other prominent forensic psychologists have also expressed caution about this decision; Bersoff (1993) questioned, "What will the effect of this decision be on such controversial forensic testimony as the prediction of violence, the use of battered spouse, rape, trauma, and child sexual abuse accommodation syndromes, the limitations of eyewitness identification, or the presence of sex stereotyping and harassment in employment settings?" (pp. 6–7).

Quotations from two sets of psychologists reflect the concerns comprehensively; first, Bottoms and Davis (1993), writing about the case, said:

Few would argue the wisdom of allowing judges the option of ignoring a consensus of

"experts" in favor of the individual integrity of evidence, or the prudence of asking questions about the sample, procedures or statistics behind a relevant finding. However, that legal experts, not scientists, will answer such questions should be of concern. Although this ruling opens the door for "well-grounded and innovative" but unpublished evidence, it also potentially opens it for testimony based on questionable techniques that are unrecognized by the scientific community for good reason—reason not necessarily discernible by fact-finders untrained in scientific methodology. (p. 14)

More recently, Kovera and Borgida (1998) wrote:

We argue that the *Daubert* decision is not well informed by psychological science. Empirical research has demonstrated that other legal safeguards presumed to be effective may not be (e.g., Stinson, Devenport, Cutler, & Kravitz, 1996). Moreover, psychological evidence already on the shelf suggests that Daubert's safeguards do not provide effective means for discrediting any unreliable expert evidence that may be admitted at trial. (p. 203)

As one attorney noted, "In a sense, the real losers in this case are trial judges" (quoted by Angier, 1993, p. A8). They will have to consider the acceptability not only of the conclusions but of the methods used by those submitted to be scientific experts. And, according to a follow-up report (Slind-Flor, 1994), federal judges have a sense that they "don't measure up well" when dealing with science and technology. Within months of the *Daubert* decision, a training program for judges was established under the direction of the Carnegie Commission on Science, Technology and Government and the Federal Judicial Center to educate judges as active evaluators of expert testimony (Sherman, 1993). A reference manual for judges was distributed by the Federal Judicial Center in 1994. Psychologists should be involved in such efforts to aid legal professionals in the challenge to discriminate good science from bad; if they do, they will benefit science *and* the law, by exhorting their colleagues "to do competent science before becoming compensated experts" (Faigman, 1995, p. 979).

Since the *Daubert* decision, the Supreme Court has acted on two more cases dealing with the limits of the admissibility of expert testimony. These decisions, too, have implications for the testimony of psychologists. In the case of *General Electric Co. v. Joiner* (1997), the Court ruled that if an "analytical gap" existed between a scientific expert's knowledge and the conclusions expressed in the expert's testimony, that testimony could be excluded from evidence. Thus, once again, the judge was expected to be a vigilant "gatekeeper" who assessed the linkages in experts' testimony.

The second decision, *Kumho Tire Co. Ltd. v. Carmichael* (1999), extended the *Daubert* ruling to nonscientific expert witnesses who claimed specialized knowledge. In the original trial, a Japanese tire company had been sued. The plaintiff claimed that a flaw in the tire's design was the cause of a fatal car accident involving an Alabama family. The evidence the Carmichael family wanted to introduce included the testimony of an engineer, a "tire-failure expert," but his methodology was questioned by the judge, who doubted whether the engineer's procedures could accurately determine the cause of the tire's failure. In a unanimous decision, the Supreme Court concluded that in federal courts, judges should apply the same standards (such as the presence of peer review or an analysis of error rates), so that, for example, handwriting or fingerprint experts whose testimony is based on dubious methodology and which does not meet the standards of legal reliability might well be rejected (see Risinger & Saks, 1996; Saks, 1998).

A recent research project at the University of Nevada, Reno (Gatowski, Dobbin, Richardson, Ginsburg, Merlino, & Dahir, 2001) has taken a look at how the *Daubert* trilogy has affected actual judges. These researchers conducted an extensive telephone survey of some 400 state court judges, asking their opinions about the case, its utility as a decision-making guideline, their level of understanding of the case, and how the case is applied to various types of expert testimony. By and large, judges endorsed the *Daubert* reasoning, but were divided on whether the intent was to raise the standard of admissibility or to lower it—which suggests that we should see quite a bit of variability in judges' decisions on specific sorts of expert testimony for some time to come (see Groscup, Penrod, Studebaker, Huss, & O'Neil, 2002; Penrod, Fulero, & Cutler, 1995). However, many judges readily noted their concern that they lacked the scientific expertise and education to make the sorts of decisions that they are required to make in cases involving experts, echoing the worries discussed earlier and making educational programs for judges even more critical.

SPECIFIC ROLES: PRESENTATION OF PSYCHOLOGY TO COURTS AND LEGISLATURES

The efforts of Münsterberg and his contemporaries to bring scientific psychology into the courts sought to produce results that would be influential at the trial level. Münsterberg apparently never tried to influence the decision of an appellate court or to testify before legislatures for or against proposed laws. This role, specifically the preparation of **amicus curiae briefs** to accompany appeals and the presentation of psychological issues to legislative committees or others with power to institute legal change, has become an important example of the role of forensic psychologists, especially in the last two decades (Acker, 1990; Wrightsman, 1999). Two of the most recent efforts are an *amicus* brief by a group of social scientists and law professors with regard to the *Kumho Tire* case just described (Vidmar et al., 1998, 2000), and the eventual adoption by the attorney general of the state of

New Jersey of guidelines for lineups and photo spreads in eyewitness identification cases (Farmer, 2001).

An ad hoc group of psychologists, sociologists, and law professors headed by Vidmar (1998, 2000) prepared the *amicus* brief in *Kumho Tire*. It was a **science-translation brief,** and its impetus was a set of other *amicus* briefs that made allegations that, in the opinion of the psychologists, drew conclusions about jury behavior that were unsupported by empirical research. Its goal was to present objectively the substantial body of research findings on issues related to the competence and diligence of juries. For example, research has determined that juries (contrary to the allegations of the other briefs) typically are not easily confused by expert evidence and do not quickly defer to experts. Furthermore, juries do not routinely sympathize with plaintiffs in personal injury cases when experts testify for the plaintiff; in fact, they may be skeptical of plaintiffs' claims (Vidmar et al., 1998, 2000). This was not the first time that social science research was used in briefs in order to present scientific findings from our field to appellate-level courts. In its historic decision that racially segregated schools were "inherently unequal" (*Brown v. Board of Education,* 1954), the Supreme Court cited, in the famous Footnote 11, research by psychologists Kenneth Clark and Mamie Clark and a statement by a group of prominent social scientists titled "The effect of segregation and the consequences of desegregation: A social science statement." It is uncertain just how much the justices, in overturning school segregation, were influenced by the social scientists' statement (Cook, 1984). However, consider such statements as "the policy of separating the races is usually interpreted as denoting the inferiority of the Negro group," or "A sense of inferiority affects the motivation of a child to learn." These statements from the Court's opinion are quite consistent with the conclusions drawn from the well-publicized doll study by Kenneth Clark and Mamie Clark (1952). Consistent with conclusions, yes, but how consistent with results?

The Clarks showed a set of dolls to 134 Black children (ages 6 to 9) in the segregated schools of Pine Bluff, Arkansas, and 119 Black children in unsegregated schools in Springfield, Massachusetts. The children were requested to do certain things, such as:

Give me the doll you like the best.
Give me the doll that looks like you.
Give me the doll that looks bad.

The segregated Southern children, the Clarks wrote, were "less pronounced in their preference for the white doll"; when asked to hand their questioner "the doll that looks like you," 39% of the unsegregated Springfield children picked the White doll compared to only 29% in the segregated Arkansas schools. When asked for the nice doll, 68% of the Springfield children chose the White doll, while only 52% of the Pine Bluff children did. Which doll "looked bad?" More than 70% of the desegregated children chose the Black doll, whereas only 49% of the segregated children did. What are we to make of these findings? Do they, as the Clarks concluded, show invidious effects of segregation? The straightforward conclusion, for critics of the Clarks' conclusions (cf. van den Haag, 1960), was that if the tests demonstrate damage to Black children, then they demonstrate that the damage is *less* with segregation and *greater* with desegregation.

Kenneth and Mamie Clark's interpretation of the results was, as you might expect, opposite. Essentially, they were that "black children of the South were more adjusted to the feeling that they were not as good as whites, and because they felt defeated at an early age, did not bother using the device of denial" (quoted by Kluger, 1976, p. 356). Surely the Clarks' interpretation is not the most parsimonious one. Did they predict this finding before the data were collected? The research report does not say so. The Clarks stated that some children, when asked which doll they resembled, broke down and cried: This type of behavior, they reported, "was more prevalent in the North than in the South" (p. 560). Research results that are subject to conflicting interpretations—especially when the result is not consistent with a desired explanation—demand that the researchers begin with a theory that produces testable hypotheses. Fortunately, the Supreme Court in 1954 concluded that school segregation is inherently unequal, and it did not have to rely on research data to so conclude.

If the data were so subject to a multitude of interpretations, why did the Supreme Court not simply note that school segregation, on the face of it, induced an assumption of inferiority leading to a response of humiliation? It may have been "precisely because the Court knew it was backing a firm precedent and entering a heated debate, that it wished to garner *all* the supporting evidence that was available. Without data, there was a danger that the arguments on both sides might merely have become so much moral posturing and empty assertions" (Perkins, 1988, p. 471). As Thurgood Marshall noted in 1952, the earlier separate-but-equal "doctrine had become so ingrained that overwhelming proof was sorely needed to demonstrate that equal educational opportunities for Negroes could not be provided in a segregated system" (quoted in Rosen, 1972, p. 130).

Turning from Clark and Clark's data to the statement by the social scientists that was part of the *Brown amicus* brief, we should note that some psychologists also disagree about its desirability. Stuart Cook (1979), 25 years later, concluded that the information in the statement was sound, but Harold Gerard (1983) felt that the statement was based "not on hard data but mostly on well-meaning rhetoric."

In the *Brown* case, the values of the psychologists were consistent with the values of the justices—especially of Chief Justice Warren—but not necessarily with a straightforward interpretation of the research results. In the brief submitted by the APA in the case of *Lockhart v. McCree* (1986) regarding death-qualified jurors (see Bersoff, 1987), we find a different combination, specifically a conflict in values between the majority of psychologists and the majority opinion of the Supreme Court.

In *Lockhart v. McCree,* the Court rejected three decades of social science research that had shown that the exclusion of prospective jurors opposed to the death penalty, done before the trial starts, produces a jury that is conviction-prone (Cowan, Thompson, & Ellsworth, 1984; Fitzgerald & Ellsworth, 1984; Thompson, 1989b). The brief also observed that such **death-qualified juries** are unrepresentative, because they exclude a higher percentage of certain types of people. The Court rejected both claims, and the conflict between social science and the law was never more sharply represented than in Chief Justice Rehnquist's majority opinion:

> We will assume for purposes of this opinion that the studies are both methodologically valid and adequate to establish that "death-qualification" in fact produces juries somewhat more "conviction-prone" than "non-death-qualified juries." We hold, nonetheless, that the Constitution does not prohibit the states from "death-qualifying" juries in capital cases. (*Lockhart v. McCree,* 1986, p. 1764)

Several value conflicts are present here; one is the priority given to empirical research findings. As Thompson (1989b) observed, the Court's decision may have rested primarily on pragmatic considerations. But a political ideology conflict exists, too. Those social scientists who are political liberals are concerned about decisions like *McCree* because they create a trial jury that is slanted toward conviction, by excluding those opposed to the death penalty. But those Supreme Court justices who are politically conservative (the majority when McCree's case was decided) are concerned that if those prospective jurors who are adamantly opposed to the death penalty were left on the jury, they would slant the trial toward acquittal.

Once more, on the acceptability of submitting the specific brief on death-qualified jurors, we find inconsistency not only between disciplines but within the field of psychology (Finch & Ferraro, 1986). Research psychologist Rogers Elliott (1991a, 1991b) has raised two questions:

(1) Are the data consistent enough to transmit to the Court (and, if consistent, are they developed enough to be useful in setting policy)? and (2) Can briefs communicate the research results adequately? Elliott criticized the methodological adequacy of the studies cited by the APA brief in the *Lockhart v. McCree* appeal and argued that "the data in the brief are insufficient to its claims and cannot do more than justify a verdict of *not proven*" (1991b, p. 62, italics in original).

Should a psychologist become an expert witness or aid in the preparation of an *amicus curiae* brief? What accounts for the sometimes volatile differences in reactions of psychologists on specific issues and specific cases? Kassin and Wrightsman (1983) proposed that jurors, contemplating evidence in a criminal trial, possessed varying degrees of either pro-prosecution or pro-defense biases; they found that a measure constructed to assess juror bias could predict the direction of the juror's verdict in most types of criminal trials. This analysis may be extended to differences in psychologists' reactions to involvement in the court system. How consistent should a phenomenon be to declare it reliable? And, how is consistency measured: A box score of different studies' results? The percentage of variance accounted for? A meta-analysis? Elliott, as implied earlier, sought a high **standard of reliability;** in his view, psychologists should reflect "organized skepticism" (1991b, p. 75). Self-descriptions of those who insist on an exceedingly high standard for reliability include "cautious" and "prudent." It would seem that for such psychologists, the state of knowledge must approach certainty. Does this mean that there is no situation in which they would endorse involvement with the courts? Elliott's response: "The claim made here is not that scientific organizations should not or may not (or should or may) take moral positions. Rather, it is that, if they do so, they should not affect to base them on scientific foundations when such foundations are insufficient to bear the argument constructed on them" (1991b, p. 74).

In contrast, those psychologists who have testified and submitted *amicus* briefs, while de-

manding a clear pattern of research findings, have different standards regarding reliability. Many of them endorse the "best available evidence" argument, which proposes that it is appropriate for psychologists to testify even if their conclusions must be tentative (see Loftus, 1983). Yarmey (1986) argued that an expert's statements should conform to the criterion of scientific respectability, but that absolute certainty is not required. He suggested this criterion: Is the evidence clear, convincing, reliable, and valid, or is it sufficiently ambiguous that experts could find support for whatever position they wished to defend? Ellsworth (1991), in response to Elliott's criticisms, wrote, "To keep silent until our understanding is perfect is to keep silent forever" (p. 77), and "I think we should file briefs when we believe that we have something to say that would improve the quality of the courts' decision making" (p. 89). (Ellsworth, in contrast to Elliott, concluded that the set of studies on the conviction-proneness of death-qualified jurors is quite consistent in the direction of its findings and that the effect is of sufficient magnitude to be of practical importance.) Fulero (1987), in discussing the question of pretrial publicity effects and expert testimony, proposes a similar standard: "If, in the view of the expert, the research literature demonstrates 'to a reasonable degree of scientific probability' that an effect exists, then the literature ought to be presented to the trier of fact in a legal context" (pp. 262–263).

Another example: Bersoff (1987), in describing the *McCree* brief, turned the question around to the critics: What state of the data would *ever* be strong enough to persuade critics and skeptics to testify? This leads to consideration of another dimension. Psychologists differ in their perception and weighing of conflicting facts, just as jurors do. Bermant (1986) proposed that these assessments of the strength of the available evidence are major causes of the disagreement about the propriety of expert testimony. Part of the difference in evidence interpretations results from the degree to which psychologists are concerned about avoiding erroneous convictions.

Perhaps, then, Fulero's (1987) criterion allows these differences to be aired in the context of expert testimony.

Does all this have to do with the political orientations of psychologists? As Ring (1971) observed three decades ago, most social psychologists are politically liberal, but not all are (and indeed, things may have changed in psychology as they have in American society in general). A major concern of politically liberal psychologists is that some defendants will be wrongfully convicted, imprisoned, and executed. Some psychologists do not see this as a major problem. McCloskey and Egeth (1983) argued that wrongful convictions from mistaken eyewitness testimony reflected only a "small fraction of the 1% of cases in which defendants were convicted at least in part on the basis of eyewitness testimony" (p. 552). Konecni and Ebbesen (1986) approvingly quoted this argument and concluded from it "that in the state of California one person is wrongfully convicted approximately every three years because of mistaken eyewitness testimony" (1986, p. 119). Of course, we might ask how many errors of omission are we willing to make to avoid making one error of commission? Konecni and Ebbesen (1986) went on to conclude: "One wrongful conviction every three years because of mistaken identification in a state the size of California (if the estimates given above are correct) may be one wrongful conviction too many, but most reasonable people would probably regard it as well within the domain of 'acceptable risk'—acceptable because no workable system of justice is perfect" (1986, p. 119).

Other psychologists would disagree. The magnitude of error, they would say, is much greater. Fulero (1997) and Cutler and Penrod (1995) have noted that if there are 1 million felony convictions in the United States each year, and the system is 99.5% accurate and has only a .5% error rate, then there are 1,500 wrongful convictions per year—and the number of wrongful convictions goes up another 1,500 for each .5% of error you give to the system. And, they might also note that we now understand that "wrongful conviction" is a concern not just of the

politically liberal but of everyone, even political "conservatives"—because for every wrongful conviction, a guilty criminal remains at large, free to commit other crimes. Those in law enforcement at the highest levels, not generally considered "political liberals," have begun to see this as well (Technical Working Group on Eyewitness Evidence, 1999).

The *amicus* brief directed to the U.S. Supreme Court has been a frequent mechanism by which the American Psychological Association seeks its goals to promote and advance human welfare (Grisso & Saks, 1991; Wrightsman, 1999). In several instances, this device has been effective (Tremper, 1987). But in several notable cases, the majority of the Court has decided in a direction contrary to the conclusions supported by psychological theory and findings.

One of these, the *McCleskey v. Kemp* (1987) decision involving the racial bias in the death penalty, was described in chapter 1. In another decision on a different issue, in *Schall v. Martin* (1984), the U.S. Supreme Court considered the constitutionality of a New York law that provided pretrial detention of allegedly delinquent juveniles if they were felt to be likely to commit further illegal acts before a court decision. Can legal professionals or mental health professionals predict who will engage in violent or criminal acts? The Supreme Court heard a presentation reflecting the then-predominant psychological perspective, that such predictions are difficult (Ewing, 1985). Yet, the Supreme Court did not find that such preventive detention violated constitutional protections.

In another case (*Bowers v. Hardwick*, 1986), the American Psychological Association offered an *amicus* brief challenging the basis of laws that made sodomy between consenting homosexual persons illegal. A few states prohibited genital-anal intercourse between heterosexual persons; the state of Georgia, the appellant in this case, prohibited such acts only between two homosexual persons. Specifically, the brief brought psychological research findings to bear on several myths offered as justifications for such "sodomy laws": that the behaviors reflect mental illness, that they are a threat to public health, and that they are unusual (Bersoff & Ogden, 1991). Yet, the Court maintained laws (recently in effect in about one half the states, though very seldom enforced) that prohibit homosexual behavior.

At first, it appeared that psychology's intervention was unsuccessful in all three cases. But in all three cases, the Court's references to scientific data did not challenge the facts that APA had demonstrated; the Court simply said that "the psychological data were not sufficient grounds upon which to decide the legal questions" (Grisso & Saks, 1991, p. 207). The Court appeared to listen to evidence and took it seriously enough to discuss it. Indeed, in a recent case, *Atkins v. Virginia* (2002), the United States Supreme Court ruled 6 to 3 that executions of mentally retarded criminals are "cruel and unusual punishment," violating the Eighth Amendment to the Constitution. The APA submitted an *amicus* brief that clearly influenced the majority opinion and indeed it quoted research from that brief in a footnote (as noted in chapter 1, there is never unanimity within psychology; Bersoff (2002) has written critically about the APA's position in the *Atkins* case).

So, in Grisso and Saks's (1991) reasoned opinion, APA *amicus* briefs may be making two important contributions to forensic psychology. First, "they may reduce the likelihood that judicial use of spurious, unsubstantiated opinions about human behavior will establish precedent for future cases" (p. 207). Second, the *amicus* briefs may, to put it crudely, "keep the Court honest," or, to quote Grisso and Saks, "psychology's input may compel judges to act like judges, stating clearly the fundamental values and normative premises on which their decisions are grounded, rather than hiding behind empirical errors or uncertainties" (p. 208). In this light, psychology's efforts in these controversial cases appear to be more effective (see also Wrightsman, 1999).

When psychology seeks to influence the courts, it needs to go more than halfway. In a study of the Supreme Court's use of social science research in cases involving children, Hafe-

meister and Melton (1987) concluded that when secondary social science sources were cited, they typically were ones published in law reviews or government reports, not in psychology journals. The moral is clear: If we want to influence judges, we must publish our conclusions in the periodicals that they read (see also Fulero & Mossman, 1998).

What is the appropriate stance for psychologists who seek to influence court decisions? We have alluded to some of the dangers. Roesch, Golding, Hans, and Reppucci (1991) posed interesting choices:

> Should social scientists limit themselves to conducting and publishing their research and leave it to others to apply their research findings? Or do they have an ethical obligation to assist the courts and other social groups in matters relating to their expertise? If an activist role for social scientists is appropriate, what are the comparative advantages of brief writing, expert testimony, and other mechanisms of approaching the courts? (p. 2)

When psychology as an organized profession seeks to influence the law through an *amicus* brief to an appellate court, it can do so for a variety of reasons. For example, the APA may perceive a shared interest in the outcome with one of the parties in the litigation; usually the interest relates to economic benefits, powers, or prerequisites for APA's members (Saks, 1993). For example, in 1993, the APA filed an *amicus* brief in conjunction with a court case involving the confidentiality of unfunded grant applications (Adler, 1993). This "guild" interest may not be consistent with the neutral stance of some conceptions of the *amicus* brief, and may in fact harm the perception of impartiality in other presentations of scientific evidence. Indeed, Roesch et al. (1991) noted that this type of advocacy brief contrasts with the science-translation brief, or an objective summary of a body of research.

The science-translation brief reflects the second role, as an honest broker; it occurs when APA possesses knowledge that the Court otherwise might not have and that might assist the Court in deciding the case before it. Saks argued that taking this role "minimizes the temptation to fudge, maximizes the value of the knowledge to the public interest, and helps protect the integrity of the APA and of psychology" (1993, p. 243).

Even a science-translation brief will reflect the perspective and values of its writers (Roesch et al., 1991). How much interpretation should an *amicus* brief contain? Melton and Saks suggested that both the advocacy brief and the science-translation brief

> can end up misleading a reader, especially a lay reader, which is what judges are when they read these kinds of briefs. The solution, we think, is in approaching the writing with an honest desire to share with the courts a faithful picture of the available psychological knowledge, and to interpret the research only to the extent that doing so will clarify its meaning. (p. 5)

Because controversy is inevitable in science, any science-translation brief will generate some disagreement by social scientists. But "in preparing briefs, social scientists should strive to ensure, at a minimum, that briefs represent a consensual view of social scientists (i.e., what *most* experts in the field would conclude)" (Roesch et al., 1991, p. 6). Alternative explanations should be included, when appropriate. Sometimes the psychologist-authors of the brief go too far, in Saks's opinion. They may begin "to lose sight of who the client is (is the client APA or one of the parties?) or what the brief's goals are (is the goal to share relevant knowledge or to urge a particular legal conclusion?), or which kind of *amicus* role they are in (is this a guild brief or a science-translation brief?)" (Saks, 1993, p. 243).

APA's brief in the case involving Ann Hopkins and Price Waterhouse (described in chapter 1) provides a provocative example; it stated:

> Amicus concludes that sex stereotyping existed in petitioner's employment setting, was transformed into discriminatory behavior, and played a significant role in the decision of the petitioner not to select respon-

dent as a partner of the firm. (American Psychological Association, 1991, p. 1062)

Note this quotation asserts an opinion on the ultimate issue—on the facts of the case—the equivalent to a psychologist testifying that a particular eyewitness was in error when identifying the defendant. Saks's reaction to this brief: "To my eyes, this is remarkable language in a science translation brief by a non-party. . . . If the goal of the brief was to share with the Court relevant findings from the research literature on gender stereotyping or to show that Professor Fiske's testimony about that research literature was generally accepted within her field, then the quoted language goes much too far" (1993, p. 244).

THE TEMPTATIONS OF FORENSIC PSYCHOLOGY

As interest in forensic psychology continues to grow, systematic concern about codifying the ethical guidelines has increased. Division 41 (the American Psychology-Law Society) of the APA has developed a set of guidelines for forensic psychologists, under the direction of Stephen L. Golding, Thomas Grisso, and David Shapiro. These Specialty Guidelines for Forensic Psychologists, approved by the membership of APA Division 41, have been published (Committee on Ethical Guidelines for Forensic Psychologists, 1991; see the American Psychology-Law Society website at www.unl.edu/ap-ls). In late 2002, a Revision Committee was formed to consider changes to the Specialty Guidelines. The guidelines build upon the APA's Ethical Principles of Psychologists in several aspects of forensic work, including confidentiality, the relationship between psychologists and litigating parties, and procedures in preparing evaluations. Nevertheless, forensic psychologists, for various reasons, may exceed what is acceptable in their profession and even what the law theoretically permits them to do. The following are some temptations that recur throughout the roles described in the rest of this book.

Promising Too Much

Sometimes forensic psychologists who are hired by attorneys or the courts promise a level of success they cannot guarantee (see Strier, 1999). Litigation Sciences, one of the earliest and largest of the trial consulting firms, in its brochure, has claimed an impressive record of successes. "We have been involved in more than 900 cases, and our research findings have been consistent with the actual outcome in more than 95% of the matters that have gone to trial" (Litigation Sciences, 1988, p. 3). This surely must generate great optimism for any law firm that hires Litigation Sciences. Is a 95% success rate consistent with the degree to which social scientists can predict outcomes in such nonexperimental situations? Can any trial consultant—without utilizing a control group consisting of the same trial without the consultant—actually show that "success," defined by a favorable verdict, was *due to* or *caused by* the consultant's input, was *irrelevant* to the consultant's input (that is, would have occurred anyway), or occurred *in spite of* the consultant's input (that is, that the trial consultant's input was detrimental, but the jury voted for that side anyway)?

Similarly, psychologists who have developed tests and other instruments that are used in child custody evaluations or assessments of psychopathology may be tempted to claim a greater level of validity than is warranted in real-life situations. Some forensic psychologists may become committed to the use of certain tests, such as the MMPI or the Rorschach, even in situations in which their applicability is questionable (see Wood, Nezworski, Lilienfeld, & Garb, 2003; Ziskin, 1995).

Substituting Advocacy for Scientific Objectivity

When psychologists become expert witnesses, they are usually hired by one side in an adversarial proceeding. Most psychologists, in such a situation, are conscientious and try to be ethical

"even to the point of providing ammunition to the other side when the situation warrants it" (Ceci & Hembrooke, 1998, p. 1). But it is tempting to play the **advocate role,** to take sides, to become sympathetic to the arguments of the side that is paying the psychologist, and to "slant" the testimony in that direction. The shift toward partisanship may be subtle, even unconscious. Attorneys contribute to the problem by "shopping around" until they find an expert who will say what they want (Spencer, 1998; see also Box 2-2). Many people, including some judges, see the expert witness as a hired gun, willing to say whatever his or her client needs said. An apparent example of a hired gun on the stand occurred in the trial of John Demjanjuk, the alleged "Ivan the Terrible," a Nazi concentration-camp guard, at his eventual trial in Israel (see chapter 10 for details of this case). A handwriting expert who was testifying in Demjanjuk's defense concluded that a signature on a document was probably not Demjanjuk's, but the prosecution confronted the expert with an earlier public statement in which he expressed the opposite conclusion. The expert refused to explain the inconsistency on the grounds that he had a "contractual relationship" with the Demjanjuk Defense Fund, which would sue him if he explained further (Spencer, 1998). A recent, widely discussed book by experimental psychologist Margaret Hagen (1997) is a broadside attack on psychologists as hired guns (see Box 2-4).

The proper role for a psychologist as an expert witness is that of an objective scientist who reports *all* the data, even if they make a less supportive case for the side that hired the psychologist. But it is hard to avoid the seduction of taking sides. Sometimes, when the advocate role becomes paramount, the psychologist may be tempted to "create" a diagnosis to fit the behavior—examples are "Black rage" and "urban survival syndrome"—when no proof exists for the reliability or validity of the diagnostic construct (see Harris, 1997; Liggins, 1999).

Letting Values Overcome Empirical Findings

Probably none of us can escape our values as influences on the ways that we perceive the world. The temptation is to let our values determine our scientific conclusions in a court of law.

For example, a forensic psychologist is asked to do an evaluation of a pair of parents who are divorcing in order to assist the judge in making a custody decision that is in the best interests of the child. What if the psychologist discovers that one of the parents—on rare occasions when the child has uttered an expletive—washes out the child's mouth with soap? There is nothing illegal about this, and probably nothing physically harmful, but perhaps the psychologist is repulsed by the behavior. No empirical data exist that such an action is related in and of itself to the general question of appropriateness for custody, but the psychologist's recommendation could be affected by it.

In another example of this type of temptation, a psychologist serving as an **expert witness** may go beyond any legitimate scientific basis in offering conclusions about whether a group of children was sexually abused. In the late 1980s, Kelly Michaels was charged with the sexual abuse of many children under her supervision at the Wee Care Day Nursery in Maplewood, New Jersey; a psychologist testified for the prosecution that for 19 of 20 children, their testimony and conduct were "consistent with" the presence of a child sexual abuse accommodation syndrome. This expert defined *consistent with* "as having a 'high degree of correlation,' 'over point six [.6]' in numerical terms of probability" (quoted by Miller & Allen, 1998, p. 148).

Despite the ambiguous nature of this conclusion, the jury convicted Kelly Michaels of 115 counts of sexual abuse of children, and she was given a prison sentence of 47 years. But 5 years later, her conviction was overturned; there was no scientific basis for the expert witness's assertion that the testimony and conduct of the children bore any relationship to the presence of a sexual abuse accommodation syndrome (Miller & Allen, 1998). As Newman put it:

> A claim that [a child's] behavior is "consistent with" the sex abuse syndrome does not reveal causes for the behavior other than sex abuse that may exist. The symptom of headache is consistent with being hit over the head with a blunt instrument, but [blows by] blunt instruments do not cause most people's headaches. (1994, p. 196)

In another case (*Barefoot v. Estelle,* 1983), the Supreme Court opinion shows that two psychiatrists went beyond the available research on predicting dangerousness by testifying that they *knew* (to 100% certainty) that the defendant would commit crimes in the future (Lavin & Sales, 1998). One, Dr. James Grigson, was expelled from the American Psychiatric Association for his testimony in this and many other Texas death penalty cases (Lavin & Sales, 1998).

Doing a Cursory Job

A prisoner on death row in Florida, Alvin Bernard Ford, began gradually to show changes in his behavior—at first just an occasional peculiar notion, but, over time, more frequent and more extreme. He reflected obsessions that he was the target of a criminal conspiracy and delusions that he was "Pope John Paul III" who had appointed the nine justices of the Florida Supreme Court. Because a person cannot be executed unless he or she is capable of understanding the implications of the act, the governor of Florida appointed a panel of three psychiatrists to conduct a **competency hearing** to evaluate whether Ford had the mental capacity to understand the nature of the death penalty and the reasons why it had been imposed on him (Miller & Radelet, 1993).

One would imagine such an evaluation should be done thoughtfully and carefully, given the implications of its possible outcome. Yet the three psychiatrists, together, interviewed Ford for only about 30 minutes. Furthermore, this questioning was done in the presence of eight other people, including attorneys and prison officials. Each of the psychiatrists filed two- or three-page reports with the governor; each agreed that Ford met the criterion of sanity as defined by the state law, even though each gave a different specific diagnosis of the inmate. Thus, the governor signed Ford's death warrant, although the U.S. Supreme Court (in *Ford v. Wainwright,* 1986), on appeal, required Florida to redo the competency hearing. (Ford died in prison of natural causes before he could be executed.)

The unreliability of psychiatric diagnoses will recur as an issue (see chapter 6, for example). However, the temptation of concern here is to be less than thorough and professional in one's work for the courts or other authorities.

SUMMARY

The roles of forensic psychologists in the legal system are diverse, but they share certain temptations, including promising too much, substituting advocacy for scientific objectivity, letting values overcome empirically based conclusions, doing a cursory job, and maintaining dual relationships and competing roles.

Psychologists differ about the degree to which we should attempt to apply our findings to legal questions. Some believe that we do not possess findings that are sufficiently reliable to be applied to real-life decisions, or believe that their colleagues, because of their politically liberal orientations, tend to sympathize with the defendant. Those psychologists active in presenting scientific psychological findings to the courts respond by arguing that the information from our field, while not unanimous, does improve the quality of decision making in the legal system.

The courts have entered this controversy by considering just what the standard should be in admitting scientific evidence at trial. In a trilogy of decisions—*Daubert, Kumho,* and *Joiner*—the

Supreme Court applied standards of scientific acceptance, such as publication in a peer-reviewed journal, general acceptance, and reliability and validity, in order to determine admissibility of psychologists as expert witnesses.

KEY TERMS

advocate role
amicus curiae briefs
competency hearing
conduit-educator
confidentiality
death-qualified juries
dual relationships
evaluation
expert witness
fact witness
Frye test
"hired gun"
"junk science"
peer review
philosopher-ruler/advocate
psychopathy
science-translation brief
standard of reliability
summary judgment
trial consultant

INFOTRAC® COLLEGE EDITION

InfoTrac College Edition is a FREE, powerful, online learning resource, consisting of full-text articles from thousands of journals and periodicals. With each new copy of *Forensic Psychology,* Second Edition, you receive four months of free access to the InfoTrac College Edition database. By doing a simple keyword search (try using the Key Terms from the list above), you can quickly generate a list of relevant articles from thousands of possibilities and can select articles to read, explore, and print for reference or further study. InfoTrac College Edition's continuously updated collection of articles can be useful for doing reading and writing assignments that reach beyond the pages of this text!

SUGGESTED READINGS

Brodsky, S. L. (1991). *Testifying in court: Guidelines and maxims for the expert witness.* Washington, DC: American Psychological Association; and Brodsky, S. L. (1999). *The expert expert witness: More maxims and guidelines for testifying in court.* Washington, DC: American Psychological Association.

These relentlessly readable books by one of America's most respected forensic psychologists include a wealth of practical suggestions, succinctly put. An example: "With indifferent attorneys be assertive. With incompetent attorneys, decline the case or educate them" (Brodsky, 1991, p. 197).

Bruck, M. (1998). The trials and tribulations of a novice expert witness. In S. J. Ceci & H. Hembrooke (Eds.), *Expert witnesses in child abuse cases* (pp. 85–104). Washington, DC: American Psychological Association.

All forensic psychologists anticipating their first testimony are indebted to Maggie Bruck for painfully portraying the pitfalls of such an activity. She had not been warned about what to expect, but now we can know.

Dawes, R. M. (1994). *House of cards: Psychology and psychotherapy built on myth.* New York: Free Press.

The general viewpoint of this book is similar to that of Margaret Hagen's *Whores of the Court;* both books are by psychologists who are critical of their psychotherapist colleagues who use invalid psychological tests and substitute intuition for empirical findings.

Hagen, M. A. (1997). *Whores of the court: The fraud of psychiatric testimony and the rape of American justice.* New York: HarperCollins.

A few forensic psychologists love it, more hate it, and some of us say to it, "Yes, but . . . " (see Box 2-4). Certainly one of the most talked-about books in recent years.

Ziskin, J. (1995). *Coping with psychiatric and psychological testimony* (5th ed., Vols. 1–3.). Los Angeles: Law and Psychology Press.

Few of us have had such an impact that our names have become verbs within the lingo of a certain profession, but that is true of the late Jay Ziskin. When trial attorneys "Ziskinize" psychologists or psychiatrists who are testifying, they challenge them by cross-examining them *intensively* with regard to the accuracy of their statements and the validity of the procedures they have used. This three-volume set (earlier editions were prepared with David Faust) assesses the validity of a number of forensic topics; any forensic psychologist who anticipates being an expert witness needs to consult these volumes.

3

Psychology and Law Enforcement: Selection, Training, and Evaluation

Forty years ago, an influential United States government report on police organizations (President's Commission on Law Enforcement and Administration of Justice, 1967) portrayed a place for psychology in only one aspect of law enforcement: the selection of police recruits.

In contrast, this chapter attempts to show that psychology can play a significant role in almost every aspect of police work, from selection of recruits, through the training of police and other law-enforcement officers, to the evaluation of their work performance. Forensic psychologists can assist in responding to the major types of complaints about the police—corruption, racism, and brutality. Furthermore, psychology and the other social sciences have evaluated recent changes in police procedures, such as **team policing,** or the assignment of police officers to particular neighborhoods, so that they become familiar with local concerns. The purpose of this chapter is to examine what psychology has to offer in reaching our shared goal of improving law-enforcement procedures.

WHO ARE THE CLIENTELES?

Police corruption and brutality in New York City; the beating of Rodney King in Los Angeles; the arrest of three police officers in Detroit for planning the theft of $1 million in cash—these and other events have sensitized the public to the potential problems of the police (Cannon, 1998; Fields, 1993). Less acknowledged is the other side of the coin: the acts of heroism by law-enforcement officers and the risk of officers' death or injury (between 140 and 200 U.S. officers are killed in the line of duty each year). Stresses on the police can take a terrible toll: Twelve New York City police officers committed suicide in a recent year (Associated Press, 1994b; James, 1994).

In identifying the possible contributions of psychology to policing, we begin by asking: Who are the **clienteles**? To whom are forensic psy-

chologists responsible, when they seek to apply psychological knowledge to the criminal justice system? A forensic psychologist is most likely to be hired by the police or sheriff's department, most often as a consultant though sometimes as a staff member, but the forensic psychologist also has an ethical responsibility to respond to the public's concerns about the police. As we will see, achieving both these responsibilities at the same time is often challenging.

The Public

What does the public want from law-enforcement officers? Specific respondents would differ, but two wishes are a sense of respect and a lack of prejudice. The Christopher Commission that studied the Los Angeles Police Department after the officers' beating of Rodney King concluded that "too many . . . patrol officers view citizens with resentment and hostility; too many treat the public with rudeness and disrespect" (quoted by Schmalleger, 1995, p. 202). A desire for fairness is typical (Tyler & Folger, 1980; Vermunt, Blaauw, & Lind, 1998); clearly, a frequent complaint about the police is their discrimination against African Americans and other minorities. For decades, members of racial minority groups have perceived themselves to be unjustly victimized by the police and other law-enforcement officers, including highway patrol officers and sheriffs' deputies (Decker & Wagner, 1982). Blacks believe they are abused by the police far more than are Whites in several types of ways: being roughed up unnecessarily, being stopped and frisked without justification, and being the object of abusive language.

These concerns are so great that victims have sarcastically developed a crime-classification acronym, **DWB** ("driving while Black"), to reflect the tendency of some patrol officers to concentrate on minorities as possible offenders. In 1998, 11 African American motorists, with support from the ACLU and the NAACP, filed a class action lawsuit against the state of Maryland, claiming **race-based profiling** by its state troopers in their efforts to seize illegal drugs and weapons. Typically these plaintiffs reported being detained for almost an hour while being questioned. Troopers exposed luggage to a drug-sniffing dog and, on occasion, left clothes strewn on the side of the highway. (An Oklahoma trooper reportedly told an African American man, "We ain't good at repacking," Johnson, 1999, p. 4A.) The Maryland state troopers' own records over a 3-year period ending in December 1997 indicated that although 75% of the drivers on Interstate 95 in Maryland were White and 17% were Black, 70% of those pulled over and searched were Black whereas only 23% were White (Barovik, 1998; Janofsky, 1998). Similar complaints have been filed against law-enforcement agencies in other states, including Oklahoma, Indiana, Pennsylvania, Colorado, Illinois, and New Jersey (Johnson, 1999). The concerns of minority-group members are also reflected in complaint rates; for example, in Philadelphia 70% of complaints against the police were from African Americans, even though the population of the city was at the time 75% White (Hudson, 1970).

What can be done to reduce this concern? Does psychology have anything to offer? Although this topic deserves more attention, one intervention is the use of a psychologist to assist in community involvement in **police selection.** Often, the goals in selection by police departments reflect traditional criteria; they fail to recognize the goal of diversity in the makeup of law-enforcement agencies, specifically the hiring of minorities and women.

Members of special interest groups want to express their own agendas in police departments' activities. Many of these departments, however, have "resisted what they consider unwarranted interference from people whom they believe have little understanding of the nature of the job, and are, in fact, hostile to the police and their definition of the nature of their work" (Ellison, 1985, p. 77).

Katherine W. Ellison (1985) is a community psychologist who was invited to develop a new procedure for selecting police officers for the Montclair, New Jersey, police department. In doing so, she capitalized on the concept of **stakeholders,** people who have a special knowledge and interest, or a "stake," in running the department. Stakeholders included, as you would expect, officers from the department, especially patrol officers. Members of the Township Council and other township officials as well as members of the local media, the clergy, and other opinion leaders were included. But Ellison also solicited interviews from a stratified quota sample of 100 citizens from the community and included community representatives in the specific panel that interviewed candidates for police training. A side benefit, in addition to selecting officers who reflected community demographics, was an increase in the communication between the police and those members of the community who characteristically complain about the unresponsiveness of the police.

A second community concern is **police corruption.** Deviant behavior by police can vary along a continuum of seriousness; an example of such a categorization is offered in Box 3-1. In a 4-year period in the mid-1990s, more than 500 police officers in 47 cities were convicted of federal crimes (Johnson, 1998). Arrests and convictions for violations of state laws were even higher. The recent violations are different from those of earlier times, when some officers accepted bribes to ignore rampant examples of gambling, prostitution, or liquor violations. Now, the corruption is manifested in officers who are active participants in the crime; some of these, in the words of the former police commissioner of New York City, William Bratton, have "truly become predatory figures" (quoted by Johnson, 1998, p. 8A).

In some cases, officers who engage in corrupt behavior do so partly because of conflicts in achieving professional success. Big city police who are given the task of capturing drug dealers must often rely on informants, but when the police slip informants money to tattle (usually $10 to $20), their supervisors ridicule their

BOX 3-1

Types of Police Deviance by Category and Example

High-Level Corruption	*Low-Level Corruption*
Violent Crimes: The physical abuse of suspects, including torture and nonjustifiable homicide	**Role Malfeasance:** Destroying evidence, offering biased testimony, and protecting "crooked" cops
Denying Civil Rights: Routinized schemes to circumvent constitutional guarantees	**Being "Above" Inconvenient Laws:** Speeding, smoking marijuana
Criminal Enterprise: The resale of confiscated drugs, stolen property, etc.	**Minor Bribes:** Twenty dollars to "look the other way" on a ticket
Property Crimes: Burglary, theft, etc., committed by police	**Playing Favorites:** Not ticketing friends, etc.
Major Bribes: Accepting $1,000 to "overlook" contraband shipments and other law violations	**Gratuities:** Accepting free coffee, meals, etc.

Source: Modified from *Criminal Justice Today* (3rd ed.) by F. Schmalleger, 1995, Table 6-3, p. 209. Used by permission of Prentice-Hall, Inc. Upper Saddle River, NJ.

requests for reimbursement, telling them that's just part of doing business (Kramer, 1997). But temptations to become lawbreakers are also a part of chasing drug dealers. One police officer, convicted of corruption, told a reporter:

> So when we hit a place, we'd take some money to reimburse our informant payments. After a while, with so much dough sitting around, you just take more, and then you begin to get used to it. Unless you're completely nuts, you're careful. If you find 10 grand, say, you take only three or four. You can't raid a drug house and come back and not turn in some money. That'd be a sure tipoff. (quoted by Kramer, 1997, p. 83)

Michael Dowd was a New York City police officer who exemplified how corruption began with small illegal acts, such as taking money from the bodies of victims, and moved to major busts, to eventually recruiting other officers to participate in an elaborate system of bribery and extortion that netted Dowd more than $15,000 per week (McAlary, 1994). Eventually Dowd and other police began to deal cocaine to suburban Long Island youngsters. Only because of those acts was he caught, arrested, and convicted; he is now serving a 14-year prison sentence.

Why do brutality and corruption occur, given the extensive screening that is demanded of candidates for training as law-enforcement officers? Are these behaviors the result of personality characteristics, or do they develop from the presence of a subculture (a local precinct, a squad of officers) prone to corruption? These important questions have not received sufficient study. Jerome Skolnick (1966) concluded that a process of informal socialization—specifically, interactions with experienced officers—was perhaps more important than police-academy training in determining how rookies viewed their work and the public. In his classic analysis of police life, Arthur Niederhoffer (1967) claimed that the police subculture transformed a police officer into an authoritarian personality, and several studies of changes that take place from the recruit to the experienced police officer support such a tendency (Carlson & Sutton, 1975; Genz & Lester, 1976; Hageman, 1979; McNamara, 1967). Role demands may lead to increased authoritarianism and a greater willingness to use force; working in high-crime areas seemed to foster authoritarianism in the police (Brown & Willis, 1985). One empirical effort to determine if authoritarianism scores of police officers were related to the number of times they had been disciplined produced no significant relationships (Henkel, Sheehan, & Reichel, 1997), but the approach needs to be extended. Expressions of brutality and corruption may well reflect an interaction between a predisposition to lawbreaking within the individual officer, combined with being in a subculture that makes such actions easy to do and easy to get away with doing—a subculture that may even have norms that encourage such behavior.

The Police Department

A second clientele for the forensic psychologist is, of course, the police department itself. A psychologist can assist police departments and other law-enforcement agencies in answering a number of important questions; for example:

- What should be included in the training program for recruits? Does success in a training program predict effectiveness as a police officer?
- Are there ways to prevent or reduce police burnout? What are effective ways to deal with the stresses of police work?
- How effective are different strategies for combating crime? Are foot patrols more effective than police cars? Does saturated patrolling work?

Subsequent sections of this chapter identify what psychology has to offer as answers to some of these questions as well as identifying conflicts between the approaches to answers by psychologists and by the police. More detailed information relevant to these questions can be found in books on the topic of police psychology, including those by Blau (1994) and by Kurke and Scrivner (1995).

THE SELECTION OF POLICE

What should be the goals of a program to select candidates for law-enforcement training? Foremost for police chiefs has been the attempt to screen out disturbed applicants rather than to

select those with a desirable profile (Reiser, 1982c). Some psychologists (e.g., Smith & Stotland, 1973) have proposed that we should move beyond this focus on gross pathology. For example, what are the characteristics of an ideal law-enforcement officer and how are they best measured? Psychology has made strides toward answering these questions over the last 90 years but definitive answers remain elusive, partly because of the lack of agreement about the ideal and also because some desired traits cannot be reliably measured (Ainsworth, 1995).

Attainment of the goal of selecting desirable police officers for training is especially tantalizing because, in many jurisdictions, the initial pool is a large one. Rachlin (1991) has pointed out that in New York City, between 30,000 and 50,000 people take the police civil service test every time it is administered. From this large pool, those who score high enough must still go through a series of rigorous evaluations before they are selected for training at the police academy. These include (Rachlin, 1991):

1. A review of academic transcripts, tax returns, and military and employment records.
2. Background checks with the Department of Motor Vehicles, and a fingerprint check with the FBI and the New York State central fingerprint registries.
3. Interviews with neighbors, family, friends, and employers.
4. A screening medical exam, in which prospective trainees may be eliminated because of heart murmurs, high blood pressure, back problems, or impaired hearing or vision. Prospective candidates must be physically fit, and standards are quite high. For example, to pass the physical for the Chicago Police Department, a man must be able to bench-press 98% of his weight, run 1.5 miles in 13.46 minutes, and do 37 sit-ups in one minute; a woman must press 57% of her weight and run 1.5 miles in 16:21 minutes (Kaplan, 1991).
5. Psychological testing (4 hours in length).
6. Interview with a clinical psychologist.
7. A full medical examination.

Only after passing all these hurdles is the applicant chosen for training; somewhere between 500 and 1,500 applicants are chosen for the 5-1/2-month training at the New York City Police Academy. Even after this rigorous selection, about 10% drop out during the training period (Rachlin, 1991).

A History of Psychology and Police Selection

Psychologists' involvement in the evaluation of police characteristics extends back, surprisingly, to Lewis Terman, the author of the widely used Stanford-Binet intelligence test. Terman (1917), publishing in the very first issue of the *Journal of Applied Psychology*, tested the intelligence of 30 police and firefighter applicants in San Jose, California. Finding that their average IQ was 84, he recommended that no one whose IQ fell below 80 be accepted for those positions (Spielberger, 1979).

Several decades later, the emphasis shifted to personality characteristics; in the 1940s, an attempt was made to use the Humm-Wadsworth Temperament Scale as a basis for selecting police applicants in Los Angeles (Humm & Humm, 1950), despite the lack of evidence for its validity (Ostrov, 1986). Since then, psychologists have employed a variety of procedures; although they continue to use personality inventories, they also employ interviews and situational tests as tools. We evaluate each of these approaches in the next sections.

Tools for Psychological Selection

The Interview

As in the selection of people for most professional positions, the personal interview has been a central part of the selection process for law-enforcement officers. Typically, a clinical psychologist or psychiatrist conducts a brief interview. Traditionally, the approach has been to search for pathology (Silverstein, 1985). Are there personality characteristics or traits that imply abnormal behavior? Recently, however, emphasis has shifted to using the interview to assess such desirable qualities as social maturity, stability, and skill in interpersonal relations (Janik, 1993). Chandler (1990) viewed the interview as providing answers to questions about "military bearing," sense of humor, and absence of anger. The interview can provide information on characteristics not visible through other procedures; these include body language, appropriateness of emotions expressed by the interviewee, insight into one's own behavior, and an ability to convey a sense of self (Silverstein, 1985).

But the interview, as a selection device, is fraught with problems. The purpose of the clinical interview has traditionally been not so much for prediction; instead, the goal was to gain an in-depth understanding of the individual. Validity was often assessed by comparing one clinician's judgment to that of other clinicians. The literature from industrial/organizational psychology on the use of the clinical interview gives no indication that it is valid as a predictor of job performance (Ulrich & Trumbo, 1965).

Another problem is that there is no agreed-upon format for the interview. Some urge that the interview be standardized so that it always covers issues relevant to the job criteria (Hibler & Kurke, 1995); a structured approach also permits comparisons between applicants. But other psychologists and psychiatrists prefer the opportunity to probe topics of concern, as these emerge from the responses of the individual candidate. Regardless of the procedures used, it is essential that the interview be conducted in a fair and equitable way (Jones, 1995). Members of minority racial and ethnic groups who are applicants are sensitive to possibilities of racial bias by interviewers, and some commentators (Jones, 1995; Milano, 1989) have suggested that a form be prepared, specifying the topics covered in the interview.

An article by Hargrave and Hiatt (1987, p. 111) cited studies related to psychiatric interviews for selection of police officers. One of the problems the researchers noted is the strong tendency for people to portray themselves more positively in face-to-face interviews than on personality tests, resulting in an increase in the number of **false positives** (poor risks who are hired) and no impact on the goal of reducing **false negatives** (those not hired who would have displayed acceptable performance).

Two particular problems obstruct the attainment of validity for interviews in police selection, although each of these problems is characteristic of some other occupations, too (Spielberger, 1979). The first is the lack of criteria against which to judge predictors (Hargrave & Hiatt, 1987). Police and other law-enforcement officers have a great deal of autonomy in their activities; also, the number of activities they carry out daily may be quite diverse. Second, screening of applicants via a clinical interview leads to elimination of those considered unqualified; the resulting studies thus have a restricted range of candidates, from whom individual differences in effectiveness are compared with their interview results.

Hargrave and Hiatt (1987) set out to deal with the second problem by capitalizing on a rather unusual situation. Two classes of police academy trainees ($N = 105$) were individually tested and interviewed by two clinical psychologists who each rated them on suitability for the job. But these ratings were not used to exclude any candidate from training. Candidates were rated on the following: personality characteristics (anxiety, mood, anger, antisocial characteristics, and ability to accept criticism), interpersonal effectiveness (ability to communicate, assertiveness, self-confidence, and ability to get along with others), and intellectual characteristics (judgment and verbal skills). The interview used a 5-point rating scale, ranging from 1 (*unsuitable*) to 5 (*excellent*), in order to assess overall psychological suitability for the job.

The trainees then completed a 5-month law-enforcement academy. At the end of training, three performance criteria were examined: (1) attrition during training, (2) ratings of psychological suitability given by the training officers, and (3) peer evaluations. Correlations were determined between each of these and the ratings by each clinician; these are as follows:

	Clinician A	Clinician B
Academy attrition	.24**	.14
Instructors' ratings	.19	.27*
Peer evaluations	.09	.13
Composite criterion	.26**	.24**

*p<.05;
**p<.01

Although some of these correlation coefficients are statistically significant, the relationships are relatively weak and certainly too low to make confident predictions about the success of individuals.

An analysis of clinicians' dichotomized ratings of "suitable" versus "unsuitable" with the goal criterion of "successful" versus "unsuccessful" found that Clinician A correctly classified 67% of the subjects, and Clinician B, 69%. An analysis of those trainees who were rated by the clinicians as "suitable" but were "unsuccessful" on the composite criterion indicated that all but one were unsatisfactory due to attrition.

Psychological Tests

Administration of psychological tests to police trainees is a frequent selection device; the tests can be group administered, computer-scored, and easily interpreted. But do they have any validity?

The MMPI and the CPI

General personality measures, such as the Minnesota Multiphasic Personality Inventory (Hathaway & McKinley, 1983) and the California Psychological Inventory (Gough, 1975), are staples of such testing. The **Minnesota Multiphasic Personality Inventory (MMPI)** was originally designed, in the early 1940s, to identify individuals with psychotic or neurotic problems. As Blau (1994) observed, it has been the workhorse of paper-and-pencil personality assessment for more than a half century. It consists of 550 true-or-false items and usually takes an hour to complete. In the late 1980s, the MMPI-2 was developed out of a need to update and restandardize the original instrument (Butcher, Dahlstrom, Graham, Tellegen, & Kaemmer, 1989). Whether the MMPI-2 was an improvement over the original

MMPI has generated much discussion (see Blau, 1994, p. 83). One study that administered both scales to 166 police officers found that 70% of them produced normal profiles on both tests (Hargrave, Hiatt, Ogard, & Karr, 1993). But individual respondents did not always score the highest on the same subscale from one form of the test to the other.

The **California Psychological Inventory (CPI)** is similar in format to the MMPI, but its subscales reflect such personal traits as dominance, sociability, and flexibility, in contrast to the diagnostic categories (for example, Psychopathic Deviate, Hypomania) of the MMPI. A survey of 72 major law-enforcement agencies (Strawbridge & Strawbridge, 1990) found that the MMPI was by far the most frequently used instrument—in 33, or 46%, of the departments. Next most frequent was the California Psychological Inventory (in 11 of 72 departments) and the Inwald Personality Inventory (used in 5 departments). Two departments used the Rorschach Inkblot Technique, and two used a human figure drawings test; 37 (or 51%) of the departments used no test at all. This survey was done 15 years ago, and the percentage of departments using tests has probably increased as more departments have sought accreditation by the Commission on Accreditation for Law Enforcement Agencies (Blau, 1994).

Reviewing the use of psychological tests in police selection, Hargrave and Hiatt (1987) reported studies finding significant relationships between MMPI scales and police officers' job tenure, automobile accidents, supervisor's ratings, and job problems. Although the CPI has been used less often, scale scores were related to trainees' academy performance and to supervisors' ratings. (Specific studies cited are listed in Hargrave and Hiatt, 1987, p. 110, and Bartol, 1991, p. 127). In another review, Bartol (1991) was less sanguine, describing the track record of the MMPI in screening and selection of law-enforcement personnel as "mixed." However, Bartol (1991) concluded that the MMPI, despite its limitations, continues to be the most commonly used personality measure for the selection of police.

In the study of trainees described earlier that evaluated the predictive validity of the clinical interview, Hargrave and Hiatt also administered the MMPI and CPI to 105 police trainees on their first day of training. The clinicians then interpreted each trainee's scores to classify his or her suitability. These ratings were compared with the same criteria as the interview data; the results were:

	Clinician A	Clinician B
Academy attrition	.24**	.15
Instructors' ratings	.25**	.27*
Peer evaluations	.36*	.13*
Composite criterion	.34**	.24**

*p<.05;
**p<.01

Clinician A correctly classified 66% of the trainees; Clinician B, 67%. These latter predictions were not different from those by the interview data, although the correlations between test results and individual criteria are somewhat higher than with the interview. Again, the results are not strong enough to make decisions about individual applicants.

Although some of these correlations are significant, the relationships are not impressive. In a follow-up study, Hargrave and Hiatt (1989) tested 579 trainees with the CPI and found that CPI profiles distinguished between those suitable and unsuitable for training. These authors concluded that CPI profiles have a more consistent relationship with job performance by police than with police academy variables. In general, the higher-rated police officers scored higher on the measures from the so-called Class II and Class III on the CPI (Class II consists of measures of socialization, responsibility, intrapersonal values, and character; Class III consists of measures of achievement potential). The other two classes of variables on the CPI showed no replicated relationship with police performance; these are Class I (measures of poise, ascendancy, self-assurance, and interpersonal adequacy) and Class IV (measures of intellectual and interest modes).

A second approach by Hargrave and Hiatt (1989) capitalized on the evaluations given to police on the job. Forty-five officers from three municipal law-enforcement agencies, all of whom had experienced serious job problems, were compared with 45 matched controls who had not received disciplinary notices for serious job problems. (The groups were matched on gender, race, education, and length of employment; their average age was 27 years, and most had some college and had been on the job 3 years.) The job-related difficulties experienced by the problem group included providing drugs to inmates, being convicted for using illegal drugs, using unnecessary force, physically confronting other officers, and violating departmental procedures, resulting in the escape of inmates. All these police had taken the CPI as part of the job-selection process. Only on the CPI Class II scales were there significant differences between the two groups (recall that Class II measures maturity, personal values, self-control, and sense of responsibility). Individuals who score higher (T scores above 50) on the scales in Class II are seen as being careful, cautious, and controlled and as having a sense of duty and a reluctance to take risks. Those scoring low (less than 40) are more carefree, but also are opportunistic risk-takers.

The non-problem group scored higher on the CPI scales So (Socialization), Sc (Self-Control), and Wb (Sense of Well-Being). Compared to non-problem officers, four times as many problem officers had scale scores at or below a T score of 40. Thus, it appears that qualities of impulsivity, risk taking, easy boredom, lack of objectivity, and willingness to break rules contribute to problems among officers (Hargrave & Hiatt, 1989).

Hiatt and Hargrave (1988a, 1988b) used a similar procedure to assess the predictive validity of the MMPI. They followed 55 urban police officers who had received at least one performance evaluation. Those rated as unsatisfactory scored significantly higher on two MMPI scales: Pa (Paranoia) and Ma (Hypomania). Building on this procedure, Bartol (1991) followed 600 police officers from 34 small-town police departments over 13 years to determine which officers were terminated. He concluded that an **immaturity index** consisting of a combination of the MMPI

scales Pd (Psychopathic Deviate) and Ma (Hypomania) plus the L scale was a strong predictor of termination.

Bartol suggested an immaturity index cutoff score of 49 (combination of the K-corrected Pd and Ma scores plus the L score) as "suggestive of possible problems" (1991, p. 131, italics in original), especially if the Ma scale is highly elevated. Seventy percent of the terminated officers received immaturity scores of 49 or above, compared with 23% of the retained group. (If an immaturity score of 54 was used as the cutoff, 53% of the terminated group would be correctly identified, contrasted with 95% of the retained group.)

Note that the typical interpretation given a high Ma score is consistent with a low score on the CPI Cluster II—impulsive, moody, and having a low frustration tolerance. Bartol wrote, "Police administrators and peers of high Ma officers often describe them as hyperactive individuals who seek constant activity" (1991, p. 131). One terminated police officer reportedly had developed the off-duty habit of locating speed traps and then driving by at a high speed to test other officers' alertness and effectiveness in high-speed chases (Bartol, 1991).

Bartol concluded that the Pd scale from the MMPI, by itself, had limited predictive power; it was more useful when combined with a high Ma score. In general, this combination—in MMPI lingo, a 4-9 code—in individuals reflects "a marked disregard for social standards and values. They frequently get into trouble with the authorities because of antisocial behavior" (Graham, 1987, p. 109).

The 4-9 code had appreciable predictive power for Bartol's sample only when merged with the **L scale.** When the MMPI was originally developed, the purpose of the L scale was to detect a deliberate and unsophisticated attempt on the part of respondents to present themselves in a favorable light (Graham, 1987). (Those MMPI items scored on the Lie scale portray the test taker as someone who does things, such as "read every editorial in the newspaper every day," which most people would like to say they do but, in all honesty, cannot say they actually do.) Bartol (1991) noted that "police administrators continually report that high-L-scoring police officers demonstrate poor judgment in the field, particularly under high levels of stress. They seem to be unable to exercise quick, independent, and appropriate decision making under emergency or crisis conditions. They become confused and disorganized" (1991, p. 131). Based on 15 years of working with police supervisors, Bartol considered an *L* score above 8 (out of 15 items) to be one of the best predictors of poor performance as a police officer. However, he offered a titillating addition: "More recently, we have also discovered that extremely low L scale scores (0 or 1) also forecast poor performance, suggesting that the L scale may be curvilinear in its predictive power" (1991, p. 131).

The Inwald Personality Inventory
The MMPI and the CPI are, of course, general instruments. In contrast, the **Inwald Personality Inventory (IPI)** was developed for a more specific and limited purpose: to measure the suitability of personality attributes and behavior patterns of law-enforcement candidates (Inwald, 1992; Inwald, Knatz, & Shusman, 1983). This instrument is a 310-item, true-false questionnaire consisting of 26 scales (25 original scales and one validity scale) designed to measure, among other matters, stress reactions and deviant behavior patterns, including absence and lateness problems, interpersonal difficulties, antisocial behavior, and alcohol and drug use. IPI subscales also measure suspicious, anxious, and rigid characteristics. This test usually takes about 45 minutes to complete.

Another significant difference between the IPI and the previously described tests is that the IPI was developed "with the express purpose of directly questioning public safety/law enforcement candidates and documenting their admitted behaviors, rather than inferring those behaviors from statistically-derived personality indicators" (Inwald, 1992, p. 4). As Blau (1994) has noted, it is essentially a "screening out" test that seeks to assess antisocial behavior and emo-

tional maladjustments that might adversely affect police performance.

The IPI items measure both personality characteristics and behavior patterns. The scales contain statements that assess both the unusual types of behavior patterns that reflect severe problems and those that reflect less extreme adjustment difficulties. They are designed to identify, for example, "a highly guarded but naive individual as having hyperactive or antisocial tendencies based strictly on behavioral admissions" (Inwald, 1992, p. 3). The scales also have a goal of differentiating between individuals who express socially deviant attitudes and those who act on them (Inwald, 1992).

The Inwald Personality Inventory contains a validity scale (Guardedness) somewhat similar to the validity scales on some other inventories. But in contrast to the MMPI *L* scale, the 19 statements on the Guardedness scale contain minor shortcomings common to almost all people. Inwald noted, "When a candidate denies such items, a strong need to appear unusually virtuous is indicated" (1992, p. 4).

Inwald developed the IPI items after reviewing more than 2,500 preemployment interviews with candidates for law-enforcement positions. Not only did the emerging characteristics include those qualities related to effective police functioning, but they also include self-revealing statements made by applicants during actual interviews.

A factor analysis (Inwald, 1992) of the IPI scales, using 2,397 male and 147 female police officer candidates, done to determine commonalities among the responses to different items, found the following:

- Factor 1, for both sexes, measured rigid, suspicious, and antisocial behaviors. It included Rigid Type, Undue Suspiciousness, and Antisocial Attitudes.
- For the males, Factor 2 was composed of two scales, Substance Abuse and Hyperactivity, reflecting risk-taking and impulsive behavior. For the female sample, Alcohol and Depression scales also contributed to this factor.

■ For the third factor, even greater sex differences emerged. For the men, Phobic Personality, Lack of Assertiveness, Depression, and Loner Type scales loaded on the factor, but for women, these were replaced with Job Difficulties and Absence Abuse.

An early effort to validate the IPI compared it to the MMPI in a study of 716 male correction-officer recruits; criterion measures included job retention or termination, absence, lateness, and disciplinary measures in the first 10 months of service (Shusman, Inwald, & Landa, 1984). This study concluded that for most criteria, the IPI scales predicted the status of officers more often than did the MMPI scales, and that the combination of IPI and MMPI scales increased accuracy of classification. The improved performance when the two scales are used together is a consistent conclusion of those validation studies reported in the test manual (Inwald, 1992), along with the relative strength of the IPI over the MMPI (Scogin, Schumacher, Howland, & McGee, 1989).

Further validation studies (Inwald & Shusman, 1984; Shusman & Inwald, 1991a) used 329 police recruits and 246 correctional officers; again, researchers concluded that more IPI than MMPI scales discriminated successfully. For example, the IPI yielded 82% correct classifications for absences, while the MMPI produced 69% correct classifications. The two scales, when combined, increased the accuracy rate to 85%. Especially useful as predictors of problematic behavior were IPI scales measuring trouble with the law, previous job difficulties, and involvement with drugs.

Another kind of study (Shusman, Inwald, & Knatz, 1987), a cross-validation, involved 698 male police officers who completed 6 months of training in the police academy. In the validation sample ($N = 421$), the IPI scales assigned from 61% to 77% of the officers into correct group membership, based on eight performance criteria, while MMPI scales identified only between 50% and 70%. In the cross-validation sample, researchers observed slightly more shrinkage for the IPI than for the MMPI concerning most of the criteria. But even with this somewhat greater degree of shrinkage, the cross-validation classification rates for the IPI were equal to or greater than the original validation percentages from the MMPI alone for all but one of the eight criteria.

Several of the IPI items ask for admissions of behaviors that are, at the least, socially unacceptable, and often are violations of laws. Would applicants for positions in law enforcement readily admit to such behaviors? A clever study by Ostrov (1985) provided a provocative answer.

The Chicago Police Department screened two groups of approximately 200 applicants each, using the IPI. Each candidate also provided a urine sample for analysis. In the first sample, 43 candidates had positive urinalysis results; in the second sample, 34 did. These subgroups were found to differ from random samples of the other candidates (i.e., those with a negative urinalysis) on several of the Drug scale items (significant differences on 3 items for sample 1 and 5 items for sample 2). The particular items referred to both marijuana and hard drug use.

Despite some impressive validation findings, the reliability of the IPI scales is not always strong. Inwald (1992) has reported Cronbach alpha coefficients (measures of internal consistency) of .41 to .82 for male police officer candidates and .32 to .80 for female candidates. An effort to combine the original 26 scales into 12 lengthier scales to increase reliability was not successful in any meaningful degree (Shusman & Inwald, 1991b).

Situational Tests

A third approach uses **situational tests,** or small samples of behaviors like those police would show on the job. One example is the work of Dunnette and Motowidlo (1976), who sought to define the critical dimensions of job performance for each of four police jobs: (1) general patrol officer, (2) patrol sergeant, (3) detective (investigator), and (4) intermediate-level commander. Finding little in the way of assessing these specific dimensions when they began their work in the early 1970s, the researchers designed a series of simulations and standardized situational tasks, such as role-playing exercises on behaviors believed to be representative of critical police tasks; that is, they tried to assess how the recruits would respond on activities that form the criteria for effective police work. For instance, they asked recruits to intervene in a dispute between a husband and his wife, to carry out a burglary investigation, and to aid a man injured at a hotel. Selection of candidates for police training was based on performance on these and other kinds of tasks.

On other occasions, situational tests have been used in police selection. One example is the work of Mills, McDevitt, and Tonkin (1966), who administered three tests intended to simulate police abilities to a group of Cincinnati police candidates. The Foot Patrol Observation Test required candidates to walk a six-block downtown route and then answer questions about what they remembered having just observed. In the Clues Test, candidates had 10 minutes to investigate a set of planted clues about the disappearance of a hypothetical city worker from his office. They were observed as they performed this task and were graded on the information they assembled. The Bull Session was a 2-hour group discussion of several topics of importance in police work.

Performance on the Clues Test correlated significantly with class ranking in the police academy, but the scores from the Foot Patrol Observation Test did not. Although researchers did not derive independent grades for the Bull Session component, it was viewed as an important measure of emotional and motivational qualities. Additionally, Mills, McDevitt, and Tonkin (1966) discovered that the Clues Test was not correlated with intelligence—indicating the advantage of including a measure of nonintellectual abilities in a selection battery.

Although situational tests have an intuitive appeal as selection devices, they have not proven to be superior predictors of performance compared to the personality test results described in the earlier section. Because they are time-consuming and expensive, they are used mainly to supplement psychological tests.

THE TRAINING OF POLICE

All law-enforcement agencies have some form of training programs for their recruits. What roles do psychologists play in such training programs, and what do our clienteles want from psychologists here?

A forensic psychologist with training in organizational psychology can evaluate a police training program to see if it is consistent with the responsibilities and responses of police as they carry out their tasks. The typical training program has been criticized for emphasizing "narrowly defined aspects of the job dealing with criminal activity, understanding relevant laws, effective firearms training, self-defense, and other survival techniques" (Stratton, 1980, p. 38). Although these are important, psychologists are urging departments to include in training the strategies necessary for coping with job-related stress and other interpersonal and communication skills. Increasingly, police need to have human-relations skills, including awareness of diversity and ability to communicate effectively.

Activities of a Psychologist in a Police Department

It is estimated that more than 150 psychologists serve full-time or part-time as **police psychologists** (Reese, 1995). Such psychologists formed the Law Enforcement Behavioral Sciences Association (LEBSA), and a section of Division 18 of the American Psychological Association (Division of Psychologists in Public Service) is titled the Police Psychology Section. These organizations sponsor presentations and workshops at national conventions and share procedures, experiences, and data.

Martin Reiser began serving as department psychologist with the Los Angeles Police Department in 1968. He observed that police departments usually ask psychologists to participate in police training programs in two ways, as teachers and as consultants (Reiser, 1972). As a teacher, the psychologist may be asked to instruct recruits on handling mentally ill people, on human relations, on criminal psychology, or on relationships with authority figures. As a consultant, "the psychologist is expected to have some practical know how and expertise about educational processes, teaching techniques, learning systems, and technology" (Reiser, 1972, p. 33).

Psychologists serving as consultants to police departments are generally available and on call to anyone in the department. Requests might include the following (Reiser, 1982b):

- The police chief wants a survey of pursuits and shootings.
- A sergeant asks for help in developing a psychologically based program of driver training to reduce police-involved accidents.
- Homicide detectives may want consultation on a bizarre murder.
- A particular officer may need psychological counseling.

Psychologists acting as consultants to police departments need to be flexible and adaptable; they must modify their frame of reference to accommodate the variety of service requests (Reiser, 1982a, 1982b). One of the central problems for the psychologist/consultant is that of identification; is the psychologist a mental health specialist, a social change agent, an organizational staff specialist, or an employee in a hierarchy? Reiser (1982b) has proposed that the level of the organization at which the consultant "gets plugged in" will determine how he or she is seen by other members of the organization, particularly those in power.

Traditionally, police officers have been wary, if not downright antagonistic, toward psychologists. Police likely have encountered a psychologist or another mental health professional in one of four ways, all of them inhibiting the development of officers' respect for the psychological profession. White and Honig (1995, pp. 258–259) described these interactions as follows:

Watching "do-gooder" psychologists testify on behalf of criminals.

Observing psychologists apparently protecting police officers who are claiming a disability but are perceived by their fellow officers as weak or abusing the system.

Viewing the psychologist as the "enemy" who has the power to keep an officer or a potential officer off the force through the psychologist's role in police selection or fitness-for-duty evaluations.

On rare occasions, dealing with mentally disturbed psychologists who have been released after police officers brought them in for involuntary hospitalization.

Thus, an initial task for a police psychologist is to listen and learn. He or she should seek to understand the culture of the police department by participating in **ride-alongs,** asking questions, and in all ways understanding the world of law enforcement rather than "gathering ammunition to change it" (White & Honig, 1995, p. 259). A police administrator may fear that the psychologist has magical powers and that the consultant may somehow usurp the administrator's control or brainwash the police administrator in some way. Reiser (1982b) has emphasized that the personal attributes of the consultant—being pragmatic, showing adaptability—are crucial for success; what a psychologist is able to achieve is "a function of role expectations of the organization, plus what the individual consultant brings to the situation in the form of his [or her] personal attributes" (p. 28).

Each of these responsibilities may have many manifestations. Like many organizations, police departments are susceptible to adopting innovative and unique programs, partly because they are new and different. Often such programs do not receive an adequate internal evaluation, if any evaluation at all. Psychologists can play a

BOX 3-2
Criminal Justice Standards and Goals
Commission-Recommended Distribution of Training Time (Percentage per Area)

Subject Area	Recommended Percentage of Training Time
Introduction to the Criminal Justice System	8
Law	10
Human Values and Problems	22
Patrol and Investigation Procedures	33
Police Proficiency	18
Administration	9
Total	100

Source: National Advisory Commission on Criminal Justice Standards and Goals. (1973). Report on police. Washington, DC: U.S. Government Printing Office, p. 394.

useful role in evaluating the effectiveness of such innovations, whether they be team policing, sensitivity training, or community orientation sessions.

The Curriculum of Training Programs

A new police chief may ask a psychologist to design a training program for recruits. Essential questions the psychologist should ask are these: What do police do? What do they need to know and be able to do? Studies of policing have consistently found that the police role is one of providing services and keeping the peace rather than handling crime (Meadows, 1987). Yet, the training the police get may be inconsistent with their subsequent duties. Germann (1969) has noted that most entry-level police training is devoted to "crook-catching"—as much as 90% of the training time—whereas officers spend only 10–15% of their job duties on this activity.

The National Advisory Commission on Criminal Justice Standards and Goals (1973, p. 392) suggested a training program of 400 hours, organized around the following six subject areas:

1. *Introduction to the Criminal Justice System:* An examination of the foundation and functions of the criminal justice system with specific attention to the role of the police in the system and government.

2. *Law:* An introduction to the development, philosophy, and types of law; criminal law; criminal procedure and rules of evidence; discretionary justice; application of the U.S. Constitution; court systems and procedures; and related civil law.

3. *Human Values and Problems:* Public service and noncriminal policing; cultural awareness; changing roles of the police; human behavior and conflict management; psychology as it relates to the police function; causes of crime and delinquency; and police–public relations.

4. *Patrol and Investigation Procedures:* The fundamentals of the patrol function including traffic, juvenile, and preliminary investigation; reporting and communication; arrest and detention procedures; interviewing; criminal investigation and case preparation; equipment and facility use; and other day-to-day responsibilities and duties.

5. *Police Proficiency:* The philosophy of when to use force and the appropriate determination of the degree necessary; armed and unarmed defense; crowd, riot, and prisoner control;

physical conditioning; emergency medical services; and driver training.

6. *Administration:* Evaluation, examination, and counseling processes; department policies, rules, regulations, organization, and personnel problems.

The commission recommended a distribution of training time as indicated in Box 3-2. Meadows (1987) surveyed 234 police chiefs and 355 criminal-justice educators about the importance of training in each of these categories. Both groups felt a need for increased training in the law and in written and oral communication, implying that police officers may not be doing a good job of communicating with the public.

On-the-Job Training

Once the police officer is credentialed and is on the job, the need for training does not end. A chapter by White and Honig (1995) on the role of the police psychologist in training activities divided on-the-job training into three categories: wellness training, training that provides information or skills, and training that relates the individual to the organization. Each is described in Box 3-3.

Specialized Training

In addition to formal and on-the-job training, police officers may need training in specialized

---

BOX 3-3

Types of On-the-Job Training for Law Enforcement Officers

WELLNESS TRAINING

White and Honig stated that the goal of **wellness training** "is assisting the police officer toward improving his or her lifestyle through learning new, health-enhancing behaviors and ideas. Wellness training is based on the concept that how an individual manages his or her life, and the accompanying stressors, will have a significant impact on job performance" (1995, p. 260).

Job stress is a major problem for law-enforcement officers, and **burnout** may be the result. Training that deals with these issues must take into account the police culture that emphasizes the illusion of invulnerability, the suppression of emotion, and the emphasis on mental and physical toughness (Hogan, 1971; Reiser, 1974). In addition to stress management, the following specific topics are a part of wellness training:

a. *Alcohol and drug abuse:* A tradition in law enforcement is drinking with fellow officers after a shift, often known as "choir practice" (White & Honig, 1995).

b. *Relationships with one's spouse:* The literature suggests that police, compared to most other occupational groups, have great difficulties in marital relationships (Kroes, Margolis, & Hurrell, 1974; Singleton & Teahan, 1978).

c. *Surviving critical incidents:* It is estimated that 60–70% of law enforcement officers leave the force within 5 years of an episode in which a fellow officer, witness, or suspect is killed or the officer is seriously injured (Reese, Horn, & Dunning, 1991; Simpson, Jensen, & Owen, 1988).

INFORMATIONAL AND SKILL TRAINING

This type of continuing education assists police officers in performing their job duties. All the special topics listed here reflect human-behavior issues that can benefit from the participation of psychologists:

a. Managing people with mental illness.
b. Increasing cross-cultural awareness.
c. Improving communication skills.
d. Working with victims of rape and sexual assault.

Two kinds of specialized topics—responses to spouse assault and negotiating with hostage takers—are considered in this chapter.

ORGANIZATIONAL TRAINING

The goal of organizational training is to improve the functioning of the organization as a whole, and such training is especially useful for officers in supervisory and management roles (White & Honig, 1995). For example, as in any organization, police departments may face questions of sexual harassment, grief management, racial discrimination, and substance use awareness.

activities; two types are described in the following sections.

Responses to Spouse Assault

Comprehensive studies indicate that in the United States, about 10% of women are assaulted by their husband and almost 7% are assaulted repeatedly (Straus, Gelles, & Steinmetz, 1980). Only about one of every seven assaults is reported to the police (Schulman, 1979; Straus, & Gelles, 1986); one reason is that victims do not expect police to be sympathetic or helpful.

These expectations are at least sometimes realistic. In 1979, the Oakland, California, Police Department's training bulletin instructed police that a man should not be arrested for wife assault because he would "lose face" (Paterson, 1979, cited by Jaffe, Hastings, Reitzel, & Austin, 1993). Levens and Dutton (1980) found that the police had negative attitudes toward intervening in domestic disputes. Training of police by psychologists conceivably can improve how police respond and eventually whether victims choose to call for help. The work by Donald Dutton and his colleagues (Dutton, 1981, 1988; Dutton & Levens, 1977) found that training significantly increased the use by police of mediation and referral techniques.

One review (Jaffe, Hastings, Reitzel, & Austin, 1993) suggested that training programs for police should include information on the "social costs of wife assault, statistics on prevalence, information on why victims stay or return, and descriptions of local services" (p. 89). It also suggested that the police have available a manual of resources as well as business cards with 24-hour phone numbers.

Negotiating With Terrorists and Hostage Takers

Terrorism is now almost a routine part of modern industrialized society; every time we go through a metal detector at an airport, we may be reminded of the possibility. Psychologists and other social scientists are beginning to study the phenomenon systematically (Crenshaw, 1986; Friedland & Merari, 1985). As the first line of response, police, the FBI, and other public-safety agencies play a central role (Greenstone, 1995b).

Another recurring problem is the person who takes hostages. Law-enforcement officers must choose whether to negotiate with the hostage taker or use direct and physical means of intervention. An example of this dilemma occurred in Kansas City, Kansas, in 1994. A man was holding his stepson at gunpoint inside the family house. During an extended standoff with the police, the estranged wife of the hostage taker escaped from the house safely along with two other people. Police entered the house and negotiated with the hostage taker, who barricaded himself and his hostage in an upstairs bedroom. After about 3 hours, the police decided they had an opportunity to jump the hostage taker and disarm him. But as they began to do so, the hostage (a teenager) bolted from the room; a police officer—confronted by a man bursting from a room straight toward him—feared for his safety and fired. The 18-year-old was shot in the abdomen and critically wounded (Alm, 1994).

Negotiation with terrorists and hostage takers has become a well-established concept in almost all police departments in the United States, and it receives great emphasis by the FBI and many state police departments. A survey of 34 police departments found that 31 (91%) had a designated negotiation team (Fuselier, 1988). Training courses on hostage negotiation often recommend consultation with a clinical psychologist (Fuselier, 1988). What can the field of psychology offer?

Who Takes Hostages?

The law-enforcement and clinical literature differentiates four basic types of **hostage taker:** the political activist or terrorist, the criminal, the mentally disturbed person, and the prisoner. Hassel (1975, cited by Fuselier, 1988) concluded that the most frequent type is the criminal trapped while committing a crime, while Stratton (1978) identified political terrorists as the most difficult to negotiate with because of their "total commitment, exhaustive planning, and ability to exert power effectively" (p. 71). But Maher (1977) considered the mentally disturbed hostage taker as the greatest threat. These contradicting conclusions reflect, for Fuselier (1988), the need for a "systematic nationwide collection or compilation . . . of information on hostage incidents" (pp. 175–176) by law-enforcement agencies.

Why Do People Take Hostages?

Fuselier (1988) suggested four reasons political terrorists take hostages: (1) to demonstrate to the public the inability of a government to protect its own citizens, (2) to ensure increased publicity for their political agenda, (3) to create civil discontent indirectly by causing the government to overreact and restrict its citizens, and (4) to demand release of members of their groups who are in custody.

These reasons reflect planned activities; in contrast, the criminal may spontaneously take a hostage when his or her own freedom is jeopardized, thus reflecting a need for safe passage or a means to escape. Mentally disturbed people take hostages for a variety of reasons, though each stems from the hostage taker's own view of the world. Prisoners usually use hostages to protest conditions within the prison.

The Role of the Clinical Psychologist

Does the psychologist have something valuable to offer when hostages are taken? The answer seems to be a qualified yes. Those police who are best trained in the procedures of hostage negotiations are more likely to bring about a successful resolution of the incident (Borum, 1988). Success in such situations is usually defined as "a resolution in which there is no loss of life to any of those involved in the incident including police, hostage taker, and hostages" (Greenstone, 1995b, p. 358). Psychological considerations are central in evaluating progress in the negotiations; for example, Greenstone (1995a) suggested that if the hostage taker is talking more, is more willing to talk about his or her personal life, and reflects less violence in his or her conversation, progress is being achieved. Furthermore, McMains (1988) identified three roles: the

professional, who is a source of applicable behavioral science information; the consultant, who develops training programs, materials, and exercises; and the participant/observer, who makes suggestions but recognizes the authority of the law-enforcement personnel.

But experts are not in agreement; several perspectives can be identified:

1. Powitsky (1979) argued that psychologists might perform some relevant duties, such as gathering information to be used in the negotiating strategy, but that "the majority of practicing psychologists, especially those who work outside of the criminal justice system, would not be very helpful (and some would be harmful) in a hostage-taking situation" (p. 30).
2. Poythress (1980), who described himself as a "guarded optimist," offered that "mental health professionals may have something to offer in the hostage situation, but probably less than the field commanders might hope for" (p. 34). He listed three reasons why the responsible police officer should not enlist a psychologist's opinion on the decision to negotiate rather than attack:
   a. Psychologists have little formal training on this topic, little research has been done, and few psychologists have had much field experience in it. In the two decades since Poythress wrote this, a modest beginning has occurred in providing assistance to negotiations (see, for example, Fowler, DeVivo, & Fowler, 1985; Soskis, 1983; and Yonah & Gleason, 1981). The FBI's training academy at Quantico, Virginia, has developed a 30-hour Basic Hostage Negotiations training module (Greenstone, 1995a).
   b. Predictors of the probable dangerousness of a given person in a given situation are notoriously bad (Poythress, 1980).
   c. As Meehl (1954) showed many years ago, statistical (i.e., actuarial) methods are more accurate than clinical judgment in general predictions of outcome.

3. More positive in his view was Reiser (1982a, 1982b), who saw the psychologist contributing as a backup and adviser to the negotiation team as well as providing training on the topics of assessment of the hostage taker's motives and personality, the development of communication skills, and the challenge of dealing with stress and fatigue.

4. Fusilier (1988), author of a useful review, accepted the value of psychologists as consultants, but only after they have received training in hostage negotiation concepts. After attendance at a hostage negotiation seminar, the psychologist "can assist in both determining whether a mental disorder exists and deciding on a particular negotiation approach" (p. 177). But Fusilier noted that a psychologist should not be used as the **primary negotiator;** instead, being a consultant allows the psychologist "to maintain a more objective role in assessing the mental status and performance of the negotiator" (1988, p. 177).

Psychologists, if not primary negotiators, can play a role by offering a post-incident critique of the team as well as counseling for the police and victims. The effects on police of participation in a hostage negotiation may be similar to those in other stressful situations: anxiety, somatic responses, and a subjective sense of work overload (Beutler, Nussbaum, & Meredith, 1988; Dietrich & Smith, 1986; Zizzo, 1985).

The Role of the Psychologist as Evaluation Researcher Another role with respect to hostage negotiations is the psychologist as evaluation researcher. What works and what doesn't work? Allen, Cutler, and Berman (1993) collected the types of responses used by the police tactical teams in all 130 situations reflecting hostage taking or suicide attempts in Miami, Florida, for 5 years; they focused on the 48 cases in which some form of negotiation was used. Face-to-face negotiation (compared to use of a bullhorn, a public address system, or a telephone) was the least effective

method of apprehending the hostage taker. Police often see face-to-face negotiation as a "last resort." The analysis also indicated that hostage takers under the influence of drugs were much less likely to come out without violence.

EVALUATING EFFECTIVENESS OF POLICE ACTIVITIES

Many evaluations of police activities and innovations in police policies are carried out by people not trained in the methodology of psychology and the social sciences. Psychologists, however, can play a major role in the evaluation of police activities. We provide two examples here: one at the level of the individual police officer (the fitness-for-duty evaluation), and the other at the level of general policy innovation (community policing).

Fitness-for-Duty Evaluations

After participating in critical incidents involving the death of a partner or an injury during a chase or shoot-out, the law-enforcement officer may exhibit emotional or behavioral reactions that prompt his or her supervisor to request a **fitness-for-duty evaluation** (Inwald, 1990). Complaints against the officer, such as charges of brutality, may also lead to an investigation of the officer's emotional stability. A psychologist may be called on to conduct the evaluation (Delprino & Bahn, 1988). Robin Inwald (1990) offered a set of guidelines for such evaluations, which include the following:

1. They shall be done only by qualified psychologists or psychiatrists who are licensed in that state.
2. The evaluator should be familiar with research on testing and evaluation in the field of police psychology.
3. As far as possible, the evaluation should *not* be done by a psychologist or psychiatrist

who provides counseling within the same department.

4. Issues of confidentiality should be made explicit in writing prior to conducting the fitness-for-duty evaluation, and a consent form should be obtained from the officer.

5. The fitness-for-duty assessment should include at least one interview with the officer; a battery of psychological tests; interviews with supervisors, family members, and coworkers; and a review of any past psychological and medical evaluations.

6. The fitness-for-duty evaluator should provide a written report documenting the findings of the evaluation along with specific recommendations regarding continued employment and rehabilitation. (Two examples of such reports may be found in Blau, 1994, pp. 134–138 and pp. 140–142.)

Community Policing

The 1970s and 1980s saw increases in drug usage and resultant crime, along with the continued decay of many inner cities in the United States. Like other concerned institutions, law-enforcement agencies sought new ways to deal with these problems. The concept of **community policing** was developed as a response; as the name implies, its goal was to reunite the police with the community (Peak & Glensor, 1996). One author defines community policing as "an extension of the police-community relations concept which envisions an effective woring partnership between the police and members of the community in order to solve problems which concern both" (Schmalleger, 1995, p. 200). For example, residents of some neighborhoods are outraged by the proliferation of "crack houses" on their streets and drug traffickers in the public parks; in community policing, focus is on improving the quality of life and being responsive (even proactively) to citizens' concerns.

Community policing has been implemented in different ways in different cities (Skolnik & Bayley, 1986). For example, in San Francisco,

police began riding on city buses; in other cities, police began athletic programs for young people in high-crime areas, established bicycle patrols or reestablished foot patrols, or started neighborhood police stations.

Anecdotal evidence for the effectiveness of these programs was encouraging, but a more reliable evaluation was more difficult to do. Often communities would initiate several changes at once and, hence, not be able to evaluate the separate impact of each. The goal of the change—was it a quicker response by the police to crimes, reduction of crime rates, higher clearance rates for crimes that were committed, or greater community satisfaction with the police and lessened fears of crime? Some citizens remain suspicious of the police and are not willing to accept a more visible presence of the police in their neighborhood (Schmalleger, 1995). Also, some police are more comfortable with traditional law-enforcement duties than with community relations (Sparrow, Moore, & Kennedy, 1990). The forensic psychologist as an evaluation researcher can aid the police department in designing interventions that permit clearer tests of their effectiveness; the evaluation researcher also clarifies the important outcome measures—how the community weighs the importance of crime control, citizen satisfaction, or job satisfaction of police.

SUMMARY

Forensic psychologists can contribute to many aspects of police work: to the procedure of selecting officers for training, to the preservice and on-the-job training of officers, and to the evaluation of the performance of individual officers and of innovative programs by law-enforcement agencies. In doing so, forensic psychologists have the difficult task of not only being responsive to the police department as a clientele but also recognizing concerns of the public about problems in some departments, including corruption, racism, and brutality.

The selection of candidates for law-enforcement training is usually an involved and extensive process. The psychologist plays a role in interviewing candidates and in advising the department about instruments to administer to candidates. Among these, the Minnesota Multiphasic Personality Inventory is the most widely used, but the Inwald Personality Inventory is worthy of consideration, as it was designed specifically for selection of law-enforcement officers.

Psychologists can contribute to the in-service training of police officers in general as well as specific areas. Wellness training is of special importance, given the high rates of stress and resulting alcoholism, burnout, and marital discord in the police as an occupational group. Forensic psychologists have also contributed to specialized training in responding to the taking of hostages and to domestic assaults. The role of the evaluation researcher enters when the psychologist is asked to assess the worthiness of a recently adopted policy, such as community policing.

KEY TERMS

burnout
California Psychological
    Inventory (CPI)
clienteles
community policing
DWB
false negatives
false positives
fitness-for-duty evaluation
hostage taker
immaturity index
Inwald Personality Inventory (IPI)
L scale
Minnesota Multiphasic
    Personality Inventory (MMPI)
police corruption
police psychologist
police selection
primary negotiator
race-based profiling
ride-alongs
situational tests
stakeholders
team policing
wellness training

INFOTRAC® COLLEGE EDITION

InfoTrac College Edition is a FREE, powerful, online learning resource, consisting of full-text articles from thousands of journals and periodicals. With each new copy of *Forensic Psychology, Second Edition*, you receive four months of free access to the InfoTrac College Edition database. By doing a simple keyword search (try using the Key Terms from the list above), you can quickly generate a list of relevant articles from thousands of possibilities and can select articles to read, explore, and print for reference or further study. InfoTrac College Edition's continuously updated collection of articles can be useful for doing reading and writing assignments that reach beyond the pages of this text!

SUGGESTED READINGS

Baker, M. (1985). *Cops: Their lives in their own words.* New York: Pocket Books.

A number of books available in paperback chronicle the lives of police in the line of duty. This book reflects interviews with 100 police officers; as you would suspect, the dramatic receives more coverage than the routine, but the book is a useful portrayal of how police describe their jobs.

Blau, T. H. (1994). *Psychological services for law enforcement.* New York: John Wiley.

A comprehensive review by a prominent police psychologist; it contains extensive practical information.

McAlary, M. (1987). *Buddy boys: When good cops turn bad.* New York: G. P. Putnam's Sons.

An expose by a former investigative reporter of organized criminal activity by certain officers in the New York City Police Department.

Peak, K. J., & Glensor, R. W. (1996). *Community policing and problem solving: Strategies and practices.* Upper Saddle River, NJ: Prentice-Hall.

A book-length analysis of the development and implementation of community policing.

Rachlin, H. (1991). *The making of a cop.* New York: Simon & Schuster.

A readable report of the transition of four recruits from the New York City Police Academy to life on the streets. Contains a detailed description of what is involved in police training.

A number of reviews of the Inwald Personality Inventory are available and are worth reading to understand what is involved in developing an effective selection device. They are

Bolton, B. (1985). Review of Inwald Personality Inventory. In J. V. Mitchell (Ed.), *The ninth mental measurements yearbook* (pp. 711–713). Lincoln, NE: Buros Institute of Mental Measurements, University of Nebraska.

Juni, S. (1992). Review of Inwald Personality Inventory. In J. J. Kramer & J. C. Conoley (Eds.), *Eleventh mental measurements yearbook* (pp. 415–418). Lincoln, NE: Buros Institute of Mental Measurements, University of Nebraska.

Swartz, J. D. (1985). Review of Inwald Personality Inventory. In J. V. Mitchell (Ed.), *The ninth mental measurements yearbook* (pp. 713–714). Lincoln, NE: Buros Institute of Mental Measurements, University of Nebraska.

Waller, N. G. (1992). Review of Inwald Personality Inventory. In J. J. Kramer & J. C. Conoley (Eds.), *Eleventh mental measurements Yearbook* (pp. 418–419). Lincoln, NE: Buros Institute of Mental Measurements, University of Nebraska.

4

Techniques of Criminal Investigation: Profiling, Psychological Autopsies, Hypnosis, and Lie Detection

CRIMINAL PROFILING AND FORENSIC PSYCHOLOGY

Is **criminal profiling** an appropriate topic for a book on forensic psychology? On the one hand, many students—some of whom will be the forensic psychologists of the future—are drawn to the field because of their desire to emulate Clarice Starling of *The Silence of the Lambs* or the main characters in such television shows as *Profiler* or *Cracker*. (Any psychology professor will tell you that a common question from students is "How can I become a criminal profiler?") The classification and capture of criminals surely offers the hope of a fascinating career.

On the other hand, many forensic psychologists would not include criminal profiling under the rubric of forensic psychology as we have defined it. Here are some of their reasons:

1. Training in criminal profiling has been controlled by the FBI, and most graduate programs in forensic psychology do not offer specialized courses on this topic. The only people who have been eligible for training by the FBI are law-enforcement officers, not psychologists.
2. The availability of jobs as criminal profilers is extremely limited. Even at its busiest, the Behavioral Science Unit of the FBI was a very small operation, with only a dozen or fewer profilers. Although there are a few positions in state crime labs, and some detectives in large-city police departments may do some profiling, the number of open positions is minuscule compared to the intense level of interest.
3. The vast majority of those who do profiling in the United States did not do graduate work in psychology; rather, they advanced through the ranks of the FBI, starting as field agents, or they went through police-academy training. (The situation is different in Great Britain, where many profilers are psychologists; Gudjonsson & Copson, 1997.)

4. Even experienced profilers acknowledge that profiling is more an art than a science. Indeed, a series of FBI Law Enforcement Bulletins on the topic of profiling make this statement repeatedly (note the potential for cross-examination under the Daubert standard for the admissibility of expert testimony!). All profilers are not in agreement about the appropriate methodology—for example, whether to use a statistical analysis of the findings or to use clinical approaches of single cases to make inferences about the perpetrator's unconscious personality processes (Bekerian & Jackson, 1997). Hence, *criminal profiling* is a broad, hard-to-pin-down term that covers a variety of procedures and operating assumptions.

For these and other reasons, expert testimony on profiling is not likely to be admitted in court, as it fails to meet the Daubert standard of merit as judged by the scientific community (see *State v. Lowe,* a 1991 Ohio case; see also Box 4-1). Testimony on crime scene analysis has been admitted, but this often occurs when no one has challenged the reliability and validity of the technique.

Despite these concerns, using the broad definition of forensic psychology introduced in chapter 1, profiling does seem to be an application of psychological concepts to the legal system, even though evidence for its effectiveness is less than overwhelming. We hope that a critical analysis of the current state of the field will increase readers' awareness of both its opportunities and its temptations.

WHY DEVELOP CRIMINAL PROFILES?

Definitions and Recurring Mysteries

Crime is always a concern in the United States. Next to crime prevention, crime detection is of the highest priority. Among the types of murderers,

BOX 4-1
John Douglas and *State of Ohio v. Lowe*

In an Ohio double murder case, the prosecution attempted to introduce testimony by John Douglas, the noted FBI profiler and author (Douglas & Olshaker, 1995, 1996, 1997, 1998). The defense filed a motion to exclude or suppress his testimony. This motion was sustained, and the court ruled as follows:

The State of Ohio appeals from a judgment entered in the Court of Common Pleas of Logan County granting a motion to suppress filed by defendant-appellee, Terry Lowe. Defendant was indicted by the Logan County Grand Jury for the aggravated murders of Phyllis Mullet and Belle Center Marshal Murray Griffin. On July 5, 1986, Phyllis Mullet was murdered in her home in Belle Center, Ohio. Mullet was stabbed multiple times in the chest area and her throat was slit. When found, Mullet's body was clad in a sweatshirt only. The body of Griffin was found in the upstairs hall of Mullet's home. Griffin **784 died from gunshot wounds which he apparently sustained at the hand of Mullet's murderer during the marshal's attempt to rescue Mullet.

In response to the defendant's request for notice of intention to use evidence at trial, the state filed a notice of intention to use "the testimony of * * * officers from the Behavioral Science Unit of the Federal Bureau of Investigation who will testify concerning crime-scene characteristics for the purposes of assisting in the identification of the Defendant as the perpetrator." The defendant responded to the state's notice of intention with a pretrial motion to suppress any testimony by any state's witness regarding "establishment of a psychological or personality profile of the perpetrator of the crimes charged, based upon crime scene analysis."

At the hearing convened upon defendant's motion, the state introduced the testimony of Agent John Douglas. Douglas is a twenty-year employee of the *406 Federal Bureau of Investigation ("FBI") who currently works within the National Center for Analysis of Violent Crime at the FBI Academy. The goal of the testimony elicited from Douglas by the state was to establish Douglas's expertise in the field of criminal-investigative analysis and psycholinguistic analysis and to determine his opinion regarding the perpetrator's motivation for the murder of Mullet, as well as the motivation for a certain writing authored by defendant. The state contended that Douglas's opinion testimony on these issues should be admitted into evidence at defendant's trial.

On direct examination, Douglas testified that criminal-investigative analysis is a process through which the crime scene is examined to determine the perpetrator's motivation for the crime. Douglas further testified that he has utilized crime-scene analysis as an investigative tool on over five thousand occasions. With respect to psycholinguistic analysis, Douglas testified that this analysis is used to discern both the underlying motivation for a particular writing and the potential for violence by the author of the writing.

As pertains to the case before us, Douglas examined the crime-scene photographs, autopsy protocols, and police reports. In addition, the agent examined a document authored by defendant which consisted of a list of women, the names of their husbands and the names of their children. The murder victim, Mullet, was included on the list of females. Although the document contained sexual language concerning at least one female on the list, there was no overt sexual language regarding Mullet.

Douglas testified that, based upon his review of the crime scene materials, he was of the opinion that the motivation for the death of Mullet was sexual. Douglas stated that his opinion in this regard was premised on the fact that Mullet's hands and feet were bound with ligatures that had been brought to the scene by the perpetrator of the crime. Douglas was of the opinion that the presence of the ligatures indicated preplanning on the part of the perpetrator. Douglas further testified that preplanning is one of several characteristics of a sexually motivated homicide.

As concerns the document that was authored by the defendant, Douglas testified that the writing was sexually motivated and represented defendant's plan or mission for power.

Upon cross-examination by defense counsel, Douglas acknowledged that his educational background consists of a bachelor's degree in physical education. Douglas also holds a master's degree in educational psychology, with an emphasis in counseling, and a doctorate in education. Douglas further acknowledged that, when concluding that an offender's motivation is sexual, he must make psychological inferences to draw those conclusions and therefore is engaging in a form of psychology. There was considerable dispute over whether Douglas was really attempting to draw a psychological profile of defendant as opposed to merely expressing investigative conclusions resulting from his analysis of **785 crime-scene evidence. In any event, Douglas conceded that none of his testimony, whether

continued

related to the motivation for the murder of Mullet or the motivation for defendant's writing, could be stated to a reasonable scientific certainty.

Additionally, defendant elicited the testimony of Dr. Solomon Fulero, who is a licensed psychologist and a professor of psychology, to rebut Douglas's testimony elicited on direct examination. Fulero corroborated the conclusion of Douglas that opinions based on criminal-investigative analysis do not rise to the level of reasonable scientific certainty that is a prerequisite to consideration as expert opinion testimony. In the case before us, the trial court suppressed the testimony of Douglas upon finding, *inter alia,* that "Mr. Douglas' opinion is an investigative tool like a polygraph; it might be used to investigate, but it does not have the reliability to be evidence." Having given careful consideration to the testimony elicited in this matter, we conclude that there is evidence in the record to support the trial court's finding that the opinion testimony of Douglas is not reliable evidence.

As a whole, the record reflects that Douglas's opinion for the most part is based on the behavioral science of clinical psychology, an area in which he has no formal education, training or license. In short, the purported scientific analytical processes to which Douglas testified are based on intuitiveness honed by his considerable experience in the field of homicide investigation. While we in no way trivialize the importance of Douglas's work in the field of crime detection and criminal apprehension, we do not find that there was sufficient evidence of reliability adduced to demonstrate the relevancy of the testimony or to qualify Douglas as an expert witness. Accordingly, the error as assigned by the state is overruled.

those who commit one murder after another are of special concern; some observers believe these serial killers and spree killers account for one third of all murders (Linedecker & Burt, 1990, p. ix). The FBI has reported that 151 serial killers have been identified and imprisoned since 1970 (Youngstrom, 1991). If we were able to develop profiles of criminals, the process would aid both of the just-mentioned goals—detection and prevention.

But what do we mean by a **criminal profile**? A "profile" of what? Some profilers emphasize the personality and motivations of the offender, including characteristic ways of committing crimes and treating their victims. But certainly physical characteristics are important—the criminal's age, gender, race, height, and weight. Whether the perpetrator is left-handed or right-handed is sometimes easily determined from an analysis of the criminal act. Because these qualities plus other demographic data (e.g., occupation, education) are sought in addition to a personality sketch of the criminal, some investigators (e.g., Holmes & Holmes, 1996) prefer the term **sociopsychological profile,** rather than the more common *psychological profile.*

False Stereotypes and Simplified Assumptions

In the novel *Evidence* (Weisman, 1980), an assistant district attorney says to an investigative reporter:

"Most crime is amazingly simple. . . . You guys always look for some kind of conspiracy. You're always writing about psychological motivation, about role modeling. . . . most perps do what they do because it's all they know. They're stupid. They hate, they want, and they do things to other people because that's what they know how to do. Robbers rob. Muggers mug. Rapists rape. That's what they do best. It's their job. All that talk about sociopathic patterns, the messed-up childhoods, the resentment of the father-authority figure, I think it's a crock. The perp is a perp. . . . They do what they know best." (p. 221)

Perhaps this oversimplified analysis applies in a few instances. But experienced criminal investigators would argue that a sophisticated psychological analysis is often required. Take, for example, the crime of stalking: The Department of Justice has estimated that as many as one million women and 400,000 men in the United States are victims of unrelenting pursuers (Brody, 1998). But stalkers reflect a variety of motives, behaviors, and psychological traits, making it difficult to develop one psychological profile that covers all, or even a majority, of them (Meloy, 1998). The procedure of profiling needs to be applied to the individual stalker, rather than to the group.

A second problem that criminal profiling must overcome is false stereotypes held by many citizens about certain types of criminals. For example, bank robbers are often considered to be clever, debonair, skillful, and glamorous; in actuality, a study of convicted bank robbers found that most were young, impulsive, high on drugs or experiencing a personal crisis, and desperate (Associated Press, 1986). Most of them repeat the crime until they get caught, and indeed most of them are—in contrast to some other types of major felonies, police solve nearly four out of every five bank robberies. In this case, crime rarely pays.

Similarly, embezzlement, as a crime, carries a false connotation. Many people assume that embezzlers are old, trusted employees who have steadfastly worked for a single firm for many years. But a survey of 23 men and 39 women convicted of embezzling (Pogrebin, Poole, & Regoli, 1986) concluded that the typical embezzler was a 26-year-old, married White woman with a high-school education who earned close to minimum wage and worked in an entry-level position for less than one year. The most frequent motivation expressed by the embezzlers was a marital or family problem.

When asked to describe what an assassin is like, many Americans would probably describe a deranged madman, a lonely loser who follows up his threats of violence with an act against his sole target (Dedman, 1998). But an analysis by the Secret Service of all 83 people who killed or tried to kill American politicians or other nationally known figures in the last 50 years challenges these stereotypes. "Fewer than half of the assassins showed symptoms of mental illness. Many shifted from one target to another, valuing the act more than the victim. No one had communicated a direct threat to the target or to law-enforcement authorities" (Dedman, 1998, p. A-15).

We also make assumptions about the backgrounds of lawbreakers. As Ressler and Shachtman (1992) observed, a common myth is that murderers come from impoverished or broken homes. Ressler, Burgess, and Douglas (1988) conducted interviews with 36 convicted murderers; more than half lived initially in a family that appeared to be intact, with both the mother and father living together with the son. As a group, they were intelligent children; although 7 of the 36 had IQ scores below 90, almost one third (11 of 36) had IQs above 120, and most were at least in the normal range. (There *were* dysfunctional aspects of these families—high rates of alcohol or drug abuse, consistent emotional abuse—but the families often appeared to be "normal.")

The D.C. Sniper Case

The D.C. Sniper case is an excellent example of "stereotypes at work." In a 23-day period in September and October 2002, the Washington, D.C., area was terrorized by a series of sniper shootings that killed 10 people and wounded 3 more, including a 13-year-old boy shot in front of his school. On October 24, 2002, the police arrested John Allen Muhammad, age 41, and John Lee Malvo, age 17, and charged them with being the snipers. The car used in the shootings had been described as a white minivan, but the car in which Muhammad and Malvo were eventually apprehended was a blue 1990 Chevrolet Caprice. In the media frenzy surrounding the case, profilers and criminologists were all over the airwaves discussing their theories and profiles in the case (Gettleman, 2002, p. A-23). The descriptions and profiles given ranged widely and were at times contradictory. Various profilers said that the killer did not have children—Muhammad had four. Army veterans insisted that the killer was definitely not in the military—Muhammad was a Gulf War veteran with

11 years of military service. The killer was thought to be a local resident, because of the well-planned acts and escapes. He was not. Candice DeLong, a former FBI agent and profiler who is often a media commentator, insisted that the sniper would be a firefighter or construction worker—Muhammad was an unemployed drifter (Gettleman, 2002, p. A-23). Based on data from a database compiled by James Alan Fox, a criminologist at Northeastern University and one of the most widely quoted profilers in the media, the average age of a sniper killer is 26, with 91% being under age 40. Most work alone (those who predicted two snipers in this case were right, but that prediction was primarily based on initial descriptions of the white minivan with two people inside). Bo Dietl, a retired New York City police detective and admitted "profiling addict," said that he thought "all along" that a "pair of twerpy teens" were involved, and then he claimed success: "It's like I picked the right team and won the World Series" (Gettleman, 2002, p. A-23).

But the most important and interesting feature was that virtually no one predicted that the sniper(s) would be African American. Fox's data showed that 55% of snipers were White. After the case, Candice DeLong said "A Black sniper? That was the last thing I was thinking" (Gettleman, 2002, p. A-23). Even Clarence Page, a noted African American columnist, said "Still, I confess, I also figured the sniper would be White" (Page, 2002, p. B-9).

This case illustrates the pitfalls, problems, and dangers of criminal profiling. Some have become quite disillusioned with the technique. Richard Ofshe, a sociologist at the University of California, Berkeley, has said, "All this profiling has gotten to be nonsense. The statistical methods are shoddy. Maybe it's time to say we don't know, I don't know, end of story" (Gettleman, 2002, p. A-23). It has been pointed out that profiles can even lead to rigidity in criminal investigations: Jack Levin, a criminologist, points out that if the police were looking for a White man in a white minivan, they could easily have let the real sus-

pects through roadblocks: "I wouldn't be surprised if the suspects just passed right by" (Gettleman, 2002, p. A-23).

WHAT *IS* CRIMINAL PROFILING?

Definitions

The origins of criminal profiling are unclear, but for centuries, elements of society have tried to pinpoint those physical or psychological qualities linked to criminal or deviant behavior (Pinizzotto, 1984). Even literary works, such as Shakespeare's *Julius Caesar* ("yon Cassius has a lean and hungry look") and Edgar Allan Poe's "The Murders in the Rue Morgue," reflected attempts to profile unacceptable behaviors by use of physical attributes (McPoyle, 1981, cited by Pinizzotto, 1984).

Criminal profiling has been described as an educated attempt to provide specific information about a certain type of suspect (Geberth, 1981) and as a biographical sketch of behavioral patterns, trends, and tendencies (Vorpagel, 1982, cited in Douglas, Ressler, Burgess, & Hartman, 1986). The basic premise of criminal profiling is that the way a person thinks directs the person's behavior; it is important to recognize that profiling does not provide the specific identity of the offender (Douglas et al., 1986).

Similarly, not all types of crimes are susceptible to successful criminal profiling. Holmes and Holmes (1996) concluded that such crimes as check forgery, bank robbery, and kidnapping are not good candidates for profiling. A single act of murder, especially if it is spontaneous, is more difficult to interpret than is a series of crimes that reflect similar actions or locations. In the latter instance, the consistencies in crime scenes and treatment of victims permit the police to get a better handle on the nature of the perpetrator. Or the nature of the victim's wounds might give clues to the personality and experience of

BOX 4-2
A Killer's View of His Own Crimes

"First of all, any investigative onlooker to my crime scene would have immediately deduced that the offender was extremely sadistic in nature. The visible markers of bondage, and the nature of the victims' wounds—the evidence of unhurried, systematic abuse—would have indicated that sadistic acts were not new to the offender; he had committed such brutality in the past, and would likely continue this pattern of victimization in the future.

"From these points, it could have then been correctly assumed that, although brutally violent, the offender was nevertheless intelligent enough to attach method to his madness—as well as cautious and aware enough with regard to his surroundings—to make sure he proceeds unseen in the commission of his deeds.

"Further, . . . [because] such a brutal offense was unprecedented in this area, it could have been correctly assumed that the offender was very new to the city; if he was a drifter, he was at least someone who very possibly could deem to leave town as suddenly as he arrived (which is exactly what I did)."

Quoted in Holmes & Holmes, 1996, p. 41, from the first author's files.

the attacker. Holmes and Holmes (1996) suggested that some serial killers are aware of the "trace" they leave at a crime scene or even do so intentionally (see Box 4-2 for an example).

Three Approaches to Criminal Profiling

Three different approaches can be included under the rubric *criminal profiling* (or *offender profiling*, the term used in Europe to describe this process). Even though each has a different procedure, the general intent is the same. We describe all three approaches in the following sections.

Distinguishing the "Evil" Person

Understanding the behavior and motivations of individuals who play a role in important events reflects one goal of profiling. In the 9 days between his murder of Gianni Versace and his own suicide, spree killer Andrew Cunanan became the target of nationwide questions about his motivations and personality (Orth, 1999). Whether a person's effects are broad and perverse, like Hitler's or Stalin's, or futile, like those of Frank Corder (the man who was killed in 1994 as he flew his small plane into the trees surrounding the White House), his or her actions lead us to ask, "Why?" When a national leader dies suddenly and is replaced by a newcomer—as occurred,

for example, when North Korea's longtime dictator Kim Il Sung died in 1994 and was replaced by his son Kim Jong Il—the CIA seeks to develop a personality profile that will predict the new leader's behavior while in power.

Adolf Hitler

The practical purposes of profiling a specific person were tested by the World War II effort of the U.S. government's Office of Strategic Services (OSS) to profile the personality of Adolf Hitler. In 1943, a practicing psychiatrist, Walter C. Langer, assembled material to provide a psychological description of Hitler's personality, a diagnosis of his mental condition, and a prediction of how he would react to defeat. Two decades after the war, Langer published a book detailing all his conclusions (Langer, 1972).

Langer employed a psychodynamic profile of Hitler, in which the nature of Hitler's childhood relationship with his parents was seen as quite influential on his future behavior. Apparently, Hitler saw his father as brutally cold and cruel in his relationship with his wife and children. In contrast, his mother was long-suffering and affectionate; young Adolf developed a strong emotional attachment to her. But, while Hitler was still an adolescent, his mother died a painful death from cancer. Langer concluded that Hitler could not develop an intimate personal relationship that survived adversity because he judged people to be untrustworthy. At the same time, he saw himself as infallible and omnipotent. Through his leadership of a powerful Germany, he could somehow prove his manhood to his deceased mother.

With regard to predictions, Langer's analysis offered several possibilities for Hitler's approach to adversity. Langer doubted that Hitler would seek refuge in another country; more likely, he would lead his troops into a final, futile battle. Langer concluded as quite plausible the possibility that in the face of inevitable defeat, Hitler would commit suicide. He noted that Hitler had threatened to take his own life on earlier occasions and had said to an associate, "Yes, in the hour of supreme peril I must sacrifice myself to the people" (quoted by Langer, 1972, p. 216). As we know, Langer was right.

It is unlikely that the profile of Hitler transmitted to the U.S. government had any discernible effect on the conduct of the Allied foreign policy or the outcome of the war; even Langer (1972, p. 25) doubts that it did. It simply came too late.

Saddam Hussein

The quest to understand the personality and behavior of "evil" world leaders is never-ending. During the Gulf War, officials in the U.S. government sought to "profile" Saddam Hussein. (They may have done so recently as well, with respect to the Iraq War, but there is no published evidence about this.) Psychiatrist Jerrold M. Post of George Washington University testified before the Armed Services Committee of the U.S. House of Representatives in December 1990, and his testimony was later published (Post, 1991).

Disabusing the government officials of the popular labels for Saddam Hussein, such as "madman of the Middle East," Post stated that "there is no evidence that he is suffering from a psychotic disorder. He is not impulsive, only acts after judicious consideration, and can be extreme-ly patient; indeed he uses time as a weapon" (1991, p. 283). However, Post concluded that Saddam was often *politically* out of touch with reality; he possessed a "political personality constellation—messianic ambition for unlimited power, absence of conscience, unconstrained aggression, and a paranoid outlook" (1991, p. 285), which made him quite dangerous. Post predicted that Saddam Hussein would not "go down to the last flaming bunker" if he had a way out, but that he would "stop at nothing if he is backed into a corner" (1991, pp. 288–289). Post's predictions—in light of events since the Gulf War of early 1991 and the recent war in Iraq, along with Saddam's capture in 2003—are interesting, to say the least.

David Koresh

The analyses of Hitler and Saddam Hussein were based on a wealth of material about these public figures, developed over extended periods. Sometimes, in contrast, a crisis erupts suddenly, requiring a quicker decision.

After a 51-day siege of the Branch Davidian compound in Waco, Texas, led by David Koresh, the FBI decided to attack, based on reports that children inside were being abused. The result, as we now know, was a disaster. As many as two dozen cult members, including Koresh, were shot as fire engulfed the 86 people in the compound on April 19, 1993 (Verhovek, 1993).

The actions of Koresh and the people in the compound have raised questions about the adequacy of the psychological profile of Koresh assembled by the FBI. William Sessions, then director of the FBI, was quoted as saying: "We had been assured, both from our own evaluations of David Koresh, from the psychologists, from the psycholinguists, from a psychiatrist, from his writings, from his assertions himself, repeatedly, that he did not intend to commit suicide" (quoted by Lewis, 1993, p. A19). One of those apparently referred to by Director Sessions was Murray S. Miron, then a professor of psychology at Syracuse University and a specialist in psycholinguistics. Miron was quoted as telling the FBI that suicide "was not part of his (Koresh's) agenda" (*Los Angeles Times,* 1993).

Determining Common Characteristics

Far different from focusing on specific influential individuals is the second approach, which seeks consistencies in the personalities, backgrounds, and behaviors of offenders who carry out similar crimes. Are all bank robbers alike? Do rapists have similar personalities? One benefit of the extensive amount of profiling done in the last 20 years is the generation of new, and sometimes surprising, relationships. For example, as Heilbroner has noted, "serial killing turns out to be an immensely sexual process" (1993, p. 147); for many serial killers—Ted Bundy, Jeffrey Dahmer—their victims are simply bodies on which they enact their sexual fantasies.

The goal of constructing a descriptive profile of a crime classification is not new. Over 40 years ago, Palmer (1960) studied 51 murderers serving sentences in New England. His "typical murderer" was 23 years old at the time of the murder, from a lower socioeconomic status, and unsuccessful in both education and occupation. The typical murderer's mother was well-meaning but maladjusted, and the murderer had experienced psychological frustrations and physical abuse while a child.

Childhood Experiences

Many methods exist for seeking answers to questions about consistency in criminals' backgrounds. One approach is to determine whether similar childhood experiences characterize offenders of a particular type. For example, do sexual murderers have a history of having been sexually abused as children? Unfortunately, many of the highly publicized answers to this question are based on conclusions drawn from self-reports of convicted rapists and pedophiles; for example, Murphy and Peters wrote, "There is a good deal of clinical lore that a history of being sexually victimized is predominant in the backgrounds of sex offenders" (1992, p. 33). When Robert R. "Roy" Hazelwood of the FBI's Behavioral

Sciences Unit interviewed 41 men who had raped at least 10 times each, he found that 31 of them reported they had been sexually abused as children (reported in Sullivan & Sevilla, 1993).

Ressler, Burgess, Hartman, Douglas, and McCormack (1986) classified 36 murderers as having committed sexually oriented murders, by using such observations as the victim's attire or lack of attire, exposure of sexual parts of the victim's body, positioning the victim's body in a provocative way, and evidence of sexual intercourse or insertion of foreign objects into the victim's body cavities. When questioned about prior sexual abuse, 43% of the sexual murderers indicated they had been the recipients of such abuse in childhood, 32% in adolescence, and 37% as adults. Three fourths reported having been psychologically abused, and 35% witnessed sexual violence as a child. Those murderers who had been abused themselves reported a wider variety of symptoms of maladjustment in childhood, including everything from cruelty to animals to rape fantasies. Those who were sexually abused in childhood tended to mutilate the body after killing, as contrasted with those murderers who raped and then killed. The authors of the study speculate that "undisclosed and unresolved early sexual abuse may be a contributing factor in the stimulation of bizarre, sexual, sadistic behavior characterized in a subclassification of mutilators" (Ressler, Burgess, Hartman et al., 1986, p. 282). That is, they concluded that murderers with a history of sexual abuse will first kill the victim to achieve control before they carry out sexual intercourse, masturbation, or other, sexually symbolic activities. But differences between the two groups only approached statistical significance, and no effort was made to verify these self-reports by the use of independent sources.

To presume that having been sexually victimized as a child is a predominant cause of becoming a sexual offender is risky. It is important to emphasize that the vast majority of such victimized children do not become offenders as adults (Murphy & Peters, 1992).

MMPI Profiles

Another approach to the search for common characteristics is the use of personality inventories to develop psychological profiles of offender types. The Minnesota Multiphasic Personality Inventory and its revision, the MMPI-2, are the most widely used assessment devices for detecting psychopathology. A number of studies have looked at the typical MMPI profiles of various types of offenders. How specific and diagnostic are the results of these studies? Controversy exists. Using, as an example, studies of sex offenders who target children, we note that several find that this group has an elevated score on MMPI scale 4, which measures Psychopathic Deviance (Langevin, Paitich, Freeman, Mann, & Handy, 1978; Swenson & Grimes, 1969); these results suggest that these offenders were rebellious, impulsive, self-centered, and defiant of authority. But other studies (reviewed by Murphy & Peters, 1992) find no differences between types of offenders, or basically normal profiles.

Two problems exist in the quest for useful information from such an approach. First, many of the studies use only convicted offenders; often the control groups are nonexistent or unsatisfactory. The second problem is that use of average elevation of each scale may imply greater homogeneity in the group than is actually warranted. Three studies with large groups, reviewed by Murphy and Peters (1992), were consistent in finding the 4-8 profile as the most frequent. But the actual percentages of child molesters with 4-8 as the elevated profile were the following:

1. Erickson, Luxenburg, Walbek, & Seely, 1987: $N = 498$ offenders, 13%
2. Hall, Maiuro, Vitaliano, & Proctor, 1986: $N = 406$ offenders, 7%
3. Hall, 1989: $N = 81$ offenders, 17%

Among these 900-plus sex offenders, researchers found almost every imaginable MMPI profile; of the 45 possible 2-scale elevated profiles, researchers observed 43 different combinations

(Murphy & Peters, 1992). A similar study (Duthie & McIvor, 1990), using a cluster analysis of MMPI profiles of child molesters, found eight identifiable clusters.

Extracting Specific Characteristics

A crime has been committed. Are there psychological or physical characteristics that can be extracted from the crime scene to a draw a profile of the criminal? Specifically, does the pattern of behaviors resemble patterns from other cases? This is the application of the term *criminal profiling* currently used by the FBI (Ressler & Shachtman, 1992).

Douglas and Munn (1992) made a distinction between the MO (**modus operandi,** or standard procedure) of a criminal and his or her "signature." A burglar may begin a criminal life by breaking a basement window to gain entry. Realizing the danger of being caught as a result of the noise, the perpetrator uses glass-cutting tools for subsequent crimes; the MO is refined to lower the risk of apprehension. In contrast, the **signature** reflects unique, personal aspects of the criminal act, often the reflection of a need to express violent fantasies. (See Box 4-3 for John Douglas's elaboration of the distinction.) For example, a rapist may consistently engage in the same specific order of sexual activities with each of his victims. Douglas and Munn (1992) concluded that "the signature aspect remains a constant and enduring part of each offender . . . it never changes" (p. 5).

PROCEDURES USED IN CRIMINAL PROFILING

Contemporary law enforcement seeks to do more than describe the typical murderer or child molester. Rather, investigators use the crime scene to generate hypotheses about the type of person who committed the crime; then they seek specific individuals who possess the characteristics of this type.

BOX 4-3
Modus Operandi versus Signature

John Douglas offered a vivid description of the difference between a criminal's MO and a signature:

> MO is what an offender has to do to accomplish a crime. It's learned behavior and gets modified and perfected as the criminal gets better and better at what he does. For example, a bank robber's accomplice might realize after one or two jobs that he ought to leave the getaway car's motor running during the robbery. This would be an aspect of modus operandi. The signature, on the other hand, is something the offender has to do to fulfill himself emotionally. It's not needed to successfully accomplish the crime, but it is the reason he undertakes the particular crime in the first place. . . .
>
> I worked on two cases, with two different offenders working in two different states, yet both did a similar thing during [a bank] robbery. In a case in Grand Rapids, Michigan, the robber made everyone in the bank undress—take off everything—and stay that way until he had left with the money. In another case in Texas, the bank robber also made his victims undress, with one variation: he posed them in degrading sexual positions and then took photographs of them.
>
> . . . the first case is an example of an MO, while the second is an example of signature.
>
> In the Michigan case, the robber had everyone strip to make them uncomfortable and embarrassed so they would not look at him and be able to make a positive ID later on. Also, once he escaped, they would be preoccupied with getting redressed before calling the police or reacting in any other way. . . . So this MO greatly helped the offender accomplish his goal of robbing money from that bank.
>
> In the Texas case, having everyone strip so he could take pictures of them had nothing to do with accomplishing the robbery; in fact, quite the opposite, it slowed him down and made him easier to pursue. But it was something he felt a need to do for his own emotional satisfaction and completeness. This is a signature—something that is special (possibly even unique) to that particular offender.

From Douglas & Olshaker, 1998, pp. 90–92.

In some ways, modern criminal profilers resemble such legendary detectives of fiction as Hercule Poirot, Sherlock Holmes, Charlie Chan, and Miss Marple. As Box 4-4, which presents an example of Sherlock Holmes's style, indicates, attention to detail is the hallmark of these investigators (Douglas et al., 1986); similarly, not the smallest clue at the crime scene escapes the attention of the profiler (Douglas & Olshaker, 1995). In contrast to some detective novels, however, the modern profiler analyzes all clues and crime patterns. As Rossi (1982) has suggested, criminal profiling can be thought of as a collection of leads.

Crime Scene Analysis and the Generation of Psychological Profiles

Crime scene analysis is an important part of the profiling process. Detailed analysis may generate many specific questions. For example, in dealing with a case in which a 67-year-old woman was found tied up in her bathroom and beaten to death, an FBI agent asked his associates: "Why so many loops in the rope? You don't need that many to control an old woman. . . . Why is she in the bathroom? It's a closed-in space—is he after security, or is he secretive? . . . Were the cuts on the body made before or after she died?" (quoted by Toufexis, 1991, p. 68).

Crime Scene Analysis

Many are familiar with psychological profiling, but another, perhaps less well known approach to criminal profiling places somewhat greater emphasis on the dynamics of the crime scene. The goals are the same, and in both approaches, the profilers make hypothetical formulations, or educated guesses, based on their past experience. Douglas et al. (1986) defined a *formulation* as "a concept that organizes, explains, or makes investigative sense out of information, and that influences the profile hypotheses" (p. 405).

BOX 4-4

Sherlock Holmes's Deductive Skills

Behavior is there for everyone to see. But the consummate criminal profiler notices and interprets things that others neglect. Sometimes works of fiction can provide examples more efficiently than can real life. Sherlock Holmes, for example, once remarked, "Perhaps I have trained myself to see what others overlook" (Doyle, 1892, p. 42). In *The Man With the Twisted Lip,* the challenge to Holmes was to determine the status of a missing husband. A clue surfaces in the form of a letter:

> Holmes: "I perceive also that whoever addressed the envelope had to go and inquire to the address."
>
> *Mrs. St. Claire:* "How can you tell?"
>
> Holmes: "The name, you see, is in perfectly black ink, which has dried itself. The rest is of the grayish color which shows that blotting

paper has been used. If it had been written straight off, and then blotted, none would be of a deep black shade. This man has written the name, and there has then been a pause before he wrote the address, which can only mean that he was not familiar with it." (Doyle, 1892, p. 89)

A small point, perhaps, but often an accumulation of details permits the investigator to narrow the possibilities to a manageable area of inquiry.

Modern fictional examples of police investigators using criminal profiling in their work include three novels by Thomas Harris—*The Red Dragon*(1981) is more detailed than the more famous *Silence of the Lambs* (1988) and the more recent *Hannibal* (1999)—as well as Caleb Carr's *The Alienist* (1994) and *The Angel of Darkness* (1997) and Lawrence Sanders's *The Third Deadly Sin* (1981).

The Criminal Profile Generating Process

Investigators used criminal profiles infrequently until 1978, when the FBI established a psychological profiling program within its Behavioral Science Unit in Quantico, Virginia. Since then, investigators at this facility have developed a **criminal profile generating process** with five main stages; apprehension of a suspect is the goal and the final step in the process. This criminal profile generating process involves the following steps (Pinizzotto, 1984, p. 33):

1. A comprehensive study of the nature of the criminal act and the types of persons who have committed like offenses in the past.
2. A detailed analysis of the crime scene.
3. An in-depth examination of the background and activities of the victim or victims.
4. A formulation of possible motivating factors for all parties involved.
5. The development of a description of the perpetrator based on overt characteristics from the crime scene and past criminals' behavior.

Initial information gathered in the **crime investigation stage** includes evidence from the crime scene, knowledge of the victim, and specific forensic evidence about the crime (cause of death, nature of wounds, autopsy report, etc.). Photographs of the victim and crime scene are included. Efforts are made to understand why this person, in particular, was the victim. Information about possible suspects is *not* included, so as not to subconsciously prejudice the profilers (Douglas et al., 1986).

The second stage emphasizes decision making, by organizing and arranging inputs into meaningful patterns. Classifications are established; for example, the crime may be a **mass murder** (defined as anything more than three victims in one location and within one event). Family murders are distinguished from so-called classic murders: John List, an insurance salesperson, killed his entire family (his wife, his mother, and three teenage children) on November 9, 1972. In contrast are the "classic" murders by Charles Whitman, the man who barricaded himself at the top of the University of Texas Tower and killed 16 people, wounding 30 others. Two other classifications are the **spree murder** (killings at two or more locations with no emotional cooling-off period between homicides) and the **serial murder,** involving three or more separate events with a cooling-off period between homicides (Douglas et al., 1986).

The next step is to reconstruct the sequence of events and the behavior of both the perpetrator and the victim. One important distinction is that between **organized** (or nonsocial) and **disorganized** (or asocial) **criminals.** Hazelwood and Douglas (1980) first applied this classification to murders motivated by lust, but it has since been expanded to other types of crimes. In their book *Sexual Homicide* (1988), Ressler, Burgess, and Douglas extended the classification but deleted the terms *asocial* and *nonsocial.*

Organized murderers are those who plan their murders, target their victims (who are usually strangers), show self-control at the crime scene by leaving few clues, and possibly act out a violent fantasy against the victim, including dismemberment or torture (Douglas et al., 1986; Jackson & Bekerian, 1997a). According to this classification scheme, Ted Bundy was a clear example of the organized rapist-murderer. He planned his abductions, usually using a ruse, such as feigning a broken arm in order to get assistance. He selected victims who were young and attractive women, similar in appearance. He used verbal manipulation and then physical force, and sexually abused them after he killed them.

The disorganized murderer "is less apt to plan his crime in detail, obtains victims by chance, and behaves haphazardly during the crime" (Douglas et al., 1986, pp. 412–413). Herbert Mullin was an example of the disorganized murderer. Between October 1972 and February 1973, Herbert Mullin killed 13 people in or near Santa Cruz, California. No pattern existed to his victims: a derelict, a hitchhiker, a priest in a church, four teenage campers (Lunde & Morgan, 1980). Once, he was "instructed by voices" to kill a man he had never seen before.

Ressler, Burgess, Douglas, Hartman, and D'Agostino (1986) analyzed the crime scene differences in cases involving 36 convicted serial murderers. Those who consented were interviewed extensively by FBI agents (but note the small sample size, and the biased sample—only those who agreed to the interview were included, and the sample does not include those who were not caught and imprisoned). Two thirds, or 24, were classified by the FBI agents as organized offenders, and the other 12 were placed in the disorganized group. In looking at aspects of the crime scene, the researchers found that organized offenders were more apt to:

a. plan
b. use restraints
c. commit sexual acts with live victims
d. emphasize control over the victim by using manipulative or threatening techniques
e. use a car or truck

Disorganized offenders were more likely to:

a. leave a weapon at the crime scene
b. reposition the dead body
c. perform sexual acts with a dead body
d. keep the dead body
e. try to depersonalize the body
f. not use a vehicle (Ressler, Burgess, Douglas et al., 1986, p. 293)

The final step usually generates a profile that follows a standard format, including hypotheses about the perpetrator's age, race, educational level, marital status, habits, family characteristics, and type of vehicle, plus indications of psychopathology.

Research on Convicted Offenders

In 1981, the FBI established the Violent Criminal Apprehension Program, or **VICAP.** The success of this program and that of the Psychological Profiling Program generated congressional legislation that established a National Center for the Analysis of Violent Crime (NCAVC) in 1984; the center is based at the FBI Academy as a subdivision of what was originally called the Behavioral Science Unit. The profiling procedures used in other countries, including Canada, Great Britain, and the Netherlands, have reflected the FBI's approach (Jackson & Bekerian, 1997a). Also, advances in computer technology permitted each of these countries to develop databases on characteristics of specific crimes and procedures for sharing information between agencies (Stevens, 1997).

How Effective Is Criminal Profiling?

It is a mistake to assume that the solution of a crime is the only indication of the usefulness of criminal profiling. A survey in Great Britain indicated that profiling led to identification of the offender in only 5 (or 2.7%) of 184 cases, but police frequently reported other benefits: Profiling "furthered understanding of the case or the offender" (61% of cases), "reassured their own conclusions" (52%), and "offered a structure for interviewing" (5%). In 32 of these cases, or 17%, the police concluded that the profiling information was not useful (Gudjonsson & Copson, 1997).

Profiling generates hypotheses, but its conclusions should not be treated as final. A problem is that police sometimes "lock in" to certain characteristics and prematurely apprehend an innocent person because he or she fits the profile.

On other occasions, the profile may be misguided, as in the Boston Strangler case described in Box 4-5 and in the D.C. Sniper case discussed earlier. We have already seen the dangers of using the MMPI or other personality tests to claim homogeneity in personality among offenders. In addition, descriptions of criminal profiling can sometimes report too much homogeneity. Earlier, we discussed the distinction between organized and disorganized offenders; the following is Vernon Geberth's evaluation of characteristics of the organized offender:

a. *Age:* This offender is approximately the same age as his victim.
b. *Marital status:* Married or living with a partner. This type of offender is sexually competent and usually has a significant relationship with a woman.
c. *Automobile:* Middle-class vehicle. May be a sedan or possibly a station wagon. The auto may be dark in color and may resemble local police cars. This vehicle will be clean and well-maintained. (1990, pp. 504–505)

BOX 4-5
A Profile Gone Awry—The Boston Strangler Case

For a period of a year and a half—from June 1962 through January 1964—the city of Boston was paralyzed by the murders of 13 women—in all cases by strangulation. Most of the first victims were older (from age 55 to 75), but most of the later ones were in their 20s or younger. The crime scenes reflected hate and chaos—and enough general similarities to justify the construction of a criminal profile. For example, 19-year-old Mary Sullivan, the last victim, was found nude in her bed with a broom handle inserted in her vagina. Both breasts were exposed, the murderer had ejaculated on her face, and a card reading "Happy New Year" had been placed next to her left foot.

A profiling committee, composed of a psychiatrist with knowledge about sex crimes, a physician with experience in anthropology, a gynecologist, and others, was established; James Brussel of "Mad Bomber" fame was also a member. The "psychiatric profile" that they developed suggested two different perpetrators for different strangulations. According to the majority opinion, one killer was raised by a domineering and seductive mother; he was unable to express hatred toward his mother and thus directed anger toward other women, especially older women. It was predicted that he lived alone. The committee report proposed that the younger victims had been killed by a homosexual man who knew his victims. Dr. Brussel filed a minority view, that one killer committed all the murders.

Albert DeSalvo was eventually arrested and convicted, after he confessed to the crimes. Married and living with his wife, DeSalvo had an insatiable sexual appetite, demanding sex from his wife five or six times a day. He was sentenced to life in prison. He showed no signs of the detailed predictions in the profile—no consuming rage toward his mother, no lack of sexual potency, no Oedipus complex.

Sources: Frank, 1966; Holmes & Holmes, 1996.

Geberth went on to list 40 "general behavior characteristics" of organized offenders, including "high birth order status, may be first born son," "methodical and cunning," "travels frequently," and "dates frequently" (1990, pp. 506–507). How many people would fit these criteria?

The opposite type of temptation also exists—to assume that if a person possesses several characteristics of a criminal profile, he or she must be guilty. For example, the profile of drug couriers describes them as dark-skinned; hence, innocent members of minority groups are frequently stopped, searched, and harassed by the police. At the Buffalo, New York, airport in 1989, federal agents detained 600 people as potential couriers; only 10 were arrested (Bovard, 1994). Yet drug courier profiling—which has been approved by the Supreme Court—allows police to search almost anyone they please. Similar complaints have been voiced recently in the wake of September 11 and the Iraq war by Middle Eastern men in relation to terrorism.

FBI agents themselves try not to exaggerate the powers of profiling (Toufexis, 1991). "It's a myth that a profile always solves the case," stated Robert Ressler, former FBI agent and now an author and consultant. "It's not the magic bullet of investigations; it's simply another tool" (quoted by Toufexis, 1991, p. 69). And sometimes police can be misled when they rely too heavily on the conclusions from FBI profiling. In 1993, police on Long Island, searching for missing 10-year-old Katie Beers, complained that they had been distracted by an FBI profile that said pedophiles didn't usually hide their victims in their homes (Rosenbaum, 1993).

Are Professional Profilers Better?

Another way to assess the effectiveness of profiling is to determine if professional profilers do better in a controlled test than do those less experienced in this task. Pinizzotto and Finkel (1990) sought to determine if the process used by professional profilers differs, as well as the outcome. They submitted the same materials to 28 persons divided into five categories:

1. Group A, Experts/Teachers ($N = 4$): profiling experts who had trained police detectives in profiling at the FBI Academy in Quantico, Virginia. Each was or had been an FBI agent; they had between 4 and 17 years of profiling experience.
2. Group B, Profilers ($N = 6$): police detectives from different police agencies across the country who had been specially trained in personality profiling, through a one-year program at the FBI headquarters. These 6 profilers had from 7 to 15 years' experience as police detectives and from 1 to 6 years in profiling.
3. Group C, Detectives ($N = 6$): detectives from a large metropolitan police department who were experienced investigators but had no training in personality profiling. Individual experience in criminal investigation ranged from 6 to 15 years.
4. Group D, Psychologists ($N = 6$): practicing clinical psychologists naive to both criminal profiling and criminal investigations.
5. Group E, Students ($N = 6$): undergraduate students from a large metropolitan university, naive to both personality profiling and criminal investigations. Their average age was 19.

Two actual cases were used, one a homicide and one a sex offense. The materials for the homicide case included 14 black-and-white crime scene photographs, information about the victim, autopsy and toxicology reports, and crime scene reports. For the sex offense, the material included a detailed statement by the victim/survivor, crime scene reports by the first officer on the scene and the detectives, and a victimology report.

The researchers collected a variety of responses from the subjects after the subjects had reviewed the two case materials. Each subject wrote a profile of the offender in each case. For both cases, the profiles written by the professional profilers were richer than those of the nonprofiler groups of detectives, psychologists, and students. Measures with significant differences between groups included the time spent writing the report, the length of the report, and the number of predictions made. The number of *accurate* predictions made by the professional profilers was twice as high as that of the detectives, three times that of the psychologists, and almost five times that of the students. However, the sex-offense case accounted for the majority of the differences; accuracy of predictions and correctness of lineup identifications did not differ very much between groups with respect to the homicide-case materials. In fact, with regard to the homicide case, students on average got 6.5 questions correct out of 15, while the profilers got only 5.3 correct (a nonsignificant difference).

What superiority the profilers demonstrated in this study was certainly a reflection of their expertise, but the level of motivation to do well on the task may also have differed between groups. This is hard to assess because the case materials had been sanitized to protect the identities of the parties involved and the police agencies. This meant that some material ordinarily available to profilers (such as maps of the geographical area and the neighborhood) was not included. (All the profilers spontaneously mentioned that some of the usual types of information was missing; no other subjects did.) The profilers did not appear to process the material in qualitatively different ways from the nonprofilers (Pinizzotto & Finkel, 1990, p. 229), but they did recall more information. The researchers concluded that the profilers' greater ability to extract and designate more details made the difference in predictive accuracy.

An Evaluation of Profiling

As noted earlier, profiling is an art; Holmes and Holmes (1996) concluded that a good profiler develops a "feel" for certain types of crimes, reflecting the intuitive quality of an art. Often, when profilers perceive patterns in behavior, they can't describe *how* their processes work; "they just do." No two profilers will necessarily produce the same profile (Bekerian & Jackson, 1997; Stevens, 1997).

The introduction of a profile can increase the efficient use of the detective's time. But profiling is not a panacea; rather, it should be viewed as an instrument to facilitate the work of investigators and detectives, by evaluating suspects and providing useful advice on investigation and interviewing (Jackson, van den Eshof, & de Kleuver, 1997; Stevens, 1997).

PSYCHOLOGICAL AUTOPSIES

Often, the cause of a person's death is a matter of forensic concern even if no criminal act is assumed to be involved. Even when the cause of death is certain, issues related to the mental state of the person prior to his or her death lead to the application of a psychological analysis; Ogloff and Otto (1993) suggested several types of situations:

a. The need to determine whether the person was competent to draw up a will (called the decedent's **testamentary capacity**).
b. In workers' compensation cases, claims may be made that stressful working conditions contributed to the person's premature death.
c. In a criminal case, the defendant, on trial for murder, may claim that the victim was a violent person who instilled such fear in the defendant that the act was truly one of self-defense.

The term **psychological autopsy** refers to the investigative method used by psychologists or other social scientists to help determine the mode of death in equivocal cases (Ogloff & Otto, 1993; Selkin & Loya, 1979); it is estimated that between 5% and 20% of all deaths that need to be certified are equivocal deaths. The beginnings of psychological autopsies grew out of the frustration of the then Los Angeles County Chief Medical Examiner and Coroner, Dr. Theodore J. Curphey, in 1958; he was faced with a number of drug-related deaths for which the **mode of death** (how the death occurred) was uncertain. Curphey invited Edwin S. Shneidman and Norman Farberow (1961), codirectors of the Los Angeles Suicide Prevention Center, and Robert Litman to assist him in analyzing these equivocal cases (Shneidman, 1981). This effort led Shneidman to coin the term *psychological autopsy* (1981, p. 327). The psychological autopsy technique is currently used to answer three distinct questions: Why did the individual do it? How and when did the individual die (that is, why at that particular time)? and What might be the most probable mode of death?

Selkin (1987) concluded that the most common inquiry in a psychological autopsy concerns whether the death was an accident or a suicide. A basic job of medical examiners is to certify whether a death could reliably be classified as natural, accidental, suicidal, or homicidal (Jobes, Berman, & Josselson, 1986a); this classification—the so-called **NASH classification** (Shneidman, 1981)—reflects the four traditional modes in which death is currently reported. But probably the most frequent distinction to be made is between suicide and homicide.

As an example, on July 20, 1993, the body of Vincent Foster, deputy White House counsel and a former law partner of Hillary Rodham Clinton, was found in a Virginia park across the Potomac River from Washington, D.C. Law-enforcement officials, including the park police, concluded that the death from a gunshot wound was self-inflicted. But speculation persisted, not only about why Foster died but even about where he died. "Who killed Vincent Foster?" the *Washington Times* asked in a front-page story. Probably the most persistent of the speculations was that the White House aide had been murdered (Isikoff, 1994); supporters of this latter view described Foster's body as lying gently on an incline with a .38-caliber revolver in one hand. They claimed that contrary to the usual mess from a suicide by gunshot, only a "thin trickle of blood" came from the corner of Foster's mouth (Ruddy, 1997). Actions by the White House staff immediately after the discovery of Foster's body—such as controlling and curtailing the search of Foster's White House office—and

the discovery several days later of a shredded suicide note doubtless contributed to the conspiracy theories, despite the fact that a park police investigator stated that Foster's shirt was still wet, there was blood on the ground, and black powder burns were found on his hand and mouth.

In early 1995, Kenneth Starr, the special prosecutor handling the investigation of President Clinton's Whitewater land deals, announced that he was reopening some aspects of the investigation of Foster's death, and it was not until July 1997 that Starr announced a reaffirmed conclusion that suicide was the mode of death. This saga only verifies the need to carry out a thorough and competent initial investigation of any suspicious death, including an inquiry into the psychological state of the person before his or her death.

The addition of a psychological autopsy to the standard examination by a coroner or medical examiner may uncover new facts about the case, information that had not been used by the medical examiner. An empirical study (Jobes, Berman, & Josselson, 1986b) demonstrated this. The researchers used as subjects 195 medical examiners drawn from the population of 400 practicing examiners in the United States; all were MDs and members of the National Association of Medical Examiners. The examiners were given two kinds of cases: in one, the death was considered *typical* (i.e., the manner of death was not difficult to certify); in the other, the death was *equivocal* (i.e., the cause of death was less clear).

To determine generalizability of results, researchers used five different pairs of cases, ranging from a single-car accident to the death of a child to a Russian roulette death. For half the cases, in addition to the standard information, the medical examiner received psychological autopsies that included information about the dead person's lifestyle, personality, and demographics, as well as a psychological interpretation of the death.

As expected, the availability of the psychological-autopsy information did not influence the manner of death certification in most of the *typical* cases, but it did influence reactions to two of these cases (psychotic and Russian roulette cases). In the *equivocal* cases, however, the *psychological*-autopsy information had a statistically significant impact on the determination of the manner of death in four of the five types of cases, with a trend toward significance in the fifth (the Russian roulette case).

Consider, for example, the single-car death. In the *typical* case, examiners were told that a woman had lost control of her car on a mountain road; her blood alcohol content was 0.21%. All but one examiner agreed that the case should be certified as an accidental death, and the inclusion of psychological-autopsy information had no effect on these decisions.

The *equivocal* single-car death produced different results. Here, a man's car collided head-on with a truck. The incident occurred late at night on a winding road, and the victim's car swerved into the path of the oncoming truck. The car left only a few short skid marks. Those examiners who received no additional information were about equally divided as to cause of death between accident, suicide, and undetermined (with slightly more favoring suicide). The psychological autopsy added that the victim was depressed, had anxiety attacks, and recently suffered a significant loss. Examiners given this added information almost unanimously (90%) ruled that suicide was the cause of death.

Perhaps such results are not surprising. Given the extra information—and especially in the context that these were not real-life cases for these examiners—the outcome may be inevitable. More research is needed to determine the extent of receptiveness by medical examiners to psychological evidence in cases for which they are responsible for the certification.

Guidelines

A 16-item instrument has been designed to assist medical examiners in their investigations of possible suicides (Jobes, Casey, Berman, & Wright, 1991). The Empirical Criteria for Determination of Death (ECDD) instrument lists 16 behavioral descriptions in the form of a checklist. The medical examiner checks all those applicable to the particular case and follows the instructions; the results indicate whether the death was suicidal or accidental. To test the instrument's validity, its authors applied its scoring and criteria to 63 cases; the empirical criteria were able to identify correctly 100% of the previously certified suicides and 83% of the previously certified accidents.

A Specific Case

The USS *Iowa* Incident

Between 1979 and 1993, the deaths of more than 3,300 members of the U.S. armed services were classified as suicides, but in more than 60 of these cases, surviving family members challenged the military's official conclusion (Biddle, 1994). The case of Clayton Hartwig is, however, unique.

On April 19, 1989, an explosion occurred in one of the gun turrets of the USS *Iowa*. Five bags of gunpowder ignited while being loaded into the open breach of a 16-inch gun, causing the death of 47 sailors. After extensive investigation, the Navy attributed the explosion to the irrational act of one sailor, Gunners Mate Clayton Hartwig. (Hartwig was among those killed in the explosion.) The Naval Investigative Service (NIS) collected a mass of archival data (letters, bank account balances, personal writings of Hartwig) plus interviews with his friends, family, and shipmates. These data were provided to agents at the National Center for the Analysis of Violent Crime at the FBI headquarters. The evaluation by the FBI, called an **equivocal death analysis,** led to an unequivocal conclusion: Hartwig had acted intentionally and was the solitary agent of cause.

The Armed Services Committee of the U.S. House of Representatives studied the FBI report and the Navy's conclusions, and it then asked the American Psychological Association to review these independently and comment on the conclusions reached by them.

The 14 APA panelists rejected the conclusion reached by the Navy, leading the Congressional Committee to characterize the Navy's effort as "an investigative failure" (quoted by Poythress, Otto, Darkes, & Starr, 1993, p. 10). Receiving particular criticism were the unequivocal, bottom-line statements of Hartwig's guilt offered by the FBI; these "are not defensible within the technical limitations of our science" (Poythress et al., 1993, p. 12). Also, Navy authorities, in testimony before Congress, responded that they were "better than 99%" sure that Hartwig was responsible for the explosion.

But the APA committee, as a group, was not willing to go so far as to conclude with certainty that the explosion was *not* a result of Hartwig's suicide attempt. Committee members had different reactions to the data. When asked by a congressional committee staff member if Hartwig was a suicidal murderer, Norman G. Poythress, chair of the APA committee, replied:

> "My answer would be couched in the manner that I think psychologists are able to answer that question, in relative probability terms. I think it a relatively low probability, but I can't dismiss it out of hand." (quoted by Jeffers, 1991, p. 214)

Four members of the APA panel concluded that Hartwig did not commit suicide. Others, like Poythress, were unsure. Some committee members leaned in the direction of the FBI's conclusions. Here are two examples:

> *Kirk Heilbrun:* "After reviewing the letters and interviews, as well as the equivocal death analysis . . . the suicide explanation does strike me as the most plausible. I am comfortable reaching a conclusion about its likelihood based on the available evidence." (quoted by Jeffers, 1991, pp. 215–216)

> *Elliott M. Silverstein:* "Assuming all the evidence presented is true, the psychological profile drafted by the FBI is very plausible." (quoted by Jeffers, 1991, p. 216)

The different reactions by psychologists may illustrate the problems with the reliability of a psychological autopsy. Randy Otto and his colleagues (Otto, Poythress, Starr, & Darkes, 1993) examined the similarity in conclusions of the committee members and, adopting broad criteria of agreement, still found only "moderate agreement" among the 14 psychologists and psychiatrists. However, a cluster analysis reflected clear majority and minority opinions: The majority was critical of the approach used and the conclusions reached by the FBI, while a minority of three psychologists felt that the conclusions in the Navy's report were appropriate.

So, the results of an "equivocal death analysis" are sometimes equivocal, too. When answers cannot be provided with certainty or great confidence, perhaps it is best simply to remain equivocal.

Expert Testimony Based on a Psychological Autopsy

Expert testimony based on a psychological autopsy has not readily been admitted in criminal cases (though see *Jackson v. State,* 1989, for a case in which such testimony was admitted). In their review, Ogloff and Otto (1993) found that in only one case out of five—the *Jackson* case—was the testimony admitted without restrictions; in one other case, it was admitted with restrictions. In civil cases, in which the mental state of the dead person is central to the issue at hand, testimony based on a psychological autopsy is more likely to be admitted. Ogloff and Otto's final words are sobering:

> In considering whether to admit psychological autopsy testimony, courts have paid surprisingly little attention to analyzing the validity/foundation of testimony regarding psychological autopsies. Courts should certainly evaluate and consider more carefully the expert testimony . . . before deciding on its admissibility. (1993, p. 646)

Given the introduction of the Daubert standard, expert testimony on psychological-autopsy results will certainly continue to be intensively scrutinized in the federal courts and most state courts.

HYPNOSIS IN CRIMINAL INVESTIGATIONS

The use of hypnosis by police grew rapidly during the 1970s, partly facilitated by the rules in most states at that time, which permitted wide admissibility of hypnotically induced memories (Steblay & Bothwell, 1994). Martin Reiser (1980), a psychologist with the Los Angeles Police Department, started the Law Enforcement Hypnosis Institute (LEHI) in the mid-1970s so that police officers could be trained as forensic hypnotists. His 32-hour course taught law-enforcement officers to become what he called "hypno-technicians" (Scheflin & Shapiro, 1989, p. 67). Within its first 7 years, more than 1,000 police officers received training at LEHI (Serrill, 1984). Reiser's approach has been adopted by police departments throughout the United States.

In actuality, hypnosis has been used by the legal system for more than 100 years (Spiegel & Spiegel, 1987), but the topic has always been fraught with mystery and controversy. Even today, experts disagree about whether hypnosis is effective in recovering memories and whether it is unduly suggestive (Hibler, 1995; Scheflin, Spiegel, & Spiegel, 1999).

Advocacy: Martin Reiser's Position

Reiser (1985) reported data from more than 600 major crime cases at the Los Angeles Police Department, claiming that interviews using hypnosis had enhanced "investigatively useful recall in approximately three-fourths of the cases" and that "accuracy levels of the hypnotically elicited information were around 90%" (p. 155).

Other experts were not nearly so sanguine or positive. Martin Orne, who was both a psychologist and psychiatrist, urged judges to use caution when considering the admissibility of hypnotically assisted testimony (cited in Scheflin & Shapiro, 1989). Orne's own research led him to conclude that the probative value of such testimony was overcome by the risks of false confidence and distorted recollection (see, for exam-

ple, a study by Orne, Soskis, Dinges, & Orne, 1984).

Most police assume that, in most instances, what is recalled under hypnosis is "the truth," at least as the person remembers it. But this kind of "truth" is not the same thing as accuracy. Despite this distinction, some observers can become convinced that whatever hypnosis generates is, in and of itself, accurate. Such trust fails to recognize that the reports of witnesses may be influenced by later events, including the way those witnesses are questioned. An even greater danger is that an expert who is convinced about the efficacy of hypnosis will come to believe a "hypnotically induced" testimonial that actually is an elaborate deception. One such example comes from the so-called Hillside Strangler case (O'Brien, 1985).

The Hillside Strangler Case

A primary focus of this chapter is on the benefits and dangers of using hypnosis with victims and witnesses to uncover more information about the crime. The use of hypnosis with Kenneth Bianchi does not fit this category; he was a suspect, not a victim. But his ability to manipulate psychologists and psychiatrists who were hypnosis experts was so powerful that his story can serve as a caution about putting too much weight on the powers of hypnosis.

Between October 1977 and February 1978, 10 young women were raped, tortured, and strangled to death; their bruised and stripped bodies were found on various hillsides northeast of downtown Los Angeles. In January 1979, a suspect was arrested in Washington State, but he denied everything. Then, under hypnosis, the suspect—Kenneth Bianchi—began to display the classic manifestations of **multiple personality.** In addition to his normal-state "Ken" personality, there emerged an alter ego, "Steve," who took responsibility for having committed the murders. A third personality later emerged, and possibly a fourth and fifth. Kenneth Bianchi claimed that he knew nothing of the murders, and thus his lawyers filed a plea of not guilty by reason of insanity.

A psychiatrist, Glenn Allison, and a psychologist, John Watkins, separately hypnotized Bianchi; each was convinced of the legitimacy of a multiple-personality diagnosis in this case; each supported Bianchi's claim that he was not responsible for his actions. But other people, including the police detectives, were dubious. They recruited Martin Orne, as another expert on forensic hypnosis, to examine Bianchi. Orne interviewed Bianchi and found that while the suspect was supposedly hypnotized, he overreacted; Bianchi did things during his "hallucination" that were clearly inconsistent with actual reactions of people in a hypnotized state. Orne concluded that Bianchi was malingering; his demonstration led to Bianchi pleading guilty to five of the hillside rape-murders (as well as two in the state of Washington). In exchange for his plea of guilt prior to a trial, Bianchi avoided the death penalty; he is now serving a life sentence in a California prison.

How could experts on hypnosis be so misled by Bianchi's performance? The author of a book on this case offers the following:

> A key lies in Dr. [John] Watkins' comment to the skeptical BBC producer that Bianchi could not have possibly known enough about hypnosis and psychology to fake multiple personality syndrome. Dr. Watkins said Bianchi would have to have had "several years of study in Rorschach [tests] and graduate study in psychology for him to be able to do that." So great is the belief of some professionals in the intricacy and obscurity of their specialty that they can become blind to the obvious. Nor was Dr. Watkins impressed by Bianchi's library of psychology texts. After all, Bianchi did not have a degree. (O'Brien, 1985, pp. 274–275)

The moral: Recognition as an expert may lead the forensic psychologist to forget that even laypeople often have access to the same knowledge and insights, or at least enough to make a convincing case. Our expertise always must be tempered by skepticism and common sense.

Hypnosis of Witnesses and Victims

The use of hypnosis with suspects is not limited to the Bianchi case; it has been used—and abused—to obtain information from a defendant about a crime (see, for example, *Leyra v. Denno*, 1954, in which hypnosis was used in an attempt to elicit a confession from a suspect). But much more frequent is the attempt to aid a witness in remembering more about a crime. Being the victim of a violent crime—a rape, a mugging—is so traumatic that the person may not remember many important details. Can, under hypnosis, more information be recalled? As noted, police certainly assume that it can and will cite anecdotal support for their expectations. Similarly, psychotherapists using hypnosis anecdotally report many cases in which, "within a therapeutic relationship, they were able to elicit many new and apparently valid memories through hypnosis" (Watkins, 1989, p. 80). But within the scientific community there remains "insufficient consensus . . . that the product elicited is reliable" (Spiegel & Spiegel, 1987, p. 493; see also Reiser, 1989). In the following section, the claims are presented and evaluated.

Research Reviews

The profusion of laboratory and field research in the last 25 years has led to several reviews and evaluations (Brown, Scheflin, & Hammond, 1998; Geiselman & Machlovitz, 1987; Smith, 1983). Steblay and Bothwell (1994) identified 19 studies: Three found hypnotized subjects to be more accurate than nonhypnotized subjects, 5 reported the opposite conclusion, and 11 found no statistically significant difference. Steblay and Bothwell carried out a **meta-analysis**—a procedure that statistically combines the results of various studies and determines an overall probability of statistical significance—to determine if certain moderator variables explained the variety of outcomes. They concluded:

> The hypothesized increase in recall accuracy for hypnotized subjects has not been substantiated by research to date. Even with the

most straightforward scenario, in which non-leading prepared questions were asked of the eyewitness, hypnotized subjects show only a minimal, unreliable edge over control subjects. When leading questions are used, the research evidence in fact demonstrates the reverse: a (nonsignificant) recall deficit in hypnotized subjects compared to controls. The recall performance of hypnotized subjects shows wide variability, suggesting that any gains in recall that might be achieved through hypnosis are easily compromised by moderator variables.

Unfortunately, at this time, the research has not presented a clear identification of the moderator variables which, when implemented in the hypnosis procedure, might guarantee the success of hypnosis in a forensic setting. A statistically significant difference between hypnotized and control subjects was found when the time delay between a subject's viewing of the event and subsequent recall event was considered. . . . [H]ypnotized subjects do show greater recall accuracy for delays of 24 hours or more. However, the strength of this finding must be tempered with three considerations: (1) Leading questions even in the delay condition reduce the effect size and eliminate the significant difference between groups. (2) The confidence intervals for these effect sizes are quite large and encompass zero; thus there is substantial variability in effect size yet accounted for. And (3) although an increased interval between event and recall attempt does appear to favor hypnotized subjects, this benefit is limited to delays of 1 to 2 days. Even a 1-week delay reverses the effect to favor control subjects. (Steblay & Bothwell, 1994, p. 648)

Among the clearest of conclusions from the meta-analysis was that hypnotized subjects are more confident about the accuracy of their recall. Even more reason for skepticism about the use of hypnosis was the fact that confidence and susceptibility to hypnosis were found to be related.

Conclusions

The conservative conclusion at this time is that the costs of using hypnosis to aid in memory recall outweigh the benefits, and its use in a court of law to convict a defendant is to be discouraged. Authorized reviews by panels from professional organizations on the issue of hypnotically refreshed memory are consistent with this conclusion. For example, a panel convened by the Council on Scientific Affairs of the American Medical Association concluded that no evidence exists that hypnosis enhances recall of meaningless material; when hypnosis is used to facilitate recall of meaningful past events, it elicits a mixture of accurate and inaccurate information (Orne, Axelrad, Diamond, Gravitz, Heller, Mutter, Spiegel, Spiegel, & Smith, 1985). Similarly, Orne (1979) argued that the use of hypnosis can "profoundly affect the individual's subsequent testimony" and "since these changes are not reversible, if individuals are to be allowed to testify after having undergone hypnosis to aid their memory, a minimum number of safeguards are absolutely essential" (p. 335).

Court Decisions

Given the preceding cautions, what is the position of the courts on the admissibility of hypnotically refreshed memories? The answer is not a simple one; by now, over a thousand state and federal appellate decisions have dealt with the legal rights and clinical practice of hypnosis. However, three positions can be identified: admit hypnotically assisted memories into evidence, prohibit them completely, or admit them only if certain guidelines are followed in carrying out the hypnosis.

Currently, only a very few states permit unlimited admissibility of such testimony. About two thirds of the states follow the **per se exclusionary rule,** meaning they prohibit hypnotically assisted testimony in all cases. The remaining states, plus the federal courts, consider the administrative procedures and, if proper safeguards were met, admit the testimony. This latter approach is called the **totality of circum-stances test;** it was endorsed in the decision of *State v. Hurd* (1981) in New Jersey and has been adopted by about one third of the states as well as the federal government *(Borawick v. Shay,* 1995). It is important to note that the preceding rules apply to hypnosis to recover memories of witnesses and victims. With regard to its use with defendants, the courts have been more willing to admit such testimony (see *Rock v. Arkansas,* 1987).

Guidelines

Given the concerns about the accuracy of **hyp-notically assisted memory,** a prime function of the forensic psychologist is to offer and encourage guidelines for the use of hypnosis. For example, if memories produced by hypnosis should not be used as evidence in court, can the police seek them during the early stages of a crime investigation? As noted earlier, many states have begun to place restrictions on the use of hypnosis in crime investigations; the New Jersey decision in *State v. Hurd* (1981) is a model. Several reviewers offer guidelines similar to these; Spiegel and Spiegel (1987) provided the following:

1. *Qualifications of the person using hypnosis.* Traditionally, police officers have conducted the hypnosis of witnesses, but the Society for Clinical and Experimental Hypnosis has proposed that only trained psychiatrists or psychologists—independent of the police department—should conduct a forensic hypnosis and questioning. One benefit of this approach is a possible reduction in the use of leading or suggestive questions.

2. *Prehypnosis records.* It is important to keep separate what the witness knew before the hypnosis and what he or she remembered as a result of it.

3. *Electronic recording of hypnosis session.* All the interactions between the examiner and the subject should be recorded electronically, preferably on videotape. If the latter is used, focus should be on both the subject *and* the

hypnotist, to detect any subtle influences in the interaction.

4. *Measurement of hypnotizability.* One guideline suggested by Spiegel and Spiegel (1987) is not found in the court decisions, such as *State v. Hurd* (1981), that proscribe limits; it is that the level of **hypnotizability** of the subject should be determined by use of one of the standardized hypnotizability scales, in order to document the subject's degree of responsivity, if any. These scales include the Hypnotic Induction Profile (Spiegel & Spiegel, 1978); the Stanford Hypnotic Susceptibility Scales (Weitzenhoffer & Hilgard, 1959); the Stanford Hypnotic Clinical Scale (Hilgard & Hilgard, 1975); or the Barber Creative Imagination Scale (Barber & Wilson, 1978–1979). If the subject does not show any hypnotic responsivity during pretesting, Spiegel and Spiegel suggested that "the person conducting the session would be well advised to forgo any further hypnotic ceremonies since the subject is unlikely to respond, and the problems inherent with the appearance of having induced hypnosis can be avoided" (1987, p. 501).

   What about the subjects at the other end of the continuum, the subjects who are highly hypnotizable? This small group of subjects should receive special concern, because they may be highly responsive to manipulation, to leading questions, and to suggestions, whether or not hypnosis has been used. Procedures described in chapter 6 for questioning of witnesses by police are especially relevant for such subjects.

5. *Prehypnosis briefing.* The hypnotist should not give the subject any indication that the subject will recall new information or that the memory of the relevant experience will be any clearer. An effort should be made to determine exactly what memories were held *before* hypnosis (Scheflin, Spiegel, & Spiegel, 1999).

6. *Management of the hypnotic session.* Spiegel and Spiegel suggested that the person con-

ducting the session should provide "a setting in which the subject can remember new facts if there are any, but in which none is introduced in the questioning" (1987, p. 501). They proposed that initially, the person should be allowed to review the events as they occurred, with little prompting. Prompting is best done through nonleading questions, such as "And then what happens?"

7. *Selective use.* Spiegel and Spiegel noted that forensic hypnosis should never be used as a substitute for routine investigative procedures.

Recall that these are guidelines for the use of hypnosis during the crime-investigation stage. The inherent dangers in hypnotically assisted memories mean that if police choose to hypnotize a victim at this early stage, the authorities should exert great caution in allowing this same person to testify at the trial, because of the suggestibility involved in the procedure and the risk of producing false memories.

THE POLYGRAPH TECHNIQUE

Police also use devices to question suspects and other people. Primary among these is the **polygraph** technique, or the so-called lie detector. Two typical uses of the polygraph are to assess the honesty of exculpatory statements given by criminal suspects and to review periodically the status of employees whose work involves international security.

Use of the Polygraph in Interrogation

When suspects are questioned by the police, they may be asked to complete a polygraph examination if they maintain their innocence. Polygraph examiners assume that changes in physiological reactions in response to incriminating questions are indications that the suspect is lying (Bull, 1988). Police believe in the accuracy of the polygraph; are their assumptions verified by empirical research findings?

Unfortunately, the scientific conclusions about the polygraph do not encourage its use. According to a review by Anthony Gale (1988), the truth "that we do not know the full truth about polygraph lie detection" (p. 2). The British Psychological Society, the leading organization of research and applied psychologists in that country, authorized a study of available research literature; it concluded that the evidence supporting the use of the polygraph test was "very slender," its reliability and validity were in question, and a need existed for more research on the topic, since much of the existing research was inadequate.

More specifically, the report criticized the typical polygraph procedure on the following grounds:

a. It involved the use of nonstandardized procedures.
b. Examiners often misled subjects about how accurate the test was.
c. Sometimes efforts were made to create anxiety in subjects, in order to encourage confessions.
d. The subject's privacy could be violated. Very personal questions about a subject's sexual, political, or religious preferences may be asked (Lykken, 1998).

The report concluded: "In such circumstances, it is difficult to see how members of the Society could engage in work as polygraphic interrogators and claim that their conduct is consistent with the Society's current Code of Conduct" (British Psychological Society, 1986, p. 93).

A Psychological Analysis

In evaluating the polygraph procedure, two potential sources of inaccuracy emerge. First, physiological measures do not directly measure lying; their changes only reflect shifts in emotional reactivity. Thus any conclusion about lying is an *inference*. It is essential that responses to the critical questions (e.g., "Did you steal the car?") be compared to responses to some other type of question. Two types of polygraph testing, discussed in the following paragraphs, use different comparisons.

The **Control Question Technique (CQT)** typically consists of about 10 questions. Relevant questions deal with the issue at hand; control questions deal with possible past behaviors that might generate emotion on the subject's part (Iacono & Patrick, 1987). An example: "Before the age of 24 did you ever try to hurt someone to get revenge?"

Note the crucial assumption: If the subject is guilty or is not telling the truth, the questions on the issue at hand will generate more emotional reactivity than will the control questions. The control questions provide a baseline measure for *that person's* level of reactivity. Those control questions must be chosen with care and pretested with the individual subject; it is essential that those questions chosen for the actual examination will elicit lying by the subject and, hence, a physiological response. The rationale behind the Control Question Technique is that an innocent person will respond as much to the control questions as to the crime-related ones (or will react even more to the control questions); in contrast, the guilty person will show more physiological responses to the crime-related questions than to the control questions. Any "score" that emerges from this procedure is thus a **difference score.**

The **Relevant-Irrelevant Test** was the first widely used polygraph test of deception. Here, the relevant questions are similar in form and content to the relevant questions in the control question procedure, but the irrelevant questions reflect a different type. They are essentially innocuous: "Are you sitting down?" or "Is your birthday in April?" The basic assumption of the Relevant-Irrelevant Test is that

a person who is deceptive in answering the relevant questions will be concerned about being discovered, which will cause involuntary autonomic reactions to occur with greatest strength in response to questions that

one answered deceptively. Thus, guilty individuals are expected to show their strongest reactions to relevant questions, whereas truthful subjects are expected to show no difference in their reactions to relevant and neutral questions. Therefore, the polygraph examiner looks for heightened reactivity to the relevant questions, and the presence of such patterns of reactions leads to the conclusion that the subject was practicing deception on the relevant issues. If no difference in reactions to relevant and neutral questions is observed, the examiner concludes that the subject was truthful in answering the relevant questions. (Raskin, 1989, pp. 250–251)

The assumptions reflected in such procedures as the Relevant-Irrelevant Test have been called simplistic and naive (Podlesny & Raskin, 1977). Most polygraph examiners have discarded this procedure, recognizing that "even an innocent person is much more likely to display more physiological activity when (truthfully) responding to the relevant questions than to the irrelevant ones" (Bull, 1988, p. 13). That is why the preferred method, the Control Question Technique, employs as its unrelated questions those that will generate emotion and lead to a response that denies culpability.

A second problem of polygraph examination deals with the task of translating the physiological responses (as operationalized by sweeping waves of recordings) into quantified measures. The goal is to classify the subject's set of responses as "truthful" or "deceptive"; a label of "inconclusive" is reserved for cases of uncertainty.

Many polygraph examiners are former police officers; few are trained as psychologists in measurement procedures (Bull, 1988). Some simply look at the charts and base their conclusions on such global, or "eyeball," impressions. Even those who are more precise may still be quite subjective; many polygraph examiners "decided which questions had occasioned the largest responses by merely looking at the charts without bothering to measure each response" (Bull, 1988, p. 17).

Examiners might even use their expectations based on the preexamination interview, along with the examinee's physiological reactivity, as determinants of their global classification. This type of subjectivity is the very antithesis of the scientific measurement model by which psychology seeks objective, replicable observations.

Even when the polygraph examiner attempts to quantify the physiological responses, the task is far from completely reliable. Raskin (1989) stated that in his procedure, a score is assigned for each of the physiological parameters for each question-pair; the score can range from −3 to +3, and "it represents the direction and magnitude of the observed difference in the reactions elicited by the relevant question and its nearby control question" (p. 260). If the observed reaction is stronger in response to the relevant question, a negative score is given; positive scores are assigned when the reaction is stronger to the control question. A value of 0 is assigned to comparisons where no difference is observed, 1 to a noticeable difference, 2 to a strong difference, and 3 to a dramatic difference. Raskin noted that most assigned scores are 0 or 1; scores of 2 are less common, and scores of 3 are "unusual." After this is done for the first pair, the procedure is repeated for other pairs of questions so that a total score can be obtained. Just how different do the reactions to the two types of questions have to be in order to conclude that the subject is deceptive? That is a matter for debate.

Note that these scores are subjectively based on a visual inspection of graphic data; certainly there is room for error. Raskin (1989) reported that the correlations among the total numerical scores assigned by the original examiner and by blind raters "tend to be very high" (p. 261). In both laboratory studies using mock crimes and in field studies, his inter-rater reliabilities were typically above .90. But these consistencies do not always hold up in real-world cases. Furthermore, a psychometrically oriented psychologist would react negatively to this procedure for a variety of reasons, not the least of which is its reliance on difference scores. Difference scores—

and in its broadest sense, the polygraph output is a difference between responses to two types of questions—are notoriously less reliable than are the scores on which they are based.

Finally, in the Control Question Technique, "it is extremely difficult to devise control questions that ensure the eliciting of stronger reactions in an innocent person than would the relevant questions relating to the crime of which they had been accused" (Bull, 1988, p. 14). Bull also noted that professional polygraphers try to minimize this problem, but for many subjects it may defy a satisfactory solution. This difficulty in selecting adequate control questions may be a reason for the Control Question Technique leading to more **false positives** (classifying truthful people as liars) than **false negatives** (classifying liars as truthful) (Carroll, 1988).

RESEARCH EVALUATION

Often, examiners who make their living by administering polygraph tests do not question the validity of what they are doing (Bull, 1988). An experienced examiner once testified before the Minnesota legislature that he had administered more than 20,000 polygraph examinations in his career and had never once been proven wrong (Lykken, 1981). David Raskin and Robert Hare have stated that "the accuracy of lie detectors on hardened criminals behind bars is 95.5%" (1978, p. 133).

Criticisms of the Polygraph

The psychologist most critical of the polygraph test is David Lykken (1981, 1985, 1988, 1998). Part of his criticism centers on his position that the lie detector is stressful and intrusive; furthermore, he has noted that polygraph examiners often rely on deceit to convince the subject that the test is accurate (Lykken, 1988, p. 112). But his central concern—and our focus here—is whether the polygraph is, in actuality an acceptably valid instrument.

Researchers have used two types of studies to evaluate the accuracy of the polygraph. In *laboratory studies,* researchers have the advantage of knowing whether subjects are actually lying or not, but the limitation of laboratory studies is one of ecological validity, specifically "the difficulty of inducing in subjects the degree and type of emotional concern experienced by guilty or by innocent suspects being tested in real life" (Lykken, 1988, p. 114). Lykken concluded that the laboratory studies that ask volunteer college students to "commit a crime" and lie during an interrogation are creating in such subjects more a state of excitement than a state of guilt.

A better way of assessing accuracy is through a *field study,* but certain criteria must be met. These include gathering a representative sample of polygraph tests administered under real-life circumstances; having the charts independently scored by polygraph examiners who have only the charts to guide their decisions (i.e., blind scoring); and, finally, comparing these scores with a criterion that is independent of the polygraph findings (that is, it is necessary to know which subjects actually did commit a crime).

Lykken (1988, 1998) concluded that many field studies did not meet these criteria; in fact, only three did (Barland & Raskin, 1975; Horvath, 1977; and Kleinmuntz & Szucko, 1984). The results of each of these studies will be described later, but, overall, 84% of the guilty subjects were judged to be lying; only 53% of the innocent subjects were judged to be truthful. Is this "accurate enough"? With these studies as our guide, our conclusion must be that the procedure is seriously biased against the truthful subject (Lykken, 1988, p. 124).

One of the most comprehensive reviews of the other type of validity check, the laboratory experiment, was carried out by the Office of Technology Assessment of the U.S. Congress (1983). It found that on average, 88.6% of the guilty were correctly classified, and 82.6% of the innocent were correctly classified. But a more ecologically valid review used the results of only those laboratory studies whose methodology close-

ly resembled the use of the Control Question Technique in the field (Carroll, 1988). The first three of these studies had guilty subjects engage in a mock crime. The Waid, Orne, and Orne (1981) study had guilty subjects conceal certain code words from the examiner, and Barland (1981) had guilty subjects lie about a biographical detail. (This is closer to a preemployment examination than to a crime-detection one.) The average success rate at detecting guilt was 85.4%, but the average for correctly detecting the innocent was lower—76.9%. However, these results reflected the examiners' using data beyond those provided by the polygraph. When blind scoring was used (i.e., only the polygraph records), the accuracy rate dropped some, particularly for innocent subjects.

Field studies produce more of a challenge, as Lykken (1988) noted; how does one find a criterion of guilt or innocence independent of a polygrapher's judgment? Two procedures have been used. In one procedure, Barland and Raskin (1975) asked five experienced attorneys to ascertain guilt or innocence based on evidence in the files; then Barland conducted the polygraph examination and Raskin, blind to the case files, analyzed the charts. Of the 92 original cases, the lawyers agreed sufficiently on 64 so they could be used. Of these, Raskin found the polygraph results to be inconclusive in 13 cases; the data are based on the remaining 51 cases.

In the second procedure, the criterion for guilt was a confession of guilt, and for innocence, a confession of guilt by another person. Horvath (1977) located 28 examples of each type from police files and gave the polygraph charts to 10 trained polygraph examiners for a blind evaluation. Five of these examiners had more than 3 years' experience; five had less, but the experience levels of the examiners did not significantly affect their accuracy. Kleinmuntz and Szucko (1984) also used actual suspects—the polygraph charts of 50 confessed thieves and 50 innocent people who, while originally suspects in these crimes, were cleared because of the confessions of the actual thieves. Six professional polygraph examiners made blind evaluations of guilt or innocence. Average accuracy in identifying guilty subjects was 83%, but for innocent subjects only 57%.

Carroll (1988) summarized the results as follows:

> These data largely speak for themselves; overall accuracy is generally low, and the rate of false positive judgments staggeringly high. Thus polygraph data per se would seem to be remarkably insensitive, particularly to a suspect's innocence. Expressed another way, the "blind" evaluation studies strongly imply that the polygraph contributes nothing of worth to traditional means of establishing innocence. In fact, the data it provides probably mislead. (p. 27)

Carroll concluded that whatever accuracy the polygraph examination provides in field tests comes from conclusions by the examiner of the subject's general demeanor rather than his or her chart responses. This evaluation is a harsh one; we prefer to frame the question of the forensic applicability of the polygraph examination within the legal instruction for determining guilt. Fact-finders—juries, judges—are not to rule for guilt unless they are convinced "beyond a reasonable doubt." Although judges are loathe to translate this instruction into a percentage, usually it is seen as an 85–90% likelihood. While the assignments of guilt or innocence based on polygraph examinations produce results that are above chance, they do not achieve this standard.

The Current Legal Status

Federal appeals courts have gone both ways on admissibility of polygraph evidence (see *United States v. Crumby*, 1995, for a case admitting a polygraph test, and *United States v. Lech*, 1995, for one that did not). Most recently, the United States Supreme Court recently considered the admissibility of polygraph findings in the case of *United States v. Scheffer*, 1998. The appeal challenged the constitutionality of President Bush's application of Military Rule of Evidence 707, which made the results of polygraph tests inadmissible in all military courts martial. (Prior to this pronouncement, the results of polygraph tests were admissible at a court martial if the judge so decided.) In this case, the defendant, Airman Edward G. Scheffer, was given a polygraph examination by the Air Force Office of Special Investigations and passed. (Two days earlier, a urine sample had tested positive for methamphetamine.) Scheffer claimed a defense of "innocent ingestion" and moved to have the polygraph results admitted at court martial but was denied. After he was convicted, he appealed; the decision eventually worked its way to the Supreme Court for review. At the oral arguments before the Court, a deputy U.S. Solicitor General argued that a blanket prohibition was justified because the "underlying scientific validity" of polygraphs was still very much in question, a matter of "extreme controversy" and "extraordinary scientific polarization." (quoted in Greenhouse, 1997, p. A14.)

In March 1998, the Supreme Court ruled, by an 8 to 1 vote, that the polygraph results were not admissible. In his majority opinion, Justice Clarence Thomas concluded that military rules of evidence call for only reliable evidence to be admitted and that scientists and legal experts are in dispute about the reliability of polygraph results. His opinion cited a survey of experts by Iacono and Lykken (1997) that concluded accuracy rates to be little above chance. Whether such a decision will be generalized to nonmilitary settings remains to be seen.

THE ROLE OF THE FORENSIC PSYCHOLOGIST

If polygraph examiners want their examinations to produce accurate results, psychologists can provide expertise regarding the psychometric qualities of adequate testing instruments. Particularly important are the phenomena of reliability, validity, and freedom from bias, and, as we have seen, the polygraph procedure often falls short of the standards for these (Blinkhorn, 1988). Bull (1988) noted that many polygraphers have "at best only a rudimentary understanding of all the physiological and psychological factors involved" (p. 18).

Another role for the psychologist is as an evaluation researcher. For example, controversy exists over the claim that subjects can be trained to engage in thoughts or acts that affect the validity of the polygraph responses. Most examiners don't think they can. What does the research conclude about the use of **countermeasures?**

What if a subject wants to present a false self-picture? Could he or she influence the responses by using one or more countermeasures during the examination? The most thorough review of this issue is by Gisli H. Gudjonsson (1988), a researcher/clinical psychologist and former police officer experienced in the use of the lie detector in criminal investigations.

What kinds of deliberate countermeasures might be used by subjects? Gudjonsson (1988) identified three different physical ways that have been offered in order to "fool" the polygraph technique:

1. Suppressing physiological responses to relevant questions.
2. Augmenting physiological responses to control questions, thereby increasing the baseline measure of the subject's emotional response. Gudjonsson observed that it is usually easier for subjects to augment responses to this type of question than to suppress responses to the crime-related questions.
3. Suppressing the overall level of physiological activity by, for example, taking drugs.

Gudjonsson expressed doubt that drugs are generally effective as a countermeasure; perhaps when the level of arousal or concern is low they might. And it is unlikely that a drug would differentially affect responses to the crime-related and control questions, and that difference is central to the diagnosis of truth-telling or lying.

In addition to taking tranquillizers or other drugs, subjects may use other physical means, such as inducing either physical pain or muscle tension. Gudjonsson wrote, "For example, biting one's tongue in response to the control questions may create sufficient pain or discomfort to elicit an artificial physiological response indistinguishable from that of a genuine one. Similarly, pressing the toes against the floor or the thighs against the chair the individual is sitting in have been shown to be effective techniques under certain circumstances" (1988, p. 129).

Do these procedures work? Early research was inconsistent in its conclusions; later laboratory studies (reviewed by the Office of Technology Assessment, 1983, and by Gudjonsson, 1988) suggested that

1. Countermeasures may result in an "inconclusive" diagnosis, rather than the "truthful" diagnosis aspired to by the deceptive subject using the physical countermeasures (Honts & Hodes, 1982a).
2. Using several physical countermeasures at the same time is more effective than using only one (Honts & Hodes, 1982b).
3. Special training and practice in their use are necessary; simply providing subjects with information about such countermeasures is ineffective (Honts, Raskin, & Kircher, 1984).
4. Some of the physical countermeasures used by deceptive subjects are not easily detected by visual observation or by the equipment ordinarily available to polygraph examiners; they require special electromyograph recordings (Honts, Raskin, & Kircher, 1983). Some polygraph examiners can monitor gross bodily movements through the use of pneumatic sensors built into the back and the seat of the subject's chair (Reid, 1945), but these do not detect subtle responses.

In addition to using physical countermeasures, subjects may employ certain kinds of mental countermeasures. Specifically, subjects can use three types of practices:

1. Artificially producing responses to control questions (for example, by thinking of an earlier erotic or painful experience).
2. Attenuating responses to relevant questions, perhaps by trying to calm themselves down when this type of question is posed.
3. Mentally dissociating, often by attempting to distract themselves, focusing their attention on some irrelevant object or thought. They may try to answer questions "automatically" in a uniform way.

For subjects who wish to be deceptive, the advantage to using mental rather than physical countermeasures is that they cannot be detected by observation or even sensitive equipment. But Gudjonsson concluded they are less effective: "The available evidence suggests that mental counter-measures are generally less effective in defeating polygraph tests than physical counter-measures, although some subjects can successfully apply such techniques" (1988, p. 131). The most effective of the mental countermeasures seems to be for deception-motivated subjects to think of emotionally arousing thoughts while being asked the emotional-baseline-generating questions.

Gudjonsson offered the following tentative conclusions:

The use of different classes of counter-measures has been reported in the literature. The available evidence shows that mental counter-measures and the use of pharmaco-logical substances (such as tranquillizers) are only moderately effective at best, whereas physical counter-measures can be highly effective under certain conditions. Two conditions appear important to the effective use of physical counter-measures. First, employing multiple counter-measures simultaneously improves the person's chances of defeating a polygraph test, at least as far as the control question technique is concerned. Second, physical counter-measures appear relatively ineffective unless people are given special training in their use. It is generally not sufficient to provide people with instructions about polygraph techniques and counter-measures.

Although there are clear individual differences in the ability to apply counter-measures effectively, training by experts in the use of physical counter-measures poses a potentially serious threat to the validity of the polygraph techniques. For this reason it becomes very important that the use of counter-measures is readily identified by polygraph examiners. Unfortunately subtle and effective counter-measures are not readily observable without special expertise and equipment which are not generally available to field examiners. (Gudjonsson, 1988, pp. 135–136)

SUMMARY

Criminal profiling is an educated attempt to provide specific information about a certain type of suspect, but several types of activities fall under the general label. For example, attempts to determine the psychological makeup of a specific person posing a threat to national security, such as Adolf Hitler in the 1940s or Saddam Hussein more recently, reflect one approach to profiling. Other approaches include determining if people who commit a particular type of crime reflect a common set of characteristics and extracting characteristics from a particular crime or set of crimes in order to identify the criminal.

The latter approach is typical of the criminal profiling procedures used by the FBI. A thorough analysis of the crime scene is carried out, in search of a "signature" left by the criminal. A distinction is made between organized and disorganized offenders.

The effectiveness of criminal profiling has yet to be firmly established. Some cases reflect remarkable accuracy in predicting specific characteristics of the offender, but other cases, reveal a high level of inaccuracy. An empirical study of effectiveness found only weak support for a conclusion that experienced profilers generated more information and more accurate information about the perpetrator from an examination of the files than did other types of law-enforcement officials, clinical psychologists, and students.

A psychological autopsy is a special type of profile, carried out after the subject's death in order to determine the mode of death (accident, suicide, homicide, or natural causes). In such cases of equivocal deaths, the psychologist collects a variety of information about the individual's state of mind prior to his or her death. The case of *Jackson v. State* led to a ruling that psychiatrists and psychologists can testify about their findings in a psychological autopsy.

When crime victims or witnesses cannot recall many details of a crime, police may use hypnosis as a memory aid. A suspect claiming to be innocent may be asked to take a polygraph examination. These two activities reflect the use of psychological procedures in crime investigation and are considered in this chapter.

Psychologists differ as to whether hypnosis, as an investigative tool, offers benefits beyond its costs. Under hypnosis, some victims and witnesses may be able to recall some information they could not remember in a waking state, but being in a hypnotized state makes one quite suggestible and leads to the production of false memories. Given the concerns about the accuracy of hypnotically assisted memory, the forensic psychologist can suggest guidelines for its use, especially with respect to the qualifications of the person doing the hypnosis and the procedures followed during the hypnosis session.

Polygraph tests are usually administered by an employee of the police department, not by a psychologist. Although the specific procedures may vary, a frequently used one, the Control Question Technique, compares the subject's physiological responses to questions about the crime to his or her responses to other questions (called control questions) designed to create

guilt. If the crime-related questions elicit the more extreme response, examiners conclude that the suspect is lying. But these responses are by no means perfectly reliable, and research findings conclude that although the success rate of the polygraph procedure in detecting guilt is above chance, it is not so high as to achieve a legal goal of "guilt beyond a reasonable doubt."

KEY TERMS

Control Question Technique (CQT)
countermeasures
crime investigation stage
crime scene analysis
criminal profile
criminal profile generating process
criminal profiling
difference score
equivocal death analysis
false positives
false negatives
hypnotically assisted memory
hypnotizability
mass murder
meta-analysis
mode of death
modus operandi
multiple personality
NASH classification
organized versus disorganized criminals
per se exclusionary rule
polygraph
psychological autopsy
psychological profile
Relevant-Irrelevant Test
serial murder
signature of a criminal
sociopsychological profile
spree murder
testamentary capacity
totality of circumstances test
VICAP

INFOTRAC®
COLLEGE EDITION

InfoTrac College Edition is a FREE, powerful, online learning resource, consisting of full-text articles from thousands of journals and periodicals. With each new copy of *Forensic Psychology,* Second Edition, you receive 4 months of free access to the InfoTrac College Edition database. By doing a simple keyword search (try using the Key Terms in the list above), you can quickly generate a list of relevant articles from thousands of possibilities and can select articles to read, explore, and print for reference or further study. InfoTrac College Edition's continuously updated collection of articles can be useful for doing reading and writing assignments that reach beyond the pages of this text!

SUGGESTED READINGS

Brussel, J. A. (1968). *Casebook of a crime psychiatrist.* New York: Bernard Geis Associates.

A readable description of the so-called "Mad Bomber" case, plus others by an early forensic psychiatrist.

Douglas, J. E., & Olshaker, M. (1995). *Mindhunter: Inside the FBI's elite serial crime unit.* New York: Scribner.

The first of several books describing some of John Douglas's classic cases of criminal profiling, this one is especially valuable because it is also a form of autobiography that describes how Douglas became a highly regarded profiler.

Fowler, R. D. (1986, May). Howard Hughes: A psychological autopsy. *Psychology Today,* pp. 22–33.

After the death of Howard Hughes, the flamboyant millionaire-turned-recluse, numerous people claimed to be inheritors of his estate. Raymond Fowler, the chief executive officer of the American Psychological Association, was asked to complete a psychological autopsy of Hughes, focusing especially on his testamentary capacity.

Gale, A. (Ed.). (1988). *The polygraph test: Lies, truth, and science.* London: Sage.

A set of contributed chapters by psychologists on the polygraph, reflecting the views of the British Psychological Society.

Hammond, D. C., Garver, R. B., Mutter, C. B., Crasilneck, H. B., Frischholz, E., Gravitz, M. A., Hibler, N. S., Olson, J., Scheflin, A. W., Spiegel, H., & Webster, W. (1995). *Clinical hypnosis and memory: Guidelines for clinicians and for forensic hypnosis.* Des Plaines, IL: American Society of Clinical Hypnosis Press.

A detailed set of guidelines for forensic hypnosis, authorized by the American Society of Clinical Hypnosis.

Harris, T. (1981). *The red dragon.* New York: Putnam.

A novel in which the hero, a criminal profiler, is based on the life and work of John Douglas.

Iacono, W. G., & Patrick, C. J. (1999). Polygraph ("lie detector") testing: The state of the art. In A. K. Hess & I. B. Weiner (Eds.), *The handbook of forensic psychology* (2nd ed., pp. 440–473). New York: Wiley.

A recent, critical examination of claims of accuracy for the polygraph.

Jackson, J. L., & Bekerian, D. A. (Eds.). (1997). *Offender profiling: Theory, research and practice.* New York: John Wiley and Sons.

A thorough, critical evaluation of criminal profiling, with chapters written by experts from the United Kingdom, the Netherlands, and Canada. Chapter 2 provides a classification of crime motives, with case histories; the final chapter describes criticisms of profiling. Highly recommended.

Lykken, D. T. (1998). *A tremor in the blood: Uses and abuses of the lie detector.* New York: Plenum.

An extensively revised version of a book first published in 1981, by one of the leading critics of the use of the polygraph to determine guilt. Contains a history of attempts at lie detection, plus reviews of the Control Question Technique, the Relevant-Irrelevant Test, and voice stress analysis. Highly recommended.

Meloy, J. R. (Ed.). (1998). *The psychology of stalking: Clinical and forensic perspectives.* San Diego, CA: Academic Press.

Fifteen contributed chapters by research psychologists, clinicians, and other experts in the field deal with classifications of stalkers, victims, explicit and implicit threats, and other related topics.

Michaud, S. G., with Hazelwood, R. (1998). *The evil that men do: FBI profiler Roy Hazelwood's journey into the minds of sexual predators.* New York: St. Martin's Press.

A very readable description of many of the cases investigated by former FBI profiler Roy Hazelwood, who developed the organized/disorganized crime classification. The cases described include the fatal explosion on the USS *Iowa* and the Atlanta child murders. Also includes some controversial conclusions about the effects of pornography, not shared by all psychologists.

O'Brien, D. (1985). *Two of a kind: The hillside stranglers.* New York: New American Library.

An account, available in paperback, of the Hillside Strangler case. A highly readable example of the "true crime" genre.

Ressler, R. K., & Shachtman, T. (1992). *Whoever fights monsters.* New York: St. Martin's Press.

A vivid description of how Robert Ressler used interviews with convicted serial killers to develop the procedure now known as criminal profiling.

Scheflin, A. W., & Shapiro, J. L. (1989). *Trance on trial.* New York: Guilford Press.

An erudite examination of the history and contemporary forensic uses of hypnosis.

Scheflin, A. W., Spiegel, H., & Spiegel, D. (1999). Forensic uses of hypnosis. In A. K. Hess & I. B. Weiner (Eds.), *The handbook of forensic psychology* (2nd ed., pp. 474–498). New York: Wiley.

A chapter on the uses of hypnosis in law enforcement, written by experts who support the use of hypnosis but recognize the necessity that it be done only by well-trained clinicians.

5

Insanity and Competency

The determination of a person's mental state, both at the time of the offense (the insanity defense) and at the time of trial (competency to stand trial), is one of the most challenging tasks given to the forensic psychologist by the courts. And throughout these assessments lurks this question: Is the person **malingering;** that is, is the defendant simulating a serious mental disorder in order to avoid a guilty verdict or a prison sentence?

INSANITY DETERMINATION

One of the most important tasks facing forensic psychologists is assisting the courts in making a determination of insanity. And this task is one of the most difficult—some would say that it is impossible. One purpose of this chapter is to examine this process, by considering some recent cases and matching the behavior of defendants with the definitions of insanity used in the courts.

The Difficulty in Determining Insanity

The sources of difficulty are multitudinous. First, it is important to remember that **insanity** is a legal concept, to be decided by the triers of fact, and not a medical or psychological one; as the following example of John Salvi illustrates, a person may demonstrate psychotic behavior and still not fulfill the legal definition of insanity (this is why, contrary to popular belief, the insanity defense is not a haven for the faker, but instead a situation in which people with severe psychological and psychiatric problems often end up in prisons rather than hospitals; see Borum & Fulero, 1999). Second, the legal definition of "insanity" may vary from jurisdiction to jurisdiction. Third, the forensic psychiatrist or psychologist faced with the difficult task of assessing insanity must make a retrospective assessment of the person's mental state at the time of the offense, several months or years before. It is no wonder that reasonable professionals can, and sometimes do, disagree.

Insanity versus Psychosis

In a very few cases, a person—based on consistent and extreme behavior—may be clearly characterized as both psychotic and insane. But in the cases that come before the courts for adjudication—John Hinckley, Jr., Lorena Bobbitt, Jeffrey Dahmer, Theodore Kaczynski (the Unabomber), and Andrea Yates are all highly publicized examples—it is not so easy to make a judgment of insanity. (Contrary to another popular myth, the defense of not guilty by reason of insanity is not limited to those who commit major offenses, and in fact it is most often used by those who have committed less serious and less publicized acts [Borum & Fulero, 1999]; almost one third of those making the claim had committed nonviolent acts [Silver, Cirincione, & Steadman, 1994].) Not only do many offenders who claim insanity demonstrate contact with reality, but the definitions given to insanity and the instructions about the burden of proof are not the same in every jurisdiction. These issues are described here.

Definitions

It is part of Western moral and legal tradition that a person who is unaware of the meaning of his or her acts should not be held criminally responsible for them. In the legal system, the presence of **mens rea,** or "a guilty mind," is essential to the classification of an illegal act. A determination of guilt and a punishment, as evaluations and responses, should ensue only if there is free will and intent to do **harm** (*Durham v. United States,* 1954). **Guilt** in a criminal sense requires not only the commission of an illegal act but a concurrently existing state of mind reflecting awareness of the act's implications. But how do we define the state of those people who commit acts but should not be held responsible for them? Currently in the various jurisdictions, several definitions of insanity are operative.

Those criminal defendants who are found *not* to be criminally responsible are judged "not guilty by reason of insanity," or **NGRI;** they are usually committed to a psychiatric hospital and remain there as long as they—in the judgment of the psychiatric staff—fit the criteria for possession of serious psychiatric disorders. Most spend extended periods in confinement, sometimes longer than if they had been found guilty and sentenced to prison (Borum & Fulero, 1999; Rodriguez, LeWinn, & Perlin, 1983). John Hinckley, Jr., for example, is still, after over 20 years, confined to St. Elizabeth Hospital in Washington, D.C.

The M'Naghten Rule

Approximately half the states in the United States now use the **M'Naghten rule** in defining insanity; this definition developed as a result of a trial in England more than 100 years ago, involving Daniel M'Naghten (also spelled McNaghten, McNaughton, and several other ways). It contains three elements; a person should, according to the definition, be judged insane if the following are present:

1. The defendant was suffering from "a defect of reason, from a disease of the mind."
2. As a result, the defendant did not "know" the "nature and quality of the act he was doing."
3. As a result, the defendant did not know that "what he was doing was wrong" (Ogloff, Roberts, & Roesch, 1993).

The M'Naghten test is called a **cognitive test of insanity** because it emphasizes the quality of the person's thought processes and perceptions of reality at the time of the crime (Low, Jeffries, & Bonnie, 1986).

The Irresistible Impulse Standard

Criticism of the M'Naghten standard for its narrow focus on the defendant's cognitive knowledge led to it being supplemented—temporarily—by what was called the **irresistible impulse exemption.** If a defendant demonstrated cognitive knowledge of right or wrong, he or she could still be found not guilty by reason of insanity if his or her free will was so destroyed or overruled that the person had lost the power to choose between right and wrong (Ogloff, Roberts, & Roesch, 1993). When referring to this loss of ability to control one's behavior, the courts sometimes refer to the **volitional aspect of insanity.**

The Durham Test

Continued criticism of the M'Naghten standard's cognitive focus caused the courts to abandon reliance on the irresistible impulse exception and to seek broader definitions. In the case of *Durham v. United States* (1954), Judge David Bazelon developed a new definition, which came to be called the Durham rule; it stated that the accused was not criminally responsible if his or her unlawful act was a product of mental disease or defect. First seen as a progressive step because it moved the legal definitions closer to psychiatric concepts, the Durham rule soon became a problem. Mental health experts, who increasingly were testifying in trials involving the insanity plea, interpreted the term *mental disease* to mean any familiar clinical-diagnostic label (Ogloff, Roberts, & Roesch, 1993). The Durham standard is currently used in only one state, New Hampshire.

The ALI Standard, or Brawner Rule

Criticisms of the Durham rule led to one further attempt at modification. The American Law Institute (ALI) developed a new definition that received acceptance in the case of *United States v. Brawner* in 1972; this innovation, now called the **ALI standard,** sought comprehensiveness. It stated: "A person is not responsible for criminal conduct if at the time of the action, as a result of mental disease or defect, he [or she] lacks substantial capacity either to appreciate the criminality (wrongfulness) of his [or her] conduct or to conform his [or her] conduct to the requirements of the law" (American Law Institute, 1962, p. 401). As used in this statement, the term *mental disease or defect* does not include an abnormality manifested only by repeated criminal or otherwise antisocial conduct.

Several aspects are worth noting in this attempt at a comprehensive definition:

First, note it states "substantial capacity" rather than total incapacity; for example, a 5-year-old can know that it is wrong to kill someone but not fully appreciate the wrongfulness of it. Second, the ability to "appreciate" wrongfulness rather than to "know" it connotes volitional or affective as well as cognitive understanding, and fits better with modern psychiatric perspectives (Ogloff, Roberts, & Roesch, 1993). Thus, the ALI standard can be thought of as including two aspects, or prongs—a cognitive one ("can't appreciate the wrongfulness") and a volitional one ("can't conform his or her conduct").

Currently, 21 states in the United States use the ALI standard. Wisconsin, the site of Jeffrey Dahmer's trial, has a unique procedure that combines elements of the M'Naghten and ALI standards. Thus, psychologists who carry out insanity evaluations need to have a working knowledge of the definition of insanity in their jurisdiction (Rogers & McKee, 1995).

The Guilty but Mentally Ill Verdict

A decision that combines recognition of mental illness in defendants but still holds them guilty has been adopted as a supplement to the insanity-defense standards in several states. For example, in 1996, millionaire John duPont was charged with killing one of his staff members. There was no question about duPont having done the killing in a calculated manner, but also it seemed clear that he suffered from a paranoid schizophrenic psychosis. At his trial, the Pennsylvania jury found him to be mentally ill but also guilty of murder. Thirteen states provide for this type of verdict, abbreviated **GBMI,** for "guilty but mentally ill" (Borum & Fulero, 1999). After such verdicts, the defendant is provided treatment at a state mental hospital until he or she is declared to be sane; then the defendant is sent to prison.

One of the original purposes of the GBMI legislation was to provide treatment within a correctional setting for those criminal defendants with psychiatric disorders. But a number of criticisms of the concept have emerged (Slobogin, 1985; Steadman, 1993); for example,

1. The definition of GBMI and the provisions for incarceration and treatment differ from state to state.
2. It is sometimes difficult for jurors to distinguish between the concepts of NGRI and GBMI. A claim of "not guilty by reason of insanity" is an **affirmative defense** to a crime: The defendant has argued that he or she meets the insanity defense standard; thus, "he or she is determined to be 'not guilty' (or 'not responsible') in the eyes of the law and is then subjected to *civil* proceedings for their confinement, but not to *criminal* incarceration or punishment" (Borum & Fulero, 1999, p. 124, italics in original). But GBMI is not a defense; it is a *verdict,* implying that the defendant is criminally culpable and eligible for criminal sanctions. The inclusion of "but mentally ill" denotes the possession of a mental disorder but does not absolve the person of guilt or criminal responsibility (Borum & Fulero, 1999).
3. The adoption of a GBMI option by a state has not necessarily led to the expected reduction in rate of NGRI acquittals; it appears that most of those found GBMI came from a population of those who would have been found guilty, rather than from the population of those NGRI (Borum & Fulero, 1999).
4. Most important, the employment of the GBMI verdict does not ensure that such offenders will get effective treatment (Perlin, 1996). In Georgia, for example, only 3 of 150 defendants found GBMI during the period under review were being treated in hospitals (Steadman, 1993). More generally, reviewers have concluded that the GBMI prisoner is not even given treatment "beyond that available to other offenders" (Slobogin, 1985, p. 513).

Currently, five states (Idaho, Montana, Nevada, Kansas, and Utah) make no provision for an affirmative insanity defense, although the defense attorney can introduce evidence of the defendant's mental status to try to disprove the *mens rea* element of the charged offense (Borum & Fulero, 1999). In contrast, the federal government uses a variation of the ALI standard, stating the person "lacks capacity to appreciate the wrongfulness of his conduct" but in operation, the rule resembles the M'Naghten definition. The jury's verdict that John Hinckley—charged with the attempted assassination of President Reagan—was not guilty by reason of insanity not only incensed the public but it motivated Congress to radically overhaul the federal laws regarding the determination of insanity (Caplan, 1984). Congress passed the Insanity Defense Reform Act of 1984, removing the volitional prong of the ALI rule, leaving it substantially like the M'Naghten rule, with focus on the accused's cognitive "appreciation." Congress also removed "substantial" as a modifier, so the federal insanity test now instructs the fact finder to decide whether or not the defendant "lacks capacity to appreciate the wrongfulness of his conduct."

The Burden of Proof

The definition of insanity was not the only aspect affected by the unpopular verdict in the Hinckley trial. Before his case, the only assassin or would-be assassin to escape conviction for attacking a sitting president was an underemployed house painter named Richard Lawrence, who attempted to kill Andrew Jackson in 1835 (Taylor, 1982). Lawrence's two pistols inexplicably failed to fire. At the trial, Lawrence proclaimed he was the king of England, the United States, and Rome, and that President Jackson had denied him his throne and fortune. Several physicians noted that he had insane delusions. It took the jury only 5 minutes to return a verdict of not guilty by reason of insanity.

Jurors at John Hinckley's trial had a more complicated case. Not only was there conflicting testimony, but the judge instructed the jury that the **burden of proof** was on the prosecution to prove beyond a reasonable doubt that Hinckley was not insane. After announcing the verdict, several jurors said that, given this instruction, the evidence was too conflicting for them to conclude that Hinckley was guilty. As a result, Congress shifted the burden of proof in federal trials; it is now on the defendant to prove insanity by clear and convincing evidence, rather than on the prosecution to disprove insanity. Almost all the state courts now also place the burden of persuasion on the defendant to prove his or her insanity, although the vast majority uses a different standard, "preponderance of the evidence" rather than "clear and convincing evidence" (Callahan, Mayer, & Steadman, 1987). A few states still require the prosecution to prove the defendant's sanity beyond a reasonable doubt.

The Example of John Salvi

On December 30, 1994, John C. Salvi III walked into the Planned Parenthood clinic in Brookline, Massachusetts, and shot and killed a receptionist, firing two times at close range. He also wounded three other people. He immediately went to another abortion clinic 2 miles away, the Preterm Health Services clinic, and again killed the receptionist and injured two other staff members. He then fled the scene, and got as far as Norfolk, Virginia, before he was captured.

John Salvi was examined by psychiatrists and diagnosed as possessing paranoid schizophrenia. He was driven by persecutory delusions; he had accused his mother of trying to poison him, and he once interrupted the Christmas mass at his local church by marching to the altar and lecturing the congregation on the failures of the Catholic Church (Swartz, 1997). He denied that he had any problems, but while he was incarcerated prior to his trial, he didn't eat much of the food, claiming that it was poisoned. But was he a zealot or was he insane? Massachusetts uses the ALI standard. The jury, in a March 1996 trial, convicted him on two counts of first-degree murder and five counts of armed assault with intent to murder, and he was sentenced to life in prison. In November of the same year, he was found dead in his prison cell, an apparent suicide. His death led to renewed discussion about the nature of criminal responsibility, although prison officials denied that he had shown any indications of suicide proneness.

THE PSYCHOLOGIST'S ROLES IN INSANITY CASES

The forensic psychologist plays several roles when insanity is used by a defendant as a defense. Prior to trial, the clinical/forensic psychologist may be asked to assess the defendant; then, at the trial, the psychologist may testify about his or her findings.

Assessment of Criminal Responsibility

In deciding whether offenders were aware of the implications of their actions, psychologists have traditionally used interviews; often these were unstandardized and unstructured. A more reliable procedure was needed. Developed for this purpose, the Rogers Criminal Responsibility Assessment Scales (or R-CRAS) attempt to apply the logic of diagnostic structured interviews to the forensic assessment of criminal responsibility (Rogers, 1984, 1986; Rogers & Cavanaugh, 1981; Rogers & Ewing, 1992; Rogers, Wasyliw, & Cavanaugh, 1984). The scales transfer the ALI definition of insanity into 25 quantifiable variables, grouped into five topics of psycho-legal relevance: organicity, psychopathology, cognitive control, behavioral control, and the reliability of the report. Each R-CRAS item requires the examiner to rate a specific psychological or situational variable on the delineated criteria; Box 5-1 gives examples of these items.

The authors have reported high interjudge reliabilities for assignment of scores to the five topics and for a final judgment of insanity; mean rate of agreement was over 90% (Nicholson, 1999; Rogers, Dolmetsch, Wasyliw, & Cavanaugh,

1982). Also, there is a high correspondence between the examiners' ratings and the final legal adjudications (Rogers, Cavanaugh, Seman, & Harris, 1984), although these data are derived from examiners who "work closely with one another in specialized forensic evaluation centers, and whose reports and testimony are well known to and influential in local courts" (Ogloff, Roberts, & Roesch, 1993, p. 171).

The review of the R-CRAS by Ogloff et al. (1993) concluded that it is a useful device; these reviewers saw as one of its benefits the requirement that forensic psychologists be comprehensive and explicit about the contributing factors in their judgments about the presence of insanity. Other reviewers have not been as accepting of the R-CRAS; Golding and Roesch (1987) were quite critical and questioned whether the inter-rater reliability coefficients were any higher than those resulting from unstructured interviews. Robert Nicholson (1999), in evaluating various reviews of the R-CRAS, noted that its variable rate of acceptance may partly reflect differences of opinion about the goal of forensic assessment; specifically, does it seek to provide an *ultimate opinion* regarding the insanity of the individual, an issue reviewed in detail later in this chapter.

A second instrument for assessing criminal responsibility, the Mental Screening Evaluation, or MSE (Slobogin, Melton, & Showalter, 1984), has a more modest goal: to "screen out" those defendants whose law-breaking actions clearly were not caused by a mental abnormality. The MSE includes questions about the defendant's general psychological history, questions about the alleged offense, and an evaluation of the defendant's present mental state. For example, in the first section, the psychologist is asked to determine: "Does the defendant have a history of prolonged bizarre behavior (i.e., delusions, hallucinations, looseness of association of ideas . . . [or] disturbances of affect)?" (Slobogin, Melton, & Showalter, 1984, p. 319).

A purpose of the MSE is to sensitize psychological examiners to the kinds of informa-

BOX 5-1

Sample Items from the R-CRAS

Two of the 25 items from the Rogers Criminal Responsibility Assessment Scales (R-CRAS) are the following:

Item 10. Amnesia about the alleged crime.
(This refers to the examiner's assessment of amnesia, not necessarily the patient's reported amnesia.)

(0) No information.

(1) None. Remembers the entire event in considerable detail.

(2) Slight; of doubtful significance. The patient forgets a few minor details.

(3) Mild. Patient remembers the substance of what happened, but is forgetful of many minor details.

(4) Moderate. The patient has forgotten a major portion of the alleged crime but remembers enough details to believe it happened.

(5) Severe. The patient is amnesic to most of the alleged crime, but remembers enough details to believe it happened.

(6) Extreme. Patient is completely amnesic to the whole alleged crime.

Item 11. Delusions at the time of the alleged crime.

(0) No information.

(1) Absent.

(2) Suspected delusions (e.g., supported only by questionable self-report).

(3) Definite delusions, but not actually associated with the commission of the alleged crime.

(4) Definite delusions which contributed to, but were not the predominant force in the commission of the alleged crime.

(5) Definite controlling delusions, on the basis of which the alleged crime was committed.

Source: Rogers, Wasyliw, & Cavanaugh, 1984, p. 299.

tion required when addressing the legal question of the defendant's mental state at the time of the lawbreaking behavior. But there is no standardized administration or formal scoring procedure, and empirical evidence on the evaluation's validity is limited (Grisso, 1986; Nicholson, 1999; Rogers & Shuman, 2000). Further, some have criticized the MSE on the ground that there should be no "screening" in such cases, and that all defendants deserve a full evaluation on a question of insanity (Foote, 2000).

Testifying as an Expert Witness

In making decisions on issues beyond their knowledge, jurors often pay attention to the testimony of expert witnesses. But the forensic psychologist who testifies for the defense that the defendant meets the definition of insanity faces several challenges. First, the prosecution is likely to have expert witnesses of its own, with conflicting conclusions. Second, in some jurisdictions, defense experts are prevented from expressing an opinion about the particular case and can only express opinions about general matters. Finally, any expert witness is likely to face a withering cross-examination. On the latter point, the volumes prepared by the late forensic psychologist Jay Ziskin (1995), a highly publicized article in *Science* by Faust and Ziskin (1988), and recent books by Dawes (1994), Hagen (1997), and Wood, Nezworski, Lilienfeld, and Garb (2003) all challenge the claim that the assessments done and tests used by clinical psychologists and other mental health professionals possess adequate levels of validity and reliability for use in court (see Nicholson, 1999, pp. 125–131, for a critique of Ziskin's efforts). In the following sections, we explore several trials that illustrate the concerns about testifying; most important, these trials illustrate the differing assessments by defense and prosecution experts when the question is the defendant's mental state.

The John Hinckley Trial

In the mid-1980s, Caplan (1984) noted that there were 30,000 American psychiatrists, fewer than 1,000 were forensic psychiatrists, and only about 125 of these testified regularly in insanity cases (it is not clear what these numbers are today, nor do they include forensic psychologists). The trial of John W. Hinckley, Jr., utilized expert psychiatrists on each side. When Hinckley went on trial 15 months after the shooting, his lawyers did not dispute the evidence that he had planned the attack, bought special bullets, tracked the president, and fired from a shooter's crouch. But they claimed that he was only responding to the "driving forces" of a diseased mind. Their claims were supported by the testimony of psychiatrist William Carpenter, who said that Hinckley did not "appreciate" the consequences of his act, had lost the ability to control himself, and was suffering from process schizophrenia. The defense also tried to introduce the results of a CAT scan of Hinckley's brain to support its contention that he was schizophrenic.

The psychiatrists testifying for the prosecution conceded that Hinckley had strange fantasies but said he did not have schizophrenia; rather, he exhibited only a few relatively mild and commonplace mental disorders. They stated that he had no delusions or psychoses; he was always in touch with reality, including the reality that actress Jodie Foster would never feel affection for him. The real motives, they said, had been to win fame and to give Ms. Foster and his parents a jolt (Caplan, 1984).

A prominent forensic psychiatrist testifying for the prosecution, Park Dietz, diagnosed Hinckley as having a borderline personality disorder with depressive neurosis. He concluded that Hinckley's goal of making an impression on Jodie Foster was indeed reasonable, because he accomplished it (Caplan, 1984). Even though his were not the reasonable acts of a completely rational individual, no evidence existed that he was so impaired that he could not appreciate the wrongfulness of his conduct or conform his conduct to the requirements of the law.

The jury found Hinckley not guilty by reason of insanity, at least in part because the burden of proof at that time was on the prosecution to show that Hinckley was sane beyond a reasonable doubt. The verdict provoked a storm of criticism and even some legislative attempts to change the insanity defense (Fulero & Finkel, 1991). In December 2003, Hinckley was granted out-of-hospital visits to his parents, which provoked another storm of controversy.

The Jeffrey Dahmer Trial

The 1992 trial of Jeffrey Dahmer is unusual for more than the reason that he had admitted killing and dismembering 17 young men over a 10-year period. Some bodies he cannibalized; others he tried to turn into "zombies" who could remain with him for companionship (Berlin, 1994). The purpose of the trial was to determine if he could be absolved of responsibility by reason of insanity, in that he had already conceded that he had committed the acts. Hence, the jury was given two different characterizations of the defendant. His attorney told the jury, "This is not an evil man; this is a sick man." The prosecuting attorney disagreed, claiming that Dahmer "knew at all times that what he was doing was wrong."

The trial was also unusual in that in addition to the expert witnesses introduced by each side, the presiding judge asked two experts to testify, one psychiatrist and one psychologist.

The defense experts, who testified first (in Wisconsin, the burden of proof concerning insanity rests with the defense) included the following:

1. Dr. Fred S. Berlin: A psychiatrist from Johns Hopkins University School of Medicine, Dr. Berlin diagnosed Dahmer's psychiatric disorder as **necrophilia** (a type of **paraphilia,** or abnormal sexual behavior), reflecting sexual urges that caused him to kill young men and then preserve their body parts in an effort to

maintain sexual intimacy. Dahmer used such terms as "overpowering" in describing the strength of his cravings; hence, Dr. Berlin felt that Dahmer lacked "substantial capacity" to control his actions. In a subsequent article (1994), Dr. Berlin concluded that Dahmer came to believe it was his destiny to kill, even though he often felt miserable, alone, and despairing. Dr. Berlin also testified that Dahmer would become erotically aroused by the thought of having sex with dead male bodies. Dahmer was frequently impotent and unable to sustain an erection when relating to those who were still alive (Berlin, 1994).

In his article on the case, Dr. Berlin stated: "I did not feel uncomfortable defending the position that an individual who recurrently experiences much more powerful urges to have sex with a corpse than with a living human being is an individual who is afflicted with a mental disease or defect" (1994, p. 14). Of all the expert witnesses, he came closest to the layperson's view when he said, "If this isn't mental illness I don't know what is."

2. Dr. Judith Becker: A clinical psychologist and professor at the University of Arizona, Dr. Becker offered a sexual history of Dahmer and described Dahmer's fantasies about capturing young men and building a kind of "temple" in his apartment from the body parts, skulls, and skeletons of his victims (Norris, 1992). She, too, felt that Dahmer suffered from the sexual disorder necrophilia and that he lacked control of his urges. She did not diagnose him as psychotic, although she felt that some of his behavior was "psychotic-like."

3. Dr. Carl Wahlstrom: A psychiatrist, Dr. Wahlstrom, on cross-examination, acknowledged that he had not yet passed his board certification and that this was his first defense testimony (Norris, 1992). He proposed that Dahmer killed in order to avoid abandonment; Dr. Wahlstrom was the only defense witness to conclude that Dahmer had a bor-

derline personality and was psychotic, even though he lacked hallucinations.

The prosecution countered with two experts:

1. Dr. Frederick Fosdal: A forensic psychiatrist from the University of Wisconsin Medical School, Dr. Fosdal noted that Dahmer's acts were not brutal or sadistic. Furthermore, Dahmer was able to refrain and had some control as to when he followed through on his sexual desires.

2. Dr. Park Dietz: Formerly on the faculty at the University of Virginia but now a full-time forensic psychiatrist (Box 5-2 elaborates on his background), Dr. Dietz had also testified in the Hinckley trial. Perhaps the most effective of the seven expert witnesses, Dr. Dietz pointed to Dahmer's capacity to exert methodical control as an indicator of his sanity and premeditation (Norris, 1992). Furthermore, "the mere fact that Dahmer disposed of his bodies efficiently, planned different methods of disposal, was able to control his murderous urges for years between crimes, and was able to fool his probation officer and policemen on different occasions proved that the man knew exactly what he was doing" (quoted by Norris, 1992, p. 281). Dr. Dietz offered two diagnoses: alcohol dependence, of a mild to moderate nature, and paraphilia (sexual deviation). These two interacted; Dahmer would drink to overcome his inhibitions against killing and dismemberment. Thus, Dr. Dietz concluded that Dahmer did not meet the Wisconsin standard of insanity.

The two court-appointed expert witnesses were

1. Dr. George Palermo: A psychiatrist who read his report to the jury, Dr. Palermo, for several reasons, was not an effective witness. He concluded that Dahmer was not insane, that he had a serious personality disorder and was driven by obsessive fantasies, but that he knew what he was doing.

BOX 5-2
Park Dietz—Expert Witness for the Prosecution

Among forensic psychiatrists who testify in murder cases in which the defense is a claim of insanity, Park Dietz is clearly the most consistently effective. Always meticulously prepared, he is able to provide jurors with plausible explanations of defendants' behavior that do not involve insanity or psychosis. In both the Hinckley trial and the Dahmer trial, Dr. Dietz effectively related the specifics of the defendant's behavior to show qualities in conflict with the local definition of insanity.

In another highly publicized case, Dr. Dietz testified in the trial of Joel Rifkin, a New York landscape gardener who picked up 17 prostitutes whom he later strangled and dismembered. The psychiatrist interviewed Rifkin extensively prior to the trial, and Rifkin told him that at times he would speak to the corpses, "saying reassuring things as he drove with them" (McQuiston, 1994, p. B16); he said "whispers" had told him to strangle his victims. Are these whispers hallucinations? Do they indicate psychosis? Do they contribute to a judgment of insanity? On the stand, Dr. Dietz characterized these "whispers" as nothing more than an "internal dialogue," just as "everyone makes decisions" (p. B16). Under intense cross-examination, he remained unwilling to call them hallucinations or symptoms of paranoid schizophrenia.

Park Dietz characteristically testifies for the prosecution. He holds little sympathy for defense lawyers; he

has written: "Criminal defense lawyers routinely withheld evidence of their clients' guilt, at least until confident that the government has the evidence" (1996, p. 159). In contrast, "I have known the prosecution to withhold important evidence on only one occasion, and it was in the context of a court-ordered evaluation" (1996, p. 159).

To what extent is Dr. Dietz's interpretation of behavior related to his political ideology? While an undergraduate at Cornell University, he was president of the Conservative Club (Johnson, 1994). He has no clinical caseload. Defense attorneys, not surprisingly, believe that he sees things through the eyes of the prosecutor. Dr. Dietz, when he agrees to take a case, warns the prosecutor that he might well end up forming an opinion that would prevent him from testifying against the defendant. But in the cases of John W. Hinckley, Jr., Jeffrey Dahmer, Betty Broderick, Arthur Shawcross, Joel Rifkin, and others, he has concluded that the behavior did not meet the definition of insanity. In the opinion of one observer, "in his view, when criminal charges are heavy, truth is rarely to be found on the side of a defense attorney's client. Dietz's predilection for the prosecutor's side does not seem unconnected to his conservative politics or to his profound alienation from the physician's role in traditional psychiatry" (Johnson, 1994, p. 48).

---

2. Dr. Samuel Friedman: A psychologist in independent practice, Dr. Friedman, in response to a question, waxed philosophical about the nature of mental illness. He agreed with Dr. Dietz and Dr. Palermo that Dahmer had a personality disorder and that he was not psychotic; in that respect, Dr. Friedman's testimony aided the prosecution, but he probably was not very effective because of his self-deprecatory manner ("My understanding of the literature is not the most sophisticated").

In Wisconsin, a unique version of the ALI rule is used to define insanity; consequently, to have found Dahmer insane, the jury would have had to conclude first, that he had suffered from a mental disorder or defect that made him unable to know right from wrong, and second, that, as a consequence, he lacked substantial capacity to

control his conduct. In a split decision, acceptable by Wisconsin rules, the jury concluded that Dahmer did not suffer from mental disease, perhaps because of the evidence that Dahmer was careful to kill his victims in a manner that minimized his chances of getting caught; such a degree of cautiousness suggested that he appreciated the wrongfulness of his behavior *and* could control this behavior when it was to his advantage to do so. Thus, Dahmer was sentenced to over 900 years in prison, where he was bludgeoned to death by another inmate in 1994.

Ultimate-Issue Testimony

As noted earlier, one of the roles of the expert is "to explore carefully, and to explain to the court, how psychopathological processes at the time of the crime might have influenced the defendant's then-existing perceptions, motivations, cognitions, intentions, and behaviors" (Ogloff, Roberts, & Roesch, 1993, p. 172). This retrospective evaluation has to be expressed in terms of likelihood rather than finality, and it is subject to several sources of error, including examiner bias, possible malingering, and undetected defensive covering of genuine paranoid pathology, among other factors (Ogloff et al., 1993).

How far should a psychologist or psychiatrist be allowed to go, when testifying in a case involving an insanity defense? Is it proper for an expert to express an opinion about whether the defendant was sane or insane at the time of the offense? Psychologists are divided on this issue; some strenuously oppose the court's questioning of mental health experts about the status of the specific defendant, while others do not (Bonnie & Slobogin, 1980; Morse, 1978). Some of the concerns stem from a belief that it is the jury's role, not that of the psychiatric expert, to determine sanity or insanity of the defendant. In keeping with the issues that introduced this chapter, we need to remember that the judgment of insanity is a legal one, not a psychological one, and we, as experts, should stop at the limits of our expertise. But some psychologists have gone farther in their criticisms, questioning whether psychology and psychiatry have any valid viewpoints on such issues, and challenging their colleagues to provide supporting evidence for claims of their accuracy in forensic opinions (Dawes, Faust, & Meehl, 1989; Hagen, 1997; Ziskin, 1995; Ziskin & Faust, 1988).

One solution is to prevent the expert from expressing an opinion on the ultimate issue of legal insanity itself. This **ultimate-issue, or ultimate-opinion, testimony** was one of the targets of the Insanity Defense Reform Act of 1984, passed by Congress after John Hinckley's trial outcome. It modified federal law specifically to prohibit mental health experts from testifying about ultimate legal issues. As amended, Federal Rule of Evidence 704(b), which generally allows ultimate-issue testimony, now states:

No expert witness testifying with respect to the mental state or condition of the defendant in a criminal case may state an opinion or inference as to whether the defendant did or did not have the mental state or condition constituting an element of the crime charged or of the defense thereto. Such ultimate issues are matters for the trier of fact alone.

Note that this proscription applies to *federal* cases; Jeffrey Dahmer's trial, as are the vast majority of trials using the insanity plea, was a state matter. Some state courts have permitted experts to testify as to the ultimate issue of insanity, but have instructed jurors that they may give such testimony as much or as little weight as they wish. Some countries (Great Britain, South Africa) permit ultimate-opinion testimony, at least in some types of cases (Allan & Louw, 1997).

This ruling has led to consternation and confusion in the federal courts. Supposedly, the expert could describe a defendant's mental condition and the effects it could have had on his or her thinking and behavioral control, but the expert could not state conclusions about whether the defendant was sane or insane. Some commentators have speculated that this exclusion may lead to the omission from the trial of clinical information quite relevant to the case (Braswell, 1987; Goldstein, 1989; Rogers & Ewing, 1989, cited by Ogloff et al., 1993). For example, Ogloff et al. (1993) observed:

If the revised rule were applied strictly, an expert could not testify as to whether a given defendant was legally sane or insane and whether he or she had a "mental disease," "intended" to do great bodily harm, "knew" the probable consequences of his or her act, "knew" what he or she was doing, "appreciated" the criminality of his or her conduct, and so forth. Yet the same expert is literally being asked by the courts to give testimony that bears directly on such psychological constructs. (p. 172)

Furthermore, as forensic psychologists whose expertise is in evaluating policy changes, we need to ask if this prohibition solves any problems, or is it, in the words of Rogers and Ewing (1989), merely a "cosmetic fix" that has few effects?

(Similarly, Fulero, 1998, sees it as a "semantic" issue only; personal communication, May 14, 1998.) A study by Fulero and Finkel (1991) was designed to answer this question. Mock jurors read one of several versions of a murder trial, in which the defendant claimed that he was insane at the time of the offense. Some mock jurors were told that expert witnesses had testified but had only given diagnostic testimony, specifically, that the defendant suffered a mental disorder at the time of the offense; other jurors were told about the effects of this disorder on the degree to which the defendant understood the wrongfulness of his act; and a third group of jurors heard ultimate-opinion testimony about whether the defendant was sane or insane at the time of the act. In this study, the type of information the mock jurors heard from the expert witnesses did *not* significantly affect whether they found the defendant guilty or not guilty by reason of insanity. Does this mean the prohibition is unnecessary? Further research is needed. Let us say that a psychologist testifies that the defendant did not know the difference between right and wrong and was not able to appreciate the wrongfulness of his or her actions. If the expert is allowed to testify thus (and stops there), the jury probably has a good idea of the expert's opinion on the ultimate question.

ASSESSING COMPETENCY

After Russell E. Weston, Jr., was charged with killing two police officers inside the U.S. Capitol during the summer of 1998, he was evaluated to determine if he was competent to stand trial. Dr. Sally Johnson, a U.S. Bureau of Prisons psychiatrist who also had evaluated John Hinckley, Jr., and Theodore Kaczynski, examined and interviewed Weston, concluding that he "suffer[ed] from a mental disease or defect rendering him mentally incapable of assisting in his defense" (Associated Press, 1998, p. A7). She recommended that he be hospitalized indefinitely.

Forensic psychologists as well as psychiatrists assist in assessing the competency of de-

fendants who come before the court. In general, **competency,** or "competence," refers to the person's ability to understand the nature and purpose of court proceedings, and it is applicable at every stage of the criminal justice process, from interrogations and pretrial hearings to trials and sentencing hearings. Competency is especially an issue when a defendant goes to trial, when he or she plea bargains a guilty plea, and if the defendant is sentenced to death.

A fundamental principle of the criminal justice system in the United States is that criminal proceedings should not continue against any person who is not able to understand their nature or purpose. Thus, an evaluation is relevant at several points: the decision how to plead, the decision to stand trial, and the decision to testify in one's own behalf. Also, part of the preceding principle is that no defendant's life should be taken if he or she does not understand the implications of his or her acts.

For example, when Theodore Kaczynski was scheduled to be tried for the Unabomber killings, he first had to be evaluated to see if he was fit to stand trial. Thus, he was examined by Dr. Sally Johnson before his trial; her 47-page report concluded that Kaczynski was, indeed, competent to go on trial and competent to represent himself. In fact, Kaczynski was lucid and very involved in his defense. Yet his case is an excellent example of the point that competency does not necessarily mean an absence of insanity; one point of view, based on analyses of his extensive journals and his responses to a battery of neuropsychological tests, is that the diagnosis of paranoid schizophrenia is defensible (Finnegan, 1998). This latter issue was denied full examination in court, because in January 1998, Kaczynski suddenly pleaded guilty to all charges and disclaimed all appeals in exchange for a life sentence.

Competency to Plead Guilty

Defendants who, at their arraignment, decide to plead guilty have, in effect, waived several of their constitutional rights, including the right to a jury trial and the right to confront their accusers. In a 1938 decision, *Johnson v. Zerbst,* the Supreme Court declared that such a waiver must be "knowing, intelligent, and voluntary." How is this determined?

The judge questions the defendant on these issues, using as a template the test developed in *Dusky v. United States* in 1960, which determines that the defendant first, understands the criminal process, including the role of the participants in the process, and second, is able to function in that process, through consulting with his or her counsel in the preparation of a defense. The defendant's attorney may seek the assistance of a psychologist or psychiatrist to assess this state; in doing a **competency evaluation,** the mental health professional usually focuses on several issues; for example, why does the defendant want to plead guilty? Does the defendant understand the implications of this decision, including the relinquishing of certain rights? The psychologist or psychiatrist then prepares a report for the attorney, either stating reasons why the defendant is competent to plead, or, if the judgment is that the defendant is incompetent to plead, suggesting what possible treatments might render the defendant competent to plead.

Competency to Stand Trial

Each year in the United States, at least 25,000 criminal defendants are referred for evaluation of their competency to participate in legal proceedings (Steadman & Hartshorne, 1983). Theoretically, the evaluation for competency to stand trial is not as exacting as that for competency to plead guilty (Wrightsman, Greene, Nietzel, & Fortune, 2002), as defendants at trial need only to be aware of how the proceedings work and to be able to cooperate with their attorneys to prepare a defense. But in most jurisdictions, the same standard—the previously mentioned Dusky standard—is used in both evaluations, and in 1993, the U.S. Supreme Court reaffirmed the procedure in its *Godinez v. Moran* decision. The criterion in the determination of competency here is the *present* level of ability of the defendant, not his or her state at the time of the

offense; thus the focus differs from the evaluation of the defendant's sanity. As is typical with appellate court pronouncements, the *Dusky* decision did not operationalize how competency to stand trial was to be evaluated, so local jurisdictions have generated some specific factors; these include the defendant's ability to relate to his or her attorney, the defendant's understanding of the charges and the range of penalties, and his or her ability to manifest appropriate courtroom behavior and to testify in a relevant fashion.

Defense attorneys have concerns about their clients' competency to stand trial in about 10–15% of their cases (Hoge, Bonnie, Poythress, & Monahan, 1992; Poythress, Bonnie, Hoge, Monahan, & Oberlander, 1994). If, as in the case of competency to plead, a question is raised about the defendant's competency to stand trial, the judge will order an evaluation of the defendant. One review (Roesch & Golding, 1980) estimated that in 30% of these referrals, the defendant was actually found to be incompetent, though more recent estimates lower this to 10–15% (Melton, Petrila, Poythress, & Slobogin, 1997). Most evaluations are completed on an inpatient basis, although some psychologists have questioned the necessity of this costly procedure and have recommended that it be done on an outpatient basis (Melton, Weithorn, & Slobogin, 1985; Roesch & Golding, 1987).

The judge, of course, decides whether the defendant is competent to stand trial. But studies consistently find that judges often defer to the opinion of the examining psychologist or psychiatrist, with judge–examiner rates of agreement at 90% or higher (Hart & Hare, 1992; Reich & Tookey, 1986; Williams & Miller, 1981, reviewed by Skeem, Golding, Cohn, & Berge, 1998).

The basic question to be answered in such an evaluation is this: If the defendant has an impairment, does it affect his or her ability to participate knowingly and meaningfully in the trial and to cooperate with the defense attorney? The procedure in the competency evaluation is subject to the usual problems of subjectivity of clinical examinations; thus, psychiatrists and psychologists have designed competency assessment instruments that seek greater objectivity. Five of these are described here; although some are called "tests," they are semistructured interviews.

The Competency Screening Test (CST)

This is a 22-item sentence-completion task, developed by Lipsitt, Lelos, and McGarry (1971) as an initial screening test for incompetency. The scale is reproduced in Box 5-3.

Each answer by the defendant is scored 2 (*competent*), 1 (*marginally competent*), or 0 (*incompetent*); thus, the range is from 0 to 44. A score of 20 or below indicates that the respondent should be given a more comprehensive evaluation.

This procedure is an improvement over the traditional, rather unstructured interview that led to seat-of-the-pants conclusions and a global, un-

quantified indication of competency (Golding, 1990). But the CST still has some subjectivity, especially in the scoring of responses (Roesch & Golding, 1987). For example, for the statement "Jack felt that the judge_____," a response of "was unjust" receives 0 points. The CST had the lowest predictive validity index of the instruments reviewed by Melton et al. (1997). Even though the inter-rater reliability coefficients on the CST appear to be high—generally .85 or better—these are apparently derived from raters who have had extensive training and have used the instrument frequently (Melton, Petrila, Poythress, & Slobogin, 1987). Studies that seek to identify a factor structure have found inconsistent results (Ustad, Rogers, Sewell, & Guarnaccia, 1996). Of greater concern is the outcome of a study (Felchlia, 1992) that sought to determine

---

BOX 5-3
Competency Screening Test

1. The lawyer told Bill that_____
2. When I go to court, the lawyer will_____
3. Jack felt that the judge_____
4. When Phil was accused of the crime, he_____
5. When I prepare to go to court with my lawyer_____
6. If the jury finds me guilty, I_____
7. The way a court trial is decided_____
8. When the evidence in George's case was presented to the jury_____
9. When the lawyer questioned his client in court, the client said_____
10. If Jack had to try his own case, he_____
11. Each time the DA asked me a question, I_____

12. While listening to the witnesses testify against me, I_____
13. When the witness testifying against Harry gave incorrect evidence, he_____
14. When Bob disagreed with his lawyer on his defense, he_____
15. When I was formally accused of the crime, I thought to myself_____
16. If Ed's lawyer suggests that he plead guilty, he_____
17. What concerns Fred most about his lawyer is_____
18. When they say a man is innocent until proven guilty_____
19. When I think of being sent to prison, I_____
20. When Phil thinks of what he is accused of, he_____
21. When the jury hears my case, they will_____
22. If I had a chance to speak to the judge, I_____

Source: From Lipsitt, Lelos, and McGarry, 1971.

if a relationship existed between the constructs that the CST claimed to assess and measures of parallel psychological constructs. The results were disappointing; for example, assessments of the defendant's ability to cope with events in the trial, as indicated by CST responses, were not significantly related to psychological measures of adaptive and coping potential.

The Competency Assessment Instrument (CAI)

The Competency Assessment Instrument is a structured interview, lasting about one hour, that explores 13 aspects of competent functioning (Laboratory of Community Psychiatry, 1974). The defendant's response is rated with a score ranging from 1 (*total incapacity*) to 5 (*no incapacity*). The judgments ask the mental health worker to appraise where the defendant stands on a number of qualities, including how he or she relates to the attorney, the defendant's ability to testify relevantly, appreciation of the charges and the possible penalties, and the defendant's ability to realistically assess the outcome of the trial; many of these are, of course, similar to the goals of the earlier-described measure.

Little research exists on the reliability of this system; in a review of research done between 1991 and 1995, Cooper and Grisso (1997) reported no published articles on the CAI. The administration and scoring are not standardized. The CAI was revised by John A. Riley (1998), along with colleagues Craig Nelson and John Gannon, at Atascadero State Hospital in California; it takes about 30 to 45 minutes to administer and assesses 14 aspects of functioning. These aspects include understanding of the charges against the accused, appreciation of the penalties, ability to cooperate with counsel, and capacity to cope with incarceration while awaiting trial. The subject's responses are evaluated for their adequacy on a 1-to-4 scale.

Fitness Interview Test-Revised (FIT-R)

The Fitness Interview Test-Revised (originally named the Interdisciplinary Fitness Interview) was developed by Roesch and Golding (1980; Golding, Roesch, & Schreiber, 1984). The revised version includes questions on three main topics: understanding of the proceedings, understanding of the consequences of the proceedings, and the defendant's ability to communicate with counsel (Roesch, Webster, & Eaves, 1994; Roesch, Zapf, Eaves, & Webster, 1998; Zapf & Roesch, 1997). The revised version responded to criticisms of the earlier version and reflected changes made in the Canadian criminal code. It appears to work well as a screening device to assess fitness to stand trial in Canada (Nicholson, 1999).

Georgia Court Competency Test (GCCT)

The Georgia Court Competency Test, or GCCT (Wildman, Batchelor, Thompson, Nelson, Moore, Patterson, & DeLaosa, 1978), consists of 21 questions. Although it is limited in coverage, its reliability appears to be good (Bagby, Nicholson, Rogers, & Nussbaum, 1992). It has demonstrated the same factor structure in two samples (Nicholson, Briggs, & Robertson, 1988)—specifically, general legal knowledge, courtroom layout, and specific legal knowledge, although a more recent study suggests that the two legal knowledge factors can be combined into one (Ustad, Rogers, Sewell, & Guarnaccia, 1996).

The original form of the GCCT was modified by psychologists at Mississippi State Hospital by adding four questions, changing the weighting of some answers, and making scoring criteria more explicit (Johnson & Mullett, 1987). Studies using this revision, the GCCT-MSH, have found significant correlations with independent criteria of competency (Nicholson, 1999); one of these validity studies concluded that performance on the GCCT-MSH "made a significant, independent contribution to prediction of competence status beyond that based on diagnosis, intellectual functioning, offense type, and background characteristics" (Nicholson & Johnson, 1991, quoted in Nicholson, 1999, p. 139).

The MacArthur Competence Assessment Tool-Criminal Adjudication (MacCAT-CA)

The most recently developed competency-assessment device is the MacArthur Competence Assessment Tool-Criminal Adjudication, abbreviated MacCAT-CA (Poythress, Bonnie, Hoge, Monahan, & Oberlander, 1994; Hoge, Poythress, Bonnie, Monahan, Eisenberg, & Feucht-Haviar, 1997). Its purpose is to measure the person's competence to proceed to adjudication—that is, his or her ability to plead guilty as well as the ability to go to trial. It is a more structured measure than the CAI and uses an objective, theory-based scoring system. In keeping with four kinds of abilities seen as relevant to the competency evaluation, questions are grouped into four categories:

1. Understanding of charges and trials (including understanding of general trial issues, competence to assist to counsel, understanding whether to plead guilty, and understanding whether to waive a jury and request a bench trial).
2. Appreciation of the relevance of information for a defense.
3. Reasoning with information during decision making, or an assessment of logical problem-solving abilities.
4. Evidencing a choice.

Most of the MacCAT-CA contains hypothetical situations about which the defendant is questioned (see Box 5-4). Administration time is from 25 to 55 minutes. The instrument discriminates well between those adult defendants whom the court has judged to be incompetent and those defendants for whom competence was never an issue (Hoge et al., 1997), and possesses construct validity in that it shows the expected patterns of relationships with cognitive ability, psychopathology, and judgments by clinicians of the degree of impaired competency (Otto, Edens, Poythress, & Nicholson, 1998). Its results show strong agreement with those of the FIT-R (Zapf, 1998).

The MacCAT-CA clearly reflects a "new generation" of instruments; Melton et al. (1997) were quite positive about its promise:

> It taps legal domains related to both the general capacity to assist counsel and competence for discrete legal decisions, simultaneously examining multiple competence-related

abilities such as understanding, reasoning, and appreciation, both before and after competency instruction. It retains the relative efficiency of existing measures, yet it offers standardized administration and, for most of its submeasures, objective, criterion-based scoring that should minimize the subjectivity that plagues existing comprehensive measures. (1997, pp. 149–150)

Much work needs to be done by forensic psychologists to improve the process of judging competency to stand trial. Research indicates that many attorneys do not follow through when they have fears about their clients' passivity and failure to understand (Hoge, Bonnie, Poythress, & Monahan, 1992; Poythress, Bonnie, Hoge, Monahan, & Oberlander, 1994). We grant that attorneys often face a dilemma; if they raise the question of their client's competency, they may sacrifice their client's trust (Gould, 1995).

The Competency Assessment to Stand Trial for Defendants with Mental Retardation (CAST-MR)

Everington and Luckasson (1992) developed the CAST-MR for use with defendants who may be mentally retarded. The CAST-MR is a standardized instrument for forensic evaluators to assess the competence of persons with mental retardation to stand trial. Based on criteria in *Dusky v. United States,* the CAST-MR has separate sections called Basic Legal Concepts, Skills to Assist Defense, and Understanding of Case Events. The examiner reads each question aloud and records the client's response in a booklet. A reusable subject form allows the client to follow along as the examiner reads the question. The CAST-MR has quite good reliability and validity data (see Everington, 1990; Everington & Dunn, 1995), and was favorably reviewed by Cooper and Grisso (1997).

Competency of Juveniles

Children can be involved in the court system in some of the same roles as adults—as witnesses or as defendants. Special concern is devoted to the

BOX 5-4

The MacArthur Competence Assessment Tool-Criminal Adjudication

The MacArthur instrument uses hypothetical situations and asks the defendant questions about them. For example:

> Two men, Fred and Reggie, are playing pool at a bar and get into a fight. Fred hits Reggie with a pool stick. Reggie falls and hits his head on the floor so hard that he nearly dies. (quoted by Melton et al., 1997, p. 146)

Defendants are asked a number of specific questions; for example, to measure understanding, the subject is told:

> Fred may plead not guilty and go to trial, or Fred may plead guilty. Now, if Fred pleads guilty to

attempted murder, he would give up some legal rights and protections. What are they? (quoted by Melton et al., 1997, p. 146)

To measure the defendant's ability to identify relevant information, the defendant is asked to choose between the following:

A. At the bar, there was a country and western band playing in the room next to the pool room.

B. Fred himself called the ambulance because he could see that Reggie was hurt very badly.

Thus the MacArthur instrument strives to provide an objective assessment of competency.

---

question of their competency. The decision of the U.S. Supreme Court in the case of Gerald Gault (*In re Gault*, 1967) meant that juvenile courts had to provide the same due process rights to juveniles as were provided in criminal proceedings involving adults. Although this decision was not explicit about an evaluation of the child's competency to stand trial, the states gradually began to recognize the right (Grisso, Miller, & Sales, 1987). But should the Dusky standard be applied routinely to juveniles? Grisso (1997, 1998) proposed that research from developmental psychology is relevant:

> Competence to stand trial inquiries focus on *cognitive* abilities (a) to *understand* information that is provided to defendants regarding the trial process and (b) to *reason* with the information that they acquire or bring to the situation. Developmental theory and relevant research tell us these capacities are still developing in most youths prior to age 14. In general, however, "average" adolescents at around age 14 and above are no less capable than "average" adults in their ability to understand matters pertaining to trials or to perform the mental processes that are required when one engages in decision making about trial-related options. These results, however, are true only for "average" adolescents. Current

research suggests that the risk of difficulties in abilities related to trial competence is a good deal greater for youths 14 and above who have mental and emotional disorders or cognitive disabilities that produce delays in their development of capacities for comprehension and reasoning.

> In addition to cognitive functions, *psychosocial* factors related to development raise important hypotheses about youths' abilities in the trial process. Very young adolescents, or middle adolescents with developmental delays or mental disorders, will vary in the degree to which they have worked through relatively normal developmental issues concerning self-concept and self-control, relationships with adults in authority, and a capacity for an extended time perspective when making decisions (Cauffman, 1996; Scott, 1992; Scott et al., 1995; Steinberg & Cauffman, 1996). Such factors may influence their judgment about the meaning and relevance of the trial process so that their decisions as juvenile defendants might not be the decisions they would make if they had attained their eventual level of maturity. (Grisso, 1998, pp. 96–97, italics in original)

Grisso and his colleagues (Grisso et al., 1987) suggested that the question of a juvenile's competency to stand trial should be evaluated when any one of the following conditions is present:

1. Age 12 years or younger.
2. A prior diagnosis of or treatment for a mental illness or mental retardation.
3. A "borderline" or lower level of intellectual functioning, or a recorded "learning disability."
4. Observations by others that suggest deficits in memory, attention, or interpretation of reality.

Grisso (1998) concluded that some of the instruments just described for adults are appropriate for adolescents, but those that are oriented only to court situations and those that require defendants to respond to closed-end questions may lack validity. We reserve examination of the competency of children *as witnesses* for chapter 8, dealing with sexual abuse of children.

MALINGERING

A special problem in assessing the mental state of individuals is to determine whether their statements are truthful or are the result of **malingering.** In the *Diagnostic and Statistical Manual of Mental Disorders, 4th edition, Text Revision,* or DSM-IV-TR, (American Psychiatric Association, 2000), malingering is defined as "the conscious fabrication or gross exaggeration of physical and/or psychological symptoms, done in order to achieve external goals such as avoiding prison or receiving monetary compensation" (p. 683).

Richard Rogers and his colleagues (Rogers, 1990; Rogers, Sewell, & Goldstein, 1994) distinguished among three types of malingerers:

1. The pathogenic: People who are motivated by underlying pathology. These people are genuinely disturbed, and Rogers and his associates assume that "the voluntary production of bogus symptoms will eventually erode and be replaced by a genuine disorder" (Rogers, Sewell, & Goldstein, 1994, pp. 543–544).
2. The criminological: People with an antisocial or oppositional motivation; they may

feign mental disorders to obtain outcomes they do not deserve.
3. The adaptational: The person who makes "a constructive attempt, at least from the feigner's perspective, to succeed in highly adversarial circumstances" (Rogers et al., 1994, p. 544).

Individuals may be stimulated to fake mental illness at several points in the criminal justice process, including determining competency to stand trial, pleading not guilty by reason of insanity, and attempting to influence the sentence (Iverson, Franzen, & Hammond, 1993). But detection of malingering is also central to a variety of other forensic psychological tasks. Claims of injuries and disabilities, such as lower back pain, a head injury, or post-traumatic stress disorder, may require a check for malingering. Claims of amnesia or other kinds of memory impairment have increasingly involved neuropsychologists assessing malingering (Arnett, Hammeke, & Schwartz, 1993; Bernard & Fowler, 1990; Lee, Loring, & Martin, 1992; Wiggins & Brandt, 1988).

There are indications that psychologists are poor at detecting malingering during forensic evaluations; Silverton, Gruber, and Bindman (1993) cite the classic study by David Rosenhan (1973) as an example. Rosenhan and seven other normal people gained admission to various mental hospitals by complaining that they heard voices repeating the word "one." No other complaints were reported. Seven were diagnosed as schizophrenic, and the eighth as manic–depressive. Immediately after being admitted, the pseudo patients stopped saying they heard voices. None of the pseudo patients was detected as a malingerer by the hospital staff; in fact, the only people who sometimes recognized the pseudo patients as normal were the other patients.

Dissatisfied with traditional procedures, psychologists have begun to use scales and other assessment devices to effectively detect malingering. Two strategies have been used: applying existing measures and developing new ones.

As a traditional measure, the Minnesota Multiphasic Personality Inventory-2 (MMPI-2) has a Lie scale of 15 items measuring social desirability, but this is a rather unsophisticated measure of malingering. Furthermore, the person who "fakes" on these items is attempting to communicate an unduly *favorable* impression, while the malingering of concern to the courts is often the opposite type. The original MMPI also included an *F* scale, designed to assess inconsistent or deviant answering. On the newer MMPI-2, an *Fb* scale seeks to detect malingering or a "fake bad" response style; this procedure seems promising in differentiating between people instructed to malinger and actual psychiatric patients (Iverson, Franzen, & Hammond, 1993), but research needs to move beyond such analog designs.

A second approach is to construct new instruments; a number of these have been constructed in the last 20 years. Some, including the Malingering Probability Scale, by Silverton and Gruber (1998), are available only through commercial publishers. Frequently used is the Structured Interview of Reported Symptoms, or SIRS (Rogers, 1988), a 16-page structured interview covering signs of malingering. Although this procedure has produced some encouraging results (Rogers, Gillis, Bagby, & Monteiro, 1991), it requires an extended administration time and a trained examiner (Smith & Burger, 1993).

A self-report measure, the M test (Beaber, Marston, Michelli, & Mills, 1985) is a 33-item inventory composed of three separate scales: the Confusion scale, the Schizophrenia scale, and the Malingering scale; the latter scale is composed of 15 items tapping unusual or rare symptoms that would be expected to be endorsed only by malingerers (for example, atypical hallucinations and delusions, or extremely severe symptoms). Another assessment device is the Malingering Scale, or MS (Schretlen, 1986); it is lengthy (150 items) and requires judgment calls on the part of the test administrator (Smith & Burger, 1993). A replication is needed to confirm the high detection rates reported in the initial study. For people suspected of malingering memory impairments, the Test of Memory Malingering (TOMM) may be employed (see Rees, Boulay, & Tombaugh, 2001). For people suspected of malingering cognitive impairments, the Rey tests of memorization and dot-counting have been used (see Lee, Boone, Lesser, Wohl, Wilkins, & Parks, 2000).

SUMMARY

One of the most important tasks of the forensic psychologist is to aid the court in its determination of the mental state of individuals who come before the court; this chapter reviews three relevant concepts: the legal term *insanity,* competency, and malingering.

Although insanity is a legal concept and not a psychiatric one, forensic psychologists are often called on to make judgments related to the presence or absence of legal insanity at the time of the alleged offense. The problem is compounded by the use of different definitions of insanity in different jurisdictions, as well as different assignments of the burden of proof. The difficulty in achieving consistent diagnoses is illustrated by the trial of Jeffrey Dahmer, in which seven psychiatrists and psychologists gave conflicting judgments about whether Dahmer's state of mind met the definition of insanity.

A related activity of the forensic psychologist is assessing the competency of those who come before the court. In general, *competency* refers to the person's ability to understand the nature and purpose of court proceedings. Competency is relevant to the decision to stand trial and the decision whether to plead guilty, and is of special concern when juveniles appear before the court. Several devices are available for assessing competency, including the Competency Screening Test, the Competency Assessment Instrument, the Fitness Interview Test-Revised, the Georgia Court Competency Test, the MacArthur assessment procedure (MacCAT-CA), and the CAST-MR.

Finally, when assessing the mental state of people appearing before the court, the possibility of malingering is always a concern. Several instruments are currently available for the assessment of malingering.

KEY TERMS

affirmative defense
ALI standard
burden of proof
cognitive test of insanity
competency
competency evaluation
GBMI
guilt
harm
insanity
irresistible impulse exception
malingering
M'Naghten rule
mens rea
necrophilia
NGRI
paraphilia
ultimate-issue, *or* ultimate-opinion, testimony
volitional aspect of insanity

INFOTRAC®
COLLEGE EDITION

InfoTrac College Edition is a FREE, powerful, online learning resource, consisting of full-text articles from thousands of journals and periodicals. With each new copy of *Forensic Psychology*, Second Edition, you receive 4 months of free access to the InfoTrac College Edition database. By doing a simple keyword search (try using the Key Terms in the list above), you can quickly generate a list of relevant articles from thousands of possibilities and can select articles to read, explore, and print for reference or further study. InfoTrac College Edition's continuously updated collection of articles can be useful for doing reading and writing assignments that reach beyond the pages of this text!

SUGGESTED READINGS

Borum, R., & Fulero, S. M. (1999). Empirical research on the insanity defense and attempted reforms: Evi-

dence toward informed policy. *Law and Human Behavior, 23,* 117–135.

A very useful article that examines many of the myths and current misconceptions about the use of the insanity defense. Various "reforms," including the authors' proposal of carefully developed, intensively monitored release programs for defendants found NGRI, are described and evaluated.

Grisso, T. (1998). *Forensic evaluation of juveniles.* Sarasota, FL: Professional Resource Press.

Excellent, comprehensive, sensible coverage of mental health issues—competency to stand trial, risk of violence, and others—as applied to juvenile offenders.

Nicholson, R. (1999). Forensic assessment. In R. Roesch, S. D. Hart, & J. R. P. Ogloff (Eds.), *Psychology and law: The state of the discipline* (pp. 121–173). New York: Kluwer Academic/Plenum Publishers.

An up-to-date, detailed assessment of instruments for assessing competency, criminal responsibility, and child custody.

Rosenberg, C. E. (1968). *The trial of the assassin Guiteau: Psychiatry and the law in the Gilded Age.* Chicago: University of Chicago Press.

The trial of the assassin of President Garfield in 1881 included the use of 24 expert witnesses who debated the nature of insanity. It reminds us that concerns over a self-defeating "battle of the experts" are not just a modern phenomenon.

Sales, B. D., & Shuman, D. W. (Eds.). (1996). *Law, mental health, and mental disorder.* Pacific Grove, CA: Brooks/Cole.

A collection of contributed review chapters by legal scholars; of relevance to this chapter are those on the insanity defense by Michael L. Perlin, competency by Bruce J. Winick, and expert witnesses by Maureen O'Connor, Bruce D. Sales, and Daniel W. Shuman.

Swartz, M. (1997, November 17). Family secret. *New Yorker,* 90–107.

A readable description of the life of John Salvi, relevant to this question: What is the proper disposition of a lawbreaker who has the mental state that Salvi had?

Woychuk, D. (1996). *Attorney for the damned: A lawyer's life with the criminally insane.* New York: Free Press.

A first-person account by a lawyer who represented a variety of patients at a mental hospital for the dangerously mentally ill in New York City. Useful examples of competency evaluations, assessments of risk, and the temptation to form a false conclusion.

6

From Dangerousness to Risk Assessment: Violence, Sexual Offending, Domestic Violence, Child Abuse, and Suicide

RISK ASSESSMENT AND PREDICTIONS OF DANGEROUSNESS

The term *risk assessment* generally refers to the process of conceptualizing various hazards in order to make judgments about their likelihood and the need for various preventative measures (see McNiel, Borum, Douglas, Hart, Lyon, Sullivan, & Hemphill, 2002). This could, in its broadest sense, refer to such processes as weather forecasting (Fischhoff, 1994), the determination of insurance premiums (Hayakawa, Fischbeck, & Fischhoff, 2000a, 2000b, 2000c), and decision making in medical contexts about diagnosis and treatment (see Haynes, 1985). The concept of "risk" is quite complex and multifaceted (Bernstein, 1996). It has been suggested that the concept of risk includes judgments of the nature of the hazard, the likelihood of occurrence, the frequency of occurrence, the seriousness of the consequences, and the imminence of occurrence (Janus & Meehl, 1997).

In a sense, the primary goal of psychological assessment is to attempt to make predictions about future behavior based on some set of factors that are combined in some fashion into a predictive scheme. Morris and Miller (1985) have specified three sorts of predictive schemes: **clinical prediction,** in which the prediction is based on clinical experience and judgment; **actuarial prediction,** in which the prediction is based on a statistical scheme or formula; and **anamnestic prediction,** in which the prediction is based on a specific analysis of how a particular person has acted in the past in similar situations.

Surely, most of the sorts of behavioral predictions that are made in the legal context—predictions of future **dangerousness** for purposes of the imposition of the death penalty; predictions of the likelihood of reoffending for purposes of probation, parole, sex offender status, and so on—are made on the basis of clinical judgment. Yet, interestingly, such judgments are the most intuitive, anecdotal, and subjective of

all predictions, and they are subject to a variety of biases and heuristics (see Grove & Meehl, 1996). It is not surprising, then, that in the debate over the relative accuracy of "clinical" and "actuarial" predictions, actuarial predictions fare better virtually every time (see, e.g., Dawes, Faust, & Meehl, 1989; Garb, 1998; Grove & Meehl, 1996; Poythress, 1992; Quinsey, Harris, Rice, & Cormier, 1998). Ironically, however, the courts have been quite hospitable and even favorable toward clinical predictions, presumably because the courts have assumed that mental health professionals have expertise and accuracy rates that are higher than those of laypersons. And this is likely true, because people tend to assume that experience improves accuracy (Bartol & Bartol, 2004; Garb, 1998). Indeed, Dawes, Faust, and Meehl (1989) conclude that "in virtually every one of these studies, the actuarial method has equaled or surpassed the clinical method, sometimes slightly and sometimes substantially" (p. 1669).

Not all have agreed with this position, however, and some have seemed to call for either a more anamnestic approach, or what is sometimes called "structured clinical judgment" (Hart, 1998a; 1998b; Webster, Douglas, Eaves, & Hart, 1997). Litwack (2001) has argued that even actuarial methods require some form of clinical judgment in their application (for example, in scoring). Some researchers (Borum, 1996; Litwack & Schlesinger, 1999) have even proposed guidelines for decision making in predictive contexts. Indeed, the work of the Research Network on Mental Health and Law established by the John D. and Catherine T. MacArthur Foundation in 1988 (discussed later in this chapter) has set forth an approach to risk assessment that takes the form of a structured clinical judgment.

When looking at judgments of risk of recidivism, and when evaluating research on predictions of risk, it is important to note that there is a host of problems in drawing conclusions about such things. First, what *is* recidivism? It can, after all, be defined in several ways. Do technical parole violations, such as not reporting on time, count? What about rehospitalization but for nonviolent or noncriminal actions? What about minor criminal violations? Second, studies that examine the risk of reoffense by following those who are released cannot, by definition, include those who are never released (such as mass murderers or those who assassinate political leaders; see Quinsey et al., 1998). And if police records are used, there is surely an underestimate, because many crimes are not reported and many perpetrators are not caught.

THE "FIRST GENERATION" OF RESEARCH

Research on **predictions of dangerousness** throughout the first part of the 20th century was sparse at best, and follow-up studies were difficult. Most studies looked at the relationship between mental illness and violence, and the conclusions were generally that the mentally ill were less prone to violence and had lower arrest rates than the general population (see Quinsey et al., 1998). In 1974, a landmark book (Steadman & Cocozza, 1974) gave a great boost to the field. In 1966, the United States Supreme Court had decided the case of *Baxstrom v. Herold*. In that case, Baxstrom had been held in the Dannemora State Hospital, a New York maximum-security psychiatric correctional hospital, after his criminal sentence had expired. The Supreme Court ruled that this was a violation of equal protection, because though he was being held for mental illness, he had not been provided with any of the legal safeguards that existed for civil or noncriminal commitments to the institution. As a result of this decision, 967 offenders were released to other hospitals in New York, and many to the community quite soon after that. Surprisingly, they had very low rates of reoffending—within one year, of 176 patients discharged to the community, only 7 had returned to security hospitals. After nearly 5 years, more than half had been discharged to the community, but less than 3% had been returned to hospitals. Only two men were reconvicted for violent crimes. A later study of a similar situation in Pennsylvania (Thornberry & Jacoby, 1979) found essentially the same thing.

After these widely publicized studies, and particularly after the seminal publications of John Monahan (1981; Monahan & Steadman, 1983), it was generally assumed in the scientific community that mental health professionals could not predict dangerousness or violence with any satisfactory degree of accuracy. Indeed, Monahan himself concluded, based on his review of research findings from the 1960s and 1970s, that "psychiatrists and psychologists are accurate in no more than one out of three predictions of violent behavior over a several-year period among institutionalized populations that had both committed violence in the past (and thus had a high base rate for it) and who were diagnosed as mentally ill" (1981, p. 77).

Despite this, courts have actually invited such predictions, and indeed have at times ignored warnings from mental health professionals that such predictions were problematic. *Barefoot v. Estelle* (1983) was an important case in point. On November 14, 1978, Thomas Barefoot was convicted of the capital murder of a police officer in Bell County, Texas. A separate sentencing hearing before the same jury was then held to determine whether the death penalty should be imposed. Under Texas law, the jury was asked to determine whether "there [was] a probability that the defendant would commit criminal acts of violence that would constitute a continuing threat to society." The state introduced into evidence Barefoot's prior convictions and his reputation for lawlessness. The state also called two psychiatrists, John Holbrook and James Grigson, who, in response to hypothetical questions, testified that Barefoot would probably commit further acts of violence and represent a continuing threat to society. The jury answered the question put to them in the affirmative, a result that required the imposition of the death penalty. (It is worth noting that Dr. Grigson rendered his opinion without ever meeting or evaluating

Barefoot; this eventually led to his ouster from the American Psychiatric Association on ethical charges; see Wrightsman, Greene, Nietzel, & Fortune, 2002).

The United States Supreme Court eventually heard Barefoot's appeal. He argued that psychiatrists, individually and as a group, are incompetent to predict with an acceptable degree of reliability that a particular criminal will commit other crimes in the future and so represent a danger to the community. The American Psychiatric Association actually submitted an *amicus* brief in the case, supporting this argument. However, the Supreme Court upheld Barefoot's death sentence:

> The suggestion that no psychiatrist's testimony may be presented with respect to a defendant's future dangerousness is somewhat like asking us to disinvent the wheel. In the first place, it is contrary to our cases. If the likelihood of a defendant's committing further crimes is a constitutionally acceptable criterion for imposing the death penalty, which it is, *Jurek* v. *Texas*, 428 U.S. 262 (1976), and if it is not impossible for even a lay person sensibly to arrive at that conclusion, it makes little sense, if any, to submit that psychiatrists, out of the entire universe of persons who might have an opinion on the issue, would know so little about the subject that they should not be permitted to testify. In *Jurek*, seven Justices rejected the claim that it was impossible to predict future behavior and that dangerousness was therefore an invalid consideration in imposing the death penalty. Justices Stewart, Powell, and Stevens responded directly to the argument, *id.*, at 274–276:
>
> "It is, of course, not easy to predict future behavior. The fact that such a determination is difficult, however, does not mean that it cannot be made. Indeed, prediction of future criminal conduct is an essential element in many of the decisions rendered throughout our criminal justice system. The decision whether to admit a defendant to bail, for

instance, must often turn on a judge's prediction of the defendant's future conduct. Any sentencing authority must predict a convicted person's probable future conduct when it engages in the process of determining what punishment to impose. For those sentenced to prison, these same predictions must be made by parole authorities. The task that a Texas jury must perform in answering the statutory question in issue is thus basically no different from the task performed countless times each day throughout the American system of criminal justice. What is essential is that the jury have before it all possible relevant information about the individual defendant whose fate it must determine. Texas law clearly assures that all such evidence will be adduced." (at p. 887)

Clearly, the Supreme Court believed that whether or not mental health professionals felt that they could make such predictions accurately, such predictions would be made anyway. In addition, it appears that the Court also did not accept the argument that mental health professionals were no better than laypersons, and they reasoned that even if this were true, mental health professionals were no worse than laypersons (although if they are no better, then they are no help, and therefore their testimony would be irrelevant or not admissible under the rules governing expert testimony, since experts are to "help" the trier of fact).

MOVEMENT FROM PREDICTION OF DANGEROUSNESS TO RISK ASSESSMENT

As the concept of "dangerousness" began to fall into disfavor in the scientific community, a new "risk assessment" model began to emerge. This model was based not on the legal conceptions of violence and "dangerous" offenders, but rather on a model influenced by public health, such that violence was seen not just as a crime but as a health problem like cancer (McNiel et al., 2002). This change in focus was also spurred by a recognition that "dangerousness" had been conceptualized as a dichotomous variable (i.e., dangerous or not dangerous), whereas risk could be conceptualized on a continuum (i.e., from low to high).

At the same time, by the early 1990s, mental health professionals and scholars began to reassess the earlier conclusions drawn by Monahan (1981) and others that predictions and risk assessments could not be accurately made. Increasingly, a so-called second generation of studies (Otto, 1992) focused on the cues or factors that are predictively associated with risk, including demographic and personal factors, dispositional or personality factors, clinical factors, and contextual factors (McNiel et al., 2002). So, for example, it is clear that a history of previous violence is strongly predictive of future violence (see Klassen & O'Connor, 1989; McNiel, 1998). The dispositional factor of psychopathy (Hare, 1991; 1996) has been strongly linked to increased future risk of various types of problematic behavior, such as violence and sexual offending (see the following sections). Similarly, certain clinical symptoms, such as command hallucinations (Link & Steuve, 1994), and contextual factors, such as neighborhood, have also been found to be predictive of violence (see Silver, Mulvey, & Monahan, 1999). Eventually, the consensus shifted to the opinion that risk assessments can be made with "moderate to good" levels of accuracy under certain conditions (Otto, 1992; Borum, 1996).

As part of this movement away from prediction of dangerousness and toward the concept of risk assessment, a number of new instruments have been developed that are specific for certain types of behaviors, such as interpersonal violence, child abuse, domestic violence, and sexual offending. We turn to each of those behaviors, and the instruments designed to measure the risk of each, in the next two sections.

PREDICTION OF VIOLENCE

Is there a relationship between mental disorder and a tendency to be violent toward others? Certainly the public believes there is; psychologists have been more skeptical, although prominent psychologists (see, for example, Monahan, 1992) now believe that a consistent but small relationship may be present (see Monahan, Steadman, Silver, Appelbaum, Robbins, Mulvey, Roth, Grisso, & Banks, 2001, for a comprehensive look at this question by the MacArthur group).

If such a relationship exists, can forensic psychologists specify which people are at risk of harming others? Monahan (1992) has concluded that only those who are experiencing psychotic symptoms are at an increased risk of violence; he wrote: "Being a former patient in a mental hospital—that is, having experienced psychotic symptoms *in the past*—bears no direct relationship to violence" (1992, p. 519, italics in original). The vast majority of people who have mental disorders to a significant degree are not violent. With a low probability that any one individual in a population will commit a violent act against another, it becomes very difficult to assess risk, because of the base rate problem described in the section Prediction of Suicide (later in this chapter).

In fact, the validity of predictions of violence made by mental health professionals generally—over and above the issue of mental illness and its relation to violence—has been described by reviewers as "modest." One recent review concluded that the rate of accuracy of such predictions was only slightly above chance (Steadman, Robbins, Monahan, Appelbaum, Grisso, Mulvey, & Roth, 1996). Another (Garb, 1998) concluded that clinical psychologists make "moderately valid" short-term and long-term predictions of violence, although their accuracy rates remain below those using statistical prediction (Mossman, 1994).

Rejuvenated interest in risk assessment with regard to violence, spurred by the MacArthur Foundation's financing of a massive study by the Research Network on Mental Health and Law (see Monahan et al., 2001), has spurred the use of better methodology in more recent studies, which has increased the rate of accuracy. For example, older research studies often used only limited ways for assessing violence (i.e., only arrest records), while more recent research relies also on self-reports and other outcome variables. The increased use of actuarial methods has also improved the accuracy of predictions (Monahan & Steadman, 1994). An example of contemporary risk assessment reflecting this approach is the work by Vernon L. Quinsey, Grant T. Harris, Marnie E. Rice, and their colleagues (Quinsey et al., 1998; Rice & Harris, 1995). For example, Harris, Rice, and Quinsey (1993) used 12 variables coded from institutional files of 618 men at a maximum-security forensic hospital in Canada. These variables included scores on the Hare Psychopathy Checklist (Hare, 1991), separation from parents before the age of 16, never married, early reports of maladjustment, presence of alcohol abuse, injuries to victims, and DSM (Diagnostic and Statistical Manual) classifications. The criterion for subsequent violence was any new criminal charge for a violent offense or return to the institution for such acts, with the typical follow-up period being 7 years. The actuarial combination of predictor variables led to a multiple regression coefficient of .46 with violent recidivism. The use of actuarial procedures is improving prediction, but current estimates are that predictions may still be inaccurate as much as 40% to 50% of the time (Slobogin, 1996).

A recent review of risk assessment research by Douglas and Webster (1999) has identified 20 variables that seem to be related to the risk of violence. These predictor variables are classified as static predictors, dynamic predictors, and risk management predictors. **Static predictors** are features of an individual, or historical events that are not changeable. **Dynamic predictors** are things that do change over time and situation (Andrews & Bonta, 1998; Andrews, Bonta, & Hoge, 1990). **Risk management predictors** focus on the nature of the situation or environment in which the person lives or will live in the future. Ten of the 20 predictor variables are static: a history of prior violence, young age, a history of relationship instability or hostility, a history of employment instability, a drug or alcohol abuse history, a major mental disorder, a diagnosis of antisocial personality disorder or psychopathy, early maladjustment in home or school settings, a history of attempted or actual escapes, and a diagnosis of any personality disorder. Another five of the 20 predictors are dynamic factors: a lack of insight into one's capacity for violent behavior; a tendency to be angry and hostile in interpersonal situations; psychotic symptoms, such as delusions or hallucinations; impulsivity and unstable negative emotions; and resistance or lack of response to treatment. The last five of the 20 predictors are risk management variables: a lack of supervision and monitoring after release; easy access to victims, drugs and alcohol, and weapons; a lack of social support or resources; noncompliance with medication or treatment; and a great deal of stress in family, employment, and peer relations.

Several risk assessment instruments have been based on these variables. For example, in 1997, Webster, Douglas, Eaves, & Hart (1997) developed the **HCR-20** (i.e., the 20 historical, clinical, and risk management variables) as a means of predicting violent behavior in released psychiatric patients. The **Violence Risk Appraisal Guide (VRAG)** was developed by Harris et al. (1993) to predict violent recidivism (see Quinsey et al., 1998). The VRAG was based on data from 618 male patients at the Oak Ridge Building of the Mental Health Centre Penetanguishene in Canada. This is a maximum-security facility that assesses and treats people sent from Canadian courts, prisons, and other hospitals (see Quinsey et al., 1998). The VRAG consists of 12 variables: separation from parents before the age of 16, elementary school maladjustment, a history of alcohol abuse, marital status, criminal history for nonviolent offenses, failure on prior conditional release, age at current offense, seriousness of victim injury, female victim, meeting the DSM criteria for personality disorder or schizophrenia, and psychopathy.

In fact, the best predictor of violence recidivism was psychopathy, as defined by the score on the **Psychopathy Checklist Revised (PCL-R;** Hare, 1991). The concept of **psychopathy** is an interesting one, because it has repeatedly demonstrated a robust relationship to risk of repeat criminality and violence in offender and patient populations (see Hart & Hare, 1997; Walters, 2003), as well as general criminality, nonsexual violence, and sexual violence and offenses (see Hanson & Bussiere, 1998; Rice & Harris, 1997; Hart & Dempster, 1997; Hart, 1998a, 1998b; Webster et al., 1997). Generally, *psychopathy* refers to people who repeatedly commit criminal acts for which they feel little or no remorse. Psychopaths are characteristically superficial in their interpersonal rela-

tionships. They seem to lack empathy and are selfish and irresponsible. They blame others for their misfortunes and offer excuses for their behavior. They are deceitful and manipulative, yet appear charming and glib at the same time. Serial killer Theodore Bundy has often been cited as an example of the psychopath (see Rule, 1989; Michaud & Aynesworth, 1991; see also Box 6-1).

Hare (1991) developed the Psychopathy Checklist Revised (PCL-R) to measure psychopathy. The research base on the PCL-R is massive and impressive, and the reliability and validity of the test are quite good (see Fulero, 1995). On the PCL-R, subjects are rated and scored on 20 variables. Scores on the PCL-R range from 0 to 40, with each item being scored either 0, 1, or 2. Scores of 30 and higher indicate the presence of psychopathy; scores of

BOX 6-1
The Strange Case of Theodore Bundy

As an illegitimate child born in 1946 to a young girl from a rigidly puritanical family, Theodore Bundy spent the first 4 years of his life posing as his mother's brother to hide the family's shame. After his mother married, Bundy discovered his parentage, a fact that would haunt him for the rest of his life. Allegedly molested as a small child by a male relative, and shown no affection by his mother, he began to mutilate animals and spy on local girls. Still, the future looked good for the exceptionally bright, handsome young man. He graduated from high school and entered college. He was a volunteer worker at a suicide hotline and dated a society girl. When she called off their engagement, Bundy was crushed. In 1972, he began to stalk women on the street. In 1974, he inflicted serious injuries on a sleeping woman in her apartment. A few weeks later, he attacked another sleeping woman and took her to a remote spot, where he raped, battered, and killed her. Posing as a student or security guard, sometimes asking for help with his arm in a sling, he killed 14 women, mostly college students who resembled his ex-fiance, in Washington, Oregon, Utah, and Colorado. Witness reports coupled with Bundy's reckless driving led to his arrest in 1975. Extradited to Colorado, he escaped in 1977 and fled to Florida where, in 1978, he raped and

killed two coeds and wounded three others. With the law on his trail, he abducted, raped, and killed his final victim, an 11-year-old girl, and was captured a week later. In 1979, Bundy was convicted of the Florida murders, in a trial in which he defended himself. Claiming complete innocence, he was married on death row, and executed in the electric chair in 1989 after several failed appeals. Before his death, he spoke at length to Dr. James Dobson (Dobson, 1995; see also Rule, 2001, for more information).

Interestingly, following Bundy's arrest, authorities in Seattle were convinced that Bundy's first victim was 15-year-old Kathy Devine, who had disappeared on November 25, 1973, and whose mutilated corpse was found less than a month later. Although Bundy freely confessed to every one of his murders prior to his death, he always maintained his innocence in that particular case. Regardless, authorities labeled the girl a "Bundy victim" and gave the case little more thought. However, on March 8, 2002, a man named William E. Cosden, Jr., 55, was arrested after DNA evidence, which had been preserved from Devine's body, linked him to her murder. Cosden has subsequently been tried and found guilty of the crime.

21–29 indicate possible or partial psychopathy, and scores of 20 or lower indicate no psychopathy. More recently, a "screening version" of the test, the **Psychopathy Checklist: Screening Version (PCL:SV),** has been developed (Hart, Cox, and Hare, 1995), with cutoff scores of 18 and higher, 13–17, and 12 and lower, respectively.

PREDICTION OF SEXUAL OFFENDING

Another common task for forensic psychologists is to assess a sex offender's degree of risk to the community. How likely is this person to commit another sex offense? Such decisions have tremendous implications both for public safety and for the liberty of the person in question. Virtually all jurisdictions in the United States and Canada now have laws governing the disposition of sex offenders. Generally, if a sex offender meets a certain criterion, such as "likely to commit a similar offense in the future" (see, for example, Ohio Revised Code Section 2945.50), then certain procedures, such as registration with the local police or community notification of a person's sex offender status, will take place.

These laws, by necessity, set forth certain criteria for how these judgments are to be made, such as "likely to commit" (see the preceding paragraph). Therefore, these laws must be related in some way to the empirical literature on the prediction of recidivism (see Quinsey, Lalumiere, Rice, & Harris, 1995). This literature, with regard to sex offenders, has been growing over the last decade. One way to establish a relationship is to perform follow-up studies of convicted sex offenders in order to estimate the proportion who are likely to relapse, or the *base rate*. Convicted rapists and convicted child molesters both have been studied this way (see Quinsey et al., 1995, for an excellent summary of this work). For convicted rapists, the weighted average sexual reconviction rate was 22.8%, with a range of 10% to 36%. Generally, sexual recidivists had more serious sexual offense histories, higher scores on measures of psychopathy, and more phallometrically measured sexual interest in violence against women (phallometers measure penile erection). For child molesters, the weighted average sexual reconviction rate was 20.4%, with a range of 4% to 38%. The sexual reconviction rate for homosexual child molesters was nearly double that of heterosexual child molesters (35.2% to 18.3%), while the reconviction rate for incest offenders was 8.5%.

Overall, as Quinsey et al. (1995) noted, although these numbers have their problems (for example, they refer to reconviction rates and so measure only offenses that are discovered), they do show a rate of recidivism high enough to make individual assessments of relative risk potentially fruitful. By careful analysis of various risk prediction factors, measured and then validated across samples of offenders, it might be possible to construct risk prediction instruments. Several attempts have been made to do just that, and these instruments have become commonplace in forensic work in which the question is the risk of reoffense by a sexual offender.

The first of these risk prediction instruments is the **Rapid Risk Assessment of Sexual Recidivism (RRASOR;** Hanson, 1997). The RRASOR is a four-item actuarial instrument rated from official records. It was intended to be a relatively brief screening instrument for predicting sexual offense recidivism (Hanson, 1997) and is based on meta-analytic research and reanalysis of existing data sets from Canada. Items were weighted according to their ability to predict likelihood of recidivism over periods of 5–10 years. Total scores range from 0–6, with most offenders receiving scores that range between 1 and 4. The items are prior sex offenses (not including the current offense), age at release (current age), victim gender, and relationship to victim. In the reported development and validation samples (see Hanson & Thornton, 2000), the RRASOR achieved some predictive accuracy (see Sjostedt & Langstrom, 2001). Unfortunately, the RRASOR has its problems. First, there is no manual, and few peer-reviewed published studies have examined its reliability and validity. Also, the RRASOR focuses on static variables and does not consider personality, treatment compliance, or other dynamic variables.

The second instrument is the **Sex Offender Risk Appraisal Guide (SORAG;** Quinsey et al., 1998). This instrument is discussed in detail in Quinsey et al. (1998). The instrument is a modification of the Violence Risk Appraisal Guide (VRAG; Quinsey et al., 1998). The SORAG is a 14-item actuarial instrument, with a range of scores from 1 to 9. Unlike the RRASOR, it includes both static and dynamic factors. The SORAG items are: living with biological parents until age 16, elementary school maladjustment, history of alcohol problems, marital status, nonviolent offense history, violent offense history, sexual offense history, sex and age of the victim, failure on prior conditional release, age at the time of the current offense, DSM-III criteria for any personality disorder, DSM-III criteria for schizophrenia, phallometrically measured deviant sexual interests, and PCL-R score for psychopathy.

Again, the SORAG has its critics. For example, at least four of the included factors have received little empirical support (history of alcohol abuse; history of nonviolent offenses; marital status; diagnosis of schizophrenia). Also, the sample used contained Canadian subjects only, and the applicability of the results has been questioned. Finally, later research (Rice & Harris, 1997) indicated that when the SORAG was cross-validated, it performed relatively poorly, and the instrument was subsequently revised (see Quinsey et al., 1998). As Boer, Hart, Kropp, and Webster (1997) noted, "although they are promising, there is no evidence at this time that the SORAG and RRASOR have predictive validity with respect to sexual violence. No published research has administered these tests to sex offenders at release from an institution and then determined the accuracy of violence predictions based on the test" (p. 4). It is likely that the research design of the validation studies along with the statistical methods used for developing the scoring algorithms resulted in an overestimation of these instruments' predictive accuracy (see Janus & Meehl, 1997).

A third sex offender classification tool is the **Minnesota Sex Offender Screening Tool Revised (MnSOST-R;** Epperson, Kaul, & Hesselton, 1998). This is a 16-item actuarial instrument that incorporates both historical and institutional information, such as treatment participation. Scores are divided into four categories, with estimated recidivism rates from 16% to 88% over 6 years. A fourth tool is the **Sexual Violence Risk-20 (SVR-20;** Boer et al., 1997), developed in a fashion similar to that of the HCR-20 for risk of violence (see earlier in this section).

The last of the sex offender classification tools is the **Static-99** (Hanson & Thornton, 1999). This is another actuarial instrument consisting of 10 items: prior sexual offenses, prior sentencing dates (i.e., the number of distinct occasions on which the offender has been sentenced for criminal offenses of any kind), any conviction for noncontact offenses, the presence of nonsexual violence in the current case, prior nonsexual violence, any unrelated victims, any stranger victims, any male victims, young age (18 to 25), and single marital status. The Static-99 shows moderate predictive accuracy for sexual recidivism and violent (including sexual) recidivism, but shows only small improvements over the original two scales from which it was adapted (i.e., the RRASOR [see above] and the Structured Anchored Clinical Judgment scale; Grubin, 1998).

PREDICTION OF DOMESTIC VIOLENCE AND CHILD ABUSE

Domestic Violence

Courts are often faced with decisions about the risk of battering in a domestic situation, whether the decision comes in the context of a restraining order, or a sentencing context, a treatment context, or even a custody context. Although the science of predicting spousal assault (it is worth noting that generally, the research has been focused on the battering of wives by husbands rather than the reverse) has been called "quite inexact" (Saunders, 1995), it is nonetheless true that assessments of risk must still be made. At this point, there is a still-growing literature on the so-called risk markers for domestic violence. Two excellent reviews of this literature are those of Hotaling and Sugarman (1986) and Tolman and Bennett (1990).

First, men who batter their spouses have often experienced family violence in their childhoods. Indeed, it seems that the effect of witnessing violence is even stronger than the effect of being the target of the violence, though those who suffer both are even more likely to batter a spouse (Hotaling & Sugarman, 1986). Second, though spousal assault occurs in all socioeconomic strata, it appears that men with less education and lower income are more prone (Hotaling & Sugarman, 1986). Demographic differences between partners also increase the risk (for example, differing religious backgrounds or the woman's having higher occupational status or more education). Third, high rates of alcohol use or abuse are also markers of domestic violence (Tolman & Bennett, 1990). Fourth, about half the men who batter their wives also batter their children (Saunders, 1994, 1995). Batterers report lower self-esteem (Hotaling & Sugarman, 1986). Studies that have looked at such factors as anger, stress, and depression have yielded surprisingly mixed results. Anger as measured on such instruments as the **Novaco Anger Scale** does not appear to be related to wife assault; stress (with the exception of work stress) also does not appear to be directly related as a risk factor. Batterers often test higher on depression, but it is not clear that the depression is a cause of the battering; rather, it appears to be an effect of the arrest and separation that often follow (Saunders, 1995). Traditional sex-role attitudes are also surprisingly unrelated to battering (Saunders, 1995).

Of course, predictions of wife assault would be better if there were test instruments that could be used. There are several reviews of the literature on spousal abuse instruments (Roehl &

Guertin, 1998, 2000; Trone, 1999; Dutton & Kropp, 2000).

One of the most commonly used instruments is the **Conflict Tactics Scale** (**CTS;** Straus, 1979). This instrument is essentially a checklist of behaviors that can be completed by either the batterer or the victim regarding actions that amount to psychological abuse, physical abuse, or life-threatening violence. The instrument is usually used in an assessment along with a comprehensive clinical interview focusing on the demographic and other variables discussed earlier (Saunders, 1995). Alcohol abuse can be tested with such instruments as the **Michigan Alcohol Screening Test** (**MAST;** Selzer, 1971).

Other commonly used instruments include the **Danger Assessment** (**DA;** Campbell, 1995); the **Domestic Violence Screening Inventory** (**DVSI;** Williams & Houghton, in press); and the **Kingston Screening Instrument for Domestic Violence** (**K-SID;** Gelles & Tolman, 1998). The DA consists of structured guidelines for assessing the risk of lethal domestic violence. It identifies 15 risk factors coded on the basis of interviews with survivors. The items are coded 0 or 1 and then summed to yield total scores ranging from 0 to 15. No cutoff scores have been identified. The DVSI is a more actuarially based instrument for assessing risk for repeated violence; it identifies 12 risk factors, which are coded 0–2 or 0–3 from case history information. Items are then summed to yield total scores, ranging from 0 to 30. The K-SID is another actuarial instrument for assessing the risk of repeated domestic violence. It was based on interviews with offenders and survivors and on police reports. It has three parts: a "poverty chart," a severity and injury index, and 10 risk markers. The parts and items are coded and combined to yield a risk rating (low, moderate, high, or very high).

Each of these instruments has its difficulties and problems, ranging from a lack of a scoring manual to weaknesses in reliability and validity data. More recently, Kropp, Hart, and their colleagues (see Kropp, Hart, Webster, & Eaves, 1998; Kropp & Hart, 1997, 2000) have developed the **Spousal Assault Risk Assessment (SARA) Guide.** This instrument is a set of structured guidelines for assessing the risk of repeated violence, which is coded from interviews and case history data. It identifies 20 risk factors, each coded 0–2. There are also critical items, coded as present or not, and a summary risk rating (low, moderate, or high). The factors include assault of family members or of strangers or acquaintances; violation of conditional release; relationship problems; employment problems; being the victim of or witness to family violence; substance abuse; suicidal or homicidal ideation/intent; psychotic or manic symptoms; diagnosed personality disorder; physical or sexual assault; the use of weapons or threats of death; an escalation in the severity or frequency of spousal abuse; any violations of no-contact orders; minimization or denial; and attitudes that support or condone spousal assault.

To validate the SARA, researchers collected ratings from adult male offenders in Canada. Ratings were available for 2,681 offenders: 1,671 provincial probationers (1,424 consecutive admissions with a history of spousal abuse, and 247 who were court-ordered to attend treatment). There were also ratings for 1,010 federal Canadian prisoners (638 consecutive admissions with a history of spousal abuse, and 372 consecutive admissions with a suspected history of spousal abuse that subsequently was determined to be absent).

In summary, the SARA is the only risk assessment guide available that has been validated empirically, and the findings thus far support the reliability, validity, and utility of the instrument (see Kropp & Hart, 2000). The SARA shows promise for use in forensic, clinical, treatment, and court settings.

Child Abuse

In the United States, almost 3 million reports of child maltreatment were filed in 1992 (McCurdy & Daro, 1993). If physical child abuse is confirmed, caseworkers must at some point estimate the likelihood of future abuse, when decisions must be made about leaving the child in the home, returning the child to the home, or removing the child. Milner (1995) notes that assessment of risk for child abuse has been traditionally important in the context of prevention programs that either attempt to prevent child abuse before it occurs (so-called secondary prevention) or attempt to reduce the risk of recurrence of child abuse after it has already taken place (so-called tertiary prevention). Belsky (1980, 1993) has described four ecological levels of risk factors for child abuse: (a) the *ontogenic level,* which refers to individual factors and parent characteristics, such as being a young single parent of lower socioeconomic status; (b) the *microsystem level,* which refers to family factors, such as marital discord; (c) the *ecosystem or community level,* which includes such factors as social support and employment stress; and (d) the *macrosystem or cultural level,* which includes such factors as cultural values (see Milner, 1995). Belsky attempted to articulate how these factors form "contexts of maltreatment" that can influence the likelihood of child maltreatment, and Milner (1995) described some of these factors in more detail.

Although attempts have been made to predict child abuse with traditional clinical instruments, such as the MMPI and the Rorschach, these attempts have been largely unsuccessful (see Milner, 1995). Only one measure specific to child abuse, the **Child Abuse Potential Inventory (CAPI)** has been found to have acceptable reliability and validity data (though there are several others, including the Michigan Screening Profile of Parenting, the Conflict Tactics Scale, and the Parenting Stress Index). The original CAPI was a 160-item, self-report questionnaire answered in a forced-choice, agree-disagree format. It has now been reduced to a 77-item physical child abuse scale (Form VI; see Milner, 1995, and the references therein for more detail).

While no one measure will predict or assess risk for child abuse by itself, the CAPI offers a means to include an actuarial measure in an overall or comprehensive risk assessment protocol that could include parent interviews and direct observations. Currently, the National Center on Child Abuse and Neglect (NCCAN) is supporting the development and testing of risk assessment protocols. Future work in this area should be important and interesting.

PREDICTION OF SUICIDE

Kurt Cobain of the band Nirvana was an immensely talented but troubled musician who took his life in April 1994. Can forensic psychologists predict which people will attempt suicide? As you might expect, the accuracy rate of suicide prediction is not high. If it were, we would be more successful at preventing it, and indeed lawsuits against mental health professionals for failing to predict it would be more successful (see Bongar, Berman, Maris, Silverman, Harris, & Packman, 1998). The most important reason for the low rate of accuracy in suicide prediction is that clinicians often fail to consider fully the effect of base rates. The **base rate** is the rate with which a specified event occurs within the population at large. If the base rate is not taken into account, clinicians are likely to predict that a higher percentage of patients will commit suicide than the actual rate in the population, which is very low. Indeed, because the rate is so low, one would actually make more correct predictions by predicting zero suicides, unless an instrument could be sensitive both to false negatives (predictions of no suicide that are wrong) *and* to false positives (predictions of suicide that are wrong).

For example, Pokorny (1983) studied the progress of 4,800 people who were psychiatric inpatients in Veterans Administration hospitals. During a 5-year period, only 67 of the 4,800 people committed suicide, a base rate of 1.4%. Given this base rate, the predictive task for the clinician would be a nearly impossible one: Which one out of every 100 patients is most likely to commit suicide? And, if a predictive

factor (say, depression) increased the risk tenfold, the risk in Pokorny's sample would increase to 14%, meaning that predictions of suicide in a sample of depressed patients would still overestimate the risk of suicide. A more recent review of the literature (Garb, 1998) has concluded that predictions of suicide generally have not been valid. Even predictions of suicide risk (as opposed to the actual behavior) seem to have little or no validity (Janofsky, Spears, & Neubauer, 1988).

Recently, attempts have been made to develop scales for prediction of suicide. There are nearly 20 such scales. One is the **Suicide Probability Scale** (**SPS;** Cull & Gill, 1982; 1999). This scale was developed based on a sample of 1,158 people and focuses on a history of suicide attempts, current depression and stress, and cognitive variables. The scale is composed of 36 items, and the respondent indicates how often each statement applies to him or her on a 4-point scale (the test form does not mention suicide in the title). The scale yields a probability score that ranges from subclinical to severe risk of suicide behavior, and links to risk management strategies. There are also four subscales, for hopelessness, suicide ideation, negative self-evaluation, and hostility.

One of the most impressive scales is the **Suicidal Intent Scale** (**SIS;** Beck, Schuyler, & Herman, 1974; Dear, 2003; Eyman & Eyman, 1992; Rothberg & Geer-Williams, 1992). This scale is designed as a semistructured interview, to be used with patients who have attempted suicide in the past. There are 15 items, each coded 0–2, presented in two sections. The first nine items examine circumstances related to the suicide attempt (such as whether the person was alone). The second section, containing the last six items, consists of self-reports about such issues as whether or not the person thought that death would actually occur. SIS scores have been shown to have significant correlations with the medical seriousness of suicide attempts (Hamdi, Amin, & Mattar, 1991) and even with subsequent suicide (Pierce, 1981; 1984). Scores on the scale were more strongly associated with feelings of hopelessness than with depression (Beck et al., 1974). This is consistent with other research showing that hopelessness as measured on the Beck Hopelessness Scale is a more robust predictor of suicidal behavior than is depression (Beck et al., 1974).

SUMMARY

The primary goal of psychological assessment is to attempt to make predictions about future behavior based on some set of factors that are combined in some fashion into a predictive scheme. In the area of prediction of problematic behaviors, such as violence, sexual offending, domestic violence, child abuse, and suicide, there has been an evolution of theory and an explosion of research over the past half-century. From models of "predictions of dangerousness" to models of "risk assessment," psychologists have focused on studies of outcome and on risk factors, and have attempted to guide predictions and assessments by the development of assessment tools.

KEY TERMS

actuarial prediction
anamnestic prediction
base rate
Child Abuse Potential Inventory (CAPI)
clinical prediction
Conflict Tactics Scale (CTS)
Danger Assessment (DA)
dangerousness
Domestic Violence Screening Inventory (DVSI)
dynamic predictors
HCR-20
Kingston Screening Instrument for Domestic Violence (K-SID)

Michigan Alcohol Screening Test (MAST)
Minnesota Sex Offender Screening Tool Revised (MnSOST-R)
Novaco Anger Scale
predictions of dangerousness
psychopathy
Psychopathy Checklist Revised (PCL-R)
Psychopathy Checklist: Screening Version (PCL:SV)
Rapid Risk Assessment of Sexual Recidivism (RRASOR)
risk assessment
risk management predictors
Sex Offender Risk Appraisal Guide (SORAG)
Sexual Violence Risk-20 (SVR-20)
static predictors
Spousal Assault Risk Assessment (SARA) Guide
Static-99
Suicidal Intent Scale (SIS)
Suicide Probability Scale (SPS)
Violence Risk Appraisal Guide (VRAG)

INFOTRAC® COLLEGE EDITION

InfoTrac College Edition is a FREE, powerful, online learning resource, consisting of full-text articles from thousands of journals and periodicals. With each new copy of *Forensic Psychology,* Second Edition, you receive 4 months of free access to the InfoTrac College Edition database. By doing a simple keyword search (try using the Key Terms in the list above), you can quickly generate a list of relevant articles from thousands of possibilities and can select articles to read, explore, and print for reference or further study. InfoTrac College Edition's continuously updated collection of articles can be useful for doing reading and writing assignments that reach beyond the pages of this text!

SUGGESTED READINGS

Borum, R. (1996). Improving the clinical practice of violence risk assessment: Technology, guidelines, and training. *American Psychologist, 51,* 945–956.

An important summary of the risk assessment literature as it advanced in the 1990s.

Campbell, J. C. (1995). Assessing dangerousness: Violence by sexual offenders, batterers, and child abusers. Thousand Oaks, CA: Sage.

A very readable edited book with chapters on assessing dangerousness in various contexts.

Dawes, R. M., Faust, D., & Meehl, P. E. (1989). Clinical versus actuarial judgment. *Science, 243,* 1668–1674.

A seminal and critically important article in the debate between those who champion the use of actuarially based instruments and those who believe "clinical judgment" has a rule in clinical decision-making.

Hotaling, G., & Sugarman, D. (1986). An analysis of risk markers in husband to wife violence: The current state of knowledge. *Violence and Victims, 1,* 101–124.

An interesting but somewhat dated article focusing on risk assessment in spousal abuse.

Monahan, J. (1981). *Predicting violent behavior: An assessment of clinical techniques.* Beverly Hills, CA: Sage.

The seminal work on predictions of dangerousness.

Monahan, J. (1992). Mental disorder and violent behavior: Perceptions and evidence. *American Psychologist, 47,* 511–521.

A later article by Monahan in which he modifies his earlier conclusion that predictions of dangerousness could not be made with any degree of accuracy.

Quinsey, V. L., Harris, G. T., Rice, M. E., and Cormier, C. A. (1998). *Violent offenders: Appraising and managing risk.* Washington, D.C.: American Psychological Association.

An up-to-date and important summary of the state of the art in risk assessment with violent offenders of various sorts.

Steadman, H. J. & Cocozza, J. S. (1974). *Careers of the criminally insane: Excessive social control of deviance.* Lexington, MA: Lexington Books.

An interesting account of what happened to a large group of mental patients released from a hospital into the community.

7

"Syndrome" Evidence: Battered Woman Syndrome and Rape Trauma Syndrome

THE BATTERED WOMAN SYNDROME (BWS)

How extensive is the problem of domestic violence in the United States and Canada? Victims' advocates offer alarming statistics, although some of their conclusions about incidence rates are generalized from small and unrepresentative samples.

Among claims supporting the severity of the problem are the following:

1. "Battering is currently the leading cause of injury in American women, sending more than 1 million every year to doctors' offices or emergency rooms for treatment" (Jones, 1994a, p. 9A; see also Quindlen, 1994).
2. Every 12 seconds in the United States, a man batters his current or former wife or woman friend (Jones, 1994b).
3. Spousal violence contributes to one fourth of all suicide attempts by women (Jones, 1994a).
4. Thirty-seven percent of all obstetric patients are battered during pregnancy (Jones, 1994a).
5. Roughly one out of every four women seen in America's hospital emergency rooms was injured by her male friend or spouse (Quindlen, 1994).
6. Fifty percent of the homeless women and children in the United States are fleeing from male violence (Jones, 1994a).

These statistics sometimes reflect reports by victims, while others use crime reports. Some of the conclusions are based on small, unrepresentative samples; others—including the suspected cause of injuries reported to emergency rooms—reflect the stance that, when the records fail to state the cause of a facial injury, the case should be classified as "probable" domestic violence. The extent of abuse against spouses is serious enough without its being exaggerated; the FBI has reported that each year about 1,400 women (or 6% of all murder victims) are killed by their partners (Brott, 1994).

Lenore Walker (1992, p. 332) has estimated that between one third and one half of all women in the United States will be abused at some point in their lives. However, other estimates are somewhat lower, with some form of physical aggression occurring in one quarter to one third of all couples (Straus & Gelles, 1988). The latter conclusion was based on a systematic survey, and it is important because Straus and Gelles made a distinction between types of violence. In the 16% of families that do experience violence, it usually takes the form of slapping, shoving, and grabbing. In 3% to 4% of all families, the dangerous violence exists—kicking, punching, and use of a weapon. Although this percentage is smaller, it accounts for almost 2 million families, and an estimated 188,000 women are injured severely enough to require medical attention (Brott, 1994).

Despite these disturbing statistics, many elements of society have been slow to respond, and many myths about battered women still abound (see Box 7-1). The United States has three times as many animal shelters as battered women shelters (Goodman, 1994). The most controversial aspect of the defense of battered women who kill is the use of the battered woman "syndrome." Although the claimed presence of this syndrome is not a legal defense in and of itself, it can be used as a justification for arguing, as a defense, either self-defense or insanity.

What Is a Syndrome?

A **syndrome** is usually defined as a group of symptoms that occur together and characterize a disease. The **battered woman syndrome** is defined as a woman's presumed reactions to a pattern of continual physical and psychological abuse inflicted on her by her mate (Walker, 1984a; 1984b). The choice of the term *syndrome* assumes that the symptoms or responses are consistent from one woman to another. But are they?

Mary Ann Dutton (1993) noted that we need to recognize that battered women's psy-

> ### BOX 7-1
> ### Some Myths About the Battered Woman
>
> In introducing her study of battered women, Lenore Walker (1979) described 21 myths about these women, their batterers, and the relationship among them. These are:
>
> Myth No. 1: The battered woman syndrome affects only a small percentage of the population.
>
> Myth No. 2: Battered women are masochistic. The prevailing belief has always been that only women who "liked it and deserved it" were beaten (p. 20).
>
> Myth No. 3: Battered women are crazy. This myth is related to the masochism myth in that it places the blame for the battering on the woman's negative personality characteristics (p. 21).
>
> Myth No. 4: Middle-class women are not battered as frequently or as violently as are poorer women.
>
> Myth No. 5: Minority-group women are battered more frequently that Anglos.
>
> Myth No. 6: Religious beliefs will prevent battering.
>
> Myth No. 7: Battered women are uneducated and have few job skills.
>
> Myth No. 8: Batterers are violent in all their relationships.
>
> Myth No. 9: Batterers are unsuccessful and lack resources to cope with the world.
>
> Myth No. 10: Drinking causes battering behavior.
>
> Myth No. 11: Batterers are psychopathic personalities.
>
> Myth No. 12: Police can protect the battered woman.
>
> Myth No. 13: The batterer is not a loving partner.
>
> Myth No. 14: A wife beater also beats his children.
>
> Myth No. 15: Once a battered woman, always a battered woman.
>
> Myth No. 16: Once a batterer, always a batterer.
>
> Myth No. 17: Long-standing battering relationships can change for the better.
>
> Myth No. 18: Battered women deserve to get beaten. The myth that battered women provoke their beatings by pushing their men beyond the breaking point is a popular one (p. 29).
>
> Myth No. 19: Battered women can always leave home (p. 29).
>
> Myth No. 20: Batterers will cease their violence "when we get married."
>
> Myth No. 21: Children need their father even if he is violent—or, "I'm only staying for the sake of the children."
>
> Source: Adapted from Walker, 1979, pp. 19–30.

chological realities vary considerably from each other and, in fact, do not fit only one profile.

In a study of battered women seeking help at a counseling program, five distinct profile types generated from the MMPI were identified, indicating different patterns of psychological functioning among them, including some profiles that were considered "normal" (Dutton-Douglas, Perrin, & Chrestman, 1990). Dutton also observed that confusion about the battered wo-

man syndrome has resulted from testimony by expert witnesses that is not limited to the psychological reactions to domestic violence. Often the expert witness testifies about the nature of physical violence and offers explanations for puzzling behavior by the victim and for behavior that may have been introduced by the prosecution to suggest that the battered woman is not the "typical" battered woman (e.g., prostitution, abuse of her children, her violent reactions).

Components of the Battered Woman Syndrome

Despite the conclusions that victims may show different symptoms, some psychologists have proposed the existence of a common set of components to the battered woman syndrome. These include (Walker, 1984a, 1984b):

1. **Learned helplessness,** or a response to being exposed to painful stimuli over which victims have no control and finding that no avenue readily exists for escape.
2. Lowered self-esteem, or an acceptance of continued feedback from the abuser about one's worthlessness.
3. Impaired functioning, including an inability to engage in planful behavior.
4. Loss of the assumption of invulnerability and safety: Previous beliefs that "things would turn out all right" or "this wouldn't happen to me" dissipate in the onslaught of abuse and violence.
5. Fear and terror, as reactions to the batterer, based on past experiences.
6. Anger/rage.
7. Diminished alternatives: Of 400 battered women interviewed by Walker (1993), 85% felt they could or would be killed at some point. Also, as a part of the diminished-responsiveness reaction, battered women focus their energies on survival within the relationship rather than exploring options outside (Blackman, 1986).
8. The **cycle of abuse** or cycle of violence: The Jekyll-and-Hyde nature of batterers has been proposed as a contribution to the battered woman syndrome. A man may be loving, nurturing, giving, and attentive to the woman's needs during courtship and perhaps early in the marriage. But then there is a **tension-building phase**—more criticism, verbal bickering, increased strain, and perhaps minor physical abuse. This is followed by the violent step in the cycle: an **acute battering incident,** in which the batterer explodes into an uncontrollable rage, leading to injuries to the woman.

When the dark side appears, the woman may be too involved with the man to break off the relationship. Also, she may remember the good times and believe that if she can find the right thing to do, he will revert to his earlier behavior; thus, she often blames herself for his actions. As reflected in her list of myths (Box 7-1), Walker (1992) proposed, "Research has demonstrated that this is a **contrite phase** in which the batterer's use of promises and gifts increases the battered woman's hope that violence occurred for the last time" (page 328; bold added). The batterer expresses regret and apologizes, perhaps promising never to lose control again. But eventually the cycle starts once more (Walker, 1984a; 1984b).

According to the theory of the cycle of violence, the woman feels growing tension during phase one, develops a fear of death or serious bodily harm during phase two, and anticipating another attack, defends herself by retaliating during a lull in the violence (Walker, 1984a; 1984b). Not all battering follows this cycle (Dutton, 1993); in fact, of the 400 women interviewed by Walker (1979), involving 1,600 battering incidents, only two thirds reflected this cycle.

9. Hypervigilance to cues of danger: Other components of the battered woman syndrome are less obvious; **hypervigilance** is one of the more important. As a result of being battered, women notice subtle things—things that others don't recognize as dangerous. The woman may notice her husband's words come faster, or she might claim that his eyes get darker. She may make a preemptive strike before the abuser has actually inflicted much damage.
10. High tolerance for **cognitive inconsistency** (Blackman, 1986): Battered women often express two ideas that appear to be logically inconsistent with each other. "For example, a battered woman might say, 'My husband only

hit me when he was drunk,' but later describes an episode during which he was not drunk and yet abusive. I believe this tolerance for inconsistency grows out of the fundamental inconsistency of a battered woman's life: that the man who supposedly loves her also hurts her" (Blackman, 1986, pp. 228–229).

The Relationship of BWS to Post-Traumatic Stress Disorder (PTSD)

What is the relationship of the battered woman syndrome to **post-traumatic stress disorder (PTSD)**? PTSD is included in the *Diagnostic and Statistical Manual of Mental Disorders–Revised (DSM-III-R)* as a clinical diagnosis. Walker (1992) viewed BWS as a subcategory of the generic PTSD. She wrote:

A good many of the reactions battered women report are similar to those of catastrophe victims. Disaster victims generally suffer emotional collapse 22 to 48 hours after a catastrophe. Their symptoms include listlessness, depression, and feelings of helplessness. Battered women evidence similar behavior. They tend to remain isolated for at least the first 24 hours, and it may be several days before they seek help. (1979, p. 63)

But Lenore Walker and Mary Ann Dutton seem to disagree about the usefulness of PTSD. Walker (1992) wrote: "In presenting the BWS to a judge or jury it is often useful to demonstrate using the PTSD criteria chart. . . . Most battered women easily meet these criteria" (p. 329). But Dutton (1993) has emphasized the variety of reactions, as has Blackman (1986): "For example, it is entirely possible for a battered woman to have a constructive, effective work style outside the home—for her to show no signs of learned helplessness" (p. 230). Also, there is the objection that such women will be misclassified as mentally ill. These experts urge: Don't "over-clinicalize" the victims of abuse.

Role of the Forensic Psychologist in the Assessment of BWS

An important role for clinical forensic psychologists is the careful assessment of the responses of a woman who has killed her husband. What symptoms does she report? Is there corroborating evidence for them? Diane Follingstad (1994b) has identified several procedures to be followed by forensic psychologists who assess the status of women who report abuse and battering and are charged with homicide. First, there should be a thorough psychological examination that explores the history of the relationship, the history of abuse, the attempts to leave the relationship, and the woman's feelings about the deceased. The examination needs to be done in a nonjudgmental manner. Box 7-2 gives a detailed outline.

The psychologist should seek verification of self-reports through medical records and interviews with others. He or she may use a survey instrument to systemize the nature of the abuse; one possible measure is Dutton's (1992) Abusive Behavior Observation Checklist. It is an interviewer-administered listing of specific physical, sexual, and psychological actions that incorporates psychological abuse items from the Power and Control Wheel (Pence & Paymor, 1985) and physical violence items from the Conflict Tactics Scale (Straus, 1979).

The **Power and Control Wheel** lists eight categories of psychological abuse:

1. coercion and threats (threaten to kill or injure wife or children, threaten to burn the house down or steal the car)
2. intimidation (display weapons, give a look that instills fear)
3. emotional abuse (humiliating name calling, insults, restriction from personal hygiene [bath, toilet], forced nudity)
4. isolation (restrict access to mail, TV, phone, friends, family; demand accounting)
5. minimization, denial, and blaming (deny that abuse happened, blame victim for abuse)

BOX 7-2
Data to Collect for Elements of Self-Defense

Diane Follingstad (1994b) provided a detailed list of issues to be considered when preparing a battered woman defense:

I. Seriousness of threatened harm

Past history of abuse.

Types of abuse previously occurring.

Worst episodes in terms of type of force and injuries—hospital records, doctors' records.

Extent of threats—content of these; whether he has carried out threats in the past; believability of threats.

Man's reputation for assaulting others in the past.

Specific cues that signaled severe episodes.

The woman's reactions and thought processes that led her to believe this episode could be lethal or cause grievous bodily harm.

Whether man has ever killed anything before, e.g., pets.

Changes in recent times that signaled that this was a more dangerous period Pattern of escalation of abuse over time.

II. Imminence

Content of the threats.

Specific cues signaling a dangerous episode was going to occur.

Changes in the man's behavior/reactions recently that signaled this was a more dangerous period.

Changes in the man's behavior/reactions recently that signaled that the man's behavior felt unpredictable.

Past patterns of abuse that would make an episode appear imminent.

Likelihood that the man would remain dangerous for hours/days based on history.

If the man was killed while his back was turned or he was sleeping, find out if and why the woman felt that was the only available time to defend herself.

Determine whether the woman had difficulty in knowing exactly when the man would carry out a threat.

III. "Overt act" as necessary for self-defense response

Careful detailing of incident.

Specific content of verbal threats.

Specific description of nonverbal cues used in intimidation and signals that violence was at hand.

IV. Rule of retreat

This area of information should be established specifically for the incident in which the woman killed the man as well as generally regarding why the woman remained in the relationship.

Prior escape attempts and results of these.

Prior use of community resources and results of contacts with societal agents.

Likelihood the man would come after her.

Analysis of her options that night and her thought processes about those options.

Specific threats as to dire consequences for leaving.

Factors preventing leaving that night, e.g., not daring to leave young children behind with the man, lack of transportation and isolated rural location of the home, no money to go anywhere, nowhere to go.

Whether woman was paralyzed by fear, too scared to run.

Likelihood that the man will remain dangerous for hours/days.

Woman's sense of isolation/learned helplessness.

Woman's perceived alternatives and resources if she left.

View of the man as omnipotent.

Beliefs as to why she should not leave.

Psychological dilemmas regarding leaving.

V. Freedom from any responsibility for provoking the confrontation

History of the woman's use of physical force in the relationship.

Reasons for any use of physical force in the relationship.

Careful detailing of everything leading up to the killing.

VI. Equal force rule

If the man was unarmed, get history of extent of injuries and force man could inflict just using hands, feet.

continued

Man's personal history outside the relationship that supports the idea of the extent of his aggressiveness without using weapons.

Size of the man versus size of the woman.

Physical strength of the man versus physical strength of the woman.

Any formal fight training for the man (e.g., military training, martial arts).

Man's knowledge of the use of guns and any history of collecting guns.

VII. Force not to exceed force necessary to disable the attacker

Woman's awareness of shooting more than one shot.

Woman's thought processes of what it would mean if the man was only injured, i.e., what would happen to her.

Woman's knowledge of firearms and whether woman had any idea what would be necessary to stop the man versus killing him.

VIII. Reasonableness

Abuse in history.

Woman's perceptions of what was likely to happen to her.

Patterns of abuse.

Man's threats and history of carrying them out.

Woman's past ability to keep abuse episodes from occurring.

Man's reputation for aggression.

Woman's thought processes leading up to the situation.

Likelihood that the man would cause grievous bodily injury or kill her.

Woman's level of fear during the killing incident.

Source: From Follingstad, 1994b, Appendix A. Used by permission of the author.

---

6. use of children to control the woman (threaten to kidnap or abuse, relay threatening messages through the children)
7. use of "male privilege"
8. economic/resource abuse (require "begging" for money, steal money from partner, destroy credit cards, control access to transportation)

THE BWS IN COURT

The next section of this chapter describes the use of the battered woman syndrome as part of a defense. In other words, the focus is now solely on those women who kill their abusers.

Battered Women Who Kill

More than 10% of the homicides in the United States are committed by women, and a significant percentage of these women have killed an abusive partner (Browne & Williams, 1989; Jones,

1981). Most of the women in prison for murder convictions are abuse victims (Bauschard, 1986), and some of the 47 women currently on death row killed their husbands or lovers.

A fundamental question examines the difference between battered women who kill and those victims who don't. Why? Again, we find differences in emphasis between experts. Walker (1992) wrote: "In my case, the differences between those battered women who kill and those who do not have more to do with the man's behavior than with the woman's. Most battered women are more sensitive than the nonbattered woman in perceiving the imminent danger to which they respond" (p. 333). Ewing (1990) has offered a different opinion: "It appears that battered women who kill are subject to more severe abuse, are somewhat older and less well-educated, and have fewer resources for coping with that abuse than do battered women in general" (p. 583). Any response to abuse is a function of both the extremity and consistency of violent acts and the nature of, and resources available to, the victim. By placing emphasis on the man's behavior, Walker implies that victims do not significantly differ, which is in conflict with empirical findings about the range of personality dynamics in abuse victims.

Possible Defenses

It is important to recall that BWS is not a defense in and of itself (Aron, 1993). In cases in which the battered woman kills her husband or lover, she must show coercion or at least temporary insanity. Two options exist: the **self-defense defense** and the insanity defense.

Self-Defense

The **battered woman self-defense,** as it is called, rests on the justification of the act as a necessary one in order to protect the woman or someone else (usually the children) from further harm or death (Walker, 1992). **Self-defense** is defined in most states as the use of equal force or the least amount of force necessary to repel danger when the person reasonably perceives that she or he is in **imminent danger** of serious bodily damage or death. Its key components are include a reasonable perception of imminent danger and a justified use of lethal force.

In contrast, the **insanity defense,** as applied here, argues that the woman was unable to tell the difference between right and wrong, "because she was mentally incompetent (perhaps harmed by head injuries or driven crazy by the abusive behavior of her husband) and therefore should be excused from any culpability" (Walker, 1993, p. 236).

How Widely should the Self-Defense Defense Be Applied?

In the last two decades, the breadth of application of the self-defense defense has been provocative. Walker (1992) wrote:

> In the late 1970s and early 1980s, what became known as the *battered woman self-defense* achieved acceptance within the case law of numerous states. As this defense gained

in popularity, attorneys and mental health professionals became more familiar with the dynamics of battering and its psychological impact on victims. Its use broadened to include battered children who killed abusive parents, battered men who killed their partners (usually male), battered women who killed their women partners, rape victims who killed their attacker, and even battered roommates! Soon the expert testimony was applied to cases where other criminal acts were committed by victims of abuse under duress from their abusive partners. Participation with a violent co-defendant in homicides involving strangers also have been explained, in part, by the duress the woman was under to comply with the man's demands. Testimony has also been introduced in cases of child abuse that resulted in the violent man's killing the child (often called "murder by omission" because of the battered woman's inability to protect the child). Crimes involving money and property such as embezzlement, forgery, burglary, robbery, and those that are drug related may well have been committed by a woman at the demand of her batterer. (p. 322, italics in original)

As just one example, Lisa Dunn was convicted of kidnapping and murder charges in Kansas in 1985; she was the accomplice of Daniel Remeta, who also was convicted. Remeta was later executed in Florida, for another of the murders during their cross-country crime spree. Dunn appealed her conviction, claiming that she had been a brutally abused woman who had been forced by Remeta to participate in the crimes. She was granted a new trial, in which expert testimony was included, and in 1992, was found not guilty of the charges (Landon, 1992).

Justification of the Self-Defense Defense

To justify a self-defense defense and therefore acquit the woman, the statutes of most states and Canada prescribe that the jury must be convinced that at the time of the incident she had a reasonable apprehension of imminent, life-threatening danger. Although such a defense is the primary one chosen by such defendants, it faces several obstacles. The first is the "masculine" nature of the defense.

The legal concept of self-defense developed in response to two basic kinds of situations in which men found themselves: a sudden assault by a murderous stranger (for example, a robbery attempt with a threat to kill), or a fist fight or brawl between two equals that gets out of hand and turns deadly. Thus, "classic" self-defense action is stranger-to-stranger assault between two males (Blackman, 1986).

But there certainly is variation, and research findings have led some researchers (Finkel, Meister, & Lightfoot, 1991) to conclude that more community support exists for the self-defense defense by battered women than the preceding would imply. Consider the following case: In the mid-1970s, Inez Garcia was raped by two neighborhood men who told her they were going to come back and rape her again. She went home, got a gun, and after several hours had passed, she found one of the men and shot him dead. She was acquitted at her second trial, a trial in which the court permitted evidence of self-defense even though the actual rape had taken place several hours earlier and there *was* an intervening time between the act and Garcia's responses. The court decided that the threat of further abuse was sufficient to raise her perception of danger to the imminence standard (Bochnak, 1981; Schneider, 1986).

The most fundamental element of the self-defense claim requires that at the time of the killing, the defendant honestly and reasonably feared unlawful bodily harm at the hands of her assailant. This principle is reflected in the *subjective definition* of self-defense, used in some states; for example, in New York, one of these states, a judicial decision (in *People v. Torres,* 1985) made explicit this subjective definition:

> The standard for the evaluation of the reasonableness of the defendant's belief and conduct is not what the ordinary prudent man would have believed or done under the same

circumstances. The test is, rather, whether the defendant's *subjective* belief as to the imminence and seriousness of the danger was reasonable. It is the defendant's state of mind and sense of fear which is critical to a justification defense.

> In this regard, proof of violent acts previously committed by the victim against the defendant as well as any evidence that the defendant was aware of specific prior violent acts by the victim upon third parties is admissible as bearing upon the reasonableness of defendant's apprehension of danger at the time of the encounter. (*People v. Torres,* 1985, p. 360, italics in original)

In contrast, the *objective definition* of self-defense refers to the average person, assumed by the courts to be a man. In some states, a distinction is made between an honest plus reasonable perception and an honest but unreasonable perception. The latter is used as a mitigating factor to lower criminal responsibility to involuntary manslaughter because the woman honestly believed that she was in danger but that perception was unreasonable from the facts of the situation (Walker, 1992, p. 324, citing Ewing, 1987, and Schneider, 1986).

The Psychological Self-Defense

As we have seen, most battered women who kill are convicted, even though they use the self-defense defense, because requirements of the current self-defense law equate "self" with only the *physical* aspects of personhood (Ewing, 1990, p. 580). That is, most do not kill at the moment they are being battered or directly threatened. Charles Patrick Ewing's survey of well-documented homicides by battered women found only about one third took place during an act of battering. Thus, Ewing proposed a new concept—the **psychological self-defense** defense; he wrote:

> In brief, my position is that failure to meet these narrow legal requirements does not mean that a battered woman did not kill in defense of self. I argue that many, perhaps

most, battered women who kill their batterers do so in *psychological* self-defense—that is, to protect themselves from being destroyed psychologically—and that under certain circumstances the law should recognize *psychological* self-defense as a justification for the use of deadly force. (Ewing, 1990, p. 581, italics in original)

Ewing, a psychologist, attorney, and law professor, wrote further:

> Should a battered woman—or anyone else—who uses deadly force to prevent that result, to avert what reasonably appears to be the threat of psychological destruction, be branded a criminal and sent to prison? I think not, but that is precisely what is happening in many cases under current self-defense law. Contrary to current law, I suggest that the use of deadly force to avoid such a dire fate is a legitimate form of self-defense and should be recognized as such by the criminal law. In short, I believe that, under certain circumstances, psychological self-defense should be a legal justification for homicide.
>
> The legal doctrine I am proposing is not a battered woman defense. Such a defense would not only arguably violate constitutional guarantees of equal protection, but would be unsound as a matter of public policy. Attaining the status of battered woman or even battered person is not and should not by itself be justification for homicide. Stated most simply, the proposed doctrine of psychological self-defense would justify the use of deadly force where such force appeared reasonably necessary to prevent the infliction of extremely serious psychological injury. *Extremely serious psychological injury* would be defined as gross and enduring impairment of one's psychological functioning that significantly limits the meaning and value of one's physical existence. (1990, p. 587, italics in original)

The major criticism of the use of psychological self-defense as a defense came from Stephen Morse (1990); his major objections were the following:

The proposal to justify homicide by psychological self-defense rests on an insecure scientific foundation and would be legally mischievous. The core concepts are unacceptably vague and lack rigorous empirical support. The proposed defense is better characterized as an excuse than as a justification because rational victims of purely psychological abuse do have socially preferable alternatives to homicide, and the proposal is inconsistent with modern criminal law that limits justifications for homicide. The defense would create substantial administrative problems and would facilitate adoption or expansion of related undesirable doctrines. The best response to abhorrent physical and psychological abuse is not unnecessary further violence, but the creation of adequate deterrents and alternative solutions for victims. (1990, p. 595)

The psychological self-defense remains untested in the courts.

The Insanity Defense

As Follingstad (1994b) has pointed out, possessing components of the battered woman syndrome does not support an insanity defense in and of itself. Furthermore, in many cases, the insanity defense is likely to be unsuccessful. Juries acquit a very small percentage of battered women based on a rationale of not guilty by reason of insanity. Defense attorneys should seriously question whether they want to propose that the defendant should not be held responsible for her actions because the beatings rendered her insane at the time of the offense. In fact, many advocates for battered women feel it is demeaning for a woman to be declared insane when acting to save her own life (Walker, 1993). Research using jury simulations comparing the use of an insanity defense and the other, preceding defenses is inconsistent; mock jurors given a self-defense option were sometimes more likely to find the woman not guilty than were mock jurors exposed to an insanity defense (Follingstad, Polek, Hause, Deaton, Bulger, & Conway, 1989), but another study using an "automatism" plea (which proposed that the woman's head injury created a dissociated state so that she could not form an intent) found that the insanity plea produced more acquittals than did a self-defense plea (Kasian, Spanos, Terrance, & Peebles, 1993).

THE USE OF A PSYCHOLOGIST AS AN EXPERT WITNESS ON THE BATTERED WOMAN SYNDROME

Testimony by an expert witness on the battered woman syndrome was first introduced in United States courts in 1979 (*Ibn-Tamas v. United States*). Several years ago, Walker (1993) estimated that expert witnesses had been allowed to testify in at least 500 trials in the United States. She wrote:

My own work as an expert witness in almost 300 of these trials in the United States began in 1977 when I was asked to evaluate Miriam Griegg, a Billings, Montana, woman who had been seriously assaulted during most of her marriage. One night she shot and killed her husband with six hollow point bullets from his own Magnum .357 gun. During an argument, he threw the gun at her and ordered her to shoot him or else, he threatened, he would shoot and kill her. When the police arrived, Miriam Griegg warned them to be careful as she knew her husband would be very angry. Obviously, her emotional state caused her to be unaware that he was dead; any one of the six bullets would have killed him instantly. She made it perfectly clear, however, that she shot him because she believed that he would have killed her otherwise, a straightforward self-defense argument. After listening to her testimony and mine—I explained the context of the relationship and how Miriam Griegg knew in her own mind that she would die if

she did not do what he ordered her to do—the jury agreed that she was not guilty. (pp. 233–234)

But, as described in detail later in this chapter, the empirical research on the effect of an expert witness does not lead to a solid conclusion about overall effectiveness of psychologists who testify for the defense.

Reasons for Use of the Expert Witness

Basically, the purpose of the expert witness is to provide fact finders with another perspective, or a "social framework" (Monahan & Walker, 1988) for interpreting the woman's actions. Mary Ann Dutton (1993) described different purposes for testimony by a psychologist:

Typically, expert testimony concerning the battered woman's psychological reactions to violence has been used to address a number of different issues. Within a criminal context, the testimony is used to bolster a standard defense (e.g., self-defense or duress), not provide a separate defense, *per se*. Issues toward which the psychological testimony is applied include, for example, whether the victim's perception of danger was reasonable (e.g., self-defense), the psychological damage resulting from domestic violence (e.g., civil tort), the basis for sole custody or restriction of child visitation (e.g., child custody), and why the battered woman engaged in seemingly puzzling behaviors (e.g., remained with or returned to the battering partner, expressed anger toward the batterer in public, left children alone with batterer, recanted testimony regarding occurrence of past violence).

It is, of course, necessary to establish that the particular aspects of a battered woman's experience of violence (and its aftermath) toward which the testimony is addressed are directly relevant to specific legal issues at hand in order for its application to be both helpful and admissible. It is essential that this link be made explicit to the fact finder, otherwise the relevance of the expert witness testimony may not be clearly understood or missed altogether. (1993, p. 1216)

The expert witness can describe three types of reaction to trauma:

1. psychological distress or dysfunction
2. cognitive reactions
3. relational disturbances

One of the most important contributions is to confront questions that jurors might be phrasing in their heads. For example, jurors ask, "Why didn't she leave?" This question, while a frequent one, assumes that there are viable options for alternative behavior; that is, it assumes that leaving will stop the violence. The law is explicit: You have no obligation to rearrange your life in order to avoid a situation in which the need to act in self-defense might arise. The expert witness needs to deflect the assumption that if the battered woman didn't leave after the abuse, she wasn't bothered by it. The witness can bring out strategies the woman used to stop the violence (Follingstad, 1994b). These form three types:

1. *Personal strategies:*
   Complying with the batterer's demands in order to "keep the peace"

   Attempting to talk with abuser about stopping the violence

   Temporarily escaping

   Hiding

   Physically resisting

2. *Informal help-seeking:*
   Soliciting help from neighbors and others in escaping from the batterer

   Asking others to intervene in attempt to get him to stop

3. *Formal help-seeking efforts:*
   Using legal strategies—calling the police, prosecuting, getting a lawyer, going to a shelter

The expert can point out that the battered woman's lack of economic resources makes it impossible for her to leave. But the expert also needs to alert the jury to the fact that different victims use different strategies and to the reasons any one option is not frequently used.

A second question jurors ponder is this: "Why did she attack when he was asleep?" The expert witness can inform the jury of the reasonableness of the battered woman's perception of danger. Walker argued, "Many women know that their abusive partner is still dangerous even while he is asleep, frequently forcing his sexual demands upon waking and immediately beginning another attack. Often these men do not sleep for long periods of time, waking early, especially if she is not right by his side as he frequently orders" (1992, p. 325).

In further support of this position, Crocker (1985) suggested:

The battered woman perceived an imminent danger of physical injury even though there was no overt act of violence. Defendants offer battered woman syndrome expert testimony to explain why their perception of danger was reasonable—why they acted in self-defense after a "reasonable man" would have cooled off or before he would have acted. The testimony may demonstrate how repeated physical abuse can so heighten a battered woman's fear and her awareness of her husband's physical capabilities that she considers him as dangerous asleep as awake, as dangerous before an attack as during one. (p. 141)

Blackman (1986) emphasized that for a self-defense plea to be viable, the woman must be acting under the reasonable belief that her life or the life of someone else is at risk. An example is given in Box 7-3 in the case of *People v. Diaz* (1983).

Cross-Examination

Regarding the prosecution's strategies in trials in which a battered woman is accused of homicide, it is typical to try to discredit the opposing case by characterizing the defendant as "unfeminine or man-like," "not a good mother," or "promiscuous" (Basow, 1986). Gillespie (1989) observed:

BOX 7-3

The Case of *People v. Diaz*, 1983

Keeping in mind the elements required for self-defense, consider the case of Madelyn Diaz, a 24-year-old New York woman, who fired twice into the body of her husband as he slept. Ms. Diaz had been married for 5 years and had two children at the time of the killing. Her husband was a police officer who frequently used his gun to get her to comply with his wishes. He had beaten her frequently during the course of their marriage. On one occasion, she suffered a broken nose. He had also used his gun to force her to have sexual intercourse with a stranger in the back seat of their car. He watched while this invited stranger raped his wife. When they got home, he refused to allow Madelyn to bathe and insisted that she have sex with him.

The night before she killed him, Madelyn and her husband had an argument. He was drunk and wanted to have sex with her. She refused. He insisted that she change her attitude toward him. He said that if she did not change by the following day, he would "blow the baby's brains out." He took his gun and placed it against the head of their 6-month-old daughter as he made this threat. Madelyn felt certain that she would not be able to change enough to satisfy him and believed him to be capable of acting on his threat. Following this exchange, they both went to sleep. In the morning, Madelyn woke up before her husband. She

dressed her children and took them outside to the car to go grocery shopping. She then realized that she had forgotten her money. She went back into the apartment and went to the drawer where they kept their money. Her husband's gun was in the same drawer. She took the gun from the drawer; as she did, she relived the moment of his threat against their daughter. She later reported that she could see him holding his gun to the baby's head—something he had never done before, a novel form of violence for him. She fired twice into his sleeping body, took the gun out of the apartment with her, and gave it to a neighbor to hide. She then took the children and went grocery shopping. She purchased things that her husband particularly liked. When she got home about 3 hours later, she discovered that the apartment door was ajar. She walked into the bedroom and discovered her husband's body. She became hysterical and called the police. She reported that a robbery had occurred and that her husband had been killed by the intruder. Three days later, when a police officer who had worked with her husband came to give her the first of the pension checks to which she was entitled, she remembered what had actually happened and said, "I can't take this check. I killed my husband." She was indicted for murder in the second degree.

Ms. Diaz was found not guilty.

Source: Blackman, 1986, pp. 236–237.

"The trial courtroom provides a forum for a biased or cynical prosecutor to trot out every myth and stereotype and his [or her] misconception about women that could conceivably inflame a jury against the defendant and that could encourage the jurors to ascribe the worst possible motive to her actions" (p. 22).

One example cited by Jenkins and Davidson (1990) came from the cross-examination of the defendant:

Q. How old was Scott when you married him?

A. 20

Q. And how old were you?

A. 28

Q. You'd been divorced twice before?

A. Yes

Q. Did you tell Scott you were pregnant before you married him?

A. I was not pregnant.

Q. Huh?

A. I was not pregnant.

Q. Did you tell Scott you were pregnant before you married him?

A. I was not pregnant. . . . No. (p. 164)

The authors observed that three aspects of this exchange—that the defendant was older than her husband, that she was a divorced woman, and that she lied to entrap him in marriage—

produce for the jury a stereotypically negative connotation of the woman defendant.

Also, the prosecution may try to minimize the injuries of the defendant. Jenkins and Davidson quoted one closing argument:

> [An eyewitness] gets up on the witness stand and she tells you [she] witnessed him beating her in the Tarver Pancake Kitchen. These beatings once a week that she suffered for five years, I don't know. If you've ever seen a boxer that's been in the game too long, it gets punch-strong [sic], and the movements get slower, the speech gets slower, and he can't get around. . . . If that woman incurred a beating a week for five years, that's the way she would look. She wants you to believe that she was beat that bad because that's her only chance. . . . That didn't happen. (1990, p. 167)

PROCEDURAL AND ETHICAL ISSUES REGARDING THE USE OF EXPERT WITNESSES

The use of a psychologist as expert witness in cases in which the battered woman syndrome is introduced is fraught with both procedural and ethical questions.

Admissibility of Expert Testimony on BWS

The rationale for many court decisions to admit expert testimony is that such testimony bears upon a crucial issue of fact that is "beyond the ken" of the average layperson or jury member (Ewing, Aubrey, & Jamieson, 1986). A decision by the Supreme Court of New Jersey is illustrative; in *State v. Kelly* (1984), this court wrote:

> The crucial issue of fact on which this . . . testimony would bear is why, given such allegedly severe and constant beatings [the] defendant had not long ago left decedent.

> [C]ommon knowledge tells us that most of us, including the ordinary juror, would ask himself or herself just such a question. And our knowledge is bolstered by the expert's knowledge, for experts point out that one of the common myths, apparently believed by most people, is that battered wives are free to leave, that the battered wife is masochistic [and] that the "beatings" could not have been too bad for if they had been, she certainly would have left. The expert could clear up these myths. (*State v. Kelly,* 1984, p. 372)

The trend has been toward admitting psychologists as expert witnesses, but testimony about the battered woman syndrome is subject to the constraints made explicit in the *Daubert* and *Kumho* decisions, described in chapter 2.

The Stance of the Expert Witness— Objectivity or Advocacy?

It is hard for psychologists testifying in such cases to remain objective. Lenore Walker even questioned the wisdom of such a stance:

> It is important to understand the *ineffectiveness* and *danger* of a professional taking an objective and neutral stance with a battered woman who comes for help since it is not unusual for the abuse to escalate to homicidal proportions after the separation and during the divorcing period. One of the areas of damage that frequently occurs after repeated trauma is the victim's inability to perceive neutrality. Battered women evaluate everyone with whom they have a significant interaction as either being with them or being against them. This means that professionals who attempt to act in a neutral and objective manner will be misperceived as being against the woman which then gets translated into being likely to cause her danger or further harm. (1992, pp. 332–333)

Although it is unclear whether Walker was talking about a therapeutic relationship or the role of expert witness (or both), her statement reflects an allegiance to the woman on trial as her only client. Throughout this book, a recurring viewpoint is that forensic psychologists have responsibilities to society in general and to their field as an objective science. Those who testify in court must remain neutral, even if "danger" (to use Walker's term) is the result.

JURORS' REACTIONS TO BWS AS A PART OF DEFENSE EVIDENCE

But what *is* the effect of expert testimony? Does it change jurors' verdicts? If so, how? Several jury-simulation studies are relevant (Blackman & Brickman, 1984). Regina Schuller has completed three studies (Schuller, 1992; Schuller, Smith, & Olson, 1994). In the first, 108 mock jurors (Canadian college students) read about a homicide trial in which a battered woman had killed her husband. The transcript, based on an actual case, was 50 pages in length. Three versions of the trial were used: In one, an expert witness presented only general research findings on the battered woman syndrome. In the second version, the expert went farther, concluding that the defendant's behavioral and emotional characteristics fit the syndrome. A third group of subjects read a transcript in which no expert testimony was presented. Compared to the control condition, jurors exposed to the transcript with the specific expert gave interpretations that were more consistent with the woman's account of what occurred and more consistent with verdicts that were more lenient.

Schuller's (1992) second study, which substituted an hour-long audiotape for the transcript, had the jurors deliberate (131 subjects were divided into 30 juries). In this study, compared to the control condition, each expert-witness condition led to a moderate shift in verdicts from murder to manslaughter. If they had heard the testimony of an expert witness, the jurors—during deliberations—discussed the defendant and her actions in a more favorable light.

A third study in Schuller's program of research (Schuller, Smith, & Olson, 1994) collected subjects' beliefs about sexual abuse 2 months before their participation as mock jurors in a study that used the same audiotape as the prior study. The presence of testimony by an expert witness again influenced verdicts but especially in those mock jurors whose earlier responses had reflected more informed attitudes about domestic abuse. These jurors attributed less responsibility to the defendant and more responsibility to the alleged abuser, compared to control subjects.

A jury simulation by Greenwald, Tomkins, Kenning, and Zavodny (1990) sought to evaluate Ewing's "psychological self-defense" defense. A total of 196 college undergraduate subjects read two trial vignettes. The instructions given to the jury varied: psychological self-defense only, physical self-defense only, psychological and physical self-defense, or none of these. Instructions were given after the vignettes, so that elements of self-defense were the last thing given to the jurors. Only the psychological self-defense instructions significantly influenced verdict patterns, primarily by shifting would-be voluntary manslaughter convictions to acquittals.

However, not all studies have concluded that testimony by a psychologist-expert is that effective. A study by Diane Follingstad and her colleagues (Follingstad et al., 1989) varied the level of force directed by the husband prior to his wife's killing him, as well as the presence or absence of an expert witness (who testified about the relationship of the defendant's actions to battering relationships in general). The presence of the expert witness had no direct influence on the jurors' verdicts, although 80% of the jurors in the expert-witness condition reported that it was influential. The factor that had the greatest impact was maximum force—that is, the condition in which the husband was described as advancing toward the woman with a weapon.

Similarly, a study by Finkel et al. (1991) manipulated the degree of threat posed by the husband as well as the presence or absence of expert testimony. As in Schuller's first study, two types of expert testimony were offered: Either the expert diagnosed the defendant as having the battered woman syndrome and described the symptoms of the syndrome, or the expert supplemented the diagnosis with an opinion about the woman's perceptions at the time of the killing. As in the study by Follingstad and her colleagues, the only variable that influenced the mock jurors' verdicts was the level of force used by the husband; that is, verdicts of guilt were rendered more often when the woman acted without being directly provoked by the man.

Thus, the research results give no consistent answer to the question of effectiveness of expert testimony. Methodological differences among the studies just described may account for the differences in results; Schuller (1994) suggested that it may be necessary for the woman's account of what happened to be challenged (as it is in a real-life trial) for the expert witness to have any impact.

CRITICISMS OF THE USE OF THE BATTERED WOMAN SYNDROME AND THE BATTERED WOMAN DEFENSE

Both the battered woman syndrome and the **battered woman defense** have received criticism from within and outside the field of psychology. The defense has been challenged as portraying women in an unfavorable light, while the battered woman syndrome has been questioned with regard to its validity as an empirically established concept.

Defense of Women at Trial

One of the problems in the use of the battered woman defense at trial is the behavior of the attorneys representing the woman. In one of the trials analyzed by Jenkins and Davidson (1990), the defense attorney, throughout the trial, referred to the 23-year-old defendant as a "little girl," once stating "she's a nice little girl and everything, but she's not a genius" (p. 164). A second problem is that the defense may cause to resurface those emotions expressed by the woman during and immediately following the homicide, contributing to the culturally held notion that women show their emotions more than men and that the defendant's emotional response is quite relevant to the case (Jenkins & Davidson, 1990). Sometimes the defense attorney will even ask a police officer on the stand, "She was in shock when you talked to her, wasn't she?" (Jenkins & Davidson, 1990, p. 165).

During witness preparation, attorneys sometimes advise the defendant to look more feminine, exploiting gender stereotyping to try to win the case. Sanders's article (1989) reflected two aspects of such stereotyping: with respect to impression management, Sanders advised other attorneys:

> Before trial, work with your client, if necessary, to soften her appearance. Have her look as "feminine" and "defenseless" as possible . . . . [A]sk your wife, a female lawyer, your secretary, or someone whose opinion about such things you respect. . . . [M]y litigation assistants and secretaries sometimes work with female clients on clothing, make-up, behavior, posture, and other things. (1989, p. 44)

With regard to jury selection, Sanders reflected some of the stereotypes of lawyers described in chapter 12, but here they are especially egregious in that they contribute to a simplified distinction between the two genders:

> As a generalization, at least, I prefer male jurors when defending a female defendant. Men . . . have protective impulses toward women. Women tend to be more negatively judgmental toward other women. (1989, p. 44)

Perpetuating the Battered Woman Stereotype: The Passive, Helpless Woman

Psychologists view the use of the battered woman defense as a mixed blessing. Crocker wrote: "The fundamental problem with the battered woman stereotype is that it allows the legal system to continue considering the defendant's claim based on *who she is*, not on *what she did*" (1985, p. 149, italics in original). The "who she is" manifested by the use of a syndrome is a sufferer of a disability; that is, it can be argued that the use of the BWS "pathologizes" battered women, many of whom have reacted justifiably to their plight (Browne, 1987).

The Scientific Validity of the Battered Woman Syndrome

Criticisms have centered on the quality of the empirical basis for the cycle of violence theory and the application of the concept of learned helplessness. To test the theory of a cycle of violence, Walker and her colleagues conducted interviews with 400 "self-identified" battered women from six states; each was asked about four battering incidents: her first, the second, one of her worst, and the most recent. No control group was used. Faigman (1986); Faigman & Wright, (1997) listed the following as among the flaws of this study:

1. The interview technique permitted the subjects to guess easily the hypotheses of the study.
2. Interviewers knew the "correct" answer.
3. Interviewers did not record the subjects' answers, only their interpretations of the subjects' answers.
4. The research did not give any time frame to the cycle; it could be a few minutes, several hours, or many weeks.
5. As noted earlier in this chapter, in only 65% of the cases was there evidence of a tension-building phase prior to the battering; in only 58% of the cases was there evidence of loving contrition afterward (Walker, 1984b, pp. 96–97). It is not clear from the report how many women reported all three phases of the cycle.

With regard to learned helplessness, scholars (cf. Schuller & Vidmar, 1992) have questioned the application of Martin Seligman's (1975; Seligman & Maier, 1967) original theory and research on dogs to battered women. Seligman's dogs were rendered helpless and immobile by receiving noncontingent electric shocks; therefore, "one would predict that if battered women suffered from learned helplessness they would not assert control over their environment; certainly, one would not predict such a positive assertion of control as killing the batterer" (Faigman & Wright, 1997, p. 79).

THE RAPE TRAUMA SYNDROME

A young woman—a student at a college in the Midwest—leaves a private club with a man whom she has met only one-and-one-half hours and two drinks earlier. After accompanying him to his apartment, the woman is forced to engage in sexual intercourse and oral sodomy. Because she resists, she is threatened with death unless she complies. After returning to her home, she informs the police, and she is taken to a hospital. A laceration is found near the opening of her vagina, but no other bruises or marks are noted (Bristow, 1984).

The woman decides to press charges against her attacker. He refuses to plead guilty; a jury trial is held, and he is convicted of rape and aggravated sodomy. In the view of many experts, this is the type of case that often is not prosecuted or, if it is, the jury may conclude that not enough evidence exists to convict the defendant. In the opinion of one observer (Bristow, 1984), what made the difference in the outcome in this case was the testimony of an expert witness, psychiatrist Herbert Modlin, that the woman suffered from the rape trauma syndrome.

What Is the Rape Trauma Syndrome?

As described earlier, a *syndrome* is defined as a set of symptoms that may exist together, such that they may be considered to imply a disorder or disease. Not all the symptoms have to exist in every subject, and, in fact, the criteria for how many must be present are unclear.

More than 20 years ago, a psychiatric nurse and a sociologist, Ann Wolbert Burgess and Lynda Lytle Holmstrom (1974), coined the term **rape trauma syndrome (RTS)** to describe the collection of responses reported by 92 women who had been raped or subjected to other sexual abuses. Each of these survivors was interviewed within 30 minutes of her admission to a hospital and reinterviewed a month later. Burgess and Holmstrom were struck by the fact that a variety of sources—self-reports by those raped, descriptions by psychotherapists and trained social-service workers, and reactions by friends and family of those who had been attacked—showed great uniformity of responses. Some typical self-descriptions of those who survived a rape are reported in Box 7-4. (Because the vast majority of those raped are women, the clinical and empirical literature has focused on their reactions, and much less information is available on male survivors; Koss & Harvey, 1991.)

It should be noted that not all the survivors suffer from the same severity of symptoms. In support of this finding, Koss and Harvey (1991) used an ecological model of response to having been raped that emphasized that a variety of personal, event, and environmental factors could influence the recovery from a sexual assault. They wrote:

> Person variables of particular relevance include the age and developmental stage of the victim; her or his relationship to the offender; the ability of the victim to identify and make use of available social support; and the meaning that is assigned to the traumatic event by the victim, by family and friends, and by others including police, medical personnel, and victim advocates with whom the victim has had contact in the immediate aftermath of trauma. Relevant event variables include the frequency, the severity, and the duration of the traumatic event(s) and the degree of physical violence, personal violation, and life-threat endured by the victim. Environmental variables involve the setting where the victimization occurred, including home, school, workplace, or street. Other

BOX 7-4
Self-Descriptions of the Reactions of Rape Survivors

Each person who has been raped has a different story to tell, but they all share reactions of personal intrusion and lifelong impact. Each has to come to terms with being assaulted; here are some reactions:

■ "Early on, I realized the way to make the pain less was to separate my mind from my body and not permit myself to feel" (quoted by Kraske, 1986, p. 8A).

■ "I can recall many landmarks in my recovery, beginning with the moment I picked myself up off the kitchen floor and got myself to a hospital. There was the first night, weeks after the attack, when I didn't wake up crying or screaming. I remember the first time I said to someone—outside of my close friends and family who knew me when the assault occurred—'I was raped.' And the first time I disclosed 'my secret' to a man with whom I was beginning a relationship" (Kaminker, 1992, p. 16).

■ "For a long time I thought I could deal with my anger and hostility on my own. But I couldn't. I denied that it had affected me, and yet I was so frantic on the inside with other people: I needed to be constantly reassured. It wasn't until I started seeing myself self-destructing that I realized I needed help. To realize how angry I was and to ask for help—those were the stepping stones. There's a part of me that wants to be stoic and very strong. I had to realize that the attack wasn't directed at me, as Kelly. It was random. I was at the wrong place at the wrong time. That was the first step toward getting rid of all those hostile feelings I had about it. Still, when you're a victim of a violent crime—when somebody has taken control over your life, if only for a moment—I don't think you ever fully recover" (actress Kelly McGillis, quoted by Yakir, 1991, p. 5).

Source: Blackman, 1986, pp. 236–237.

environmental variables are the degree of safety and control that are afforded to victims post-trauma; prevailing community attitudes and values about sexual assault; and the availability, quality, accessibility, and diversity of victim care and victim advocacy services. (p. 45)

A middle-class college student who has been raised in a family that values daughters as much as sons and who is well-informed about rape and able to avail herself of the supportive resources of an active feminist community will respond to sexual assault quite differently than will a teenage girl whose pre-rape beliefs were basically victim blaming and whose key support figures continue to believe that "an unwilling woman can't really be raped." Similarly, individuals who experience violence and abuse in isolation from others and who feel obliged to recover from their experience in continued isolation will adjust differently over time than will those individuals whose suffering has been shared and/or those who have access to and are able to make use of helpful support figures.

Burgess and Holmstrom (1974) divided the rape trauma syndrome into two phases, an **acute crisis phase** and a **long-term reactions phase.** The first phase may contain reactions that last for days or weeks, and these are likely to be quite severe. They can affect all aspects of the survivor's life, including physical, psychological, social, and sexual aspects. The second phase is a more reconstructive one and includes survivors' coming to terms with their reactions and attempting to deal with the hurt and sadness in an effective way.

Phase I: Acute Crisis Phase

Initiated immediately after the act, the acute crisis phase is one of much disorganization in the survivor's lifestyle; it is often described by survivors as a state of shock, in which they report that everything has fallen apart inside. Many reexperience the attack over and over again in their minds. Even sleep, when it finally comes,

does not reenergize; instead, it is a vehicle for nightmares about the rape. Those raped in their own beds are particularly affected by insomnia (Burge, 1988).

When victims were asked to complete a checklist of their reactions only 2 or 3 hours after having been raped, interviewers found high degrees of similarity in response: 96% reported feeling scared, a similar percentage were anxious or worried, and 92% said they were terrified and confused (Veronen, Kilpatrick, & Resick, 1979). "Thoughts were racing through my mind," said more than 80% of those who had been attacked.

Cognitive accounts of anxiety were not the only frequent reactions; physiological exemplars of fear or anxiety often included:

- shaking or trembling (reported by 96% of respondents)
- a racing heart (80%)
- pain (72%)
- tight muscles (68%)
- rapid breathing (64%)
- numbness (60%).

Although these manifestations of fear and anxiety are the most frequent, a number of other consequences appear. Nearly one half of survivors scored as moderately or severely depressed on the Beck Depression Inventory (Frank & Stewart, 1984). One study reported suicide attempts by 19% of a community sample of women who had been raped (Kilpatrick, Best, Veronen, Amick, Villeponteaux, & Ruff, 1985). The person's previous sense of invulnerability dissipates in a decrease of self-esteem. Allison and Wrightsman (1993), in reviewing reports, classified these phase-one reactions as follows:

1. *Denial, shock, and disbelief:* "This couldn't have happened *to me*" was a common response. One victim, later recounting her thoughts during the attack, said, "Thoughts pounded through my head as I tried to understand what was happening. Was this a joke? Was this someone I know being cruel? It couldn't be real?" (Barr, 1979, p. 18). Survivors may question

their family and friends about how the rape could have happened.

2. *Disruption:* Changes in sleeping and eating patterns are typical. To varying degrees, survivors may display personality disorganization (Bassuk, 1980). Some may appear to be confused and disoriented while others do not exhibit such easily observable behavioral symptoms, but the latter type may be dazed and numb, and hence unresponsive to their environment.

3. *Guilt, hostility, and blame:* When learning that a friend has been raped, others may react by **blaming the victim,** or by assuming that the rape could have been avoided or otherwise attributing responsibility for having been raped to the person who was raped. Psychoanalytic theory unfortunately proposed that the essence of femininity included masochism, and the belief persists that women not only invite, but enjoy, sexual aggression (Bond & Mosher, 1986). Thus, it is not surprising that victims, too, respond with guilt and self-blame.

Janoff-Bulman (1979) suggested that a **self-blaming response** may be the second most frequent one after fear. "If only I had locked that window" or "If only I had taken an earlier bus home" are examples of reactions in which the survivors blame their own actions for the rape, or at least imply that different behaviors on their part could have avoided it. A distinction has been made between this type of self-blame, behavioral self-blame, and a characterological self-blame, which refers to attributions by the survivor to stable and uncontrollable aspects of the self, such as her personality (Frazier, 1990; Janoff-Bulman, 1979). In some victims, self-blame can be so strong that they believe the rape was their fault or that the man cared for them. Cases are reported of survivors who even married the men who raped them (Warshaw, 1988).

Other survivors may direct their aggression and blame at men in general, or at society for permitting sexual assaults to occur. Meyer and Taylor (1986) reported that 11% of rape victims reacted in this manner, by agreeing to statements like "Men have too little respect for women" or "There is never a policeman around when you need him." In this sample of survivors, only a little more than half (56%) assigned blame to the rapist.

4. *Regression to a state of helplessness or dependency:* People who have been raped often report the feeling that they no longer are independent individuals. A sense of autonomy or competence is replaced with one of self-doubt. Survivors are overwhelmed with feelings that they no longer have control over their lives and what happens to them. They have to rely on those close to them to make even the most insignificant decisions. One told Warshaw (1988): "Deciding what to wear in the morning was enough to make me panic and cry uncontrollably" (p. 54).

5. *Distorted perceptions:* Distrust and pessimism—even paranoia—are frequent reactions to being the recipient of a sexual assault. The world becomes a scary place in which to live; in one survey, 41% of those college students who were acquaintance-rape survivors believed that they would be raped again (Koss, 1988).

Phase II: Long-Term Reactions

In the second phase of the rape trauma syndrome, survivors face the task of restoring order to their lives and reestablishing a sense of equilibrium and the feeling of mastery over their world (Burgess & Holmstrom, 1985). The task is not an easy one; if, indeed, completion of the task occurs, it usually takes anywhere from a few months to years. Most of the improvement occurs somewhere between 1 and 3 months after the rape (Kilpatrick, Resick, & Veronen, 1981), but only 20% to 25% of survivors reported no symptoms one year after the attack. Burgess and Holmstrom (1985) reported that

25% of the women they studied had not significantly recovered several years after the rape. Regression can occur, with some reporting being worse on some measures a year after the rape, compared to 6 months afterward. Among the responses that may reoccur are specific anxieties; guilt and shame; catastrophic fantasies; feelings of dirtiness, helplessness, or isolation; and physical symptoms (Forman, 1980).

Thus, often life activities are resumed, but they are "undertaken superficially or mechanically" (Koss & Harvey, 1991, p. 54). One of the challenging quests during this phase is for survivors to understand what has happened to them and what they are feeling as a process of restoration moves forward (Bard & Sangrey, 1979). Their cognitive development may be impeded by being "constantly haunted" by vivid, traumatic memories (Neiderland, 1982, p. 414). One survivor reported, "I can't stop crying . . . and sometimes I feel a little bit overwhelmed. All these things flashing, all these memories" (quoted by Roth & Lebowitz, 1988, p. 90). It is not uncommon to experience contradictory feelings: fear, sadness, guilt, and anger all at the same time. A temptation is to assume "once a victim, always a victim." Four months after having been raped, a woman wrote, "I am so sick of being a 'rape victim.' I want to be me again" (Barr, 1979, p. 105). Following a cognitive explanation, Koss and Harvey (1991) noted a change of schema, or organizing structure, as the rape led to shifts in beliefs about trust, safety, and intimacy.

Allison and Wrightsman (1993) described the following as among the major symptoms of this second phase:

1. *Phobias:* A **phobia** is an irrational fear, the possession of which interferes with affective adaptation to one's environment. A one-year follow-up of women who had been raped found frequent reports that they were still expressing phobias and other manifestations of fear and anxiety (Kilpatrick et al., 1981). A rape can be viewed as a **classical conditioning stimulus,** and thus anything associated with the rape will come to be feared (Kilpatrick et al., 1981). The phenomenon of *stimulus generalization* means that if a knife was used in the attack, the survivor may develop a negative reaction to all types of knives. Recipients of sexual assaults may become afraid of being alone or of going out at night.

As Allison and Wrightsman observed:

These fears may force the victim into what seems to be a no-win situation. If she stays home alone, she is afraid. If she goes out, she is also afraid. Many victims leave the lights on in their homes 24 hours a day. Clearly the nature of the conditional associations to the rape leads victims to alter their lives in many ways. (1993, p. 156)

2. *Disturbances in general functioning:* Carrying out routine aspects of life is often a challenge during the second phase. Changes in eating patterns and sleeping patterns remain a problem. For some, the quality of intimate relationships may deteriorate, as the survivor restricts opportunities to take advantage of what previously were seen as positive experiences. One survivor wrote:

Jon and I had known for months that he would have to make a business trip to California in December. Originally, before things had changed, we had all planned to go. I loved California, I wanted to go away with Jon, I didn't want to be left alone, but as the trip approached we had to face the reality. . . . I didn't think I could leave the little security I found in my house, for strange motels. Camping was out of the question. We gave up the idea and I tried to think about how I would survive a week without Jon. (Barr, 1979, p. 83)

3. *Sexual problems:* Rape has a strong negative effect on the survivor's sexual life. But several studies concluded that the difference

between those women who had been raped and a comparable group who had not was not the *frequency* of sexual activities but, rather, the subjective quality of such experiences (Feldman-Summers, Gordon, & Meagher, 1979; Orlando & Koss, 1983). Rape survivors reported that they did not enjoy sex with their partner as much as they had before they were raped, and this level of satisfaction was not as high as that of the control group for almost every type of intimate relationship. The only exceptions were of two types: those activities considered primarily as affectional rather than sexual (such as hand-holding or hugging) and masturbation; frequency and satisfaction for both of these types of activities were unaffected by the rape. But rape survivors reported less desire to engage in sexual activity (Becker, Skinner, Abel, Axelrod, & Treacy, 1984).

4. *Changes in lifestyle:* Some survivors of a sexual assault may restructure their activities and change their jobs and their appearance (Warshaw, 1988). Changing their phone numbers is typical. Moving to another residence or even another city is not unusual.

The Relationship of RTS to PTSD

A number of researchers have pointed to many possible parallels between the rape trauma syndrome and post-traumatic stress disorder, or PTSD (Follingstad, 1994a). The *DSM-III-R* first recognized the presence of a psychological disorder that was a direct result of a stressful event; this disorder, termed *post-traumatic stress disorder,* was defined as "the development of characteristic symptoms following a psychologically distressing event that is outside the range of usual human experience" (American Psychiatric Association, 1987, p. 247). The *DSM-III-R* further suggested that PTSD is "apparently more severe and longer lasting when the stressor is of human design" than if it were a disaster of nature or war combat (1987, p. 248). The major symptoms used to demonstrate the presence of PTSD are

(a) a repeated experiencing of the traumatic event (for example, intrusive thoughts or recurrent nightmares) or, in contrast, an avoidance of those situations, ideas, and feelings that were related to the rape, and (b) a **psychic numbing** or reduced responsiveness to the environment.

In addition to these primary symptoms, the *DSM-III-R* diagnosis specified that a person must be experiencing at least two of the following:

1. Difficulty falling or staying asleep.
2. Irritability or outbursts of anger.
3. Difficulty concentrating.
4. Hypervigilance.
5. Exaggerated startle response.
6. Physiological reactivity upon exposure to events that symbolize or resemble an aspect of the traumatic event (American Psychiatric Association, 1987).

Several of these symptoms were amplified or revised in the fourth edition of the *DSM.*

Several researchers have documented that PTSD is present in survivors of rape, and some have concluded that survivors of rape are the largest single group of PTSD sufferers (Foa, Olasov, & Steketee, 1987, cited by Koss & Harvey, 1991; Steketee & Foa, 1987). Horowitz, Wilner, and Alvarez (1979) developed the Impact of Event Scale (IES) to measure the first primary symptom associated with PTSD. Later, Kilpatrick and Veronen (1984) administered this scale to survivors whose rapes had occurred earlier (either 6 to 21 days before, 3 months, 6 months, 1 year, 2 years, or 3 years before). Regardless of the length of time since the rape, most survivors reported experiencing aspects of both primary symptoms. With regard to the second symptom, the numbed responsiveness and reduced involvement with the environment, Kilpatrick et al. (1981) found in a longitudinal study that fear stemming from having been raped caused survivors to restrict their daily activities and lifestyles dramatically.

With respect to the other six PTSD criteria just listed, several studies identified some of or all these symptoms in specific survivors of rape (Burgess & Holmstrom, 1985; Kilpatrick, Veronen, & Best, 1985). More frequently, the symptoms are avoidance behaviors, hypersensitivity, difficulties in maintaining concentration, and intensification of symptoms whenever exposed to rape-related cues.

WHAT CAN A PSYCHOLOGIST DO?

When a person reports having been raped and becomes a witness in a criminal trial against her or his alleged attacker, one task for a forensic clinical psychologist is an assessment of the survivor's claims and responses. Later, at the trial, a forensic psychologist can be called on to testify about the presence of the rape trauma syndrome in order to support the survivor's claim of rape, especially if there is no corroborating evidence to support the claim (Follingstad, 1994a). These roles are described in the next sections.

Assessment

Follingstad (1994a) has identified a number of activities for the psychologist in this role:

1. Document the survivor's level of psychological, social, and physical functioning both before and after the sexual assault.
2. Assess the survivor's changes in identity, including loss of self-esteem and dignity, increased difficulty in decision making, and changes in feeling about her appearance.
3. Interview the survivor and administer self-report measures to determine the presence of phobias as well as generalized and specific fears.
4. Determine social adjustment, level of sexual functioning, and coping mechanisms, and identify other stressors around the time of the rape.
5. Interview others (family members, friends, roommates, spouse or significant other) to corroborate the survivor's report, as well as obtaining their evaluations of the survivor's truth telling.

6. Determine if the survivor has experienced previous sexual assaults.

Psychologists need to exercise great care in the way they question rape survivors. Dean Kilpatrick (1983) urged that the psychologist not be judgmental and that an effort be made to normalize the experience. That is, recognize that survivors often are reluctant to disclose or describe the assault and give them support when interviewing them. Suggested introductory statements include: "Some things happen to many women that are not pleasant kinds of sex."

A number of rating scales and self-report measures are available to document the victim's level of trauma. Follingstad (1994a) and Koss and Harvey (1991) have described the following:

1. Sexual Assault Symptom Scale (Ruch, Gartrell, Amedeo, & Coyne, 1991): a 32-item self-report scale, administered to the survivor as soon as possible after the rape. Measures four factors, including Disclosure Shame, Safety Fears, Depression, and Self-Blame. A difficulty is that many survivors are unable to complete the scale because of their emotional state, exhaustion, or intoxication.
2. Clinical Trauma Assessment (Ruch, Gartrell, Ramelli, & Coyne, 1991): a rating scale, completed by the clinical psychologist; useful in assessing the severity of the trauma. The survivor first participates in a structured interview. Then, the psychologist rates her or him on each of 16 specific trauma symptoms; examples include depression, tension/rigidity, and loss of trust in people. A factor analysis revealed three mean factors, labeled as Controlled Emotional Trauma Style, Cognitive Trauma, and Expressed Emotional Trauma Style.
3. Rape Trauma Syndrome Rating Scale (DiVasto, 1985): a scale designed to assess the severity of eight symptoms of the trauma of sexual assault; ratings are done by the interviewers, after they ask open-ended questions about each symptom (e.g., "Has your appetite changed in any way?"). The scale distinguishes between survivors and a

control group of women who had not been raped.

4. Impact of Event Scale, or IES (Horowitz, Wilner, & Alvarez, 1979): a 15-item self-report scale, separated into two subscales, designed especially to measure symptoms of intrusion and avoidance. Respondents think of the last week and rate the items according to how much trouble they have had. The IES was able to detect changes in distress in rape survivors after treatment (Kilpatrick & Amick, 1985).

Also, a number of clinical instruments are available to assess PTSD, including scales developed from the MMPI; these are reviewed by Wilson and Keane (1997).

Testimony as an Expert Witness

One justification for the testimony of a psychologist as an expert witness in a rape trial is that jurors do not fully understand the nature of rape; they may misinterpret the reactions of the survivor, and they may believe a number of **rape myths,** or incorrect assumptions about the causes and consequences of rape. Although a number of specific myths abound, they may take three general forms: (a) Women cannot be raped against their will; (b) women secretly wish to be raped; and (c) most accusations of rape are faked (Brownmiller, 1975). Specific knowledge about the rape trauma syndrome is often lacking. A survey about rape and post-traumatic stress disorder, completed by laypersons and by psychologists, found that the laypersons were not well informed on many relevant issues (Frazier & Borgida, 1988).

Consider a typical set of circumstances: A woman reports to the police that she has been raped and identifies her attacker. The district attorney concludes that enough evidence exists to hold a trial. The defendant's position is that sexual intercourse occurred between the two parties, but it was consensual. This set of events is fairly typical; most rapes are acquaintance rapes, not rapes by strangers. Thus, when the case goes

to trial, the jury essentially is faced with answering this question: "Who do you believe?"

Given such circumstances, a forensic psychologist as an expert witness may be helpful to the prosecution with regard to several issues (Block, 1990).

On the Issue of Consent or Lack of Consent

Is a complainant's behavior consistent with having been raped? Faigman, Kaye, Saks, and Sanders (1997) concluded that "by far the most accepted use of RTS in rape prosecutions" was to demonstrate that the alleged victim's behavior was consistent with that of victims in general" (1997, p. 406). A number of courts have permitted psychologists and other mental health professionals to testify about trauma in the survivor as evidence of a lack of consent, or to refute defense claims that the alleged victim's behavior was inconsistent with that of someone who had been raped. One of the first such cases in which admissibility was granted was *State v. Marks* (1982). The defendant, Marks, met a woman at a bar and persuaded her to return to his home where—she later alleged—he drugged her, raped her, and forced her to have oral sex with him. The prosecution introduced the expert testimony of a forensic psychologist who had examined the survivor 2 weeks after the encounter and concluded "that she was suffering from the PTSD known as rape trauma syndrome" (*State v. Marks,* 1982, p. 1299). The defendant was convicted.

On Questions About the Behavior of the Alleged Victim

As noted earlier, some jurors may believe myths or have incorrect assumptions about the nature of rape and survivors of rape. Survivors may delay in reporting the attack; when they testify, they may make inconsistent statements or reflect a lack of memory. The defense attorney may use these behaviors to attack the credibility of the alleged victim, and hence the testimony of a psychologist about the presence of the rape trauma syndrome in the witness may educate the jury about the real reactions and feelings of rape survivors as well as disabusing them of misconceptions (Block, 1990). Thus, here, the expert would testify as a rebuttal witness, after the survivor's credibility has been challenged, either on cross-examination or during the defense's direct examination (McCord, 1985).

In a Civil Suit to Support a Claim of Damages

On occasion, a survivor may sue an alleged attacker in a civil action to recover damages, or a third party may be sued for failure to provide protection. A psychologist's testimony may be introduced to support the claim; for instance, in *Alphonso v. Charity Hospital of Louisiana at New Orleans* (1982), the court considered whether $50,000 was an adequate amount of damages for the negligence of the hospital that allowed a mental patient to be raped by another patient. A psychologist found that the plaintiff was suffering from a post-traumatic stress disorder and testified in support of her claim of severe emotional injuries.

As a Defense for Culpable Behavior by a Rape Survivor

What if a woman feared for her life when she later encountered the man who had raped her, and thus attempted to murder him? In the case of *People v. Mathews* (1979), this occurred a month after the rape. At her trial, the defendant's claim that she was suffering from rape trauma syndrome was supported by expert testimony, and she was acquitted of the charge of attempted murder.

ADMISSIBILITY OF PSYCHOLOGICAL TESTIMONY ON RTS

In not all cases has the testimony about the common aftereffects of rape been admitted. When it has been admitted at trial but later challenged, appellate courts have sometimes concluded that the rape trauma syndrome is unreliable, prejudicial, or unhelpful to the jury (Block, 1990). That is, these particular courts concluded that (a) psychologists cannot accurately determine whether a rape occurred, (b) the testimony would improperly bolster the testimony against the defendant, and (c) the testimony is not beyond the common knowledge of the jury.

Some of these criticisms have also been leveled against the admissibility of evidence about the battered woman syndrome as discussed earlier, but testimony about the rape trauma syndrome is different in that it is used—by the prosecution—to show that the behavior (i.e., the rape) actually occurred. Thus, to admit such evidence can mean "the expert is essentially corroborating the complainant's claims and is therefore offering an opinion on the woman's testimony" (Follingstad, 1994a, p. 6). Judges are protective of the jury's right to be the fact finder regarding the credibility of any witness. Critics also have noted that using the term *rape* in testimony about the rape trauma syndrome implies that a rape has occurred, even if the psychologist does not directly testify that it did (Follingstad, 1994a).

In summary, once the courts began to consider the rape trauma syndrome in the early 1980s, they became quite inconsistent in decisions whether to admit expert testimony (Borgida, Frazier, & Swim, 1987; Faigman et al., 1997; Frazier & Borgida, 1985). As noted earlier, in *State v. Marks* (1982), the decision was favorable to psychologists, concluding that (a) rape trauma syndrome was a generally accepted reaction to a rape, (b) testimony about rape trauma syndrome is relevant when the defendant claims that the sexual activity was consensual, and (c) testimony about rape trauma syndrome does not invade the province of the jury. Sometimes a master's degree and extensive clinical experience are sufficient (*State v. McCoy*, 1988), but a number of decisions have gone the other way. For example, the Kansas Supreme Court held that only psychiatrists could testify about a diagnosis of RTS or PTSD (*State v. Willis*, 1993).

Sometimes the courts have placed limits on the use of RTS testimony. In the case of *People v. Bledsoe* (1984), the defendant used the defense of consent. A rape counselor who had treated the survivor testified that she exhibited a number of emotional symptoms after the rape and that these qualified as the rape trauma syndrome. But the court ruled that, because the concept of rape trauma syndrome was not designed to determine whether, in a legal sense, a rape had actually occurred, testimony from an expert witness was inadmissible if the intention was to prove that a rape occurred. Similarly, in the case of *State v. McCoy* (1988), the court responded to expert testimony with the following:

> We . . . must draw a distinction between an expert's testimony that an alleged victim exhibits post-rape behavior consistent with rape trauma syndrome and expert opinion that bolsters the credibility of the alleged victim by indicating that she was indeed raped. (p. 737)

Box 7-5 presents another case in which such testimony was rejected.

The *purpose* of the testimony is crucial with regard to decisions about its admissibility. A recent review concluded that "in every case in which the testimony has been found to be scientifically unreliable, it is because the court has ruled that the testimony cannot reliably determine, or *prove*, that a rape occurred. . . . In contrast, courts that have found the testimony reliable focus on whether RTS is a generally accepted response to sexual assault" (Faigman et al., 1997, p. 408, italics in original).

The U.S. Supreme Court's ruling in the case of *Daubert v. Merrell Dow Pharmaceuticals, Inc.* (1993) has implications for the admission of testimony about rape trauma, just as it does for the battered woman syndrome and other psychologically related concepts and evidence. The Daubert requirement that scientific evidence, in order to be admitted, must meet standards of reliability may reduce the willingness of some trial judges to admit testimony about the exis-

---

BOX 7-5
The Case of *State v. Saldana* (1982)

An early but important case, *State v. Saldana* reflects one position on the admissibility of psychological testimony about the rape trauma syndrome. The defendant in this Minnesota case, charged with first-degree "criminal sexual conduct," claimed that the complainant had consented to sexual intercourse. To rebut this claim, the prosecuting attorney called a rape counselor as an expert witness. Not only did the expert describe the usual behavior of rape victims, but she also testified that she definitely believed the woman had been raped and that she did not believe the rape was a fantasy.

After the defendant was convicted, he appealed, and the Minnesota state appellate court, in a thorough discussion of the issues, considered the following criteria:

- *Scientific status:* The court held that the evidence was not established to a sufficient degree in the medical or psychiatric community for it to be admitted. The court concluded that "rape trauma syndrome is not a fact-finding tool, but a therapeutic tool useful in counseling" (*State v. Saldana*, 1982, p. 230).

- *Helpfulness to the jury:* The court ruled that even if such evidence were reliable, it would not be helpful to the jury because it was not "the type of scientific test that accurately and reliably determines whether a rape occurred" (*State v. Saldana*, 1982, p. 229). Furthermore, the court held that "evidence concerning how some, or even most, people react to rape is not helpful to the jury; rather, the jury must decide each case on the basis of the facts at hand" (quoted by Frazier & Borgida, 1985, p. 986).

- *Prejudicial effects:* The statement that the expert believed the complainant had been raped was seen as unfairly prejudicial in that it involved making a legal conclusion. "Credibility judgments, such as testimony that the rape was not fantasized, are regarded as within the province of the jury and are allowed only in unusual circumstances (for example, in the case of a mentally retarded witness)" (quoted by Frazier & Borgida, 1985, p. 986).

The Saldana case was retried and the defendant acquitted.

tence of the rape trauma syndrome. However, many courts are not well informed about the current state of scientific knowledge on RTS (Frazier & Borgida, 1992). Even worse, some courts seem to be confused about the proper terminology; two examples are the following:

1. In *State v. Saldana* (1982), described in Box 7-5, the court concluded that RTS is "not the type of scientific test that accurately and reliably determines whether a rape has occurred" (p. 229).
2. In *State v. Alberico* (1993), the court concluded that "PTSD is generally accepted by psychologists and psychiatrists as a valid technique for evaluating patients with mental disorders" (p. 208).

But RTS is a general term for the aftereffects of rape, and PTSD is a diagnostic category; to refer to them as tests or techniques "is both inaccurate and misleading" (Faigman et al., 1997, p. 412).

As Frazier and Borgida (1992) noted, the term, *rape trauma syndrome* refers to a loose collection of symptoms; some critics have already argued that the term's generality removes any meaning (Lawrence, 1984). Furthermore, it is a term that may have several specific definitions. Their careful review of the scientific literature led Frazier and Borgida to conclude that the recent literature, which has used standardized assessment measures and carefully matched control groups, has established that "rape victims experience more depression, anxiety, fear, and social adjustment problems than women who have not been victimized . . .[and] that many victims experience PTSD symptoms following an assault" (1992, p. 301).

At the same time, experts need to be careful to limit their testimony to verifiable statements; sometimes the specific testimony by the expert is not an accurate reflection of the state of scientific knowledge. Expert witnesses have described symptoms that have not been documented empirically, and, on occasion, they have general-

ized findings from adults to children (Faigman et al., 1997). Frazier and Borgida (1992) also cited several examples of experts' claims that have not been found in research—for example, that it is "very common" for a victim to ask the rapist not to tell anyone about the rape. Boeschen, Sales, and Koss (1998) classified possible testimony into five levels; these levels are summarized in Box 7-6 and are a useful summary for the limits of testimony.

THE STATUS OF RESEARCH ON RTS

Given the sometimes misleading testimony and inconsistent court decisions, what is the current status of research on the rape trauma syndrome? Frazier and Borgida, in a section of the relevant chapter of Faigman et al.'s (1997) handbook on scientific evidence, provided a useful review of recent research. The two central questions are these: What symptoms do rape victims experience? Do rape victims differ in their set of symptoms from those who are not victims? The reviewers identified several symptoms, with the following conclusions:

1. *Depression:* As noted earlier, depression is one of the most commonly reported symptoms of rape victims. The review identified seven studies that compared depressive symptoms of groups of rape victims and nonvictims, with depression assessed through the highly regarded Beck Depression Inventory (see Groth-Marnat, 1990). All seven studies found the average scores of the rape victims to be significantly higher than those of the nonvictims, with scores for the victims being in the mild to moderately depressed range. Across studies, between 18% and 45% of the victims were moderately to severely depressed, while only 4% to 23% of the subjects in the nonvictim control groups were (Faigman et al., 1997).

BOX 7-6
The Levels of Testimony by an Expert Witness

Boeschen, Sales, and Koss (1998) proposed five levels of testimony, in evaluating the appropriateness of admitting scientific testimony on the trauma of having been raped.

Level 1: Testimony on specific behaviors of rape survivors that are described as "unusual" by the defense. "Testimony at this level is used by the victim's counsel in both criminal and civil trials to rebut the perpetrator's argument that a victim exhibited an unusual behavior following a rape" (Boeschen et al., 1998, p. 424). The courts generally have found this testimony helpful; it counteracts stereotypes held by some jurors, and empirical work has confirmed that such behaviors (delay in reporting a rape, failure to identify the attacker) are not that unusual.

Level 2: Testimony on the common reactions to rape and the general diagnostic criteria of RTS or PTSD. The expert describes common reactions; he or she has not examined the alleged victim and does not discuss the specific victim's behaviors. This type of testimony is generally considered to be appropriate, with the qualifier that the term *rape trauma syndrome* is sometimes excluded because of its prejudicial nature.

Level 3: Expert gives an opinion about the consistency of a victim's behavior or symptoms with RTS or PTSD. Boeschen and her colleagues noted: "This type of testimony is much more controversial than that of

Level 1 or 2 because it permits the expert to go beyond the general, educational information and apply it to a specific case" (1998, p. 426). Some courts have found it too prejudicial, but these authors believe that it is a valid use of expert testimony, since the psychologist "does not appear to unfairly comment on the victim's credibility" (p. 427).

Level 4: Testimony stating that the victim suffers from RTS or PTSD. The expert describes the complainant's symptoms and states that these meet the criteria for a diagnosis of PTSD, but the expert does not state that the complainant was raped. Some courts have permitted this level of testimony (an example is *State v. McQuillen,* 1984), noting that the defense is allowed to cross-examine this witness or provide its own expert witness. But resolution of the issue remains difficult, especially with RTS testimony. Any psychologist who is allowed to testify has the ethical obligation to state the limitations on the concepts he or she introduces.

Level 5: Expert opinion that goes beyond a diagnosis. At this level, the expert testifies that the victim is telling the truth and that she was raped. Almost all states refuse to admit this level of testimony; as noted in chapter 5 with regard to testimony on insanity, this is ultimate-opinion testimony that invades the role of the fact finder.

2. *Fear:* Self-report studies using the Veronen-Kilpatrick Modified Fear Survey (Veronen & Kilpatrick, 1980) found differences between victims and nonvictims up to one year after the rape. One study found that recent rape victims were more fearful than victims of other crimes. However, the duration of the fear was unclear, with some studies reporting differences several years after the rape, while other studies concluded that victims' fear had subsided by then.

3. *Anxiety:* Difficulties in concentrating and avoidance of certain situations because of anxiety were present more often in rape victims than in nonvictims, for at least a year after the rape. In one study, 82% of the rape victims met the criteria for a diagnosis of generalized anxiety disorder.

Despite the consistent findings for these specific symptoms, the question remains whether there is virtue or even validity to suggest the presence of a "syndrome." The next section offers a substitute for the use of RTS in expert testimony.

SUBSTITUTING PTSD FOR RTS

As we have seen, the concept of rape trauma syndrome was originally based on the commonly shared experiences of rape survivors interviewed in hospital emergency rooms; its original purpose was to aid psychotherapists in treatment. Some careful reviewers (cf. Frazier & Borgida, 1992) believe that the evidence is sufficient that certain reactions differentiate women who have been raped from those who have not. But is this strong enough to justify introduction of RTS testimony in the courtroom? The previous section reviewed the conflicting reactions by judges to its proposed admissibility, and the application of the Daubert standard may increase the judicial resistance.

Recently Boeschen, Sales, and Koss (1998) have proposed that the post-traumatic stress disorder be substituted for the rape trauma syndrome in the courtroom. PTSD has the following advantages:

1. It is the primary trauma-related diagnosis included in the *Diagnostic and Statistical Manual of Mental Disorders*. (The term *RTS* is not found in the current *DSM-IV* or in any earlier editions.)
2. As described earlier, a diagnosis of PTSD reflects six rather specific criteria, each with an understandable, operational definition.
3. The PTSD criteria reflect "the intense fear that many rape survivors experience, as well as the desire to avoid situations that are reminders of the rape experience" (Boeschen et al., 1998, p. 418).
4. A variety of tools are available to assess PTSD, including objective tests, structured diagnostic interviews, and trauma-specific self-report measures (Wilson & Keane, 1997).
5. The use of PTSD in the courtroom avoids employing the word *rape* in the diagnosis. As noted, some courts have considered admitting testimony on RTS as too prejudicial. For example, in the case of *State v. Horne* (1986), the court allowed the expert to provide a general description of the common responses of rape survivors but not a description of RTS because its language might lead jurors to conclude that the complainant must have been raped (Boeschen et al., 1998).

However, it should be noted that many of the reactions common to rape survivors—depression, anger, sexual dysfunction, and disruption of basic values—are not included in the PTSD criteria (Faigman et al., 1997). Some have suggested a "complex PTSD categorization" (Herman, 1992) that would create a consolidated diagnosis for those reacting to rape.

SUMMARY

In recent years, the extent and seriousness of domestic violence in the United States have been increasingly publicized. Useful typologies of men who abuse have been developed. Some psychologists have proposed that the responses of women who have been continually abused by their partners are consistent enough to qualify as a syndrome, called the *battered woman syndrome*. Among these reactions are learned helplessness, lowered self-esteem, loss of a feeling of invulnerability, a sense of diminished alternatives, and hypervigilance. Lenore Walker proposed that the interaction between the batterer and his partner goes through a set of observable phases—a tension-building phase, an acute battering incident, and then a contrite phase; she called this the *cycle of abuse* or *cycle of violence*.

Psychologists can play several roles when a battered woman reacts by killing her husband or lover. Assessment of the presence of the battered woman syndrome includes a comprehensive interview and the collection of medical records and court reports. At the trial, the forensic psychologist may be permitted to serve as an expert witness. Note that the battered woman syndrome is not a legal defense in and of itself; usually the woman's defense is either to claim that she acted out of self-defense or to claim insanity. The psychologist, at trial, can deal with many of the myths about battered women and their batterers and respond to prevalent concerns of jurors, such as "Why didn't she leave?" and "Why did she act when he was asleep?" However, results of empirical studies on the effectiveness of such expert testimony are inconsistent.

Criticisms of the use of the battered woman syndrome take two forms: first, that it portrays women as emotional, passive, and helpless, and second, that it lacks the proper theoretical and research background to justify its admissibility at trial.

The term *rape trauma syndrome* (RTS) was first developed more than 20 years ago to account for the relative uniformity of responses by survivors of rape. Burgess and Holmstrom divided the RTS into two phases, an acute crisis phase and a long-term reactions phase. The first phase included cognitive and physiological reactions, including denial, disruption of normal activities, guilt, and regression to a state of helplessness or dependency. The second phase dealt with restoration to a sense of equilibrium and mastery over the world, but many problems continued or reoccurred in this second phase.

Two roles for psychologists are salient with regard to the use of the rape trauma syndrome. First, the psychologist may assess the survivor's claims and responses. In doing so, the psychologist interviews the survivor and others and administers several self-report measures. Second, at the trial, the forensic psychologist might be called on to testify about the presence of the rape trauma syndrome in order to support the survivor's claims, especially if no corroborating evidence exists to support the claim and if the defendant counterclaims that consensual sexual intercourse occurred. Specifically, as an expert witness, the psychologist might testify about the presence of RTS, which is indicative of lack of consent, or, in a civil suit, the psychologist might testify to support a claim of damages.

Courts have disagreed on the admissibility of such testimony. Some courts have concluded that (a) psychologists cannot accurately determine whether a rape occurred, (b) the testimony would improperly bolster the testimony against the defendant, and (c) the testimony is not beyond the common knowledge of the jury.

Because of problems with the conceptualization of RTS, it has been suggested that, instead, psychologists testify about the applicability of the post-traumatic stress disorder, which overlaps some with RTS but contains more clearly defined criteria.

KEY TERMS

acute battering incident
acute crisis phase
battered woman defense
battered woman self-defense
battered woman syndrome
blaming the victim
classical conditioning stimulus
cognitive inconsistency
contrite phase
cycle of abuse
hypervigilance
imminent danger
insanity defense
learned helplessness
long-term reactions phase
phobia
post-traumatic stress disorder (PTSD)
Power and Control Wheel
psychic numbing
psychological self-defense
rape myths
rape trauma syndrome (RTS)
self-blaming response
self-defense
self-defense defense
syndrome
tension-building phase

INFOTRAC®
COLLEGE EDITION

InfoTrac College Edition is a FREE, powerful, online learning resource, consisting of full-text articles from thousands of journals and periodicals. With each new copy of *Forensic Psychology,* Second Edition, you receive 4 months of free access to the InfoTrac College Edition database. By doing a simple keyword search (try using the Key Terms in the list above), you can quickly generate a list of relevant articles from thousands of possibilities and can select articles to read, explore, and print for reference or further study.

InfoTrac College Edition's continuously updated collection of articles can be useful for doing reading and writing assignments that reach beyond the pages of this text!

SUGGESTED READINGS

Barnett, O. W., & LaViolette, A. D. (1993). *It could happen to anyone: Why battered women stay.* Thousand Oaks, CA: Sage.

The layperson's most frequent question is "Why doesn't she leave?" This book examines contemporary theories about why women remain in abusive relationships.

Boeschen, L. E., Sales, B. D., & Koss, M. P. (1998). Rape trauma experts in the courtroom. *Psychology, Public Policy, and Law, 4,* 414–432.

A recent review of the scientific legitimacy of using expert testimony on the rape trauma syndrome in the courtroom.

Brekke, N., & Borgida, E. (1988). Expert scientific testimony in rape trials: A social-cognitive analysis. *Journal of Personality and Social Psychology, 55,* 372–386.

Empirical studies on the limits of the impact of an expert witness testifying about RTS on jury deliberations and verdicts.

Browne, A. (1987). *When battered women kill.* New York: Free Press.

An analysis of the causes for the actions of 42 women charged with killing or seriously injuring their partners. Case studies are sensitively presented. Recommended.

Dutton, D. G. (1995). *The domestic assault of women: Psychological and criminal justice perspectives* (Rev. ed.). Vancouver, B.C., Canada: UBC Press.

A comprehensive examination of the causes and effects of spousal assault, with a detailed classification of types of violent men and an analysis of the dynamics of the victim–abuser relationship.

Ewing, C. P. (1987). *Battered women who kill: Psychological self-defense as legal justification.* Lexington, MA: Lexington Books.

A thorough review of the psychological plight of the battered woman, plus an exposition of the author's proposal of a defense of psychological self-defense.

Faigman, D. L., Kaye, D. H., Saks, M. J., & Sanders, J. (1997). *Modern scientific evidence: The law and science of expert testimony.* St. Paul, MN: West.

The best law school text on expert testimony, and worth reading by psychologists as well as judges and lawyers.

Frazier, P. A., & Borgida, E. (1992). Rape trauma syndrome: A review of case law and psychological research. *Law and Human Behavior, 16,* 293–311.

Organized around the legal issues of scientific reliability, helpfulness, and prejudicial impact, this review considers the psychological research findings relevant to each of these concerns.

Pekkanen, J. (1976). *Victims: An account of a rape.* New York: Popular Library.

Based on one case, this book traces a rape from the attack, through hospital procedures, the survivor's delayed reactions, the rapist's background, his trial, and the outcome of the case.

Walker, L. E. A. (1979). *The battered woman.* New York: Harper and Row.

A detailed analysis of the components of the battered woman syndrome and the cycle of violence, with examples from the author's interviews and case studies.

8

Child Sexual Abuse

THE MCMARTIN PRESCHOOL CASE

In the last 20 years, allegations have been made about the sexual abuse of children while they were at certain day care centers in the United States, Canada, and Europe. The first to gain wide publicity was the McMartin Preschool case in Manhattan Beach, California. Because a great deal is known about that case, and especially about the interviewing of the children, it will serve well as an illustration of the issues involved.

The Charges and the Trials

On August 12, 1983, the mother of a 2½-year-old boy at the school called the local police to tell them that she believed that her child had been molested by a teacher, Raymond Buckey. (Buckey also was the grandson of the school's 82-year-old founder, Virginia McMartin.) According to the child's mother, the child reported that he was forced to drink blood, he witnessed the head of a live baby being chopped off, and "Mr. Ray" was able to fly.

Shortly thereafter, the McMartin Beach police sent a letter to 200 parents, asking if their children had reported any incidents of molestation at the school. The letter indicated that the police investigation had discovered possible criminal acts including oral sex, sodomy, and fondling of genitals. Raymond Buckey was even named in the letter as a prime suspect.

As you would expect, receipt of the letter created panic in many of the parents; many sent their children for assessment to a social-service agency under contract with the prosecutor's office, the Children's Institute International (CII). Of the 400 children interviewed by CII staff, at least 350 were judged to have been abused. A grand jury subsequently indicted Raymond Buckey, his mother (Peggy McMartin Buckey), and five other teachers on charges of sexually abusing children. In June 1984 (almost a year after the initial charges), a preliminary hearing began; it lasted an incredible 17 months. After another year's delay, charges against five of the teachers

were dropped, but in April 1987, jury selection was begun for the trial of Raymond Buckey and his mother (*People v. Buckey*, 1990).

The jury reached its verdicts in January 1990, after the longest criminal trial in United States history. The Buckeys were acquitted on 52 of the counts; the jury was deadlocked on 13 other counts against Raymond Buckey. Five months later the state began a second trial against Raymond Buckey on those 13 counts. Mercifully, this second trial was a shorter one; in July 1990, the second jury announced its verdicts: Not guilty on all counts. An investigation that began with a single complaint in July 1983 was resolved almost 7 years later.

But not everyone was satisfied by the outcome. Prosecutors remained convinced that *someone* had sexually abused children who attended the McMartin Preschool. A number of the children appeared on talk shows to maintain steadfastly that they had been sexually abused. And some scholars and observers still believe that the claims in the McMartin case and similar cases, such as that of Margaret Kelly Michaels, are true (Faller, 1996; Manshel, 1990).

The Issue

As we know, the McMartin case is not the only one that, despite its resolution in the courts, has left participants in disagreement over the correctness of its outcome. Cases in many places, including North Carolina, New Jersey, Florida, Massachusetts, and Saskatchewan, Canada, have all dealt with claims of the abuse of children in day care centers; most of these cases, in contrast to the McMartin trial, led to convictions of school staff members or owners of the day care center. (Convictions in some of these cases, but not all, were overturned on appeal.)

Although this type of case receives national publicity, there is a second type of charge that is more frequent: the claim that a child has been sexually abused by a parent, another member of the family, or a family friend. What can forensic psychologists provide in the way of expertise in understanding both types of claims?

ROLES FOR PSYCHOLOGISTS

This chapter describes four roles for forensic psychologists that are specifically in response to claims that children have been sexually abused. Each of these is introduced in this section and then described in detail in the remaining sections of this chapter. Equally important, but more general, is the task of carrying out systematic research on the nature of sexual offenders. Particularly important is the assessment of future risk in such offenders; beginning with the state of Washington in 1991, a number of states have adopted laws that permit the state to confine sexual offenders after completion of their prison sentences if they are assessed to remain a threat. Such laws were upheld by the United States Supreme Court in *Kansas v. Hendricks* (1997). All sexual predators are not alike; Becker and Murphy (1998) have reviewed the backgrounds of such offenders and have concluded that there appears not to be a consensus on what causes them to become sexual offenders. Some clearly suffer from a **paraphilia,** a recognized mental disorder that involves sexual deviancy; recall (from chapter 5) that several expert witnesses concluded that Jeffrey Dahmer fit such a diagnosis. But other offenders do not demonstrate mental abnormalities other than their sexual preferences and behavior. Similarly, the likelihood of recidivism by sexual offenders remains a question difficult to answer with precision (see, e.g., Heilbrun, Nezu, Keeney, Chung, & Wasserman, 1998), though some work has been done in this area, and actuarial instruments have been developed to assist in prediction (see, e.g., Quinsey, Harris, Rice, & Cormier, 1998). The efficacy of treatment for sex offenders is not clear, either (see, e.g., Rice & Harris, 1997).

Evaluating the Child

Sometimes, in the midst of a contested child custody case, one of the child's parents may claim that the other parent abused the child. Or, as in the McMartin case's instigation, a parent may tell authorities of unusual activities at preschool. Evaluating claims, whatever their source, is an exceedingly difficult task; no one feels comfortable responding about acts that invaded their privacy, and young children are quite limited in their ability to express what happened or to separate truth from fantasy. Clinical psychologists and social workers have used **anatomically detailed dolls** and other materials in addition to interviews to assess the presence of abuse.

In the last two decades, a number of adults have come forward with claims that they were sexually abused while children (usually by the father or by both parents) and that they have repressed memories of this abuse until recently. The frequency of **repressed memories** or **recovered memories** of having been abused as a child remains a controversy that divides psychologists. The American Psychological Association, in an effort to bring its professional scrutiny to the issue, left the matter as unsettled as before, as Box 8-1 reflects.

Assessing Competency to Testify

If a conclusion is made by the authorities that sexual abuse did occur and charges are made, the child may be called on to testify at preliminary hearings and at a trial. Although the courts have their methods of determining the child's competency to testify, judges may consult with psychologists, who may use modifications of some of the procedures used in courts for adults.

Preparing the Child to Testify

Some children face trial, especially about abuse, with trepidation. (Other children may find that testifying is a source of catharsis or vindication.) The prosecuting attorney may ask a psychologist to assist in making the apprehensive child as comfortable as possible. On a broader front, several of the states have developed innovative procedures that try to mitigate the stress when a child testifies about sexual abuse. Psychologists can evaluate the strengths and limitations of

BOX 8-1

Do Repressed Memories Exist? The APA's Position

Because of the publicity and controversy over questions of the nature and frequency of repressed or recovered memories, the Council of Representatives of the American Psychological Association, in 1993, established a working group to review the relevant scientific literature and produce a report. This working group was composed of six APA members, with differing backgrounds and perspectives. The initial report of this Working Group on the Investigation of Memories of Childhood Abuse stated the following as the key points of agreement among its members:

■ Controversies regarding adult recollections should not be allowed to obscure the fact that child sexual abuse is a complex and pervasive problem in America that has historically gone unacknowledged.

■ Most people who were sexually abused as children remember all or part of what happened to them.

■ It is possible for memories of abuse that have been forgotten a long time to be remembered. The mechanism, or mechanisms, by which such delayed recall occurs is not currently well understood.

■ It is also possible to construct convincing pseudo memories for events that never occurred. The mechanism, or mechanisms, by which these pseudo memories occurs is not currently well understood.

■ There are gaps in our knowledge about the processes that lead to accurate and inaccurate recollections of childhood abuse (see Pezdek & Banks, 1996, pp. 371–372).

these innovations, with regard to their stated goal of reducing trauma.

Testifying as an Expert Witness

Each side could conceivably use a psychologist as an expert witness in a trial involving the sexual abuse of children. A prosecutor could employ a psychologist to testify about the legitimacy of the phenomenon of recovered memories, or, more generally, the validity of children's memories, to try to overcome the reluctance of many jurors to believe the testimony of children. The defense attorney could use a psychologist to testify about the problems of eyewitness accuracy and the **suggestibility** of children.

Each of these roles is described in subsequent sections of this chapter.

ASSESSING ALLEGATIONS BY THE CHILD

A parent reports that her son has told her that one of the teachers at his day care center has played with his penis and repeatedly inserted a thermometer in his rectum. As a part of the investigation, psychologists or social workers are asked to interview the child.

Interviewing Techniques

One of the temptations in interviewing young children is the use of **leading questions,** or questions that assume a particular answer. The dilemma is that, without the use of such questions, the child may be reluctant to respond at all, but the nature of the question may cause the child to answer in the suggested way, even if the answer does not reflect the child's real feelings or beliefs.

The interviewing procedures used by the staff of Children's Institute International in the McMartin Preschool case have been subjected to severe criticism by several psychologists and social workers (Ceci & Bruck, 1995; Mason, 1991), and the availability of the transcripts of these interviews (thanks to the Department of Psychology at McGill University) has permitted the identification of specific problems. Five questionable procedures have been identified by James M. Wood, Sena Garven, and their colleagues

(Wood, Schreiber, Martinez, McLaurin, Strok, Velarde, Garven, & Malpass, 1997; Garven, Wood, Malpass, & Shaw, 1998). These procedures include:

1. *The use of suggestive questions*
   This device is more than simply asking the child a set of leading questions. The technique of **suggestive questions** consists of "introducing new information into an interview when the child has not already provided that information in the same interview" (Garven, Wood, Malpass, & Shaw, 1998, p. 348). For example, a CII interviewer asked a McMartin preschooler, "Can you remember the naked pictures?" when no picture taking or nudity had been mentioned (quoted by Garven et al., 1998, p. 348). Suggestive questions reduce the accuracy level of children's reports (Ceci & Bruck, 1993); even the responses of adults are susceptible to being altered by such questions (Loftus, 1975).

2. *The implication of confirmation by other people*
   What Wood et al. (1997) called the technique of Other People involves telling the child that the interviewer has already obtained information from another child or children regarding the topic at hand. For example, as one interview began, the CII staff member told the child that "every single kid" in a class picture had already talked to her about a "whole bunch of yucky secrets" from the school (quoted by Garven et al., 1998, p. 348). Such actions create conformity pressures in the respondent, just as do similar police interrogation techniques, used with suspects and described in chapter 11. As in the preceding, the memory of adults as well as that of children can be substantially affected by the purported statements of another witness (Shaw, Garven, & Wood, 1997).

3. *Use of positive and negative consequences*
   Wood et al. (1997) noted frequent use of positive and negative reinforcement in the McMartin interviewing. The psychologists labeled the technique of giving or promising praise and other rewards as Positive Consequences; for example, after a series of suggestive questions led one child to agree that a teacher had photographed some children while they were naked, the interviewer responded, "Can I pat you on the head . . . look at what a good help you can be. You're going to help all those little children because you're so smart" (quoted by Garven et al., 1998, p. 349). The technique called Negative Consequences reflected criticism of a statement by a child or a general indication that the child's statement was inadequate or disappointing. Wood, Garven, and their colleagues found striking examples in the transcripts; for example, one child denied any wrongdoing by the McMartin staff, and the interviewer's response was, "Are you going to be stupid, or are you going to be smart and help us here?" (quoted by Garven et al., 1998, p. 349). Although these psychologists noted that the effects of positive or negative reinforcement on children's accuracy have not been explored in forensic settings, wide acceptance exists for their general impact.

4. *Repetitious questioning*
   Imagine you are a child and the interviewer keeps asking you a question you have unambiguously answered a few minutes earlier. Would this procedure cause you to change your answer? Wood and his colleagues called this the Asked-and-Answered procedure; research generally has found that children will change their answers to repeated forced-choice questions but not to repeated open-ended questions; the interpretation is that children assume that their first answer to a forced-choice question was incorrect and so they change it to please the interviewer (Siegal, Waters, & Dinwiddy, 1988).

5. *Inviting speculation*
   The procedure that Wood et al. (1997) called Inviting Speculation asked the child to "pretend" or "figure something out" and was used by interviewers when other procedures

had failed to produce confirmations of wrongdoing. (Again, it is remarkably similar to a technique used by police detectives with suspects, when they ask the suspects to role play or answer a question, such as, "Assume you did kill her—how *would* you have done it?") In effect, this procedure lowered the threshold for producing incriminating statements that later could be "confirmed" by the use of some of the earlier-described procedures, especially positive reinforcement and repeated questioning.

Garven, Wood, Malpass, and Shaw (1998) investigated the impact of these techniques in a field experiment, using children ages 3 to 6. While at their day care center, the children had a visit from a storyteller; they were interviewed about these happenings a week later. Even though the interview was brief (2 to 5 minutes long), responses of many of the children were influenced by the use of reinforcement and social influence techniques. In fact, close to 60% of the children's responses reflected errors because of these interview techniques. Garven et al. concluded that those techniques that effectively elicit false statements from children and adults "fall into four overlapping but distinguishable categories, represented by the acronym SIRR: (a) suggestive questions, (b) social influence, (c) reinforcement, and (d) removal from direct experience" (1998, p. 355). The last of these refers to such procedures as Inviting Speculation (just described) and the interviewer's use of a puppet and a "pretend" instruction to question the child. The latter may provide the child an "escape hatch" when pressured to make false allegations; that is, the child can comply with the interviewer's insistence and still feel that he or she did not tell a lie.

Using the Criterion-Based Content Analysis Technique

Often the purpose of the interview appears to be to get the child to provide more about the abuse, which the interviewer assumes to have happened. We need to step back and acknowledge that allegations can be either truthful or entirely manufactured (or something in between). Do psychologists have procedures to distinguish between children's truthful statements and fanciful or false ones?

The **criterion-based content analysis (CBCA) technique** was developed as a clinical procedure in Germany to distinguish between children's truthful and fabricated allegations (Undeutsch, 1982, 1984, 1989). The CBCA is one component of a more comprehensive procedure, called **statement validity assessment (SVA),** that consists of three parts: a structured interview with the child witness, the CBCA, and the application of the Statement Validity Checklist that assesses other characteristics of the interview process, the witness, and the investigation (Raskin & Esplin, 1991). A description of these follows:

> The structured interview portion consists of an extensive interview with the alleged child victim, with the use of leading questions. The purpose of this portion of the SVA is to create rapport and assess the child's cognitive, behavioral, and social skills. The second portion of the SVA consists of the CBCA. In this portion, a set of criteria is applied to the verbal content of the child's statement and used to provide an estimate of the statement's veracity. The presence of a criterion is an indication that the child is telling the truth. During this analysis, it may be important to consider the child's age, experience, and skill level when applying the criteria (e.g., younger children's verbal statements may contain less detail, which is one of the CBCA criteria). . . .
>
> The last portion of the SVA consists of applying the Statement Validity Checklist, which contains statement-related factors that assess the validity of several other characteristics related to the interview, the witness, and the investigation. . . . These characteristics include, for instance, the child's psychological

status and things about the interview that may have influenced the content. On the basis of the integration of the results of these three parts of the SVA, an overall evaluation is made of the statement's veracity. (Ruby & Brigham, 1997, p. 708)

A list of the criteria typically used is found in Box 8-2. The procedure has been used in more than 40,000 cases in Germany, where it is carried out by psychologists who are appointed as expert witnesses by the trial judge, and it is beginning to be used in courts in Canada and the United States (Honts, 1994). Some prominent psychologists, including Charles Honts, David Raskin, and John Yuille, have encouraged its wider use, but two careful reviews of research on its validity, done by Steller and Koehnken (1989) and by Ruby and Brigham (1997), suggested caution. The latter reviewers concluded that the technique "shows some promise in enabling raters to differentiate true from false statements" (Rudy & Brigham, 1997, p. 705) but that its validity still needs to be proved before it is applied to decisions about individual cases.

Using Anatomically Detailed Dolls

To evaluate the reports of sexual abuse by children, psychologists and other mental health professionals have sought to use procedures beyond the usual interview, including the use of puppets, drawings, dollhouses, and—especially—anatomically detailed dolls (sometimes called "anatomically correct dolls") (Conte, Sorenson, Fogarty, & Rosa, 1991). Dolls were introduced in the late 1970s and apparently have become "*the* assessment tool" (White, 1988, p. 472, italics in original) and have even received endorsement from the American Psychological Association's Council of Representatives to the effect that they "may be the best available practical solution" (Fox, 1991, p. 722) to the problem of validating allegations of abuse.

Anatomically detailed dolls include, ideally, a mature male with a penis, scrotum, and pubic hair; a mature female with developed breasts, a vagina, and pubic hair; a young male with a penis and scrotum but no pubic hair; and a young female with a vagina but without developed breasts and pubic hair (Skinner & Berry, 1993). Several companies have manufactured these dolls. The justification for the use of anatomically detailed dolls reflects not only a belief that they permit children to reveal aspects of abuse that they wouldn't reveal verbally but also an assumption that sexually abused children will manifest "inappropriate" sexual behavior when playing with such dolls—especially precocious play—that is a result of abuse (Skinner & Berry, 1993, p. 401).

The research tests of this latter assumption led to mixed results (Skinner & Berry, 1993). On the one hand, the doll play of 25 nonabused children was found to differ from that of 25 sexually abused children; the latter were more likely to comment about specific sexual acts and demonstrate such acts (White, Strom, Santilli, & Halpin, 1986). Several studies indicated that the use of anatomically detailed dolls increased the reporting of genital contact when such contact had occurred. Gail Goodman and her colleagues (Goodman, Quas, Batterman-Faunce, Riddlesberger, & Kuhn, 1997) used the setting of a medical examination to determine if those 3- to 10-year-olds who had been touched during the exam would indicate so when later questioned with the dolls; the researchers found that the children were more likely to disclose the touching with the dolls than when posed a free-response question. Another study that also used the setting of a medical examination found that use of the dolls increased reporting of touching of private parts, but also some children who had not been touched reported that they had, when questioned with the dolls (Saywitz, Goodman, Nicholas, & Moan, 1991).

In contrast, a study of 2- to 3-year-olds found that questions using the dolls did not generate more accurate responses than did questions that asked the children to demonstrate the touching on their own bodies (Bruck, Ceci, Francouer, & Renick, 1995). And some comparisons of abused children and those who had not been abused

BOX 8-2

Criteria for Analyzing the Content of Children's Accounts of Abuse

Marxsen, Yuille, and Nisbet (1995) have suggested that 19 criteria are more likely to be found in truthful than untruthful statements. The first five listed here are considered essential; the remaining 14 add to the credibility of the child's report. The researchers stated, "A common rule of thumb is that a credible statement must include the first 5 and any 2 of the remaining 14" (1995, p. 455). The criteria are:

1. Coherence: Does the statement make sense?

2. Spontaneous reproduction: Does the child's presentation of the account seem rigid and rehearsed, or is it reasonably natural?

3. Sufficient detail: Does the child give as much detail in discussing the abusive incident as he or she does in describing a nonabusive incident?

4. Contextual imbedding: Is the account embedded in a distinct spatial-temporal context?

5. Descriptions of interactions: Is there an account at all?

6. Reproduction of conversation: Is verbatim dialogue reported spontaneously?

7. Unexpected complications during the incident: Did an interruption or complication arise during the abuse?

8. Unusual details: Does the child spontaneously supply any details that would be considered unusual for a child to have made up?

9. Peripheral details: Does the child spontaneously include details peripheral to the abusive incident?

10. Accurate reported details misunderstood: Does the child spontaneously incorrectly describe a detail he or she misunderstood during the incident (e.g., saying that the abuser "peed white and sticky and that must have hurt 'cuz he groaned when it happened")?

11. Related external associations: Does the child spontaneously include something from outside the abusive event that is somehow connected to that event?

12. Accounts of subjective mental state: Does the child spontaneously describe his or her emotion and thought during the abusive event?

13. Attribution of perpetrator's mental state: Does the child spontaneously infer the abuser's emotion and thought during the abusive incident?

14. Spontaneous corrections: Does the child make any spontaneous corrections in his or her account?

15. Admitting lack of memory: Does the child spontaneously admit that he or she does not recall some details of the abusive event?

16. Raising doubts about one's own testimony: Does the child spontaneously express the unlikelihood of his or her own story?

17. Self-depreciation: Does the child spontaneously suggest that he or she may have some responsibility for the abuse taking place?

18. Pardoning the perpetrator: Does the child spontaneously attempt to excuse the abuser?

19. Details characteristic of the act: Does the child spontaneously describe the details of child sex abuse that may not be common knowledge?

---

found no differences in response to the dolls (Cohn, 1991; McIver, Wakefield, & Underwager, 1989).

The use of the dolls can be a modeling and learning experience for a child. Interviewers model handling the dolls, suggest that they be undressed (or undress them for the child), and label them for the child. They ask the child to show with the dolls what the accused did and may even place the dolls in sexually explicit positions for the child. This is a teaching experience for the child. Several studies suggest that some nonabused children engage the dolls in sexual play (Dawson & Geddie, 1991; Dawson, Vaughan, & Wagner, 1992; Everson & Boat, 1990; McIver, Wakefield, & Underwager, 1989).

A further limitation is demonstrated when the dolls are evaluated as a measuring instrument. The APA's Committee on Psychological Testing and Assessment has concluded that anatomically detailed dolls are "a psychological test and are subject to the standards [of test construction and validation] when used to assess individuals and make inferences about their behavior" (Landers, 1988, p. 25). How well does the doll procedure stack up psychometrically? Not well at all. For example, any valid test should be standardized; that is, the materials, testing conditions, instructions, and scoring procedures should remain constant. In contrast, wide variation exists in the specific design of the dolls; as they became widely used, more than 15 firms began to manufacture and distribute them (White & Santilli, 1988). Furthermore, some psychologists use other dolls—genitally neutral dolls, such as Barbie dolls, or incompletely modified ones (e.g., Cabbage Patch dolls with breasts or a penis sewn on) (Skinner & Berry, 1993).

An additional problem is that no standardization exists in administration of the dolls—for example, whether to present them dressed or undressed, how to introduce them into the interview, and just when to use them. No manual is available to provide scoring procedures; one study (Boat & Everson, 1988) found wide variation among examiners as to what was meant by particular types of responses (especially, avoidance and anxiousness). It follows that no norms exist that permit psychologists to know the likelihood of certain types of responses (see also Wolfner, Faust, & Dawes, 1993).

White and her colleagues (White, Strom, Santilli, & Halpin 1986) developed a structured protocol for the use of the dolls, but this protocol has not been validated or accepted in clinical practice. Realmuto, Jensen, and Wescoe (1990) used this protocol and found that their raters were unable to correctly classify the children as abused or nonabused.

It should be clear that if anatomically detailed dolls are to be used at all, they should be used only with the greatest of caution (Everson & Boat, 1994). After reviewing a number of studies, Ceci and Bruck (1995) wrote:

Although the data, taken together, do not present persuasive evidence for the value of dolls in forensic and therapeutic settings, there are small pockets of data that would appear to provide some support for the validity of doll-centered interviews. . . . However, we feel that these types of studies are not very relevant . . . because these interviewing procedures bear little relationship to the procedures used in actual interviews with children suspected of sexual abuse. In the latter situation, children are rarely observed for over an hour in a free play situation, nor are these children merely asked to undress a doll and name its body parts. Rather, children are asked direct, leading, and misleading questions about abuse with the dolls, and they are often asked to reenact alleged abusive experiences. (p. 174)

Guidelines for the use of dolls include the following:

1. The dolls should not be used to make an initial diagnosis of abuse.
2. Mental health professionals who use the dolls should first be trained about proper interview techniques and the limitations of the procedure.
3. Investigators should be aware of the interpersonal factors, including age of the child and his or her cultural background and socioeconomic status, that can affect responses (Goodman, Redlich, Qin, Ghetti, Tyda, Schaaf, & Hahn, 1999; Koocher, Goodman, White, Friedrich, Sivan, & Reynolds, 1995).
4. Videotaping interviews with the child and the administration of the doll technique has been suggested, so that independent fact finders can assess whether suggestive procedures were used.

Futhermore, it is unlikely that a psychologist who used anatomically detailed dolls in the evaluation of alleged sexual abuse would be allowed to testify at trial, according to the present federal admissibility standards, which have also been adopted by the majority of the states (Kovera & Borgida, 1998). For example, a California appeals court, in the case of *In re Amber B* (1987), ruled that the use of the dolls did not meet the Frye standard for admissibility. The Supreme Court of Utah (*State v. Rimmasch,* 1989) deemed use of the dolls to be among techniques that are not accepted in the scientific community and that cannot be used to bolster the truth of a witness's testimony. The U.S. Ninth Circuit Court of Appeals (*United States v. Gillespie,* 1988) held it was reversible error to admit expert testimony based on the use of the dolls without evidence for their scientific reliability.

Suggestions for Improving Procedures

Each of the preceding procedures has been criticized; thus, what *should* be done? Interviewing techniques that have not been subjected to the criticisms just discussed are available (Saywitz, Geiselman, & Bornstein, 1992; Saywitz & Snyder, 1996). A number of suggestions for an acceptable procedure have been offered by Saywitz and Dorado (1998):

1. Interviewers must talk to children in language the children understand; thus, interviewers should listen to a sample of the child's speech to determine the language level. Subsequent questioning should reflect this language level.
2. Documentation is essential; if not taped, questions and answers should be recorded verbatim whenever possible. The CBCA categories *are* useful here, in judging the validity of the child's statements.
3. Questioning should begin with general, open-ended questions. If a narrative results, interviewers can prompt children to elaborate. But highly leading questions should be avoided.

DETERMINING IF THE CHILD IS COMPETENT TO TESTIFY

Should children be allowed to testify in court? Or should some assessment be made to determine their competency to testify? The courts have answered yes to the second question, but often have used a particular age as an up-or-down indication of competency. First, psychologists can provide information to the court that aids in the decision whether to permit testi-

mony, particularly by younger children. Second, research findings about the memory abilities of young children can be provided to jurors or other fact finders as they assess the credibility of a child who has been permitted to testify.

Traditionally, the age at which a child has been presumed to be incompetent varied from one jurisdiction to another. For example, a state statute might specify that a child below the age of 7 or 10 or 12 is presumptively incompetent unless the trial judge determines through questioning the child that the child possesses the capacity to testify. More recently, emphasis has shifted, with younger children, to assessment of the following criteria:

1. Does the child know the difference between truth and falsehood?
2. Does the child understand the events he or she witnessed? Can the child describe the events?
3. Does the child have sufficient memory for the events?
4. Is the child able to testify in court?

To answer the first question, some states employ an oath taking as a means to ensure the witness's understanding of the obligation to testify truthfully. The majority of children even at the age of 3 have a grasp of the difference between truth and falsehood and of the duty to tell the truth in court (Johnson & Foley, 1984). Still, it is important to consider each child's age and stage of moral development when assessing his or her comprehension of the obligation to be truthful (Perry & Wrightsman, 1991). Understanding of courtroom procedures and of the functions of courtroom personnel also show improvements as children get older; certainly children under the age of 7 need to be questioned on these topics to determine their level of understanding (Perry & Wrightsman, 1991, pp. 99–106, review these topics).

On the issues of children's understanding and memory of events, extensive research exists; it has been reviewed by several groups of psychologists (Goodman et al., 1999; Melton, Goodman, Kalichman, Levine, Saywitz, & Koocher,

1995). Of special concern is the degree to which children are suggestible, because many judges and jurors assume the worst when children on the witness stand are questioned. The following conclusions seem appropriate:

1. Children are more susceptible than adults, at least under some circumstances (Ceci & Bruck, 1993). But children are not as suggestible as many adults believe them to be, especially when questioned about salient events in their lives.
2. Qualities that lead to increased suggestibility in adults—a relatively weak memory to begin with, or a high-status interviewer—also lead to increased suggestibility in children (Ceci, Ross, & Toglia, 1987).
3. When initial memory is strong, age differences in suggestibility diminish or may not be a factor; even 3-year-old children are quite capable of resisting false suggestions when their memory is solid (Goodman et al., 1999).

CHILDREN'S RIGHTS WHEN TESTIFYING

It can be argued that for *any* victim of sexual abuse or rape, whether an adult or a child, the experience of facing the alleged attacker in court is potentially stressful. The legal system, in recent years, has become increasingly concerned about the possible traumatic effects upon children as witnesses in court. The trauma is compounded if opposing attorneys view children as especially susceptible to intimidation during cross-examination and judges remain oblivious to efforts to "break down" the child on the witness stand. Some defense attorneys may use questions with complex grammatical structure in order to confuse the child; they may accuse the child of having been coached or use other "dirty tricks" to discredit the child. In the McMartin Preschool trial, one child was questioned by the prosecutor for one-half hour and then cross-examined by a defense attorney for

15½ hours. Trial judges have great discretion to terminate or restrict cross-examination; yet this child was subjected to more than two days of questioning before being released from the witness box.

Do children possess any special rights to protection against these stresses? And if they do, can the defendant's rights to a fair trial still be preserved? Can those psychologists who are advocates for children advise the courts about ways to preserve the child's self-esteem? In addressing these questions, many courts have instituted innovative procedures that seek to protect children from undue traumatization; for example, courts have used child-sized witness chairs and have even permitted children to testify while sitting on the floor (Walker, Brooks, & Wrightsman, 1998). Dolls or drawings have been allowed to supplement the child's oral testimony; screens have been introduced to shield the child from the defendant, and children have testified over closed-circuit television.

Not all these innovations have withstood appeals by defendants who were convicted when they were used. Perry and Wrightsman (1991) summarized the decisions:

> Courts generally have been sympathetic to courtroom and procedural changes that make the experience of testifying less traumatic for children, as long as defendants' rights are not unduly compromised in the process. Recent decisions by the Supreme Court suggest that the essence of the right to confrontation must be maintained, including physical presence of the child, administration of the oath, cross-examination by defense counsel, and observation of the child's demeanor by the trier of fact. Moreover, the Court has stated clearly that there must be an individualized finding of need when alteration of standard procedures is requested. (p. 173)

The use of a semitransparent screen, placed between the defendant, John Avery Coy, and the child, was not approved by the Supreme Court (*Coy v. Iowa,* 1988); specifically, the Court concluded that use of the screen was inconsistent with a clause of the Sixth Amendment of the U.S. Constitution that permits defendants to confront their accusers. Justice Scalia, in the majority opinion, wrote that a witness "may feel quite differently when he has to repeat his story looking at the man whom he will harm greatly by distorting or mistaking the facts" (*Coy v. Iowa,* 1988, p. 1019).

But two years later, in the case of *Maryland v. Craig* (1990), the Court reached a different decision; it ruled that the testimony by a child transmitted via closed-circuit television was permissible when it had been demonstrated to the trial judge that the particular child who was to testify would be unduly traumatized by giving testimony publicly. (Sandra Ann Craig owned a day care facility; she was accused of sexually abusing several of the children under her care.) In Craig's trial, four children, ages 4 to 7, and the two attorneys were in a different room; the defendant, the jury, and the judge remained in the courtroom and viewed each child's testimony on a television monitor; thus, the children could not see the defendant, but the defendant could see the children. The defense attorney could object to testimony or carry out a cross-examination as in any other trial. The defendant communicated with her attorney via a telephone, and she had to speak loudly enough for her attorney to hear her voice from the telephone receiver.

In this case, the Court held that before an alternative form of testimony could be employed for a child witness, the prosecutor must convince the judge that the use of the procedure was necessary. To establish this, the prosecutor must show (a) the alternative procedure was necessary to protect the welfare of the child witness; (b) the child would otherwise be traumatized by testifying in front of the defendant, in contrast to merely testifying in a courtroom setting; and (c) the trauma or stress resulting from testifying in the presence of the defendant would produce more than mere nervousness or reluctance to testify. Thus, in this groundbreaking decision, the Court held that the Constitution allowed for exceptions to the right of con-

frontation when competing interests of the state were overriding. In the *Maryland v. Craig* decision, in contrast to the *Coy* case, Justice Scalia was in the minority, and he wrote a vigorous dissent; the decision has also been criticized by legal experts because of its "tinkering with admissibility standards" (Kohlmann, 1996, p. 399) and its "disturbing erosion of confrontation and due process rights" (p. 420).

Psychologists played an influential role in the *Maryland v. Craig* decision (see chapter 16). An *amicus curiae* brief, prepared by a committee of the American Psychology-Law Society on behalf of the American Psychological Association, was submitted to the Supreme Court as it considered the appeal in Sandra Craig's case. (Portions of this brief were reprinted in an article by its drafters, Goodman, Levine, Melton, and Ogden, 1991.) The APA's brief argued that some but not all children might be sufficiently disturbed by the trial procedures as to warrant some limitation on the defendant's right to confront them. The Court agreed, by a 5 to 4 vote, but it remanded the case back to Maryland for a new trial, instructing the judge to determine beforehand whether those children serving as witnesses would suffer emotional distress when testifying.

In reflecting a concern for the child who must testify, the majority opinion, written by Justice O'Connor, referred to large sections of APA's brief. For example, APA's brief stated: "Requiring child witnesses to undergo face-to-face confrontation, therefore, may in some cases actually disserve the truth-seeking rationale that underlies the confrontation clause" (quoted by Goodman et al, 1991, p. 14).

Justice O'Connor's opinion was very similar: "Indeed, where face-to-face confrontation causes significant emotional distress in a child witness, there is evidence that such confrontation would in fact *disserve* the confrontation clause's truth-seeking goal" (*Maryland v. Craig,* 1990, p. 3169, italics in original).

However, not all psychologists have supported APA's position in the *Craig amicus* brief or the majority opinion of the Court that the trauma for the child must be centered on the presence of the defendant rather than the court-room in general and that the distress must be more than a minor one. Ralph Underwager and Hollida Wakefield (1992) concluded that this creates an impossible situation; they wrote:

> This ruling appears to demand that there will be an evidentiary hearing, prior to the trial, at which there will be testimony, most likely by experts, about the effect on the specific child of testifying in the presence of the person accused. This puts psychologists in an extremely difficult position. No professional can respond to this requirement with anything other than subjective opinion. There is no research that separates out the single factor of the defendant's presence from all other factors in assessing the effects of courtroom testimony on a child. Nobody knows how to determine whether the single factor of the presence of the defendant, by itself, causes serious emotional distress. However, the Supreme Court's ruling may require an expert to predict that the presence of a defendant alone will cause emotional harm. (1992, pp. 239–240)

It would seem that this claim has some merit, that it would be difficult to tease out and distinguish between the specific sources of a young child's distress. But in a rejoinder to Underwager and Wakefield, those psychologists who drafted APA's brief disputed the claim that no studies existed that focused specifically on the psychological effects of testifying in front of the defendant (Goodman, Levine, & Melton, 1992). Five studies were cited in the APA brief; also, they noted that clinical literature supported the viability of their conclusion. A comprehensive review concluded, "When children are required to give evidence from the courtroom, seeing the accused and fear of retribution from him are major causes of distress" (Spencer & Flin, 1990, p. 293).

Canada and at least 33 states of the United States now permit closed-circuit televising of children as witnesses, when the judge concludes there is justification. And recent work has explored the effects of such technology on child witnesses and on jurors (Goodman, Tobey, Batterman-Faunce, Orcutt, Thomas, Shapiro, & Sachsenmaier, 1998).

PSYCHOLOGISTS AS EXPERT WITNESSES

In light of the recent publicity regarding numerous claims of sexual abuse—either within families or by child-care providers—probably the testimony of children does not receive the degree of skepticism it once did (Goodman, 1984). Yet publicity about such cases can vary; in the early 1980s, the dominant theme was children as victims, but more recent portrayals have once more cast doubt on the accuracy of memories, at least in cases of adults reporting recent awareness of abuses during their childhood (Berliner, 1998). Psychologists can play an important role as expert witnesses, by being knowledge brokers in the courtroom and providing reviews of the scientific literature on topics of relevance. This is an important function, for potential jurors have been found to disagree significantly with psychologists on many items in a questionnaire designed to determine knowledge about sexual abuse (Morison & Greene, 1992).

Types of Testimony for the Prosecution

Berliner (1998) has identified several types of testimony by psychologists as expert witnesses in sexual abuse cases:

1. Social framework testimony.
Social framework testimony or the "use of general conclusions from social science research in determining factual issues in a specific case" (Walker & Monahan, 1987, p. 570). (Such testimony can also be given in other types of cases covered in this book, including rape trauma, the battered woman syndrome, and racial discrimination.) This type of testimony provides a context for evaluating the evidence in the case; it can "tell jurors something they do not already

know or disabuse them of common but erroneous misconceptions" (Walker & Monahan, 1987, p. 583). Examples suggested by Berliner (1998) included the nature of sexual abuse of children, the reactions of victims, and the memory abilities and suggestibility of children; a law review article by J. E. B. Myers and his colleagues amplified on these issues (Myers, Bays, Becker, Berliner, Corwin, & Saywitz, 1989). Courts have accepted as admissible this type of testimony, done to educate jurors or correct misapprehensions.

2. Testimony about the similarities between a particular child witness and the general class of sexually abused children.

As Berliner noted, "Although the expert may rely on general social science knowledge, the opinion is specifically linked to the child witness" (1998, pp. 13–14). Here things get more questionable, as the following indicates.

Margaret Kelly Michaels was charged in June 1985 with sexually abusing 20 children at the Wee Care day care center in Maplewood, New Jersey, where she had worked, first as a teacher's aide and then as a teacher of a prekindergarten class. At her trial, several children testified to

> having blades of knives inserted into their rectums, vaginas, and penises. Children also reported having had sticks and wooden spoons inserted into their various orifices. One child said that Michaels put a light bulb in her vagina. Others told of the tine end of forks being inserted into their vaginas while the back end of the silverware was inserted into their rectums. (Rosenthal, 1995, p. 252)

As part of the prosecution's case, Eileen Treacy, an expert witness described as authoritative in child psychology and the treatment of sexually abused children, testified, despite objections by the defense. Treacy's letterhead stated that she provided "psychological and consultation services," but she did not have a doctoral degree and was not licensed to practice psychology (Rosenthal, 1995). She testified about a variation of the **child sexual abuse accommodation syndrome** that included five phases, or characteristics common to many situations of abuse—engagement, sexual interaction, secrecy, disclosure, and suppression. She told the jury that if those five characteristics could be identified in cases in which abuse was suspected, the abuse had in fact occurred (Rosenthal, 1995). She based her testimony on her interviews with 18 of the Wee Care children and a checklist of 32 "behavioral symptoms" for each child. She told the jury that the existence of 5 to 15 of her indicators established the existence of sexual abuse; when she was asked by Michaels's defense attorney how she had arrived at the "5 to 15" figure, the trial judge refused to allow the question (Rosenthal, 1995).

For Treacy, the behavioral symptoms were evidence for the presence of the five phases of the child sexual abuse accommodation syndrome; for example,

> where children denied that abuse occurred, Treacy instructed the jury that the denials were exhibitions of the "suppression phase." In fact, she found that all 19 of the children who testified at trial exhibited the suppression phase as well as the other four "phases." That the children initially told investigators and their parents that they liked Michaels, Treacy said, was evidence of the "engagement phase," during which the abuser ingratiates herself with the children. Statements elicited from the children regarding the alleged pile-up games and sexual contact between Michaels and the children were evidence of a "sexual interaction" phase. The "secrecy phase," she testified, was found in the absence of complaints or indications of abuse at Wee Care until the interviews with the children began. And, the statements elicited from the children during and about the interviews constituted the exhibition of the "disclosure phase." Treacy testified that, on the basis of her theories, every child's denials, recantations, and unresponsive answers were proof of victimization. (Rosenthal, 1995, pp. 259–260)

Treacy concluded that in all the children but one, the indicators were "consistent with" having been sexually abused. Although she acknowledged that other factors in children's lives could have caused some of the behavioral symptoms—for example, birth of new siblings, severe illness of family members, a turbulent relationship between parents—she was able to conduct a "confounding variable analysis," the results of which led her to conclude that for all but one of the children, these "confounding variables" could not have been responsible for the appearance of the "behavioral indicators."

Although Kelly Michaels was found guilty of 155 counts of sexually abusing these children and sentenced to 47 years in prison, her conviction was later negated by a New Jersey appellate court, which ruled that the expert went beyond acceptable limits in leaving an impression with the jury that particular children had been abused (*State v. Michaels,* 1993). After some delay, the district attorney decided not to retry Michaels and she was released from custody. An *amicus* brief by a group of social scientists played a role in the appeal of the conviction (see Box 8-3).

Is the type of testimony exemplified in this case effectively different from ultimate opinion testimony (to be described next)? Psychologists Gary Melton and Susan Limber (1989) have taken the position that a psychologist testifying that a child has been abused is the same as testifying that the child is telling the truth. Similarly, the New Hampshire Supreme Court ruled, "We see no appreciable difference between [a statement that the children exhibited symptoms consistent with those of sexually abused children] and a statement that, in her opinion, the children were sexually abused" (*State v. Cressey,* 1993, p. 699).

3. Ultimate opinion testimony.

As in the case of determination of insanity, courts have generally been adamantly opposed to admitting **ultimate opinion testimony** about the credibility of a particular witness—in this case, a child who has reported having been sexually abused. An Oregon appellate judge put it forcefully:

> We have said before, and we will say it again, but this time with emphasis—we really mean it—no psychotherapist may render an opin-

BOX 8-3
The *Amicus* Brief in the *State v. Michaels* Appeal

The conviction of Kelly Michaels was seen as an injustice by some journalists (Nathan, 1987; Rabinowitz, 1990) and by a number of social scientists. The journalists brought the public's attention to the case by publishing articles in widely read periodicals. The social scientists, led by Maggie Bruck and Stephen J. Ceci (1993), prepared an *amicus* brief accompanying Michaels's appeal. The brief presented a summary of research findings on children's suggestibility and cited examples from interviews with the Wee Care children that increased the risk that the children's responses were more a function of suggestibility than reflective of accuracy. As just one example, interviewers often began the interview with an assumption of guilt; here are some examples:

■ "There's a couple of things I'd like to let you know before we start. Alright? That is, Kelly said a lot of things to scare kids and I think she might have said them to you, too."
■ "All your friends that I told you about before were telling us that Kelly, the teacher we are talking about, was doing something they didn't like very much. She was bothering them in a kind of private way and they were all pretty brave and they told us everything, and we were wondering if you could help us out too, doing the same thing."
■ "Some of your friends were hurt and they told us just about everything." (Bruck & Ceci, 1995, p. 284)

The procedures used by the interviewers in this investigation capitalized on intimidation and social influence, just as the interviewers in the McMartin case.

ion on whether a witness is credible in any trial conducted in this state. The assessment of credibility is for the trier of fact and not for therapists. (*State v. Milbradt,* 1988, p. 624)

Still, J. E. B. Myers (1992) has distinguished between testifying on the ultimate *legal* issue and on the ultimate *factual* issue, which may be permitted. Berliner (1998) noted that some courts have agreed, citing as an example an Idaho court that ruled that "if a proper foundation has been laid, it is proper for the expert to testify whether a person has been sexually abused" (*State v. Lewis,* 1993, p. 409). But it remains the fact that it is very difficult for psychologists to assess whether sexual abuse took place; even physical evidence, such as a ruptured hymen, can occur in young girls through natural causes. No checklist of automatic indicators exists; in fact, a review of the literature found that no symptom was reported to be present in more than half of sexually abused children (Kendall-Tackett, Williams, & Finkelhor, 1993).

Testimony for the Defense

Most of the testimony by psychologists in child sexual abuse cases has been offered in support of the prosecution (Mason, 1998), but several aspects of such cases cause psychologists to be expert witnesses for the defense. Among these are the following:

1. An expert can testify about the suggestive nature of the questions in the interview, as illustrated in the description of types of questions by the McMartin Preschool interviewers. The expert could inform jurors about the influence of misleading information on the accuracy of the child's self-report (McAuliff & Kovera, 1998).
2. Psychologists can testify about research findings on the causes and extent of suggestibility in children and the sometimes vulnerable nature of memory. In cases claiming repressed or recovered memory, a defense witness can testify about successful demon-

strations of how false memories can be implanted in children and adults (Loftus, 1993b; Loftus & Hoffman, 1989; Loftus & Ketcham, 1994; Loftus & Rosenwald, 1995; Pezdek & Banks, 1996).
3. Psychologists can refute the testimony of prosecution witnesses, and, particularly, they can question whether the procedures used by prosecution experts meet the standards for admissibility of scientific testimony specified in the *Daubert v. Merrell Dow* (1993) decision. (See Kovera & Borgida, 1998, and Mason, 1998, for detailed reviews of the limits of testimony under *Daubert.*) For example, even the psychiatrist who first introduced the child sexual abuse accommodation syndrome questioned its use to "prove a child was molested" (Summit, 1992, p. 160), and Treacy's use of "behavioral symptoms" and her procedure of doing a "confounding variable analysis" did not meet scientific standards of verifiability and validity.

In another example, in 1984, Ben Bussey, Jr., was found guilty of the sexual abuse of a child after a psychiatrist testified that the alleged victim exhibited symptoms of the child sexual abuse accommodation syndrome, or CSAAS (Fisher & Whiting, 1998). The Supreme Court of Kentucky overturned the conviction on the grounds that the CSAAS was not an accepted scientific concept (*Bussey, Jr., v. Commonwealth,* 1985) that met the Frye standard then operative in that state (*Frye v. United States,* 1923).

SUMMARY

Charges of the sexual abuse of children usually take one of two forms: either a number of children have allegedly been abused by a day care provider, or an individual child has been abused by a member of the child's family or a close friend. In the latter type, sometimes adults reported they only recalled the attack long after it happened.

Psychologists can participate in several ways when charges of sexual abuse of children are advanced. They can assess the nature of the abuse (including whether, in fact, it did occur); they can advise the court about the child's competency to testify; they can assist the prosecutor in preparing the child to testify and, especially, make recommendations to the judge about whether the trauma of testifying justifies innovations; and they can testify as expert witnesses, either for the prosecution or the defense.

In assessing the validity of claims of abuse, psychologists face a challenging task. Sometimes, to gain information from children, interviewers have used suggestive questions and other procedures that create legitimate questions about the accuracy of the children's answers. The use of anatomically detailed dolls, though a well-meaning procedure, lacks the precision required of psychometric instruments and should not be used to diagnose the presence of abuse.

Psychologists have testified on either side in trials of alleged abusers of children. For the prosecution, testimony in general is in support of the validity of claims of abuse, although ultimate opinion testimony is usually not permitted. Psychologists testifying for the defense may focus on the inadequacies of interviews with children, the suggestibility of young children, or the limitations in the procedures used by those psychologists who concluded that abuse was present.

KEY TERMS

anatomically detailed dolls
child sexual abuse accommodation syndrome
criterion-based content analysis (CBCA)
    technique
leading questions
paraphilia
repressed memories or recovered memories
social framework testimony
statement validity assessment (SVA)
suggestibility
suggestive questions
ultimate opinion testimony

INFOTRAC® COLLEGE EDITION

InfoTrac College Edition is a FREE, powerful, online learning resource, consisting of full-text articles from thousands of journals and periodicals. With each new copy of *Forensic Psychology*, Second Edition, you receive 4 months of free access to the InfoTrac College Edition database. By doing a simple keyword search (try using the Key Terms in the list above), you can quickly generate a list of relevant articles from thousands of possibilities and can select articles to read, explore, and print for reference or further study. InfoTrac College Edition's continuously updated collection of articles can be useful for doing reading and writing assignments that reach beyond the pages of this text!

SUGGESTED READINGS

Bruck, M., Ceci, S. J., & Hembrooke, H. (1998). Reliability and credibility of young children's reports: From research to policy and practice. *American Psychologist, 53,* 136–151.

A succinct review of the issues and research findings with regard to interviewing young child witnesses, written by some of the leading experts in the field.

Ceci, S. J., & Hembrooke, H. (Eds.) (1998). *Expert witnesses in child abuse cases.* Washington, DC: American Psychological Association.

Includes a number of valuable contributed chapters, all devoted to issues relevant to the psychologist called to serve as an expert witness in child sexual abuse cases. Contains chapters by Michael Lavin and Bruce D. Sales, Margaret Bull Kovera and Eugene Borgida, Lucy McGough, and others. Highly recommended.

Kuehnle, K. (1996). *Assessing allegations of child sexual abuse.* Sarasota, FL: Professional Resource Press.

Provides a comprehensive model for assessing multiple sources of information in assessing claims of sexual abuse.

Perry, N. W., & Wrightsman, L. S. (1991). *The child witness: Legal issues and dilemmas.* Thousand Oaks, CA: Sage.

A review of research and legal issues when children are called as witnesses in court.

Pezdek, K., & Banks, W. P. (Eds.). (1996). *The recovered memory/false memory debate.* San Diego: Academic Press.

A number of contributed chapters, reviewing both sides of the debate about the existence and frequency of repressed memories or recovered memories of childhood sexual abuse. Covers childhood memory and suggestibility also.

Sales, B. D. (Ed.). (1995). Special issue of *Psychology, Public Policy, and Law, 1(2),* pp. 243–520.

This journal issue concentrates on the case of Margaret Kelly Michaels, charged with the sexual abuse of children at the Wee Care day care center in Maplewood, New Jersey. Contains the *amicus* brief prepared by a committee of concerned social scientists, headed by Maggie Bruck and Stephen J. Ceci; a chronology of the case by Michaels's defense attorney; and commentaries by psychologists, attorneys, and social workers.

Winick, B. J., & LaFond, J. Q. (Eds.). (1998). Special theme: Sex offenders: Scientific, legal, and policy perspectives. *Psychology, Public Policy, and Law, 4,* 1-570.

This special journal issue examines the assessment, future dangerousness, and treatment of sexual offenders. Legal issues are considered in light of the Supreme Court's decision in *Kansas v. Hendricks* (1997) regarding the right to confine sexual offenders beyond their prison sentence if they remain a risk to community safety.

9

Child Custody and Related Decisions

Dr. Lenore E. Walker is a prominent forensic psychologist who has worked extensively with many types of clients, including battered women and rape victims. Speaking at the 1998 American Psychological Association convention, she told the audience, "No area in forensic psychology requires more skills than child custody. It is my least favorite area. Psychologists are treated with the greatest disrespect in Children's Court" (Walker, 1998). Frequently, it is a thankless job, in part because of the overwhelming desire of each parent to maintain custody of the children. Four diverse examples, though not typical cases, reflect the intense feelings often present:

1. After a bitter divorce from his wife a year earlier, Stephen Fagan kidnapped his two young daughters in October 1979, moved to Palm Beach, Florida, from suburban Boston (where he held a part-time job at Harvard's Legal Aid Clinic), and took on a new identity as "Dr. William Martin," supposedly a Harvard-educated psychiatrist. He told his daughters—then ages 4 and 2—that their mother had died in a car crash. He maintained this charade for almost 20 years, until May 1998, when a relative told the authorities of his true identity. His daughters, ages 23 and 21 when he was apprehended, maintained loyalty to their father and denied that they desired to see their mother (Parker, 1998). After he was identified, Mr. Fagan said that everything that he had done for the last 20 years was for his girls and that their mother was unfit to care for them because of her abuse of drugs and alcohol. But he was transported to Massachusetts, where he later pleaded guilty to several counts of kidnapping and was given a sentence of probation and a $100,000 fine.

    Fagan's act was just one of the 350,000 abductions of children by their parents that occur each year, according to the National Center for Missing and Exploited Children (Lopez, 1998). At least half of these—163,200 in a recent year—were character-

ized as ones in which the abductors planned to keep the child indefinitely (Katel, 1998). The problem is so extensive that at least some police departments and sheriff's offices have established departments dedicated to finding children abducted by their parents. And forensic psychologists have begun to identify qualities that increase the risk of an abduction (Plass, Finkelhor, & Hotaling, 1997). Parents who kidnap tend to have strong ties with their children, a view of the other parent as incompetent, and a distrust of child protection agencies or courts as ways to provide justice (Greif & Hegar, 1993). The majority are male.

2. Sometimes, the intensity of the custody conflict extends beyond children. A divorced couple even went to court after each claimed five frozen fertilized eggs that they created in an effort to have children. (After numerous failures, the couple participated in the type of fertility treatment known as in vitro fertilization.) New York's highest court, the Court of Appeals, ruled that the woman, Ms. Maureen Kass, could not use the frozen embryos to impregnate herself without the consent of her former husband, Steven Kass (Hernandez, 1998). Prior to their divorce, the couple had signed a contract stating that each had to give consent before the five embryos could be used and that in the case of their divorce, ownership of the eggs would be determined through either a property settlement or a court decision. After the divorce, Ms. Kass went to court seeking sole custody of the embryos, leading to the decision.

3. After he was found not guilty of the murder of his former wife and Ronald Goldman, O. J. Simpson sought the custody of his children, 11-year-old Sydney and 8-year-old Justin. During the trial, the children were kept by the parents of Nicole Brown Simpson, but in December 1996, a judge ruled that the Browns must relinquish the children to their father. Central to Judge Nancy Wieben Stock's decision was a 16-page

court-ordered report by psychologist Jeffrey M. Lulow, who (it is reported) wrote, "Remaining at the home of their grandparents is likely to reinforce the impression [that] their father is either dangerous, uncaring, inadequate or emotionally distant from them" (quoted by Associated Press, 1997, p. 5A). Psychologist Lulow also analyzed O. J. Simpson's test results and concluded that he could be impulsive but that his capacity for empathy was higher than that of either Louis or Juditha Brown. (Two years later, a California appeals court overturned the judge's decision and ordered a new trial under a different judge, who was told to consider evidence regarding O. J. Simpson's culpability in the murder of the children's mother. Simpson eventually retained custody.)

4. In 2000, Elian Gonzalez, a 6-year-old Cuban boy, was rescued off the coast of Florida after his mother drowned during an attempt to reach the United States. Although Elian's father lived in Cuba and seemed clearly entitled to custody, the mother's relatives in Florida attempted to gain custody of Elian in the Florida courts, arguing that it was not in the boy's best interests to be returned to a Communist country. Numerous emotional scenes were played out in the media, but after psychological evaluations and a court ruling in favor of the father, Elian was returned to Cuba by the U.S. government.

WHAT ROLES CAN PSYCHOLOGISTS PLAY?

When a marriage fails—or shows signs of beginning to fail—a psychologist can play a number of roles in working with one member of the couple, with the couple together, or with the children. Only *some* of these roles reflect actions of a *forensic* psychologist. However, for a complete picture of the process of determining child custody, each role is briefly identified in this section.

Marriage Counselor

Many psychotherapists, whether they be psychologists, psychiatrists, or social workers, work with troubled couples. If a couple has sought help for their marriage but then decides to divorce, their marriage counselor should not be given the responsibility of advising the judge about the best custody arrangements for the couple's children. Such a situation would create a conflict of interest; the psychologist would have a **dual relationship.** Matters that were revealed in the privacy of the counseling relationship should remain there.

Mediator

Once a couple decides to divorce, they face the task of determining custody of the children. If the parents cannot agree on custody, a court may order mediation. As an alternative to litigation, mediation provides several attractions:

1. It is more informal; rules of evidence do not have to be followed, and court personnel and adversarial lawyers are not present (however, specially trained lawyers may serve as mediators).
2. The sessions are usually held in private, and the proceedings are confidential.
3. Participants in mediation are more satisfied with the process and the outcome than are parents who use the courts (Gould, 1998).
4. Cases are settled more quickly than if they were to go through court (Emery, 1994; Katsh, 1998).

Psychologists as well as attorneys have become mediators in a variety of disputes (Emery & Wyer, 1987). The allocation of material resources in a divorce proceeding is an important matter, and whatever decisions are made have implications for child custody decisions. For example, if the husband is the sole wage-earner and the wife is granted custody, is the allocation of income sufficient to provide for the children?

The **mediator's** job is to try to help the parties resolve their differences through an agreement. The mediator explores options with the couple and provides a safe environment for communication; many mediators believe confidentiality to be a necessity if the mediation is to succeed (Stahl, 1994). Mediators ensure that the parents focus on the needs of their children and not on themselves. They seek agreements about plans for the children that can be put in writing, even though mediators do not have the power to enforce binding rulings. The goal often is to develop an acceptance of the nature of the co-parenting relationship; that is, each parent must agree to cooperate with the other parent in raising the children, regardless of his or her feelings about the other parent (Stahl, 1994).

Psychologists can facilitate the realization of several benefits through mediation; for example,

1. The mediator can distinguish between demands and needs. Melton and his colleagues noted, "In performing custody evaluations, we have been struck by the number of times the spouses' disagreements—on which they are expending substantial time and money—are objectively rather insignificant (e.g., a difference of one or two hours a week in how much time each parent has the children)" (1997, p. 485).

An examination of underlying needs sometimes can resolve these disputes.

2. As noted earlier, mediation provides the opportunity, in a less-charged atmosphere, to discuss how property will be divided, how custody will be structured, and how visitations will be implemented (Lemmon, 1985; Friedman, 1993).
3. The process may increase the emotional acceptance of divorce by the two parties (Wallerstein & Kelly, 1980).
4. Mediation may be able to achieve an atmosphere that helps the former spouses to establish a new working relationship that is essential for the co-parenting of their children.

In situations in which one parent is passive and not standing up for his or her parental rights, achieving the goals of mediation becomes more challenging. Although it has been suggested that

the mediator can assist in balancing the power in a couple (Haynes, 1981, pp. 122–123), the mediator cannot become an advocate for one side. In such families, litigation may be necessary.

On the question of the effectiveness of mediation in such disputes, the thorough review by Melton and his colleagues is less optimistic than are advocates of the process; these authors concluded that:

> mediation (especially when compulsory) is not necessarily beneficial. It has been asserted that, relative to litigation, mediation will likely reduce competition between parents, improve children's adjustment, reduce relitigation, and increase compliance with agreements. . . . Although the majority of studies on particular hypothesized benefits of mediation have confirmed the hypotheses, research to the contrary is also available on virtually every point. No study has shown mediation, relative to litigation, to have the hypothesized ultimate benefit: better post-divorce adjustment by children. Indeed, mediation—especially when conducted in a high-conflict divorce—may actually increase the strength of association between parental and child problems (1997, p. 486).

Despite this less-than-encouraging evaluation, these commentators see the movement toward compulsory mediation of custody disputes as likely to continue to grow, because of a powerful reason—it reduces the workload of the courts.

Child Therapist

Another role for the psychologist is as a psychotherapist for children experiencing the trauma of family conflict and incipient divorce. For example, Philip Stahl (1994) has posed the following dilemma:

> Johnny, age 11, is your client in psychotherapy. You have seen him for a year for school problems and difficulties in his family relationships. During the course of therapy, you have had frequent contact with Johnny's

mother but little contact with his father. His parents have had a tumultuous marriage and have finally decided to get a divorce. Johnny's mother and her attorney ask you to make a statement to the court about Johnny's poor relationship with his father and to recommend rather limited visitation with him. What do you do? (p. 2)

The answer is simple; you refuse. Again, as in the first role, the psychologist serves as a counselor, and to ask this person to serve also as an evaluator in court places an undue burden on the psychologist. However, it is possible that the psychologist could testify as a **fact witness** (not as an expert witness). That is, it might be appropriate for the psychotherapist to testify about Johnny's mother's commitment to his mental health, while avoiding any recommendation about custody.

Court-Appointed Evaluator

When custody of children surfaces as an issue in a divorce case, and the matter cannot be settled through mediation, the presiding judge will sometimes ask a clinical or counseling psychologist to serve as a **court-appointed evaluator** to make an evaluation and then a recommendation of the best custody arrangement. (For a recent and comprehensive child custody evaluation protocol and an up-to-date review of the literature, see Benjamin & Gollan, 2003.) Do the two parents differ in their expression of good and bad parenting behaviors? Which parent is more competent to respond to the needs of the children? (In some jurisdictions, psychologists may be employed by the state as Court Services Officers, with similar functions.) Because the final decision is which parent retains the legal authority over the child, the judge makes the ultimate determination. Even though this is the topic on which mental health professionals feel that they are most useful to the courts, psychologists and other mental health professionals are not routinely consulted by judges (Melton, Petrila, Poythress, & Slobogin, 1997). Box 9-1 provides an elaboration of this conclusion and

some reasons for it. Nevertheless, the role is a crucial one, and a subsequent section of this chapter explores the activities of the evaluator in depth.

Despite occasionally succumbing to the temptation to oversell their offerings, psychologists do have something to offer judges. For example, Melton et al. noted that "clinical impressions about alliances and conflicts within the family and their bases might present judges with a useful framework for consideration of which child goes where" (1997, p. 485). Similarly, an investigation of the level of marital conflict might aid in the judge's success in predicting whether, for the couple, joint custody might work.

Thus, if appointed to do a **custody evaluation,** the psychologist must approach the task "unburdened by any particular point of view or preset conclusions" (Schutz, Dixon, Lindenberger, & Ruther, 1989, p. 50). The prime duty of the evaluator is to investigate, to gather facts for the judge; the clinical or counseling psychologist's strength is "talking with children and families under stress and gathering information from diverse sources about the life of the family" (Melton et al., 1997, p. 485). The psychologist as evaluator then prepares a report for the judge; in some jurisdictions—but not all—copies of the report are available to the attorneys for each parent, and, in some jurisdictions, even family members get copies. Stahl (1994) has listed the desired characteristics of such a report; it should

1. Focus on the issues and problems of the family,
2. Be credible, well-reasoned, clear, and thoughtful,
3. Be fair, balanced, and neutral, avoiding advocacy of one parent and accentuating positives when possible,
4. Avoid jargon and diagnosis, yet remain behaviorally focused, and
5. Contain recommendations that are focused and that clearly flow from the material in the report (1994, p. 75).

BOX 9-1

Why Don't Judges Consult Psychologists?

Should clinical or counseling psychologists be involved in the resolution of most child-custody disputes? Melton, Petrila, Poythress, and Slobogin (1997) conclude no, for several reasons.

At present, most custody decisions are made during a period of mediation or bargaining between the spouses and do not require a Solomon-like judge to make the decision (even though the judge must ratify whatever decision is made by the parents). Even when the decision goes to trial, only a few include an evaluation by a mental health professional. In a nationwide survey, summarized by Melton et al. (1997), about half the judges reported that they consulted mental health experts in fewer than 10% of the custody cases they decided; none reported eliciting such evidence in more than three fourths of their cases. In another survey (Felner, Rowlison, Farber, & Primavera, 1987), only 2% of the judges included the opinions of mental health professionals among the five leading factors in their custody decisions.

Melton and his colleagues go on to offer a provocative explanation: "Mental health professionals may have little expertise that is directly relevant to custody disputes" (1997, p. 483). Their arguments for this conclusion include the following:

1. Psychologists have no special expertise with respect to some of the factors related to the child's best interests, including moral guidance and parental "responsibility" (Lowery, 1981).

2. The amount of scientific evidence on some issues to be decided by the judge is limited. One example is the relative benefit of various custody arrangements (see Box 9-4).

3. In the past, some psychologists have not endeared themselves to judges by testifying and drawing conclusions from clinical data that are irrelevant to the legal questions in dispute (Melton et al., 1997, p. 484). In fact, one of the most distinguished forensic psychologists, Thomas Grisso, has written, "Mental health professionals do not have reason to be proud of their performance in this area of forensic assessment" (1984, pp. 8–9).

Modern custody options differentiate legal custody from physical custody. *Legal custody* refers to the right to make major decisions about a child's life; *physical custody* refers to where the child resides on a day-to-day basis. In a *sole custody arrangement,* one parent obtains both legal and physical custody, with visitation by the other parent. In a *joint custody or shared custody arrangement,* legal custody is shared, with one parent typically being designated as the primary residential parent for purposes of physical custody. Finally, *divided custody* refers to the situation in which one parent gains sole custody of one or more of the children, and the other parent gains sole custody of any other(s); for example, if there are two children, the mother gets custody of the daughter and the father gets custody of the son.

It is worth noting that although many would assume that joint or shared parenting is always a better arrangement for the children, the research does not support such a conclusion. Instead, the research shows that children do best with parents who can work together and cooperate, regardless of the custody arrangements. Joint custody arrangements are best when voluntarily chosen. If they are mandated by courts, joint custody arrangements can be detrimental to a child's post-divorce adjustment (see Pruett & Santangelo, 1999).

Expert Witness

After providing an evaluation to the court, the psychologist usually participates as an **expert witness** in a hearing. Sometimes the psychologist is hired by one side, rather than appointed by the court. The examination of the psychologist by attorneys representing each of the two parents is likely to be an intense one; hence, a section of this chapter deals with the trials and tribulations of the expert witness.

Psychologists may carry out other functions as expert witnesses. For example, a psychologist may be called upon to testify about the effects on child rearing if a divorced parent is gay or lesbian, a topic discussed later in this chapter.

Applied Researcher

A separate role exists for the forensic psychologist as an **applied researcher** in evaluating general claims and assumptions about the nature of custody. As we know, for many years mothers typically received custody of the children, but in recent years joint custody has come into vogue. Is the latter a better arrangement with regard to the adjustment and satisfaction of children? And, standing back from the effectiveness of various custody arrangements, the applied researcher asks, What are the long-term effects of divorce on children?

If the child's wishes are a factor in determining custody, at what age are children competent to participate in the decision making? Forensic psychologists can provide the research findings to guide judges; one study (Garrison, 1991) found that even elementary-school-age children were able to give adultlike reasons, at least in response to hypothetical questions about preferences for custody arrangements.

WHAT DO CLIENTELES WANT?

Throughout this book, an organizing question is: What interests is the forensic psychologist serving? The answer depends on the particular role. With regard to child-custody evaluations, there are three interested groups: the children, their parents, and the presiding judge. What does each want, and have a right to expect, from the forensic psychologist?

The Children

As often-powerless pawns in a dispute, children deserve empathy and concern. The psychologist can help children examine their feelings about their parents and divorce. But the primary responsibilities of the forensic psychologist are to be fair, thorough, and professional. The psychologist should enter into an evaluation free of biases favoring one parent and make a recommendation about the best interests of the child based on an objective evaluation of a variety of data.

The Parents

In often-acrimonious child-custody disputes, each parent wants to "win." In only 10% of divorces do the two parents contest custody, and only a minority of these contested cases go to trial (Hedrick, 1998). Thus, those parents with whom the psychologist interacts are an extreme, intense group. They want vindication in that they want the experts to conclude that they are better parents—even that they are better human beings!—than their ex-spouses, and that the other is at fault for the family's problems. Needless to say, a psychologist cannot provide satisfaction to most parents entrenched in emotional disputes. But disputants also seek procedural justice, whether they win or not; that is, they want to have assurance that they have been treated fairly, that all those contributing to the decision have listened to their side with openness and fairness (Thibaut & Walker, 1975; Lind & Tyler, 1988).

A field study of 71 couples who either mediated or litigated their child custody disputes (Kitzmann & Emery, 1993) found that the relative fairness of the proceedings influenced overall satisfaction felt by the participants, especially by those who felt that they were in a disadvantaged position (usually, the fathers).

The Judge

Some judges feel poorly trained with regard to understanding the dynamics of family relationships (Stahl, 1994). As noted earlier, judges seek relevant information about family dynamics from the psychologist. Like the other participants, judges want fairness and objectivity, and they expect an awareness of the court's role and the limits of the law with regard to the resolution of custody disputes. In a word, judges expect the psychologist always to act in a professional manner.

But sometimes judges may not realize what is unprofessional and unethical for a psychologist. Some judges will quiz psychotherapists about what is best for the child they are treating, inadvertently pressuring the psychologists toward dual relationships. Especially in small communities, where "everybody knows everybody else," psychologists need to remind others of their professional limits.

THE COURT-APPOINTED EVALUATOR

The most "forensic" of the various activities described earlier are the evaluations of the parents and the children and the recommendations to the judge. Thus a major portion of this chapter examines the role of the court-appointed evaluator.

Standards for Resolution of Custody Disputes

Two hundred years ago, if a married couple decided to divorce, the rights of their children were irrelevant to the decision to assign custody to one parent or the other. Until the early 1900s, only one person in a family had any legal rights (Drinan, 1973); only the husband had the right to make a contract or have legal status. Children were treated as property and, like the rest of the property, automatically assigned to their fathers. In fact, in William Blackstone's influential 18th-century commentaries on the law, children were considered "prized possessions" of their fathers. But early in the 20th-century, sentiment shifted, reflecting a belief that mothers were better caregivers. Typically, the mother was given custody of the child, unless strong countervailing factors prevailed.

The Best-Interests-of-the-Child Standard

Around 1970, another shift occurred, placing the **best interests of the child** at the forefront (see Krauss & Sales, 2001). A child is treated as a distinct person and is to be accorded, by law, individual rights in the child custody proceedings (Woody, 1977). At present, in most states, child custody statutes give the judge the power to make custody decisions "as justice requires," generally using some version of the "best interests" test (Sales, Manber, & Rohman, 1992, p. 23). Neither parent is now presumed to have a superior right to the child, according to current laws in most states (Wyer, Gaylord, & Grove, 1987). Section 402 of the Uniform Marriage and Divorce Act, passed by Congress in 1970, describes the following as among the factors a judge may consider in reaching a custody decision:

1. The mental and physical health of all individuals involved.
2. The child's adjustment to his or her home, school, and community.
3. Each parent's ability to provide food, clothing, medication, and other remedial care and material benefits to the child.
4. The interaction and interrelationship of the child with parents or other individuals who might affect the child's best interests (thus, in a general sense, the parents' lifestyles).
5. The wishes of the parents and the wishes of the child (Sales et al., 1992).

Congress thus outlined some broad characteristics, but it was intended for judges to operationalize the terms. As Gould (1998) noted, terms were left undefined; furthermore, in some and maybe most states, case law was used to define what was meant. For example, Melton et al. (1997) asked this question: Is the best-interests standard present-oriented or future-oriented? Judges have great discretion when it comes to evaluating the lifestyle of each competing parent. Perhaps the most provocative example of how judges' values can affect their decisions was the case of *Painter v. Bannister* (1966), described in Box 9-2.

With respect to the child's preferences, the Uniform Marriage and Divorce Act of 1970 directs judges to consider the child's wishes. Some states specify an age, typically 12 or 14; others consider the maturity of the child's cognitive and emotional development. For instance, in the case of *In re Marriage of Rosson* (1986), the California court concluded that a child of sufficient age and capacity to reason well enough to form an intelligent custody preference has the right to have that preference seriously considered. But consensus is lacking about how much weight is to be given to the child's preferences, and sometimes the child's choice is considered only when other factors balance out the choice between parents (*Sharp v. Sharp*, 1973). The highly publicized case of "Gregory K.," who decided to "divorce" his parents and was allowed to do so, is a very specialized one and should not be taken as any legal landmark (see Walker, Brooks, and Wrightsman, 1998, Box 5.5, pp. 96–97, for a description). Recently, Crosby-Currie (1996) surveyed attorneys and mental health professionals in several states to see how often children are asked for their opinions in custody cases; in Virginia, judges reported asking children for preferences in 33.4% of cases, and in Michigan, 69.9% of cases. Most said that the age of the child was important, with judges in Virginia saying that they were likely to ask a child starting at about age 12, while in Michigan, it was at about age 8.

One observer noted, "In all matters where children are involved, courts have said with tedious regularity that the welfare of the child is the supreme goal to be obtained" (Drinan, 1973, p. 40). As a moral principle, the best interests of the child would seem to be a step forward over previous rationales for custody determination. But who determines what is in the child's best interests? Rarely is the child given the final choice in the exercise of his or her rights (Sales et al., 1992); for example, if the state concludes that several children have suffered incalculable harm in the custody of their parents, the state may intrude into the family relationship and remove the children (Walker, Brooks, & Wrightsman, 1998). Some advocates, including Hillary Rodham Clinton (see Rodham, 1974, p. 512) have seen the "best interests" standard as a rationalization by decision makers to justify their judgments about the child's future.

The Tender-Years Doctrine

Another phenomenon that impedes the impact of children's preferences upon custody determinations is the widespread acceptance of the **tender-years doctrine,** which presumes that the best interest of all children regardless of their gender and the best interest of girls (regardless of their age) are best served by awarding custody to the mother, assuming she is fit (Okpaku, 1976). The assumption that "a mother is the natural custodian of a child of tender years" (*B v. B.*, 1978, p. 251) was based on the theory that the father was unable to provide "that tender care which nature requires, and which it is the

---

BOX 9-2
Painter v. Bannister: **Values in Conflict**

After 7-year-old Mark Bannister's mother died, an Iowa judge awarded custody to his grandparents (his mother's parents) rather than to his father—apparently because his father possessed liberal political values and agnostic religious ones. Living in an unpainted house in Northern California, the father would—in the expressed opinion of the judge—have provided Mark with an "unstable, unconventional, arty, Bohemian, and proba-

bly intellectually stimulating" home (*Painter v. Bannister,* 1966, p. 156). In contrast, the grandparents were churchgoers who would provide a "stable, dependable, conventional, middle-class mid-west background" (p. 154). The judge did not question the basis for his decision, stating, "We believe security and stability in the house are more important than intellectual development in the proper development of the child" (p. 156).

peculiar province of the mother to supply" (*Miner v. Miner*, 1849, p. 49). With its presumption that the mother was best for rearing the young child, the tender-years doctrine put the burden of proof on the father to show that the mother was unfit (Wyer, Gaylord, & Grove, 1987).

Custody Determinations in Mixed-Race Cases or in Cases Involving a Parent With a Homosexual Orientation

As noted, judges have great discretion in awarding custody. Even though psychologists are sometimes consulted by the courts and asked to carry out evaluations about the child's welfare, the judge is not required to follow them. Judges' decisions may reflect their own fuzzy thinking, blatant prejudices, and stereotyped beliefs about what is in the child's best interests, and these may or may not agree with conventional wisdom or with empirical findings. An example is illustrated by the case of *Palmore v. Sidoti* (1984). The trial judge transferred the custody of a White child from her mother to her father because her mother had married an African American man. Upon appeal, the judge's decision was upheld by the Florida Circuit Court, which concluded that the child in a mixed marriage would "inevitably" be vulnerable to "social stigmatization." It required an appeal to the U.S. Supreme Court to get the judge's decision overturned.

In two types of cases, divorce in a mixed-race family and custody when a parent's sexual orientation is homosexual, conflicts are likely to surface.

Custody After the Divorce of a Mixed-Race Couple

What if a husband and wife of different races, who have had children together, decide to divorce? Some judges have assumed that such children's interests are best served by "placement with the potential custodian whom the child most closely resembles in terms of physical racial attributes" (Sales et al., 1992, p. 31). But some commentators have been critical of this determination. In their extensive review, Sales et al. (1992) found no empirical studies on this specific topic, but they concluded from the findings on adoptions by White families of non-White children that the procedure does not jeopardize the non-White child's racial awareness or identity.

Custody When a Parent's Orientation Is Homosexual

Sharon Bottoms is openly homosexual in orientation; she lives with another woman and, on occasion, with her child, Tyler. But in 1993, Sharon Bottoms's mother sued for custody of Tyler, claiming that her daughter's sexual orientation made her unfit as a mother. A circuit court judge in Virginia agreed, citing a 1985 state law saying that a parent's homosexuality is a valid reason for losing custody, and awarded custody of the 2-year-old child to his grandmother. Other judges' actions have reflected similar values; Falk (1989) identified seven unverified assumptions that guided those judges who have decided that a mother's lesbian orientation was contrary to the child's best interests:

1. Homosexuality is associated with mental illness.
2. Lesbians are less maternal than heterosexual women.
3. Children reared by lesbian mothers are at risk for mental health problems.
4. Children reared by homosexual parents are more likely to be subjected to sexual molestation.
5. Children reared by lesbian mothers may have difficulty in establishing a clear gender identity.
6. Children reared by homosexual parents are more likely to become homosexual themselves than if they are cared for by heterosexual parents.
7. Children living with lesbian mothers are likely to be stigmatized, especially by their peers, and teased and ostracized as a result.

The trial judge in the Bottoms case ruled the way he did despite testimony by a psychologist as expert witness that children suffer no untoward effects from growing up in a family in which the caregivers have a homosexual orientation. Available research supports the conclusion by the psychologist (American Psychological Association, 1995; Patterson, 1992; Tasker & Golombok, 1995); a review of relevant research by Cramer (1986) concluded that "the evidence to date suggests that gay parents raise children who are emotionally and sexually similar to those raised by heterosexual parents" (p. 506). No research exists finding that the sexual orientation of a lesbian couple significantly influences the sexual orientation of any children in the home (Sales et al., 1992; Buxton, 1999). The American Psychological Association has filed several *amicus* briefs in homosexual custody cases (all APA *amicus* briefs are available for review at www.apa.org, the APA's website).

The decision in the Bottoms case was the first known instance in which a judge awarded a third person the custody of a child because the parent is gay (Howlett, 1993). However, later in 1993, a Virginia appellate court overruled the judge and awarded custody to Sharon Bottoms. In contrast, an increasing number of lesbian mothers are being permitted to have custody by the lower courts (e.g., *Doe v. Doe,* 1981), and at least 10 states have statutes or case law holding that homosexuality should not be a factor in determining custody. Most of the recent decisions hold that homosexuality, taken alone, is not sufficient grounds to change custody and that there also has to be a showing of emotional or physical harm to the child. But sometimes judges still deny custody simply because the other parent is heterosexual or because the judge anticipates that the child might encounter future prejudice by a disapproving society.

Ethical Issues and Temptations

As psychologists increasingly are called upon to perform child custody evaluations, the potential for making mistakes and taking unethical actions increases; in the first 5 years of the 1990s, between 7% and 10% of the cases examined by the APA Ethics Committee dealt with custody evaluations (Morris, 1995; see also Benjamin & Gollan, 2003). This number has increased. In 1994, the APA developed a set of guidelines for child custody evaluations in divorce proceedings (APA, 1994). This section discusses some of the potential problems in doing these evaluations and suggests ways to overcome them.

Recognizing One's Limits and Biases

Each of us has biases; for some of us, these have a potential to influence evaluations significantly and detrimentally. Does the psychologist have a strong preference for, say, joint custody over mother-only custody? Sometimes the biases of the evaluating psychologist may be more subtle; he or she may look unfavorably upon a parent who lives in a trailer, or one with a low IQ. If the psychologist cannot avoid his or her biases when playing a determinative role, the psychologist should withdraw from the case.

Marsha Hedrick (1998), who has conducted more than 300 divorce/custody evaluations, suggested that potential evaluators need to know what their "hot buttons" are. What behaviors cause knee-jerk reactions in the psychologist: domestic violence? Being lied to by a client? Sex abuse? Psychologists also need to recognize that if they are "people-pleasers," carrying out such evaluations may not be their activity of choice. "You must tolerate people hating you," she said; "If you say one negative thing about some parents, you're scum."

Avoiding Dual Relationships

This chapter has described the various roles for the psychologist as a part of the child custody process. The American Psychological Association's code of ethics notes the strong danger of an ethical violation when the same psychologist carries out several roles; Morris has put it succinctly: "A psychologist should avoid conducting a custody evaluation involving a family when he or she has seen a member(s) of the family at some previous time in individual psychotherapy or family therapy" (APA, 2002). But is it improper for a psychologist to enter into a therapeutic relationship with a parent he or she has previously evaluated? Although some psychologists are uncomfortable with this kind of dual relationship, other psychologists have argued that sometimes the previous contact facilitates achieving the goals of therapy and that the ethical questions need to be reviewed on a case-by-case basis (L. Greenberg, personal communication, November 17, 1998).

Violating Confidentiality and Informed Consent

Both the APA ethics code and the law require psychologists not to reveal any information conveyed to them by their clients, without those clients' expressed written consent. But in child custody evaluations, the very nature of the evaluation means that the information will be shared with others, certainly with the judge responsible for the decision (Morris, 1995). The legal tradition of admitting all relevant evidence into court runs counter to confidentiality and privilege (Knapp & Vandecreek, 1985). Given these phenomena, parents need to be informed in advance of the special circumstances, or what the APA Code of Ethics refers to as the "limits of confidentiality"; Morris even recommended obtaining written permission from the parents reflecting their awareness of those parties who will be assessed or interviewed and those who will receive the report.

In informing parents and gaining their consent, Morris proposed that parents should be told about each step in the evaluation process, including what tests are going to be administered to each person, who will be interviewed, whether observations will include home visits, what legal or medical documents will be examined, and how long the evaluation will take (1995, p. 8). Informed consent should also be extended to each child being evaluated. Even if the evaluation is court ordered, all parties need to sign a consent form (Gould, 1998). Often, these forms are available from other psychologists or even from attorneys versed in mental health law and practice.

Custody Evaluations Versus Psychological Evaluations

Clinical psychologists, when doing custody evaluations, are not doing "pure" psychological evaluations. The goal in a custody evaluation is to assist the trier of fact in the determination of what is in the best interest of the child, not to diagnose all the personality inadequacies of each parent. Assessing parenting skills is relevant, but too often the evaluation assesses the lifestyle of each parent rather than focusing on the wants and needs of the child (Melton et al., 1997). If the evaluator insists on diagnosing the personality of parents, he or she needs to be explicit about what this means with respect to parenting skills. To say that a mother has a bipolar disorder is not enough; the psychologist should be explicit that the disorder, in her case, means that she can't manage routines or consistently respond to the child's needs (Hedrick, 1998). Grisso (1984) elaborated on this point:

> Too often we still evaluate the parent but not the child, a practice that makes no sense when the child's own, individual needs are the basis for the legal decision. Too often we continue to rely on the assessment instruments and methods that were designed to address *clinical* questions, questions of psychiatric diagnosis, when clinical questions bear only secondarily upon the real issues in many child custody cases. Psychiatric interviews, Rorschachs, and MMPIs might have a role to play in child custody assessments. But these tools were *not* designed to assess parents' relationships to children . . . [or their] child rearing attitudes and capacities, and *these* are often the central questions in child custody cases (1984, pp. 8–9, italics in original).

But judges can also be faulted here. Lowery, after her survey of judicial practices, wrote, "According to the results of this study, the court, on its own, is more likely to ask, 'Which parent is the better adult?', using relatively apparent and verifiable indices of competence such as health, financial status, and reputation in the community" (1984, p. 379). Psychologists need not only to move beyond their own biases but also to educate judges about needs of the child and appropriate parenting skills.

The Technique of Custody Evaluation

Not all forensic psychologists carry out custody evaluations in the same way, and certainly they do not completely agree on what specific procedures should be used. A number of books are available that can give a forensic psychologist guidance in the area of custody evaluations (e.g., Stahl, 1994, 1999a, 1999b; Gould, 1998; Ackerman, 1994, 2001; Benjamin & Gollan, 2003). Most psychologists who do these evaluations make sure to interview each parent and each child and to observe each child in interaction with each parent; many include the administration of psychological tests (see Keilin & Bloom, 1986, and Ackerman & Ackerman, 1997, for surveys on custody evaluation practices, and also see Otto, Edens, & Barcus, 2000, and Otto, Buffington-Vollum, & Edens, 2003, for an up-to-date and complete review). A typical characteristic of poor-quality evaluations is the failure to be comprehensive. The most common complaint concerns making a recommendation about a person the psychologist has not evaluated. For example, the negligent psychologist may write a report saying "the father needs domestic violence therapy" without ever observing or interviewing the father (Hedrick, 1998).

Scope of Evaluation

The scope of the evaluation should reflect a functional assessment of the skills and values of the parents and their congruence with the assessed needs of the child; the APA Guidelines note that this necessarily requires a wide range of information sources and methods of gathering data. Thus, the psychologist needs to obtain a picture from all perspectives; it is recommended that the psychologist interview all parents and guardians alone as well as together (APA, 1994, pp. 678–679). But many other sources should be consulted in a *comprehensive* evaluation procedure; see Box 9-3 for a listing.

Observation Procedures

As Yogi Berra once reportedly said, "You can observe a lot by just watching." Observation of a child interacting with each of his or her parents has the attraction of being a slice of "real" behavior, and forensic psychologists have used observation techniques in child custody evaluations, while recognizing the potential for error (Marafiote, 1985). Some might doubt that the interactions under the scrutiny of an observing psychologist are really that "real," but most parents and especially most children soon accommodate to the presence of an observer. Sometimes what happens in real life is surprising; psychiatrist Robert M. Galatzer-Levy (1997) wrote,

> As a part of a clinical assessment in custody evaluations I have been impressed by how much information is often readily apparent in observed interactions and incidentally how convincing material from such interactions can be to finders of fact. What is often astonishing is how blatant some of the behavior can be, including being unresponsive to the child, striking the child, the child's unresponsiveness to reasonable attempts at interaction, etc. When blatant interactions occur, they are so striking that issues of validity and reliability or concerns that the difficulties of the situation brought them on are of little relevance. The behavior speaks for itself (personal communication, December 27, 1997)

As a structured observation technique, Vicky Campagna (personal communication, July 29, 1998) suggested the following:

> What I do is buy a math workbook and an English workbook from the local school supplies store. They're cheap enough (usually about $3.50 each) so that I can have one for whatever age child I'm evaluating. (They have different workbooks for each age.) Then I choose a workbook that's a year or so beyond where the child is in school and ask the parent to

> **BOX 9-3**
> **Steps in the Evaluation Process**
>
> The clinical inquiry in custody evaluations should include the following; each parent and each child should be assessed:
>
> - Parent's description of marital relationship and family structure.
> - Parent's attitude and concerns regarding the other parent, his or her access to the children, nature of visitation, etc.
>   - Discussion with children about the separation and divorce.
>   - The parent's communications with the children about the other parent.
>   - The parent's goals for visitation and decision making should he or she be awarded custody.
> - Parent's prior and current relationship with the children and responsibility for caretaking.
>   - Reaction to pregnancy and childbirth, and impact of these on relationship and functioning outside the family.
>   - Early caretaking.
>   - Current caretaking.
>   - Punishment.
>   - Leisure and social activities.
>   - Interactional style.
>   - Allegations of abuse/neglect.
> - Parent's current, anticipated living and working arrangements.
>   - Who is living in the home.
>   - Significant others.
>
> - Day care, babysitting.
> - Schools and school districts.
> - Parent's emotional functioning and mental health.
>   - Prior or current substance abuse/dependence and treatment.
>   - Prior or current mental health problems and treatment.
>   - Emotional response to the divorce.
>   - History of domestic violence (several states now have laws that discourage awarding custody to anyone with a history of spouse-battering; Drozd, 1998).
> - Child's attitude and preference regarding the parents, current living arrangements, visitation, and future placement.
> - Child's depictions and conceptualization of relationship with each parent.
>   - Punishment.
>   - Leisure and social activities.
>   - Interactional style.
>   - Allegations of abuse/neglect.
> - Child's emotional functioning and mental health.
>   - Prior or current substance abuse/dependence and treatment.
>   - Prior or current mental health problems and treatment.
>   - Emotional or behavioral responses (i.e., problem behaviors) to the divorce.
> - Child's social, academic, and vocational functioning prior to and after divorce.
>
> Source: Adapted from Melton, Petrila, Poythress, & Slobogin, 1997, Table 16.1; and from Otto, 1996.

teach the child one of the pages in each workbook. Since the subject matter is beyond what the child's already learned, I get a nice snapshot of how the parent teaches the child new material, how they interact in a stressful situation, etc.

Such procedures may generate useful hypotheses, but observations by one individual need some demonstration of interobserver reliability. Yet experienced custody evaluators often rely on them.

Jerry Nims (1998) has a systematic procedure, the NIMS Observation Checklist, which he uses in his home visits. Five aspects of the situation are broken down into specific behaviors that are rated. The five general characteristics are

1. Safety and environment
2. General behavior toward the child
3. Teaching and training
4. Control
5. Child-initiated behavior

Within each category, Nims rates more specific aspects on a 1 to 5 scale; for example, within "General behavior toward the child," the parent is rated on the degree to which he or she has eye contact, strokes the child, is patient with the child, smiles, cuddles, and hugs appropriately. The rating, Nims states, is done according to *his* value system, and there are no norms. He assumes that the behavior is reliable and consistent but recognizes that it is not always true. Nevertheless, he reports that judges appreciate his system, doubtless because the characteristics he rates are clearly important and Nims has a solid, no-nonsense manner about him. But does Nims's procedure achieve the standard set forth in the *Daubert* decision?

Psychological Tests and Scales

If an evaluation is going to be comprehensive, why not include scales to assess the behaviors and attitudes of parents and of children? This sounds like a good idea, but achieving such goals well is not so easy to do (Heinze & Grisso, 1996; Otto, Edens, & Barcus, 2000).

The most widely used test administered to parents in custody evaluations is one not designed for that purpose: the Minnesota Multiphasic Personality Inventory, now updated as the MMPI-2 (Butcher, Dahlstrom, Graham, Tellegen, & Kaemmer, 1989). Other instruments that are also frequently administered to each parent, such as the Rorschach Inkblot Technique, the Millon Inventories, and projective techniques involving drawings, were developed without custody determinations in mind; their main purpose is the assessment of the likelihood of neurosis or psychosis; some claim to measure neurological malfunctioning. Stahl (1994) concluded, "The Rorschach can provide a good understanding of the adult's affect, organization skills, and reality testing, but, except for the most dysfunctional parent, it will not do much to answer questions about day-to-day parenting" (p. 55). On the other hand, Wood, Nezworski, Lilienfeld, and Garb (2003) provided a devastating critique of the Rorschach that attorneys would do well to read in considering a Daubert challenge to the reliability and validity of conclusions based on Rorschach testing (for more discussion

of *Daubert* in the context of custody evaluations, see Krauss & Sales, 1999).

Despite these reservations, some of these instruments are used almost as frequently as interviews with the parents. LaFortune and Carpenter (1998) surveyed 165 practitioners; among the information solicited was a listing of the procedures used in custody evaluations. Respondents rated the frequency of their usage of each on a scale of 1 (*never*) to 5 (*always*). Mean ratings for interviewing significant parties were, as expected, quite high: Interview mother = 4.98; Interview father = 4.91; Interview younger child = 4.65; Interview older child = 4.91; Observe mother with child = 4.82; Observe father with child = 4.80. But the *next most frequent* activity was to administer the MMPI-2 to the parents; its average rating of 4.19 meant that it was used quite frequently. The scales specifically developed to assess parenting—to be described later in this section—were used only about half the time (average rating of 3.28, although there was wide variation among respondents in their reported use). Thus, the survey supported the conclusion of reviewers Randy K. Otto and Robert P. Collins (1995) that "the MMPI/MMPI-2 is the psychological assessment instrument most significantly used [with parents] in child-custody evaluations today" (p. 246).

Is it a good idea to rely on an instrument not designed for the specific purpose? Does the degree to which each parent's responses conform to the scales of, for example, Schizophrenia or some form of neuroticism, say much about what is best for the child? Otto and Collins's (1995) review concluded that the Minnesota instruments can play a role in a much broader inquiry by the psychologist. They can

> assess the emotional functioning and adjustment of the parents, other persons who may significantly affect the child (e.g., stepparents, live-in relatives, or others), and (adolescent) children. The MMPI-2/MMPI-A will also prove of some relevance to child custody evaluations to the degree that they offer a description of, and inform the court about,

the parents' (or other potential caretakers') and (adolescent) child's traits and behavior (Pope, Butcher, & Seelen, 1993). Finally, the MMPI/MMPI-2 also may prove to be of some value with respect to assessing the overall test-taking set that parents, other potential caretakers, and (adolescent) children have adopted with respect to the evaluation process. To the degree that minimization or denial of problems and shortcomings is a potential concern in child custody evaluations, the Minnesota tests' validity scales may also prove of some value. (pp. 234–235)

Pope, Butcher, & Seelen (1993) provided a comprehensive guide to the use of the MMPI, MMPI-2, and MMPI-A in court settings.

As noted earlier, several devices have been developed specifically to assist psychologists in making child custody evaluations (see Otto, Edens, & Barcus, 2000; Otto, Buffington-Vollum, & Edens, 2003). This section reviews five that have received attention in the various books published within the past 15 years on child custody evaluations (Ackerman, 1994, 2001; Bricklin, 1995; Gould, 1998; Kissel & Freeling, 1990; Schutz, Dixon, Lindenberger, & Ruther, 1989; Skafte, 1985; Stahl, 1994, 1999a; and Weithorn, 1987). Most of these scales are distributed by commercial test publishers.

The ASPECT Procedure

The Ackerman-Schoendorf Scales for Parent Evaluation of Custody (ASPECT) is really more than a scale or even a set of scales; it is a comprehensive procedure that uses testing, observation, and interviews with each parent and child.

Thus, the ASPECT procedure (Ackerman & Schoendorf, 1992; Ackerman, 1994) receives good marks for its thoroughness; in addition to a set of 68 questions (mostly open-ended) responded to by each parent, it includes a consideration by the evaluating psychologist of the parents' responses on various standard psychological tests, and the psychologist's own responses to evaluations of each parent. The Parent Questionnaire is composed of questions about custody arrange-

ments, living arrangements, and child-care arrangements, the children's development and education, and the relationship between the two parents and between each parent and the children. It also seeks information about the parents' background, including substance abuse, psychiatric treatment, and legal problems. Based on the variety of information, the psychologist answers a series of questions about each parent, leading to scores on three subscales: the Observational Scale, the Social Scale, and the Cognitive-Emotional Scale. The first assesses the quality of each parent's self-presentation during the evaluation process. The Social Scale seeks to measure each parent's quality of interpersonal relationships and concerns about the family, while the Cognitive-Emotional subscale evaluates each parent's affective and cognitive capabilities in relation to child rearing. These lead to an overall score on a Parenting Custody Index (PCI), considered to be a global measure of parenting effectiveness.

The psychologist is encouraged to assess the quality of each parent's interaction with the children and the manner in which each parent communicates with the child. Also, does the parent recognize the present and future needs of the child? Can the parent provide adequate discipline?

Each parent thus emerges with an ASPECT score, and if one of the parents' score is 10 points or more from the other parent's score, the scale authors believe that there exists a significant difference in custodial effectiveness. Among 30 couples who had a 10-point difference or greater, in 28 of these (93%) the ASPECT results were consistent with the judge's decision about custody (Ackerman, 1994).

In a chapter reviewing the use of the MMPI in child custody evaluations, Otto and Collins (1995) evaluated the ASPECT because the ASPECT procedure includes items from the MMPI-2. They were not favorable in their review; they wrote,

> The authors' presentation of validity data on the ASPECT is confusing and incomplete. The authors report that predictive validity was assessed by comparing recommendations

made on the basis of the ASPECT with the parents in the normative study to their judges' final custody decisions. Although the test manual is unclear, apparently, in 59 of the 100 sample cases, results of the ASPECT were conclusive enough to recommend custody for one parent or the other and this recommendation was offered to the court. The authors report that the ASPECT correctly "predicted" the judges' custody decisions in about 75% of the cases (Ackerman & Schoendorf, 1992, p. 53). This, of course, is not true predictive validity because the results of the ASPECT presumably formed the basis of the examining psychologists' opinions that were presented to the court. (pp. 231–232)

The Parent-Child Relationship Inventory (PCRI)
The PCRI (Gerard, 1994) includes 78 items that form seven content subscales and two validity subscales; these subscales are titled: Satisfaction with Parenting, Autonomy, Limit Setting, Involvement, Communication, Parental Support, Role Orientation, and the two validity scales, Social Desirability and Inconsistent Reporting. Each parent independently responds to the items, using 4-point Likert-type choices. The PCRI provides information about the parents' disciplinary styles and feelings of competence, self esteem, and social support. Clinicians who have administered the PCRI report that in about half the couples, the scores do not differentiate between the two parents (Gerard, 1994), a finding consistent with our belief that often the task of the evaluator is not an easy one, *if* the evaluator sees his or her role as making a distinction between the desirability of the two parents.

A Set of Scales Developed by Barry Bricklin (1994)
Bricklin (1994) has developed an interlocking set of scales, including the Bricklin Perceptual Scale (BPS), Perception-of-Relationships-Test (PORT), Parent Awareness Skills Survey (PASS), and the Parent Perception of Child Profile (PPCP). As described in his handbook (Bricklin,

1995, chapters 4–7), these have the following purposes:

- BPS: Sixty-four items (32 about the mother and 32 about the father) are posed to the child. The child is asked how well each item describes each parent; the author considers it appropriate for use with children over 6 years of age. The goal is to assess the child's perceptions of each parent on each of four characteristics: competence, supportiveness, follow-up consistency, and possession of admirable character traits. Not only does the child provide an oral response about how well each parent performs each activity but the child is also instructed to use a nonverbal response (pushing a stylus through a black line with end points of *very well* and *not so well*); the latter procedure, according to the author, reflects "unconscious mental sources" (Bricklin, 1995, pp. 77–78). It is only this latter nonverbal response that is scored; Bricklin believes that children's verbal expressions are often defensive or distorted (Schutz et al., 1989).
- PORT: With the goal of assessing the degree of closeness the child feels toward each parent, this measure primarily uses projective drawings by the child. Bricklin has designed this measure for administration to children 3 years of age and older.
- PASS: This scale measures each parent's awareness of factors important in determining his or her response to 18 issues related to child care. The scoring reflects the interviewer's assessment of the quality of the parent's answers to questions, including follow-up ones that probe the parent's feelings.
- PPCP: This procedure asks for information from each parent about his or her perceptions of each child; more than 120 questions (plus probes) are used.

As can been seen, some of the preceding measures use responses from the child, some from the parents; some are self-report questionnaires, some structured interviews, and some use projective techniques. To varying degrees, the psychologist makes his or her own interpretation of the responses and behaviors of the participants. The whole collection makes for a lengthy evaluation, and, unfortunately, no norms exist. However, Bricklin (1994) reported an 89% agreement rate between the "preferred parent" based on the BPS measure and the judge's eventual choice of the primary caretaker (but is this the best measure of test validity?). A recent survey (Ackerman & Ackerman, 1997) found that the BPS was the most frequently administered test to children.

Parenting Stress Index
The fourth measure reflects a different goal—a less direct one; its purpose is to assess the type and severity of stresses associated with the child-rearing role (Abidin, 1990, 1998). Its author made a candid disclaimer: "I would like to make it clear that I am not a forensic psychologist and that in developing the PSI I never envisioned that it would be used for forensic purposes" (1998, p. 1). Both a 101-item self-report scale, used by parents of children ages 3 months to 10 years, and a 36-item short form exist. Various subscales are related to the child or children in the family (for example, the children's adaptability, mood, demandingness, and hypersensitivity) and to the parent's feeling of his or her own competence, social isolation, depression, attachment, and relationship with spouse.

Parenting Satisfaction Scale
Another, relatively new scale that focuses on parenting is the Parenting Satisfaction Scale (Guidubaldi & Cleminshaw, 1998), which consists of 45 self-report items in three domains: satisfaction with the parenting done by the spouse or ex-spouse, satisfaction with one's own parent–child relationship, and satisfaction with one's own performance as a parent. Sample items include:

- "I wish I did not become so impatient with my children."
- "My spouse has sufficient knowledge about child development that makes him/her feel comfortable as a parent."

One application of the scale is to assess judgments of compatibility for shared parenting.

Evaluating These Scales
The various books on child custody evaluations differ in how much enthusiasm they express for using these measures (for an advocate of the instruments, see Podrygula, 1997). The published reviews of the psychometric properties of these scales are, in contrast, almost uniformly critical (see Krauss & Sales, 2000; Otto & Heilbrun, 2002); among the limitations cited are the following:

1. Inclusion of unrealistic or untested assumptions, including the reduction of complex constructs to narrow behavior samples (Melton, 1995; Shaffer, 1992).
2. Use of small samples, or inappropriate clinical samples, or inadequate descriptions of the sample (Hagin, 1992; Carlson, 1995; Hiltonsmith, 1995).
3. Frequent absence of norms (Carlson, 1995).
4. Lack of evidence of reliability or validity (Arditti, 1995; Conger, 1995; Bischoff, 1995; Hiltonsmith, 1995).

A more detailed critique of these devices may be found in the reviews by Heinze and Grisso (1996); Borum (1998); Melton et al. (1997, pp. 503–504), Krauss and Sales (2000); Otto, Edens, & Barcus (2000); Otto, Buffington-Vollum, & Edens (2003); and Otto and Heilbrun (2002). Our view of the best use of these is reflected in the summary by Melton and his colleagues:

> We join with other reviewers who recommend caution in the use of these commercially available "child custody" measures. Although some of these measures may facilitate gathering useful responses regarding parents' attitudes, knowledge, or values with respect to raising their children, the lack of adequate reliability and validity studies counsels against use of formal indices they yield. Certainly these indices do not identify "scientifically" the parent of choice or indicate other dispositional conclusions, matters

which are properly reserved for the court. (Melton et al., 1997, p. 504)

THE EXPERT WITNESS ROLE

A judge who handles many child custody cases, Samuel G. Fredman (1995), offered the following specific advice to psychologists who are testifying:

1. Be prepared. Be ready to give the judge your point of view. Show the judge you know your subject. "Convince me . . . that some of my long-held thinking should fall by the wayside because of your testimony" (p. 4).
2. Provide your expert opinion. "We want to know, having satisfied ourselves as to your background and experience and knowledge, what you think we ought to do in a given situation" (p. 4).
3. Reflect objectivity. "When the court appoints a psychologist, the court expects the neutrality which such designation underscores. We would like to feel we are getting that same kind of objectivity" (pp. 4–5).

Ultimate-Opinion Testimony

The APA Guidelines (APA, 1994) do not say that you cannot give an opinion on the ultimate issue, and psychologists need to recognize that judges differ in the degree that they want **ultimate-opinion testimony.** Some judges are explicit about wanting a recommendation regarding the custody determination and will not reappoint a psychologist who won't give such an opinion (Gould, 1998). On the other hand, for some judges, their authority and rule making are paramount. Judge Fredman, in speaking to psychologists, stated, "*You* are not making the custody or visitation decision: I am. We want merely advice and counsel" (1995, italics in original).

Some psychologists (Melton et al., 1997; Schutz et al., 1989; Weithorn & Grisso, 1987) have concluded that it is inappropriate for custody

evaluators to give testimony on the bottom-line question. Instead, the focus should be on the quality of the relationship between parents and the child.

Mario Dennis (personal communication, May 8, 1998), a psychologist, wrote,

I think there are ways of addressing the ultimate issue without giving a final opinion on it. I generally list the advantages and disadvantages of placing the children with each parent, and relate those to the test data, parenting experience, relationships between the parents and children, environment, etc. I also factor in the potential consequences of disrupting the status quo, whatever that may be.

Regardless, the psychologist as expert witness should resist the temptation to express an opinion that goes beyond his or her information or competence, whatever the pressures from the judge or the attorneys to do so.

Ethical Considerations

The ethical responsibilities upon any psychologist testifying as an expert witness apply here. The APA Guidelines for Child Custody Evaluations (APA, 1994) emphasize that any recommendation should reflect the best interests of the child. The psychologist should be informed on a variety of topics: the applicable legal standards, the effects of divorce on children, and child psychopathology (Ackerman, 1994).

THE EVALUATION RESEARCHER ROLE

Forensic psychologists who are on the "firing line" need to be aware of research findings on relevant issues. Psychologists reflecting the evaluation researcher role have provided useful findings on two topics: the effects of divorce on children, and the effects of type of custody arrangement.

Effects of Divorce on Children

The decision to divorce is a complicated one, and considerations abound. Some divorcing couples partially justify the decision to divorce by assuming that any detrimental effects on their children will gradually dissipate. This self-serving assumption that "children are resilient; they will eventually get over it" is challenged by a 15-year longitudinal study by Wallerstein and Blakeslee (1989). Their participants were 131 children and adolescents from 60 divorced families in Marin County, California. Only about one tenth of the children in this study felt relieved when the quarreling parents separated, and these tended to be the older children who had been observers or recipients of physical abuse from one or both parents.

Judith Wallerstein, one of the authors of the study, stated, "Almost half of children of divorces enter adulthood as worried, underachieving, self-deprecating, and sometimes angry young men and women" (quoted by Toufexis, 1989, p. 61). Wallerstein and Blakeslee described a "sleeper effect" on females; many of them seemed to have adjusted to their parents' divorce well into adulthood, at which point they suffered "an intolerable level of anxiety about betrayal." They then might drop out of college, become promiscuous, or trap themselves in unsatisfactory relationships—all, according to the authors, to protect themselves from rejection, abandonment, and betrayal. The researchers reported that this reaction occurred in two thirds of the women between the ages of 19 and 23. Of children whose mothers remarried, half said they did not feel welcome in the new family. Ten years after the divorce, more than one third reported having poor relationships with both parents.

These results are disturbing, but whether they apply to a more representative sample of divorced families may be questioned. The subjects were recruited through the offer of counseling, leading some reviewers (cf. Melton et al., 1997, p. 492) to expect them to differ from a broader set of families who were coping with marital separation.

Another major study presents more optimistic conclusions about the effects of divorce on children. The longitudinal study by Hetherington and her colleagues (Hetherington, 1979, 1989, 1993; Hetherington, Stanley-Hagan, & Anderson, 1989) was a quasi-experimental study of 72 White, middle-class 4- and 5-year-old children and their divorced parents. (In all these families, mothers received custody of the children.) Focus was on the changes in the relationships; for example, the first year after the divorce is conflict-ridden, as everyone deals not only with anger and loss but also with practical problems of separate households. Results often differ from family to family; general trends are summarized by Thompson (1983) and by Melton et al. (1997).

Effects of Type of Custody

The most consistent innovation by the courts regarding divorce in the last three decades is **joint custody;** statutes in an increasing number of states have come to favor it as an alternative (Rohman, Sales, & Lou, 1990), and, in some recent statutes, such custody must be ordered by the judge unless the evidence exists that such an arrangement would be harmful to the child (Scott & Derdeyn, 1984). In some states, joint custody has become the judicial determination in as many as 80% of the cases (Byczynski, 1987). But definitions of joint custody differ widely from state to state. In some instances, the amount of time the child is in the physical custody of each parent is split relatively equally; in other instances, the child lives mainly with one parent, but both parents retain legal decision making with respect to the child's education, health, and welfare (Felner & Terre, 1987). Simply put, joint legal custody does not necessarily mean shared physical custody (Maccoby & Mnookin, 1992).

During the period of peak interest in the procedure, joint custody was seen as a panacea to the problem of custody, because children could maintain their relationship with both parents, divorced fathers could maintain influence over the lives of their children, and mothers could avoid the burden of being the sole disciplinarian (Press, 1983). Two other reasons for the enthusiasm for joint custody have been offered: (a)

Fathers who continued to share custody of their children were more likely to make child-support payments, and (b) co-parenting would reduce the conflict between divorced parents (Weitzman, 1985).

BOX 9-4
How Beneficial Is Joint Custody? A Task for Evaluation Research

A review of findings about the effects of joint custody upon children (Felner & Terre, 1987, pp. 126-134) provides mixed conclusions.

On the positive side are the following findings:

1. Luepnitz (1982) compared joint-custody arrangements with single-custody homes. All the children in the joint-custody arrangements reported that they preferred that system; about half the children in the single-custody homes wished for more contact with the other parent. In a follow-up of 43 of her 50 families, Luepnitz (1986) concluded that joint custody, at its best, is superior to single custody at its best, but by no means was one always better than the other.

2. Shiller (1986b) concluded that children in joint custody retain more appropriate and realistic feelings about each parent.

3. In another study, Shiller (1986a) found that boys have fewer behavioral difficulties in joint-custody arrangements.

Less optimistic were the findings of a study by Steinman (1981), who interviewed 24 families, all of whom had agreed to a joint-custody arrangement. Although many of the parents and children thrived under this system, about one fourth of the 32 children reported having a difficult time shifting back and forth between the two homes. One third of these children seemed "overburdened" and were having noticeable adjustment problems. In fact, the child's need for environmental stability is considered by some as the major obstacle to greater use by judges of the joint-custody arrangement (Clingempeel & Reppucci, 1982).

Given that sometimes joint custody is helpful to children and sometimes it is harmful, can we identify factors that increase the likelihood of a beneficial result? Yes. If the parents have an amicable relationship, joint custody seems to have no adverse effect on the emotional health of the children (Kline, Tschann, Johnston, & Wallerstein, 1989). But a continuing conflict-riddled relationship between parents can be detrimental to the

children in a joint-custody arrangement. Sales, Manber, and Rohman summarized the research findings as follows:

Factors that have been identified as important for joint custody to work beneficially for the children include the parents' willingness to share custody and cooperate; their motivation to provide continued access to the other parent; and their ability to separate their own feelings and issues about the other parent from the child's needs and feelings, to empathize with the child, to respect the other parent's bond with the child, to trust in the other parent's parenting skills, and to maintain objectivity through the divorce process (Keilin & Bloom, 1986; Steinman, Zemmelman, & Knoblauch, 1985; Shiller, 1986a; Volgy & Everett, 1985). The importance of the quality of the interparental relationship for the success of the joint-custody arrangement fits with Koch and Lowery's (1984) findings regarding non-custodial fathers; continued involvement of fathers with their children after divorce is predicted by the relationship between the divorced parents rather than by the parent-child relationship (1992, p. 33).

As this review implies in its last statement, the specific custody arrangements may be less influential on children's adjustment than the parents' emotional stability and the amount of continuing conflict between them (Grych & Fincham, 1992). In summary, as the review by Felner and Terre (1987) concluded,

Perhaps the clearest statement that can be made is that no particular custody arrangement is "best." Arguments in favor of a resumption of one form over another are ill-suited to the realities of family life and development. The contention of Goldstein et al. (1979) that the child's relationship with the custodial or "psychological parent" may be damaged by the continued coequal involvement of the noncustodial parent does not appear to be necessarily true in all cases. However, neither is the contention by joint custody advocates that joint custody is the best alternative for all children (p. 140).

But then second thoughts surfaced; for example, it has been claimed that joint custody strains the ideal of "psychological parenting" after divorce. The concept of psychological parenting was advanced by Goldstein, Freud, and Solnit (1979), who defined such a parent as "one who, on a continuing, day-to-day basis, through interplay, and mutuality, fulfills the child's psychological needs for a parent, as well as the child's physical needs" (p. 98). Also, the early expectations about the unqualified beneficial effects of joint custody upon the children have been tempered by research findings that are mixed. Box 9-4 reviews these findings.

As noted earlier, the anticipated benefits of joint custody extend beyond the satisfaction level of children and include possible increased compliance with child-support mandates and a reduction in conflict between the two parents. The detailed review by Sales, Manber, and Rohman (1992), on which we have relied heavily in this chapter, concludes that results are also mixed for each of these. For example, some studies conclude that those fathers who are participating in joint-custody arrangements are less often late or delinquent in paying child support (Luepnitz, 1982, 1986; Waddell, 1985), but another study reports no difference between joint-custody and maternal-custody arrangements (Lowery, 1986).

Likewise, it is not clear that joint custody reduces the level of antagonism between divorced parents (Sales, Manber, & Rohman, 1992, p. 32). Hauser (1985), in an extreme view, concluded that "simply having the designation of joint custody does little, if anything, to ameliorate conflict; nor does it promote, support, or make possible appropriate communication, adequate to children's needs in a population of chronic litigators" (p. 581). It is the case that other studies report no difference in conflict levels from different custody arrangements (Albiston, Maccoby, & Mnookin, 1990), but many studies report the opposite, including greater cooperation between parents and a lower rate of further lawsuits (Shiller, 1986a; Luepnitz, 1986; Ilfeld, Ilfeld, & Alexander, 1982).

SUMMARY

As a part of the decision making when a couple divorces and contests the custody of their children, forensic psychologists can play several roles, including that of marriage counselor, mediator, child therapist, court-appointed evaluator, expert witness, and applied researcher. In such activities, the forensic psychologist needs to avoid the possibility of dual relationships of, for example, serving as a therapist for the child and later serving as a consultant to the court on the best disposition for the child.

When the forensic psychologist carries out an evaluation at the request of the court, several procedures are typically included; each parent and each child are separately interviewed and each child is often observed interacting with each parent. Usually, the parents are asked to complete a questionnaire or even a battery of psychological assessment techniques. The most frequently used instrument is the MMPI-2, although several instruments have been devised specifically for child custody evaluations.

Upon completion of the evaluation, the forensic psychologist prepares a report for the judge. In some jurisdictions, the report is made available to the parents' lawyers and to the parents. The psychologist may then testify at a hearing; judges differ in their desire to hear ultimate opinion testimony from the psychologist.

A separate role exists for the forensic psychologist in evaluating general claims and assumptions about the nature of custody as well as the long-term effects of their parents' divorce on children.

KEY TERMS

applied researcher
best-interests-of-the-child standard
court-appointed evaluator
custody evaluation
dual relationship
expert witness

fact witness
joint custody
mediator
tender-years doctrine
ultimate-opinion testimony
"Ziskinize"

INFOTRAC®
COLLEGE EDITION

InfoTrac College Edition is a FREE, powerful, online learning resource, consisting of full-text articles from thousands of journals and periodicals. With each new copy of *Forensic Psychology,* Second Edition, you receive 4 months of free access to the InfoTrac College Edition database. By doing a simple keyword search (try using the Key Terms in the list above), you can quickly generate a list of relevant articles from thousands of possibilities and can select articles to read, explore, and print for reference or further study. InfoTrac College Edition's continuously updated collection of articles can be useful for doing reading and writing assignments that reach beyond the pages of this text!

SUGGESTED READINGS

Ackerman, M. J. (1994, 2001). *Clinician's guide to child custody evaluations.* New York: John Wiley.

A detailed description of the comprehensive ASPECT procedure.

Gould, J. W. (1998). *Conducting scientifically crafted custody evaluations.* Thousand Oaks, CA: Sage.

State-of-the-art application of forensic techniques to child custody evaluations. The author reviews applicable literature from child development.

Greenberg, S. A., & Shuman, D. W. (1997). Irreconcilable conflict between therapeutic and forensic roles. *Professional Psychology: Research and Practice, 28,* 505–557.

An article that analyzes 10 critical differences between the role of the psychotherapist and the forensic evaluator.

Liss, M. B., & McKinley-Pace, M. J. (1999). Best interests of the child: New twists on an old theme. In R. Roesch, S. D. Hart, & J. R. P. Ogloff (Eds.), *Psychology and law: The state of the discipline* (pp. 339–372). New York: Kluwer Academic/Plenum.

A chapter-length review of applications of the best-interests-of-the-child standard not only to custody after divorce but also to adoption cases.

Melton, G. B., Petrila, J., Poythress, N. G., & Slobogin, C. (1997). *Psychological evaluations for the courts* (2nd ed.). New York: Guilford Press.

Chapter 16, on "Child Custody in Divorce" (pp. 483–505), is a sobering but thoughtful treatment of the psychologist's varied roles.

Otto, R. K., Buffington-Vollum, J., & Edens, J. F. (2003). Child custody evaluations: Research and practice. In A. Goldstein (Ed.), *Handbook of Psychology: Vol. 11. Forensic Psychology.* New York: Wiley.

An up-to-date and complete discussion of the issues in child custody evaluations.

Schutz, B. M., Dixon, E. B., Lindenberger, J. C., & Ruther, N. J. (1989). *Solomon's sword: A practical guide to conducting child custody evaluations.* San Francisco: Jossey-Bass.

A brief guide for the forensic psychologist with useful examples of interview questions for parents and for children and behavioral observations. Contains a section on how the psychologist as expert witness should respond when **"Ziskinized,"** or aggressively questioned during cross-examination.

10

Improving Eyewitness Identification Procedures

HOW IMPORTANT IS EYEWITNESS TESTIMONY IN CRIMINAL CASES?

A central goal of police work is to solve, or "clear," crimes. In their effort to solve crimes, police are more likely to be successful if at least one eyewitness was present. Fisher (1995) cited a 1975 Rand Corporation study of the process of crime investigation that concluded that the major factor determining whether a case would be solved was the completeness and accuracy of the eyewitness's account. In fact, those crimes that were most likely to be cleared were those in which the offenders were captured within minutes or those in which an eyewitness provided a *specific* relevant piece of information—a license plate number, a name, an address, or a unique identification. If one of these was not present, the chances that the crime would be solved were less than 10% (Greenwood & Petersilia, 1976).

The conclusion that eyewitness evidence is crucial in the outcome of cases is supported by the work of Lavrakas and Bickman (1975). These researchers surveyed 54 prosecutors regarding their opinions of "what makes a good witness." The prosecutors were asked to consider what effect a set of witness attributes would have on the outcome of a case. Ratings were made on a 5-point scale, from *this attribute is totally unrelated to the outcome* to *this attribute is very related to the outcome*. Results showed that witness attributes such as race, sex, age, or socioeconomic status made virtually no difference in the prosecutor's ratings of importance. On the other hand, the victim's availability for testimony, the victim's ability to testify, and the witness's assertion of a "good memory" and clarity of recall were central to the prosecutors' ratings. Clearly, the presence of "good" and available eyewitness evidence is seen as an important determinant of case outcome.

CAN EYEWITNESS TESTIMONY CONTRIBUTE TO WRONGFUL CONVICTIONS?

The importance of the eyewitness's memory in reconstructing events from the past does not end with the arrest of a suspect. At a trial, the testimony of an eyewitness who incriminates the defendant is—along with the presence of a confession—usually the most influential evidence (Lavrakas & Bickman, 1975). If a jury or a judge believes eyewitnesses who have testified in good faith (and why doubt them?), the belief leads to a conclusion of guilt. Alibis, circumstantial evidence, even masses of physical evidence favoring the defendant's innocence, can wither away in light of an eyewitness's courtroom identification.

Of course, the essential problem is that eyewitnesses are not infallible. We know this from a variety of sources, primarily from studies of cases of known wrongful convictions (Rattner, 1988; Huff, Rattner, & Sagarin, 1996). But the most important such studies have emerged from the recent availability of DNA technology to analyze claims of wrongful conviction. Wells (1993) concluded that eyewitness errors provide the single most frequent cause of wrongful convictions, and two recent examinations of such cases provide strong evidence for that assertion. In 1996, the United States Department of Justice published an analysis of the first 28 cases of individuals in the United States who were convicted of crimes but later exonerated on the basis of DNA testing (Connors, Lundregan, Miller, & McEwan, 1996). Of those, 24 involved mistaken eyewitness identification, some with multiple witnesses (as many as five in one case). A later analysis found that in the first 40 of these cases, 36 (or 90%) were cases in which one or more eyewitnesses falsely identified the innocent person (Wells, Small, Penrod, Malpass, Fulero, & Brimacombe, 1998). Another even more recent review, extending the number of DNA cases to over 100, found that eyewitness error was involved in 84% of the cases of wrongful conviction (Scheck, Neufeld, & Dwyer, 2000).

HOW CAN FORENSIC PSYCHOLOGISTS HELP POLICE OBTAIN USEFUL INFORMATION FROM EYEWITNESSES?

Can forensic psychology assist in reducing the error rate? As chapter 1 described, the field of experimental psychology has a long history of the study of memory and especially errors in memory, tracing back to a century ago with the work of Hermann von Ebbinghaus and Hugo Münsterberg. Eyewitness accuracy was one of the earliest topics in experimental psychology (e.g., Cattell, 1895). But in the last 15 years there has been an explosion of research on this topic (see Cutler & Penrod, 1995; Wells et al., 1998), and psychologists now possess extensive information on how eyewitness evidence can be improved in actual cases (Wells, 1993; Technical Working Group on Eyewitness Evidence, 1999, 2003).

The act of a witness describing or identifying a suspect involves more than memory alone; it invokes reasoning processes, suggestibility and social influence, self-confidence, authoritarian submission, conformity, and a host of other social processes. Wells (1995) has pointed out that "*memory testimony* and *memory* are not identical twins. **Memory testimony** is the witness's statement of what he or she recalls of a prior event. These statements can be influenced by more than just memory processes" (p. 727, italics in original, boldface added).

The examples of problematic police witness interview procedures—to be described in a later section—illustrate the distinction between memory and memory testimony and some of the determinants of inaccurate conclusions. Ideally, an eyewitness's identification will be a product solely of his or her memory rather than a product of the identification procedures used by the police (Technical Working Group on Eyewitness Evidence, 1999, 2003). Studies in the psychological laboratory or controlled field studies that simulate a crime and then determine the degree of accuracy of eyewitnesses confirm the fear that false identifications by bystanders occur with frightful frequency (Brigham, Maass, Snyder, & Spaulding, 1982; Buckhout, 1974; Cutler, Penrod, & Martens, 1987; Ellis, Shepherd, & Davies, 1980; Leippe, Wells & Ostrom, 1978; Wells, 1984b; Wells, Lindsay, & Ferguson, 1979). In those crime simulations in which subjects believed the crime was real and their identification would have consequences for the accused, high rates of false identification still occurred (Malpass & Devine, 1980; Murray & Wells, 1982). Studies that have looked at actual eyewitnesses in actual crimes (after the fact, of course, since crimes cannot ethically be created by researchers) have generally found similar results (see Behrman & Davey, 2001). How high a rate of inaccuracy? In some studies, as many as 90% of responses were false identifications; in others, only a few subjects erred. The extreme variation exemplifies a central theme of this chapter: The degree of accuracy can be partly determined by the specific procedures used by the police to collect eyewitness evidence during a criminal investigation.

System Variables Versus Estimator Variables

Those who study eyewitness identification emphasize that rather than being satisfied simply to point out that the reports of eyewitnesses are often inaccurate, we should recognize that the degree of accuracy is often influenced by the procedures used by the police and other members of the criminal justice system (Wells & Seelau, 1995). Wells (1978) referred to these as

system variables. These variables include the type of questioning done by the police, the nature of the lineup or photo array, and the presence or absence of videotaping of procedures. These variables are the focus of this chapter, because when they contribute to eyewitness inaccuracy, they are *preventable errors* (Wells, 1993); in fact, psychologists could aid in the construction of lineups and the development of interviewing procedures that reduce inaccuracy.

The other determinants of an eyewitness's accuracy—what Wells called **estimator variables**—are not controllable by the criminal justice system and, hence, not reviewed in detail in this chapter, given that the chapter's topic is working with the police to improve their crime investigation (see Box 10-4 for examples of estimator variables that psychologists commonly testify about; see also Wrightsman, Greene, Neitzel, & Fortune, 2001, for a more detailed discussion; Wells & Loftus, 2002). Estimator variables include environmental factors (for instance, length of time the witness saw the target, stress, weapons focus, cross-racial identification) and within-the-person variables (the witness's mental state, physical condition, eyesight, etc.). Estimator variables are determined before the police respond. For example, the degree of violence that is a part of a crime affects the witness's ability to recall the event; Clifford and Scott (1978) reported that subjects who witnessed a nonviolent act were able to remember aspects with more detail and correctness than were those who witnessed a violent act. But what's done is done here, and nothing the police can do can increase or decrease the accuracy of this aspect, other than being more cautionary in assuming the accuracy of reports by victims of violence.

Thus, the distinction of importance between these two types of variables is that errors in system variables can often be reduced and can sometimes be prevented. We can do nothing about poor lighting conditions or the brevity of exposure to the criminal, but police can work to eliminate practices that have been shown to lead to further inaccuracies in reports.

Examples of Problematic Police Procedures

Wells (1995, p. 727) has observed that police use great caution and care when collecting physical evidence at the crime scene, but "these same police . . . do not seem to accept the premise that memory traces can also be contaminated." A number of police departments in the United States and Canada have written guidelines for use in identifications, but these are not always consistent with what psychologists would recommend (Wells, 1988; Wells et al., 1998). Variations from acceptable procedures identified by Wells (1988, p. 727) include

1. Asking witnesses poorly constructed questions immediately upon discovering the crime.
2. Allowing one eyewitness to overhear the responses of other eyewitnesses.
3. Taking "spotty" notes of witnesses' answers (and not recording the actual questions asked).
4. Failing to use any theory of a proper memory interview.
5. Using investigators who have little training in interviewing or the psychology of memory (or as Fisher, 1995, noted, generalizing interviewing procedures from those they use to interview *suspects*).

Compounding the problem is the fact that, as Fisher (1995) noted, many interviews with eyewitnesses are conducted under the worst conditions imaginable: witnesses who are agitated and/or injured; time pressures that demand rapid-fire questioning; and background conditions characterized by distractions, confusion, and noise. On top of this, police supervisors often goad officers to file their reports rapidly.

An even broader concern is the motivation of police in questioning witnesses. A temptation of police investigators is to act prematurely in forming a conclusion about the likely perpetrator; this too-early hunch then guides the investigator toward those questions and procedures that validate the belief (Fisher, 1995). So, in interviewing eyewitnesses, police may be tempted to ask leading questions or offer subtle confirmation of their hunches; they may construct biased **lineups** or **photo arrays** to aid in identifying the "correct" suspect (Lindsay, 1994).

In a decision more than 30 years ago (*Simmons v. United States,* 1968), the Supreme Court recognized that dangers exist from the ways that police sometimes use lineups and photo arrays to question victims and witnesses. But, amazingly, in two important cases regarding eyewitness identification, the Court decided—rather than rejecting certain police practices as improper—to try to deal with the problem by supporting the suspect's right to counsel during a lineup. In the first case (*United States v. Wade,* 1967), Wade was accused of bank robbery and placed in a lineup with five prisoners. Both eyewitnesses later reported that they had seen Wade standing in the hall with a police officer before the lineup (in which they picked him out as the perpetrator). In the second case (*Gilbert v. California,* 1967), the lineup was conducted in an auditorium; 100 people who had been victims of one robbery or another were present. These eyewitnesses talked to each other and called out numbers of the men they could identify; all in all, the procedure was very poorly controlled. Although the Court expressed some concern about each of these procedures, the emphasis in both decisions was on the right of the defense attorney to be present during the lineup to help reveal the biased procedures to the trial jury. Rather than ruling against the use of such procedures, the Court concluded that the right to counsel was a safeguard against unfair effects of such practices. But why not try to prevent those practices from occurring at all as well as attempting to protect defendants' rights if damage is still done?

The following are a few of the cases in which errors by the police have been documented; Box 10-1 provides another. They provide raw material for the sorts of guidelines advocated by psychologists who all too frequently see this kind of case in their forensic work:

The Steve Titus Case

Steve Titus was stopped for questioning by police because his car's license plate and description were both generally similar to those given by a rape victim. He willingly cooperated with the police when they asked him if they could take his photograph. When the 17-year-old victim was shown Titus's two photographs, they had been placed on a sheet with the profile and full-face shots of five other men who resembled Titus. But the two photographs of Titus were of a different size from the others, and they were not separated by a black line as the other pairs were. There were other "hints" in the presentation that Titus was the person to be selected; for example, the jurisdictional designation under Titus's photos was different from the one under the photos of the other five men.

Further violations of acceptable procedures in this investigation included the instruction that the police officer gave to the victim: "Tell me which one raped you." After staring at the photographs for five minutes, the victim finally, hesitantly, said—pointing to Titus's photos—"This one is the closest" (Olsen, 1991, p. 169). On this basis, Titus was brought to trial and convicted of rape. Only the work of an investigative reporter with the *Seattle Times* led the authorities to question this verdict. Eventually, the real rapist came forward and confessed. When the victim was shown his photo, she immediately recognized her mistake and broke down and cried.

The John Demjanjuk Case: Was He Ivan the Terrible?

In the 1980s, John Demjanjuk, a retired automobile worker living in Cleveland, Ohio, was accused of having been, during World War II, a Nazi collaborator who was a guard at a concentration camp where thousands of German and Polish Jews were annihilated. With the cooperation of the U.S. government, he was deported to Israel, where he was put on trial as a war criminal in February 1987.

BOX 10-1
The Howard Haupt Case

Howard Haupt was charged with the abduction and murder of a young boy from a Nevada hotel-casino. Several eyewitnesses to the abduction were questioned by the Las Vegas County police; among them was John Picha. The interview was audiotaped.

Loftus and Ketcham (1991) described the questioning:

The interviewer then turned to John Picha, asking him to go through the photos, beginning with number 1. "Definitely not," he said to numbers 1 and 2. At number 3 he hesitated and said, "I'm stuck on . . . no, that one is too old. He didn't seem to be that old."

"Well, other than that?" the interviewer said. "I mean, is it similar?"

"Yeah."

Picha looked at numbers 4 and 5. Both were definite no's. At number 6 he said, "The face has a resemblance and the glasses I think, but the hair doesn't."

"So the only two in here that kind of ring your bells are number 6 and number 3?"

"Well, actually if you put that type of hairdo"—Picha pointed to number 3—"with that type of face"—he pointed to number 6—"I think you would come up with a clue."

"You like number 3's hair?"

"Yeah, I think that's . . ."

"How about the glasses on number 3?"

"It was more this type of glasses," Picha answered, pointing to number 6.

"You want number 6's glasses on number 3?"

"Yeah."

"Okay, and you think number 3 is too old. How old do you think number 3 is?"

"In his forties."

"What is your estimate of the age of number 6?"

"In his thirties."

"Okay. So what rules out number 3 to you is just that he looks too old?"

"And the sideburns. I don't remember because this guy was pretty much clean shaven."

"But his hair is similar configuration?"

"The hair, yeah, from the color too."

"That's another thing about the color. What do you think about the color on number 3's hair?" the interviewer asked.

"That's what I'm saying. I can't tell from this picture."

"It's difficult I know."

"Pictures are just so hard."

"But you don't see anyone there that you are positive of?"

"No. Number 1 I know it is not. Number 2 I know it isn't. Number 5. Number 6 . . . I've seen so many, it's starting to get foggy. It's just so foggy now that I've seen so many things and so many people."

"Okay."

"But I'd say number 3 would be closest." (From Loftus & Ketcham, 1991, pp. 171–173)

The demand characteristics operating on the eyewitness are rampant here. As Loftus and Ketcham noted:

The cops had a firm suspect—number 3. The eyewitness hesitated at number 3 but then rejected him as being too old. If the suspect had been number 6, number 3 would have been forgotten and the conversation would have focused on number 6. All of these questions focused the eyewitness's attention on number 3. How many times did the interviewer need to repeat "number 3" before his witness got the idea that . . . "number 3 is the guy I'm supposed to pick." (1991, p. 173)

Howard Haupt went to trial but was acquitted.

Incredibly, several survivors of the concentration camp at Treblinka identified him after examining his 1951 visa photo; note that these identifications reflect the assumption of accurate memories of interactions that occurred more than 30 years earlier. For example, Yossef Czarny survived the Treblinka camp and later was freed from the camp at Bergen-Belsen; when he examined a photo album of Ukrainian suspects, he immediately pointed to Demjanjuk's photo and exclaimed:

"This is Ivan, yes. It is Ivan, the notorious Ivan. Thirty years have gone by, but I recognize him at first sight with complete certainty. I would know him, I believe, even in the dark. He was very tall, of sturdy frame, his face at the time was not as full and fat from gorging himself with food, as in the picture. However, it is the same face construction, the same nose, the same eyes and forehead, as he had at that time. A mistake is out of the question." (quoted by Wagenaar, 1988, pp. 110-111)

Czarny and other survivors testified at Demjanjuk's trial, but cross-examination of the Israeli police investigator, Miriam Radiwker, revealed that she did not think it was wrong to direct the survivors' attention to one particular photo during the questioning. She admitted having used this very suggestive procedure. Furthermore, the photos of **foils** presented to the survivors did not fit the description of Ivan the Terrible; his picture was the only one that could be described as balding, with a round face and short neck (Wagenaar, 1988, p. 133). Also, in their report to the court, investigators did not mention that some survivors failed to recognize Demjanjuk.

Even though Demjanjuk was convicted of war crimes in April 1988, the Supreme Court of Israel 5 years later overturned the conviction, basing its conclusion on the inconsistency of evidence, which created a reasonable doubt as to the identity of Demjanjuk as Ivan the Terrible.

The Case of Father Bernard T. Pagano

The false identification of a Catholic priest, Father Bernard Pagano, as an armed robber reflects several improper procedures. After several armed robberies around Wilmington, Delaware, with similar characteristics, the state police drew upon eyewitnesses to prepare a **composite drawing** of the robber. Publication of this drawing led to several anonymous calls pointing to Father Pagano, the assistant pastor of a church in Bethesda, Maryland (Ellison & Buckhout, 1981). He was placed under surveillance; in fact, the police took two eyewitnesses to a health club so that they could get a good look at him. Later, they placed a 10-year-old photo of him in a photo array; the photographs of the eight other men who served as foils differed from him in several respects, including hair style, clothing, and age. Furthermore, the background of Pagano's photo

was distinctly different from the others. In a third procedure, the police used a recent photograph of Father Pagano and the photos of several foils. Pagano was 53 years old; none of the foils was more than 32. His clothing was different, and his photo had the profile on the left, in contrast to all the foils (Ellison & Buckhout, 1981). Father Pagano was placed on trial, and it was likely that the jury would have found him guilty, but during his trial the true robber came forward and confessed. The true criminal, Ronald Clouser, bore a striking resemblance to Father Pagano.

QUESTIONING WITNESSES (INFORMATION GENERATION)

Police conduct a variety of activities in a crime investigation. This section focuses on the task of eliciting descriptions from victims and bystander witnesses; we make no distinction between these two types of eyewitnesses, while acknowledging that victims are more likely to be aroused than bystanders.

As in the work of the Department of Justice's Technical Working Group on Eyewitness Evidence (1999, 2003), the goal of this section is to propose techniques that improve the quality of the methods police use to interview witnesses. In doing so, it is necessary to assess the current state of police interviewing techniques (see Fisher, 1995). Unfortunately, the picture is a rather bleak one.

Lack of Training

First, police receive surprisingly little instruction on how to interview cooperative witnesses (Fisher, 1995, p. 733). Only the larger departments and major training centers offer what Fisher called "reasonably adequate training" (p. 733). Furthermore, the handbooks and textbooks used in police training "either omit the issue of effective interviewing techniques or provide only superficial coverage" (Fisher, 1995, p. 733).

Interview Content

Despite this lack of training, the interviews carried out by different police officers possess some consistencies (Fisher, Geiselman, & Raymond, 1987):

1. After an introduction, the interviewer asks the witness to describe, via a narrative, what happened in the crime.
2. Police then tend to ask brief, direct questions that elicit equally brief responses ("How tall was he?").
3. Other than ending the interview with a broad request for additional information ("Is there anything else you can remember about the event?"), the police interviewer gives little or no assistance to enhance the witness's recollection (Fisher, 1995).

Three types of errors occurred almost universally: interrupting the witness, asking too many short-answer questions, and using an inappropriate sequence of questions (Fisher, Geiselman, & Raymond, 1987). The average interview had three open-ended questions and 26 direct ones; the latter were asked in a staccato, rapid-fire style, usually a second or less after the witness's answer to the previous question.

Failure to Recognize the Dynamics of the Interview

Police appear to be insensitive to the dynamics of the situation when an eyewitness is interviewed by a police officer. The witness is often seeking confirmation or justification; the **demand characteristics** of the situation may elicit pressures to give a "right answer" to an authority figure, or at least to avoid appearing ignorant when asked a specific relevant question. Thus, when asked "Was he wearing jeans?", victims may be reluctant to acknowledge that they didn't notice. (Even more serious is the failure by the

police to evaluate if a victim-witness is lying; see an example in Box 10-2).

Psychologists are, we assume, more aware of the dangers of post-event suggestion (for example, asking "Did he have a mustache?") than are police investigators. More controversial is this question: How often do police ask **leading questions** or make subtle suggestions while interviewing witnesses? Martin Reiser (1989), a longtime psychologist with the Los Angeles Police Department, concluded that the phenomenon is seen more often in laboratory studies than in real-world questioning. Fisher (1995) acknowledged that the empirical evidence about actual use of leading questions "is meager and, at best, difficult to interpret" (p. 740). A laboratory study (Geiselman, Fisher, MacKinnon, & Holland, 1985) found very few leading questions offered, but a field study that tape-recorded the actual interviews by British police officers concluded that one out of every six questions was leading (George & Clifford, 1992). Fisher's conclusion: "[A] cautious approach is to assume that leading suggestions do occur with some regularity" (1995, pp. 740–741).

Police also seem to be unaware that a witness's previous exposure to the *photograph* of a suspect can increase the eyewitness's likelihood—when shown the photograph again at a later time—to identify the suspect as the culprit. Brown, Deffenbacher, and Sturgill (1977) carried out an experiment that manipulated this experience, using a one-week time interval between viewings; around 20% of subjects who had been shown an earlier photograph wrongly identified a suspect (see also Gorenstein & Ellsworth, 1980; Brigham & Cairns, 1988; Hinz & Pezdek, 2001). That is, people may remember a face but forget where they saw it—an example of the phenomenon called **unconscious transference.**

Also, police officers seem to be insensitive to types of errors in their own interviews. Although most recognized that it was a poor interviewing technique to interrupt a witness repeatedly and denied that they did so in their own interviews, many of these same officers made this error at

BOX 10-2

Are Police Able to Detect Deception in Reports of Witnesses and Victims?

When a victim reports a crime, police tend to believe the victim; even rape victims are increasingly being believed by the police. The issue of detecting lying on the part of claimed "victims" has not received sufficient attention.

The case of Cathleen Crowell is illustrative; in 1979, she accused Gary Dotson of having raped her after a party. First she gave a description of her rapist to the police; then she picked out his photograph from a set shown her by the police. No physical evidence linked Dotson to the crime, but despite that and his vehement protests of his innocence, he was convicted and sentenced to 25 to 50 years in prison. Then, 6 years later, suddenly the "victim" (now married, Cathleen Crowell Webb) announced that she had lied; fearing rejection by her foster parents after having had sexual relations with her boyfriend, she manufactured the story that she had been raped (Webb & Chapian, 1985).

Despite a public outcry, the trial judge refused to release Dotson from prison; he did not believe Webb's denial. Finally, in 1987, James Thompson, the governor

of Illinois (and a former law professor and prosecutor), commuted Dotson's sentence to the time already served and Dotson was released from prison. But the governor refused to grant him a pardon, asserting his belief that Crowell's original testimony was accurate and that Dotson was a rapist. Finally, after a prison term for parole violation, Dotson was cleared of the rape charge in 1989, when a DNA test excluded him as the rapist (Yant, 1991).

We do not advocate that police investigators typically doubt the reports of victims of rape; in the matter of rape, the percentage of claimed victims who falsify their claims is quite low (5% or less) and equal to the false-report rate of other major crimes (Allison & Wrightsman, 1993). But further interest should be devoted to the issue of assessing the ability to distinguish between people who tell the truth and those who falsify. The issue is relevant not only to witnesses and victims but also to suspects interrogated by the police, as described in chapter 11.

---

an alarmingly high rate (Fisher, Geiselman, & Amador, 1989). Fisher (1995) observed: "I have witnessed countless times in training workshops detectives who claim at the outset that they already know the principles of effective interviewing from earlier training programs, only to make the same interviewing mistakes as those who have never had any formal training" (p. 757).

Another interviewing technique fraught with potential danger is to ask the same question several times or more during the same interview (Fisher, 1995). If the witness failed to answer the question the first time, the repeated questioning may create a demand characteristic to respond *in some way*, even if it means that the witness lowers his or her standard of confidence. If the witness did answer the first time questioned, the repetition may communicate that the answer was not satisfactory to the police-authority figure, creating social pressure to substitute another response (Fisher, 1995). The latter result is especially likely with witnesses who are young children (Geiselman & Padilla, 1988). Although we do not know how often police use repeated

questions, laboratory research concludes that such a procedure increases a witness's mistakes in recollection (Poole & White, 1991).

Similarly, the use of multiple-choice questions may encourage guessing. Unless witnesses are clearly told that they shouldn't respond unless they are sure—an admonition rarely offered by the police—such a procedure may lead to an increase in information apparently uncovered, but at a cost in accuracy (Lipton, 1977). (See Fisher, 1995, pp. 748–749, for a discussion of the difficulty in comparing the accuracy levels of open-ended and forced-choice questions.)

Ways to Improve the Accuracy of Information Elicited From Witnesses

Fisher's (1995) thorough review details a number of procedures specific to the questioning process that can either increase the memory retrieval of a witness or improve the witness's conversion of a conscious recollection into a statement to the interviewer. Many of these suggestions are quite straightforward; for example,

1. *Slow down the rate of questioning.* When asked a specific question, witnesses may need to search through their memory store; police should not impatiently interrupt the search with another question.

2. *Re-create the original context.* A staple of the **cognitive interview,** this principle proposes that, before answering any questions about the crime, witnesses should be told to re-create, in their own minds, the environment that existed when the crime happened. They should focus on how things looked and sounded and smelled, what they were doing, how they felt, and what was happening around them.

3. *Tailor questions to the individual witness.* Many police routinely plod through a standardized checklist of questions (Fisher, Geiselman, & Raymond, 1987). Instead, Fisher encourages the investigation to be sensitive to each witness's unique perspective.

4. *Make the interview witness-centered rather than interviewer-centered.* Often, the interview is structured so that the witness sits passively waiting for the police officer to ask question after question (Fisher, Geiselman, & Raymond, 1987). Investigators even apply their aggressive, controlling, intimidating style for questioning *suspects* to the interviewing of cooperative witnesses. For the latter, police should use more questions of the open-ended type and tell the subject that he or she should do most of the talking. Similarly, police officers need to convey what they need from the witnesses more explicitly than the typical "Tell me what happened," because the detailed, extensive responses wanted from witnesses go beyond the level of precision typical of ordinary discourse. For example, witnesses should be told *not* to edit their thoughts, but rather to pour forth all of them.

5. *Be sensitive to the distinction between correct and incorrect responses.* How do we know when someone is giving us false information? Common sense suggests that when a witness is slow to respond, is less confident in his or her answers, or is inconsistent in answering from one situation to another, the response is less likely to be an accurate one. Psychological research has confirmed that those subjects who take longer to respond make incorrect responses (Sporer, 1993).

6. *Be sensitive to temptations to form premature conclusions.* The beginning of the chapter noted that one problem is the bias of the police interviewer who may have already formed a conclusion about the identity of the perpetrator. Several ways of dealing with the resulting bias have been suggested; these will be described in detail later in the chapter. For example, Wells (see Fisher, 1995, p. 754, n. 5) proposed that police interviewers be given only general knowledge about the crime (e.g., that a bank was robbed) before doing their witness interviews. A second suggestion is to videotape interviews and provide them to both the prosecution and the defense (Fisher, 1995; Kassin, 1998b).

The most basic suggestion is to provide proper training for police interviewers. Although it is true that some police have better interviewing skills than do others, psychologists have been able to improve the skills of both recruits and experienced detectives (Fisher, Geiselman, & Amador, 1989; George & Clifford, 1992). And, more recently, a number of Fisher and Geiselman's suggestions have been incorporated into specific guidelines in order to help police collect better eyewitness evidence (Technical Working Group on Eyewitness Evidence, 1999, 2003).

USE OF LINEUPS AND PHOTO ARRAYS

When the police have a suspect, they usually ask any victim or other eyewitness to identify him or her through the use of a lineup (called an **identity parade** in Great Britain) or a photo array (also called a photo spread). The use of photo arrays is now more frequent than the use of live lineups, perhaps because the suspect has no right to counsel when witnesses look through a "mug book" (in contrast to suspects' rights to have an attorney present when they are placed in a lineup). Then, too, it is easier for the police to assemble a photo spread than it is to arrange for a live lineup in which four to seven innocent persons bear some resemblance to the suspect (Wells & Seelau, 1995). Despite an assumption that live lineups should be more effective than photo arrays, a meta-analysis of research findings indicates no consistent difference (Cutler, Berman, Penrod, & Fisher, 1994), and the conclusion of prominent researchers is that the principles governing the responses of the eyewitness are the same (Wells, Seelau, Rydell, & Luus, 1994; see also Box 10-3).

As an aside, it should be noted that the Supreme Court does not see the processes as similar. In a decision on the right to counsel during a photo spread session (*United States v. Ash,* 1973), the Court decided that the right to counsel applied only in situations in which the defendant had a right to be present; the Court stated that "a photographic identification is quite different from a lineup, for there are substantially fewer possibilities of impermissible suggestion when photographs are used" (*United States v. Ash,* 1973, p. 324; see also Wells & Cutler, 1990); thus, there was no right to counsel when the police used a photo array rather than a lineup.

A special mention should be made of the procedure called the **showup**—essentially a lineup composed of only one person. Both psychologists and the courts have assumed that showups are inherently more suggestive than lineups that include 4, 5, or 6 foils (*Stovall v. Denno,* 1967, p. 302), though courts commonly allow eyewitness evidence obtained with showups anyway. In fact, experimental psychologists who study the accuracy of memory are quite strong in their belief that the procedure is prejudicial (Malpass & Devine, 1983; Wells,

---

BOX 10-3
Lineups Versus Photo Arrays

The greatest threats to the accuracy of identifications—regardless of which procedure is used—may come from the actions of the police questioner. But the medium is still worthy of study. Cutler, Berman, Penrod, and Fisher (1994) have noted that an inherent distinction between a lineup and a photo array is image quality; "common sense tells us that live lineups produce the clearest image" (p. 163). Furthermore, photo arrays do not provide information about the behavior of the criminal, including his or her voice and gait. But many advantages actually exist for the photo array or photo spread approach (Cutler et al., 1994):

1. Immediate availability and selection of foils.

2. Portability.

3. Control over the behavior of lineup members. (In a live lineup, a possibility always exists that a suspect will act in some way to draw the eyewitness's attention, which can invalidate the lineup.)

4. Opportunity to examine a photo array repeatedly and over extended lengths of time.

5. Less eyewitness anxiety when they use a mug book, in contrast to viewing their potential attacker through a one-way glass.

As noted in the text of the chapter, the careful analysis by Cutler and his colleagues of studies using different procedures concluded that "given the apparent comparability of lineups and photo arrays, it is not worth the trouble and expense to use live lineups" (1994, p. 180). However, a newer development may offer promise. Videotaping lineups is increasingly popular in police departments. Cutler et al. noted that the use of videotaped lineups has advantages not present in either live lineups or photo spreads: With the use of large monitors, faces can be blown up larger than life. With the use of jog-and-roll dials, lineup members can be shown moving in slow motion, even on a frame-by-frame basis. Videotaped lineups can be paused on a specific frame, showing a lineup member in a specific bodily position. In addition, videotaped lineups can be shown repeatedly and for an unlimited amount of time (Cutler et al., 1994, p. 179).

Leippe, & Ostrom, 1979; Yarmey, Yarmey, & Yarmey, 1996; Yarmey, 1979; though see Gonzalez, Ellsworth, & Pembroke, 1993; Davis & Gonzalez, 1996).

It is easy to see why lineups and photo spreads should be a better procedure for law enforcement to use. Used effectively, a lineup will serve two purposes: to determine whether a suspect is in fact the perpetrator observed by the witness, and to assess the reliability of the witness. Picking someone other than the suspect suggests the latter—unreliable witness memory—and discredits the witness rather than the suspect. The lineup witness who selects a foil may rightly be considered an unreliable source for subsequent identification evidence. On the other hand, the showup witness has no foil options. A witness who rejects the showup retains police trust as a reliable witness, even in the case in which the witness incorrectly says it is not the perpetrator. Therefore, if foil choices are considered useful indications that witnesses are willing to identify innocent people, lineups and photo spreads may have an important evidentiary advantage—one that actually transcends the rates of correct identification or errors in the two procedures (see Steblay, Dysart, Fulero, & Lindsay, 2003). This reinforces the practical recommendation made by Daniel Yarmey and his colleagues (1996) that showup encounters not be used, except when a witness is dying. It is also worth noting that in today's world, one could imagine a time when a photo lineup could be generated by a police officer in his or her car in minutes, using a digital camera and photos obtained over the police car's computer, effectively rendering the showup technique obsolete.

Common Errors

Ellison and Buckhout (1981), psychologists with a great deal of experience in actual cases, reported that the most biased lineup they ever encountered "was composed of five White men and one Black man in an actual murder investigation in which a Black suspect had been arrested. The excuse given was that the police wanted to make the lineup representative of the town's population, which had few Black people! Another 'justification' was that there were no other people in the building" (p. 115). Certainly, improper procedures used by the police can have the same effect on witnesses' reactions, regardless whether the witness is viewing a lineup or scanning a mugbook (Lindsay, 1994). The Steve Titus case illustrated how such procedures can have a deleterious effect. We can summarize the frequent kinds of errors as follows:

1. Implying that the criminal is definitely one of the stimulus people.
2. Pressuring the witness to make a choice (i.e., creating a demand characteristic).
3. Asking the eyewitness specifically about the suspect while not asking those same questions about the foils (or what Wells and Seelau, 1995, call a **confirmation bias**).
4. Encouraging a loose recognition threshold in the eyewitness by asking the witness if there is "anyone familiar," or "anyone who looks like the person."
5. Leaking the police officer's hunch, by making it obvious to the eyewitness which is the suspect (Wells & Seelau, 1995, pp. 767-768).
6. Telling the eyewitness, after a selection, that his or her choice is the "right" one. Studies have shown that the confidence level of witnesses' reports as well as their memories of the circumstances of their view of the event can be manipulated by giving them feedback that their choice is correct, such as by telling them that another witness identified the same person (Luus & Wells, 1994; Luus, 1991; Semler, Brewer, & Wells, in press; Wells and Bradfield, 1998, 1999; Bradfield, Wells, & Olson, 2002; Wells, Olson, & Charman, 2003).

The fact that eyewitnesses are highly susceptible to the powers of suggestion from police is admirably demonstrated in a study by Wells and Bradfield (1998), who showed undergraduate-student subjects a grainy videotape made by a Target store surveillance camera; it portrayed a man entering the store. Subjects were told to notice the man as they would be asked questions about him later. After viewing the tape, they were informed that the man engaged in a robbery that went wrong and that a store security guard had been killed. Each subject was then shown a five-person photo spread that did *not* contain the photograph of the man who had been seen in the surveillance tape. Each individual subject selected someone from the photo spread as the person in the video. Upon making this response, the subject was told either "Good, you identified the actual suspect" (called confirming feedback), or "Actually, the suspect is No. __" (disconfirming feedback); one third of the subjects were given no feedback. Immediately thereafter, each subject answered a long set of questions, some of which assessed the effect of the feedback. Those who had been told, "Good, you identified the actual suspect" were far more confident in their choices than were those who were told the suspect was someone else; the latter feedback had a moderate detrimental effect on the subject's confidence. The mean confidence ratings were: Confirming feedback, 5.4; No feedback, 4.0; Disconfirming feedback, 3.5. In addition, those given positive feedback felt they had a better view of the perpetrator, reported paying greater attention to the videotape, had an easier time making the identification, and were more willing to testify about their identification. Clearly, the nature of feedback from an authority distorts the witness's reports, across a wide variety of phenomena.

The use of such responses by police questioners is particularly disturbing, given the emerging conclusion from psychological research that the act of lineup-identification is largely governed by a **relative judgment process** (Wells, 1984b, 1993; Wells et al., 1998). That is, the witness selects the stimulus person who most resembles, in the witness's memory, the perpetrator of the crime. If the real culprit is present, this procedure is effective, but *if the lineup contains only foils,* an innocent person who resembles the perpetrator is likely to be chosen. For example, Malpass and Devine (1981) carried out a study in which they staged a crime and then asked eyewitnesses to pick out the culprit from a lineup. When the actual culprit was *not* in the lineup and when witnesses were *not* warned of this, 78% of the subjects chose one of the innocent people. When warned about the possibility of the perpetrator's absence, only 33% chose someone from the culprit-absent lineup. The latter figure is important; in fact, other research (Wells, 1993) confirmed that about one third of witnesses or more select an innocent person in a culprit-absent photo spread or lineup, even when told that the culprit might not be present. The problem with the relative judgment process, in the words of Wells and his colleagues, is "that it includes no mechanism for describing that the culprit is none of the people in the lineup" (Wells et al., 1998, p. 614). In addition, the relative judgment process has implications for the use of photo spreads that present all the photos at one time, rather than sequentially (discussed later in this chapter).

Operational Rules

It is clear that the procedures used by some police have the potential of increasing the rate of false identifications (Loftus, 1993b). Wells and his colleagues (Wells & Seelau, 1995; Wells et al., 1998) have suggested that the application of four straightforward rules can reduce such errors, rules that have now become part of the material found in the eyewitness evidence guide and manual developed by the Technical Working Group on Eyewitness Evidence (1999, 2003):

Rule 1: "The person who conducts the lineup or photo spread should not be aware of which member of the lineup or photo spread is the suspect" (Wells et al., 1998, p. 627).

Customarily, the detective who has handled the case administers the lineup. The problem is that this officer, knowing who is the suspect, may communicate this knowledge, *even without intending to do so.* A variation in eye contact with the witness, a subtle shift in body position or facial expression, or the tone of voice may be enough to communicate feedback to the witness, who often is unsure and hence seeks guidance and confirmation from the detective. And, as we know, some detectives are not reluctant to tell witnesses when their choices identified the suspect. But if a **double-blind procedure** were to be used, in which the lineup administrator is unaware of the "correct" answer, neither subtle nor overt communication would be made, and a purer estimate of the accuracy of the witness's memory and his or her confidence level could be determined.

Rule 2: "Eyewitnesses should be told explicitly that the perpetrator might not be in the lineup or photo spread and therefore eyewitnesses should not feel that they must make an identification. They should also be told that the person administering the lineup does not know which person is the suspect in the case" (Wells et al., 1998, p. 629).

Consider the reaction of an eyewitness when he or she is shown a lineup; it probably is something like this: "They wouldn't have gone to this trouble unless they have a suspect. So one of these guys must have done it." If the lineup is seen as a "multiple-choice" question without the option "none of the above," the question is an easier one, and, in fact, an eyewitness could use the "relative judgment" strategy, comparing his or her memory to the person who "looks" most like the one remembered. Thus, it is essential for the investigator to *emphasize* that the culprit might not be in the photo array or lineup, by means of an instruction that states clearly that the perpetrator "may or may not be in the set of photos you are about to view." Empirical studies, analyzed by Steblay (1997), find that an explicit warning such as this significantly reduces the rate of incorrect identifications when the offender is *not* in the lineup.

Rule 3: "The suspect should not stand out in the lineup or photo array as being different from the distractors based on the eyewitness's previous description of the culprit or based on other factors that would draw extra attention to the suspect" (Wells et al., 1998, p. 630).

In previous lineups, the suspect stood out in the following ways:

1. He or she was the only one who fit the verbal description that the eyewitness had given to the police earlier (Lindsay & Wells, 1980).
2. He or she was the only one dressed in the type of clothes worn by the perpetrator (Lindsay, Wallbridge, & Drennan, 1987).
3. The suspect's photo was taken from a different angle than were the foils' photos (Buckhout & Friere, 1975, cited by Wells & Seelau, 1995).

Wells and his colleagues emphasize that distractors should not necessarily be selected to look like the police detectives' prime suspect; instead, they should be chosen to *match the description of the criminal given by the witness.* Note that this recommendation goes against the common procedure in which police choose foils to resemble the suspect, rather than resembling the witness's description of the offender.

Rule 4: "A clear statement should be taken from the eyewitness at the time of the identification and prior to any feedback as to his or her confidence that the identified person is the actual culprit" (Wells et al., 1998, p. 635).

Repeated questioning by authorities (police, investigators, prosecutors) may increase the confidence of the witness's answers (Shaw, 1996; Shaw & McClure, 1996). By the time witnesses reach the witness box at the actual trial, they may act quite differently than they did initially. The initial levels of confidence should be recorded. In response to the preceding guidelines (and especially rule 4), suggesting that they do not go far enough, Kassin (1998b) has suggested one more rule—that the identification process (especially the lineup and the interaction between the detective and the witness) be videotaped, so that attorneys, the judge, and the jury can later assess for themselves whether the reports of the procedure by police are accurate (see also Judges, 2000). Unfortunately, since videotaping is rarely done, the attorneys, judge, and jury see only the product of an identification procedure, rather than the actual collection of the eyewitness evidence.

A fifth and important "rule" not included in Wells et al. (1998), but strongly advocated by eyewitness researchers and mentioned in the eyewitness evidence guide (discussed later in this section) is this: "Scientific research indicates that identification procedures such as lineups and photo arrays produce more reliable evidence when the individual lineup members or photographs are shown to the witness sequentially— one at a time—rather than simultaneously" (Technical Working Group on Eyewitness Evidence, 1999, p. 9). Standard police lineups have traditionally used simultaneous procedures. However, under those conditions, eyewitnesses tend to compare lineup members to each other to determine which one most closely resembles their memory of the perpetrator, a process called *relative judgment* (discussed earlier). Lindsay and Wells (1985) devised an alternative lineup presentation technique, sequential presentation, that reduces or eliminates relative judgment by essentially forcing the witness to use an absolute criterion on each picture (yes or no) before seeing the next one. This sequential presentation technique has been shown to reduce the rate of false alarms with little or no effect on correct identification rates (Lindsay, Lea, and Fulford, 1991; Steblay, Dysart, Fulero, & Lindsay, 2001).

Since the publication of these rules, there has been a clear acceptance of their worth and importance in psychology, law enforcement, and the courts. In October 1999, the United States Department of Justice published a set of guidelines or recommendations for the collection and preservation of eyewitness evidence, entitled *Eyewitness Evidence: A Guide for Law Enforcement* (Technical Working Group on Eyewitness Evidence, 1999; a training manual for law enforcement was released later; see Technical Working Group on Eyewitness Evidence, 2003). The guide covers interview techniques, such as those discussed in this chapter, and recommends procedures for the collection of eyewitness evidence by use of lineups, photo spreads, and so

on, including double-blind and sequential techniques. In 2001, the attorney general of New Jersey, John Farmer Jr., ordered the official adoption and implementation of the recommendations of the guide for all lineups and photo spreads in that state (see Kolata & Peterson, 2001). It is worth noting that Kebbell (2000) suggested that the law in England and Wales comports reasonably well with the recommendations in Wells et al. (1998) and thus in the guide.

CHILDREN AS EYEWITNESSES

Because of commonly held beliefs and research findings about their heightened suggestibility and chance of error, children as eyewitnesses pose particular challenges to investigators who seek information from them (Ceci & Bruck, 1993; Ceci, Toglia, & Ross, 1987; Lindsay, Pozzulo, Craig, Lee, & Corber, 1997). The recommendations noted earlier in questioning adult eyewitnesses would, of course, apply to the questioning of children, also. Special problems with respect to the questioning of children and procedures for reducing suggestibility were covered in chapter 8, which deals with forensic responses to sexual abuse of children.

PUBLIC POLICY ISSUES

Chapter 1 noted that psychology and the law are often in conflict and that psychology's attempts to have an impact on the legal system have often failed. At present, neither the police nor the courts have been very responsive to input from psychological research. Wells confirms this conclusion: "To date, the scientific literature on witness memory has not been a driving force behind the legal system's assumptions, procedures, and decisions regarding witness memory" (1995, p. 730). One way to have an influence is to bring about changes in legislation or more enlightened court decisions. This section discusses three approaches to changes in public policy: recent changes in statute-of-limitation laws in recovered memory or child sexual abuse cases, trial judges' decisions on admitting psychologists as expert witnesses, and relevant Supreme Court decisions.

Recent Changes in Statute-of-Limitation Laws in Recovered Memory or Child Sexual Abuse Cases

A clear example of legislative decisions made without regard for the complexity of psychological viewpoints is the extensive nature of changes made in the United States and Canada with regard to the **statute of limitations** for claims of sexual abuse of children. Many cases involve claims that the alleged victims of abuse as children have "repressed" or do not recall the abuse until their adolescence or adulthood. Previously, such claims had to be brought forward within a specific time after the act in order to be responded to by the criminal justice system. Legislators and judges have accepted the concept of **delayed discovery** (Bulkley & Horwitz, 1994; Boland & Quirk, 1994); in one Canadian case (*Regina v. Norman,* 1993), the court "apparently gave additional weight to the complainant's recovered memory testimony because a friend of the victim testified that she witnessed the alleged rape and claimed that she also repressed and then recovered memories of it" (Lindsay & Read, 1995, p. 886).

The goal of this liberalization of the statute of limitation was to provide opportunities for reporting delayed but legitimate claims of child abuse. But in light of the recent heightened concern about such abuses, the legal changes may instead encourage false reports to be brought forward. Some psychologists (Ernsdorff & Loftus, 1993; Bulkley & Horwitz, 1994) have proposed several changes, ranging from complete exclusion of those cases that are based on claims of recovered memory to the imposition

of a higher burden of proof ("clear and convincing evidence" rather than "a preponderance of evidence") in civil cases.

Judges' Decisions on the Admissibility of Expert Testimony

Chapter 1 recounted the efforts of Hugo Münsterberg almost 100 years ago to educate trial judges about the relevance of psychological expertise when fact finders evaluated how accurate eyewitnesses were. But consider that Münsterberg arrogantly wrote, "It seems indeed astonishing that the work of justice is ever carried out in the courts without ever consulting the psychologist and asking him (*sic*) for all the aid which the modern study of suggestion can offer" (1908, p. 194). It is not surprising that the legal community (e.g., Wigmore, 1909) treated such advocacy with disdain then, and—if not disdain—at least with ambivalence now.

In fact, in trials in which the testimony of an eyewitness is potentially pivotal and eyewitness accuracy is an issue, psychologists have often been denied the opportunity to testify. Buckhout (1983) reported that, in New York by that time, "I have testified before juries in about 10 cases and been kept out too many times to count" (1983, p. 67). Fulero (1988) concluded that by 1988, psychologists had been allowed to testify about eyewitness accuracy for the defense in at least 450 cases in 25 states, but some states still prevent them from doing so (see, e.g., *Commonwealth v. Abdul-Salaam,* 1996).

Why not? Some judges fear that an eyewitness expert's testimony will be so powerful that it will usurp the jury's role as fact finder in the case. A second reason is that judges may fear a "battle of the experts." Yet a third is that judges may feel that psychology does not possess information beyond the common knowledge of ordinary people, and therefore eyewitness expert testimony would not meet the usual criteria for expert testimony. These latter two reasons can be collapsed because psychology has generated research, the conclusions of which experts generally support; at the same time, controversy exists within the field over the propriety of testifying and the appropriate role. Each of these issues is discussed here.

Kassin, Ellsworth, and Smith (1989) surveyed 63 experts on eyewitness testimony. At least 80% of these experts agreed that research results on each of the following topics were consistent enough to present in court: the relationship between accuracy and confidence, the lineup instructions, the impact of exposure time, and unconscious transference as well as other topics. More than 70% of the experts believed that the tendency to overestimate the duration of the event, the cross-racial identification bias of White witnesses, and lineup fairness generated consistent research findings. This survey was recently repeated in 2001 (Kassin, Tubb, Hosch, & Memon, 2001) with quite similar results.

Such experts have often testified as expert witnesses in criminal and civil cases around the country and even in other countries (see Buckhout, 1983; Loftus, 1983; Wells, 1986; Penrod, Fulero, & Cutler, 1995; Leippe, 1995). But others have proposed that the research is not sufficiently conclusive or applicable (Konecni & Ebbesen, 1986; McCloskey & Egeth, 1983; McCloskey, Egeth, & McKenna, 1986). Some of these psychologists have testified to that effect (see *People v. Legrand,* 2002, for example), though judges increasingly appear to be convinced of the scientific merit of such expert testimony (see *United States v. Smithers,* 2000; *United States v. Norwood,* 1996; *State v. Echols,* 1998; *People v. Smith,* 2002; see also Penrod et al., 1995).

Despite that, we believe that expert witnesses have a good deal to offer with respect to helping jurors understand how the variables affecting eyewitness reliability work (Leippe, 1995; Penrod et al., 1995). Indeed, by now, we estimate that psychologists have testified in about 1,000 cases in the United States (Penrod et al., 1995; Cutler & Penrod, 1995), and this number is increasing as case law becomes more amenable to eyewitness expert testimony (see, e.g., *United States v. Smithers,* 2000; *State v. Echols,* 1998).

Expert testimony about the determinants of eyewitness accuracy is an example of what Monahan and Walker (1988) called **social framework testimony;** that is, it presents "general conclusions from social science research" to assist the fact finder (whether that is judge or jury) "in determining factual issues in a specific case" (Monahan & Walker, 1988, p. 470). As noted in chapter 2, a judge's decision to admit or exclude scientific testimony is usually based on a combination of four criteria: the scientific nature of the work, the relevance of the work, the general agreement among experts in the area, and the extent to which the expert might unduly influence the jury (Wells, 1995, p. 729). But in real life, matters are not so straightforward: "From a legal and public policy perspective . . . there is a problem to the extent that the variation in admissibility decisions is attributable more to ambiguity in the criteria for admissibility, the idiosyncratic views of the trial judge, or the characteristics of the jurisdiction than it is to the specific characteristics or needs of the case" (Wells, 1995, p. 729).

How can psychologists convince trial judges of the importance of the psychological findings? Two important points emerge from the research findings: the tendency for fact finders not to be adequately informed on the topic, and the high level of consistency in the conclusions drawn by experts in this area. Recent United States Supreme Court case law (*Daubert v. Merrell Dow Pharmaceuticals, Inc.,* 1993; see chapter 2) reinforces the importance of the expert's helpfulness to the jury by providing information that is not "within the ken of the average layperson," and of the scientific reliability and validity of the information that is to be provided (see Penrod et al., 1995).

How Accurate Is the Knowledge of Jurors?

Until the mid-1970s, expert testimony in such cases was rarely offered or admitted; among reasons given by judges for exclusion were that "jurors already know all this" and that experts would "waste the court's time" (Leippe, 1995,

p. 912; see also Penrod et al., 1995). But jurors are often in error in two respects: They overestimate the level of accuracy of eyewitnesses, and they do not appreciate the impact of either estimator or system factors on reducing accuracy. Laypersons usually begin with the assumption that the memory of an adult eyewitness is accurate (Leippe, 1995), and, hence, they expect a far greater percentage of witnesses to be accurate than are found in the field studies that create a mock crime and determine actual levels of eyewitness accuracy (Brigham & Bothwell, 1983; Wells, 1984a; Wells & Leippe, 1981; Lindsay, Wells, & Rumpel, 1981).

An assumption that "jurors already know all this" is clearly unwarranted. Four different surveys came to the same conclusion: "Much of what is known about eyewitness memory—that eyewitness experts might talk about in court—is not common sense" (Leippe, 1995, p. 921). Specific findings of these surveys documented this conclusion:

1. Deffenbacher and Loftus (1982) gave a set of multiple-choice questions on variables associated with eyewitness accuracy to college students and nonstudents with and without jury experience. At least half the respondents chose the wrong answer (i.e., an answer in conflict with the direction of empirical findings) on questions about the confidence–accuracy relationship, cross-racial bias in identification, and weapon focus.
2. Using law students, legal professionals, undergraduate students, and adults as participant subjects, Yarmey and Jones (1983) found that respondents did not recognize the empirically derived relationships between level of accuracy and such factors as the eyewitness's confidence, the presence of a weapon, and the status of the witness (i.e., that police are no better at identification than are other witnesses).
3. Using those 13 empirical findings deemed by experts to be reliable enough to testify about, Kassin and Barndollar (1992) found

that significantly fewer students and adults than experts considered the findings reliable. In 4 of the 13 reliable findings, the majority of the students and adults disagreed with the experts.
4. Brigham and Wolfskeil (1983) surveyed trial attorneys and found, not surprisingly, that prosecutors were much more likely to believe that eyewitnesses were accurate than were criminal defense attorneys.

How Consistent Are the Experts?

A second argument important in order to persuade judges to admit psychological testimony is the consistency of agreement among experts on the phenomenon. A survey by Kassin, Ellsworth, and Smith (1989, 1994; repeated by Kassin, Tubb, Hosch, & Memon, 2001) of 63 active psychological researchers determined just which specific phenomena, in their opinion, were reliable enough to testify about in court. Box 10-4 describes those findings that at least 70% of this sample felt were reliable, in both 1989 and 2001. These conclusions are not idle speculations; they are based, for most of the findings, on a multitude of studies using a variety of methods and types of subjects. As Leippe (1995) observed, "In matters of reliability, a number of eyewitness research findings score highly. They are replicable, the opposite findings (as opposed to simply null findings) are seldom reported, the research has high internal validity, and the settings and measures often have high mundane realism in terms of approximating certain eyewitness situations. A strong argument can be made for reliability and validity" (Leippe, 1995, p. 918).

Of course, as in any other field of endeavor, not all experts agree with the preceding statement. A few psychologists, including Rogers Elliott (1993), Vladimir Konecni and Ebbe Ebbesen (1986), and Michael McCloskey and Howard Egeth (1983; Egeth, 1993), have been critical for several reasons, including their assertion that the findings have not reached a level of consistency necessary for application in the

BOX 10-4
What Is Reliable Enough to Testify About?

The following are the findings that at least 70% of the researchers and experts surveyed by Kassin, Ellsworth, and Smith (1989) and by Kassin, Tubb, Hosch, & Memon (2001) rated as reliable enough to include in courtroom testimony (1989 and 2001 percentages):

1. Wording of questions: An eyewitness's testimony about an event can be affected by how the questions put to that witness are worded. (97%; 98%)

2. Lineup instructions: Police instructions can affect an eyewitness's willingness to make an identification and/or the likelihood that he or she will identify a particular person. (95%; 98%)

3. Postevent information: Eyewitnesses' testimony about an event often reflects not only what they actually saw but information they obtained later on. (87%; 94%)

4. Accuracy and confidence: An eyewitness's confidence is not a good predictor of his or her identification accuracy. (87%; 87%)

5. Attitudes and expectations: An eyewitness's perception and memory for an event may be affected by his or her attitudes and expectations. (87%; 92%)

6. Exposure time: The less time an eyewitness has to observe an event, the less well he or she will remember it. (85%; 81%)

7. Unconscious transference: Eyewitnesses sometimes identify as a culprit someone they have seen in another situation or context. (85%; 81%)

8. Showups: The use of a one-person showup instead of a full lineup increases the risk of misidentification. (83%; 74%)

9. Forgetting curve: The rate of memory loss for an event is greatest right after the event and then levels off over time. (83%; 83%)

10. Cross-racial/White: White eyewitnesses are better at identifying other White people than they are at identifying Black people. (79%; 90%)

11. Lineup fairness: The more the members of a lineup resemble the suspect, the higher is the likelihood that identification of the suspect is accurate. (77%; 70%)

12. Time estimation: Eyewitnesses tend to overestimate the duration of events. (75%; not asked)

13. Stress: Very high levels of stress impair the accuracy of eyewitness testimony. (71%; 60%)

14. Weapons focus: The presence of a weapon impairs an eyewitness's ability to accurately identify the perpetrator's face. (57%; 87%)

15. Hypnotic suggestibility: Hypnosis increases suggestibility to leading and misleading questions. (69%; 91%)

16. Confidence malleability: An eyewitness's confidence can be influenced by factors that are unrelated to identification accuracy. (not asked; 95%)

17. Mug shot-induced bias: Exposure to mug shots of a suspect increases the likelihood that the witness will later choose that suspect in a lineup. (not asked; 95%)

18. Child suggestibility: Young children are more vulnerable than adults to interviewer suggestion, peer pressures, and other social influences. (not asked; 94%)

19. Alcoholic intoxication: Alcoholic intoxication impairs an eyewitness's later ability to recall persons and events. (not asked; 90%)

20. Presentation format: Witnesses are more likely to misidentify someone by making a relative judgment when presented with a simultaneous (as opposed to sequential) lineup. (not asked; 81%)

21. Child accuracy: Young children are less accurate as witnesses than are adults. (not asked; 70%)

22. Description-matched foils: The more that members of a lineup resemble a witness's description of the culprit, the more accurate an identification of the suspect is likely to be. (not asked; 71%)

Percentages of experts rating the statement as "reliable enough" are given in parentheses beside each statement. Data from Kassin, Ellsworth, and Smith (1989), and Kassin, Tubb, Hosch, and Memon (2001).

courts. But these psychologists are clearly very much in the minority, and sometimes the issue of dispute is more a matter of philosophical disagreement about how and when psychological research findings should be presented in court settings, rather than whether a stable body of research exists or what conclusions are being drawn from the research studies.

Supreme Court Decisions

The U.S. Supreme Court has made several other decisions beyond the right-to-counsel one that reflect legal assumptions vastly different from the empirical findings of psychologists. One dealt with the question of when suggestion becomes so strong that it intrudes on rights of defendants to fair treatment. In the case of *Stovall v. Denno* (1967), a man named Paul Behrendt was stabbed to death in the presence of his wife; she was so severely wounded that her survival was questionable. Stovall, a suspect, was brought to Ms. Behrendt's hospital room in handcuffs, two days after the crime, and in this showup condition, the victim identified him as the perpetrator. This procedure was justified by the authorities because it was uncertain whether the victim would survive, and, under such conditions, the victim could not come to the police station. Stovall appealed his conviction, but the Supreme Court ruled that the procedure was not a violation of due process because—although the procedure was suggestive—it was not "unnecessarily" suggestive. That is, a showup procedure would be excluded if it were "unnecessary" (if the circumstances had permitted the use of a lineup as a viable alternative). Although we may be able to agree about the justification in this case, the Court has not taken a position on how suggestive procedures can be reduced or avoided; in fact, as Wells and Seelau (1995) observed: "The Court has not articulated some simple and effective minimal requirements for lineups and photo spreads for the vast majority of cases for which there is no necessity for suggestive procedures" (p. 785).

The second difference between the Supreme Court and experimental psychology deals with the relationship of eyewitnesses' accuracy levels and their levels of confidence. In *Neil v. Biggers* (1972), the Court concluded that even the pressure of unnecessarily suggestive procedures by the police didn't mean that the testimony of the eyewitness had to be excluded from the trial *if* the procedure did not reflect a substantial possibility of a mistaken identification. (The rape victim identified her attacker in a showup 7 months after the crime occurred.) The criteria that the Court, in the preceding decision and in *Manson v. Braithwaite* (1977), felt increased the likelihood of an *accurate* identification were

1. The opportunity for witnesses to view the criminal at the time of the crime.
2. The length of time between the crime and the later identification.
3. The level of certainty shown by the witnesses at the identification.
4. The witness's degree of attention during the crime.
5. The accuracy of the witness's prior description of the criminal.

For example, if little time had passed since the crime, then even a suggestive procedure should not have had an impact, and it could be assumed that the witness was on target. Most of these criteria reflect plausible assumptions, but they are questionable ones, for several reasons. First, leading questions (e.g., "You had a pretty long time to look at him, did you?") can alter the witnesses' responses about their degree of attention and opportunity to view the criminal—and, indirectly, their level of confidence. Second, the initial relationship between different witnesses' levels of accuracy and their levels of confidence about their own accuracy is quite low (Cutler & Penrod, 1989, 1995). In a comprehensive review, Bothwell, Deffenbacher, and Brigham (1987) completed a meta-analysis of 35 studies that used staged crimes to assess eyewitnesses' accuracy and confidence. The average correlation was only an *r* of .25, suggesting that "witnesses who are highly confident in their identifications are only somewhat more likely to be correct as compared to witnesses who display little confidence" (Penrod & Cutler, 1995, p. 823).

A third reason for concern about the Supreme Court's criteria is that—contrary to the assumptions of most jurors—the confidence of a witness is malleable; that is, events that happen after the initial identification can cause the eyewitness to become more or less confident (Wells et al., 1998). It was found in the studies by Luus and Wells (1994) and by Wells and Bradfield (1998) that certain of the suggestive procedures used by the police can increase the confidence of eyewitnesses without changing their accuracy (Wells, Rydell, & Seelau, 1993). If a police officer tells an eyewitness that his or her choice from the lineup is "the guy we think did it," such a reaction quite likely increases that eyewitness's confidence without affecting accuracy. And once the confidence of the witness is heightened by the feedback, the witness's assessments of some of the other criteria are endangered; recall the Wells and Bradfield (1998) subjects who received positive feedback reported that they had paid more attention to the video. Such feedback could color witnesses' self-reports about several of the *Neil v. Biggers* criteria.

Thus, witness confidence should be considered a system variable (i.e., police questioning procedures can affect it) as well as an estimator variable. But jurors are ordinarily not aware of this; in fact, "jurors appear to overestimate the accuracy of identifications, fail to differentiate accurate from inaccurate eyewitnesses—because they rely so heavily on witness confidence, which is relatively nondiagnostic—and are generally insensitive to other factors that influence identification accuracy" (Wells et al, 1998, p. 624). This has led some psychologists to criticize the *Neil v. Biggers* criteria as outmoded and in need of revision (Bradfield & Wells, 2000).

SUMMARY AND A CAUTIONARY EVALUATION

This chapter attempts to demonstrate that the field of psychology has much to offer police and the legal system to help ensure the most reliable use of eyewitness evidence. Some of the suggestions in this chapter stem from the conclusions of empirical research; others reflect commonsense derivations from observation of the ways that police conduct investigations. Some police detectives will object to representatives from another discipline "telling them how to run their business," and psychologists always need to remember the pressures and constraints on police conducting crime investigations. In fact, the field of psychology would benefit from feasibility studies to determine what affects how receptive the police are to suggestions from psychologists, though the publication of the Technical Working Group's guide and manual suggests that things are changing. Of course, it is important to remind law enforcement that indeed, the goals of everyone who works in the system are the same—because if the wrong person is apprehended and convicted, the right one remains free to commit other crimes.

Psychologists must also remember that the goals for the forensic application of their findings may differ from the goals of testing a theory in the laboratory, and they must be careful in what they say in a courtroom setting. For example, experimental psychologists find that very high levels of stress inhibit accuracy of memory. However, that finding may conflict with the experience of police officers, who sometimes find that real eyewitnesses often have good recall for many of the details of armed robberies, such as the weapons used and statements made by the criminals (Christiaanson & Hubinette, 1993). Although stress may have an adverse effect on identification accuracy, it may improve the recall for specific *relevant* information (Kebbell & Wagstaff, 1997), and it is important to note the difference.

The research findings described in this chapter are often only a beginning to the task of providing directions for the police to improve their procedures. For example, the Wells and Bradfield (1998) procedure of "Good, you identified the suspect" needs to be extended to other types of subjects in other types of situations, and particularly to actual crime victims who are given disconfirming feedback by the police investigator.

The **evaluation research** role of psychologists is also relevant to other means that police use to generate information from eyewitnesses. Victims and eyewitnesses may be asked to describe the perpetrator, after which a sketch artist will draw the criminal's appearance based on this description. Most of these artists will first have the witness go through the FBI's Facial Identification Catalogue, a collection of noses, eyebrows, and other facial characteristics. Traditionally, police have used the **Identikit,** another collection of various facial characteristics from which witnesses can choose to put together the lips, the eyes, and the hair of the criminal. More recently, computer-generated faces have replaced the Identikit.

The problem with these procedures is that it is much harder than we think to recall individual facial features of a person, especially after only a limited opportunity to observe his or her features. Furthermore, features interact; when using the Identikit, a nose will look different when the witness changes the eyes. Wells (1993), in reviewing the literature on this issue, concluded that the identification of faces by an eyewitness is a **holistic process** rather than an analysis of component features. By *holistic process* we mean that face recognition is an act in which the relationship of features and the general appearance serve as determinants so that piecemeal analyses are not productive. Psychologists should continue to evaluate such procedures and advise police departments on their effectiveness.

KEY TERMS

cognitive interview
composite drawing
confirmation bias
delayed discovery
demand characteristics
double-blind procedure
estimator variables
evaluation research
foils
holistic process
identity parade
Identikit
leading questions
lineup

memory testimony
photo array
relative judgment process
sequential lineup procedure
showup
social framework testimony
statute of limitations
system variables
unconscious transference

INFOTRAC® COLLEGE EDITION

InfoTrac College Edition is a FREE, powerful, online learning resource, consisting of full-text articles from thousands of journals and periodicals. With each new copy of *Forensic Psychology,* Second Edition, you receive 4 months of free access to the InfoTrac College Edition database. By doing a simple keyword search (try using the Key Terms in the list above), you can quickly generate a list of relevant articles from thousands of possibilities and can select articles to read, explore, and print for reference or further study. InfoTrac College Edition's continuously updated collection of articles can be useful for doing reading and writing assignments that reach beyond the pages of this text!

SUGGESTED READINGS

Cutler, B. L., & Penrod, S. D. (1995). *Mistaken identification: The eyewitness, psychology, and the law.* New York: Cambridge University Press.

The authors present a comprehensive account of psychological research on eyewitness accuracy, and a good description of errors in estimator variables (not covered in this chapter) as well as system variables.

Devenport, J. L., Penrod, S. D., & Cutler, B. L. (1997). Eyewitness identification evidence: Evaluating common sense evaluations. *Psychology, Public Policy, and Law, 3,* 338–361.

This useful review evaluates the safeguards developed by the legal system to protect defendants from being convicted falsely on the basis of mistaken identifications. The article concludes that many of these safeguards are not as effective as the legal system assumes them to be.

Fisher, R. P. (1995). Interviewing victims and witnesses of crime. *Psychology, Public Policy, and Law, 1,* 732–764.

This is the definitive article on the ways that psychologists can assist the police to improve the quality of their interviews with crime witnesses.

Loftus, E. F., & Ketcham, K. (1991). *Witness for the defense: The accused, the eyewitness, and the expert who puts memory on trial.* New York: St. Martin's Press.

This immensely readable account covers some of the cases (including those of Steve Titus, Ted Bundy, and Ivan the Terrible) for which Elizabeth Loftus, premiere researcher/expert witness, was asked to testify for the defense regarding the inaccuracy of eyewitnesses' testimony.

Sporer, S. L. (1993). Eyewitness identification accuracy, confidence, and decision times in simultaneous and sequential lineups. *Journal of Applied Psychology, 78,* 22–33.

In contrast to the standard lineup procedure, a **sequential lineup procedure** has the witness view only one person at a time, deciding whether that person is the offender before seeing the remaining members of the lineup. This article is one of several that find that sensitivity to the presence or absence of the culprit in the lineup is greater when the sequential procedure is used rather than the traditional simultaneous procedure.

Technical Working Group on Eyewitness Evidence (1999). *Eyewitness evidence: A guide for law enforcement.* Washington, DC: United States Department of Justice, National Institute of Justice, Document No. NCJ178240 (available on the Web at www.ojp.usdoj.gov).

This historic document published by the Department of Justice takes psychological research on eyewitness reliability out of the laboratory and into the police station (see also Wells, Fisher, Lindsay, Turtle, Malpass, & Fulero, 2000, for an account by the six psychologists on the panel of their experiences).

Wells, G. L., & Seelau, E. (1995). Eyewitness identification: Psychological research and legal policy on lineups. *Psychology, Public Policy, and Law, 1,* 765–791.

Among the many authoritative articles by Gary Wells, this one applies what forensic psychologists know to recent court decisions and legislative acts.

Wells, G. L., Small, M., Penrod, S., Malpass, R. S., Fulero, S. M., & Brimacombe, C. A. E. (1998). Eyewitness identification procedures: Recommendations for lineups and photospreads. *Law and Human Behavior, 22,* 603–647.

The first Scientific Review Paper of the American Psychology-Law Society, this article provides a detailed rationale for its four recommendations for improving the construction and administration of lineups and photo arrays.

11

Interrogations and Confessions

A **confession** by a defendant—an admission of guilt—is the most damaging evidence that can be presented at the defendant's trial (Kassin, 1997). Because of its impressive impact, the courts need to be wary about the circumstances under which a confession was obtained. In a minority opinion, Supreme Court Justice William Brennan voiced his distrust about relying on confessions because of their decisive leverage; he wrote, "No other class of evidence is so profoundly prejudicial. . . . Triers of fact accord confessions such heavy weight in their determinations that the introduction of a confession makes the other aspects of a trial in court superfluous, and the real trial, for all practical purposes, occurs when the confession is obtained" (*Colorado v. Connelly,* 1986, p. 182).

The quest for a confession from a suspect by police and prosecutors is fierce and, on occasion, even frenzied. In their zeal to obtain an admission of guilt, police may intimidate innocent suspects. In addition, we know now that the very techniques that are designed for and taught to police officers in order to elicit confessions work too well—they elicit more true confessions, but also more false ones. Not all confessions represent the truth, and one of the tasks of the forensic psychologist—one of the most difficult ones we will have—is to convince law-enforcement authorities to reexamine their interrogation procedures. The need is exemplified by the case of the "Central Park jogger," in which five individuals confessed in 1989—falsely, it turned out—only to have the real rapist admit to the crime in 2002 (see Kassin, 2002).

This chapter deals with one of the most acrimonious topics in forensic psychology, one that seems to divide some psychologists from law-enforcement officials. The chapter examines how police use interrogations to obtain confessions, what the courts permit police to do and prohibit them from doing, and what the psychological field has to apply to the police detective's task.

THE PAUL INGRAM CASE

When people confess to crimes, sometimes questions persist about the accuracy of the confession; false confessions occur for a number of reasons, as this chapter illustrates. Perhaps the suspect was overly suggestible or simply too fatigued or anxious. Perhaps excessive pressure was placed on the suspect to confess. And we must realize that it is not always easy to separate false confessions from authentic ones; some confessions, such as the one described here, are equivocal.

The Charges

In 1988, Paul Ingram was a deputy sheriff in the state of Washington, a position he had held for almost 17 years. He was married, the father of five children, and a central member of a local Pentecostal church. Apparently the paragon of mainstream values, he was even the chair of the Thurston County Republican Party. He spent many of his working hours in schools, warning children of the dangers of drug use (Wright, 1994).

But suddenly his life changed, as he was charged with a number of incredibly heinous crimes: sexual abuse, the rape of his own daughters, and participation in hundreds of satanic cult rituals that included the slaughter of some 25 babies. Even more amazingly, these charges stemmed from allegations by his eldest daughter Ericka, aged 22 at that time, who claimed that her father had repeatedly molested not only her but also her sister. The abuse had ended in 1979, Ericka said, when she was 9 and her sister Julie was 5. But Julie later reported that she had been molested as recently as 5 years before, when she was 13.

Ericka first made the charges public in the summer of 1988 at a church camp where she served as a counselor. As she talked to police later, the allegations built in extremity and detail: She had caught a disease from her father; he had led satanic rituals in which live babies were sacrificed; a fetus had been forcibly removed from her body when it was almost full-term. Contrary to her first revelations, Ericka now told the police that the last incidence of abuse had happened just 2 weeks earlier.

After Ericka came forward with these claims, Julie provided further allegations; the police acquired two letters that Julie had written a teacher 5 or 6 weeks before. One stated:

> I can remember when I was 4 yr. old he would have poker game [sic] at our house and a lot of men would come over and play poker w/ my dad, and they would all get drunk and one or two at a time would come into my room and have sex with me they would be in and out all night laughing and cursing. I was so scared I didn't know what to say or who to talk to (quoted by Wright, 1994, p. 36).

Interrogation Procedures

Even though he was a law-enforcement officer, Paul Ingram had no experience with interrogations (Ofshe & Watters, 1994). After his arrest, he was kept in jail for 5 months and interrogated 23 times during that period. At first, he denied any knowledge of the claims. He was hypnotized and given graphic crime details; mystified by his inability to remember any details of these acts, he was told by a Tacoma forensic psychologist, Richard Peterson, that sex offenders often repress memories of their offenses, because they were too horrible to acknowledge. His pastor—who urged him to own up to the claims—told him the charges were probably true, because children did not make up such things. Even while Ingram's response was that he could not remember having ever molested his daughters, he added, "If this did happen, we need to take care of it" (Wright, 1994, pp. 6–7).

Ingram's Response

Leading questions by the police and the psychologist attempted to cause Ingram to visualize scenes involving group rapes and satanic cult activities. His response began to change from "I didn't do it" to "I don't remember doing it" (Ofshe & Watters, 1994, p. 167). After further questioning, he told the police, "I really believe that the allegations did occur and that I did violate them and abuse them and probably for a long period of time. I've repressed it, probably very successfully from myself, and now I'm trying to bring it all out. I know from what they're saying that the incidents had to occur, that I had to have done these things. . . . my girls know me. They wouldn't lie about something like this" (Ofshe & Watters, 1994, p. 167). Yet, at that point he could not recall *any* specific incidents of abuse.

Later, Ingram was able to visualize scenes the detectives had suggested, and he did confess in detail, but in a rather detached and almost remorseless manner; for example, he would describe events by saying, "I would have . . ." rather than "I did. . . ." The admissions—given after relaxation exercises by the psychologist—were devastating; they included having sex with each of his daughters many times (beginning when Ericka was 5 years old) and having taken Julie for an abortion of a fetus he had fathered, when Julie was 15. For a time, he came to believe the accuracy of the charges. He "recalled" the crime scenes to specification and admitted guilt; for example, he reported seeing people in robes kneeling around a fire and cutting out a beating heart from a live cat, as well as watching another of the sheriff's deputies having sexual intercourse with Ingram's own daughter.

Evaluating the Accuracy of Ingram's Confession

A social scientist, as an expert witness, played a unique role in this case. Richard Ofshe (1992) is a social psychologist and professor of sociology at the University of California at Berkeley. Even though he was called as a witness by the prosecution, he came to conclude—after interviewing Ingram—that through hypnosis and "trance logic,"

Ingram had been "brainwashed" into believing that he had been part of a satanic cult. Ofshe decided to try a daring experiment with Ingram. He suggested that Ingram had forced one of his sons and one of his daughters to have sex with each other, and watched them while they did. (No one had ever brought that accusation against Ingram before.) After repeated questions and suggestions by Ofshe, Ingram began to "remember" and acknowledged that he had done that, too, and even embellished details of the act. He prepared a three-page, excessively detailed description of the incestuous act. Thus, Ofshe (1992) began to have serious doubts "that Ingram was guilty of anything, except of being a highly suggestible individual with a tendency to float in and out of trance states and a . . . rather dangerous eagerness to please authority" (Wright, 1994, p. 146); Professor Ofshe became an advocate of Ingram's innocence.

The Outcome

But it was too late. Ingram had not only pleaded guilty but had plea-bargained to six counts of third-degree rape. There was no trial. He was sentenced to a 20-year term in prison, with the possibility of parole after 12 years. Although he has been moved to a prison in a different state, some 15 years after his conviction he remains incarcerated.

Yet no physical evidence exists that he was a Satanist or a child abuser. Ingram no longer believes that he was, and his attorneys have appealed, unsuccessfully, to withdraw his guilty plea. The Washington State Supreme Court rejected his appeal in September 1992.

THE FORENSIC PSYCHOLOGIST AND POLICE INTERROGATIONS

What is the appropriate role of the forensic psychologist when asked to evaluate the procedures or results of a police interrogation? The short answer is: There is more than one role. Dr. Ofshe, first asked to be an expert witness by one side, came to play an active role for the other. This chapter examines possible roles by considering the clienteles to whom the psychologist might be responsive. For example, acting as a consultant or an employee of a police department, a psychologist might seek to educate police detectives about the possibility of false confessions. If the clientele is the judiciary, the psychologist could serve as an expert witness or author of an *amicus* brief about how the use of coercion and trickery by the police contributes to false confessions. Last, the forensic psychologist may feel that his or her ultimate responsibility is to society in general and, hence, may try to educate the public about the dangers of misleading interrogations. This chapter considers each of these roles, but first we examine why false confessions occur.

THE PSYCHOLOGY OF FALSE CONFESSIONS

People assume that most confessions are spontaneous and that almost all are truthful. In reality, many confessions are negotiated, and 20% are **recanted;** that is, the suspect who has made an incriminating statement to the police later states that it was false. Among the reasons that people confess is the desire to escape further interrogation; they may assume, "I'll tell the police whatever they want, to avoid this terrible situation, and deny it later." Sometimes they may come to believe what the police have told them, as some observers concluded that Paul Ingram temporarily did.

Three Types of False Confessions

Recanted or disputed confessions are not necessarily false confessions. With regard to those that *are,* Kassin and Wrightsman (1985; Wrightsman

& Kassin, 1993)—relying on Kelman's (1958) analysis of opinion change—identified three types of false confessions (see also Gudjonsson, 2003):

1. **Voluntary false confessions** are offered willingly, without elicitation. They may be instigated by a desire for publicity or by generalized guilt, or they may reflect some form of psychotic behavior. Every highly publicized crime generates people who come forward, claiming to have committed the crime. When the baby son of the Lindberghs was kidnapped in 1932, more than 200 people falsely confessed (Note, 1953).

Kassin (1997) described a case for which he was contacted as a possible expert witness by the defense attorney: A young Wisconsin woman had falsely implicated herself and a group of motorcyclists in a local murder. She later told the police that she had lied about participating in the murder, because she craved the notoriety and attention.

2. **Coerced-compliant confessions** are those in which the suspect confesses, even while knowing that he or she is innocent; coerced-compliant confessions may be given to escape further interrogation, to gain a promised benefit, or to avoid a threatened punishment. The person does not privately believe that he or she committed the criminal act. In general, *compliance* refers to an inconsistency between one's public behavior and one's private opinion, a phenomenon reflected in Asch's (1956) classic study of the impact of others' false estimates in a line-judging task.

In the fall of 1974, the Irish Republican Army (IRA) placed bombs in two public houses in Guildford in the county of Surrey, England, and Birmingham, England. Five people were killed in one bombing, 21 in the other; more than 150 were injured. Police, under great pressure to make arrests, questioned four Irishmen about one bombing and six other Irishmen about the other. After intense questioning, the four men questioned in the Guildford bombing and four of the six men interrogated about the other bombing made written confessions,

although they all recanted their confessions at trial. They said that their confessions had been beaten out of them (Mullin, 1986). One, Paddy Hill, claimed that he had been kicked, punched in the side of the head, and kneed in the thigh. "We're going to get a statement out of you or kick you to death," was the threat that he later reported (Mullin, 1986, p. 100). Those claims were rejected by the jury, which found the Irishmen guilty; they were sentenced to life in prison.

One of the Irishmen, Gerry Conlon of the Guildford Four, was the subject of a 1993 movie, *In the Name of the Father*. Both sets of defendants spent close to 15 years in prison before their convictions were overturned because the English courts acknowledged that the police had coerced the defendants to confess by subjecting them to psychological and physical pressure (Gudjonsson, 1992, 2003).

Gisli Gudjonsson (1992, 2003) was able to later interview and administer suggestibility scales to one member of the Guildford Four and each of the Birmingham Six. The most dramatic finding from the responses of the Birmingham Six was the difference in personality test scores between those two defendants who did not confess and the four who did. Thirteen years after their interrogations, those two who didn't make written confessions "scored exceptionally low on tests of suggestibility and compliance" (Gudjonsson, 1992, p. 273). Gudjonsson concluded that all eight of the defendants who made self-incriminating written statements reflected the coerced-compliant type.

Certainly the **"third-degree" tactics** that were commonplace all over the world 100 years ago—such as extreme deprivation, brutality, and torture—led to many coerced-compliant confessions (see *Brown v. Mississippi*, 1936, for an example). But do they still? In at least some communities and at least with selected suspects, such tactics may still be used in the United States. In the mid-1980s, four New York City police officers were arrested and accused of extracting confessions from suspects by jolting them with a stun gun; one of the victims was found to have 40 burn marks on his body (Huff, Rattner, & Sagarin, 1996). Lawyers for Barry Lee Fairchild, an African American man with an IQ score of 62, claimed that he confessed to the murder of a White nurse only after Pulaski County (Arkansas) sheriffs' deputies "put telephone books on the top of his head and slammed downward repeatedly with blackjacks" (Lacayo, 1991, p. 27). Such actions cause excruciating pain but leave no marks as evidence of coercion. The sheriff of Pulaski County denied Fairchild's claims, but 11 other African American men brought in for questioning about that time reported almost equally intimidating procedures; three said they had pistols placed in their mouths, with officers pulling the triggers of the unloaded guns (Lacayo, 1991). A former sheriff's deputy even came forward and testified that he had seen the sheriff and some deputies abuse various suspects (Annin, 1990).

More frequent are procedures that more subtly seduce suspects. Now popular among police interrogation procedures are psychologically oriented ploys, such as apparent solicitousness and sympathy, the use of informants, and even lying to suspects (Leo, 1992). When a bomb went off during the 1996 Summer Olympics in Atlanta, the FBI brought in for questioning a man named Richard Jewell, because he fit their criminal profile of someone intrigued with law enforcement; although Jewell was certainly a suspect, the FBI got his initial cooperation by telling him they needed his help in preparing a training film. He willingly came in; the next thing he knew, the FBI, with a search warrant, was going through his apartment and plucking hair from his head (Brenner, 1997).

When the two sons of Susan Smith were found in the family car, drowned in a South Carolina lake, Mrs. Smith first told the sheriff that a Black man had hijacked her car and had kidnapped her children. The Union County sheriff, Howard Wells, noted inconsistencies in her story and her behavior, doubted her story, and—after extensive questioning—tricked Mrs.

Smith by telling her that his deputies had been working a drug stakeout at the very crossroads at the very time that Susan Smith claimed the abduction had occurred. "This could not have happened as you said," he told her, upon which she broke down in tears and confessed to driving the car into the lake (Bragg, 1995, p. A1).

Richard Jewell was innocent and did not falsely confess; Susan Smith was guilty and did eventually confess, truthfully, to the murder of her two children. In fairness, it must be acknowledged that in both of these cases "the system worked," but the willingness on the part of law-enforcement authorities to mislead suspects in the hope of eliciting a confession still creates problems for a society in which trust of the police is a concern.

3. **Coerced-internalized confessions** are those in which the innocent suspect confesses and comes to believe that he or she is guilty. Interrogation by the police is a highly stressful experience that can create a number of reactions, including a state of heightened suggestibility in which "truth and falsehood become hopelessly confused in the suspect's mind" (Foster, 1969, pp. 690–691). In this type, Gudjonsson concluded that "after confessing for instrumental gain, the persistent questioning continues and the accused becomes increasingly confused and puzzled by the interrogator's apparent confidence in the accused's guilt" (1992, p. 273; see also Gudjonnson, 2003). Richard Ofshe and some other observers of his case concluded that Paul Ingram—reflecting an extreme state of **suggestibility**—should be placed in this category (Wright, 1994), and case reports exist of other coerced-internalized false confessions (Gudjonsson & Lebegue, 1989; Gudjonnson, 1992, 2003).

At times, it is difficult to classify a specific person's response as compliant or internalized; this is especially true of the responses of children to interrogations. They will later say things like, "I was so confused; I couldn't separate what happened from what they told me happened." In Chicago in 1998, two boys—ages 7 and 8—

were arrested and charged with the sex-related murder of a young girl. They had confessed to the murder during an intensive interrogation. Later, however, the authorities concluded that the boys were not physically mature enough to produce the semen found on the victim's body, and they were released. Although no recording was made of the questioning, it appears that the boys repeated back what the detectives had told them (Kotlowitz, 1999). The validity of responses of children to questioning by authorities—whether the children are suspects, as in the Chicago case, or victims—is a matter of great concern, described in more detail in chapter 8.

How Many Confessions Are False?

Granted that in at least a few isolated cases, false confessions may occur, how extensive is the problem?

Wrongful Convictions

We cannot say in any systematic way how many people confess falsely (see Gudjonnson, 2003, for a discussion). In fact, estimates of the number of convictions in the United States that are a result of a false confession vary widely—from fewer than 35 a year (Cassell, 1996a) to 600 per year (Huff, Rattner, & Sagarin, 1996). As Kassin (1997) observed, determining the number is difficult for two reasons: (a) Even if it was coerced and the accused retracts it, a confession may be true, and (b) "a confession may be false even if the defendant is convicted, imprisoned, and never heard from again" (Kassin, 1997, p. 224). But independent evidence exists that *some* confessions are false.

Among those cases of people wrongfully convicted of crimes, several documented ones reflect an erroneous confession as the cause (Bedau & Radelet, 1987; Borchard, 1932; Rattner, 1988). For example, Rattner (1988; Huff, Rattner, & Sagarin, 1996) analyzed 205 cases of known wrongful convictions and concluded that 16, or 8%, were the result of coerced confessions. Although this percentage is low, false con-

fessions more often occur in highly publicized cases dealing with major crimes.

People's Self-Expectations

Does questioning by the police lead to false confessions, even if intimidation is absent? *Sometimes*—not always, not even most of the time, but on occasion—people admit to the police that they committed a crime when they are in fact innocent. This conclusion is hard for most of us to apply to ourselves; many even ask, "Why would anyone confess to something he or she didn't do?" Curious about the extent of this belief, Monica Fellhoelter, Amy Posey, and Lawrence Wrightsman asked 347 students in an introductory psychology class the following:

> Let us say that the police are questioning you about a certain crime. You know that you did not commit this crime. Are there any circumstances under which you would confess to the police that you committed a crime, when you actually didn't?
>
> Please check one.
>
> Yes, I might confess. __
> No, I wouldn't confess to a crime I didn't commit. __
> My answer depends on the circumstances. __

Responses were as follows:

> Yes, I might confess: 9, or 2.6%
> No, I wouldn't: 220, or 63.4%
> My answer depends: 118, or 34.0%

If combined, the "yes" and "it depends" choices garner about 37% of the responses. What is most provocative is the gender difference in responses. Do men or women more frequently acknowledge that they might confess to a crime they didn't commit? The data were as follows: Combining "Yes" (7 men and 2 women) with "My answer depends," 43% of men (70 of 161) but only 31% of women (57 of 186) reflected some possibility of a false confession; this is a statistically significant difference at the .05 level.

These results, indicating a general disbelief in the possibility of false confessions, are relevant to jury decisions in trials involving contested confession evidence; as Wakefield and Underwager wrote, "Widespread overconfidence in personal ability to resist coercion may lead jurors to give undue and erroneous weight to a coerced confession" (1998, p. 424).

False Confessions in the Laboratory

If we assume that on occasion, at least, a confession was a result of suggestibility and pseudomemories and that the suspect did not commit the crimes, this question remains: Is this an isolated case? Is there any evidence that under controlled conditions, in the psychological laboratory, people can be convinced that they committed undesirable acts that, in fact, they did not commit?

To study such a question under controlled conditions, and still protect subjects' rights and act in an ethical manner, is a challenge for research psychologists. Ethical guidelines (both internal and institutional) prevent most researchers from placing research subjects in a situation in which they may succumb to a belief that they committed a criminal act. The solution to the challenge, described here, may strike some as contrived and not generalizable to real crime-related interrogations. Yet it is a beginning.

Saul Kassin (1997; Kassin & Kiechel, 1996) developed the following paradigm to test the proposal that people can be convinced that they did undesirable acts even when they didn't. He and Kiechel had pairs of students (one subject and one confederate) participate in a reaction-time task on a computer, with the subject typing the letters on a keyboard. Before beginning the session, the participants were instructed on how to use the computer and were specifically told not to press the ALT key near the space bar. If they did, the program would crash and the data would be lost. But during the experiment, the computer did crash and the seemingly distressed experimenter accused the subject of hitting the forbidden key.

When this happened, all 75 of the subjects denied the experimenter's charge, but in half of the cases, the confederate sheepishly "admitted" that she saw the subject accidentally strike the ALT key. (This procedure was designed to reflect the use by police of false incriminating evidence, a topic described later in this chapter.) Subjects were given a chance at that point to sign a confession of wrongdoing prepared by the experimenter; all in the crucial condition agreed to do so, but perhaps that's not so surprising. By doing so, they avoided a confrontation with the professor supervising the study. But as each subject was leaving the experimental area, a waiting subject (actually another confederate of the experimenter) asked the subject what had happened. Two thirds of the subjects in the crucial condition indicated that they had erred and hit the wrong button; they didn't say, "He said I hit the wrong button," but rather said things like "I hit the wrong button and ruined the program." Thus, even under laboratory conditions, not just compliance but **internalization** occurs, and people can come to believe that they committed acts that they did not, in fact, commit. Furthermore, some of the subjects even manufactured explanations for how they had made the "mistake." These results are consistent with those of Stanley Milgram's (1974) obedience studies, in that—despite their protestations beforehand—many people conform to an authority figure when in a coercive environment.

THE ROLE OF POLICE INTERROGATIONS IN GENERATING CONFESSIONS

Throughout history every society has been concerned with violations of its laws, customs, and social expectations. Those who were suspected of such violations were often subjected to interrogations in hopes that they would confess. Many did. The first pictures ever drawn of police—found in 12th-dynasty Egyptian tombs of about 2000 B.C.—show them administering the third-degree to a suspect. In light of the videotape of the treatment given Rodney King by the Los Angeles police, it is provocative to note that in one of the drawings, "a man is being beaten with a stick by one of the policemen, while his legs and arms are being held by three others; a fifth officer looks on, supervising the proceedings" (Franklin, 1970, p. 15).

Most police and sheriffs' department officers recognize that intimidating actions like those claimed by Barry Fairchild are illegal and often counterproductive, as "confessions" created by such coercion will usually not stand the scrutiny of a judge in a preliminary hearing. Police and legal experts differ about whether the **Miranda warnings** are a good idea (and see Kassin & Norwick, 2004, for the interesting argument that those most likely to waive their Miranda rights, and thus to place themselves into an interrogation situation alone, are those who know they are innocent!). As Box 11-1 describes, it is claimed that the presence of the warning has decreased the conviction rate. But police see themselves as members of a profession that has an agreed-upon set of rules deriving partly from the law, partly from common sense, and partly from tradition. These rules are systematized in several handbooks developed for the use of police and described in Box 11-2. Also, police are briefed about new laws and court decisions that affect what is and is not acceptable procedure.

If the goal of the forensic psychologist is to improve the accuracy rate of confessions, then it is appropriate to examine just what procedures the police use in questioning suspects.

The Goals of Interrogations

Police question suspects for two reasons: to get more information about the case and to induce suspects to confess. Contrary to the stereotype held by some, police handbooks state that the main goal for the **interrogation** of suspects by the police is to gain information that furthers the investigation; "interrogation is not sim-

ply a means of inducing an admission of guilt," wrote O'Hara and O'Hara (1980, p. 111), who included a number of other specific goals, including the location of physical evidence, the identity of accomplices, and details of other crimes in which the suspect participated. Royal and Schutt have agreed: "The real objective of interrogation is the exploration and resolution of issues, not necessarily the gaining of a written or oral confession" (1976, p. 25). Inbau, Reid, and Buckley (1986; also Inbau, Reid, Buckley, & Jayne, 2001) advised, "Avoid creating the impression of an investigator seeking a confession or conviction. It is far better to fulfill the role of one who is merely seeking the truth" (p. 36). That may well be, but if a suspect does confess, the police do not look a gift horse in the mouth.

As Irving and Hilgendorf (1980) observed, sometimes a police manual conflicts with itself about the primary goal of interrogation. Lloyd-Bostock (1989) summarized this viewpoint:

Inbau and Reid are working with a dual notion of the causality of confessions and therefore are sometimes inconsistent in their advice. On the one hand they see confession as resulting from the suspect coming to believe that confession is the reasonable course of action but, on the other, they also sometimes view confession more in terms of ["breaking"] the suspect. But overt threats, a build up of stress and pressure, and displays of force tend to be counterproductive as a means of extracting a confession. There is a danger that the suspect will become over-aroused and this can produce a boomerang effect. When people (or animals) become very frightened, they respond by retreating or attacking. Similarly, an over-aroused suspect may withdraw cooperation in panic, or aggressively defy the interrogator. (p. 28)

Sometimes, experts have advocated keeping the pressure on suspects who, close to the point of deciding to confess, begin to fidget and dither and show confusion. But on other occasions, they have proposed what Lloyd-Bostock calls a

BOX 11-1
Has the Miranda Warning Affected the Conviction Rate?

The Miranda warnings were instituted more than 30 years ago (*Miranda v. Arizona,* 1966). Some law-enforcement officials immediately decried the decision, claiming it would hamper the police and the arrest of lawbreakers (Donahue, 1998). Currently, about 20% of arrestees invoke the right to remain silent during questioning (Schulhofer, 1999).

Has the existence of the Miranda warning affected police procedure and trial outcomes? Three viewpoints exist. One argues that judicial decisions have eviscerated the impact of the ruling (Garcia, 1998). Furthermore, some police introduce it so casually that suspects waive their rights without full knowledge; other police continue to question the suspect even if he or she refuses to answer. The view that Miranda is impotent is so strong among some of its believers that a proposal has been made to "Mirandize" Miranda—that is, to require that all suspects in custody be provided an attorney prior to questioning (Ogletree, 1987).

But the other two positions continue to clash. Paul Cassell (1996a, 1996b; Cassell & Hayman, 1996), while a law professor at the University of Utah and a former law clerk to Justice Scalia, accumulated extensive findings about the reduced clearance rates after the advent of Miranda, meaning that a greater percentage of suspects (or, in the eyes of the police, *criminals*) are out on the streets. Cassell has concluded that Miranda "has resulted in a lost confession in one out of every six cases" (1996b, p. 417). He has also claimed that the problem of false confessions is largely limited to those suspects who are mentally retarded or disturbed (Cassell, 1999). Another law professor, Joseph Grano (1993), of Wayne State University, has argued not only this point but also that the Miranda decision by the Supreme Court was not supportable by the Constitution; Grano would abolish the warnings and leave it up to the jury to decide if a resultant confession was coerced or voluntary.

Others have disagreed, arguing that Cassell's conclusions are based on selective cases and that the actual declines are not so large (Schulhofer, 1996); further-more, it is claimed that the majority of suspects waive their Miranda rights anyway (Leo, 1996c). In fact, one of the goals of many interrogations is to stop the suspect from invoking his or her right to an attorney under Miranda (Simon, 1991).

As Kassin (1997) has observed, debate on this question reflects both data and the ideological viewpoints of its advocates; these viewpoints are reflected in an ongoing exchange in the literature (Cassell, 1998, 1999; Leo & Ofshe, 1998; Markman & Cassell, 1988; Ofshe & Leo, 1997). Although we all seek a society in which most criminals are apprehended and convicted, we differ with regard to the costs and sacrifices we are willing to pay to achieve this goal. Richard Leo (1996a) has argued that the presence of a Miranda rule has had a "civilizing" effect on police practices and has increased the public's awareness of defendant's rights. The contrast between his position and those of Professors Cassell and Grano is reminiscent of the distinction introduced in chapter 2 between those who wish to avoid any false convictions and those who are willing to accept a higher rate of false convictions in order to put a greater number of real lawbreakers behind bars.

The viability of the Miranda warnings has finally been tested in the courts. In 1999, a panel of the Fourth Circuit Court of Appeals ruled (in *United States v. Dickerson*) that a relatively unknown law enacted by Congress in 1968 (18 U.S.C. 3501) superseded *Miranda* so that federal prosecutors could use a confession at trial even if the suspect had not been read his or her rights, as long as the confession was judged to be a voluntary one. That is, the panel, by a 2 to 1 vote, held that the 1968 law (generally unenforced since it was passed) was a valid exercise of Congressional power (Schulhofer, 1999), thereby making Miranda warnings unnecessary. However, in a much-anticipated decision, *Dickerson v. United States* (2000), the United States Supreme Court reversed the Fourth Circuit's decision by a 7 to 2 vote (Justices Scalia and Thomas dissenting). The *Miranda* decision remains good law, and police are still required to give Miranda warnings.

more promising approach to dealing with the suspect's conflict over making a decision; in these situations, experts have suggested that the interrogator lead the suspect away from the ultimate choice and thus take the pressure off, so that the suspect is not faced with making the critical choice until the optimum point in the questioning.

Police need to recognize that suspects confess for a variety of reasons, some of which may be unreliable. The greatest value of obtaining a confession may be that it leads to other incriminating

BOX 11-2
Police Handbooks That Offer Instruction on Interrogations

Police interrogators are very experienced and skilled at what they do (Leo, 1996c). After spending a year with homicide detectives in Baltimore, Simon described the typical interrogator as "a salesman, a huckster as thieving and silver-tongued as any man who has ever moved used cars or aluminum siding, more so, in fact, when you consider that he's selling long prison terms to customers who have no genuine need for the product" (1991, p. 213). One reason interrogators are so effective is the wealth of information available to them.

It is not difficult to find advice from police experts about how their colleagues ought to conduct interrogations. Among the numerous books with guidelines on criminal investigation are the following:

1. *The Gentle Art of Interviewing and Interrogation: A Professional Manual and Guide,* by Royal and Schutt (1976). This informal and readable manual concentrates on interviewing and interrogation. Some of the procedures proposed are controversial and may be surprising, but the authors cannot be faulted for failing to express their opinions.

2. *Fundamentals of Criminal Investigation,* by O'Hara and O'Hara (1980). In its fifth edition, this 900-page

handbook devotes almost 100 pages to interrogations, confessions, and appropriate procedures by the police.

3. *Criminal Interrogation and Confessions,* by Inbau, Reid, Buckley, and Jayne (2001). Now in its fourth edition, this widely quoted text falls between the preceding two books in its length and style. It contains a detailed set of steps for questioning and eliciting confessions from suspects. Its authors facilitated the development of the polygraph, and the senior author was the John Henry Wigmore Professor of Law, Emeritus, at Northwestern University.

4. *The Confession: Interrogation and Criminal Profiles for Police Officers,* by Macdonald and Michaud (1987). The authors of this manual are a psychiatrist and a police detective. Containing a number of fascinating examples, the manual concentrates on interrogations leading to confessions.

5. *Police Interrogation: Handbook for Investigators,* by Walkley (1987). This was the first manual designed for police officers in the United Kingdom.

evidence. But even false statements are useful, because "the subject who lies is then committed to the psychological defense of a fantasy" (Royal & Schutt, 1976, p. 25).

What Can Police Do and What Can't They Do?

As noted, the police handbooks emphasize the need to be professional in conducting investigations and interrogations. Beyond the previously described reasons for restraint, too much pressure may put the accused in such an emotional state that his or her capacity for rational judgment is impaired. Some manuals suggest opening with a positive statement: "We're investigating an armed robbery and we think you can help us" (Macdonald & Michaud, 1987, p. 19). But these questions remain: What other kinds of

devices do police use in questioning suspects? What are the limits?

The public has very limited knowledge about the broad limits given to police during interrogations; we will return to this point later when we consider the forensic psychologist's role in working with society in general as a clientele. Police can use **trickery,** and they can lie to suspects and otherwise mislead them. A more detailed list of police tactics that *have not been ruled to be illegal* by the courts is found in Box 11-3.

Methods of Interrogation

The term *interrogation* is used generally to describe all questioning by police, regardless of whether it is conducted in custody or in the field, before or after arraignment. The term is preferred over *interviewing* because it implies a much more active role by the police detective (Macdonald & Michaud,

BOX 11-3
What Is Legal During Interrogations

The following is a list of examples of interrogation tactics that are allowed:

1. Misrepresentation of the facts of the case.

   - Falsely telling the suspect that another suspect has named him as the gunman (*Michigan v. Mosley*, 1975).

   - Falsely telling the suspect that his wife has confessed to possessing and importing cocaine (*United States v. Castaneda-Castaneda*, 1984).

   - Subjecting the suspect to a staged identification procedure in which he is picked out as the culprit (*People v. McRae*, 1978; *Commonwealth v. Graham*, 1962).

   - Misleading a murder suspect into believing that the victim is still alive (*Collins v. Brierly*, 1974).

2. Use of techniques that take unfair advantage of the emotions, beliefs, or medical condition of the defendant.

   - Telling the suspect that if he does not confess, the police officer might lose his job and his family would suffer (*Spano v. New York*, 1959).

   - Feigning friendship with, or sympathy or concern for, the suspect (*Lathan v. Deegan*, 1971).

   - Misrepresenting the reason for professional assistance to an ill suspect (*Leyra v. Denno*, 1954).

   - Disguising informers as fellow prisoners (*Yong v. United States*, 1939).

   - Using fellow prisoners to trap the accused (*People v. Lopez*, 1963).

   - Playing on the superstitions of the accused (*Denmark v. State*, 1928).

   - Promising secrecy (*People v. Stadwick*, 1962).

3. Failure to inform the suspect of some important fact or circumstance that might make the suspect less likely to confess.

   - Failing to inform the suspect that an attorney has called (on behalf of the suspect's sister), inquiring if the suspect is to be questioned (*Moran v. Burbine*, 1986).

   - Pretending that evidence favorable to the defendant is nonexistent (*State v. Rossell*, 1942).

Sources: Sasaki, 1988; Slobogin, 1997; and Thomas, 1979

Note: Sasaki (1988) defines police trickery as the presence of any of these three elements; Thomas defines it as "any police attempt to confront a suspect with evidence of his guilt when no such evidence exists" (1979, p. 1169), a narrower definition than Sasaki's.

1987). Despite the persistence of controversy surrounding this aspect of criminal investigation, surprisingly little exists in the way of empirical documentation of interrogation practices.

In 1931, the U.S. National Commission on Law Observance and Enforcement published a report of its findings and confirmed the worst fears about police abuse, noting that the use of severe third-degree tactics to extract confessions was at that time "widespread" (p. 153). As examples, the commission cited as commonplace the use of physical violence, methods of intimidation that capitalized on the youth or mental abilities of the accused, refusals to give access to counsel, fraudulent promises that could not be fulfilled, and prolonged illegal detention. A few decades later, in an effort to characterize the interrogation process, the Supreme Court in its *Miranda v. Arizona* (1966) decision—lacking direct observational or interview data—turned for evidence of what transpired to reported cases involving coerced confessions and to review of the most popular manuals then available for advising law-enforcement officials about successful tactics for eliciting confessions (cf. Aubry & Caputo, 1965; Inbau & Reid, 1962; Inbau, Reid, & Buckley, 1986; Inbau, Reid, Buckley, & Jayne, 2001; O'Hara & O'Hara, 1956). Essentially, the Court concluded from its inquiry that "the modern practice of in-custody interrogation is [now] psychologically rather than physically oriented" (p. 448) but that the degree of coerciveness inherent in the situation had not diminished. The Court's majority opinion in

Miranda, written by Chief Justice Earl Warren in 1966, noted "the use of physical brutality and violence is not, unfortunately, relegated to the past" (p. 446). Have matters changed in the four subsequent decades?

Manipulative Tactics

Inbau and Reid (1962; Inbau, Reid, & Buckley, 1986; Inbau, Reid, Buckley, & Jayne, 2001) described in considerable detail 16 overlapping strategies through which confessions could be elicited from initially recalcitrant suspects. From these, three major themes emerge.

1. *Minimization.* **Minimization** is reflected in the "soft sell" techniques in which the interrogator offers sympathy, face-saving excuses, or moral justification (Kassin & McNall, 1991). Thus the detective reconceptualizes for the suspect the attributional implications of his or her crime by seemingly belittling its seriousness (e.g., "It's not all that unusual" or "I've seen thousands of others in the same situation"), or by providing a face-saving external attribution of blame (e.g., "on the spur of the moment you did this"). The interrogator might, for example, suggest to the suspect that there were extenuating circumstances in his or her particular case, providing such excusing conditions as self-defense, passion, or simple negligence. Or the blame might be shifted onto a specific person, such as the victim or an accomplice. Often, the suspect is asked if the act was victim-precipitated.

For example, Inbau and Reid (1962; Inbau, Reid, & Buckley, 1986; Inbau, Reid, Buckley, & Jayne, 2001) offered the following instance of how such attributional manipulation has been used successfully as bait: A middle-aged man, accused of having taken indecent liberties with a 10-year-old girl, was told that "this girl is well-developed for her age. She probably learned a lot about sex from boys . . . she may have deliberately tried to excite you to see what you would do." In another documented instance, a detective told a breaking-and-entering suspect that "the guy should never have left all that liquor in the window to tempt honest guys like

you and me" (Wald, Ayres, Hess, Schantz, & Whitebread, 1967, p. 1544).

2. *Maximization.* From an entirely different angle, an alternative strategy is to use "scare tactics" to frighten the suspect into confessing (Kassin & McNall, 1991). One way to accomplish **maximization** is by exaggerating the seriousness of the offense and the magnitude of the charges. In theft or embezzlement cases, for example, the reported loss—and hence the consequences for a convicted defendant—might be exaggerated. In a variation of the scare tactic, the interrogator presumes to have a firm belief about the suspect's culpability, based on independent, supposedly "factual" evidence. A variation of this procedure is to falsify the magnitude of the crime in the hope of obtaining a denial that would implicate the suspect—for example, accusing the suspect of stealing $80,000 when only $20,000 was taken.

Police manuals are replete with specific suggestions about how to use what is referred to as the **"knowledge-bluff" trick.** Using this technique, the interrogator could pretend to have strong circumstantial evidence, such as the suspect's fingerprints at the crime scene; the interrogator might even have a police officer pose as an eyewitness and identify the suspect in a rigged lineup. Another technique is to focus the suspect on his or her physiological and nonverbal indicators of an apparent guilty conscience, such as dryness of the mouth, sweating, fidgety body movements, or downcast eyes.

"Baiting questions" are sometimes employed if the preceding approach is chosen. Such questions are not necessarily accusatory in nature but still convey to suspects that some evidence exists that links them to the crime. For example, the detective may ask, "Jim, is there any reason you can think of why one of Mary's neighbors would say that your car was seen parked in front of her home that night?" Without waiting for an answer, the interrogator would then say, "Now, I'm not accusing you of anything; maybe you just stopped by to see if Mary was at home" (Inbau, Reid, & Buckley, 1986, p. 69). Sometimes baiting questions carry the strong implication that the answer is already known to the police, when in fact it is not.

3. *Rapport-building.* The third type of approach is based on the development of a personal rapport with the suspect. Referring to such **rapport-building** as the emotional appeal, police manuals advise the interrogator to show sympathy, understanding, and respect through flattery and such gestures as the offer of a drink. Having established an amicable relationship, the interrogator might then try to persuade the suspect that confessing is in his or her own best interest. In a more elaborate version of this strategy, two detectives enact a **"Mutt and Jeff"** (or "good-cop, bad-cop") **tactic** in which one comes across as hostile and relentless, while the other gains the suspect's confidence by being protective and supportive. This technique is quite common (Zimbardo, 1967). Rachlin (1995) described a New York City detective who used a combination of rapport-building and minimization: "He appealed to his human feelings, he occasionally made gentle body contact, he tried to make Turner believe that, yes, people do make mistakes sometimes and the detectives understood and wanted to help him" (1995, p. 182).

In addition to these various specific strategies, the literature reviewed by the Supreme Court in the *Miranda* decision contained several consistently demonstrated procedures, the most important of which is "an oppressive atmosphere of dogged persistence." For example, police detectives emphasize the need to maintain pressure on the suspect. One told Rachlin:

> You put your suspect on a rail. . . . You push him forward, then back up a little. But once you get any kind of statement, he is committed to that statement. You back off a little, but stay on the rail. If your suspect feels he's losing control, he'll back off. You let that aspect go for a while, go on to something else, then come back. And ask another question that will incriminate him. He'll finally put the

pieces together and realize you've nailed him. (Rachlin, 1995, p. 183)

Not surprisingly, the Court concluded from its findings that unrestricted interrogation practices were inherently coercive. As noted later in this chapter, the viewpoint of the more recent Supreme Court justices is less adamant.

Direct Observational Data

Are the admittedly indirect and poorly sampled data culled by the Supreme Court an accurate depiction of the interrogation process or do they portray only the most atypical and extreme forms of coercion? David Simon's year-long observations of Baltimore detectives (the inspiration for the TV series *Homicide*) led him to characterize such tactics as routine, "limited only by a detective's imagination and his ability to sustain the fraud" (1991, p. 217). In an empirical study, Wald, Ayres, Hess, Schantz, and Whitebread (1967) observed 127 interrogations over the course of 11 weeks in the New Haven, Connecticut, Police Department. In addition to recording the frequency with which various tactics were used in these sessions, the investigators interviewed the police officers and attorneys involved as well as some former suspects.

Overall, this research revealed that one or more of the tactics recommended by Inbau and Reid and their colleagues were employed in 65% of the interrogations observed, and that the detectives used an average of two kinds of tactics per suspect. The most common approach was to overwhelm the suspect with damaging evidence, to assert a firm belief in his guilt, and then to suggest that it certainly would be easier for all concerned if the suspect admitted to his role in the crime. This latter appeal was often accompanied by a show of sympathy and concern for the suspect's welfare. Most of the other methods cited in the manuals were also used with varying frequency, including the "Mutt and Jeff" routine, playing off suspects against each other, minimizing the seriousness of the offense, shifting the blame for the crime to external factors, and alerting the suspect to his or her signs of nervousness that reveal a guilty conscience. The researchers reported that the detectives used no undue physical force, but they did observe the frequent use of promises, such as offers of lowered bail, reduced charges, and judicial leniency, plus vague threats about harsher treatment. In three instances, suspects were told that the police would make trouble for their families and friends if they refused to cooperate.

Wald et al. (1967) concluded from their observations that the New Haven detectives employed most of the persuasive techniques listed by Inbau and Reid, thus justifying, to some extent, the Supreme Court's fears. When these tactics were combined with a generally hostile demeanor and lengthy interrogation, they often appeared to be successful. Moreover, it is reasonable to speculate that because the mere presence of observers at the sessions could have inhibited the use of stronger forms of pressure, these results might underestimate the coercion employed during interrogation.

In the United Kingdom, Barrie Irving and Linden Hilgendorf (1980) carried out a similar study, by observing interrogations carried out by the CID at Brighton. They classified police interviewing techniques based on how well they altered the suspect's view of the consequences of confessing or not confessing. These outcomes are utilitarian ones, social consequences, or effects on the suspect's self-esteem. For example, if the interrogators chose to downgrade the seriousness of the crime, it could affect the utilitarian consequences for the suspect who thus confessed. Interrogators were observed telling suspects that if they made a clean breast of things, it would increase the likelihood of their receiving lenient treatment in court. (In the United Kingdom, the Police and Criminal Evidence Act of 1984 changed the rules regarding acceptable procedures, by limited police tactics and requiring the taping of all interrogations.)

Other police interrogators skillfully develop a relationship with suspects, so that the interrogator's own approval has social consequences for the suspect. The police officer might express sympathy, understanding, or empathy with the suspect's actions, thus downplaying the negative social outcomes that might follow a conviction (Lloyd-Bostock, 1989). Or, the interrogator may attempt to alter the way a suspect views himself or herself by emphasizing the suspect's good sense or likeable nature, or by pointing out how much better the suspect would feel to get things off his or her chest, thus attempting to affect the suspect's self-esteem (Irving & Hilgendorf, 1980).

Richard Leo (1996b) observed 182 interrogations, either live or videotaped, in three police departments, all in the state of California. Typically, five or more different tactics were used in an interrogation; detectives would note contradictions in the suspect's statements, and confront the suspect with incriminating evidence (some of it faked), but they also used minimization and positive incentives such as praising the suspect. Leo's observations led him to characterize the interrogation as a **confidence game** that involved the well-developed use of deception and manipulation, and thus the betrayal of trust (Leo, 1996c).

What Is Allowable?

The preceding discussion implied that the police have much greater leeway in the interrogation of suspects than most people assume. For example, the following tactics are allowed:

- Misrepresentqtion of the facts of the case.
- Use of techniques that take unfair advantage of the emotions or beliefs of the suspect.
- Failure to inform the suspect of some importatnt fact of circumstance that might make the suspect less likely to confess.

A Specific Example

The case of *State v. Jackson* (1983) is an example of the courts' reluctance to curtail interrogation techniques (Heavner, 1984). James Jackson was a murder suspect who was *falsely* told by the police that bloodstains from the victim were on his pants, his shoes matched footprints at the crime scene, and a witness saw him at the crime scene. In addition to telling the suspect these lies, the detective tried to generate a confession through other forms of intimidation, such as reminding Jackson that death was the maximum penalty for murder and threatening to testify falsely that Jackson, an African American man, had raped and killed a White woman. He even fabricated evidence; he put blood and fingerprints on a knife that resembled the murder weapon, photographed it, and told James Jackson that the fingerprints were his.

Jackson gave a confession, but it was quite an implausible story; then he retracted the confession on grounds that it was coerced. But the North Carolina Supreme Court ruled that the confession was voluntary and that it should not be invalidated by the use of trickery. "After all," wrote the court, "Jackson was not physically restrained, not promised a light sentence and not directly threatened."

But is it correct that a promise of leniency was not implicit in the interrogation? Kassin (1997) has suggested, "Perhaps Jackson reasonably inferred from his interrogation that he would be convicted despite his denials and that a confession might draw leniency in sentencing" (p. 224). Kassin and McNall (1991) found that the use of minimization techniques implied an offer of leniency, and detectives are skilled at *suggesting* leniency without overtly offering it.

The Current Status in Appellate Courts

Not all state appellate courts have been reluctant to exclude confessions obtained by trickery (on due process grounds), and some courts have expressed serious dissatisfaction with deceptive interrogation techniques. (Thomas, 1979, pp. 1187–1188, reviewed examples.) Perhaps the best summary of the current state of affairs remains Thomas's conclusion:

> It is not suggested that these cases represent a substantial "trend" against the use of trickery in custodial interrogations. The cases are cited merely to suggest that at least a detectable amount of judicial approval of deceptive interrogation practices exists. Under the pres-

ent state of law, trickery is a "quasi-legal" form of police behavior.

> Although courts do not approve of it, and *Frazier* [to be described later] dictates that it is a "relevant factor" in a due process claim, the practice does not seem offensive enough to warrant the exclusion of confessions induced by such trickery. Trickery seems particularly palatable when an appellate court is dealing with it in the context of a defendant who has already been convicted and is undoubtedly guilty of the crime charged. No appellate court, however, has ever considered that tolerating trickery in the case of an obvious criminal enhances the likelihood that innocent persons will also be subjected to deceptive interrogation practices because the police know they have nothing to fear by using such techniques. (Thomas, 1979, p. 1188)

The Supreme Court

Perhaps surprisingly, the Supreme Court has had little to say about police trickery. The "closest scrutiny" (Sasaki, 1988, p. 1607) was in the case of *Frazier v. Cupp,* in 1969, a murder case in which police employed at least two forms of trickery in encouraging the suspect to confess. At the time of the murder, Martin E. Frazier was 20 years old and a U.S. Marine, home on emergency leave because of his mother's funeral. After the service, he and his cousin, Jerry Rawls, went to a bar, where they were seen with the murder victim. The victim was later found dead of strangulation. Several days afterward, the police, acting on a tip from a member of the family, picked up Frazier. They then lied to him, telling him that Rawls had been arrested and had confessed to involvement in the crime; they also told him, "You couldn't be in any more trouble than you are now" (*Frazier v. Cupp,* 1969, p. 738). But Frazier remained "reluctant to talk" (p. 737). The detective then sympathetically suggested that the victim had started a fight with Frazier by making homosexual advances. At that point Frazier began to confess. He was convicted but appealed his conviction to the

U.S. Supreme Court, claiming that his confession was involuntary, partly because of the trickery employed by the police detectives. But the Supreme Court ruled that the confession was admissible; Justice Thurgood Marshall wrote the majority opinion, to wit:

> The fact that the police misrepresented the statements that Rawls had made is, while relevant, insufficient in our view to make this otherwise voluntary confession inadmissible. . . . These cases must be decided by viewing the "totality of the circumstances" and on the facts of this case we can find no error in the admission of petitioner's confession. (*Frazier v. Cupp,* 1969, p. 739)

As Thomas (1979, pp. 1184–1186) and Sasaki (1988, p. 1608) both noted, several aspects make the *Frazier* decision a particularly bad case for a definitive ruling on police trickery. These include:

1. Other than the two instances of trickery above, the interrogators' behavior was exemplary. Questioning lasted only 45 minutes, immediately after Frazier was brought to the police station, and the interrogation was tape-recorded.
2. Telling the suspect that his cousin had confessed—a lie—did not seem to have induced Frazier's confession.
3. Frazier's involuntariness claim was not the major thrust of his appeal (the thrust was on the police denial of his request to see an attorney; this case occurred in the interlude between the *Escobedo* and *Miranda* decisions). Only three sentences were devoted to the claim of "deliberate misrepresentation."

So the *Frazier* case was "a particularly unfavorable opportunity to proscribe police trickery" (Sasaki, 1988, p. 1608). What is important now, however, is that later courts have interpreted it as definitively ruling that police trickery is "a mere factor to be included in a court's assessment of a confession's voluntariness under a totality of the circumstances analysis" (Sasaki, 1988, p. 1608). And Professor Inbau (1976), of police handbook fame, regarded the *Frazier* decision as "tacit approval" of trickery (p. 251).

Why Are Such Tactics Not Uniformly Excluded?

Two reasons lie behind court decisions when they rule that a confession is inadmissible because it was coerced: Such confessions violate due process, and they may be unreliable because of the possibility that people might confess to crimes they didn't commit. When the police lie to a suspect, the courts apparently assume that such lying would be counterproductive with truly innocent suspects. That is, if a suspect is told that he was seen at the crime location, and the suspect knew that he had never been there, the suspect would recognize that the police were lying to him and refuse to confess. But things are not that simple, and forensic psychologists can try to educate the police about the power of the interrogation process to get innocent suspects to convince themselves that the false feedback they received is true.

Tactics That Are Illegal

The Standard or Criterion

Both physical and psychological **coercion** are of concern to the courts, because either can cause innocent suspects to confess. Generally, the types of tactics that are illegal include physical force, abuse, and torture; threats (even implicit ones) of harm or punishment; prolonged isolation or deprivation of food or sleep; promises of leniency; failure to notify the suspect of his or her *Miranda* rights; and certain types of psychological influence (Kamisar, LaFave, & Israel, 1994; Kassin, 1997). For example, in *Rogers v. Richmond* (1960), the Supreme Court dealt with a case in which the police pretended to place a telephone call to other police officers, directing them to arrest the suspect's wife. The court ruled that this action psychologically coerced the suspect, possibly rendering his subsequent confession involuntary. "Obliquely suggesting the prospect of harm to the suspect, his relatives, or his property can be interpreted as psychological abuse even though these suggestions do not assume the form of explicit threats" (O'Hara & O'Hara, 1980, pp. 142–143). The question is: Does the suspect reasonably think he or she is in sufficient danger? Examples include telling a suspect he will be turned over to a mob unless he confesses and threatening to "throw the book at him" if he doesn't.

As a rule, for a promise to invalidate a confession, it must have reference to the suspect's escape from punishment or the mitigation of his or her punishment. A promise to the suspect that if she confesses she will be released from custody, that she will not be prosecuted, that she will be granted a pardon, or that she will receive a lighter sentence than the law prescribes will invalidate a confession (Inbau, Reid, & Buckley, 1986; Inbau, Reid, Buckley, & Jayne, 2001). Such invalidation holds even if the interrogator merely states that he will do whatever he can to induce the proper authorities to grant such immunity or reduction of a sentence. Likewise, a kind of plea bargain—telling the subject who is accused of a number of crimes that if he confesses to one, he will not be prosecuted for the others—nullifies the confession.

Most people considering the manipulative techniques described earlier would probably rank as the most unpalatable the following, in ascending order: promises, threats, and lies. State and federal appellate courts have, since *Miranda*, ruled on each of these procedures, but a guideline is to ask: "Is the action something that is likely to cause the suspect to make a false confession?" If it is, it should not be employed.

Psychological Assumptions by the Courts

It is apparent that the courts have made several psychological assumptions; one is that when a suspect is physically abused or tortured, he or she may give in to the pressures and admit to guilt, even when innocent, to avoid further pain. Most of us would probably agree that the courts' assumption is valid here. But the earlier assumption that innocent suspects will not confess when they are lied to is less acceptable to psychologists. Several case decisions reflect the conflict.

1. *Davis v. North Carolina* (1966). A classic example of the conflict between judicial and psychological assumptions was the decision in *Davis v. North Carolina* (1966). The police held Davis incommunicado for 16 days; there was even a notation on his arrest sheet that he was not allowed to have visitors or to use the telephone. After 16 days, he confessed. Both the North Carolina appellate courts and the lower federal courts found his confession to be voluntary, concluding there was no evidence that his confession was unreliable.

2. *Ashcraft v. Tennessee* (1944). As an aside, it should be noted that even the decisions by the Supreme Court as to what is coercion are subjective and inconsistent. Sixty years ago, E. E. Ashcraft (*Ashcraft v. Tennessee,* 1944) was questioned continuously by the police for 36 hours, in connection with his wife's death. Interrogated by police officers in relays, he was given only 5 minutes' respite from questioning during this entire period. Supreme Court Justice Hugo Black, in reviewing this case, declared that the intensity and duration of the interrogation constituted a "situation . . . so inherently coercive that its very existence is irreconcilable with the possession of mental freedom by a lone suspect against whom its full coercive force is brought to bear" (*Ashcraft v. Tennessee,* 1944, p. 154). Justice Black's view served as the majority opinion in this case, but not all the justices agreed. Justice Robert Jackson wrote a minority opinion in which he reflected a traditional assumption that suspects possessed the ability and will to withstand even this pressure. A minority opinion, and hence of no impact? Here's where we see that the Court's decisions are both subjective and inconsistent.

3. *Lyons v. Oklahoma* (1944). The case of *Lyons v. Oklahoma* (1944), decided by the same court just a little more than a month after *Ashcraft,* had a radically different outcome. Justice Jackson's view prevailed, and the majority decision upheld the use of continued questioning as long as the

individual suspect possessed "mental freedom" at the time of his or her confession.

The use of prolonged questioning of suspects continues to this day. In the case in which six Thai Buddhist monks were massacred in a Phoenix, Arizona, temple, one suspect was interrogated for 21 hours without respite.

The Fulminante Decision

The preceding material leads to a conclusion that self-incriminating statements are worthy of concern to the courts. The decision by the U.S. Supreme Court in the case of *Arizona v. Fulminante* (1991) has heightened their importance. Prior to 1991, if a coerced confession had been admitted into testimony by mistake, that wrong decision by the presiding judge was grounds, in and of itself, to throw out any conviction resulting from the trial. But in the *Fulminante* decision, the Supreme Court ruled that a coerced confession could be considered as **harmless error** if there was sufficient other evidence to convict the defendant.

To some, this seems like a sensible decision. If the defendant is guilty anyway, why should an improper ruling by a judge stand in the way of a jury voting to convict? But this rationale fails to recognize that the presence of a confession may convince jurors of the defendant's guilt, even when the jury is fully aware that the confession was involuntarily produced (Kassin & Sukel, 1997; Kassin & Wrightsman, 1985).

WHAT CAN PSYCHOLOGISTS CONTRIBUTE?

The responsibilities of the forensic psychologist with respect to the use of police interrogations are diverse and often conflicting.

The Police as a Clientele

Police and psychologists maintain a complex relationship, as the previous chapter illustrated. Psychologists want to assist police in improving their interrogation procedures when they lead to authentic confessions, but at the same time, many psychologists are appalled by the coercive procedures often used and are concerned that the use of manipulation and falsehoods will lead to an increase in false confessions. How may the two professions work together to achieve common goals? A number of ways are suggested in this section; some, such as psychologically strengthening the interrogation process, reflect an effort to improve the achievement of the goals held by the police; others, such as videotaping of interrogations, reflect the psychologists' concern about the validity of confessions.

The Concept of Interrogative Suggestibility

Police tend to believe that almost all suspects are guilty and that they confess only if they *are* guilty; thus, interrogators may extract confessions that are false without realizing it (Leo, 1996a). Psychologists need to introduce to police the concept of coerced-internalized false confessions; police need to be sensitive to the fact that some suspects are subject to **interrogative suggestibility;** that is, because they are anxious or lacking a strong self-concept or for other reasons, they actually come to believe what the police are telling them. Gisli Gudjonsson (1984, 1989, 1992, 1997, 2003) developed a procedure to identify those subjects high in interrogative suggestibility. The subject first is read a narrative paragraph; then he or she is asked to provide a free recall of the story and to answer 20 memory questions, 15 of which are misleading. After being told—in a firm voice—that he or she made several errors, the subject is then retested, and shifts in the subject's answers are studied. A distinction is made between the number of shifts in memory and the number of responses that reflect yielding to the misleading questions. Subjects who score high on interrogative suggestibility also tend to have high levels of anxiety, low self-esteem, poor memories, and a lack of assertiveness (Gudjonsson, 1992, 2003). Among criminal suspects, those who confessed to the police but later retracted their statements scored higher than the general population

(Gudjonsson, 1991). Although in the preceding description interrogative suggestibility is portrayed as a trait, it also has qualities of a temporary state; for example, sleep deprivation increases scores on interrogative suggestibility (Blagrove, 1996).

How to get police to be aware of such problems is a challenge. First of all, police don't consider these as "problems," and police detectives do not routinely solicit advice from a psychologist to improve the accuracy of their interrogation techniques. Police detectives don't see the use of false evidence during the interrogation as unfair (Skolnick & Leo, 1992), for most of them believe that if the suspect is innocent, he or she won't "bite" on the false information. Such techniques, for Inbau, Reid and Buckley, are not "apt to make an innocent person confess" (1986, p. xvii). And, as noted earlier in the chapter, the actual number of innocent people who confess under such an inducement remains controversial (Ofshe & Leo, 1997; Cassell, 1998; Slobogin, 1997; Gudjonnson, 2003).

Prior Planning

Police are always interested in ways to improve their ability to get suspects to cooperate and reveal information. Part of the prevalent stereotype of police interrogation is the belief that the criminal is usually driven to confessing after having been trapped by the piercing brilliance of the police interrogator (Deeley, 1971). "In reality," states a Scotland Yard detective, "there is no sudden blinding shaft of light. You pick a villain [the English equivalent of "suspect"] up on something he said yesterday. . . . Usually it's a matter of wearing a person down. You may consider that a form of duress, but that's what it amounts to—wearing them down by persistence, like water dripping on a stone. Not brilliance" (quoted by Deeley, 1971, p. 139).

Prior planning is one facilitator of a successful crime investigation. Psychologists can aid by encouraging detectives to ask themselves if the questioning of a suspect is potentially the most valuable means of getting the desired information under the existing circumstances (Royal & Schutt, 1976). If it is decided to question suspects, the police officer should first read all the investigation reports and statements already taken, then visit the scene of the crime, check out suspects' alibis, examine any previous criminal records of suspects, and make inquiries of other people who may have relevant information (Macdonald & Michaud, 1987; Royal & Schutt, 1976). One detective has commented, "The more you know about the man you are going to interrogate the better position you are in to know his weak points. I had a case where I could have talked till hell froze over and this guy wouldn't have confessed. But another policeman had supplied me with a tiny scrap of information beforehand which opened him up" (quoted by Deeley, 1971, p. 142).

The Physical Setting

Whether they like it or not, social psychologists have a number of concepts and research findings that are helpful to police as they seek to generate confessions. Consider, for example, what we know about the effects of the physical setting on behavior. Police manuals agree with social psychologists in urging officials to employ a specifically constructed room that is psychologically removed from the sights and sounds of everyday existence and to maintain rigid control over the ecology of that room. The novelty of this facility serves the function of promoting a sense of lack of control and social isolation and hence gives the suspect the illusion that the outside world is withdrawing farther and farther away (Aubry & Caputo, 1980). Inbau, Reid, and Buckley (1986; Inbau, Reid, Buckley, & Jayne, 2001) go so far as to conclude that privacy—being alone with the suspect—is "the principal psychological factor contributing to a successful interrogation" (p. 24).

To further minimize sensory stimulation and remove all extraneous sources of distraction, social support, and relief from tension, the manuals recommend that the interrogation room be acoustically soundproofed and bare, without furniture or ornaments—only two chairs and perhaps a desk (see, for example, Macdonald & Michaud, 1987, p. 15). Also critical, of course, is that the accused be denied communicative access to friends and family. Finally, the interrogator is advised to sit as close as possible to the subject, in armless, straight-backed chairs, and at equal eye level. Such advice reflects the psychological hypothesis that invading the suspect's personal space will increase his or her level of anxiety, from which one means of escape is confession.

Both O'Hara and O'Hara (1980) and Inbau et al. (1986, 2001) instruct police interrogators to dress in regular clothes—and conservative ones, at that: "Civilian dress is more likely to inspire confidence and friendship in a criminal than a uniform. The accouterments of the police profession should be removed from view. The sight of a protruding gun or billy may arouse enmity or a defensive attitude on the part of the criminal" (Inbau et al., 1986, p. 114).

Establishing Authority

In keeping with the preceding constraints, psychological principles would advise police interviewers to avoid letting the suspect establish the ground rules. The most common procedure is the **stipulation,** in which the detectives stifle attempts by the suspects to set down ground rules for the questioning. A suspect may say, "I will answer any questions about 'X' or 'Y' or 'Z' but not others" (Royal & Schutt, 1976, p. 67). Female suspects may use seductive behaviors or may cry, in order to try to control the situation. In response, the interviewer must display firmness and authority without reflecting arrogance.

Emphasis in the police manuals on establishing authority is consistent with the findings of psychological research. As Lloyd-Bostock (1989) observed, the relationship between an individual and someone in authority can generate quite dramatic psychological effects. As mentioned earlier, Stanley Milgram's (1974) series of studies showed the appalling degree to which ordinary people would obey the instructions of an experimenter who had established a position of authority. Many subjects in Milgram's studies were willing to follow instructions to administer painful and dangerous shocks to other subjects. Lloyd-Bostock (1989) concluded that subjects

being interrogated can become, like Milgram's subjects, just as acquiescent to the demands of the interrogator who has carefully established control over the situation.

Police and the Ability to Detect Deception

Psychologists have carried out extensive research on the accuracy of people in detecting deception and the cues that indicate deception. These research findings can be applied to the task of the police detective in assessing the truth-telling of a suspect.

Police Assumptions About Their Accuracy

Police believe they can spot the liar in the interrogation room. Inbau and his colleagues (1986, 2001) claimed that it is possible, using a variety of cues from the suspect, to distinguish between guilt and innocence. For example, they proposed that the innocent suspect will give concise answers because "he has no fear of being trapped" (p. 48). In contrast, guilty suspects wouldn't make "direct eye contact" (p. 51) and would be "overly polite" (p. 47).

Harvey Rachlin (1995) was given permission by the New York City Police Department to observe police detectives at work. He has provided an example of how these detectives form impressions of suspects immediately:

> Detectives often wanted to appraise how compliant their subject would be, and there was one simple method that gave them a good clue right from the start. When the detective shook hands with the subject at the time of introduction, in grasping the subject's hand, the detective pivoted his own around clockwise. If the subject's hand followed [quite] easily, it could be interpreted to mean he would be tractable and forthcoming; if not, it was an indication he might be resistant and different. (1995, p. 180)

Interrogators also had their devices for detecting deception:

> The so-called **scan technique** involved asking the subject to describe his [or her] activi-

ties the day of the crime, covering a period from several hours before to several hours after. The detective would listen to the entire recital without interrupting, paying attention to the degree of denial. If the person provided explicit particulars of events up until the time of the actual crime, then glossed over what he was doing at the time of the crime and concluded with a detailed post-crime accounting of events, it was a signal to the detective that the subject was trying to conceal the criminal behavior that was the focus of the interview. (Rachlin, 1995, p. 181)

Psychological Research on the Ability to Detect Deception

Psychological research does not support people's assumptions that they are good judges of lying (Zuckerman, DePaulo, & Rosenthal, 1981). Even those people who are experienced and hence assumed to be proficient—polygraphers, psychiatrists, police investigators—have high rates of error (Ekman & O'Sullivan, 1991; Frank & Ekman, 1997), probably because they have erroneous beliefs about the indicators of truth or falsity (Akehurst, Kohneken, Vrij, & Bull, 1996). Indeed, in a recent study by Kassin and Fong (1999), examiners were found to be generally unable to distinguish between truthful and deceptive suspects. Those who were trained in interrogation methods were more confident of their decisions, but not correct any more often.

Videotaping of Interrogations

Given that police often use manipulation and trickery in interrogations and that some suspects are susceptible to making false confessions, it is essential that some independent record of the proceeding be made available to the judge and jury (Cassell, 1996b; Gudjonsson, 1992; Kassin, 1997; Leo, 1996a). In England, the Police and Criminal Evidence Act requires that all interrogations be taped. The state supreme courts of Minnesota and Alaska have ruled that defendants' statements obtained without taping are generally inadmissible (Leo, 1996a). In 2003, the state of Illinois passed legislation mandating such

taping in murder cases (Davey, 2003). A national survey (Geller, 1993, cited by Kassin, 1997) estimated that one third of all large police and sheriffs' departments in the United States do some videotaping of interrogations, but often what is shown to jurors is only the defendant's final confession.

Furthermore, the way the interrogation is videotaped can affect jurors' reactions to it. Judgments of the voluntariness of videotaped confessions have been found to be systematically affected by something as subtle as the camera angle (Lassiter & Irvine, 1986). Subjects watched a tape of an interrogator from one of three angles; for a third, the interrogator was visually salient; for a third, only the suspect was; and for a third, both participants were. Judgments of coercion were lowest when the suspect was salient, highest when the interrogator was salient, and intermediate when the two were equally visible. The research results are consistent with social-psychological tests of **correspondent inference theory** (Jones & Davis, 1965; Jones & Harris, 1967), which deals with the decision to infer whether a person's actions reflect (or "correspond to") an internal characteristic. A camera focused on the suspect increases the attribution by observers that the suspect's response was determined by his or her internal predispositions rather than by any coercive nature of the situation.

The Courts as a Clientele

On the matter of suspects' confessions, the forensic psychologist can play a role in advising trial judges as well as the police. Appellate courts have, over the years, made a number of decisions relevant to the admissibility of confession evidence and, more recently, the admission of expert testimony on false confessions; these are reviewed in this section.

What Do the Courts Want to Know?

In determining whether to admit a confession into evidence, the fundamental question asked by judges is whether it was voluntary (Rutledge,

1996). The U.S. Supreme Court has ruled that the **voluntariness** of a confession must be determined by the "totality of circumstances" (*Culombe v. Connecticut,* 1961). Involuntary confessions, usually generated by coercion, are seen as false by the courts and hence are inadmissible. But where do we draw the line between involuntary and voluntary? We may agree that physical brutality or torture contribute to an involuntary confession, but often the police and the defendant will disagree as to whether such actions by the police took place.

The decision by the Supreme Court in the case of *Lego v. Twomey* (1972) is illustrative. The following description is taken from the Court's opinion (pp. 480–481); note that the fact finder is presented with conflicting testimony from the defendant and the police regarding what occurred during the interrogation:

> Petitioner Lego was convicted of armed robbery in 1961 after a jury trial. . . . The court sentenced him to prison for 25 to 50 years. The evidence introduced against Lego at trial included a confession he had made to the police after arrest and while in custody at the station house. Prior to trial Lego sought to have the confession suppressed. He did not deny making it but did challenge that he had done so voluntarily. The trial judge conducted a hearing, out of presence of the jury, at which Lego testified that police had beaten him about the head and neck with a gun butt. . . . Lego introduced into evidence a photograph that had been taken of him at the county jail on the day after his arrest. The photograph showed that petitioner's face had been swollen and had traces of blood on it. Lego admitted that his face had been scratched in a scuffle with the robbery victim but maintained that the encounter did not explain the condition shown in the photograph. The police chief and four officers also testified. They denied either beating or threatening petitioner and disclaimed knowledge that any other officer had done so. The trial judge resolved this credibility problem in favor of the police and

ruled the confession admissible. (*Lego v. Twomey,* 1972, pp. 480–481)

Such conflicts often occur, and the fact finder is forced to choose in a "who-do-you-believe" case. In the preceding decision, the Court not only affirmed the conviction but established a rather low standard (the **preponderance of evidence standard**) for admitting such "gray-area" confessions into evidence. In general, judges rarely conclude that the police trickery was so severe that it undermined voluntariness (Young, 1996). The research by Kassin and Wrightsman (1980, 1981; Wrightsman & Kassin, 1993) suggests that judges need to exert more caution in admitting such disputed confessions into evidence. When told that a suspect confessed, mock jurors do not always consider the circumstances or give much weight to the possibility that coercion caused the confession (Kassin & Neumann, 1997; Kassin & Sukel, 1997); rather, they tend to reflect an application of the **fundamental attribution error,** accepting a dispositional attribution of a person's actions without fully accounting for the effects of situational factors (Jones, 1990).

Forensic psychologists can serve the court as expert witnesses by pointing out how judicial assumptions about the abilities of jurors are sometimes in conflict with the findings of psychological research. The previously mentioned *Arizona v. Fulminante* (1991) decision is a case in point, in that the decision assumed that jurors can "correctly" weight the value of a coerced confession in their decision making (Kassin & Neumann, 1997). The conclusion of the research program by Saul Kassin and his colleagues (see especially Kassin & Sukel, 1997) is that "confession evidence is inherently prejudicial and that people do not discount it even when it was logically and legally appropriate to do so" (Kassin & Neumann, 1997, p. 471).

It is true that when a defense attorney attempts to introduce the testimony of a psychologist regarding the circumstances that led to an allegedly false confession, the trial judge may not admit such testimony. But such efforts should continue, if for no other reason than it establishes grounds for an appeal. And such appeals have begun to be successful (see Fulero, in press, for a full discussion of the current case law). For example, in *United States v. Hall* (1996), the Seventh Circuit Court of Appeals reversed a trial judge's decision not to admit the testimony of Dr. Richard Ofshe. The court ruled that

> once the trial judge decided that Hall's confession was voluntary, the jury was entitled to hear the relevant evidence on the issue of voluntariness. . . . This ruling [by the trial judge] overlooked the utility of valid social science. Even though the jury may have had beliefs about the subject, the question is whether those beliefs were correct. Properly conducted social science research often shows that commonly held beliefs are in error. Dr. Ofshe's testimony, assuming its scientific validity, would have let the jury know that aphenomenon known as false confessions exists, how to recognize it, and how to decide whether it fits the facts of the case being tried. (*United States v. Hall,* 1996, pp. 1344–1345)

Cases in state courts are also beginning to allow experts on false confessions to testify (see Fulero, in press, for a review of cases).

Society as a Clientele

The typical layperson does not think very much about confessions of suspects until a highly publicized case brings a claimed confession into question. But people have expectations and standards for how the police should behave when interrogating suspects, and some people are concerned when judges permit the admission of evidence that unfairly convicts a defendant.

Lying to Suspects by the Police

Deceit is generally repugnant in our society. Police manuals differ about its acceptability during interrogations. Macdonald and Michaud advise police, "Do not make any false statements. Do not tell him his fingerprints were found at the scene if they were not found at the scene. Do not tell him he was identified by an eyewitness if he was not identified by an eyewitness. If he catches you in a false statement, he will no longer trust you, he will assume that you do not have sufficient evidence to prove his guilt, and his self-confidence will go up" (1978, p. 23).

But, as we have seen, many police interrogators disregard such admonitions. Furthermore, some police manuals conclude that without the use of some trickery—leading the suspect to believe that the police have some tangible or specific evidence of guilt—many interrogations would be totally ineffective. Documented cases exist of police telling the kinds of lies that Macdonald and Michaud warn against; such behavior may even be the norm (Aronson, 1990). In a Hawaii case, a police officer testified that he lied at the interrogation because he had been told to do so at a police seminar (Wakefield & Underwager, 1998).

Do people subscribe to such tactics? Research (Engelbrecht & Wrightsman, 1994) indicated that when mock jurors were told that police carried out improper activities during an interrogation, they were less likely to find the defendant guilty than were mock jurors who were told that the police acted appropriately. The effect of the improper police tactics on verdicts was just as strong whether or not the suspect had confessed during the interrogation. Similarly, Skolnick and Leo (1992) asked college students to respond to a brief vignette that described a suspect who was confronted with false evidence by the police; only 36% of the students felt that the tactic was fair. The addition of a fabricated scientific report reduced the sense of fairness; only 17% of the students now rated the procedure as fair.

At a broader level, betrayal in the interrogation room not only taints the police but our society in general, a society built on relationships of trust (Paris, 1996; Slobogin, 1997). A general distrust of police interrogators creates unwillingness on the part of innocent, law-abiding citizens to cooperate with law-enforcement authorities (Stuntz, 1989).

SUMMARY AND CONCLUSIONS

The goals of the interrogation of suspects by the police are the elicitation of further information about the crime and a confession of wrongdoing by the suspect. Confessions, as evidence at trial, are extremely influential; however, an uncertain number of confessions are false. These can be of three types: voluntary, coerced-compliant, and coerced-internalized. Of these, the coerced-compliant type is probably the most frequent; suspects confess—perhaps to get relief from the persistent questioning—even though they know they are innocent.

Police use a number of techniques during interrogations that reflect psychological principles; these include maximization and minimization, "baiting questions," and rapport-building. Courts have been reluctant to overrule the use of lying and trickery by the police, apparently on the assumption that innocent suspects would not succumb to such ruses and confess falsely.

One contribution that can be made by forensic psychologists is to emphasize to police that their procedures can produce false confessions and that some suspects are susceptible to what has been called interrogative suggestibility; these suspects will sometimes come to believe false information about their role in the crime. It is recommended that police videotape the entire interrogation, so that judges and jurors can observe the procedures used by the interrogators and the style and content of the suspect's responses.

Psychologists can be called by defense attorneys to testify as expert witnesses with regard to the coercive effects of certain interrogation techniques; a recent appellate decision upheld the admissibility of such testimony. Forensic psychologists also serve society as a clientele by evaluating the public's reaction to the use of trickery in interrogations. General distrust of police interrogators erodes the willingness of innocent citizens to cooperate in investigations.

KEY TERMS

"baiting questions"
coerced-compliant confessions
coerced-internalized confessions
coercion
coercive-reactive confession
compliance
confession
confidence game
correspondent inference theory
fundamental attribution error
harmless error
internalization
interrogation
interrogative suggestibility
"knowledge-bluff" trick
maximization
minimization
Miranda warnings
"Mutt and Jeff" tactic
preponderance of evidence standard
rapport-building
recanted confession
scan technique
stipulation
suggestibility
"third-degree" tactics
trickery
voluntariness
voluntary false confession

INFOTRAC® COLLEGE EDITION

InfoTrac College Edition is a FREE, powerful, online learning resource, consisting of full-text articles from thousands of journals and periodicals. With each new copy of *Forensic Psychology,* Second Edition, you receive 4 months of free access to the InfoTrac College Edition database. By doing a simple keyword search (try using the Key Terms in the list above), you can quickly generate a list of relevant articles from thousands of possibilities and can select articles to read, explore, and print for reference or further study. InfoTrac College Edition's continuously updated collection of articles can be useful for doing reading and writing assignments that reach beyond the pages of this text!

SUGGESTED READINGS

Ekman, P. (1985). *Telling lies: Clues to deceit in the market place, politics, and marriage.* New York: Norton.

Can people tell when someone else is lying? Most cannot, using customary procedures. But psychologist Paul Ekman has developed a system that analyzes brief, specific muscle movements, such as a fleeting grimace that may momentarily precede a liar's smile; these are quite difficult to fake.

Gudjonsson, G. H. (1992). *The psychology of interrogations, confessions and testimony.* New York: John Wiley; Gudjonsson, G. H. (2003). *The psychology of interrogations and confessions: A handbook.* New York: John Wiley.

Comprehensive state-of-the-art reviews of the interrogation and confession process, by one of the world's leading authorities.

Inbau, F. E., Reid, J. F., and Buckley, J. P. (1986). *Criminal interrogation and confessions* (3rd ed.). Baltimore, MD: Williams and Wilkins; Inbau, F. E., Reid, J. F., Buckley, J. P., and Jayne, B. (2001). *Criminal interrogation and confessions* (4th ed.). Baltimore, MD: Williams and Wilkins.

The most frequent sources for what the police are told regarding how to conduct an interrogation of a suspect.

Kassin, S. M. (1997). The psychology of confession evidence. *American Psychologist, 52,* 221–233.

An outstanding article that discusses, in depth, many of the issues introduced in this chapter.

Kotlowitz, A. (1999, February 8). The unprotected. *New Yorker,* 42–53.

A disturbing account of the threats to validity when children are interrogated as crime suspects.

McCann, J. T. (1998). A conceptual framework for identifying various types of confessions. *Behavioral Sciences and the Law, 16,* 441–453.

This article proposes a fourth type of false confession, called the **coercive-reactive confession,** that reflects coercion from sources other than the police; for example, a teenager is threatened with death by his gang members unless he admits responsibility for a crime actually committed by the gang leader.

Shuy, R. W. (1998). *The language of confession, interrogation, and deception.* Thousand Oaks, CA: Sage.

An examination of criminal confessions through the use of linguistic analysis. Many examples from actual cases are provided. Highly recommended.

Wakefield, H., & Underwager, R. (1998). Coerced or nonvoluntary confessions. *Behavioral Sciences and the Law, 16,* 423–440.

An article that covers a number of topics from this chapter, including types of false confessions, police interrogation procedures, and the admissibility of psychologists as expert witnesses. Specific cases are described in detail.

Young, D. (1996). Unnecessary evil: Police lying in interrogations. *Connecticut Law Review, 28,* 425–477.

A law review article that documents how standards in U.S. courts have shifted over the years regarding the admissibility of confessions elicited in those interrogations that involved questionable police tactics.

12

Trial Consultation: Jury Selection, Case Preparation, and Pretrial Publicity

OVERVIEW

This chapter deals with the activities of what are most often called **trial consultants.** Hired by trial attorneys (or—rarely—appointed by the court), trial consultants assist attorneys in preparing for the trial, evaluating the effectiveness of the trial presentation, and formulating procedures for the so-called selection of the jury.

Trial Consultants as Forensic Psychologists

Some people do not think of trial consultants when the term *forensic psychologists* is mentioned. And it is true that not all trial consultants are trained in departments of psychology or identify themselves as psychologists; almost 40% receive their education in departments of speech communication/communication studies, others in political science or social welfare (Wortz, 1999). The major organization of trial consultants, the American Society of Trial Consultants (ASTC), does not specify a particular training program or set of courses, and, in fact, no state currently licenses or certifies trial consultants. An analysis of a recent ASTC directory indicates that less than a third of the members indicate they have a doctoral degree (Mendenhall, 1998). But if we employ the definition of forensic psychology introduced in chapter 1—that it covers any application of psychological principles to the legal system—we conclude that trial consultation can be considered a full-fledged example of forensic psychology. Furthermore, the field is a rapidly expanding one, with stimulating job opportunities.

Trial Consultants: Better Thought of as Litigation Consultants?

When so-called scientific jury selection began in the early 1970s, the activities of the psychologists and other social scientists who spearheaded the effort were localized on the trial's 12 jurors. The focus was on assisting defense attorneys in their decisions about which prospective jurors

should be dismissed. As social scientists became more active as consultants, their activities broadened—to assisting in the preparation of witnesses for testifying, to directing focus groups of mock jurors to identify central issues or themes in the case, to carrying out mock trials, and even to helping attorneys develop a **theory of the case.** These duties are described later in this chapter. A recent and fascinating presentation of the activities of trial consultants is presented in Kressel and Kressel (2002).

Possible Pretrial Activities

The distinction between criminal trials and civil trials is very important when discussing what trial consultants usually do (Kressel & Kressel, 2002). Contrary to public perception, most cases in which trial consultants are involved are civil cases, because those are the ones for which attorneys have clients who are willing and able to pay the fees of these and other consultants. Perhaps the prototypic case is one in which a trial consultant assists a large corporation that is the defendant in a personal injury case—for example, an automobile manufacturer that allegedly installed a defective seat belt, or a power company with a plant at which (plaintiffs claim) human error has led to the death of several of its electrician-employees. In such cases, trial consultants may be asked to conduct **focus groups** to uncover feelings and biases held by the public. The lawyers representing the corporation may feel that some of the company's management team (who will be called on to testify) need to be assisted in preparing to testify. Composition of the jury is also a possible activity for which the trial consultant may offer advice, although in most jurisdictions the number of prospective jurors who can be dismissed, or **peremptory challenges** given each side in a civil trial, is limited (often only three per side) so that jury "selection" in civil trials has less impact than in criminal trials.

In criminal trials, other activities may take priority. If the crime has been highly publicized in the local media, the defense attorney may conclude that his or her client cannot get a fair trial locally and may request moving the trial to another jurisdiction. Trial consultants, psychologists, and forensic experts have developed procedures for determining the impact of pretrial publicity (Arnold & Gold, 1978–1979; Moran & Cutler, 1997; Nietzel & Dillehay, 1983; Pollock, 1977). Although the use of mock juries and focus groups is considered desirable by some criminal defense attorneys, often their clients are indigent and not able to afford the costs of such activities; similarly, jury selection has to be done on a minimal budget.

Ethical Issues

Trial consultants are employed by attorneys who assume that they will subscribe to the attorneys' code of "zealously" representing their client. Yet, even though they are a part of the legal team, trial consultants have their own set of ethical principles. Those who are psychologists have the APA Ethics Code as a standard. Also, the American Society of Trial Consultants has developed a brief, one-page Code of Professional Standards; the guidelines it offers are well-meaning but, in truth, the organization has no enforcement powers. Furthermore, many trial consultants do not belong to the organization; it is estimated that more than 700 individual practitioners and 400 firms are now doing trial consulting (Strier, 1999), whereas membership in ASTC includes only about 400 individual and corporate members. Temptations to misrepresent one's qualifications, to promise too much, to fail to inform clients fully, or to violate confidentiality are not punished because there is no regulatory board.

PRETRIAL ACTIVITIES

Sometimes parties insist on going to trial. What assistance might a forensic psychologist provide an attorney when a trial is the inevitable result? The rest of the chapter considers some proce-

dures for which psychologists and other social scientists have some expertise that can aid the trial attorneys. These will include change of venue in cases involving pretrial publicity, witness preparation, organizing the case, and jury selection.

CHANGE-OF-VENUE REQUESTS IN RESPONSE TO PRETRIAL PUBLICITY

In a criminal trial, a defendant has a constitutional right to a "fair trial." The Supreme Court has, on occasion, reversed a conviction because of the impact of **pretrial publicity** on the jurors (*Irvin v. Dowd,* 1961; *Rideau v. Louisiana,* 1963; *Sheppard v. Maxwell,* 1966). After Mikail Markhasev was convicted of the murder of Ennis Cosby, the defendant's attorney blamed the conviction on the news media's infatuation with Bill Cosby's celebrity status and the resulting publicity about the case. Psychologists have methodological skills that are useful in assessing a claim that publicity has ruined the chances of a fair trial, and for more than 30 years the courts have accepted public opinion surveys into evidence (*Zippo Manufacturing Co. v. Rogers Imports,* 1963).

Origin of Requests

A particularly heinous crime has been committed, and the local television stations and newspapers have proclaimed the seamy details of the crime ad infinitum and ad nauseam. A suspect is arraigned and scheduled for trial. His attorney concludes that the pretrial publicity is such that the defendant cannot get a fair trial in this jurisdiction. The attorney requests a **change of venue.** It is conceivable that there might be a criminal case in which the *prosecution* asks for a change of venue (perhaps a highly discussed case in which a vigilante chases and kills a child rapist and the community emotionally supports the vigilante's actions), but almost always the *defense* attorney is the one making such a request. For example, such a change of venue was requested—and granted—in the Timothy McVeigh case, from Oklahoma City to Denver (see Studebaker, Robbennolt, Pathak-Sharma, & Penrod, 2000; Studebaker, Robbennolt, Penrod, Pathak-Sharma, Groscup, & Devenport, 2002). A change of venue might be requested in a civil trial, if, for example, in a product liability case the defendant's attorney believes that publicity has been so pervasive as to bias the jury against the defendant. Forensic psychologist Stanley Brodsky (1998) vividly described a change of venue survey for a civil case, in which an Alabama county was suing the architects who designed a new countywide high school.

Thus, it is essential that the attorney believes that the pretrial publicity is, first of all, pervasive, and second, of such a one-sided nature as to bias the jury against the defendant or defendants. For example, the attorneys representing the four Los Angeles police officers who beat Rodney King requested a change of venue because available data indicated that more than 95% of residents of Los Angeles County had seen the videotape of the beating, and a majority of these had formed an opinion about the impropriety of what the police had done.

The Litigation Consultant's Activities

Given such a situation, a defense attorney might approach a forensic psychologist or litigation consultant with the request to do a community survey to determine the extent of knowledge of the case and the extent of prejudgment about the guilt of the defendant. In most jurisdictions, the court will allocate an amount of money to pay for such a survey. Ideally, respondents in the local jurisdiction (usually a county) will be compared with respondents in some other jurisdiction in the same state to determine if differences exist in extent of knowledge and bias. The second jurisdiction, or county, should be some distance away, but similar in demographic qualities.

Most surveys of this sort are telephone surveys. The psychologist, working in conjunction

with the attorney, drafts a series of questions. The survey cannot be too long, or it challenges the cooperation of telephone respondents, but it needs to assess the respondent's knowledge of the case, the extent to which the respondent has formed an opinion as to the guilt of the defendant, and the respondent's ability to be open-minded. It is helpful to assess how many of the respondents have knowledge about *specific* aspects of the crime. Some typical questions from a change-of-venue survey may be found in Box 12-1. The actual phone-calling can be subcontracted to a marketing firm, which usually charges at least $8,000 to do a survey of 15–20 minutes with 300–400 respondents. The marketing firm then provides a tabulation of responses to each question to the psychologist and the lawyer.

Once the survey has been completed, the psychologist evaluates the results and prepares a report to the attorney. This report may be considered an **attorney work product** and hence is **privileged information;** that is, its contents do not have to be revealed to the other side. In the report, the psychologist advises the attorney whether to proceed on the change-of-venue request; the basic question to be answered is whether the defendant can expect an unbiased jury in this jurisdiction.

What are the criteria for deciding whether to go forward? Is there a cutoff percentage for knowledge about the case? A cutoff percentage for opinion already formed? The short answer is no; simply, the higher these percentages, the stronger a case can be made for honoring a change-of-venue request. Although there is no absolute standard, Hans and Vidmar (1982) suggested that the results can be compared with those of other change-of-venue surveys. For example, in their book *Psychological Consultation in the Courtroom,* Nietzel and Dillehay (1986) reported detailed results from a number of surveys conducted in various Kentucky counties; for example, they found that in the local counties, in five cases, the percentages of respondents assuming guilt ranged from 19% to 50%, whereas

> **BOX 12-1**
> **Some Typical Questions From a Change-of-Venue Survey**
>
> 1. Are you a resident of _____ County?
> 2. Are you 18 years of age or older?
> 3. Do you have a driver's license from the state of _____?
> 4. Are you a United States citizen?
> 5. What newspapers do you read?
> 6. How often do you watch the local news on television?
> 7. Do you recall reading, seeing, or hearing about a case that. . . ? (describe the facts of the case coming up for trial)
> 8. When did you first hear about this incident?
> 9. Can you tell me the names of any of the people involved in the crime?
> 10. Do you think that _____ is: definitely not guilty, probably not guilty, probably guilty, or definitely guilty of this crime?
> 11. Have you discussed this case with family, friends, or people at work?
>
> Note: This is only a sample of the questions. Other questions would amplify on the issues raised in these.

in alternative counties in these five cases, the equivalent percentages were only 9% to 20% (see also Nietzel & Dillehay, 1983).

If, in the judgment of the defense attorney and the psychologist, there is enough indication of extensive knowledge and bias, the psychologist then prepares an **affidavit** for the court. In some respects, this affidavit will resemble the previous confidential report to the attorney. But it differs in several important ways:

1. It needs to describe the invidious effects of pretrial publicity.
2. The methodology must be covered in a clear and detailed way.
3. Defensible conclusions are drawn.

The Effects of Pretrial Publicity

There exists an impressive body of research on the effects of pretrial publicity on jurors' verdicts, but judges are ordinarily not aware of this unless they are so informed in the psychologist's affidavit (Fulero, 1987, 2002a). Among the sources that are helpful in informing the judge

are the guidelines developed by the American Bar Association (1978; Fulero 2002a) and articles by Costantini and King (1980–1981); Kerr, Kramer, Carroll, and Alfini (1991); Moran and Cutler (1991); Otto, Penrod, and Dexter (1994); Kramer, Kerr, and Carroll (1990); Padawer-Singer and Barton (1975); and Studebaker and Penrod (1997). Recently, an entire special issue of the American Psychology-Law Society's scientific journal, *Law and Human Behavior,* was devoted to the topic of pretrial publicity (Fulero, 2002b), in both criminal cases (see, e.g., Kovera, 2002), and civil cases (see, e.g., Bornstein, Whisenhunt, Nemeth, & Dunaway, 2002).

Empirical work has reflected two methodological approaches: surveys of potential jurors in actual cases, and simulations of jury trials, using subjects who are instructed to respond as if they were jurors (Steblay, Besirevic, Fulero, & Jimenez-Lorente, 1999; Studebaker & Penrod, 1997). More recently, some researchers have turned to the Internet as a means of research in this area (Studebaker et al., 2002). The following are the general conclusions from the approach that surveys members of actual jury pools:

1. Respondents with a greater knowledge about a case were more likely to assume that the defendant was guilty (Costantini & King, 1980–1981; Nietzel & Dillehay, 1983).
2. The more media sources the respondent mentioned attending to, the more he or she knew about the case (Moran & Cutler, 1991).
3. The respondents' knowledge of the case was *not* related to their reported ability to be impartial. In fact, Moran and Cutler (1991) found that those respondents who believed there was "a lot of evidence" against the defendant were the most likely to believe they could be fair and impartial.

In the second type of research, an attempt is made to approximate the trial experience for mock jurors in a controlled experimental environment (Davis, 1986; Kramer, Kerr, & Carroll, 1990; Otto, Penrod, & Dexter, 1994; Padawer-Singer & Barton, 1975). Videotapes of trial reenactments, trial transcripts, or written summaries are used as stimulus materials. These studies, for the most part, find that the presence of pretrial publicity that is detrimental to the defendant increased the likelihood that the defendant would be convicted. Examples of detrimental publicity include reports of involvement in past crimes, prior convictions, or a confession by the defendant. In 28 comparisons, the conviction rate averaged 59% for those mock jurors in a pretrial publicity condition, compared to a 45% conviction rate for jurors in a control condition (Steblay, Besirevic, Fulero, & Jimenez-Lorente, 1999). Most of the research in this second line of study has found that pretrial publicity affects judgments *prior to* the trial. More recently, research has shifted to include the question of whether evidence presented during the trial could have a moderating effect on the biases generated by pretrial publicity. In one study, the introduction of trial evidence favoring the defendant diminished, but still did not eliminate, the effects of pretrial publicity (Otto, Penrod, & Dexter, 1994). Others have also noted that mid-trial publicity can still have prejudicial effects,

though more empirical research is clearly needed to determine the scope and direction of such effects (see Vidmar, 2002).

Testifying at a Hearing

Ordinarily after the affidavit has been submitted to the judge, the judge will schedule a preliminary hearing, at which time the psychologist will testify about the results of the survey and the recommendations. This testimony is, of course, subject to cross-examination; thus, it is vital that the psychologist or litigation consultant meet with the defense attorney prior to the hearing to review the questions that should be asked on direct examination and the anticipated questions that might be asked by the judge and the attorney representing the prosecution. For example, in such a case, the psychologist would want to bring out the following points during the direct examination:

1. The results of the survey, especially the percentage of respondents who had heard about the case, the number who already thought the defendant was guilty, and the extent of knowledge about details of the crime.
2. The conclusion that prior information can influence verdicts, especially when it is entrenched. Knowledge of details is an indication of the entrenched nature of such information. The possession of prior information colors the way that jurors process evidence presented at the trial.
3. Are jurors able to put aside prior information about a case? It depends, but in general, no. Jurors' claims that they can be open-minded do not seem verified in their behavior (Dexter, Cutler, & Moran, 1992).
4. A comparison of the results of this survey with others in previous change-of-venue appeals, emphasizing, if possible, the relatively high percentages of respondents who have formed an opinion and already assume that the defendant is guilty.

It is hard to anticipate just what questions will be asked on cross-examination, but typically, experts are asked about how they interacted with the marketing research organization, how much they were paid to testify, and how many such surveys they have conducted. They may be asked about the specific wording of questions on which the conclusions are based (see Posey & Dahl, 2002). Their reports on the research findings may be questioned on the basis of challenges to the ecological validity of the procedures. Judges may disfavor what they consider to be small samples; they need to be informed how a random sample of 300 to 400 respondents can represent the responses of a jury pool of 50,000 to 100,000 people with only a small margin of error.

The American Society of Trial Consultants is aware that change-of-venue surveys are sometimes of marginal quality and that judges usually have little or no experience in survey research and thus cannot properly evaluate the quality of the findings. The ASTC has initiated a project to establish minimum standards for such surveys (American Society of Trial Consultants, 1998). The draft of the guidelines covers a variety of issues, including the length of the interview (10 minutes is the goal), the sample size (400 respondents is typical), the use of callbacks (three or four callbacks are recommended for uncompleted calls), the question wording (open-ended questions are discouraged), and the testing of the validity of the responses (sometimes fictitious cases are used to check on the respondent's truth telling).

Sequestered Voir Dire

Sometimes a judge, when denying a request for a change of venue, may agree to conducting a **sequestered voir dire** of prospective jurors; that is, the judge will question each prospective juror individually about his or her biases, in the judge's chambers, rather than in open court (Nietzel & Dillehay, 1986). Although such a procedure may lead to more acknowledgment of bias by prospective jurors (Nietzel & Dillehay, 1982), the problem of negative effects from pretrial publicity remains. Ronald Dillehay (per-

sonal communication, February 23, 1999), a psychologist experienced in jury selection, tries to convince the judge that sequestered voir dire is not an adequate substitute for a change of venue. Ample social psychological research exists to show that prospective jurors will claim that they can be objective when often they are not (Anderson, Lepper, & Ross, 1980; Petty & Cacioppo, 1977; Sue, Smith, & Pedroza, 1975); pretrial publicity can affect verdicts even when jurors say that they can be unbiased (a testament to the ineffectiveness of the pretrial procedure in which a potential juror is "rehabilitated" by asking, "Despite your exposure to pretrial publicity, can you lay aside that knowledge and decide the case fairly and impartially?"). In the *Irvin v. Dowd* (1961) decision, the U.S. Supreme Court recognized that statements of impartiality "can be given little weight" (p. 728) when abundant other evidence exists of bias. Efforts by judges to instruct jurors to disregard pretrial publicity may boomerang. Daniel Wegner's (1989, 1994) research program on thought suppression concluded that people found it very difficult to suppress a vivid or emotionally arousing thought, especially when told to.

WITNESS PREPARATION

Another contribution of the psychologist deals with the preparation of witnesses. When they step into the witness stand and take an oath to tell the truth, many people are not as effective witnesses as they could be. They do not achieve good eye contact with the questioner or the jury, they hesitate or stutter, they wring their hands or fidget. They may not give consistent or clear responses. Can such an unsatisfactory performance be improved? If so, is it ethical to try to do so? And what are the limits on what can be done, prior to trial, with a potentially ineffective witness?

For a long time, some attorneys have been concerned with the effectiveness of their witnesses on the stand. In the 19th century, attorney William J. Fallon rehearsed witnesses in the carriage sheds near the White Plains, New York, courthouse. Publishers of contemporary books oriented specifically to trial attorneys offer publications that promise to improve the attorneys' witness-preparation skills and to help their clients avoid the mistakes witnesses often make in testifying. Some of this advice to witnesses is quite simple: "Take your time." "Don't answer a question you don't understand." "If you don't remember, say so." But witnesses don't always follow these directions; even Bill Clinton apparently failed to do so, when he gave a deposition while he was president (see Box 12-2).

Textbooks for trial advocacy courses, such as Mauet's *Fundamentals of Trial Techniques* (1992), describe in detail the techniques of **witness preparation.** Among other points, Mauet suggested that each witness be prepared individually and that all previous testimony by the witness (statements to the police, depositions, answers to interrogatories), be reexamined to determine if the witness's present recollections differ in any way from his or her previous statements. Often the lawyer reviews questions and answers with the witness in an empty courtroom. Included in this preparation is, in Mauet's proposal, a review of those aspects of the testimony that will elicit cross-examination; an associate of the attorney can play the role of the cross-examiner.

Trial consultants offer a new perspective on witness preparation (see Kressel & Kressel, 2002). They analyze both the stylistic and substantive

---

BOX 12-2
Following Witness-Preparation Guidelines When Under Oath

After President Clinton gave a deposition in January 1998, author James B. Stewart wrote the following:

> Virtually every witness who's about to be deposed gets a lecture from his or her attorney delineating the basic rules of witness deportment. Surely Bob Bennett, President Clinton's attorney in the Paula Jones lawsuit, briefed his client on the usual procedures. What, then, accounts for the President's performance? . . . Although Clinton was at times a model witness, answering questions succinctly and directly, at other times he clean forgot some of the dos and don'ts:

1) If the question calls for a yes-or-no answer, answer yes or no.

> Q. Do you know why she [Kathleen Willey] would tell a story like that if it weren't true?

The "correct" answer would seem to be a simple "no." Instead, Clinton responds at length and volunteers information that isn't asked for.

> A. I did to her what I have done to scores and scores of men and women who have worked for me or been my friends over the years. I embraced her, I put my arms around her, I may have even kissed her on the forehead. There was nothing sexual about it. I was trying to help her calm down and trying to reassure her.

2) Don't speculate. If you don't know or don't remember, say so.

> Q. When was the last time you spoke with Monica Lewinsky?

The right answer is probably "I don't know." Instead, Clinton describes a meeting he's evidently unsure of, then volunteers more unasked-for information:

> A. I'm trying to remember. Probably sometime before Christmas. She came by to see Betty [Currie, the President's secretary] sometime before Christmas. And she was there talking to her, and I stuck my head out, said hello to her.

> Q. Stuck your head out of the Oval Office?
> A. Uh-huh, Betty said she was coming by and talked to her, and I said hello to her.

> Q. Was that shortly before Christmas or—

At this juncture, Clinton interrupts, hedges his early answer, and adds gratuitous information:

> A. I'm sorry. I don't remember. Been sometime in December, I think, and I believe—that may not be the last time. I think she came to one of the, one of the Christmas parties.

Source: From Stewart, 1998, p. 43.

aspects of mock testimony; they videotape the witness on the stand so that the witness can observe his or her effectiveness. They point out the use of **powerless speech** (that is, expressions of hesitancy, uses of "uh," use of qualifiers) (O'Barr, 1982). They seek to bolster anxious witnesses and reduce expressions of arrogance and defensiveness. They may employ mock jurors to react to the mock testimony. Nietzel and Dillehay (1986), in their text on psychological consultation, noted five topics on which the psychologist may be a helpful consultant: the facts to which the witness will testify, the witness's feelings associated with the issues of the case (including the act of testifying), the courtroom environment, direct examination, and cross-examination.

What Is Proper and What Is Not

Gray areas exist in lawyer–client communication, as shown in the example in Box 12-3. Is witness preparation within the limits of an attorney's ethical duty to "zealously" represent his or her client, to the limits of the law? And if so, should psychologists and litigation consultants engage in it?

Wrightsman posed these questions to several experienced litigation consultants attending a meeting of the executive committee of the American Society of Trial Consultants in April 1992; their reactions varied. One responded, "What are the boundaries? I don't like: 'I'll work on the credibility but not change the fact pattern,' because once you work on the credibility you affect the fact pattern." But most of the consultants were less concerned with this example than Wrightsman was. Several told him that witness-preparation is proper and necessary to do, whether an attorney or someone else does it, and that it's unethical *not* to prepare a witness. First of all, witnesses put themselves in the attorney's hands; they trust the attorney to know what is best for them. It was also argued that witnesses who have "been prepared" give more valid testimony.

Some consultants seemingly bought into the attorney's goals without question; one told Wrightsman, "The trial is a justice-seeking event, not a truth-seeking event," emphasizing that the goal was to increase the witness's persuasiveness. One litigation consultant posed the dilemma succinctly: "I don't 'fix' a witness's testimony but I can enhance it." Another said, "I ask, 'What's the most colorful way you can express this?' I don't tell him what to say." Psychologists Nietzel and Dillehay, while noting that facts cannot be altered, agree with the preceding consultants that "presentation style is fair game for intervention" (1986, p. 121).

BOX 12-3
How Direct Can an Attorney Be With a Client?

In preparing for trial, attorneys go over the anticipated testimony of their witnesses. But how direct may the attorney be in clarifying matters? Successful defense attorney Leslie Abramson provides the following example; she writes,

> Sometimes, the obstinate nature of kidspeak in general (the rule: never give a straight answer to adults) can drive you crazy. And the vagaries of popular usages of words could be utterly defeating in a search for the truth. I'd ask, "Did Johnny push the guy?"

"Not really."

"Well, what do you mean, 'Not really'? Did he push him or didn't he push him?"

"I will say he didn't push him."

"You will say what happened, you got that? Now did he push him or didn't he, yes or no?"

"No, he didn't push him."

"Then when you say 'Not really,' do you mean 'No'?"

"Yeah, no. He didn't push him."

"Then say 'No,' for chrissake. Because if you say 'Not really,' it can mean 'Yes, sort of.'"

Source: From Abramson, 1997, pp. 107–108.

These responses indicate that the gray area between proper assistance to potential witnesses and the encouragement of lying on the stand is a shifting area, depending on the views of the individual consultant or attorney. We recommend that attorneys bend over backward to avoid telling the witness what to say. Videotape the "dry-run" direct examination and cross-examination and then have the witness watch the tape. Ask the witness: How effective were you? What could you do better? Put the onus on the witness to draw conclusions about how to improve his or her credibility.

ORGANIZING THE CASE

Most trial attorneys have strong beliefs about how they want to proceed with a trial, but if they ask for advice, psychological research has a number of conclusions to offer them. And psychologists can provide a good sounding board for those trial attorneys who want to test out ideas. Following the belief that "two heads are better than one," we offer several empirically based suggestions relevant to three aspects of the trial presentation: opening statements, presentation of evidence, and closing arguments.

Opening Statements

The purpose of the opening statement is to give an overview of the case. Because the opening statement is not a part of the evidence, some trial attorneys dismiss it as less important. Psychological research concludes this is a big mistake. More specifically, several decisions need to be made by the attorney with regard to the opening statement; in the following subsections, we bring to bear psychological expertise on these issues.

Goals, Length, and Style of Opening Statements

Occasionally attorneys use their opening statements simply to introduce themselves and their witnesses; this is not enough. Opening statements should be long enough to give an orientation to the case (Pyszczynski, Greenberg, Mack, & Wrightsman, 1981; Pyszczynski & Wrightsman, 1981). Given that psychological research has clearly demonstrated the impact of initial information on attitude formation, it is in the lawyer's best interest to elaborate in the opening statement. Jurors are seeking a structure by which to organize their impressions of the case; opening statements can provide one. The disclaimer that opening statements "are not part of the evidence" is not always understood or followed by jurors, who do not distinguish precisely between evidence and nonevidence.

Some attorneys prefer to present only a "bare facts" version of the case in their opening statement. Rather, the attorney needs to have a perspective for the opening statement and the case in general. For example, in a criminal trial, the defense strategy may be to tell its story to the jury (what Bennett & Feldman, 1981, call the **reconstruction strategy**). Or, the defense may "challenge" the prosecution's story, pointing out inconsistencies or missing story elements. Or, in Bennett and Feldman's **redefinition strategy,** the defense may reconstrue one or more particular elements in the prosecution's story, offering a different interpretation of the prosecution's story, based on the redefinition.

In civil trials, plaintiffs' attorneys are more likely to tell stories, while defendants' attorneys may emphasize the rules and definitions of negligence or fault (Feigenson, 1995).

Thus, communication theorists are in agreement in urging that lawyers provide opening statements that provide a narrative or a **story of the case,** as jurors remember the evidence better when they have such a structure. But the story of the case must meet the tests of narrative coherence and fidelity (Rieke & Stutman, 1990). **Narrative coherence** concerns the following issues: Does the story hang together? Does it have internal logic? Is it consistent with the jury's expectations for stories in general? Are the characters clearly defined and consistent?

Narrative fidelity deals with what Rieke and Stutman call "the logic of good reasons."

Jurors must decide "if the story of the case is accurate in terms of their sense of reality" (1990, p. 95). For example: Are the statements in the opening that purport to be facts truly facts, and what are the values embedded in them? Have relevant facts been omitted, and what (if any) distortions exist in those that are included? Do conclusions develop reasonably from the facts? Does the story address the real issues in the case?

Psychologists agree with these communication theorists about the importance of a narrative. Pennington and Hastie's (1981, 1986, 1993; Hastie, Penrod, & Pennington, 1983) story model proposes that jurors impose a narrative story organization on trial information and that they assign meaning to trial evidence by incorporating it into a plausible account of what happened. Empirical support for the story model has confirmed that jurors' memories and inferences reflected their use of stories to organize information and that these stories were directly related to the verdicts they chose (Hastie, Penrod, & Pennington, 1983; Olsen-Fulero & Fulero, 1997; see also Kressel & Kressel, 2002). When the story is introduced during the opening statement, it serves as an "advanced organizer" of the evidence that follows. Individual facts become more meaningful if a context exists in which to incorporate them.

Statements can be presented in "narrative" form, as in the story model approach, or a so-called legal-expository form, which emphasizes the judicial instructions and legal elements governing the dispute, along with how and why the evidence either supports or refutes the applicable law (Spiecker & Worthington, 2003). In a recent experiment using a simulated civil trial, Spiecker and Worthington (2003) varied both prosecution and defense organizational strategies for both opening and closing statements, using the narrative, legal-expository, and a "mixed" form. After viewing a videotaped trial, subjects were asked to render verdicts and award damages. Results indicated that a "mixed" organizational strategy, with a narrative opening statement and a legal-expository closing statement, was more effective for plaintiffs than the narra-

tive strategy alone, and that either a "mixed" or legal-expository strategy was more effective for the defense than a narrative strategy.

Timing of Defense Opening Statement

The defense has the option of giving its opening statement right after that of the prosecution or plaintiff, or delaying its opening statement until the other side has presented its evidence. This is an example of a place where psychological research can make a significant contribution, because textbooks on trial advocacy are in disagreement about the desirability of delaying. The empirical research is clear (Wells, Miene, & Wrightsman, 1985)—the earlier the better. Jurors apparently want to hear the "other side"; at the very least, presentation of the defense's opening statement right after the prosecution's alerts the jurors of the conflicts in the evidence.

Making Concessions in an Opening Statement

Attorneys generally have a good idea of the "holes" in their case and the strengths of the opposition. A basic decision is whether, in their opening statement, to concede their "weaknesses" or rather to leave it to the other side to expose them. In some highly publicized trials, the concessions made by criminal defense attorneys about their clients are sometimes amazing. In his defense of Leona Helmsley for tax evasion, her attorney told the jury that it was true his client was "a real bitch" but that didn't make her guilty of the charge for which she was on trial. When representing Claus von Bulow for the attempted murder of his wife, Herald Fahringer mentioned during jury selection that his client was an adulterer.

To concede or not to concede? Some legal theory has conflicted with the psychological theory and research findings in providing guidance to this dilemma. Most trial advocacy textbooks (see, for example, Mauet, 1992, pp. 47–48) say that if the other side will present potentially damaging evidence, you should definitely mention it first. But an approach to trial strategy called **sponsorship theory** disagrees. Klonoff and Colby (1990) claimed that criminal defense attorneys facing a decision on whether to reveal negative information about their case should almost *never* do so. Sponsorship strategy theory assumes that jurors' evaluations of evidence are strongly influenced by which side brings it up. If damaging evidence against the defense is brought up by the prosecution, this theory says that the jury may question its validity because the prosecution is attempting to persuade the jury to return a guilty verdict. But if the damaging evidence is brought up by the defense, the jury will accept its credibility without questioning it. This approach seems to place greater emphasis on the *source* of a message than psychological research findings would warrant. Although there is some research showing the importance of source credibility, it is also true that the content of what is remembered is often separated, in memory, from the source. Furthermore, research on one-sided versus two-sided communications leads to a contrasting conclusion.

Research extending back to World War II (summarized by Rieke & Stutman, 1990, pp. 207-209) has found that a two-sided argument is more effective when the audience is familiar with the issues. More recently, the superiority for the two-sided presentation has noted that it enhances a speaker's credibility and provides greater resistance to persuasive messages from the other side. This latter reason has been supported by a mini-program of research on **"stealing thunder"** from the other side (Williams, Bourgeois, & Croyle, 1993).

The underlying rationale is based on William McGuire's (1964) **inoculation theory,** which argued that when a person holds an attitude that is not buttressed by a strong cognitive arsenal, the attitude can be attacked relatively easily. If, however, there is a weak initial attack against the attitude, people will generate counter arguments to strengthen their position and will be more resistant to a subsequent strong attack. In his book *How to Argue and Win Every Time,* noted trial attorney Gerry Spence (1995) described how making a concession about a client can often establish a trial attorney's credibility: "A concession coming from your mouth is not

nearly as hurtful as an exposure coming from your opponent's" (Spence, 1995, p. 131). One of his examples is described in Box 12-4.

Kipling Williams and his colleagues, in studying the act of "stealing thunder" in the courtroom, defined it similarly to Spence's view, as "revealing negative information about oneself or one's client before it is revealed by the other side" (Williams, Bourgeois, & Croyle, 1993, p. 597; see also Williams & Dolnik, 2001). The psychologists carried out two studies, one dealing with a criminal trial and the other with a civil trial. In both cases, mock jurors were exposed to one of three conditions: A damaging piece of evidence about one of the parties was absent (the "no thunder" condition), the damaging evidence was brought up by the attorney representing that party but downplayed before it was mentioned by the other side (the "stealing thunder" condition), or the damaging evidence was only introduced by the other side (the "thunder" condition). In both types of trials, the fact that the attorney made the concession of first acknowledging evidence against his side affected the mock jurors' verdicts to a significant degree. In the civil trial, for example, when the damaging evidence dealt with a key plaintiff's witness, the percentage of mock jurors who found for the plaintiff was: Thunder condition, 43%; No thunder condition, 58%; Stolen thunder condition, 65% (Williams, Bourgeois, & Croyle, 1993). Making a concession early on does appear to weaken the damage when the other side later in the trial emphasizes the same matter. Interestingly, though, in a follow-up study, Dolnik, Case and Williams (2003) found that when the opposing counsel revealed to jurors that the "stealing thunder" tactic had been used, its effectiveness disappeared.

Presentation of the Evidence

How should lawyers order the presentation of their witnesses and evidence? Should they follow a chronological order, or should they lead with their most powerful testimony? Or maybe they should save the most effective witness for the last.

BOX 12-4
An Example of "Stealing Thunder" by Gerry Spence

An easy example of the power of concession: Many years ago I had a case in which my client, George, was drunk. He staggered across the street and was run over. But he crossed the street with the green light and was hit by a speeding motorist who ran the red. I conceded my client's drunkenness in this fashion:

"George had been to a party and he had had a pretty good time. He was, to put it plainly, drunk when he left the party. And he was drunk when he crossed the street. But George was one of those people who knew when he was drunk. You have seen them—supercautious, superslow people. Well, we can all tell such people are drunk because they are overly cautious and overly careful.

"And so George came to the crossing and the green light was with him. There is no question about that. More than half a dozen witnesses saw him crossing with the light. And, when he was

helplessly trapped in the center of the street, Mr. Majors here, the defendant, came careening and screeching around the corner at a high rate of speed, nearly tipped his car over, ran the red light, and ran poor George down like a mangy cur.

"Now, George was drunk all right. But the laws of this country were passed to protect both the drunk and the sober. One does not lose one's rights as a citizen because one crosses the street with the green light while drunk. As a matter of fact, when you think about it, a drunk man like George needed the protection of the law more than a sober man would under the same circumstances."

I could not have achieved the favorable result in the case for George had I held George's drunkenness back, tried to cover it, and objected like hell to the introduction as evidence of George's blood alcohol of .18 taken in the emergency room a half-hour after the accident.

Reprinted from Spence, 1995, pp. 131–132.

The psychological research is most consistent in answering some of these questions than others. What is clearest is that memory is not equivalent for each item on a list or for each witness in a trial. The **serial position effect** concludes that people learn and remember the first and last items in a series more quickly than those in the middle. Although it *is* more effective to place one's strongest witnesses first and last, the order of witnesses should also be sensitive to the story introduced in the opening statement.

But should the strongest evidence come first or last? The debate over the relative importance of a **primacy effect** and a **recency effect** has a history extending 50 years. Evidence presented first is potentially influential because it alters the way the listener perceives and incorporates evidence that is presented later. But the final witness and evidence, by being the most recent, may be powerful, and the longer the trial, the greater the likelihood that a recency effect will surface.

In summary, the evaluation of the relative impact of the primacy effect or the recency effect is a complex one; conclusions from relatively straightforward laboratory studies are not necessarily applicable to the courtroom, where there is an extended presentation of evidence, frequent delays, sometimes in-trial summaries, and opportunities for cross-examination.

Closing Arguments

Attorneys often place more emphasis on closing arguments (also called **summations**) than on opening statements; after all, it is their very last chance to influence the jury, and they are granted more freedom to argue their case than in their opening. Although psychologists and other social scientists would acknowledge that the closing argument is important, they would remind the attorneys that preliminary verdicts may have been formed in the minds of the jurors well before then (Matlon, 1991).

Some disagreement exists between communication theorists and psychologists as to the *nature* of the closing argument. Rieke and Stutman maintain that, like the opening statement, the closing argument should provide a narrative. "Counsel's first and primary charge is to tell a convincing story" (1990, p. 203). He or she should chronologically describe the events as they occurred, providing vivid details. The attorney should also point out ambiguities in the opponent's narrative.

In contrast, psychologist Gary McCullough (1994), using an empirical study, argued for a different kind of closing argument. McCullough concluded that the narrative approach is useful early on, in providing a structure, but as the trial winds down and jurors move toward making a decision, what he calls an **expository approach** is more effective in the closing argument. The expository approach compares two opposing views on the same issues. The focus is on answering this question: Why is our evidence better than their evidence? Thus, a chronological or narrative organization of the argument is not desirable. Using a medical malpractice case, McCullough found the expository closing argument to be more effective with mock jurors than a narrative-based one. This conclusion reflects a view of information processing in which jurors are actively evaluating information as they go through the trial, deciding which narrative better accommodates the conflicting evidence. Their task, at the time of the closing arguments, is to challenge the various claims and to make a final assessment of the validity of different narratives. In a more recent study, Spiecker (1998) found that a narrative opening statement and an expository closing argument were more effective for the plaintiff than was a consistently narrative strategy (see also Spiecker & Worthington, 2003, discussed earlier).

The expository approach in the closing argument may have another benefit. One purpose of the closing argument is to help those jurors on the attorney's side to argue with the opposing jurors during their deliberations; thus, the closing argument can provide "talking points" that jurors can use to convince their recalcitrant colleagues, for—after all—the jury deliberations represent the ultimate closing arguments.

JURY SELECTION: PSYCHOLOGY AND LAW IN CONFLICT

A theme of this book is that forensic psychologists—whatever their duties—must ask: Who is the clientele? Although psychologists serving as trial consultants must be responsive to the ethics code of the American Psychological Association (1992), they also are aware that they are advocates hired by attorneys, and conflicts between the two professions and perspectives may occur. Sometimes the only resolution of such clashes is for the trial consultant to disengage from the relationship.

Nowhere can the conflict between the law and psychology become more intense than in the task commonly called **jury selection.** (Actually, *deselection* would be a better term, as attorneys cannot select jurors; they can only prevent some from being chosen, but the common expression will be used here.) Most psychologists are committed to procedures that reflect an empirical approach; whether litigation consultants use community surveys, focus groups, or mock juries, they are exemplifying a belief that it is not enough "to fly by the seat of one's pants" or to rely on intuition or "gut feelings." As a group, trial attorneys are harder to characterize. A few are not particularly concerned with which individuals are on the jury; some of these attorneys are so self-assured and egocentric that they believe they can persuade anybody, while others may be convinced that the rightness of their case will prevail, regardless of the obstacles. Some attorneys are so confident (or lackadaisical) that they fail to exercise all their opportunities to dismiss prospective jurors.

In contrast, some trial attorneys are increasingly relying on consultants and empirical methods to advise them in making these decisions. But most attorneys have their own ingrained assumptions about who makes a good or bad juror (Fulero & Penrod, 1990; Kressel & Kressel, 2003). If they cannot hire the expertise of a trial consultant, these attorneys will employ their assumptions and stereotypes in their choices. Thus, it can be argued that the goals of trial consultants, despite their negative reputation in the eyes of the public, aren't any different from those of trial attorneys—they both seek a jury composed of people who will be open-minded about (if not sympathetic to) their side's set of facts and arguments. The difference is that litigation consultants use what is called **systematic jury selection,** or scientific procedures, rather than the seat-of-the-pants orientation of many lawyers.

Examples of Lawyers' Approaches

Examples of trial attorneys' stereotyped beliefs about jurors are the stuff of legend. Jeffrey Toobin recounted, "Early in my career as a prosecutor, when I first began selecting juries, a senior colleague warned me about men with beards. 'Guys with beards are independent and iconoclastic,' my mentor said. 'They resist authority. Get rid of them.'" (Toobin, 1994, p. 42). Master attorney Clarence Darrow believed that, as a defense attorney, he was better off with jurors of an Irish background; he avoided Scandinavians, who—he presumed—had too much respect for the law (see Fulero & Penrod, 1990). Celebrated contemporary attorney Gerry Spence said, "Women are more punitive than men by a score of about five to one" (quoted by Franklin, 1994, p. A25). And attorney Keith Mossman (1973) reported that "a nationally known trial lawyer once told me he would not accept any left-handed jurors" (1973, p. 78).

Such stereotypes may be specific to the individual lawyer and, hence, considered tolerable or even quaint. But the problem is more serious; general stereotypes are taught in law-school trial advocacy courses as well as passed down to neophyte lawyers on the job. Toobin described how, as a new member of the staff of federal prosecutors, he learned that "we preferred jurors who were old rather than young; married rather than single; employed rather than jobless. . . . We sought jurors smart enough to understand the

evidence but not so clever that they would overanalyze it; educated, but not to excess" (1994, p. 42). Stereotypes also abound for the defense bar, for whom the ideal juror was a member of the helping profession—a teacher, a social worker, a psychologist—because such folks had sympathy for the underdog. Members of racial minorities were also seen as pro-defense jurors in criminal trials, because of their more-frequent conflicts with police and other authorities in the legal system.

Should such stereotypes be dismissed as idle folklore? Or is there some basis for their evolution? Early in the psychological study of racial stereotypes, a position was advanced that came to be called the **kernel-of-truth hypothesis:** Group stereotypes may be unwisely generalized, but some basic distinctions exist between groups. A review by Brigham (1971) concluded that ethnic and racial stereotypes could have such a "kernel of truth" in the sense that different groups of respondents agreed on which traits were associated with a particular object group. (But we often lack the information to know if the object group actually possesses the traits.) Even if the kernel-of-truth proposal is accepted as a general proposition, do these stereotypes have enough predictability to be used in selecting or rejecting individual jurors? Usually not.

What Do Psychologists Do?

Psychologists have sought to determine if group differences (including racial and ethnic classifications as well as broad personality characteristics and attitudes) are predictive of verdicts. Their conclusion is not a simple one, for the verdict of an individual juror is the product of a wealth of factors, not only that juror's gender and race, attitudes and personality, but also the weight of the evidence in the case, the responses to the pressures on the juror to vote one way or another, and other factors specific to the situation. At the broadest level, we can say that jurors' verdicts can be affected by their biases, but how their biases are manifested may depend on specific aspects of the trial. For example, jurors who are relatively authoritarian *tend* to go along with the prosecution, but what if the defendant is an authority figure, such as a police officer or a physician? Then, the relationship may shift, and the authoritarian juror will side with the defense.

TWO APPROACHES TO JURY SELECTION

Given the fragile relationship between jurors' demographic classifications or internal qualities and their verdicts, psychologists have followed two pathways in advising and evaluating jury selection: a general and a case-specific approach. These approaches, described further in this section, disagree about the wisdom of a search for generality.

Broad Attitudes and Traits

A fundamental principle of social psychology is that each of us perceives the world in an idiosyncratic way. It is very difficult for us to look at a stimulus without evaluating it at the same time that we perceive it. Two different jurors will interpret the same stimulus differently, based on their past experiences and training. The phenomenon of **juror bias** refers to the assumptions that each of us makes interpretations based on experience and that these interpretations can color our verdicts.

In criminal trials, jurors' biases can be classified as favoring the prosecution or favoring the defense. That is, some prospective jurors—without knowing anything about the evidence—may assume that the defendant is guilty. Pro-prosecution bias reflects, in some jurors, the aforementioned trust of authority figures, in others a belief in a just world, in others perhaps an acquiescent response set. In contrast, a pro-defense bias often stems from a sympathy with the underprivileged

or an opposition to or suspicion of those in power.

Biases can also occur when jurors are asked to decide in a civil case. Here the biases are more varied, and it may not be possible to identify a single dimension of bias that applies to every civil suit. Some plaintiffs who sue resemble defendants in criminal trials, in that they are (sometimes powerless) individuals in opposition to a powerful organization. Consider, for example, a parent with a child injured in a car wreck who is claiming that the child seat in the car was defective. A suit by an individual against a major corporation with seemingly limitless resources evokes from some jurors a sympathy bias that resembles a pro-defense bias in criminal trials, but here, in civil trials, it reflects a **pro-plaintiff bias.** But other jurors may manifest **pro-defendant biases** (or at least **anti-plaintiff biases**); for example, some jurors feel strongly that there is too much litigation and that many lawsuits are without merit. By identifying with powerful corporations, some pro-defendant jurors in civil cases may possess some of the authoritarian orientations that pro-prosecution jurors show in a criminal case.

Several instruments have been developed to attempt to measure the basic biases. A later section reviews and evaluates these instruments. But recall that some trial consultants prefer to relate jury selection to specific issues in the case at hand, rather than trying to assess general biases.

Case-Specific Approaches

If the broad-attitude/trait approach may be said to address jury selection with a preconceived theory about dimensions of jurors that are related to their verdicts, the **case-specific approach** works in the opposite way; it looks at the particular facts and issues of the case and then tries to develop some measurable characteristics of jurors that would be related to their verdicts. In its purest form, the case-specific approach is coldly empirical; it uses the reactions of mock jurors and focus groups to identify those variables likely to be important in the actual jurors' decisions. But usually when it is used, the trial consultants have some characteristics that they hypothesize to be important. These juror qualities, however, are not as broad as the traits described in the other approach. For example, if a criminal defendant is a member of a minority group, the racial identifications or racial attitudes of jurors may be considered as case-specific variables. If a hospital patient is suing a surgeon for medical malpractice, attitudes toward authority figures and especially the medical profession become salient.

MEASUREMENT OF JUROR BIAS

As indicated earlier, the general attitudes that may be related to jurors' verdicts in criminal trials differ from those attitudes relevant to responses in civil trials; thus, different instruments have been developed to assess each type of attitude.

Criminal Trials

Two types of concepts have provided the structure for the measures of criminal juror bias: authoritarianism and the distinction between a pro-prosecution and a pro-defense orientation. Attitude scales have been developed to measure each.

The Legal Attitudes Questionnaire (LAQ) and Revised Legal Attitudes Questionnaire (RLAQ)

The Legal Attitudes Questionnaire (LAQ) was apparently the first systematic measure developed to assess jurors' biases; it was published by Virginia R. Boehm more than 30 years ago, in 1968 (see Wrightsman, Batson, & Edkins, 2004). As a pioneering instrument, it had worth, but also some of the problems often characteristic of attitude scales of that period. The LAQ contained 30 statements, arranged in 10 sets of three items. In each of these triads, one statement reflected **authoritarianism,** one reflected

equalitarianism, and one reflected, to use Boehm's term, **anti-authoritarianism.** (The instructions for the LAQ and a sample item are reprinted in Box 12-5; because the scale has been revised to reflect more contemporary measurement procedures, the entire scale is not included in this box.)

According to Boehm (1968), the authoritarian items reflected one of three topics: They either "expressed right-wing philosophy, endorsed indiscriminately the acts of constituted authority, or were essentially punitive in nature" (p. 740). In contrast, anti-authoritarian items "expressed left-wing sentiments, implied that the blame for all antisocial acts rested with the structure of society, or indiscriminately rejected the acts of constituted authority" (p. 740). The more moderate third type, equalitarian items, "endorsed traditional, liberal, nonextreme positions on legal questions or were couched in a form that indicated the questions reasonably could have two answers" (p. 740). Answering reflected a type of forced-choice procedure; for each triad, respondents assigned a + (plus) to the statement with which they most agreed and a − (minus) to the statement with which they least agreed. In scoring, these responses were treated as ratings, with the positively marked statement receiving a rating of 3; the unmarked statement, a rating of 2; and the negatively marked statement, a rating of 1. Then the ratings for each of the three subscales were totaled separately; no total score was determined. Thus, every respondent could have a score ranging from 30 (high) to 10 (low) on each of the three dimensions—authoritarianism, anti-authoritarianism, and equalitarianism. Boehm theorized that jurors with high scores on authoritarianism had a tendency to convict, that high scores on anti-authoritarianism were associated with a verdict of acquittal, and that scores on equalitarianism were not related to verdicts.

More recently, researchers at Florida International University—especially Gary Moran, David Kravitz, Douglas Narby, and Brian Cutler—have systematically examined the validity of the LAQ and have proposed revisions of it (see Wrights-

> **BOX 12-5**
> **LAQ Instructions and Sample Item**
>
> The Legal Attitudes Questionnaire was the first instrument to attempt systematic measurement of jurors' general predispositions. However, it was cumbersome to complete and to score, as is illustrated by its instructions.
>
> *Instructions:* On the following pages are ten groups of statements, each expressing a commonly held opinion about law enforcement, legal procedures, and other things connected with the judicial system. There are three statements in each group.
>
> Put a plus (+) on the line next to the statement in a group that you agree with most, and minus (-) next to the statement with which you agree the least.
>
> An example of a set of statements might be:
>
> + A. The failure of a defendant to testify in his own behalf should not be taken as an indication of guilt.
>
> B. The majority of persons arrested are innocent of any crime.
>
> – C. Giving an obviously guilty criminal a long drawn-out trial is a waste of the taxpayer's money.
>
> In this example, the person answering has agreed most with statement A and least with statement C.
>
> Work carefully, choosing the item you agree with most and the one you agree with least in each set of statements. There is no time limit on this questionnaire, but do not spend too much time on any set of statements. Some sets are more difficult than others, but please do not omit any set of statements.
>
> *Set 1*
>
> ___A. Unfair treatment of underprivileged groups and classes is the chief cause of crime.
>
> ___B. Too many obviously guilty persons escape punishment because of legal technicalities.
>
> ___C. The U.S. Supreme Court is, by and large, an effective guardian of the Constitution.
>
> Source: From Kravitz, Cutler, and Brock, 1993, p. 662; the other sets of statements may be found in Boehm, 1968; see Wrightsman et al., 2004, for a revised version of the LAQ.

man et al., 2004). As part of a meta-analysis of the effects of authoritarian attitudes on mock jurors' verdicts, Narby, Cutler, and Moran (1993) reviewed three studies using the original LAQ (Boehm, 1968; Jurow, 1971; Cowan, Thompson, and Ellsworth, 1984).

These studies, plus several others that altered the format and scoring of the original LAQ, indicated that subscale responses (at least for the authoritarian subscale) had predictive validity; that is, they were related to eventual verdicts. But this conclusion reflected **group differences,** not results that were so precise that you could, with assurance, predict an individual's verdict on the basis of his or her authoritarian score. Furthermore, the original version of the LAQ had several problems (Kravitz, Cutler, & Brock, 1993), one of which was the cumbersome scoring structure, in which the three-forced-choice response format prevented an independent assessment of

the dimensions. The format and instructions were also difficult for some respondents to understand and follow, leading to frequent invalid responses. For those and other reasons, researchers developed a revised version of the LAQ.

The Revised Legal Attitudes Questionnaire (RLAQ) was constructed by Kravitz, Cutler, and Brock (1993), who created 30 items with statements from the original LAQ. (The items on the RLAQ may be found in Box 12-6.) Further item analyses reduced the number of scored items to 23; in Box 12-6 these items are marked with an F.) This version can be administered with the usual Likert-scale response options (strongly agree, agree somewhat, etc.).

The Juror Bias Scale

In seeking to uncover attitudes that would predict jurors' verdicts, Kassin and Wrightsman (1983) chose another dimension, the bias to favor the prosecution or the defense. They noted that virtually all models of juror decision making (cf. Pennington & Hastie, 1981) assume that jurors make decisions in criminal cases that reflect the implicit operation of two judgments. The first judgment is an estimate of the **proba-**

BOX 12-6

Items of the Revised Legal Attitudes Questionnaire

The following statements comprise the Revised Legal Attitudes Questionnaire:

1. Unfair treatment of underprivileged groups and classes is the chief cause of crime. (AA, R, F)
2. Too many obviously guilty persons escape punishment because of legal technicalities. (A, F)
3. The Supreme Court is, by and large, an effective guardian of the Constitution. (E)
4. Evidence illegally obtained should be admissible in court if such evidence is the only way of obtaining a conviction. (A, F)
5. Most prosecuting attorneys have a strong sadistic streak. (AA, R)
6. Search warrants should clearly specify the person or things to be seized. (E, R, F)
7. No one should be convicted of a crime on the basis of circumstantial evidence, no matter how strong such evidence is. (AA, R, F)
8. There is no need in a criminal case for the accused to prove his innocence beyond a reasonable doubt. (E, R, F)
9. Any person who resists arrest commits a crime. (A, F)
10. When determining a person's guilt or innocence, the existence of a prior arrest record should not be considered. (E, R, F)
11. Wiretapping by anyone or for any reason should be completely illegal. (AA, R, F)
12. A lot of recent Supreme Court decisions sound suspiciously Communistic. (A)
13. Treachery and deceit are common tools of prosecutors. (AA, R)
14. Defendants in a criminal case should be required to take the witness stand. (A, F)
15. All too often, minority group members do not get fair trials. (E, R, F)

16. Because of the oppression and persecution minority group members suffer, they deserve leniency and special treatment in the courts. (AA, R, F)
17. Citizens need to be protected against excess police power as well as against criminals. (E, R, F)
18. Persons who testify in court against underworld characters should be allowed to do so anonymously to protect themselves from retaliation. (A)
19. It is better for society that several guilty men be freed than one innocent one wrongfully imprisoned. (E, R, F)
20. Accused persons should be required to take lie-detector tests. (A, F)
21. It is moral and ethical for a lawyer to represent a defendant in a criminal case even when he believes his client is guilty. (E, R, F)
22. A society with true freedom and equality for *all* would have very little crime. (AA, R, F)
23. When there is a "hung" jury in a criminal case, the defendant should always be freed and the indictment dismissed. (AA, R, F)
24. Police should be allowed to arrest and question suspicious looking persons to determine whether they have been up to something illegal. (A, F)
25. The law coddles criminals to the detriment of society. (A, F)
26. A lot of judges have connections with the underworld. (AA, R)
27. The freedom of society is endangered as much by zealous law enforcement as by the acts of individual criminals. (E, R, F)
28. There is just about no such thing as an honest cop. (AA, R)
29. In the long run, liberty is more important than order. (E, R, F)
30. Upstanding citizens have nothing to fear from the police. (A, F)

Note: Identification of subscales (A, AA, E) is given immediately following each item. Items that were reverse-coded on the overall RLAQ scale are indicated with an R following the subscale identification. Items included in the final RLAQ23 scale are indicated with an F.

Source: Kravitz, Cutler, & Brock, "Reliability and validity of the original and revised Legal Attitudes Questionnaire," *Law and Human Behavior 17*:666, 1993. Reprinted with permission of Kluwer Academic/Plenum Publishers.

bility of commission; specifically, how likely is it that the defendant was the person who committed the crime? Although jurors will base their estimates of this probability mainly on how strong the evidence is, their previous experiences will influence their interpretation of the evidence. For example, if a police officer testifies that he found a bag of heroin on the person of the defendant, some jurors, trusting police, would use this to increase their estimate that the defendant did commit a crime, but other jurors, given the same testimony, would discount or reject it based on their prior experiences and beliefs that police witnesses are dishonest.

A second judgment by the juror concerns his or her use of the concept of **reasonable doubt,** or the threshold of certainty deemed necessary for conviction. Judges always instruct jurors in criminal trials that they should bring back a verdict of not guilty if they have a reasonable doubt about the defendant's guilt. But the legal system has great reluctance to operationalize reasonable doubt, and when juries, during their deliberations, ask the judge for a definition, the judge usually falls back on the prior instruction or tells them that it is a doubt for which a person can give a reason. Left to their own devices, different jurors apply their own standards for how close they must be to certainty in order to vote guilty. Some jurors may interpret "beyond a reasonable doubt" to mean "beyond any doubt," or 100% certainty. Others may interpret it quite loosely (Dane, 1985; Kagehiro & Stanton, 1985).

Kassin and Wrightsman proposed that judgments of guilt arise when a juror's probability-of-commission estimate exceeds his or her reasonable-doubt criterion; they thus used these two factors to classify jurors as having a pro-prosecution or pro-defense bias. To determine whether bias affected jurors' verdicts, the researchers constructed a 17-statement Juror Bias Scale (JBS). (The statements, and filler items, are reprinted in Box 12-7.) The JBS gives scores on each of the two factors of probability of commission and reasonable doubt.

Evaluation of the Scales

Of what use are the Revised Legal Attitudes Questionnaire and the Juror Bias Scale to the trial consultant faced with aiding an attorney in jury selection for a criminal trial? Individual items can serve as the basis for questions to individual prospective jurors during the **voir dire,** or, if there is an opportunity to administer a supplemental juror questionnaire (to be described subsequently), prospective jurors can be asked to respond to all the statements. But the trial consultant should always remember that general traits, as measured here, have a very limited relationship to verdicts in specific cases. They are better than nothing, and they are probably better than most people's intuitions, but their predictive accuracy is low when it comes to verdicts by individual jurors.

Civil Trials

Most of the published work on assessment of jurors' pretrial biases has dealt with criminal trials. But it can be argued that the issue of civil law is most susceptible to the effects of bias by individual jurors. Traditionally, criminal cases come to trial because the prosecution believes there is a chance for conviction. The defendant may feel there is little chance of acquittal but, having refused to plea bargain, he or she is faced with only one last resort. In civil cases, however, it is necessary that *both* the plaintiff and the defendant be reasonably assured of a favorable decision. A litigant who is not so assured will, most likely, settle the issue out of court. Given this aspect of civil jury trials, in many cases the amount of evidence favoring each side will be nearly equal. But what are the basic dimensions or qualities of a pretrial bias in a juror in a civil trial? Although such trials can differ in the nature of the claim, the types of parties involved, and other specifics, some general attitudes may be useful.

General Attitudes

Biases in civil trials may not be as easily verbalized as those in criminal cases, but they can

BOX 12-7
The Juror Bias Scale

The second measure of general juror attitudes is the Juror Bias Scale. The instructions and scale items are given here.

Instructions: This is a questionnaire to determine people's attitudes and beliefs on a variety of general legal issues. Please answer each statement by giving as true a picture of your position as possible.

[Note: On the version of the scale administered to respondents, each statement is followed by five choices: 1. Strongly agree, 2. Mildly agree, 3. Agree and disagree equally, 4. Mildly disagree, and 5. Strongly disagree. To conserve space, these are deleted here.]

1. Appointed judges are more competent than elected judges.
2. A suspect who runs from the police most probably committed the crime.
3. A defendant should be found guilty if only 11 out of 12 jurors vote guilty.
4. Most politicians are really as honest as humanly possible.
5. Too often jurors hesitate to convict someone who is guilty out of pure sympathy.
6. In most cases where the accused presents a strong defense, it is only because of a good lawyer.
7. In general, children should be excused for their misbehavior.
8. The death penalty is cruel and inhumane.
9. Out of every 100 people brought to trial, at least 75 are guilty of the crime with which they are charged.
10. For serious crimes like murder, a defendant should be found guilty if there is a 90% chance that he or she committed the crime.

11. Defense lawyers don't really care about guilt or innocence, they are just in business to make money.
12. Generally, the police make an arrest only when they are sure about who committed the crime.
13. Circumstantial evidence is too weak to use in court.
14. Many accident claims filed against insurance companies are phony.
15. The defendant is often a victim of his or her own bad reputation.
16. If the grand jury recommends that a person be brought to trial, then he or she probably committed the crime.
17. Extenuating circumstances should not be considered—if a person commits a crime, then that person should be punished.
18. Hypocrisy is on the increase in society.
19. Too many innocent people are wrongfully imprisoned.
20. If a majority of the evidence—but not all of it—suggests that the defendant committed the crime, the jury should vote *not guilty.*
21. If the defendant committed a victimless crime like gambling or possession of marijuana, he should never be convicted.
22. Some laws are made to be broken.

Scoring procedures: The following are filler items and are not scored: Items 1, 4, 7, 18, and 22.

The following nine items are part of the Probability of Commission subscale: Items 2, 6, 9, 11, 12, 13 (reversed scoring), 14, 15 (reversed scoring), and 16.

These eight items are part of the Reasonable Doubt subscale: Items 3, 5, 8 (reversed scoring), 10, 17, 19 (reversed scoring), 20 (reversed scoring), and 21 (reversed scoring).

---

include several possible attitudes, which can be collapsed into a distinction between pro-plaintiff and pro-defendant jurors. These include

Attitudes Toward the "Litigation Explosion"
Whether there has truly been an increase in the amount of civil litigation in recent years, there has been ample publicity for those who claim there has (Huber, 1988; Olson, 1991). Some

prospective jurors—believing media claims of a **litigation explosion**—may have adopted beliefs that there are too many frivolous lawsuits and that people are too quick to sue, thus reflecting an anti-plaintiff bias.

Attitudes Toward Risk-Taking
Risk, as a concept, is central to the content of the law (Carson, 1988), but it has not received

the analysis it deserves. By **risk** is meant a danger of harm or loss from a plaintiff's action or behavior. Traditionally, the law has said that "a plaintiff who voluntarily encounters a known risk cannot recover" (Cox, 1991, p. 24). But in real life, things are not that simple, as demonstrated by the attempts to classify the allocation of blame implicit in contributory negligence. For example, in one case, a man sued Sears, Roebuck because he had a heart attack while trying to get his Sears lawn mower started (Cox, 1992), and most people are familiar with the elderly woman's lawsuit against McDonald's for the too-hot cup of coffee.

Jurors can differ in their attitudes toward the **assumption of risk.** Assumption of risk can be thought of as a continuum ranging from no risk to 100% risk. Particular actions by plaintiffs can be assigned values along this continuum. For example, a person who buys a package of Tylenol and takes several tablets assumes very little risk; a patient undergoing heart-bypass surgery assumes some risk; a person who mixes drugs whose interactive effects are unknown takes a higher risk. But the same action may be rated differently by different jurors.

Attitudes About Standard of Care
How stringent a standard do jurors hold with regard to the manufacture of products or the provision of services? Should a drug be 100% free of serious side effects before it is approved for sale? Viagra was instantly popular, but it apparently contributed to the sudden death of several men. How much should a new car be tested to see if it has a faulty design before it is placed on the market? How risk-free should a surgical procedure be before a doctor uses it?

Attitudes About Personal Responsibility
The public has stereotyped civil juries as proplaintiff—that is, sympathetic to claims of misfortune and willing to tap into the **"deep pockets"** of rich defendants. The empirical evidence challenges this view (cf. Vidmar, 1995) and even leads to a conclusion that an anti-plaintiff bias often emerges in jury decisions. Several causes

for this doubtless exist. One impression we have from talking to jurors after civil trials is a strong belief in personal responsibility; these jurors lack sympathy for those people with unhappy outcomes and (sometimes justified) grievances against a manufacturer, a physician, or a governmental organization. Feigenson, Park, and Salovey (1997) noted "evidence of a specifically antiplaintiff bias in responsibility judgments" (p. 600) and referred to interviews with actual jurors (Hans & Lofquist, 1992) and experimental research (Lupfer, Cohen, Bernard, Smalley, & Schippmann, 1985) supporting a conclusion that jurors often attribute the behavior of plaintiffs to undesirable motives, such as greed, rather than to legitimate grievances.

Corporate Responsibility

Attitudes toward corporations are related to some of the general attitudes just detailed, but they deserve special consideration (Hans, 1990). Some potential jurors are antibusiness, standing up for the powerless individual against the monolithic corporation. But others believe that businesses are hampered too much by government regulations. Should we hold corporations to higher standards of responsibility than individuals? Who deserved the blame when the Exxon tanker *Valdez* ran aground off the coast of Alaska, the captain or the oil company?

Hans and Lofquist (1992) constructed an attitude scale to measure potential jurors' attitudes toward business regulation. The 16 items on this scale tap attitudes about civil litigation, the benefits and costs of government regulation of business, and standards for worker safety and product safety. After reviewing this work, Wrightsman and Heili (1992) formulated additional items that might reflect jurors' biases in civil trials. These items, called the Civil Trial Bias Scale, were administered, along with Hans and Lofquist's items, to 204 undergraduate students, and the responses were factor analyzed to determine what constructs underlay the responses. The first factor that emerged in this analysis seemed to favor business and the easing of stringent requirements for safety. For example, the highest loading item, #16, from the Hans and

Lofquist set, states: "Requiring that products be 100% safe before they're sold to the public is just too expensive." The other factors emerging from this analysis also covered a variety of attitudes.

A separate analysis of the Hans and Lofquist items produced clearer results than the factor analysis of the two scales together. What emerges is one set of attitudes opposed to government regulation and another concerning the proper safety standards. But other dimensions may also be present; the separate factor analysis of the Civil Trial Bias Scale, not detailed here, found that jurors differed on assigning responsibility for bad outcomes, the inexplicability of bad events, and the value of risk-taking.

A recent instrument that shows promise here is the Attitudes Toward Corporations (ATC) scale (Robinette, 1999); it contains five subscales that measure product safety, government regulation, treatment of employees by corporations, and anti-plaintiff and anti-corporate attitudes. The original pool of items from which the ATC emerged capitalized on the items developed by Hans and Lofquist (1992), described earlier, but other items were constructed, and then the early versions of the scale were subjected to item analyses, resulting in a 15-item scale.

Medical Malpractice

The measurement of pretrial biases of jurors in medical malpractice trials is just beginning. However, it seems plausible that jurors can be distinguished based on a *tendency* to favor patients or to favor doctors. Those who favor doctors may also hold some of the attitudes about too many frivolous lawsuits illustrated in the previous section.

DOES SCIENTIFIC JURY SELECTION WORK?

The effectiveness of trial consultants in jury selection is difficult to assess. For instance, we may ask: Effective compared to what? To dismissing jurors by chance? To the traditional methods used by attorneys? The latter, as a comparison, is full of problems, because attorneys differ in how they "select" juries. A further difficulty is that real-life trials are not susceptible to an experimental manipulation in which they are repeated with an alteration of the method for selecting the jury. One study did follow that procedure, but it was a laboratory study using mock jurors recruited from the community and law students who role-played the lawyers (Horowitz, 1980). The study compared scientific jury selection with a traditional method; in the latter procedure, attorneys used their past experience, conventional wisdom, and beliefs about jurors to make their choices. Four different criminal trials were used. The results found that scientific jury selection was sometimes more effective, but not in all trials. In fact, its effectiveness seemed to be limited to those trials in which clear-cut relationships existed between jurors' personality or demographic variables and their votes.

Legal psychologists remain divided about the effectiveness of scientific jury selection (Diamond, 1990; Moran, Cutler, & DeLisa, 1994; Saks, 1976, 1987); Shari S. Diamond, after reviewing the research, concluded, "There is good reason to be skeptical about the potential of scientific jury selection to improve selection decisions substantially" (1990, p. 180). But Gary Moran and his colleagues (Moran, Cutler, & DeLisa, 1994) noted that studies that fail to find a relationship often have not used real jurors; these researchers also concluded that case-specific attitudes are better predictors of verdicts than are broad demographic variables.

In summary, as Strier (1999) concluded, "empirical studies testing the predictive value of scientific jury selection have produced inconclusive findings" (p. 101). Reid Hastie's (1991) review of his own and other studies observed:

> It remains unclear exactly which types of cases will yield the greatest advantage to the "scientific" selection methods. . . . "Scientific" jury selection surveys or attorney intuitions occasionally identify a subtle, case-specific

predictor of verdicts. It is difficult, however, to cite even one convincingly demonstrated success of this type, and these methods frequently suggest the use of completely invalid, as well as valid, predictors. . . . The predictive power of these [juror] characteristics invariably turned out to be subtly dependent on specific aspects of the particular case for which they proved valid. Due to their subtlety, prospective identification of any of these factors under the conditions that prevail before actual trials remains doubtful. (pp. 720, 723–724)

The quality of the evidence remains the clearest determinant of jury verdicts (Visher, 1987); the side with the stronger evidence *usually* wins. However, as noted, especially in civil trials, the evidence for the two sides may be close to equal. In such "close cases," scientific jury selection might be able to predict 10% or 15% of the variance in jurors' verdicts (Penrod & Cutler, 1987). Trial attorneys seek every edge they can obtain; this might be enough for them to justify the use of a trial consultant.

IS IT ETHICAL FOR PSYCHOLOGISTS TO AID IN JURY SELECTION?

John Grisham's highly entertaining novel *The Runaway Jury* (1996) begins with the surveillance of a young man who works at the computer store at the local mall. He's surreptitiously photographed by the observers; they knew he didn't smoke from watching him at his lunchtime breaks; they also knew he claimed to be a part-time college student, but a check of every college within 300 miles revealed no one enrolled under his name.

Why was he being watched? A potential security risk? A drug courier? No. Nicholas Easter was on a jury panel for an important case, and he was being investigated by a trial-consulting

firm in the employment of the defendants, a consortium of tobacco companies. Is this what trial consultants do in real life? And regardless whether they do or not, what ethical dilemmas surface for psychologists who assist in jury selection? Several are perplexing.

Juror Investigations

Although the activities described in *The Runaway Jury* are an exaggeration of what usually happens in the real world, citizens clearly have their privacy invaded when they become prospective jurors. The courts have accepted certain procedures because they subscribe to the goal that voir dire can identify those prospective jurors whose biases prevent them from being open-minded. But how far can the inquiry go?

Trial consultants do, on occasion, use out-of-court investigations to determine the attitudes and values of prospective jurors. Public records, such as house appraisals, may be consulted; the trial consultants' team may drive by the prospective juror's house, note its condition and the quality of its neighborhood, and search for any "diagnostic" bumper stickers on the juror's car. Friends and neighbors may be interviewed.

There are limits to such activities. Clearly, prospective jurors cannot be contacted outside the courtroom; **jury tampering** is illegal, and the courts have held people to be in contempt of court for communicating with jurors even though it was not clear that they sought to influence the juror (*Kelly v. United States,* 1918). A defendant was held in contempt of court for hiring a detective agency to follow jurors during a trial, even though the detective did not speak to any juror—in fact, no jurors were aware that they were being shadowed (*Sinclair v. United States,* 1929, cited by Herbsleb, Sales, & Berman, 1979). But would such rules apply to investigation of *prospective* jurors? Herbsleb, Sales, and Berman thought not; they wrote that "it seems unlikely that [such jury tampering laws as the preceding] will be applied today to hold social scientists in contempt for gathering jury information, unless some communication with the sworn jurors has occurred in or near the courtroom" (1979, p. 206).

But the dangers of out-of-court investigations remain. As Herbsleb et al. suggested,

> Suppose that as social scientists are establishing their network, one of the people contacted becomes suspicious of the investigators' motives and of the propriety of their actions. . . . [H]e may contact the prospective juror to inform him that persons of questionable character and motives are conducting an investigation into his personal affairs. The prospective juror in turn may well feel threatened or intimidated by the knowledge that someone is "checking up" on him. (1979, pp. 207–208).

What is the solution to this problem? To seek court approval for such inquiries? To inform prospective jurors that such information will be used only to exercise challenges? Although both have been suggested as remedies, they fail to recognize that out-of-court investigations by psychologists may violate APA ethical guidelines about subjects' rights. Principle 9, section c (American Psychological Association, 1992) provides that subjects are free to decline or withdraw from research participation. Herbsleb at al. offered one solution: "Have the court announce the presence of the social scientists and ask jurors if they object. If objections are voiced, the judge orders the social scientists to discontinue their research; if no objections are voiced, it is assumed that the jurors are participating voluntarily" (1979, p. 211). But the "compliance" in this situation may be a rather coerced one, not well thought out. And invasions of privacy, whether "voluntary" or not, are still invasions of privacy.

Use of Supplemental Juror Questionnaires

A better solution to the preceding problem is to avoid out-of-court investigations and substitute for them the use of a **supplemental juror questionnaire,** an extensive set of questions that prospective jurors answer in writing before the jury selection begins. Such questionnaires can cover a number of topics that might have been answered by out-of-court investigations—what newspapers and magazines the prospective jurors read, what television shows they watch, whether they are gun owners. Furthermore, attitude statements like those in the earlier described juror-predisposition measures can, with the approval of the judge, be included. The validity of information now rests on the honesty of the prospective jurors. Some invasion of their privacy remains, but it seems inevitable, given the defendant's right to a fair trial by impartial jurors.

In fact, prospective jurors have a real dilemma if the trial judge is unconcerned about the psychologist's ethical responsibility to obtain consent from subjects. If the judge has approved the administration of the questionnaire to prospective jurors, they may be punished if they refuse to answer. This happened to a Texas prospective juror, who refused to answer 12 questions (out of 100) that dealt specifically with her religion, income, and political-party affiliation. The judge cited her for contempt and sentenced her to three days in jail.

The rules in most jurisdictions do not specifically address the use of questionnaires prior to voir dire, and so the judge has discretion to permit them. However, the federal courts have recommended the use of prescreening questionnaires in highly publicized cases, and they were used in the trials of William Kennedy Smith, General Manuel Noriega, and Susan Smith, as well as in O. J. Simpson's criminal trial (Fargo, 1994). When such questionnaires have been approved, they are, in some jurisdictions, distributed by the clerk of the court at the beginning of jury selection, and jurors fill them out in the jury assembly room. Completed questionnaires are available for review by attorneys on either side. The amount of time allowed the attorneys to examine them depends on the judge and may be as brief as a couple of hours, although often the attorneys are given overnight to review them. Responses assist the attorneys and trial consultants not only in making preliminary decisions about peremptory challenges but in identifying prospective jurors who might be challenges for cause.

The use of supplemental juror questionnaires may save time during the voir dire, in that many of the questions would have been asked orally and individually during that process. They also add to the goal of fairness by giving both sides equal access to information.

Several commonsense suggestions can be made for the preparation and administration of such questionnaires (Fargo, 1994):

1. Keep the questionnaires as short as possible. Four to six pages will suffice. Follow-up questions may be allowed during voir dire.
2. The introduction to the questionnaire should explain its purpose; Fargo suggested the following:

   This questionnaire will be used only to assist the judge and the attorneys in the jury selection process. The information requested is strictly confidential and will not be used for any other purpose. Please read all questions carefully, answer them fully, and notify court personnel if you need any assistance or have any questions. Do not discuss the questions or answers with fellow jurors. It is very important that your answers be your own. You are sworn to give true and complete answers to all questions. (Fargo, 1994, p. 1)
3. Questions should be clustered by topic and arranged in a logical sequence.
4. Topics to be covered should include the prospective juror's experience with legal matters and the courts, his or her experiences related to the case at hand, and the juror's exposure to media coverage about the case. On all these topics, the experiences of the juror's immediate family and close personal friends are also relevant. Open-ended questions on these topics often work better than "yes-or-no" types.

5. At the end of the questionnaire, statements reflecting general attitudes and opinions, such as those from the instruments described in this chapter, may be included.

All the preceding implies that the trial consultant, working with the attorney, needs to be proactive in the preparation of such questionnaires. Such instruments require some time to prepare, and sometimes obstacles to scheduling may delay preparation of a final draft, especially if both sides contribute questions.

The O. J. Simpson criminal trial was an extreme example. The supplemental juror questionnaire used in that case covered more than 60 pages, reflecting questions contributed by both sides. In selecting questions for inclusion, the trial consultant for the defense, Jo-Ellan Dimitrius, used public opinion polls and focus groups (Gordon, 1997; and see Box 12-8 for some examples).

The Problem of Discovery and the Attorney Work Product

A supplemental juror questionnaire that reflects questions contributed by each side also resolves the nagging problem of **discovery.** To varying degrees, attorneys are required to provide to the other side any evidence they have that is relevant to the case. But what can be classified as an attorney work product is not discoverable; usually this includes legal research, correspondence, reports, and memoranda that contain opinions and conclusions by the attorneys. Some observers have proposed that the final rank ordering of the desirability of prospective jurors—based on an analysis of responses, psychologists' discussion with attorneys and litigants, and a sprinkling of intuition—is protected from discovery because of the attorney work product (Davis & Beisecker, 1994; Herbsleb et al., 1979). If both sides have access to the same raw material (the response of prospective jurors to the questionnaire), the issue of discovery is less important.

BOX 12-8
The O. J. Simpson Juror Questionnaire

The supplemental juror questionnaire for O. J. Simpson's criminal trial contained 294 questions, on 61 pages. Both sides contributed questions. For the prosecution, the questions were developed by the district attorney's office; Marcia Clark (1997) stated that the prosecution's trial consultant, Donald Vinson, submitted only one question. Jo-Ellan Dimitrius, the defense team's trial consultant, supervised the preparation of questions from the defense. Although prospective jurors were instructed that "each question has a specific purpose," respondents must have wondered about the relevance of some; for example,

143. Have you ever asked a celebrity for an autograph?

165. Have you ever had your spouse or significant other call the police on you for any reason, even if you were not arrested?

201. Do you have a religious affiliation or preference?

210. Have you ever given [a] blood sample to your doctor for testing?

212. Do you believe it is immoral or wrong to do an amniocentesis to determine whether a fetus has a genetic defect?

248. Have you ever written a letter to the editor of a newspaper or magazine?

257. Are there any charities or organizations to which you make donations?

Source: Daily Journal Court Rules Service, 1994.

Fairness in Jury Selection

What if one side employs a psychologist or a trial consulting firm and the other does not? Is this fair? Should the psychologist be concerned?

The position of the courts is that no legal violation has occurred when one side and only one side uses a trial consultant. A generally recognized principle of the law is that the attorneys on the two sides are "never perfectly equal in abilities or resources" (Herbsleb et al., 1979, p. 201, who cite the case of *Hamer v. United States*, 1958, which concluded, on p. 281, that "perfect equality of counsel can never be achieved"). In fact, a justification of the early participation of psychologists and other social scientists on the defense team was that the federal government, as prosecutor, had many unfair advantages in its efforts to convict war protesters.

Strier (1998) has summarized the current situation as follows:

Until clear and convincing evidence of the ability of scientific jury selection to affect verdicts surfaces, there appears no sustainable argument that its use threatens the Constitutional right to an impartial jury or the court-mandated injunction to seek cross-sectional juries. The law seeks jury representativeness. Scientific jury selection will still result in unfairly excluding some Americans from jury service; it will merely substitute exclusions based on scientific analysis for those derived from stereotypes and intuition (1998, p. 11).

Does the fact that one side may have resources that the other side does not mean that trial consulting should be banned? Fulero (in Kressel & Kressel, 2002, pp. 80–81), noting the analogy to the use of lawyers on behalf of indigent clients, stated,

You could have argued, I suppose, "I've got the solution. Since only the rich have lawyers, we'll ban lawyers. Right?" And of course, that's not what the Supreme Court did. They leveled the playing field by providing lawyers at public cost to criminal defendants who can't afford them. If . . . [trial consultants] are really effective, what you do is level the playing field. Provide them at no cost, at least in cases where it's an issue.

Even if the use of scientific jury selection and trial consultants does not violate the U.S. Constitution, or should not be banned, psychologists always have—as one of their clienteles—society in general. We need to ask: Is the "institutionalization" of jury selection in the best interests of society? Advocates of scientific jury selection will say that the process is only a more systematic version of what most trial lawyers do in a more subjective, less precise, and less thorough manner. But it may be true that the inclusion of these procedures may move actual juries farther away from the goal of a representative sample of the populace (see also Kressel & Kressel, 2002, for a discussion of these issues).

It remains the situation that in criminal trials, the defense is much more likely to use a trial consultant than is the prosecution (the Simpson case was unusual, and the services of the trial consultant were offered **pro bono**). Although no law prevents the prosecution from doing so, there is some merit to Marcia Clark's view that the government has no business doing market surveys to test the strength of its arguments. In a criminal trial, the prosecution is constrained in ways that the defense is not; it must base its argument on the evidentiary facts at its disposal. So some "unfairness" may be inevitable.

The Relationship of the Trial Consultant to the Attorney

When employed by a trial attorney, a trial consultant may formulate a theory of potentially favorable and unfavorable jurors after having conducted mock trials, focus groups, community attitude surveys, and even out-of-court investigations (Pitera, 1995). What if the trial consultant and the attorney disagree? Who makes the final decision regarding peremptory strikes?

The answer stems from the psychologist's title: trial *consultant*. Dr. Andrew Sheldon, a trial consultant, stated, "To me, the attorney's role is primary because it is the attorney and the client who are making these decisions. I am *advising* the attorney" (quoted by Pitera, 1995, p. 6, italics

in original). But conflicts in the two roles often surface. Trial consultants complain that attorneys provide short notice for complying with their requests, and then the attorneys may not provide the information necessary to complete the task effectively.

But attorneys complain that trial consultants may overstep the boundaries by trying to usurp the decision making. They may insist on their "theory of the case" or their choices for peremptory strikes. This conflict cannot always be avoided, but if each party is explicit about its expectations at the beginning, some problems can be reduced.

SUMMARY

Several activities carried out by psychologists prior to a trial are of assistance to judges and trial attorneys. The forensic psychologist, acting as a trial consultant, may assist attorneys in several ways: preparing a change-of-venue request, assisting witnesses in preparation for testifying, advising the attorney on the best way to organize his or her case, and providing data for jury selection. Psychological research findings are applicable to decisions about the timing and content of opening statements, the order of witnesses, and the type of argument used in the summation.

Some attorneys believe that trials can be won or lost based on the specific jury selected for the trial. Actually, *selected* is a misnomer, because attorneys on each side can dismiss prospective jurors but cannot ensure that any one juror is chosen, as the other side also has the opportunity to "strike," or dismiss, jurors through the use of peremptory challenges. These trial attorneys are increasingly relying on psychologists as trial consultants; in advising the attorney about jury selection, the psychologist uses information based on mock trials, focus groups, community attitude surveys, and sometimes out-of-court investigations.

Two approaches have been used. The use of broad traits or general attitudes reflects an assumption that certain predispositions of jurors may predict their verdicts in a wide variety of trials. With regard to criminal trials, two attitude scales have some limited general predictability: the Revised Legal Attitudes Questionnaire, which measures authoritarianism, and the Juror Bias Scale, which measures biases regarding probability of commission and reasonable doubt. With regard to general characteristics that may predict verdicts in civil suits, measures of risk-taking, beliefs in personal and corporate responsibility, and attitudes toward the litigation explosion are promising. Psychologists disagree about whether scientific jury selection works; one laboratory study found that it was more effective than the traditional method in some trials, but not all trials. A conservative conclusion is that the use of such procedures may account for a small degree of variance in jurors' verdicts—perhaps 10%, thus not enough to conclude that trial consultants can "rig" juries, but enough of an edge to make them useful to some trial lawyers.

The second approach works from the inside out, identifying specific aspects of a particular case and then assessing prospective jurors on those characteristics (such as racial attitudes or attitudes toward protesters).

A number of ethical issues surface when forensic psychologists assist in jury selection. Investigations of prospective jurors may violate their rights to give consent and their privacy rights. Use of supplemental juror questionnaires may reduce some of the concerns over lack of fairness.

KEY TERMS

affidavit
anti–authoritarianism
anti–plaintiff bias
assumption of risk
attorney work product
authoritarianism
case-specific approach
change of venue
"deep pockets"
discovery
equalitarianism
expository approach
focus groups
group differences
inoculation theory
juror bias
jury selection
jury tampering
kernel-of-truth hypothesis
litigation explosion
narrative coherence
narrative fidelity
peremptory challenge
powerless speech
pretrial publicity
pro bono
probability of commission
pro-defendant bias
pro-plaintiff bias
primacy effect
privileged information
reasonable doubt
recency effect
reconstruction strategy
redefinition strategy
sequestered voir dire
serial position effect
sponsorship theory
"stealing thunder"
story of the case
summation
supplemental juror questionnaire
systematic jury selection
theory of the case
trial consultants
voir dire
witness preparation

INFOTRAC®

COLLEGE EDITION

InfoTrac College Edition is a FREE, powerful, online learning resource, consisting of full-text articles from thousands of journals and periodicals. With each new copy of *Forensic Psychology*, Second Edition, you receive 4 months of free access to the InfoTrac College Edition database. By doing a simple keyword search (try using the Key Terms in the list above), you can quickly generate a list of relevant articles from thousands of possibilities and can select articles to read, explore, and print for reference or further study. InfoTrac College Edition's continuously updated collection of articles can be useful for doing reading and writing assignments that reach beyond the pages of this text!

SUGGESTED READINGS

Adler, S. J. (1994). *The jury: Trial and error in the American courtroom.* New York: Times Books.

A critique of the jury system, with attention paid to the role of trial consultants (or, as Adler calls them, "jury consultants"). Chapter 3 illustrates how the plaintiff's strategy was completely altered by the input from his trial consultant.

Bennett, C., & Hirschhorn, R. (1993). *Bennett's guide to jury selection and trial dynamics in civil and criminal litigation.* St. Paul, MN: West.

A practical description of jury selection procedures, by two of the most experienced and successful trial consultants.

Fisk, M. C. (1998, November 23). Winning: Successful strategies from 10 of the nation's top trial lawyers. *National Law Journal,* B5–B16.

An analysis of the actions of 10 of the country's most successful litigators reflects how they use opening statements, what they believe jurors to be like, and whether they believe in "stealing thunder" in the courtroom. Although anecdotal, there is much here worthy of consideration by trial consultants as well as trial attorneys.

Fulero, S. M. (Ed.). (2002). Empirical and legal perspectives on the impact of pretrial publicity [Special issue]. *Law and Human Behavior, 26*(1).

An interesting cross section of articles on the topic of pretrial publicity in criminal and civil cases, along with discussion of methodological and ethical issues and policy implications in this difficult area.

Hastie, R. (Ed.). (1993). *Inside the juror: The psychology of juror decision making.* New York: Cambridge University Press.

A series of contributed chapters reviewing different models of juror decision making, including a detailed description of the story model.

Krauss, E., & Bonora, B. (1983). *Jurywork: Systematic techniques* (2nd ed.). St. Paul, MN: West.

An indispensable reference for the professional trial consultant. It contains many examples of supplemental juror questionnaires, community opinion surveys, post-trial interviews with jurors, and other procedures.

Kravitz, D. A., Cutler, B. L., & Brock, P. (1993). Reliability and validity of the original and revised Legal Attitudes Questionnaire. *Law and Human Behavior, 17,* 661–677.

A research article illustrating the steps in constructing and validating a scale to measure prospective jurors' general attitudes.

Kressel, N. J. & Kressel, D. F. (2002). *Stack and sway: The new science of jury consulting.* Boulder, CO: Westview Press.

A fascinating inside look at the world of trial consulting.

Nietzel, M. T., & Dillehay, R. C. (1986). *Psychological consultation in the courtroom.* New York: Pergamon Press.

Chapter 3 contains wise advice about conducting a change-of-venue survey, as well as the results of several conducted by these prominent forensic psychologists.

O'Barr, W. M. (1982). *Linguistic evidence: Language, power, and strategy in the courtroom.* San Diego: Academic Press.

Characteristics of the trial witness's style can affect jurors' evaluations of the witness and later their verdict. The effects of powerless and fragmented styles are evaluated.

Rieke, R. D., & Stutman, R. K. (1990). *Communication in legal advocacy.* Columbia: University of South Carolina Press.

A valuable book that integrates findings from communications theory and social science research in order to analyze the communication process in trials. Contains chapters on opening statements, witness examination, and the closing argument.

Saks, M. J. (1987). Social scientists can't rig juries. In L. S. Wrightsman, S. M. Kassin, & C. E. Willis (Eds.), *In the jury box: Controversies in the courtroom* (pp. 48–61). Thousand Oaks, CA: Sage.

A distinguished psychologist and legal scholar suggests that trial attorneys should use psychologists to help structure the evidence to be presented at trial rather than as "jury selectors."

Schulman, J., Shaver, P., Colman, R., Emrich, B., & Christie, R. (1973, May). Recipe for a jury. *Psychology Today*, 37–44, 77–84.

A report of the trial that initiated "scientific jury selection," written by the social scientists who aided the defense. Highly recommended.

Spence, G. (1995). *How to argue and win every time.* New York: St. Martin's Press.

A prominent trial lawyer's view on the art of arguments. Contains many examples of effective witness preparation, opening statements, and cross-examination.

Strier, F. (1999). Whither trial consulting: Issues and projections. *Law and Human Behavior, 23,* 93–115.

A comprehensive article on the current status of the trial-consulting field. Techniques, including the use of community surveys, focus groups, mock trials, and jury selection at voir dire, are described. Examines the effectiveness of consultants and the ethical issues they face.

Studebaker, C. A., & Penrod, S. D. (1997). Pretrial publicity: The media, the law, and common sense. *Psychology, Public Policy, and Law, 3,* 428–460.

Most U.S. citizens had heard and seen much about Timothy McVeigh and the Unabomber before they were brought to trial. *Why* does pretrial publicity have such an irrevocable effect on jurors' verdicts? The authors review unsuccessful attempts to reduce this bias and offer ways to determine the mediating factors.

Vidmar, N. (1995). *Medical malpractice and the American jury.* Ann Arbor: University of Michigan Press.

A thorough analysis of the behavior of jurors in medical malpractice trials; it deflates claims that jurors are usually biased against the "deep-pockets" defendants.

13

Discrimination

THE TARGETS OF DISCRIMINATION

If the United States is truly a country that values diversity, Amadou Diallo—an immigrant from the African country of Guinea—appeared to be an excellent contribution to achieving such a goal. He was a devout Muslim who did not drink, smoke, or use drugs; he prayed five times a day. He spoke four languages and had never been in trouble with the law during his two years in the United States.

But about 12:45 A.M. on February 4, 1999, as he left his Bronx, New York, apartment building to get something to eat, he was shot 41 times by four White police officers, assigned to an elite Street Crimes Unit, who were searching for a serial rapist. Diallo was not armed, but the police apparently believed that he made a move toward his pocket, as if he had a gun. Two of the officers—all of whom were in plainclothes—used their 9-millimeter semiautomatic service pistols, which hold 16 rounds. They discharged their rounds in mere seconds, from a distance about 10 feet away. The other two officers, at a greater distance from the victim, fired 9 rounds.

In the ensuing days, thousands of New York citizens—including former mayor David Dinkins—protested the senseless killing, and many claimed it was an example of racial discrimination by White police officers. A criminal trial, moved to Albany, led to the acquittals of the officers. A civil lawsuit filed by the family was settled by the City of New York in January 2004 for three million dollars (Feuer, 2004).

At about the same time Diallo was killed—in early 1999—several New York City police officers were convicted of brutalizing a Haitian immigrant, Abner Louima, in 1997. In an interview on the NBC television program *Dateline* on February 24, 1999, Howard Safir, the New York City police commissioner, acknowledged that he knew of no equivalent case in which White police officers in the city had deliberately killed a White person who was found to be innocent, "although some White bystanders" had been killed by the police. Louima settled a simi-

lar civil lawsuit against the City of New York for nine million dollars (Feuer, 2004).

Are the Diallo and Louima cases examples of racial discrimination? Would Amadou Diallo still be alive if he had been White? How do we prove that an act reflects discrimination against an individual based on some personal characteristic? These are difficult questions to answer, but important ones, and ones that are worthy of study by those psychologists who wish to apply the knowledge of their profession to a solution of problems facing the legal system.

What Is Discrimination?

First, we need to be explicit about the meaning of some terms, especially because words like *prejudice* and *discrimination* are frequently used by the public and the media.

Social psychologists customarily distinguish between **prejudice** and **discrimination** by labeling prejudice as an attitude and discrimination as a behavior. That is, *prejudice* is something internal and is defined as an unjustified evaluative reaction to a member of a group that results from the recipient's membership in that group. The definition implies that the prejudiced person holds the same evaluative attitude toward the group as a whole. A prejudice is considered to be unjustified because it involves prejudgment, or because it is illogical (derived from hearsay or from biased sources), or because it leads the person to overcategorize and treat individuals based on the group with which they are identified. A prejudiced attitude can be either favorable or unfavorable, either positive or negative, but most of society's concern focuses, understandably, on the negative prejudices.

In contrast, *discrimination* is defined as a behavior—an overt, observable action—that accepts one person or rejects another based on his or her membership in a particular group. Negative actions can be ones of aggression and hostility or actions reflecting avoidance and withdrawal. Many times, discrimination is a direct reflection of prejudice, but not always. On the one hand, a person may have prejudiced attitudes and yet not be discriminatory in his or her behavior; a college student who is homophobic may not seek a transfer when he learns his new dormitory roommate is gay. On the other hand, a person may be unprejudiced in his or her attitudes and yet reflect discriminatory behavior; for example, Domino's Pizza employees —some of whom were African American—in several large cities refused to deliver to certain minority neighborhoods because the owner of the company told them not to stop in high-crime areas.

As the killing of Amadou Diallo became widely publicized, many claimed the act reflected **racism,** especially as the 41 shots were interpreted as driven by some sort of internalized hate of Blacks. Is racism a type of prejudice or a type of discrimination? The critics of the police referred to the act of shooting an innocent African American as racist, but social scientists ordinarily define *racism* as a subset of attitudes within the domain of prejudice.

Modern Racism

Strong pressures exist within the United States and Canada against the endorsement of blatantly racist remarks, and researchers agree that the expression of prejudice is often more subtle now than in the past. When respondents are asked to select those traits that are most typical of specific racial and ethnic groups, those who are willing to attribute negative characteristics to African Americans have consistently declined over the last 70 years, as the compilation done by Dovidio and Gaertner (1996), reprinted in Table 13-1, illustrates. In fact, many Whites may regard themselves as unprejudiced, but they still may reflect bias and harbor negative feelings and beliefs about certain groups. Hence, social psychologists have developed concepts to refer to a prejudice that fulfills the original definition, but is more nuanced than blatant. Applied to racial attitudes, this concept has often been called **modern racism** (McConahay, 1983, 1986), or **subtle racism,** although other terms, such as *symbolic racism* (Sears, 1988), *subtle prejudice* (Pettigrew & Meertens, 1995), *aversive racism* (Dovidio & Gaertner, 1996; Gaertner & Dovidio, 1986), and *racial ambivalence* (Katz & Hass, 1988; Katz, Wackenhut, & Hass, 1986) have also been used. These are described in Box 13-1. Scales measuring these attitudes are evaluated in a useful chapter by Biernat and Crandall (1999).

Who Are the Recipients of Discrimination?

Members of any group can be the recipients of discrimination, for sometimes the most trivial reasons. Certain groups receive protection from

---

BOX 13-1
Contemporary Views of Racism

Social psychologists have offered several conceptions relevant to the distinction between what McConahay (1986) called "old-fashioned racism" and the more nuanced type:

- McConahay and Hough (1976). *Modern racism:* "The expression in terms of abstract ideological symbols and symbolic behaviors of the feeling that Blacks are violating cherished values and making illegitimate demands for changes in the racial status quo" (p. 38). For example, the person who agrees with the statement "Blacks are getting too demanding in their push for equal rights" would reflect modern racism.

- Dovidio and Gaertner (1986). *Aversive racism:* Although White Americans want to be perceived as nonracist in keeping with current social norms, they also have a desire to express racist feelings.

- Katz and Hass (1988). *Ambivalent racism:* Among many Whites, both pro-Black and anti-Black attitudes exist jointly; hence, their attitudes are ambivalent.

- Jackman (1978). *Functional theory of modern racism:* A Marxist position, proposing that Whites wish to maintain their advantaged position in society.

Table 13-1   Percent of Subjects Selecting a Trait to Describe Black Americans (Formerly "Negroes") in 1933, 1951, 1967, 1982, 1988, 1990, 1993, and 1996

	1933	1951	1967	1982	1988	1990	1993	1996
Superstitious	84	41	13	6	2	3	1	1
Lazy	75	31	26	13	6	4	5	2
Happy-go-lucky	38	17	27	15	4	1	2	1
Ignorant	38	24	11	10	6	5	5	2
Musical	26	33	47	29	13	27	12	18
Ostentatious	26	11	25	5	0	1	1	0
Very religious	24	17	8	23	20	19	17	23
Stupid	22	10	4	1	1	3	0	0
Physically dirty	17	—	3	0	1	0	1	0
Naive	14	—	4	4	2	3	1	0
Slovenly	13	—	5	2	1	1	0	0
Unreliable	12	—	6	2	1	4	1	0
Pleasure loving	—	19	26	20	14	14	14	12
Sensitive	—	—	17	13	15	9	4	5
Gregarious	—	—	17	4	6	2	4	6
Talkative	—	—	14	5	5	8	13	9
Imitative	—	—	13	9	4	3	0	1
Aggressive	—	—	—	19	16	17	24	21
Materialistic	—	—	—	16	10	3	13	6
Loyal to family	—	—	—	39	49	41	39	39
Arrogant	—	—	—	14	7	7	5	3
Ambitious	—	—	—	13	23	16	24	18
Tradition loving	—	—	—	13	22	16	16	18
Individualistic	—	—	—	—	24	17	19	16
Passionate	—	—	—	—	14	17	19	14
Nationalistic	—	—	—	—	13	13	19	6
Straightforward	—	—	—	—	12	15	24	19
Intelligent	—	—	—	—	—	14	5	21
Sportsmanlike	—	—	—	—	—	13	8	17
Quick-tempered	—	—	—	—	—	12	13	13
Artistic	—	—	—	—	—	12	6	9
Argumentative	—	—	—	—	—	—	14	11
Loud	—	—	—	—	—	—	11	24
Progressive	—	—	—	—	—	—	11	14
Radical	—	—	—	—	—	—	10	8
Revengeful	—	—	—	—	—	—	11	5
Suspicious	—	—	—	—	—	—	10	6
Talkative	—	—	—	—	—	—	13	9
Faithful	—	—	—	—	—	—	—	15

Source: From "Affirmative Action, Unintentional Racial Biases, and Intergroup Relations," by J. F. Dovidio and S. L. Gaertner, 1996, *Journal of Social Issues, 52*(4), p. 52. Used by permission of Blackwell Publishers.

the courts, and they have received the most attention from psychological researchers; qualities defining these groups are:

1. Race, color, religion, or national origin
2. Gender
3. Age, particularly older adults
4. Disabilities (both physical and psychological)

In some jurisdictions, people with a homosexual sexual orientation are provided legal protection against discrimination, but in other jurisdictions they are not.

Overview of the Chapter

Society has raised a number of legitimate questions regarding discrimination that, though not easy to resolve, are better answered by considering the psychological perspectives. These include

1. Is the use of IQ tests valid for assigning people of different races to special education classes?
2. Do affirmative action programs achieve their goals?
3. How extensive is gender discrimination in the workplace?
4. Is legislation that mandates special penalties for hate crimes a deterrent to them?

This chapter examines four topics, reflecting discrimination, that have been studied by psychologists: (a) the use of testing to assign students to special education classes; (b) the impact of affirmative action policies; (c) employment discrimination by race and gender; and (d) hate crimes. These are, of course, only a few of the issues that reflect discrimination and that have drawn the interest of social scientists. Racial discrimination in prisons, in jury verdicts, and by judges has been studied (Foley, Adams, & Goodson, 1996; Ruby & Brigham, 1996). Additionally, social scientists have sought to determine what influences businesses' compliance with the Americans with Disabilities Act of 1990 when people with mental disabilities seek employment (Scheid, 1999). The empirical study of age dis-

crimination by employers, especially the impact of expert witnesses on jury awards, has generated useful findings (Greene, Downey, & Goodman-Delahunty, 1999).

WHAT CAN PSYCHOLOGY CONTRIBUTE?

Throughout this book, there are frequent examples of discrimination against females and members of minority racial and ethnic groups. Chapter 1 described racial differences in the use of the death penalty and gender discrimination in the workplace. Subsequent chapters illustrated racial profiling by law enforcement officers and denigration of rape victims. Chapter 14 will present an analysis of sexual harassment.

In the quest to understand and ameliorate these various manifestations of discrimination, the greatest contribution of psychology is its approach to understanding the phenomenon. More specifically, it can contribute in two ways: (a) through a conceptual analysis and (b) through the use of its methodologies. Each is described here.

Conceptual Analysis—An Example

We have already noted that psychologists have specified distinctions between prejudice and discrimination and recently focused on the more subtle forms of these. The analysis of racial discrimination began in the 1930s; in contrast, researchers have studied gender discrimination only for the last three decades, even though gender discrimination has had just as long a history in the United States, in Canada, and throughout the world.

Modern Sexism

Just as racism has often become more subtle in its expression, it can be argued that laws that give women the same rights and privileges as men have shifted the type of **sexism** most frequently expressed. Researchers have proposed that three types of sexism can be distinguished (Benokraitis & Feagin, 1986):

1. Blatant or overt sexism: "Those discriminatory actions directed against women that are quite obvious and visible" (Benokraitis & Feagin, 1986, p. 46). Examples of this type are the inequity in pay for women and men in the same jobs, the greater difficulty of women in obtaining credit and loans, and the frequency of sexual harassment of women at work.
2. Subtle sexism: "The unequal and harmful treatment of women that is visible but often not noticed because we have internalized sexist behavior as normal" (p. 30). It may take many forms, from effusive chivalry by men to discouragement and exclusion of women.
3. Covert sexism: "The unequal and harmful treatment of women that is hidden, clandestine, maliciously motivated, and very difficult to document" (p. 31).

Consider the case described in chapter 1, in which Ann Hopkins brought suit against her employer, Price Waterhouse, claiming sex stereotyping caused her to be denied a partnership (*Price Waterhouse v. Hopkins,* 1989). Recall that the partners who made promotion decisions considered Ann Hopkins to be too hard-driving, profane, and aggressive in her behavior. Is this blatant or subtle sexism? Recall that Susan Fiske, a psychologist, testified about the possible influences of sexual stereotyping on judgments, such as promotion decisions, in organizations. Some observers have concluded that her testimony "was very valuable in providing the courts with a scientific basis for holding that sex stereotyping had a subtle, discriminatory impact on the views that Price Waterhouse's partners had toward Ms. Hopkins' candidacy for partnership" (Tomkins & Pfeifer, 1992, p. 399). Yet also recall that after Price Waterhouse appealed the district court's decision that Hopkins had been unfairly treated, Supreme Court Justice William Brennan, in a majority opinion that did not support Price Waterhouse, commented that the Court

didn't need a psychologist to point out that sex discrimination had occurred. He seemed to be labeling Price Waterhouse's action as blatant, but even members of the Supreme Court differed; Justice O'Connor, in a concurring opinion, wrote that "direct evidence of discrimination is hard to come by" and that the law protects against "discrimination, subtle or otherwise" (*Price Waterhouse v. Hopkins,* 1989, pp. 1804–1805).

Regardless of these labeling distinctions, Susan Fiske's testimony stands as an example of a conceptual analysis of the characteristics of gender stereotyping and their effects on employment and promotion decisions, as chapter 1 illustrates in detail. In what other ways can psychology contribute?

Methodology

Psychologists and other social scientists are justifiably proud of the sophistication of their methodological techniques. Trial lawyers and judges are often not trained in the use of statistics, and psychologists can make a valuable contribution by the application of their methodologies to claims of employment discrimination and to the evaluation of laws that seek to provide reforms regarding, for example, hate crimes or school segregation. Two types of contributions are described in this section: the use of statistical evidence, and the application of experimental designs to assess subtle racism.

The Use of Statistical Analysis

Chapter 1, in describing the appeal of Warren McClesky (*McCleskey v. Kemp,* 1987) illustrated how a statistical analysis can be used in the courtroom. More frequently, statistical evidence has been used in employment discrimination cases (Baldus & Cole, 1980; Dawson, 1980; Kaye, 1982a, 1982b; Kaye & Aicklin, 1986), and some judges have strongly advocated its use (see an illustration in Box 13-2). For example, Justice Potter Stewart, in *International Brotherhood of Teamsters v. United States* (1977), wrote that Supreme Court opinions "make it clear that statistical analyses have served and will continue to serve an important role in cases in which the existence of discrimination is a disputed issue" (p. 339).

The courts, in discrimination suits, make a distinction between claims of disparate treatment and disparate impact. **Disparate treatment** is judged to be present when an employer treats an employee or some employees less favorably than the other employees because of race, color, religion, sex, or national origin. **Disparate impact** (also called **adverse impact**) occurs if the employer's practices appear to be neutral in the treatment of different groups but nevertheless "fall more harshly on one group than on another and cannot be justified by business necessity" (Fienberg, 1989, p. 22). Disparate treatment is more susceptible to illustration by the use of statistical analyses than is disparate impact, and appeals courts have proposed that

disparate treatment should be the model for the statistical assessment of a claim of discriminatory hiring (*Vuyanich v. Republic National Bank,* 1984).

Tomkins and Pfeifer (1992) have concluded that judges are especially uncomfortable with the use of statistical evidence, in part because it is hard for them to evaluate. They suggested that social framework evidence, as illustrated in Dr. Fiske's testimony, is more effective than statistical evidence. They wrote,

> The social science evidence that was introduced by Hopkins differed from the kind of social science evidence presented in *McCleskey.* Instead of presenting social science evidence that statistically quantified the influence of discriminatory factors on Price Waterhouse's partners' decision and that

BOX 13-2
A Judge Who Did His Statistics Homework

Although some judges shy away from statistical evidence and hence form their conclusions on personal experiences rather than empirical data, Judge Patrick E. Higginbotham's behavior, in the case of *Vuyanich v. Republic National Bank* (1984), is an example of a legal expert who sought to understand the workings of another approach.

Joan Vuyanich was an African American woman who worked as a clerk for the Republic National Bank for three months in 1969. Shortly after she was let go, she filed a charge with the Equal Employment Opportunity Commission (EEOC), claiming that she had been fired because of her race and sex, in violation of Title VII. After much delay, the case went to trial in 1979, and Judge Higginbotham took almost a year to announce his opinion. He faced a formidable task; five statistical expert witnesses testified for the plaintiff, and the defense countered with four statistical experts who presented alternative analyses and rebutted the testimony of the plaintiff's experts. Most of the data used by each side were derived from the bank's records, but the two sides chose different variables to evaluate, including different regression analyses.

During the trial, Judge Higginbotham listened to the direct examination and cross-examination of each witness, and then he questioned the witnesses himself,

usually asking about the substantive nature of the evidence. Saks and Duizend (1983) observed:

> The judge employed flexible procedures in managing the trial. On several occasions he allowed experts to conduct what in essence was an in-court seminar through which they were invited to explain in more detail their underlying conceptualizations or mathematical procedures. Although the attorneys objected to this departure from the traditional procedures for eliciting testimony, they were overruled. (1983, p. 35)

The detail in the decision was worth the wait: Almost 80 pages of the 127-page document were devoted to a review of "the mathematics of regression analysis." Judge Higginbotham subsequently observed that he and his law clerks took an entire month off from their other duties in order to understand the statistical evidence presented by the teams of expert witnesses. The judge's eventual opinion—which found for the plaintiff—contains several statistical conclusions that not all experts would agree with, but "on balance it remains a remarkable description of some basic statistical issues in a legal context, something that even the most diligent and able judges can rarely take the time to do" (Fienberg, 1989, p. 21).

was designed to make law (i.e., social authority evidence: see Monahan & Walker, 1986, 1990), Hopkins had her expert describe social science evidence in a descriptive, overview manner. The expert provided a scientific context, a framework (Walker & Monahan, 1987), for the consideration of the specific factual information related to Hopkins' term of employment at Price Waterhouse. (Tomkins & Pfeifer, 1992, pp. 398–399)

They later contrasted this approach with the statistical analysis used by Professor David Baldus in Warren McCleskey's appeal:

In contrast to Dr. Fiske's spending her time instructing the court in *Hopkins* about the substance of sex stereotyping, Professor Baldus spent a considerable amount of his time teaching the court in *McCleskey* about multiple regression and appropriate techniques for data coding, data reduction, and the like. What if Professor Baldus had been allowed to inform the court about subtle racism and the insidious effect it likely had on decision making in Georgia's criminal justice system? What if Professor Baldus had read from some of the court employees' process notes instead of coding them and regressing them on a bivariate, outcome variable? Certainly, to prove a constitutional violation is a lot more difficult than proving a statutory violation; nonetheless, there might be a greater likelihood of convincing the trial court that discrimination persists if the social science expert offers contextual (and perhaps even concrete, anecdotal evidence: see generally Borgida & Nisbett, 1977; Kahneman & Tversky, 1973; Nisbett, Borgida, Crandall, & Reed, 1982; Tversky & Kahneman, 1973) evidence to complement abstract statistical evidence or if the expert simply provides the background, the social science context, which the fact finder then can use to consider the other witnesses' evidence. (Tomkins & Pfeifer, 1992, p. 402)

Perhaps so. As Tomkins and Pfeifer acknowledged, the Court's rejection of what psycho-logists consider persuasive statistical differences in the death penalty for African Americans and Whites reflects a number of causes; for example, constitutional issues extract different considerations. It can be argued that the Court would not have been persuaded by *any* type of social science evidence in McCleskey's appeal, because tremendous problems for many states' penal systems would have been created had McCleskey's death sentence been overturned on the basis of racial disparities. Such a decision would have unleashed numerous appeals and changes in sentences throughout the country.

The Application of Research Designs to Detect Subtle Racism and Sexism

- Two men answer the same advertisement for an entry-level professional position in an engineering firm; they are of the same age and their credentials are quite similar. The White man gets the job; the African American man does not.
- Two couples respond to the "Open House" sign displayed in front of a nice house in a prestigious suburban neighborhood. When the White couple follows up by contacting the real estate agent, they are greeted with enthusiasm; when the Native American couple does the same, the agent tells them that a buyer has already made a bid on the house.
- A psychology department chairperson reviews the resumes of two applicants for an assistant-professorship position; both applicants have recently completed their Ph.Ds at rather distinguished universities, and each has several publications. The man is invited to campus for an interview; the woman is not.

Although each of these situations could well occur in real life—and often does—they also reflect the application of traditional research methodology to a new field—the identification of expressions of discrimination. Just as in any experiment, researchers make an effort to keep other factors equivalent—the credentials, the age and apparent affluence of the house-seeking couple, the job experience—while varying the race or gender. Any difference in response can then plausibly be attributed to this independent variable. Such procedures have been used by investigators working for federal agencies charged with identifying and prosecuting examples of racial or gender discrimination in employment or housing (Crosby, 1994). Even the biases of White physicians have been studied by using such procedures; actors posing as cardiac patients solicited evaluation and treatment; only the sex and race of the patients were varied. Women and African Americans—especially African American women—were far less likely to be referred for cardiac catheterization, an important diagnostic procedure, than were White men with the same symptoms (Williams, 1999).

The application of this type of methodology has produced findings that illustrate the salience of subtle racism. For example, a program of research by Samuel Gaertner and John Dovidio (1977; Dovidio & Gaertner, 1996; Frey & Gaertner, 1986) found that in a situation that was clearly an emergency, Whites who believed they were the only witnesses came to the aid of a Black person as quickly as they did for another White person. But in an ambiguous situation in which it was unclear if an injury had taken place, Whites responded less quickly to a Black person than to a White person. Furthermore, if the respondent was led to believe that other witnesses were present, the Black victim was helped only half as often as the White victim.

The use of such real-life situations often exposes subtle racism. For example, a person at home receives a phone call. It is clearly a wrong number, but the caller still describes his plight: He is stranded on the freeway and has run out of coins for the pay phone; he needs someone to call the garage for him (Gaertner & Bickman, 1971). Willingness to help is often a function of the race of the caller, even by recipients who deny any overt racial prejudice.

Results of extensive work on this general topic lead to a conclusion that racism is, indeed, subtly manifested in contemporary life. Returning to the preceding employment examples,

researchers have found that, characteristically, if information about job candidates is consistent—that is, each candidate has uniformly positive credentials—applicants of each race are treated similarly. In some studies, the African American candidate with strong credentials is rated more favorably—a kind of reverse racism. But when the information about each candidate is more ambiguous, subtle racism may favor the White (Dovidio, 1995).

Similar methodologies have been used to detect sexism. More than 30 years ago, Philip Goldberg (1968) asked respondents to evaluate the significance and writing style of articles written by either "John McKay" or "Joan McKay." The articles were, of course, the same, but the respondents rated them more favorably when they thought the author was a man. This procedure has been adapted to assess the reactions to women in the workplace, with similar results (Wallston & O'Leary, 1981). Like the results when comparing races, these results often reflect subtle biases. Especially when the criteria for evaluation are vague, subjective, and ill-defined does gender bias occur (Goddard, 1986).

RACIAL DIFFERENCES AND THE USE OF TEST RESULTS TO ASSIGN STUDENTS TO SPECIAL EDUCATION CLASSES

As Daniel Reschly (1999) has observed, the assessment of the educational abilities of schoolchildren has become a major responsibility of psychologists in the United States as well as other countries. Should IQ test results be the basis for assigning schoolchildren to special classes for those who are mentally retarded? Should such tests be used even if it is claimed that they are biased against minority children? And what should be the role of the forensic psychologist when such issues are brought before the courts for resolution?

On the issue of the fairness of using IQ results for placement of children in special education classes, two experienced federal judges considered the same evidence about the same legal issues; in fact, in both cases the defendant was the board of education, some of the expert witnesses were the same, and both trials were bench trials. Yet the two judges reached drastically different conclusions on the question of racial bias in the procedure.

The first of the cases, chronologically, was that of *Larry P. et al. v. Wilson Riles et al.* (1979), which involved litigation over a 15-year period, beginning in 1971. When the suit was initiated, more than 25% of the children in special education classes in California were African American, although less than 10% of the school population in general was of that race (Elliott, 1987). Initially, the representatives of Larry P. and four other minority students in California—concerned about "dumping" such students in these classes—sought and received an injunction that prevented the use of intelligence test results in making decisions about placement in EMR (Educable Mentally Retarded) classes in the San Francisco school district. The plaintiffs claimed that the tests were culturally biased against minorities and that the school system was acting in violation of Title VI of the Civil Rights Act of 1964, which stated that recipients of federal aid may not "utilize criteria or methods of administration which have the effect of subjecting individuals to discrimination because of their race, color, or national origin, or have the effect of defeating or substantially impairing accomplishment of the objectives of the program as respecting individuals of a particular race, color, or national origin" (*Larry P. et al. v. Wilson Riles et al.*, 1979, p. 963). Furthermore, the plaintiffs claimed that the school district moved toward the use of what they called "nonobjective" intelligence tests in the early 1970s and, in so doing, intentionally fostered the overenrollment of African American children in EMR classes. They argued that intelligence tests were not valid measures of intelligence in minority children and had not

been specifically validated as EMR placement mechanisms.

After a second injunction in 1974, the case went to trial in 1977 and lasted 8 months; the judge, Robert F. Peckham, did not announce his decision until a year later. This decision, based on reviewing more than 10,000 pages of testimony from more than 50 witnesses (mostly experts) and 200 exhibits, was a complex one. Judge Peckham acknowledged that "the court has necessarily been drawn into the emotionally charged debate about the nature of 'intelligence' and its basis in 'genes' or 'environment.' This debate, which finds renowned experts disagreeing sharply, obviously cannot be resolved by judicial decree. Despite these problems, however, court intervention has been necessary" (*Larry P. v. Riles,* 1979, p. 932). He also noted that his decision was based on the consensus of expert witnesses' testimony about what intelligence tests could and could not do, while acknowledging that the experts disagreed about the utility of intelligence testing for EMR placement.

Judge Peckham's decision affirmed almost all of the plaintiffs' contentions; he concluded that the available data were consistent with a finding of bias against African American children, that those children's subculture, socioeconomic status, or environment hampered their ability to acquire the knowledge needed to answer specific items. His ruling included the following conclusions:

1. California schools were acting in violation of federal law, including the Civil Rights Act of 1964, Section 504 of the Rehabilitation Act of 1973, and the Education for All Handicapped Children Act of 1975 (Elliot, 1987).
2. The school system used intelligence tests that were racially and culturally biased and that had a discriminatory impact on African American children.
3. These tests had not been validated for the placement of African American children into EMR classes, and the result had been the placement of children from that racial group

in disproportionate numbers into these classes, thus denying them their guarantee to a right of equal protection.

Judge Peckham's remedy was to enjoin the school system from using intelligence test results for placement of children in special education classes. This decision was appealed by the school district but upheld in 1984. And 2 years later, an injunction was issued in California that prohibited the use, statewide, of intelligence tests with African American students for *any* reason (Taylor, 1990). Furthermore, an IQ score of an African American student transferring into California would not remain as a part of his or her permanent record, nor could parents of African American children put into their child's records any privately obtained IQ scores (Elliott, 1987).

Although its locale was different, the second case was strikingly similar in many ways. Filed in 1975 and tried in 1980, the case of *PASE v. Hannon* (1980) was also a class action suit brought by the representatives of African American children; PASE stood for "People in Action on Special Education." In contrast to the earlier case, the trial lasted only 3 weeks and generated fewer witnesses and about 2,000 pages of testimony and argument. Judge John F. Grady, based in Chicago, concluded, in contrast, that the tests generally were not biased and that cultural differences had little effect on the differential performance of children of differing races; furthermore, he reached his decision in a manner entirely different from Judge Peckham's. In fact, Judge Grady stated that he was uncomfortable relying on expert testimony:

> None of the witnesses in this case has so impressed me with his or her credibility and expertise that I would feel secure basing a decision simply on his or her opinion. In some instances, I am satisfied that the opinions expressed more the result of doctrinaire commitment to a preconceived idea than they are a result of scientific inquiry. I need something more than the conclusions of the

> witnesses in order to arrive at my own conclusions. (*PASE v. Hannon,* 1980, p. 836)

Judge Grady based his decision on his analysis of specific test items; he wrote:

> It is obvious to me that I must examine the tests themselves in order to know what the witnesses are talking about. . . . For me to say that the tests are either biased or unbiased without analyzing the test items in detail would reveal nothing about the tests but only something about my opinion of the tests. (p. 836)

Almost 90% of Judge Grady's judicial opinion was devoted to a detailed armchair analysis of items and answers from the three prominent individually administered intelligence tests of that time, the Wechsler Intelligence Scale for Children (WISC), the Wechsler Intelligence Scale for Children-Revised (WISC-R), and the Stanford Binet. He judged each item as either biased or not. For example, consider this item: "Who discovered America?" Dr. Robert L. Williams, a psychologist testifying for the plaintiffs, stated that this question was insulting to Native American children because it implied that their homeland had to be "discovered"; furthermore, he said, the question was confusing because the land didn't need to be "discovered" in the first place. But Judge Grady disagreed; he wanted to know how this question discriminated against African American children (p. 838). After doing his item-by-item check, Judge Grady evaluated very few test items as being biased against any racial or cultural group. Specifically, he concluded that:

1. One item from the Stanford Binet and eight items from the WISC and WISC-R were culturally biased against African American children. These included: "Why is it better to pay bills by check than by cash?" and "What are you supposed to do if you find someone's wallet or pocketbook in a store?" (Elliott, 1987, p. 149). In Judge Grady's opinion, those few items did not cause the tests to be unfair, as they made up a small proportion and many of them were higher level questions that would

not usually be administered to a child who had the possibility of placement in an EMR class.

2. Placement in EMR classes was not decided solely by the intelligence test results; other tests were included in the battery. Furthermore, many of those who administered the tests in the Chicago area were themselves African American, and they would administer the tests in a culturally sensitive way.

3. No evidence existed that wrong placements of children into EMR classes occurred.

Not only were Judge Grady's findings and ruling opposite those of Judge Peckham, but Judge Grady went out of his way to acknowledge the differences in his opinion:

> As is by now obvious, the witnesses and the arguments that persuaded Judge Peckham have not persuaded me. Moreover, I believe the issue in the case cannot properly be analyzed without a detailed examination of the items on the tests. It is clear that this was not undertaken in the Larry P. case. (*PASE v. Hannon,* 1980, pp. 882–883)

Judge Grady's procedure was roundly criticized by several psychologists; for example, Donald Bersoff wrote, "If Judge Peckham's analysis is scanty and faulty, Judge Grady's can best be described as naive; at worst it is unintelligent and completely empty of empirical substance. It represents a single person's subjective and personal opinions cloaked in the authority of judicial robes" (1981, p. 1049). But psychologist Rogers Elliott (1987) noted that Judge Grady had pleaded with both sides to provide him with research articles concerned with item analyses; during the testimony he said, "Hasn't anybody ever, in the Chicago school system, bothered to take the scores and take the tests and see how these kids do on these various items? I just can't believe that nobody has done that" (quoted by Elliott, 1987, p. 142). But the attorneys chose to emphasize other aspects of the case.

Should judges be making decisions about the potential cultural bias of individual test items? Are they any good at it? Jerome Sattler (1991) sought to answer the latter question with respect to the judges in these two cases. He used 25 items from the WISC or WISC-R, including 11 identified as biased by either Judge Peckham or Judge Grady, and administered them to 448 randomly selected students (224 African American and 224 White) in grades 4 through 6 in various Ohio schools. Of the 25 items, 12 were found to be significantly more difficult for African American children than for White children; of these, the judges had identified only 6, or 50%. Additionally, 5 items that were singled out by the judges as being biased were found not to be harder for African American children. Neither outcome reflected a high degree of accuracy by the judges; Sattler concluded,

> The results suggest that an armchair inspection of items cannot provide reliable data about differential difficulty levels. . . . Court judges, untrained in psychometrics and without resort to data, lack the expertise required to decide which items on tests are or are not biased. Such unsupported decisions fall into the realm of personal opinion. (1991, pp. 127–128)

Perhaps Judge Grady's criticism of Judge Peckham's reliance on expert testimony should be reexamined in light of the empirical findings (Brown, 1996). But judges *are* the decision makers, and some judges, as illustrated by Judge Grady's response, are not impressed with the testimony of psychologists.

THE IMPACT OF AFFIRMATIVE ACTION POLICIES

Most citizens value the principles of equality and fairness; yet when attempts are made to apply these principles to members of diverse groups, reluctance and resistance are often the results (Skedsvold & Mann, 1996a). **Affirmative action** generally refers to any procedure that permits consideration of race, gender, disability, or national origin, along with other variables, in order to provide equal opportunity to qualified individuals who have been denied those opportunities because of past discrimination (Lasso, 1998). Social programs designed to eliminate discriminatory practices have become undesirable in the eyes of some; the term *affirmative action* has become an emotional symbol, both for its supporters and for its opponents. As the nation reconsiders its policies, can psychology contribute anything to the understanding and possible resolution of the controversy?

The Courts and Affirmative Action

Before identifying possible psychological contributions, it is useful to examine how the courts have dealt with the constitutionality of affirmative action programs. In doing so, a theme from earlier chapters—the complex, sometimes conflicting, relationship between the law and psychology—resurfaces.

Rupert Nacoste (1996) has suggested that the U.S. Supreme Court, in its evaluations of the constitutionality of affirmative action policies, has developed procedural standards that are based on reasoning that has as its goal "avoiding government actions that might have negative social psychological effects" (1996, p. 133). Specifically, he concluded that "members of the U.S. Supreme Court appear to have been influenced by an implicit theory that indicates that the use of group membership as a criterion for making personnel decisions will reinforce common, negative group stereotypes" (p. 134). Four recent cases, one from 1973, one from 1996, and two just decided in 2003, are illustrative:

Regents of the University of California v. Bakke (1978)

In 1973, Allan Bakke was one of 2,664 applicants who sought admission to the medical school at the University of California at Davis. From this overwhelming number, only 100 were accepted; 84 of these places were filled through the regular admission procedures and 16 by minority applicants who were "disadvantaged." Applicants not only were separated into two groups but were screened by different committees using different criteria. The year that Bakke applied, the 16 applicants who were selected under the special program had undergraduate grade point averages of 2.88, as compared to 3.49 for the 84 students admitted through the standard admission process. The "disadvantaged" students' scores on the MCAT (the medical school aptitude test) were also lower (Schwartz, 1988). Bakke's application was rejected, even though his credentials were stronger than those of the 16 minority students who were admitted. Bakke thus filed a lawsuit claiming that the procedure gave preferential treatment to minorities and hence was a form of racial discrimination, denying him equal protection of the law under the Fourteenth Amendment of the Constitution. After lower courts essentially agreed with Bakke, the Regents of the University of California appealed the case to the United States Supreme Court.

The majority opinion by Justice Lewis Powell reflected Nacoste's assessment; he wrote, "Preferential programs may only reinforce common stereotypes holding that certain people are unable to achieve success without special protection based on a factor having no relation to individual worth" (quoted by Nicoste, 1996, p. 134). Furthermore, Justice Powell concluded that the set-aside procedure used by the University of California at Davis led to a disregard of individual rights that were guaranteed by the Fourteenth Amendment. But he did not conclude that all affirmative action procedures were unconstitutional; for example, a policy that gave some weight to group membership, but not necessarily decisive weight, would be constitutional because the program would treat each applicant as an individual in the admission process.

Hopwood v. State of Texas (1996)

More recently, the Supreme Court decided not to hear the appeal in the case of *Hopwood v. State of Texas* (1996). The University of Texas School of Law had been using a procedure similar to the one Bakke confronted: It set lower test score standards for African American and Hispanic American applicants than for White applicants, and it provided a separate review board for minority applicants. Thus, the law school hoped to achieve a diversified student body with a goal of about 10% Hispanic Americans and 5% African Americans in the entering class. The school had already scrapped the procedure after being sued by four unsuccessful White applicants, including Cheryl Hopwood, but the procedure was rejected by the Fifth Circuit Court anyway.

When they decide not to review an appeal stemming from a decision by a lower court, the justices of the Supreme Court do not have to give a reason for their action. But the decision by the Fifth Circuit Court to strike down the procedure was certainly in keeping with Justice Powell's concern that separate admissions committees failed to protect individual rights.

Grutter v. Bollinger (2003) and Gratz v. Bollinger (2003)

In June 2003, the United States Supreme Court decided the constitutionality of affirmative action, upholding 5 to 4 the use of race as a factor to achieve "diversity" in college admissions. In a companion case, the high court struck down 6 to 3 an admissions process that automatically granted a preference to applicants from certain minority groups, claiming the specific method employed was too broad and mechanical and consequently violated the equal protection clause of the U.S. Constitution.

In the more important of the two cases, *Grutter v. Bollinger,* Associate Justice Sandra Day O'Connor wrote the majority opinion—joined by Associate Justices John Paul Stevens, David Souter, Ruth Bader Ginsburg, and Stephen Breyer—upholding the University of Michigan Law School's practice of considering the race of applicants to insure a "critical mass" of minority students. "The Equal Protection Clause does not prohibit the Law School's narrowly tailored use of race in admissions decisions to further a compelling interest in obtaining the educational benefits that flow from a diverse student body," O'Connor wrote. Chief Justice William Rehnquist and Associate Justices Anthony Kennedy,

Antonin Scalia, and Clarence Thomas dissented. In the other ruling, *Gratz v. Bollinger,* Rehnquist wrote the majority opinion, striking down the University of Michigan's undergraduate admissions policy, which assigned "points" to African American, Hispanic, and Native American applicants. Stevens, Souter, and Ginsburg dissented.

The rulings appear to resolve, at least for the time being, the intense legal dispute that has simmered in the lower courts for the 25 years that have passed since the Supreme Court issued six conflicting opinions—none commanding a majority—in *Regents of the University of California v. Bakke.* Although *Bakke* banned the use of outright racial quotas, the opinion of former Associate Justice Lewis Powell—which was not binding precedent because it received only a plurality of votes—left the door open for "narrowly tailored" policies using race to achieve diversity. The majority decision in *Grutter* effectively makes Powell's earlier opinion in *Bakke* the law of the land.

The University of Michigan Law School's admissions policy considered in *Grutter* allowed reviewers to take into account the overall "diversity" of its student body when considering whether to accept individual students, "with special reference to the inclusion of students from groups which have been historically discriminated against, like African Americans, Hispanics and Native Americans, who without this commitment might not be represented in our student body in meaningful numbers." The undergraduate admissions policy in dispute in *Gratz* was more rigid. The school used a 150-point system, in which applicants with more than 100 points were generally accepted. Applicants from an underrepresented minority group, defined as African American, Hispanic, or Native American, automatically received 20 points. This policy significantly impacted applicants in the midrange of academic achievement at both the law school and the undergraduate program. At the law school, of students with a grade point average in the 2.75–2.99 range in 1995, all 4 Black applicants were accepted, while none of 14 White applicants was accepted. Of those in the 3.0–3.24 range, 7 of 8 Black applicants, compared to 2 of 42 White applicants, were accepted. Under the undergraduate admissions procedure, most academically qualified "underrepresented minorities" were accepted to the university. In contrast, many academically qualified students who were White or Asian had a more difficult time gaining acceptance.

Each of the two cases attracted over a hundred *amicus curiae* briefs, an extraordinary number. Briefs were filed in support of affirmative action by 3M Corporation (on behalf of itself "and other leading businesses") as well as by Exxon Mobil and General Motors. In addition, a group of retired military officials led by Lt. Gen. Julius W. Becton, Jr., filed a brief in support of racial preferences. "Major American businesses," O'Connor wrote in *Grutter*, "have made clear that the skills needed in today's increasingly global marketplace can only be developed through exposure to widely diverse people, cultures, ideas, and viewpoints. High-ranking retired officers and civilian military leaders assert that a highly qualified, racially diverse officer corps is essential to national security." In all, 40 of the *Fortune* 500 largest U.S. corporations registered their support in the Supreme Court for the University of Michigan's policies. Clearly, they were worried that the elimination of racial preferences would have damaging effects. Justice O'Connor reflected that fear, writing, "In order to cultivate a set of leaders with legitimacy in the eyes of the citizenry, it is necessary that the path to leadership be visibly open to talented and qualified individuals of every race and ethnicity."

Psychological Contributions

Four potential types of contributions by psychologists to the understanding of affirmative action procedures can be identified:

Affirmative Action and the Limits of Fairness

As Opotow (1996) observed, affirmative action programs have been characterized as controversial since their introduction in 1965, when President Johnson signed Executive Order 11246, requiring federal contractors to "take affirmative action" in recruitment, training, and employment. The order required contractors to monitor their workforces to determine if non-Whites were being underutilized and, where there was underutilization, to develop concrete plans to eliminate it. Subsequently, the federal government made racial composition a factor in awarding federal contracts.

It has been suggested that the major hindrance to acceptance of affirmative action programs is that they violate a "sense of fairness" and thus run counter to Americans' endorsement of the value of equality (Chang, 1996). Opponents of these programs argue that affirmative action provides an "unfair advantage" to members of targeted groups, and the eventual result will be a form of **reverse discrimination** (Gamson & Modigliani, 1987). The perceived fairness of a procedure has an impact on the evaluation of a person associated with the procedure (Nacoste, 1985, 1987; Thibaut & Walker, 1975); thus, when an affirmative action procedure is implemented, employees are identified on the basis of their race and sex, and any perceived group differences become more salient (Chang, 1996).

To understand the diverse reactions, it is helpful to ask: What is the **psychological boundary** for those who are justified to receive fair treatment? Or, to put it another way: Who is seen as undeserving and hence outside the boundary? Opotow's analysis emphasized how this boundary between the deserving and the undeserving can shift as social and economic conditions change; for example, as minorities move into professional and managerial positions, a threatened person's boundary for recipients of justice may shrink.

An Analysis of Public Opinion about Affirmative Action

Social scientists conduct public opinion polls, but sometimes polls can lead to misleading conclusions because of their limited structure. Common wisdom says that the American public is currently not supportive of affirmative action policies, and some recent votes (such as the one on California's Proposition 209) have reflected such a conclusion. When the choices are limited to two diverse positions, such as no affirmative action versus such extreme programs as set-asides or separate admissions criteria for minorities, the public's reaction is to reject "affirmative action." But public resistance is diminished when the choices include more moderate procedures (Plous, 1996), and, if individual achievement-related characteristics are given weight as well as one's race or gender, procedures are more likely to be accepted (Heilman, 1994; Kravitz, 1995; Nacoste, 1994). Specifically, a Gallup poll found that fewer than 25% of the respondents wanted to eliminate affirmative action laws completely (Benedetto, 1995).

The Development of More Acceptable Programs

If it is the case that much of the resistance to affirmative action stems from the preceding reactions, psychologists can assist employers and admissions officers to design programs that do not threaten participants' self-images. Pratkanis and Turner (1996) have offered 12 principles to serve as a guide for improving the effectiveness of affirmative action programs and removing the stigma of preferential selection; these are described in Box 13-3.

Evaluation of Effectiveness

Psychologists and other researchers have contributed to an understanding of the acceptance and effectiveness of affirmative action policies in several ways. For example, as noted in the proposals of Pratkanis and Turner (1996) in Box 13-3, equal-status contact should be a goal when implementing affirmative action programs. A program of research by Stuart W. Cook (1971, 1978; see also Wrightsman, 1972, pp. 324–337) showed that prejudice and resentment toward African Americans was ameliorated when the interracial working conditions involved common goals, a state of cooperative interdependence

between the workers, equal status, and the endorsement of equality by the supervisors. Similarly, Elliot Aronson and his colleagues (Aronson, 1992; Aronson & Bridgeman, 1992; Aronson, Stephan, Sikes, Blaney, & Snapp, 1978), through the ingenious application of a jigsaw technique, showed that students from diverse backgrounds, when placed in learning groups that emphasized interdependence, improved their school performance, along with a reduction in the levels of prejudice expressed by the White students toward the minorities.

Recently, two distinguished academic administrators, William G. Bowen and Derek Bok (1998), studied the progress of African American and White students who entered 28 prominent colleges in 1976 and 1989, when affirmative action programs were in effect. They noted that the African American students entered these elite colleges and universities with lower test scores and high-school grades than did the Whites; furthermore, they received lower grades in college and had a lower graduation rate. But after graduation, they achieved notable success. For example, they earned advanced degrees at rates identical to those of their White classmates; they were slightly more likely to obtain professional degrees in law, business, and medicine; and they were more active than their White classmates in civic activities. Those African Americans who graduated from elite colleges earned 70% to 85% more than did African American graduates generally.

EMPLOYMENT DISCRIMINATION

The history of the United States is one that makes commonplace the denial of job opportunities for women and members of racial and ethnic groups. The expressed reasons for these discriminatory employment decisions traditionally reflected blatant racism and sexism; as we have seen, more recently, shifts toward the use of

BOX 13-3
Principles of Effective Affirmative Action

Pratkanis and Miller (1996) proposed that affirmative action can be seen as a type of help, but it is often resisted because its offer of help does not conform to society's values and implies that the recipient lacks certain abilities; thus, it creates a sense of being threatened and, as a result, produces defensive behaviors. Pratkanis and Miller suggested 12 principles, the implementation of which might reduce such reactions:

1. Focus the helping efforts away from the recipient and toward a goal of removing social barriers.

2. Establish unambiguous, explicit, and focused qualifications for use in selection and promotion decisions.

3. Communicate clearly the requisite procedures and criteria.

4. Be certain that selection procedures are perceived as fair by relevant audiences.

5. Emphasize the recipients' contributions to the organization and his or her specific competencies.

6. Develop socialization strategies that deter respondents from making attributions that they are dependent on the good graces of the organization for their jobs, status, and future advancement.

7. Reinforce the fact that affirmative action is not preferential selection.

8. Establish the conditions of equal status contact and the sharing of common goals.

9. Emphasize that change is inevitable, that participants must bring their attitudes in line with the new reality.

10. Be aware that affirmative action programs do not operate in isolation.

11. Recognize that affirmative action is not a panacea.

12. Monitor the affirmative action program to see what works and what doesn't.

---

test scores and subtle stereotypes have occurred. In the last 30 years, statistical analyses have been used to provide convincing evidence that discrimination exists, although often the figures are so extreme that tools of statistical inference are not required.

For example, consider the case of *Jones v. Tri-County Electric Cooperative* (1975), which concerned the hiring practices of a utility company. The firm had hired only one African American (for a janitorial position) from the time the 1964 Civil Rights Act became law (July 1, 1965) until the initiation of a lawsuit 7 years later. *After* the initiation of the suit, the company hired several more African Americans, but the number of newly hired people who were minorities was only 8 out of 43 hires, or 19%—sufficiently far from the 40% of the local population who were African American. The defendant was, based on this disparate impact, found to be in violation of the law.

But sometimes job qualifications, such as past experience or aptitude test scores, were used to prevent minorities from obtaining jobs.

In 1971, in the case of *Griggs v. Duke Power Co.,* the Supreme Court recognized that the lack of equal opportunity could result not only from intentional discrimination but also from practices that, though not intending to discriminate, have a disparate impact on non-Whites and women. It ruled that when a job qualification had such an impact on minorities or women, the Civil Rights Act of 1964 made such a procedure unlawful unless an employer could show that the action was a business necessity; thus, the burden of proof was on the employer. But in 1989, the Supreme Court modified the *Griggs* decision, placing the burden of proof on employees to prove that a challenged job qualification was not really related to the company's needs (Lewis, 1991).

Thus, employment discrimination continued in the sense that a differential in test scores was used as a justification that minorities were not eligible for certain jobs. But the United States Department of Labor initiated a procedure that had the goal of reducing the impact of test results on hiring; it revised the scoring system for its General Aptitude Test Battery (GATB) by using a within-group scoring procedure, usually called **race-norming.** Consider the following example:

> John Smith, a White, scores 327 on a vocational-aptitude test. Fred Jones, a Black, gets only 283. But if the two applicants are sent to a prospective employer, their test results are said to rank identically at the 70th percentile. A computer error? No. The raw score Jones earned was compared only with the marks earned by fellow Blacks. Smith's number went into a blend of scores made by Whites and "others." If a Hispanic takes the same test, his raw score is converted on a third curve reserved for Hispanics only. (Barrett, 1991, p. 57)

A fair procedure to redress past employment discrimination, or a case of reverse discrimination? Psychologists are divided on the legitimacy of the procedure, just as are members of Congress, lawyers, and even civil rights activists (Gottfredson, 1994; Sackett & Wilk, 1994). The Civil Rights Act of 1991 banned any form of "score adjustment" based on "race, color, religion, sex, or national origin" (1991, p. 1071). Perhaps the U.S. Congress, in passing such a law, did not envision its far-reaching implications (Brown, 1994); for example, should police departments that have separate physical-ability requirements for female and male applicants be required to change them?

HATE CRIMES

As Americans moved toward the new millennium, they were shocked by the news of two vicious murders, reminding them that hate directed toward "deviant groups" was still a virulent phenomenon:

- Two Jasper, Texas, White supremacists, unrepentant even after their conviction for murder, chained James Byrd, Jr., an African American, to a pickup truck and dragged him three miles to his death.

- Two men in Laramie, Wyoming, learning that Matthew Shepard was gay, enticed him into their truck, drove him to an isolated area, tied him to a fence, pistol-whipped him, and left him to die. In April 1999, one of the perpetrators, Russell Henderson, pleaded guilty to kidnapping and murder in order to avoid the death penalty.

Hate crimes are words or actions intended to harm or intimidate an individual because of his or her membership in a minority group; they may include violent assaults, murder, rape, or property crimes motivated by prejudice, as well as threats of violence or acts of intimidation (Finn & McNeil, 1987, cited by Herek, 1989). Hate crimes differ from other serious crimes in that they are based primarily on the victim's membership in an identifiable group; thus, any incident with such a victim has threatening implications for other members of that group (Craig & Waldo, 1996). A swastika burned into a synagogue door, a racial epithet scrawled on a sidewalk are actions that assail the identity of group members.

The FBI estimated that more than 8,000 hate crimes were committed in the United States in 1997. Victims of hate crimes are most often members of groups that are stereotyped in this society; Herek (1989) has concluded that lesbians and gay men are the principal targets of such crimes. Yet social science research on hate crimes is only at its beginning stages.

Meanwhile, legislation has moved forward establishing more severe penalties for such crimes. In the last decade, 40 states and the federal government have passed laws that single out crimes based on race, color, religion, or national origin, although in some of these states, including New York, these laws cover only lower level offenses, such as harassment. Other states, including Wisconsin, double or triple the minimum sentence if the perpetrator was motivated by racism, anti-Semitism, or **homophobia** (Gey, 1997). But only 19 states include the victim's sexual orientation in their hate-crime legislation, and 10 states have no hate-crime laws at all.

The legislature of the state of Wyoming, where Matthew Shepard was killed, has rejected hate-crime legislation that includes sexual orientation three times in recent years. Psychologists can contribute to the policy debate on the merits of special hate-crime legislation by carrying out evaluation research on the effects of such legislation on crime rates. Do such laws have a deterrent impact? The perpetrators of both of the heinous hate crimes that took the lives of James Byrd, Jr., and Matthew Shepard are eligible for the death penalty, even without such laws.

SUMMARY

Psychologists distinguish between prejudice and discrimination: The first is internal, an unjustified evaluative attitude toward a member of a group that results from the recipient's membership in that group. In contrast, discrimination refers to an observable behavior that accepts or rejects another based on his or her membership in a particular group. Expressions of prejudiced attitudes are less blatant than in the past, leading to the development of the concept of modern racism, or subtle racism, to refer especially to the attitudes of White people who may regard themselves as unprejudiced, while still harboring feelings of resentment toward certain groups.

Forensic psychologists can contribute to the amelioration of discrimination by the application of a conceptual analysis and by the use of several research and statistical methodologies, including evaluation research procedures that assess the effectiveness of, for example, affirmative action programs or laws that provide for more severe punishments for hate crimes.

Psychologists have contributed to judicial decisions regarding the use of IQ test results to place children in special education classes and particularly the potential bias against minority group children by the use of individualized intelligence tests in this determination. Researchers have also evaluated the effectiveness of affirmative action programs and have made suggestions for ways to improve such programs.

KEY TERMS

adverse impact
affirmative action
discrimination
disparate impact
disparate treatment
hate crimes
homophobia
modern racism
prejudice
psychological boundary
race-norming
racism
reverse discrimination
sexism

INFOTRAC®
COLLEGE EDITION

InfoTrac College Edition is a FREE, powerful, online learning resource, consisting of full-text articles from thousands of journals and periodicals. With each new copy of *Forensic Psychology*, Second Edition, you receive 4 months of free access to the InfoTrac College Edition database. By doing a simple keyword search (try using the Key Terms in the list above), you can quickly generate a list of relevant articles from thousands of possibilities and can select articles to read, explore, and print for reference or further study. InfoTrac College Edition's continuously updated collection of articles can be useful for doing reading and writing assignments that reach beyond the pages of this text!

SUGGESTED READINGS

Clayton, S. D., & Crosby, F. J. (1992). *Justice, gender, and affirmative action.* Ann Arbor: University of Michigan Press.

An application of the social psychological theory of relative deprivation to the reactions of victims of prejudice and discrimination. Includes a chapter identifying aspects of affirmative action programs that promote success.

Cole, D. (1999). *No equal justice: Race and class in the American criminal justice system.* New York: New Press.

First, a demonstration of racial bias in the United States criminal justice system, with extensive review of its applications to profiling, right to counsel, jury selection, sentencing, and other aspects. Second, a claim that the criminal justice system "affirmatively depends upon inequality." A well-written book by a Georgetown University law professor.

Elliott, R. (1987). *Litigating intelligence: IQ tests, special education, and social science in the courtroom.* Dover, MA: Auburn House.

Not only a detailed analysis of the *Larry P.* and *PASE* cases regarding the use of IQ tests for placement in special education classes but also a wide-ranging description of what happens to social science evidence in an adversary system. Written by a psychologist.

Goodman-Delahunty, J. (1999). Civil law: Employment and discrimination. In R. Roesch, S. D. Hart, & J. R. P. Ogloff (Eds.), *Psychology and law: The state of the discipline* (pp. 277–337). New York: Kluwer Academic/Plenum.

A recent survey of psychological applications to the study of employment discrimination and sexual harassment.

Kravitz, D., & Platania, J. (1993). Attitudes and beliefs about affirmative action: Effects of target sex and ethnicity. *Journal of Applied Psychology, 78,* 928–938.

Application of traditional social psychological methodology to determinants of opinions about affirmative action.

Skedsvold, P. R., & Mann, T. L. (Eds.). (1996b). The affirmative action debate: What's fair in policy and programs? *Journal of Social Issues, 52*(4), 1–160.

A special journal issue containing articles by prominent psychologists on the impact of affirmative action policies.

Tomkins, A. J., & Pfeifer, J. E. (1992). Modern social-scientific theories and data concerning discrimination: Implications for using social science evidence in the courts. In D. K. Kagehiro & W. S. Laufer (Eds.), *Handbook of psychology and law* (pp. 385–407). New York: Springer-Verlag.

An excellent review of the psychological approach to discrimination, including historical antecedent, the early research on prejudice, modern approaches to conceptualization, and applications to recent court cases.

14

Sexual Harassment

INCREASED AWARENESS OF SEXUAL HARASSMENT

Sexual harassment is any unwelcome, sex-based interaction, including verbal interaction, at work or at school, that renders harm to the recipient. But the term is not fully understood, and one of the contributions of psychology is the analysis of its meanings held by different people, especially as these are compared with the legal definition of sexual harassment (Frazier, Cochran, & Olson, 1995). As the chapter describes, psychology can also contribute to the understanding of the conditions under which harassment occurs and to an awareness of what determines whether claims of sexual harassment will be upheld.

Origins of the Term

The term sexual harassment was apparently first coined in 1974 by a group of women at Cornell University, after several female colleagues had been forced off the job by unwanted advances from their male supervisors (Brownmiller & Alexander, 1992). The first national media attention came in an article in the *New York Times* ("Women Begin to Speak Out Against Sexual Harassment at Work") by Enid Nemy, on August 19, 1975, reporting on hearings held by the New York City Commission on Human Rights, then chaired by Eleanor Holmes Norton. Three years later, Lin Farley's "breakthrough" book, *Sexual Shakedown: The Sexual Harassment of Women on the Job,* was published—after 27 publishers had turned it down. Also in the 1970s, the Equal Employment Opportunity Commission (EEOC) emerged as a major means of redress against sexually harassing actions by employers. By 1977, several appellate cases had established the harassed victim's right, under **Title VII of the 1964 Civil Rights Act,** to sue the company that employed her. (However, she is entitled to collect only back pay, not damages, if she uses EEOC; if she chooses to file a civil suit, instead, she may be embroiled in lengthy court proceedings, and even if she wins, she faces the possibility that a judge will reduce the amount awarded her by the jury; Fisk, 1998.)

Incidence Rates

Perhaps the first large-scale survey using self-reports was the one done by a federal regulatory agency and released in 1981; in a random survey of 20,000 federal employees, the agency found that 42% of the female workers had experienced an incident of sexual harassment on the job in the previous 2 years (Brownmiller & Alexander, 1992). A later survey of 13,000 government workers, done in 1994, found that 44% of the women and 19% of the men said they had been the targets of unwanted and uninvited sexual attention (McAllister, 1995). A number of more specialized surveys have provided a variety of examples of the pervasiveness of sexual harassment. For example,

1. One out of every seven female faculty members at U.S. colleges and universities has reported having experienced sexual harassment, according to a survey of 30,000 faculty members at 270 colleges (Henry, 1994).
2. More than 40% of women lawyers in large law firms answered yes to queries about being deliberately touched, pinched, or cornered in the office (Slade, 1994). Similarly, a survey of 4,500 female physicians found that nearly half (47.7%) reported having experienced some form of harassment, from being told that medicine was not a fit career for a woman to being called "honey" in front of patients; more than a third (36.9%) said they had been sexually harassed (Manning, 1998).
3. In general workplace surveys, 40% to 60% of women say they have been sexually harassed at some point in their careers (Swisher, 1994).
4. In regard to female graduate students, 60% in Schneider's (1987) survey said they had been exposed to some form of everyday harassment by male faculty members, such as sexually suggestive remarks, and 22% had been asked for dates.

5. In a survey done by the Department of Defense in 1995, approximately half the women in each branch of the armed services reported unwanted sexual attention; the percentage was highest in the Marine Corps (64%) and lowest in the Air Force (49%; Seppa, 1997).

Recall that these surveys used retrospective self-reports and that widely varying definitions of sexual harassment were used in the different surveys. Yet even the critics of the methodology have acknowledged that sexual harassment is "a very real and important problem in organizations" (Arvey & Cavanaugh, 1995, p. 50).

Highly Publicized Cases

It may be said that the decade of the 1990s contributed mightily to public awareness of sexual harassment. Over the Columbus Day weekend of 1991, many Americans watched their television sets as Professor Anita Hill recounted her claims that a Supreme Court Justice nominee had sexually harassed her. Activities at the Tailhook convention of U.S. naval officers in Las Vegas and the actions of Army drill sergeants at Aberdeen Proving Ground received national visibility. Senator Robert Packwood's advances toward several of his staff members became fodder for David Letterman's monologues. Mitsubishi Motor Corporation agreed to pay $34 million to end a lawsuit that claimed that hundreds of its female assembly-line workers at its Normal, Illinois, plant had been sexually harassed. And, in the latter part of the decade, the country faced the suit of Paula Jones against the president of the United States.

But do people agree on what constitutes sexual harassment? Can a woman be a perpetrator of sexual harassment against a man? In Michael Crichton's (1993) novel *Disclosure* (and the subsequent movie), she could. In 1997, 12% of sexual harassment charges filed with the EEOC were filed by men (Goodman-Delahunty, 1999). And when a female employer harasses a male employee, his reaction can be as extreme as that of a female who has been sexually harassed, yet the public does not view female-to-male harassment as negatively (Pigott, Foley, Covati, & Wasserman, 1998).

The 1990s also revealed that appellate courts disagreed about what constituted harassment, and some psychological research also revealed gender differences in ratings of what constituted sexual harassment in some "gray area" situations (Frazier, Cochran, & Olson, 1995; Gutek & O'Connor, 1995). During that decade, the courts sought clarification on a number of questions; for example, if the incident involves two people of the same gender, does it constitute sexual harassment? (See Box 14-1 for an exploration of this issue.)

CONCEPTUALIZATIONS OF SEXUAL HARASSMENT

Confusion Surrounding the Term

As the media made the public increasingly aware of the problem, the number of complaints by employees increased, from 5,600 in 1989 to 15,500 in 1997 (Cloud, 1998; Mauro, 1993). A significant number of these, 968 out of 10,577 in 1992, were by men against female bosses. Yet these represent only the tip of the iceberg. It is estimated that only 6% of grievances generate formal complaints to the EEOC, other agencies, or employers; many employees fear repercussions for complaining (Fitzgerald, Swan, & Fischer, 1995; Kantrowitz, 1992). Others—whether employees or students—do not label the act as harassment at the time, or may blame themselves for the interaction (Kidder, Lafleur, & Wells, 1995; Weiss & Lalonde, 1998).

The public lacks consensus as to exactly what statements or acts constitute sexual harassment (Gruber, 1992). For example, men have difficulty labeling a statement or a question as sexually harassing if it attempts to reflect a compliment or if it is intended to be humorous

BOX 14-1

Is Same-Sex Harassment Sexual Harassment?

Perhaps surprisingly, men report potentially harassing behaviors from men at least as often as they do from women (Waldo, Berdahl, & Fitzgerald, 1998). Joseph Oncale's case is an example. For 4 months in 1991, Joseph Oncale worked on an offshore oil rig. While working as part of an eight-man crew for Sundowner Offshore Services, he claimed that he was sexually pursued and threatened with rape by two of his supervisors—who were also male. Once, the two men grabbed his genitals and one of them placed his penis against Oncale's head. On another occasion, he claimed, he was sodomized with a bar of soap. He twice reported these incidents to his employer's representative at the job site, but nothing was done. His supervisors portrayed their actions as a locker-room type of horseplay. So Oncale quit. Did he have the right to sue for sexual harassment? The Fifth Circuit Court of Appeals said that Title VII of the Civil Rights Act of

1964 did not apply to same-sex encounters; several other circuits have ruled the same way (Ryan & Butler, 1996). Are such decisions justified? Critics have noted that Title VII prohibited discrimination in the workplace based on race, religion, sex, and national origin, but ignored same-sex discrimination (Landau, 1997).

But Oncale pursued his suit to the U.S. Supreme Court, and in the oral arguments held in December 1997, six of the nine justices were quite critical of the circuit court's ruling; at one point, Chief Justice Rehnquist said, "I don't see how we could possibly sustain the ruling" (quoted by Carelli, 1997, p. A-1). In its unanimous decision, the Court ruled in favor of Oncale: "Nothing in Title VII necessarily bars a claim of discrimination . . . merely because the plaintiff and the defendant are of the same sex" (*Oncale v. Sundowner Offshore Services*, 1998, p. 1001).

(Gutek, 1985; Terpstra & Baker, 1987). Thus, one of the tasks in the early years of the 1990s was to develop classifications of sexually harassing statements and actions.

Gruber's Typology of Sexual Harassment

Gruber (1992) divided harassment into three types: verbal requests, verbal comments, and nonverbal displays. Within each type, he generated several subcategories. His typology is reprinted in Box 14-2. Within each of the three categories, the subcategories ranged from more severe to less severe. For example, sexual bribery was defined as a request with either a threat or a promise of a reward, while the less severe verbal requests, labeled **subtle pressures/advances,** were exemplified by ambiguous or inappropriate questions or double entendres.

Fitzgerald's Typology

Louise Fitzgerald and her associates (cf. Fitzgerald, Drasgow, Hulin, Gelfand, & Magley, 1997;

Fitzgerald & Hesson-McInnis, 1989; Fitzgerald, Shullman, Bailey, Richards, Swecker, Gold, Ormerod, & Weitzman, 1988) have generated a classification of types of behaviors between students and professors; these are listed from less serious to more serious and include:

1. gender harassment, or generalized sexual remarks and behavior.
2. seductive behavior, or inappropriate and offensive, but sanction-free, advances.
3. sexual bribery, or solicitation by promise of rewards.
4. threat of punishment, or use of coercion.
5. sexual imposition, or gross sexual advances or assault.

These classifications, developed by psychologists, are helpful, but it was up to the courts to decide where to draw the line between borderline acceptable and unacceptable practices. Two Supreme Court cases tried to clarify such questions. These cases, *Meritor Savings Bank v. Vinson* (1986) and *Harris v. Forklift Systems, Inc.* (1993), provided some clarification but left questions unanswered.

BOX 14-2

Gruber's Typology of Sexual Harassment

A. Verbal requests
   (More to less severe)

   1. Sexual bribery
   2. Sexual advances
   3. Relational advances
   4. Subtle pressures/advances

B. Verbal comments
   (More to less severe)

   1. Personal remarks
   2. Subjective objectification
   3. Sexual categorical remarks

C. Nonverbal displays
   (More to less severe)

   1. Sexual assault
   2. Sexual touching
   3. Sexual posturing
   4. Sexual materials

Source: Adapted from Gruber, 1992, pp. 451–452

SEXUAL HARASSMENT IN THE COURTS

As the EEOC guidelines (U.S. Equal Employment Opportunity Commission, 1980) were implemented, a number of appeals were sent to state and federal appellate courts, beginning in the 1980s. Some of these courts made rulings that were inconsistent with those of other courts, partly because of their interpretations of these guidelines. The specific wording of the guidelines is as follows:

> Unwelcome sexual advances, requests for sexual favors, and other verbal or physical conduct of a sexual nature constitute sexual harassment when: (1) submission to such conduct is made either explicitly or implicitly a term or condition of an individual's employment, (2) submission to or a rejection of such conduct by an individual is used as a basis for employment decisions affecting such individual, or (3) such conduct has the purpose or effect of unreasonably interfering with an individual's work performance or creating an intimidating, hostile, or offensive working environment. (1980, p. 74677)

Two Types of Sexual Harassment

The guidelines have been interpreted to distinguish between two types of sexual harassment, one more clear-cut than the other.

Quid Pro Quo Type

In the **quid pro quo** type, sexual demands are made in exchange for employment benefits. More broadly, such harassment involves an implicit or explicit bargain whereby the harasser promises a reward or threatens punishment, depending on the victim's response (Hotelling, 1991). An example: "Sleep with me or you'll get fired." In most cases, this type of sexual harassment—often manifested by explicit propositions or physical sexual actions—is relatively easy to recognize (McCandless & Sullivan, 1991). The term can also be applied to faculty-student relationships in which the promise of a higher grade (or the threat of a failing one) is the inducement to comply.

Hostile Workplace Environment

Overt sexual behavior or **bribery** is not required for sexual harassment to have occurred. If ridicule, insult, or intimidation are severe or pervasive enough to create an abusive atmosphere or to alter the working conditions of the employee, the situation meets the second criterion of sexual harassment, the presence of a **hostile workplace environment.** Under Title VII of the 1964 Civil Rights Act, it is illegal for employers to create or tolerate "an intimidating, hostile, or offensive working environment" by use of harassment. If, for example, pornographic pictures and sexually explicit language are frequent in the workplace, the environment may—in and of itself—be considered a harassing one.

Assessing the presence of this type is more challenging (McCandless & Sullivan, 1991). Is an act a well-intentioned compliment or the creation of a difficult working arrangement? How frequently must a coworker tell obscene jokes for a hostile work environment to be present? If the only woman on a work team is given the most dangerous tasks (or the most menial ones), is this a hostile work environment? As far back as 1986, the Supreme Court, in the case of *Meritor Savings Bank v. Vinson,* recognized that sexual harassment that creates a hostile work environment violates Title VII of the 1964 Civil Rights Act. (See Box 14-3 for a description of the facts of this case.) But in the years after that decision, lower courts differed in what criteria were used to establish a "hostile workplace environment"; for example, did the victim have to suffer "psychological damage"? And what should the standard be—the perspective of the victim or that of an outside observer? Because of these ambiguities, the Supreme Court agreed to take on a second case, *Harris v. Forklift Systems, Inc.,* in 1993.

The *Harris v. Forklift Systems, Inc.* Decision

Teresa Harris held a secure and rather well paying job as rental manager of Forklift Systems, Incorporated, in Nashville, Tennessee, but her boss (also the owner of the company) persisted in making demeaning and humiliating comments to her. At first, she tried to ignore the infuriating and sexist remarks, but that didn't work. When she confronted him about them, he promised to stop, but he didn't. One especially personal comment was the last straw; after working there for 2 years, Teresa Harris quit. Eventually, she sought compensation for her lost wages, claiming that her boss's behavior had created a "sexually hostile" workplace environment.

The EEOC passed the case to a federal magistrate judge, who ruled that the boss's behavior was not offensive enough to qualify as sexual harassment, even though the boss was characterized by the judge as "a vulgar man who demeans the female employees at his work-

place" (quoted by Plevan, 1993, p. 20). The judge noted that there was testimony that Ms. Harris and her husband had socialized with the boss and his wife; furthermore, other female employees were not as offended by the boss's behavior as Ms. Harris was. Perhaps most important in his decision was the conclusion that she was still able to act effectively in this environment and suffered no "serious psychological injury," a criterion that had been used in several courts.

The district court and the U.S. Court of Appeals for the Sixth District affirmed the judge's decision, so Ms. Harris appealed to the U.S. Supreme Court. Her attorneys had noted that an inconsistency existed among the decisions of several federal circuit courts; some courts had adopted a subjective approach focusing on the impact on the plaintiff of the alleged harasser's behavior. In contrast, others used an objective definition, asking whether a reasonable person would find the environment to be abusive. That is, some courts had required proof of **psychological injury,** while others had only required plaintiffs to meet variations of a **reasonable person standard,** meaning that a reasonable person would find the harassing behavior extremely offensive in a way that affected the conditions of employment.

The Supreme Court can agree to take a case because the issue at hand has led to conflicting decisions in different parts of the country. In the previously mentioned *Meritor Savings Bank v. Vinson* case, in 1986, the Supreme Court had already ruled that a "hostile work environment" could be a determinant of sexual harassment, but at that time, the Court said that the harassment had to be "sufficiently severe or pervasive to alter the conditions of [the victim's] employment and create an abusive working environment."

The Decision in the Case

The decision by the Supreme Court came uncharacteristically quickly—only 27 days after the oral arguments. Furthermore, the decision was a unanimous one, and it covered only six pages. Essentially, it favored Ms. Harris's appeal.

> ### BOX 14-3
> ### *Meritor Savings Bank v. Vinson*
>
> A vice president of the Meritor Savings Bank and manager of one of its branches, Sidney Taylor, had hired Mechelle Vinson as a teller. Four years later, the bank discharged her because it claimed she had used excessive amounts of sick leave. (By that time, she had been promoted to assistant branch manager.) Ms. Vinson filed a suit, claiming she had been sexually harassed by her boss (she claimed he had exposed himself and had fondled her in front of other employees), and that she had agreed to have sexual relations with him out of fear of losing her job. She estimated that they had sex 40 or 50 times. The bank responded by claiming that Ms. Vinson had voluntarily agreed to her boss's advances, and hence no grounds for sexual harassment were present. The district court had found for the bank, based on her "voluntary" acquiescence. After several intervening steps, the case was accepted for review by the Supreme Court, which in
>
> 1986 ruled unanimously that Title VII forbade not only quid pro quo type of sexual harassment but also situations in which harassment created an abusive work environment. The decision was written by Justice Rehnquist, who stated that "the correct inquiry is whether respondent by her conduct indicated that the alleged sexual advances were unwelcome, not whether her actual participation in sexual intercourse was involuntary."
>
> The decision was not, however, a complete victory for those in sympathy with women who were harassed in the workplace. At the trial, the bank had introduced evidence about Ms. Vinson's style of dress and personal fantasies in support of its rejoinder that the sexual activity was voluntary. The Supreme Court ruled that it was within the domain of the trial judge to decide whether such evidence was relevant or prejudicial to the case.

The outcome was to return the case to the lower court, which was instructed to examine the ruling and decide how much back pay, if any, Ms. Harris deserved. Several months later, Forklift Systems settled with Teresa Harris, paying her an undisclosed amount of back wages.

The decision favored Ms. Harris in the sense that the Court did not require a demonstration of "psychological injury" as long as the behavior was physically threatening or humiliating or if it "unreasonably interferes with an employee's work performance." Notable in Justice Sandra Day O'Connor's opinion was her use of the "reasonable person" standard; for example, she ruled out as sexual harassment "conduct that is not severe or pervasive enough to create an objectively hostile or abusive work environment—an environment that a reasonable person would find hostile or abusive." She ignored the traditional "reasonable man" usage but also was unwilling to go so far as to adopt the subjective "reasonable woman" standard.

The Reasonable Woman Standard

The **reasonable woman standard** was apparently first used in a Ninth Circuit Court case in 1991, *Ellison v. Brady*. In this case, Ms. Kerry

Ellison, an IRS agent, was pressured to go out on dates by Stanley Gray, a coworker she hardly knew. He wrote her a series of love letters, saying things like the following: "I cried over you last night and I'm totally drained today. I have never been in such constant term oil [*sic*] . . . I could not stand to feel your hatred for another day." (In another letter:) "I know you are worth knowing with or without sex. . . . Watching you, experiencing you . . . so far away. Admiring your style and elan. . . ." (quoted by McCandless and Sullivan, 1991, p. 18).

The Ninth Circuit Court decided to focus on the perspective of the victim; thus, it used a subjective definition. The circuit court explained that "if it examined only whether a 'reasonable person' would find the conduct harassing, it would run the risk of reinforcing the prevailing level of discrimination" (quoted in McCandless and Sullivan, 1991, p. 18.) In changing the focus, this circuit court decision reflected earlier psychological research that men and women may differ, with men more likely to see sexual harassment as "comparatively harmless amusement" (see Wiener, 1995). But these gender differences should not be overestimated. A meta-analysis of more than 90 comparisons (Blumenthal, 1998) concluded that gender differences in the perception of sexual harassment were relatively small, although they were consistent across age, culture, and professional status.

With regard to the letters sent to Ms. Ellison, the circuit court concluded that a "reasonable woman" could have had the same reactions that she had, namely fright and shock. Thus, the court held that the letters and the conduct may have been unlawful; it overruled the lower court's summary judgment against Ms. Ellison and sent the case back to the district court for a trial. (A **summary judgment** is a decision by a judge in favor of one side in a civil suit, based on the judge's conclusion that the evidence is so strong that a trial is not necessary.)

The focus on "victims" in the *Ellison v. Brady* decision has drawn attention and criticism. Rosen (1993a) noted that the decision used the terms *victim* and *woman* interchangeably, as in, "an understanding of the victim's view requires, among other things, an analysis of the different perspectives of men and women. Conduct that many men consider unobjectionable may offend many women" (quoted by Rosen, 1993a, p. 14).

The Shift in Focus from *"Victims"* to *"Reasonable Women"*

In contrast, in the *Harris v. Forklift* decision, the Supreme Court shifted the emphasis away from the feelings and subjective perceptions of the complainant. In doing so, it ignored some of the psychological research reviewed in an *amicus* brief submitted by the American Psychological Association, although it was responsive to the other major input from the APA. (See Box 14-4 for details.)

Concerns about and Criticisms of the Decision

The Supreme Court's decision in the *Harris v. Forklift* case did not put to rest the issue of what constitutes sexual harassment. Exactly what makes up a "hostile environment" was not precisely specified (Plevan, 1993). Justice O'Connor's opinion painted only broad limits; sexual harassment goes beyond isolated jokes and comments—a "mere offensive utterance" is not enough—and a hostile environment emerges before the harassing conduct leads to a nervous breakdown. To assess the presence of a hostile work environment, the Court relied on its frequent focus on the "totality of the circumstances"; that is, the context in which the behavior occurs is important.

Critics, such as John Leo (1993), have focused their concern on incidents that stretch the standard, such as the banning of photos of women in scanty swimsuits. In 1993, a graduate student at a midwestern university was forced to remove from his desk a photograph of his bikini-

---

BOX 14-4

The APA Brief in the Case of *Harris v. Forklift*

The American Psychological Association was one of the 12 organizations to file an *amicus curiae* brief regarding the *Harris v. Forklift* case; in its brief, social science findings were used to argue that plaintiffs should not have to prove psychological damage to win sexual harassment suits. Having to prove psychological injuries places emphasis on the victim and his or her "ability to withstand harassment," instead of placing it on the conduct of the alleged harasser, argued the brief, which noted that plaintiffs usually suffered other losses long before they could prove that they had been psychologically hurt.

The APA brief also reviewed empirical studies on differences in women's and men's perceptions of what is and is not sexual harassment. It concluded that men were more tolerant of sexual harassment than were women, and women were more likely than men to label sexually aggressive behavior at work as harassment. Other studies cited in the brief concluded that men were much more likely to attribute the causes of harassing behavior to characteristics of the victims, in contrast to women, who were more likely to attribute them to characteristics of the perpetrator.

clad wife, because two other students reported it as a violation of the university's policies (Cloud, 1998). Leo has proposed that "what we need from the courts is a definition of 'hostile environment' that focuses sharply on harassment and harm and veers away from equating harassment with 'offensiveness'" (Leo, 1993, p. 20).

Another concern is the possible restriction on free speech (Rosen, 1993a, 1993b). To some observers, the "hostile environment" test represents "a radical exception to the First Amendment axiom that speech cannot be punished merely because it is offensive" (Rosen, 1993a, p. 12). Let us say that an employer uses profane language; he claims that his words are merely expletives and protected as free speech. Should he be punished? Should the man who directs a wolf whistle at a woman on the street? Rosen (1993a) went farther, asking, Will gender-based job titles, such as "draftsman" or "foreman," become actionable as "sexually suggestive" material? (See an article by Eugene Volokh, 1992, for a review of the free-speech issue; Volokh, a law professor, has been quoted as saying that the liberal court decisions have had a "chilling effect" on the expression of free speech at work; Cloud, 1998, p. 53).

A third concern asks about the image of women reflected in the opinion. Does it attempt to shield women and reflect a stereotype of them as needing special protection from words and images? Rosen (1993a) concluded, "The generalization that women are more likely to be offended by scatology than men also seems like the sort of romantic paternalism that Title VII was designed to erase" (p. 12). Rosen cited the statement of a female attorney at a New York City law firm, someone who specialized in employment law, who was concerned that the opinion leaves the impression that women are not as tough as men in the workplace: "While at a quick glance the idea of a reasonable-woman standard may seem quite appealing and beneficial to women, such a standard will not, in the long run, serve to promote equality for women. The adoption of this standard unfortunately

serves to affirm a long-term popular misconception—that women and men think and react differently" (Rosen, 1993a, p. 13).

Post-*Forklift* Decisions

In what was apparently the first post-*Forklift* harassment case to be decided, the Seventh Circuit Court of Appeals affirmed a summary judgment ruling in favor of the employer in a case in which a telephone company employee alleged that her supervisor had sexually harassed her (*Saxton v. American Telephone and Telegraph Co.,* 1993). Despite acknowledging that the boss's conduct was "inappropriate and unprofessional" and that the conduct of the AT&T supervisor had a sufficiently adverse effect on the employee, Judge Ilana Diamond Rovner noted that the plaintiff's Title VII claim still failed because "the objective prong" of the Supreme Court's inquiry—whether reasonable others would find the work environment hostile or abusive—was not satisfied. It was not "so serious or pervasive that it created a hostile work environment within the meaning of Title VII."

Although this was not the only decision to favor the defendant, other post-*Forklift* decisions in the Fourth, Sixth, and Eighth Circuit Courts favored plaintiffs, with the courts upholding claims of a hostile environment. The review by Sanders and Stanley (1994) provided brief summaries of all these cases, but these reviewers doubted that we may extract some principles about the differences in decisions favoring the plaintiff and the defendant.

PSYCHOLOGY'S CONTRIBUTIONS TO UNDERSTANDING AND AMELIORATING SEXUAL HARASSMENT

Although ambiguities and disagreements remain, the past decade also saw progress in understanding the nature of sexual harassment. Psychological analyses of cases and psychological research have contributed to this understanding; this section reviews several ways in which forensic psychologists can extend their contributions.

Developing Models for Causes of Sexual Harassment and for Attributions of Causality

What causes sexual harassment to occur? Do people differ in their explanations of the causes when a complaint of sexual harassment is filed? In answer to the first question, Pryor, Giedd, and Williams (1995; Pryor, 1987) employed the classic Lewinian model of social behavior—it is a function of both the person and the environment. Sexual harassment is thus social behavior that some people do some of the time. Specifically, certain people may possess proclivities to sexually harass others, but the social norms of the organization may either encourage or discourage the expression of harassment. For example, the incidence is higher in male-dominated workplaces (Gutek, 1985); these workplaces can be environments that make one's gender more salient (Deaux, 1995).

With regard to situational factors, local social norms influence the incidence rate; in some organizations, managers or local work-group leaders may condone such behavior, so that potential harassers may perceive that they are free to do so (Gutek, 1985). For example, among military personnel, women reported being sexually harassed more often in those units in which the commanding officers were perceived as encouraging sexual harassment (Pryor, LaVite, & Stoller, 1993). And it was not only the women who felt their commanders were insensitive; independent measures of the local social norms showed the same relationship between women's experiences and *others'* perceptions of management's attitudes about sexual harassment.

With regard to the second determinant in Pryor's theory, or within-the-person factors, Pryor elaborated on a methodological procedure

first used by Malamuth (1981) to study rape proclivities. Men were asked to imagine themselves in a series of scenarios in which they have power over an attractive woman. For example,

> one scenario depicts an interaction between a male college professor and a female student who is seeking to raise her grade in a class. Male subjects are asked to rate the likelihood of their performing an act of quid pro quo sexual harassment in each scenario, given that they could do so with impunity. In the professor/student scenario, for example, how likely is it that the subject would raise the student's grade in exchange for sexual favors, given that his behavior would go unpunished? (Pryor et al., 1995, p. 74)

The scale developed by Pryor, the Likelihood to Sexually Harass scale (LSH), has high reliability. Based on administration of this instrument and other self-report measures to groups of college men, Pryor drew the following conclusions about those men who report they would be likely to engage in sexual harassment:

1. They tend to believe common myths about rape, and they are more sexually aggressive in general.
2. They describe themselves as stereotypically male; they believe men should be mentally, emotionally, and physically self-reliant; they avoid stereotypically feminine occupations and activities. In summary, they view themselves as hypermasculine.
3. They think of women as sex objects, and they can readily provide justifications for actions that others would call sexual harassment. But they are also aware of the situational constraints on such behavior (Pryor et al., 1995).

In an ingenious series of studies, Pryor and his colleagues demonstrated that high-scoring LSH men did harass women "when they found themselves in a situation socially engineered such that harassing behavior was convenient and not conspicuous" (Pryor et al., 1995, pp. 80–81).

Furthermore, they tended to engage in such behaviors only when local norms encouraged or allowed such behavior.

When it comes to attributions of the cause of specific acts of harassment, a number of factors have been identified, including how flagrant the act was, how frequently it was done, and how the other person responded (Thomann & Wiener, 1987). These factors are useful in determining whether a complaint of sexual harassment will receive recognition and compensation in the courts (discussed later in this chapter).

Distinguishing Between Female and Male Victims

Box 14-1 described the *Oncale v. Sundowner Offshore Services* (1998) case, dealing with a male harassment victim. The phenomenon of a supervisor or coworker provoking a person of the same gender, referred to as **same-sex sexual harassment,** is beginning to be studied by psychologists. Several conclusions have emerged from these investigations:

1. When men report being victims of sexual harassment, the perpetrator is much more likely to be of the same sex, in contrast to complaints by women, who most often list a person of the other sex as the perpetrator. Self-report surveys have found that 40% to 50% of complaints by males report that the harassment is by another male, while only 2% of the complaints by women cite another woman (Pryor & Whalen, 1997; Waldo, Berdahl, & Fitzgerald, 1998).
2. Men and women report experiencing different types of sexual harassment. Almost all men reported crude or offensive behaviors, such as jokes or obscene gestures, as the most frequent type of offense (Bastian, Lancaster, & Reyst, 1996; Magley, Waldo, Drasgow, & Fitzgerald, 1998; cited by Foote & Goodman-Delahunty, 1999). Fewer than 2% reported sexual concern. While females were more likely to report conduct fulfilling

a quid pro quo claim, men more often reported conduct reflecting a hostile work environment.
3. The emotional impact of the harassment on men depends upon many factors, including the setting and the type of harassment. Previously, we noted that women interpret a wider range of behaviors as sexual harassment. Similarly, Foote and Goodman-Delahunty concluded that "from one perspective, men may actually experience sexual harassment as less offensive than do women" (1999, p. 133). They wrote,

> First, the harassment may be considered a more acceptable part of male culture; it is an element of men's experience as early as grade school. Second, most of the harassment experienced by men is verbal in nature, rather than sexual touching or coercive sexual behavior. . . . This "guy talk" is often derisive of women as well as men . . . and, although it disparages both genders, it enforces stereotypical male roles and behaviors. (Foote & Goodman-Delahunty, 1999, p. 133)

Measuring Beliefs

Equally important in understanding the nature of harassment is the assessment of beliefs about what does and does not constitute sexual harassment. Two measures have been developed—the Tolerance for Sexual Harassment Inventory (Lott, Reilly, & Howard, 1982) and the Beliefs About Sexual Harassment Scale (Perot, Brooks, & Gersh, 1992)—but little research has been done using them. As noted earlier, assumptions that men and women differ in their definition of harassment have been qualified in the sense that egregious cases lead the vast majority of both women *and* men to label them as harassing; gender differences emerge with respect to evaluating less clear-cut actions. As Gutek and O'Connor (1995) noted, "When the harassment is either severe or the behavior is so benign that it is clearly not harassment, the perceptual gap between the two sexes closes" (p. 156).

Predicting the Outcome of Complaints

To bring a complaint of sexual harassment against a supervisor is not easy. Is there a way to predict whether complainants who do so will be successful? Yes. Terpstra and Baker (1988, 1992), after examining a number of cases in two settings, have identified several relevant factors. First, they examined 81 sexual harassment cases filed with the Illinois State Equal Employment Opportunity Commission over a 2-year period to determine what influenced their outcome. About 30% of these cases were settled in favor of the complainant. The researchers identified nine characteristics that *might have influenced* the EEOC's decisions:

1. the perceived seriousness of the harassment behavior reported.
2. the frequency of the harassment
3. the status of the harasser (coworker, immediate supervisor, or higher-up).
4. the severity of the job-related consequences of the harassment.
5. whether the complainant had witnesses to support the charges.
6. whether the complainant had documents to support the charges.
7. the nature of management's reasons for the reported adverse employment-related consequences.
8. whether the complainant had notified management of the harassment prior to filing charges.
9. whether the employing organization had taken investigative or remedial action when notified of the problem.

Only three of these characteristics were significantly related to EEOC decisions; the sexual harassment charges were more likely to have been resolved in favor of the complainant if the harassment behaviors were serious, or if the complainant had witnesses to support the charges, or if the complainant had given notice to management prior to filing formal charges (Terpstra & Baker, 1988).

This type of analysis was repeated by the same researchers (Terpstra & Baker, 1992) for 133 cases that led to court decisions between 1974 and 1989. Of these cases, 38% were decided in favor of the complainants—higher than the 31% of the EEOC cases—even though the complainants' cases were not as strong as those heard by the state EEOC. In these cases, five of the nine aspects distinguished between winning and losing. Complainants were more likely to win their cases if (1) the harassment was severe, (2) witnesses supported their cases, (3) documents supported their cases, (4) they had given notice to management prior to filing charges, or (5) their organization took no action.

If a complainant had none of these factors in her or his favor, the odds of winning the case were less than 1%; if all five, almost 100%. Specific odds for each of the five: factor 1, 40%; factor 2, 48%; factor 3, 44%; factor 4, 49%; factor 5, 53%.

Restructuring the Workplace

As Pryor's analysis (discussed earlier) suggested, sexual harassment involves not just an individual's attitudes and beliefs but also practices in the organization, whether it is a factory, an office, or an academic department (Riger, 1991). For example, until recently, universities—as well as businesses—had no policies condemning or punishing sexual harassment.

Psychologists have played a role in designing and administering training programs that seek to educate workers about the meaning of sexual harassment. One goal of such programs is to encourage a greater percentage of victims to report the harassment. Barak (1992) suggested a two-phase workshop:

> Intensive, cognitive-behavioral workshops designed to provide women with skills to combat [sexual harassment] might be divided into two phases. The first phase could develop their awareness of the . . . phenomenon, including its process, causes, and typical consequences. By means of brief lectures, exercises, case-study simulations, and video modeling, participants could be taught to identify, detect, understand, and analyze the many forms of sexual harassment and the

ways in which they typically unfold. The second phase could teach practical coping skills. Again, with the help of a range of teaching techniques, such as live simulations and video demonstrations, participants could be taught, among other things, the multiple response options appropriate to various forms of sexual harassment, as well as how to make use of the applicable laws and grievance procedures. (p. 818)

All well and good. But why not put our emphasis on restructuring the workplace so that sexual harassment is less likely to occur, rather than dealing with ways to respond to it? A first step would be to educate members of both genders about discrepancies in what they consider sexual harassment, as Riger (1991) suggested.

SUMMARY

Awareness of the nature and frequency of sexual harassment increased during the 1990s, because of several highly publicized cases (including Anita Hill's claims about Clarence Thomas, the Tailhook convention of naval officers, and Paula Jones's suit against President Clinton). Yet the term is not fully understood, and one of the contributions of psychology is the analysis of its meaning for different people, especially as these mesh or conflict with the courts' definition of sexual harassment.

The courts have identified two types of sexual harassment, called "quid pro quo" and hostile workplace harassment. In the quid pro quo type, demands are made upon an employee that she or he provide sexual favors to the boss or employer, with threats of being fired if the employee fails to comply (or promises of increased benefits if the employee does comply). In school settings, an instructor's offer of a better grade for a student who complies with requests/demands for sexual favors reflects this type of sexual harassment.

The second type, sexual harassment emerging from a hostile workplace environment, is sometimes less clearly identified. It has been defined as the creation of "an intimidating, hos-

tile, or offensive working environment" by the use of harassment.

In the decision of *Harris v. Forklift Systems, Inc.* (1993), the U.S. Supreme Court ruled that the actions of a harasser do not have to produce the extreme effect of causing "psychological injury" to an employee to qualify as sexual harassment, as long as the behavior "unreasonably interferes with an employee's work performance." This decision was consistent with portions of the *amicus* brief submitted by the American Psychological Association.

Forensic psychologists can contribute to a better understanding of the nature of sexual harassment and to a reduction in its appearance by assessing beliefs about what does and does not constitute sexual harassment, developing models to predict whether harassment will occur, and determining the outcome of specific complaints. Psychologists have played a role in designing and administering training programs that seek to educate workers about the meaning of sexual harassment.

KEY TERMS

bribery
hostile workplace environment
psychological injury
quid pro quo
reasonable person standard
reasonable woman standard
same-sex sexual harassment
sexual harassment
subtle pressures/advances
summary judgment
Title VII of the 1964 Civil Rights Act

INFOTRAC® COLLEGE EDITION

InfoTrac College Edition is a FREE, powerful, online learning resource, consisting of full-text articles from thousands of journals and periodicals.

With each new copy of *Forensic Psychology*, Second Edition, you receive 4 months of free access to the InfoTrac College Edition database. By doing a simple keyword search (try using the Key Terms in the list above), you can quickly generate a list of relevant articles from thousands of possibilities and can select articles to read, explore, and print for reference or further study. InfoTrac College Edition's continuously updated collection of articles can be useful for doing reading and writing assignments that reach beyond the pages of this text!

SUGGESTED READINGS

Borgida, E., & Fiske, S. T. (Eds.). (1995). Gender stereotyping, sexual harassment, and the law. *Journal of Social Issues, 51*(1), 1–207.

A special issue of the *Journal of Social Issues* that includes articles on lay definitions of sexual harassment, models for predicting harassment, and the reasonable woman standard. Highly recommended.

Foote, W. E., & Goodman-Delahunty, J. (1999). Same-sex harassment: Implications of the *Oncale* decision for forensic evaluation of plaintiffs. *Behavioral Sciences and the Law, 17,* 123–139.

A recent review of research on the frequency and types of same-sex sexual harassment.

Mayer, J., & Abramson, J. (1994). *Strange justice: The selling of Clarence Thomas.* Boston: Houghton-Mifflin.

Of the several books about Justice Clarence Thomas's confirmation hearing and the claims of sexual harassment by Professor Anita Hill, this is probably the most thoroughly researched.

Pryor, J. B., Giedd, J. L., & Williams, K. B. (1995). A social psychological model for predicting harassment. *Journal of Social Issues, 51*(1), 69–84.

An article presenting a person–situation model of sexual harassment.

Wekesser, C., Swisher, K. L., & Pierce, C. (Eds.). (1992). *Sexual harassment.* San Diego: Greenhaven Press.

A collection of reprinted articles about the extent of sexual harassment, its causes, and its possible solutions.

15

Death Penalty Trials
and Appeals

Early in 1992, Ricky Ray Rector was on death row in Arkansas, scheduled for execution. Rector had killed a police officer while at his mother's house; he then turned his gun on himself, shot himself in the head, damaged his brain, but survived. Neuropsychologists estimated his resultant mental functioning as that of a 5-year-old.

Should someone who cannot understand the consequences of the punishment be executed? In early 1992, Bill Clinton, the Governor of Arkansas, was campaigning for the Democratic Party's nomination for president. He flew home to Arkansas in time to oversee the execution. As Rector was escorted to his execution, he told his guards—without a trace of irony—to say hello to Governor Clinton, whom he had just seen on television. He also asked them to save him a slice of pecan pie, which he intended to eat upon his return (Caddell & Cooper, 1998).

WHY DO FORENSIC PSYCHOLOGISTS GET INVOLVED IN DEATH PENALTY CASES?

The United States is one of the few countries (along with China, Iran, Libya, the Philippines, and a mere handful of others) still to have the death penalty; Canada and all the countries of Western Europe have abolished it. In the United States, since 1976 when the death penalty was reinstituted, 890 people had been executed as of January 2004, and over 3,500 currently line the death rows of the 38 states that permit the ultimate penalty. Also, a person can be executed if convicted of certain federal crimes in the United States; as of January 2004, there were 28 inmates on federal death row, after two executions in 2001 (Timothy McVeigh being one of those), and one in 2003. The U.S. military has its own death penalty statute; seven men are on military death row, although no executions have been carried out since 1961.

Attitudes toward or against the death penalty are often strongly held. Psychologists who strive toward the general abolition of the death penalty or toward exoneration or clemency in a specific case do so out of values of the importance of individual life and of justice, but these same values are often advocated by those who see justification in the use of the death penalty (see, e.g., Van den Haag, 1975). The intensity of feelings by proponents for each position is reflected in the ongoing controversy over the appeal by Mumia Abu-Jamal (see Box 15-1). It is worth noting that the American Psychological Association, in August 2001, unanimously passed a resolution that called for the suspension of the death penalty unless problems with its implementation could be addressed (see Box 15-2 for the text of the resolution).

ROLES FOR FORENSIC PSYCHOLOGISTS

Some psychologists opposed to the death penalty choose not to be involved as consultants or expert witnesses in cases in which the death sentence is a possibility. But those who do participate may play several roles.

An Outline of the Process and Possible Roles

These roles, in chronological order, are the following:

1. Prior to the trial, a psychologist may be asked to assess the competency to stand trial (i.e., the defendant's ability to assist in his or her defense), if the judge orders such an evaluation. (Chapter 5 describes this procedure.)

2. If the crime has been highly publicized, the forensic psychologist may be hired to complete a survey of knowledge and bias in the local community, as part of a request for a change of venue (see chapter 12).

3. If the judge rules that the defendant is competent to stand trial, and if the prosecutors

BOX 15-1

The Case of Mumia Abu-Jamal

In 1982, Mumia Abu-Jamal, an outspoken, charismatic African American journalist, was convicted of killing a White police officer, Daniel Faulkner, a few blocks from City Hall in Philadelphia. He was sentenced to death.

Since his conviction over two decades ago, the supporters of Abu-Jamal, who reflect a cross section of races and include a number of celebrities (Danny Glover, William Styron, Whoopie Goldberg), have protested his conviction and sentence, claiming that he is a political prisoner punished for his criticisms of the government. They have sponsored protests and financed full-page advertisements in prominent newspapers. Jesse Jackson has spoken in Abu-Jamal's behalf, as a part of his general opposition to the death penalty. Other supporters have claimed that his trial was a sham (with a racially unrepresentative jury, a biased judge, and an unprepared, court-appointed defense attorney) and that Abu-Jamal was persecuted because he was an outspoken critic of police brutality, he had been a member of the Black Panther party, and he had supported the radical group MOVE, which had several bitter run-ins with the Philadelphia police (Terry, 1995).

What happened the night of December 9, 1981, is, of course, contested, and it remains murky. According to the authorities, Officer Faulkner around 4:00 a.m. stopped a car driven by Abu-Jamal's brother, William Cook, for driving the wrong way on a one-way street in downtown Philadelphia. Cook began to resist when the police officer attempted to handcuff him. Abu-Jamal, moonlighting as a cab driver, came upon the scene, and—according to the authorities (Abraham, 1995)—shot Faulkner in the back. The police officer

then shot Abu-Jamal in the chest before collapsing; Abu-Jamal then approached the prostrate body of the police officer and shot him four times between the eyes. He then sat down on the curb, four feet from Faulkner; when other police arrived, almost immediately, they found a gun, registered in Abu-Jamal's name, loaded with five spent cartridge cases of the caliber and brand of bullet that killed the officer (Abraham, 1995). However, the bullets were too misshapen for ballistics experts to determine if they came from Abu-Jamal's pistol.

In prison, Abu-Jamal has continued to work as a journalist, documenting conditions on death row and publishing a book and articles in magazines and a law review. He has become a global cause célèbre (see *www.freemumia.org*). He was scheduled to be executed on August 17, 1995, but 10 days before that, the judge who had sentenced him granted him an indefinite stay of execution after a 4-week-long hearing in a courtroom sharply divided, with Abu-Jamal's supporters on one side screaming "Free Mumia," and Faulkner's widow and other relatives and members of the Fraternal Order of Police on the other, silently enraged.

The Pennsylvania Supreme Court held a hearing in 1996 to consider new evidence, but in 1998 turned down the appeal for a new trial. In 2003, the Pennsylvania Supreme Court again turned down a postconviction review of Abu-Jamal's trial and sentence (*Commonwealth v. Abu-Jamal*, 833 A.2d 719 (2003)). In March 2004, Abu-Jamal's attorney filed an appeal with the United States Supreme Court, but there has been no decision as yet.

---

announce that they will seek the death penalty (making it a **capital case**), the jury selection includes what is called a **death-qualification procedure.** Prior to the trial, prospective jurors are asked if they are so opposed to capital punishment that they would be unable to vote for the death penalty regardless of the facts and circumstances of the case. As in any trial, forensic psychologists can serve as trial consultants and advise defense attorneys on the **theory of the case.** For example, are there findings that would justify the use of insanity as a defense?

4. If the defendant is found guilty in this first phase (or **guilt-determination phase**) of what is called a **bifurcated trial,** the second phase, or **sentencing phase,** begins. The purpose of the second phase is to decide the appropriate punishment (states differ as to whether the judge determines the sentence, the jury does, or the jury makes a recommendation to the judge). Not all capital cases in which the defendant is found guilty lead to death sentences; in fact, this penalty is given in only about 20% of such cases. If the jury does the sentencing, the jurors are asked to consider whether and

BOX 15-2
APA Resolution on the Death Penalty (August 2001)

WHEREAS recent empirical research reviewing all death penalty cases in the United States concluded that two thirds of the death penalty cases from 1973 to 1995 were overturned on appeal with the most common reasons cited as incompetent counsel, inadequate investigative services, or the police and prosecutors withholding exculpatory evidence (Liebman, Fagan, & West, 2000); and

WHEREAS the recent application of DNA technology has resulted in, as of June 2000, 62 post-conviction determinations of actual innocence, with eight of these having been for persons sentenced to death at trial (Scheck, Neufeld, & Dwyer, 2000; Wells, Malpass, Lindsay, Fisher, Turtle, & Fulero, 2000); and

WHEREAS research on the process of qualifying jurors for service on death penalty cases shows that jurors who survive the qualification process ("death-qualified jurors") are more conviction-prone than jurors who have reservations about the death penalty and are therefore disqualified from service (Bersoff, 1987; Cowan, Thompson & Ellsworth, 1984; Ellsworth, 1988; Bersoff & Ogden, 1987; Haney, 1984); and

WHEREAS recent social science research reveals strong inconsistencies in prosecutors' decisions to seek the death penalty in particular cases, based on factors other than the severity of the crime. The "prosecutor is more likely to ask for a death sentence when the victim is European-American, of high social status, a stranger to the offender, and when counsel is appointed" (Beck & Shumsky, 1997, p. 534); and

WHEREAS race and ethnicity have been shown to affect the likelihood of being charged with a capital crime by prosecutors (e.g., Beck & Shumsky, 1997; Bowers, 1983; Paternoster, 1991; Paternoster & Kazyaka, 1988; Sorensen & Wallace, 1995) and therefore of being sentenced to die by the jury. Those who kill European-American victims are more likely to receive the death penalty, even after differences such as the heinousness of the crime, prior convictions, and the relationship between the victim and the perpetrator are considered. This is especially true for African-Americans (e.g., Keil & Vito, 1995; Thomson, 1997) and Hispanic-Americans who kill European-Americans (Thomson, 1997); and

WHEREAS psychological research consistently demonstrates that juries often misunderstand the concept of mitigation and its intended application (e.g., Haney & Lynch, 1994, 1997; Wiener, Pritchard, & Weston, 1995; Wiener, Hurt, Thomas, Sadler, Bauer, & Sargent, 1998), so that mitigation factors, e.g., the defendant's previous life circumstances, mental and emotional difficulties and age, have little or no relation to penalty phase verdicts (Beck & Shumsky, 1997; Costanzo & Costanzo, 1994); and

WHEREAS death penalty prosecutions may involve persons with serious mental illness or mental retardation. Procedural problems, such as assessing competency, take on particular importance in cases where the death penalty is applied to such populations (Skeem, Golding, Berge, & Cohn, 1998; Rosenfeld & Wall, 1988; Hoge, Poythress, Bonnie, Monahan, Eisenberg, & Feucht-Haviar, 1997; Cooper & Grisso, 1997); and

WHEREAS death penalty prosecutions may involve persons under 18 (sometimes as young as 14). Procedural problems, such as assessing competency, take on particular importance in cases where the death penalty is applied to juveniles (Grisso & Schwartz, 2000; Lewis et al., 1988); and

WHEREAS capital punishment appears statistically neither to exert a deterrent effect (e.g., Bailey, 1983, 1990; Bailey & Peterson, 1994; Cheatwood, 1993; Costanzo, 1997; Decker & Kohfeld, 1984; Radelet & Akers, 1996; Stack, 1993) nor save a significant number of lives through the prevention of repeat offenses (Vito, Koester, & Wilson, 1991; Vito, Wilson, & Latessa, 1991). Further, research shows that the murder rate increases just after state-sanctioned executions (Bowers, 1988; Costanzo, 1998; Phillips, 1983; Phillips & Hensley, 1984);

THEREFORE, BE IT RESOLVED, that the American Psychological Association: Calls upon each jurisdiction in the United States that imposes capital punishment not to carry out the death penalty until the jurisdiction implements policies and procedures that can be shown through psychological and other social science research to ameliorate the deficiencies identified above.

References

Bailey, W. C. (1990). Murder, capital punishment, and television execution publicity and homicide rates. *American Sociological Review, 55,* 628–633.

Bailey, W. C. (1983). Disaggregation in deterrence and death penalty research: The case of murder in Chicago. *Journal of Criminal Law and Criminology, 74*(3), 827–859.

Bailey, W. C., & Peterson, R. D. (1994). Murder, capital punishment and deterrence: A review of the evidence and an examination of police killings. *Journal of Social Issues, 50*(2), 53–74.

Beck, J. C., & Shumsky, R. (1997). A comparison of retained and appointed counsel in cases of capital murder. *Law and Human Behavior, 21*(5), 525–538.

Bersoff, D. N. (1987). Social science data and the Supreme Court: Lockhart as a case in point. *American Psychologist, 42*(1), 52–58.

Bersoff, D. N., & Ogden, D. W. (1987). In the Supreme Court of the United States *Lockhart v. McCree: Amicus curiae* brief for the American Psychological Association. *American Psychologist, 42*(1), 59–68.

Bowers, W. J. (1983). The pervasiveness of arbitrariness and discrimination under post-*Furman* capital statutes. *Journal of Criminal Law and Criminology, 74*(2), 1067–1100.

Bowers, W. J. (1988). The effect of execution is brutalization, not deterrence. In K. C. Haas and J. A. Inciardi (Eds.), *Challenging capital punishment: Legal and social science approaches* (pp. 49–89). Thousand Oaks, CA: Sage.

Cheatwood, D. (1993). Capital punishment and the deterrence of violent crime in comparable countries. *Criminal Justice Review, 18*(2), 165–181.

Cooper, D. K., & Grisso, T. (1997). Five-year research update (1991–1995): Evaluations for competence to stand trial. *Behavioral Sciences and the Law, 15*(3), 347–364.

Costanzo, M. (1997). *Just revenge: Costs and consequences of the death penalty.* New York: St. Martin's Press.

Costanzo, S., & Costanzo, M. (1994). Life or death decisions: An analysis of capital jury decision-making under the special issues framework. *Law and Human Behavior, 18,* 151–170.

Cowan, C. L. Thompson, W. C., & Ellsworth, P. C. (1984). The effects of death qualification on jurors' predisposition to convict and on the quality of deliberation. *Law and Human Behavior, 8,* 53–80.

Decker, S. H., & Kohfeld, C. W. (1984). A deterrence study of the death penalty in Illinois, 1933–1980. *Journal of Criminal Justice, 12,* 367–377.

Ellsworth, P. C. (1988). Unpleasant facts: The Supreme Court's response to empirical research on capital punishment. In K. C. Haas and J. A. Inciardi (Eds.), *Challenging capital punishment: Legal and social science approaches* (pp. 177–211). Newbury Park, CA: Sage.

Grisso, T., & Schwartz, R. G. (Eds.). (2000). *Youth on trial: A developmental perspective on juvenile justice.* Chicago: University of Chicago Press.

Haney, C. (Ed.). (1984). Death qualification [Special issue]. *Law and Human Behavior, 8*(1&2).

Haney, C., & Lynch, M. (1997). Clarifying life and death matters: An analysis of instructional comprehension and penalty phase closing arguments. *Law and Human Behavior, 21*(6), 575–595.

Haney, C., & Lynch, M. (1994). Comprehending life and death matters: A preliminary study of California's capital penalty instructions. *Law and Human Behavior, 18,* 411–436.

Hoge, S. K., Poythress, N., Bonnie, R. J., Monahan, J., Eisenberg, M., & Feucht-Haviar, T. (1997). The MacArthur adjudicative competence study: Diagnosis, psychopathology, and competence-related abilities. *Behavioral Sciences and the Law, 15*(3), 329–345.

Keil, T. J., & Vito, G. F. (1995). Race and the death penalty in Kentucky murder trials: 1976–1991. *American Journal of Criminal Justice, 20*(1), 17–36.

Lewis, D. O., Pincus, J. H., Bard B., Richardson, E., Princher, L. S., Feldman, M., & Yeager, C. (1988). Neuropsychiatric, psychoeducational, and family characteristics of 14 juveniles condemned to death in the United States. *American Journal of Psychiatry, 145*(5), 584–589.

Liebman, J. S., Fagan, J., & West, V. (2000). A broken system: Error rates in capital cases, 1973–1995. [On-line]. Available: www.TheJusticeProject.org.

Paternoster, R., & Kazyaka, A. (1988). Racial considerations in capital punishment: The failure of evenhanded justice. In K. C. Haas & J. A. Inciardi (Eds.), *Challenging capital punishment: Legal and social science approaches* (pp. 113–148). Newbury Park, CA: Sage.

Paternoster, R. (1991). Prosecutorial discretion and capital sentencing in North and South Carolina. In R. M. Bohm (Ed.), *The death penalty in America: Current research* (pp. 39–52). Cincinnati, OH: Anderson.

Phillips, D. P. (1983). The impact of mass media violence in U.S. homicides. *American Sociological Review, 48,* 560–568.

Phillips, D. P., & Hensley, J. E. (1984). When violence is rewarded or punished: The impact of mass media stories on homicide. *Journal of Communication, 34,* 101–116.

Radelet, M. L., & Akers, R. L. (1996). Deterrence and the death penalty: The views of the experts. *Journal of Criminal Law and Criminology, 87,* 1–16.

Rosenfeld, B., & Wall, A. (1998). Psychopathology and competence to stand trial. *Criminal Justice and Behavior, 25*(4), 443–462.

Scheck, B., Neufeld, P., & Dwyer, W. (2000). *Actual innocence.* New York: Harper.

Skeem, J. L., Golding, S. L., Berge, G., & Cohn, N. B. (1998). Logic and reliability of evaluations of competence to stand trial. *Law and Human Behavior, 22*(5), 519–547.

Sorensen, J. R., & Wallace, D. H. (1995). Capital punishment in Missouri: Examining the issue of racial disparity. *Behavioral Sciences and the Law, 13*(1), 61–81.

continued

continued

Stack, S. (1993). Execution publicity and homicide in Georgia. *American Journal of Criminal Justice, 18*(1), 25–39.

Thomson, E. (1997). Research note: Discrimination and the death penalty in Arizona. *Criminal Justice Review, 22*(1), 65–76.

Vito, G. F., Koester, P., & Wilson, D. G. (1991). Return of the dead: An update of the status of *Furman*-commuted death row inmates. In R. M. Bohm (Ed.), *The death penalty in America: Current research* (pp. 89–99). Cincinnati, OH: Anderson.

Vito, G. F., Wilson, D. G., & Latessa, E. J. (1991). Comparison of the dead: Attributes and outcomes of *Furman*-commuted death row inmates in Kentucky and Ohio. In R. M. Bohm (Ed.), *The death penalty in America: Current research* (pp. 101–111). Cincinnati, OH: Anderson.

Wells, G., Malpass, R., Lindsay, R., Fisher, R., Turtle, J., & Fulero, S. (2000). From the lab to the police station: A successful application of eyewitness research. *American Psychologist, 55,* 581–594.

Wiener, R., Hurt, L., Thomas, S., Sadler, M., Bauer, C., & Sargent, T. (1998). The role of declarative and procedural knowledge in capital murder cases. *Journal of Applied Social Psychology, 28,* 124–144.

Wiener, R., Pritchard, C., & Weston, M. (1995). Comprehensibility of approved jury instructions in capital cases. *Journal of Applied Psychology, 80,* 455–467.

how many **aggravating** and **mitigating factors** were present; generally, the jury has to unanimously agree that one or more aggravating circumstances were present, making the crime more heinous than usual, in order to give a death sentence. In some jurisdictions, these aggravating circumstances are specified; they are not the same in all jurisdictions, but some typical aggravating factors include:

a. murder of a law-enforcement official (a police officer, a judge, even—in some jurisdictions—a juror).
b. murder after kidnapping.
c. heinous murder; torture; "depravity of mind."
d. the defendant is dangerous or a risk to others.
e. history of violence.
f. murder for hire.
g. murder of two or more people.

Mitigating factors are those that temper or moderate the punishment; if specified, they may include the following characteristics of the defendant as well as other factors:

a. no significant prior criminal record.
b. youth of the defendant.

c. duress, coercion, or domination by another.
d. extreme emotion.
e. limited understanding of the consequences of the act.
f. mental retardation.
g. any factors the defendant believes are mitigating.

Note this last factor. In the case of *Lockett v. Ohio* (1978), the Supreme Court concluded that states' death penalty statutes must permit consideration, "as a mitigating factor, [of] any aspect of the defendant's character or record and any other circumstances of the offense that the defendant proffers as a basis for a sentence less than death" (quoted by Barrett, Ruhnke, & Goldstein, 1999, p. 49). This consideration permits the forensic psychologist or psychiatrist to carry out a **mitigation assessment,** to be described later in this chapter, that may conclude that the defendant was born addiction-prone or that the defendant's life was so traumatic that it left emotional scars.

5. If the jury or judge decides on a sentence of death, the defendant is entitled to an appeal.

After the execution is scheduled, attorneys for some defendants may appeal that those defendants are not competent to be executed. A **competency-for-execution evaluation** may include many of the procedures used in the mitigation assessment phase, although the focus is on the defendant's understanding of the implications of the death sentence.

Is the Role Necessarily That of an Advocate?

It would seem that when a psychologist participates in an appeal in response to an impending execution, he or she is reflecting the role of an advocate, as that term has been used in this book. Yet by no means do all forensic psychologists who carry out competency-for-execution evaluations see their role as an advocate for the defendant. A distinguished forensic psychologist and frequent evaluator, Alan Goldstein, has stated that he is not opposed to the death penalty and that he views his task as evaluating the competency of the defendant as objectively as possible (Barrett, Ruhnke, & Goldstein, 1999); "my obligation is to provide the attorney with all the information that I find, and then it's the attorney's job to decide how to use it." Goldstein went on to say that he is not there to "help the defendant avoid execution" regardless of what defendants or juries might think. (Despite such objectivity, the prosecution is likely to try to counter the testimony of defense-hired experts with either a cross-examination or the testimony of their own expert witnesses.)

Goldstein's position is supported by the findings of a survey of mental health professionals done by Deitchman, Kennedy, and Beckham (1991). These researchers obtained responses from 222 licensed psychologists and psychiatrists who were also forensic examiners. Not all of them were willing to participate in competency-for-execution evaluations; 49 of 71 psychiatrists (69%) and 90 of 151 psychologists (60%) were willing to do so. Those willing to participate were significantly *more* in favor of capital punishment than were the forensic examiners who were un-

willing to participate in these evaluations. However, a wide spread of attitudes regarding the death penalty existed in each group, indicating that "a large number of willing examiners do not favor capital punishment and a large number of unwilling examiners do favor capital punishment" (Deitchman, Kennedy, & Beckham, 1991, p. 296).

However, some psychologists' participation may reflect their basic belief that taking another life is wrong, even when the state does it, or may be based on an awareness that a certain percentage of sentences (including death sentences) reflect innocent people wrongfully convicted. As noted in chapter 2, a sizable number of psychologists sympathize with the powerless and are disturbed by the imbalance in resources between the prosecution and the defense in death penalty cases. Examples of inadequate counsel or prosecutorial misconduct are described later in this chapter to show the source of the motivation of some psychologists who assist the defense. Their concern about a racial bias in the application of the death penalty also reflects this sense of injustice.

Differences often concentrate on this question: Is participation in a competency-for-execution evaluation a violation of professional ethics? Stanley Brodsky (1990) questioned whether mental health professionals—given the emotional context of the death penalty issue—can be objective and neutral. But others (Bonnie, 1990; Heilbrun, 1987) noted that the death penalty is a political reality in the United States that will not go away simply because mental health professionals refuse to participate and that competency-for-execution assessments should be made by those professionals who have the training to do so.

Social-Psychological Research and Evaluation Research on the Death Penalty

Social-psychological research can play a role in understanding the decision to assign a penalty of death. For example, Haney and Lynch (1994) found that the instructions given about aggravating and mitigating factors are widely misunderstood by jurors; they wrote,

> Our data suggest that profound confusion may plague the process from the onset and implicate jurors' comprehension of the most basic features of the task itself. This confusion seems to begin with the question of what the concepts of aggravating and mitigating actually mean, and extend to disagreements about whether the specific factors they are given to weigh should tip the scales in the direction of life or death. (1994, p. 425)

Psychologists acting as evaluation researchers also have a role to play in studying the impact of the death penalty; for example, questions of the deterrence value and the cost of executions are empirical questions, the understanding of which will be improved by the use of psychological research methods. The results of research on these questions are presented in a later section of this chapter.

CONVICTIONS AND EXECUTIONS OF INNOCENT PEOPLE

Whether people support capital punishment or oppose it, they can agree that it is essential to avoid the execution of innocent people. But how many false convictions and executions occur? Psychologists and other social scientists have sought to answer this question.

Estimating the Number of Wrong Convictions

Some of the people languishing in prison steadfastly maintain their innocence. How many are innocent? A precise answer is impossible. However, we know that some exist. The advent of DNA analysis has permitted (as of January 2004) the release of 140 people falsely convicted of major crimes, some of whom were on death

row (this number is constantly updated and can be checked at *www.innocenceproject.org*). In November 1998, the School of Law of Northwestern University held a National Conference on Wrongful Convictions and the Death Penalty; among those in attendance were 28 of the 73 men and 2 women released from death rows in the last 25 years (Terry, 1998). Some of these were innocent; others were released upon appeal, after courts ruled there had been errors in the prosecution or in judicial instructions.

Social scientists have sought to estimate the number of wrong convictions, using two different approaches. First, Huff, Rattner, and Sagarin (1996; Rattner, 1988) determined an estimate of the number of wrongful convictions per year in the United States. They contacted police administrators, sheriffs, prosecutors, public defenders, and criminal court judges in Ohio and asked them what percentage of those convicted of felonies were actually innocent. (The types of crimes to be considered were the major crimes from the FBI list: murder and nonnegligent manslaughter, forcible rape, aggravated assault, robbery, burglary, larceny-theft, motor-vehicle theft, and arson.) The estimates they received ranged from zero errors to errors in 5% of the cases, with most responses near the 1% mark. (The researchers gave respondents the following choices: Never, Less than 1%, 1–5%, or 6–10%; a total of 72% of the respondents chose "Less than 1%.") The authors then concluded that it was reasonable to estimate that 0.5% of convictions were in error. Interestingly, in one state (Illinois), of 265 people sentenced to death, 13 were later released, based on evidence of their innocence, which is 4.9% (Rollin, 1998).

One can look at the estimate generated by Huff, Rattner, and Sagarin in several ways; as they wrote, it can be seen as "an impressive figure for accuracy and justice; 99.5% of all guilty verdicts in felony cases are handed down on people who did indeed commit the crimes of which they had been accused" (1996, p. 61). But from the other perspective—that of errors made—consider that in the United States, with 1½ to 2 million people convicted of such crimes, 0.5% in error would mean between 7,500 and 10,000 wrongful convictions (Fulero, 1999). Much has been made of these figures, but recall their basis. Most respondents acknowledged that errors do happen—only 5.6% chose the response "Never"—but we do not know the basis for their response. Some doubtless were thinking of cases they had personally observed, but others were simply recognizing that so massive a system inevitably made at least occasional errors.

The second approach focused on individual cases and tried to assess if they reflected errors by the legal system such that an innocent person was scheduled to be executed or was, in fact, executed. Such claims are frequently made, and, as Box 15-1 illustrates, the facts are often contested so that it is very difficult to know if an error was made. In the 70-plus years since Colonel and Mrs. Charles Lindbergh's baby was taken in 1932, various investigators have claimed that an injustice was done when Bruno Richard Hauptmann was convicted and executed for the kidnapping and murder of the child (Scaduto, 1976). In a book titled *The Airman and the Carpenter: The Lindbergh Kidnapping and the Framing of Richard Hauptmann*, Ludovic Kennedy (1985) marshaled evidence that Hauptmann had been framed by the authorities who were eager to get a conviction. And, in another book containing a detailed analysis of the case, Noel Behn (1994) speculated that a member of the Lindbergh family was the actual perpetrator of the crime.

In the second approach, the criteria for the later determination of innocence can include several factors, including a DNA analysis or another person's admitting to having committed the crime. The most systematic work here has been done by three sets of investigators, two in the United States and one in Great Britain. Both Radelet and Bedau (Bedau & Radelet, 1987; Radelet & Bedau, 1988; Radelet, Bedau, & Putnam, 1992) and Rattner and his colleagues (Rattner, 1988; Huff, Rattner, & Sagarin, 1996) studied wrongful convictions in the United States in the 20th century, while Brandon and Davies (1973) investigated 70 cases in the United Kingdom between 1950 and 1970 in which a

conviction was eventually set aside. Rattner (1988) examined 205 cases, using materials from previous reviews (Borchard, 1932; Frank, 1957; Gardner, 1952). A total of 21 of these cases, or 10%, included a sentence of death.

Radelet and Bedau chose to define innocence as occurring in "those cases in which either the crime itself never actually occurred or the convicted defendant was legally and physically uninvolved in the crime" (1988, p. 94). Amazingly, in at least seven of these cases, the victim showed up alive after a homicide conviction; this happened as recently as 1974 after two defendants in California had been convicted of murdering their daughter. Radelet and Bedau identified 400 cases that met their criteria. An analysis based on 350 of these defendants revealed the following:

1. In 309 of these cases, the state implicitly or explicitly admitted that the conviction had been in error; in 20 of these, the state made a voluntary award of indemnity to the defendant. A total of 64 defendants were pardoned with no compensation.

2. In 113 cases, the conviction was reversed on appeal and the charges were dropped; in 38 other cases, a retrial led to new evidence that contributed to an acquittal.

3. In the remaining cases, other evidence led the researchers to conclude that the initial conviction was wrong. For example, in 134 cases, the guilty person eventually confessed. In 7 cases, there was strong evidence (but not a confession) that implicated another suspect. (See the example of Julius Krause in Box 15-3.) In 6 cases, Radelet and Bedau based their assignment on the "considered judgment of a state official in a position to know" (1988, p. 98).

Finally, 15 of the 350 cases were classified as innocent by Radelet and Bedau on the basis of the preponderance of informed opinion; the researchers acknowledged that here their evidence was the weakest. The most famous of these 15 is the aforementioned case of Bruno Richard Hauptmann, and one may question whether the "preponderance of opinion" truly

BOX 15-3
"The Fugitive"—Alive and Well in the Real World?

Can a person be judged to be innocent even if the state never admitted that he or she was wrongfully convicted?

Consider the case of Julius Krause. He was convicted of first-degree murder in 1930; instead of being given the death penalty, he was sentenced to life imprisonment. Five years later, his codefendant con-fessed on his deathbed that another man, not Krause, was his actual partner. When the authorities did noth-ing to locate the man, Krause escaped from prison and located him himself. The other man was tried and con-victed; Krause voluntarily returned to prison, but—despite his innocence—he was kept there for 15 years, until he was paroled in 1951 (Radin, 1964).

considers Hauptmann to be innocent; for exam-ple, a recent and thorough biography of Charles Lindbergh (Berg, 1998) concluded that Haupt-mann was, in fact, guilty.

What can we conclude from these analyses? First, it is difficult to know absolutely when an error has been made; when another person comes forward years later and confesses to the crime, we cannot be sure that this "confession" is a true one (recall from chapter 11 the number of people who came forward as the perpetrators of the Lindbergh kidnapping). DNA analysis, if done properly, is a clear demonstration of inno-cence, but it is not feasible in every case. Sec-ond, the definition of a "false conviction" can vary from researcher to researcher; some include cases in which the conviction was thrown out because of improper procedures but the eventual guilt of the accused was never resolved (see Drizin and Leo, 2004, for an excellent discussion of this issue and a careful study of 125 false con-fession cases).

We are left with the conclusion that errors do occur; whether they account for 0.5% of the cases, or more, or less, we cannot say. And, as Arye Rattner wrote, "It is difficult to eliminate the falsely convicted from the criminal justice system entirely. A system of law that never caught an innocent in its web would probably be so narrow that it would catch few of the guilty as well" (1988, p. 291). But the next sec-tion describes some cases in which confidence increases that the wrong person was sentenced to die and was later executed.

Examples of Death Sentences for Innocent People

Numerous cases exist in which apparently inno-cent defendants were executed. For example, in 1909 in Nebraska, R. Mead Shumway was hanged for the murder of his employer's wife; a year later, the victim's husband confessed on his deathbed that he had killed his wife. Maurice Mays, a Black man, was convicted of murdering a White woman in Tennessee in 1919; 3 years later, he was executed, while still protesting his innocence. In 1926, a White woman came for-ward and, in a written confession, admitted being the murderer; she had dressed up as a Black man to kill the woman with whom her husband was having an affair (Radelet, Bedau, & Putnam, 1992).

Perhaps the most unbelievable case—certainly one of the most disturbing—is that of Jesse Dewayne Jacobs in Texas. Jacobs was executed by the state of Texas in 1995, even though the prose-cutor had conceded that Jacobs did not commit the murder for which he was convicted and sen-tenced to die (Gwynne, 1995). The story is a con-voluted one; it began in 1986 in Conroe, Texas, with the kidnapping and killing of a woman named Etta Ann Urdiales, the estranged wife of the boyfriend of Jacobs's sister, Bobbie Hogan. At first, Jacobs confessed to the killing, saying that his sister had paid him $500 to do it. But by the time of his trial, he had changed his mind and said that his sister was the killer; he had been outside the house at the time and did not even know that his sister had a gun. He did admit that he helped bury the victim. Nevertheless, he was convicted of capital murder by the jury, which—after 35 minutes of deliberations—sentenced him to die. But 7 months later, Peter Speers, the very same district attorney who had prosecuted Jacobs, charged Jacobs's sister with the same killing. At the subsequent trial of Bobbie Hogan, the prosecutor admitted that he had been wrong at the first trial; he now believed that Ms. Hogan had pulled the trigger and that Jacobs did not know she had a gun. Jacobs testified for the prosecution at his sister's trial, admitting only his involvement in the kidnapping.

Jacobs's sister was found guilty of involuntary manslaughter and sentenced to 10 years in prison (her lawyers convinced the second jury that she meant only to threaten the victim and that the gun had fired accidentally). But the state made no effort to vacate Jacobs's conviction and, incredibly, none of his appeals was successful; the appeals court for the Fifth Circuit acknowledged a disparity in the two trials, but said that "it was not for us to say" that the jury that had convicted Jacobs had made a mistake (Greenhouse, 1995). Governor Ann Richards wouldn't issue even a temporary reprieve, and the U.S. Supreme Court refused to grant a stay of execution. Thus, in 1995, Jacobs was executed, 8 years after he had been convicted.

It is true that Jacobs forcibly took Ms. Urdiales to the scene of the fatal quarrel. But would a jury, given only this charge, have sentenced him to death?

The Case of Randall Dale Adams

Why do innocent people get convicted of major crimes and sentenced to death? Often, they have inadequate representation in court; on occasion, they are victims of deliberate bias by the police, a prosecutor, or the presiding judge. (These types of errors are reviewed in subsequent sections.) If the community is consumed by racial strife or political controversy, the defendant may serve as a scapegoat to feed the community's need for vengeance. The killing of an important person in the community or of someone assigned to

maintain order, such as a police officer, can lead to errors by other participants in the legal system. Such was the case of Randall Dale Adams, who later wrote,

> Imagine you are dreaming.
>
> You have been accused of murder. You have never seen or heard of the victim. You have no knowledge of where or when it occurred. All that you know is that the punishment is death in the electric chair.
>
> Fingers point in your direction and the courtroom is filled with eyes that bore into you with hatred. State-appointed psychiatrists declare to the court that you are a vicious sociopath, beyond hope of redemption. You want to scream out, but your lawyer advises silence. You are tempted to lash out in righteous frustration, but handcuffs pin you. You think of running away, but shackles bind your ankles.
>
> In your dream, you toss and turn but you do not awaken.
>
> The words of the prosecutors echo in your mind as they describe what will happen to you: "they strap you down . . . your eyeballs explode . . . your fingernails and toenails pop off . . . you bleed from every orifice of your body."
>
> The jury files into the room and twenty-four eyes stare through you. The bailiff reads the verdict:
>
> Guilty!
>
> Finally you awaken. You are drenched in perspiration, but you are filled with relief to realize that it was just a dream.
>
> But for me, it was a real-life nightmare. (Adams, 1991, p. xiii)

In November 1976, Randall Adams was in Dallas, Texas, on the way from his hometown of Columbus, Ohio, to southern California. When his car broke down, a young man offered him a ride; they spent the day and some of the evening together. Later that evening, the police stopped the youth's car because its lights weren't on. As one of the officers approached the car, someone fired at him six times and killed him. The young man, David Harris, was aware that the car was stolen; apparently, that caused him to shoot at the police officer, but he later claimed that Adams was the killer, even though he had actually dropped Adams off at his motel 3 hours earlier. Harris was a teenager; perhaps the authorities did not want to charge him with capital murder. For whatever reason, Randall Adams was charged with the crime, and, based largely on a perjured identification by Harris and the altered testimony of an eyewitness, Adams was convicted of the murder of a police officer. He was an easy target; as he put it in the book he later wrote, he was:

> an outsider, a blue-collar worker new to Texas who presented them with the image of a long-haired pot-smoking "hippie." Another factor was the Texas political climate . . . demanding that someone should die in retaliation for Officer Woods' death. Because of his youth, David Harris could not be executed for murdering a police officer. On the other hand, a 28-year-old whom the judge himself had described as a "drifter" was a prime candidate for the electric chair. . . . If the prosecution blamed me, it had a witness who said he was sitting in the passenger's seat at the time. If it chose Harris, it had no witness. (Adams, 1991, pp. 58–59)

The results of the **penalty phase** of the trial were especially disturbing. Texas had an unusual procedure in that the jurors doing the sentencing were asked to assess whether the defendant they have just convicted will be a continuing threat to society. If their judgment is yes, then they sentence him to death. Two psychiatrists testified at Adams's sentencing hearing; based on a 20-minute examination, Dr. James Grigson testified that Adams was a sociopath without remorse, who would likely kill again if given a chance. (Dr. Grigson has testified in more than 100 death penalty cases; in all but 9 of these, the jury responded to his testimony by sentencing the defendant to death.)

Thus, Adams was put on death row where, at one point, he was only 72 hours away from being executed. However, one appeal freed him from death row (after 3½ years) but he remained in prison for 9 more years, before national media attention led to a hearing in which the witnesses were discredited and Adams was released from prison.

Trial-Related Reasons for Incorrect Convictions

Homicides and rapes deservedly receive special attention by the criminal justice system, and there is extra effort to get them solved. Two thirds of homicides are "cleared," compared to only 21% of serious crimes in general and a smaller percentage of robberies (Gross, 1997). For cases that lead to the death penalty, police and prosecutors push harder; they may err in the process.

Prosecutorial and Police Errors

Clarence Brandley, a janitor in a Texas town and a Black man, was accused of killing a White girl in 1980. A police officer, it is claimed, told Brandley and another janitor (who was White) that one of them would hang for the crime and, looking at Brandley, then offered, "Since you're the nigger, you're elected" (McCormick, 1988, p. 64). At his trial, prosecutors suppressed evidence. Brandley was convicted; an appeal got him released but only after he had spent 10 years in prison.

In a criminal trial, prosecutors are required to reveal to the defense attorneys any **exculpatory evidence**—that is, evidence that casts doubt on the guilt of the defendant. But some prosecutors test the limits; they may delay, obfuscate, or feign disorganization. In his book about the trial of his client, Timothy McVeigh, for the murders resulting from the bombing of the federal building in Oklahoma City on April 19, 1995, Stephen Jones (Jones & Israel, 1998) portrayed numerous examples of ways the prosecution obstructed the defense's access to exculpatory information; for example, he wrote,

> the government, having long ducked and delayed and stonewalled on the production

of evidence we were entitled to, took, under pressure from Judge Matsch, the very opposite tack. They drowned us with material. All at once they would cascade 302s [interviews carried out by FBI agents] on us in a great dumping—some ten thousand 302s arriving virtually at the same time—in totally helter-skelter form. There could be, for instance, four or five or six 302s pertaining to one person, but you'd never know it until you went through the whole batch, one by one. (Jones & Israel, 1998, p. 199)

Principles of fairness would seem to dictate that when it can be shown that a prosecutor has exceeded the rules, either by injecting false statements or by deliberately withholding evidence, a person convicted and sentenced to death should get a new trial. But in such cases, the appellate courts have responded, "It depends." For example, William Brooks was charged with the kidnapping, rape, and first-degree murder of a young woman in Georgia in 1977. After the jury had found him guilty, during the penalty phase the prosecutor tried to dilute the jury's sense of responsibility by telling the jurors they would not be "responsible" for Brooks's death: "Brooks himself pulled the switch on the day he murdered the victim" (quoted by Platania, Moran, & Cutler, 1994, p. 22). The prosecutor also made specific statements that the appellate court labeled as erroneous and in violation of Brooks's constitutional rights. Yet the Eleventh Circuit Court of Appeals refused to overturn the jury's sentence of death for Brooks; the majority called the prosecutor's remarks **harmless error,** in that the mistakes did not influence the outcome of the sentencing phase.

Incompetent Counsel

Perhaps the greatest source of erroneous convictions in death penalty cases is inadequate counsel for the defendant (Bright, 1994; Vick, 1995). (See Box 15-4 for an example.) Public defenders are often talented but usually overworked. When they are not available, the judge may assign a capital case to a young or inexperienced

attorney (Coyle, 1998). But the U.S. Supreme Court has ruled that states don't have to provide lawyers for the indigent when they appeal their sentences—not even in death penalty cases. So a few states don't provide funds for appeals by indigent defendants. Pay in many other states is quite low. Mississippi, for example, pays court-appointed defense lawyers $11.75 per hour, and Alabama pays them just $20 an hour—with a ceiling of $1,000—to prepare for a death penalty trial, and $40 per hour for time in court; they must pay for any expenses out of this fund. In these states, the court reporters make more per hour than do the court-appointed attorneys.

As a result, many defense attorneys do not have the resources to put on a proper defense. Such a defense often requires money for investigators or expert witnesses (Beck & Shumsky, 1997). Thought needs to be given to the theory of the defense, especially when a novice defense attorney is matched against an experienced prosecutor; Box 15-5 illustrates some of the arguments that such prosecutors use in their closing arguments.

As a result, some attorneys provide less-than-responsible preparation; one 72-year-old Texas attorney slept through portions of the trial (Aron, 1998), and another lawyer in that state provided only a 26-word statement at the sentencing: "You are an extremely intelligent jury. You've got that man's life in your hands. You can take it or not. That's all I have to say" (quoted by McCormick, 1998, p. 64). His client, Jesus Romero, was executed in 1992.

For a while, some of the slack was taken up by the availability of Post-Conviction Defense Organizations (called PCDOs) established to represent the condemned in their death penalty appeals (Coyle, 1995). Twenty resource centers were established in 1988 by the federal government, and they provided 190 attorneys (average salary, $30,000) who specialized in death penalty appeals; funding came mostly from the U.S. Congress (Wiehl, 1995). But in 1995, Congress eliminated the $20 million allocation for such centers, and the next year they abruptly shut down (Herbert, 1997).

BOX 15-4

Examining the Competence of a Death Penalty Defense Attorney

A habeas corpus hearing was held in January 1996 in Georgia to determine if Wallace Fugate was given "effective assistance of counsel" by Leo Browne during his 1992 murder trial; Fugate was convicted and sentenced to death. At the hearing, Browne, who had been appointed by a county judge to represent Fugate, was questioned by Stephen B. Bright, a lawyer for the Southern Center for Human Rights. The judge ruled against Fugate despite the testimony in the following excerpt:

STEPHEN B. BRIGHT: Do you know what the case of *Gregg v. Georgia* [the 1976 Supreme Court ruling that allowed states to once again impose the death penalty] is?

LEO BROWNE: No, I don't—I don't know what you're getting at there, no.

BRIGHT: You—you're not familiar with that case?

BROWNE: No.

BRIGHT: All right. So you don't—you don't follow Supreme Court cases.

BROWNE: Not too closely.

BRIGHT: All right. You don't know what—

BROWNE: The past few years I haven't.

BRIGHT: All right. I'm just asking you if when we say "post-*Gregg* case," do you know what *Gregg* means?

BROWNE: You mean about the—the death penalty?

BRIGHT: Well, I'm just asking you if that time frame means anything to you?

BROWNE: Not exactly, no.

BRIGHT: Now, are you familiar with the case of *Furman v. Georgia?*

BROWNE: No.

BRIGHT: Have you ever read that case?

BROWNE: I don't think I have.

BRIGHT: You familiar at all with the case of *Godfrey v. Georgia?*

BROWNE: No.

BRIGHT: Ever read any of the opinions with regard to death-penalty cases out of the Federal District Courts in Georgia?

BROWNE: I might have, but I don't—I don't recall specifically.

BRIGHT: And between the time of the Horol case [a capital case Browne worked on in 1979] and Mr. Fugate's case, you had not been involved in any death-penalty case?

BROWNE: That's correct.

BRIGHT: No death-penalty case?

BROWNE: No.

BRIGHT: Been involved in any murder cases?

BROWNE: No. Not in that length of time.

BRIGHT: Have you ever had a case where you had an expert witness?

BROWNE: You mean for the defendant?

BRIGHT: Yes, sir.

BROWNE: I don't really recall. I had one case I may have had a doctor come in and testify. But I—I can't recall specifically.

BRIGHT: Do you remember what year that was?

BROWNE: No, good God.

BRIGHT: What case?

BROWNE: Lost back there somewhere.

BRIGHT: What subject?

BROWNE: In the sixties or seventies or somewhere in there.

BRIGHT: Ever had an investigator?

BROWNE: Do what?

BRIGHT: Investigator? Ever have an investigator?

BROWNE: Oh, investigator?

BRIGHT: Yeah.

BROWNE: No. No.

BRIGHT: Do you feel like an investigator would have been of benefit to you in the defense in this case?

BROWNE: I think we discussed that at one time and decided that we really wouldn't need an investigator.

BRIGHT: Do you have any idea what you would use an investigator for if you had one?

BROWNE: I'm sure I—I'm sure I have been exposed to some of that, but I don't remember specifically.

BRIGHT: Could you just tell me, Mr. Browne, can you tell me what criminal-law decisions from any court you're familiar with? Georgia Supreme Court—

BROWNE: Well, off the top of my head I can't tell you any cases I'm familiar with. I've—from time to time I've had to refer to cases, go research cases. But I can't sit here and tell you what cases I'm actually familiar with. Can't do it.

BRIGHT: Not even one?

BROWNE: None. Not even one.

BRIGHT: All right. Thank you. Nothing further, Your Honor.

JUDGE JOHN R. HARVEY: All right. Thank you, Mr. Browne.

BROWNE: I can find you some, if you need 'em.

JUDGE HARVEY: Okay, Mr. Browne, just one last question. Do you recall how much you were, in fact, paid by the county to represent Mr. Fugate?

BROWNE: I don't recall that either.

Source: Court transcript: A lawyer without precedent. (1997, June). *Harper's Magazine,* pp. 24–26.

BOX 15-5

How Do Attorneys Argue in the Closing Arguments of Death Penalty Cases?

Chapter 12 noted that one contribution of trial consultants to attorneys preparing cases is to advise them about the possible content and structure of their closing arguments. In a capital murder case, after a defendant has been convicted and the jury must decide the punishment, both the prosecutor and the defense attorney have choices to make about the most effective arguments to present. (The defense attorney usually is aspiring for a sentence of life in prison rather than death.) Mark Costanzo and Julie Peterson (1994) analyzed the closing arguments during the penalty phase of 20 capital murder trials, to discover what themes were emphasized.

The focus of the penalty phase is often on the perpetrator's personal history, character, and motives. Prosecutors thus portrayed the defendant as a cold, remorseless killer, motivated by little more than greed, rage, or sadism; they emphasized the brutal nature of the murder, the victim's suffering, and the moral legitimacy of the jury reflecting revenge (Costanzo, 1997). Prosecutors noted the vivid nature of the murder. With regard to assessments of the character of the defendant, some psychologists (Costanzo & Costanzo, 1992; Hans, 1988) proposed that when jurors consider the penalty, they employ a kind of prototype-matching strategy; that is, they have general ideas of the type of criminals who deserve to be executed (such as Charles Manson, Ted Bundy, or Jeffrey Dahmer). Thus, the prosecutor seeks to portray the defendant's character and behavior as matching the prototype. Here is one prosecutor's statement from Costanzo and Peterson's set:

> Of all the cold-blooded murderers I have ever seen, heard about, read about, worked on their cases, or thought about, this is the worst, because it was the coldest. Because it was the least motivated by any human emotion. (1994, p. 133)

Prosecutors have an advantage, with regard to laypersons' (and jurors') explanations of the causes of behavior. Social psychological theory and research (Heider, 1958; Ross & Nisbett, 1991) has proposed that people attribute behavior to dispositional rather than situational causes; that is, we say that the defendant's criminal acts were caused by qualities within the criminal rather than by the environment surrounding the criminal. Here is the way one prosecutor capitalized on what social psychologists call the **fundamental attribution error:**

> Even though he had an abused childhood, even though he may have felt rejected, even though those problems were with him, he had the ability not to take them out on someone else just like you and I have that ability. You have that ability. Is [the defense attorney] suggesting that if you or I had

continued

The Effect of Type of Counsel

As noted, although some defendants charged with capital crimes obtain excellent representation, the general record is quite poor. In Alabama, those attorneys who represented defendants sentenced to death had been subject to disciplinary action (including disbarment) at a rate 20 times higher than other Alabama lawyers; one fourth of the inmates on death row in Kentucky had attorneys who later were disbarred or resigned to avoid such sanctions (Vick, 1995).

A prisoner on death row once said, "Capital punishment means those without capital get the punishment" (quoted by Adams, 1991, p. 175). Are those defendants who have an attorney appointed by the judge more likely to receive a death sentence than are those who were able to hire a private attorney? Beck and Shumsky (1997) examined the records of 606 homicide trials in the state of Georgia. Controlling for the effects of aggravating circumstances, they found that the type of defense counsel affected the sentence; those defendants with a private attorney were less likely to be sentenced to death. In cases in which four or more aggravating factors were present, the kind of attorney did not have much effect, but in the 103 cases for which there were a smaller number of aggravating factors, more than 20% of the defendants with appointed counsel were sentenced to death, while less than 5% of those with private counsel were sentenced to death.

Appointed attorneys are not inherently ineffective, but they need to be adequately trained and reasonably paid (Rosenberg, 1995).

continued

those same problems that we would have made the same decision, that is, the decision to kill? No, not at all. It doesn't make common sense. He has the capacity for saying no, he has the ability to say, "No, I am not going to kill another human being." (Costanzo & Peterson, 1994, p. 135)

In contrast, defense attorneys used a variety of arguments and often told a complex and textured story. (After all, they had a tougher task; the jury had already decided their client was guilty.) Some relied on the moral argument about the unjust nature of the death penalty. Others explained the murders within the context of the defendant's own background and life history, with a tragically flawed character deformed by years of neglect and abuse (Costanzo, 1997). Thus they followed Goodpaster's (1983) proposal that the central task of the defense attorney *at this point* is to humanize the defendant, or at least portray the defendant in such a way that situational attributions for his or her behavior may emerge, so that jurors may reflect some compassion or mercy. An example:

You heard about a father that beat the hell out of his mother. Beat her so badly that he choked her unconscious, hit her so hard she had to be treated for her female organs. You heard about an alcoholic father, alcoholic mother. You've heard about, worst

of all, an overbearing, arrogant, abusive, nasty, giant brute of a grandfather. . . . Or how about the grandmother that likes to go beating up people with electric extension cords. Or how about torture? How about torture? Can you imagine the terror of being closed inside a burlap sack, have a rope tied to the burlap sack, having it thrown over a limb of an oak tree, and having yourself hoisted. You can't see a damn thing. And then being smoked. . . . Can you imagine the terror of that? Does that give you a little bit of a clue of what that life must have been like? To give you a little bit of a clue why John maybe doesn't see things the way we see things? (Costanzo & Peterson, 1994, p. 135)

Often, humanizing the defendant takes the form of emphasizing attributes that serve as explanations that may mitigate the punishment:

John D. is mentally disturbed. You know it. I know it. You know it from the circumstances of the crimes that you've heard about. Carrying the body of your dead lover around a couple of weeks in your apartment, lighting fires and talking to her. Sure, any normal human being does that. He's very, very sick, and he has been for a long, long time. Death is an absolute punishment. And we, at least in this country, don't kill people that are not absolutely responsible. (p. 136)

As indicated earlier, both the U.S. Congress and the Supreme Court have not been supportive of the necessary training and funding. The next section specifically considers the role of the courts.

APPELLATE COURTS AND THE DEATH PENALTY

Those defendants who are convicted and sentenced to death may appeal these outcomes if they feel that they were inadequately represented at their trial and sentencing hearing. Exculpatory evidence uncovered after the trial may be another reason to seek an appeal. But appellate courts have often been unsympathetic to such appeals; consider the following:

- Judy Haney was convicted in 1988 of murdering her husband, who, she said, routinely beat her and their children. As noted in chapter 7, women who kill their abusive lovers are rarely sentenced to death, but Haney was. During the trial, one of her attorneys came to court so drunk that the judge halted proceedings and sent the man to jail overnight. He neglected to present to the jury the mitigating evidence about the long-time abusive nature of Haney's husband. Despite the attorney's failings, the Alabama Supreme Court upheld Haney's conviction and sentence, and she remains on death row in Alabama (Gleick, 1995).

- Larry Heath's lawyer failed to appear when the appeal of Heath's death sentence was argued before the Alabama Supreme Court. Heath was executed in 1992.

■ When John Young was on trial in Georgia, his attorney was addicted to drugs, and, shortly after Young was sentenced to death, his attorney was jailed on drug charges. The attorney told the appeals court that he had spent "hardly any time preparing the case" and had been unable to concentrate on the case "because of a myriad of personal problems" (Amnesty International, 1987, p. 46). He acknowledged that he had failed to investigate Young's life for mitigating circumstances (of which, it developed, there were many). Yet the appeals court rejected Young's contention that he received ineffective assistance; he was executed in 1985 (Carelli, 1995).

THE U.S. SUPREME COURT'S REACTION TO DEATH PENALTY APPEALS

In 1972, in the decision in *Furman v. Georgia,* the United States Supreme Court effectively outlawed the death penalty, because its arbitrary and discriminatory application qualified as "cruel and unusual punishment." Four years later, satisfied that the states had passed legislation that dealt with inequities, the Supreme Court reinstated the possibility of a death penalty (*Gregg v. Georgia,* 1976). In recent years, both the U.S. Congress and the Supreme Court have been increasingly concerned with the drawn-out nature of appeals of death penalties. Only 4 of the 62 South Carolina inmates sentenced to death since 1978 had been executed by 1995. The review process may drag on for 10, 15, even 20 years, meaning more and more people are on death row. "The leading cause of death on death row is natural causes. . . . We've got 3,000 people on death row. We are adding 250 people a year and we're only executing 30," said the attorney general of South Carolina, Charles Condon (Associated Press, 1995, p. 7F). One of Congress's objections to the federal funding of the Post-

Conviction Defender Organizations was the belief, initiated by some state prosecutors, that PCDO lawyers filed numerous petitions that lacked merit and that they otherwise manipulated the system to delay the litigation involved in their clients' claims.

In 1989, a divided U.S. Supreme Court held that neither the Eighth Amendment to the U.S. Constitution nor the due process clause required states to appoint counsel to poor death-row inmates who sought further appeals after their initial ones were unsuccessful (*Murray v. Giarratano,* 1989). Recall that in the case of Jesse Dewayne Jacobs, the Supreme Court refused his request for a stay of execution. The response to the case of *Herrera v. Collins* (1993) is further indication of the Court's desire to expedite executions.

For critics of the death penalty, the outcome of Leonel Torres Herrera's appeal is disturbing. Herrera was convicted in 1982 of killing a Texas police officer, and the next year he pleaded guilty to the murder of a second officer. In 1992, three days before he was scheduled to be executed, he filed his second federal **habeas corpus** petition (*habeas corpus* literally means "to have the body," but the term is used to refer to appeals for the dispensation of a case). His claim of innocence was bolstered by four affidavits, one of which was from an alleged eyewitness, Herrera's nephew, who reported that he was hiding in the room and saw his own father shoot the police officers. All the other affidavits also named Herrera's brother as the murderer. Note that the new evidence surfaced 10 years after the crime. The state of Texas refused to consider his claim because the state required that newly discovered evidence had to be brought before the court within *30 days* of the defendant's conviction. When Herrera's attorneys appealed to the U.S. Supreme Court, they tried to frame the issue in its most dramatic terms: "Is it constitutional to execute someone who is innocent?" But the justices resisted this approach: "We don't have an innocent person here; we have a person who has been convicted of a murder, and we have allegations that someone else may have committed the crime," Justice

Sandra Day O'Connor told Herrera's attorney during oral arguments (Lewis, 1992, p. A15).

The Supreme Court's ruling supported the Texas law. According to Chief Justice Rehnquist, claims of innocence are not, alone, a basis for federal habeas relief; it must be shown that the trial or other criminal proceedings violated the Constitution. The fact that Texas refused to hear the newly discovered evidence did not violate a fundamental principle of fairness, according to the Court, "given the historical unavailability of new trials and the practice of imposing time limits by the various states and federal courts" (quoted by Coyle & Lavelle, 1993, p. 5).

The Supreme Court's decision was announced on January 25, 1993; Herrera was executed on May 12, 1993, claiming his innocence to the end. Although the Court felt that the Texas procedure did not "violate a principle of fairness," others would question whether a deadline of 30 days after a conviction is too stringent to ensure justice.

The Supreme Court also rebuked a federal appeals court for halting the execution of a murderer, Thomas Thompson, in California, saying that the lower court's action was a "grave abuse of discretion" and that without "a strong showing of actual innocence, the state's interest in actual finality outweighs the prisoner's interest in obtaining yet another . . . delay" (quoted by Mauro, 1998, p. 1A). It also upheld the U.S. Congress's contribution to the reduction of habeas corpus rights. In 1996, Congress passed the Anti-Terrorism and Effective Death Penalty Act, which reduced the number of appeals to the federal courts by death-row inmates and made it impossible for most convicts to file more than one habeas petition unless they could show that new evidence provided "clear and convincing" proof of innocence.

SOME SPECIFIC ACTIVITIES

For those forensic psychologists who choose to be involved in death penalty appeals, the material in the foregoing sections reflects the chal-

lenges for those whose mission is to reverse a miscarriage of justice. But recall Alan Goldstein's words, that the task of the psychologist is to make as objective an evaluation as possible. This section examines in more detail some specific activities of the psychologist.

Evaluations for Dangerousness

Chapter 6 focused on risk assessment and predictions of dangerousness. These sorts of evaluations take on particular significance in death penalty cases. A recent study shows why (Texas Defender Service, 2004). In Texas, "future dangerousness" essentially refers to the extent to which these individuals will engage in violent acts while incarcerated in an institutional setting for a minimum of forty years. Thus, the institutional adjustment or ability of capital defendants to conform their behavior to a prison setting is generally the critical issue to consider when evaluating whether they actually continue to represent a threat to others. Testing the predictive reliability of expert testimony in Texas capital trials on questions of future dangerousness, the Texas Defender Service conducted original research on these predictions to determine if inmates sentenced to death did indeed pose a future danger in their communities—i.e., prisons. In doing so, they gathered disciplinary records from the Texas Department of Corrections and identified inmates who had engaged in violent behavior. They found that state-sponsored experts are much more likely to be wrong than right in their predictions of dangerousness (Texas Defender Service, 2004). Of the 155 inmates in the study, seven (5%) engaged in assaultive behavior requiring treatment beyond first aid. Thirty of the 155 inmates (19%) had no records reflecting disciplinary violations. The remaining 76% of inmates committed disciplinary infractions involving conduct not amounting to serious assaults. None of the inmates identified in this study committed another homicide and only two inmates (1%) were prosecuted by the Texas Special Prosecution's Unit, the agency responsible for charging and prosecuting crimes committed in prison. State-paid witnesses were wrong in their predictions of future dangerousness in 95% of the cases. In addition, Krauss and Sales (2001) provide disturbing evidence that jurors have difficulty in distinguishing "good" expert testimony from testimony based on less accurate scientific grounds.

Competency Examinations

Probably the most frequent activity of the forensic psychologist is the mitigation assessment. The prosecution is asking for the death penalty; are there any factors in the defendant's childhood or personality that would lead a jury to lessen the sentence?

A mental status examination, consisting of several components, is essential prior to the penalty phase of any capital case, and it should be repeated during incarceration on death row, if there is any question of the convict's competence. It is imperative to evaluate the defendant's history to determine if any traumatic debilitation or organic impairment exists, to assess the defendant's ability to assist in his or her own appeal, and to assess credibility. If the defendant has a long history of drug or alcohol usage, or has had a head injury, or has been in special education classes, he or she should be evaluated by a forensic neuropsychologist. Structural dysfunctions are likely to be found, particularly frontal lobe dysfunctions (Hart, Forth, & Hare, 1990; Kandel & Freed, 1989; McKinzey, 1995).

George Michael Newman (1999), who has conducted a number of death penalty investigations, suggested that a competent death penalty investigation takes the defendant's life back through the lives of his or her parents, at least to the time of the defendant's birth. Birth records, school records, and any information about the defendant's military, legal, marital, and occupational history should be collected. Psychological tests should be administered to the defendant; for example, Ogloff (1995) described how the MMPI has been used to determine the current

mental state in sentencing appeals, and Heilbrun (1990) tested the personality and mental competence of murderers on death row. Although there is no fixed battery, Alan Goldstein usually includes in his evaluation the WAIS-R test of intelligence (for its value as a measure of reasoning and judgment), the Hare Psychopathy Checklist (Hare, 1991), and the Rogers Criminal Responsibility Assessment Scales (described in chapter 5; Rogers, 1984), as well as the MMPI or the Millon personality inventories (Barrett, Ruhnke, & Goldstein, 1999).

This kind of evaluation is also relevant to the issue of whether the defendant is competent to assist his or her attorneys during an appeal. For example, while Ted Bundy was on death row, his attorney, Polly Nelson (1994), arranged for Dorothy Lewis, a prominent psychiatrist, to evaluate him. Dr. Lewis's diagnosis was that Bundy suffered from a bipolar disorder—his unbounded self-assurance, at times, shifted into a depressed mood. As you would expect, Dr. Lewis's testimony to this effect was strongly challenged by the prosecution, whose own expert witnesses diagnosed Bundy as a sociopathic personality, and the judge refused the claim that Bundy was not competent to assist in his own defense.

Competency to Be Executed

Heilbrun and McClaren (1988) provided a thorough outline of the procedures to be followed in assessing competency to be executed. An interview with the defendant is essential; it should include an assessment of his or her comprehension of just what the physical finality of death means and the causal link between the act of murder and the penalty (Ogloff, Wallace, & Otto, 1992; Small, 1988). The need for a careful evaluation was illustrated in the case of Alvin Ford (*Ford v. Wainwright,* 1986). While Ford was on death row in Florida, he began to display indications of a psychotic breakdown (including incoherent verbal behavior, diminished attention span, and inappropriate emotional expression), although authorities were suspicious that he was malingering in order to avoid execution. The three psychiatrists who were commissioned to examine Ford were offered a detailed set of records about him, including psychiatric and medical reports, letters he had written, and other indications of his deteriorating mental status. One of the three psychiatrists declined to accept these materials until he was leaving the prison after the brief, 30-minute, jointly conducted interview; he submitted his report the next day, and in it he included no mention of these records; it is assumed that he formed his opinion without considering them (Miller & Radelet, 1993). He concluded that Ford's "disorder" was contrived and that Ford knew exactly what was going on. The other two psychiatrists, who may or may not have used the records in their determination, also concluded that Ford was competent to be executed (for an interesting perspective on the ethics of psychiatrists' involvement in the determination of competency to be executed, see Mossman, 1992).

Mental Retardation

In 1997, the state of Texas executed Terry Washington, a brain-damaged African American man who had an IQ between 58 and 69; he could neither count nor tell time and had the social skills of a 5-year-old. In fact, since the death penalty was reinstituted, approximately 30 mentally retarded people have been executed in the United States. In Terry Washington's case, the defendant's attorney (who was assigned by the judge) did not obtain an assessment of his client's mental deficits, and the jurors doing the sentencing were not provided relevant information about his mental status (Berger, 1997). When a person who is mentally retarded is sentenced to death, psychologists believe it is legitimate—even essential—to evaluate whether the person has the mental capacity to understand the nature of the death penalty and the reasons why it was imposed. Those who are classified as mentally retarded often lack the perspective, judgment, and self-control possessed by those of average or above-average intelligence; their moral development and reasoning ability are stunted (Berger, 1997).

Some of those states that have the death penalty have passed laws abolishing it for mentally retarded defendants; Georgia was the first state to do so, in 1988. But does the execution of such a person violate the U.S. Constitution? The U.S. Supreme Court considered this issue in the case of *Penry v. Lynaugh* (1989). The facts of the case are these: In 1979, a young woman was raped and stabbed in her own home in Livingston, Texas. Before she died a few hours later, she gave a description of the assailant to the police, leading them to question Johnny Paul Penry, age 22. Penry confessed to the crime and was charged with murder.

At a hearing, a psychologist testified that Penry was mildly to moderately retarded and had a mental age of 6½ years, with an estimated IQ between 50 and 63. At his trial, Penry offered the defense of insanity and offered expert testimony about organic brain damage, moderate retardation, and poor impulse control. But the prosecution offered expert testimony that he was legally sane and instead had an antisocial personality. The jury found him guilty of first-degree murder and, concluding that he was a continuing threat to society (he had a previous conviction for rape), he was sentenced to die.

The Supreme Court reviewed Penry's case because an appeal questioned whether the execution of a mentally retarded person violated constitutional safeguards. In a split (5 to 4) decision, the Court ruled that the Eighth Amendment does not categorically prohibit the execution of mentally retarded capital murderers if they have been found to be competent to stand trial, for such a finding assumes that they understand the proceedings against them. Thus, the Court made a distinction between Penry, with supposedly mild mental retardation, and those who are profoundly or severely mentally retarded and "wholly lacking in the capacity to appreciate the wrongfulness of their actions" (*Penry v. Lynaugh,* 1989, p. 2939).

Finally, in *Atkins v. Virginia* (2002), the U.S. Supreme Court ruled 6 to 3 that executions of mentally retarded criminals are "cruel and unusual punishment," violating the Eighth Amendment to the Constitution. The ruling spared the life of convicted killer Daryl Renard Atkins, who was scheduled to be executed in Virginia. Atkins was convicted of shooting an Air Force enlisted man for beer money in 1996. Atkins's lawyers said he has an IQ of 59 and has never lived on his own or held a job.

Justice Stevens wrote the opinion, which was joined by Justices O'Connor, Kennedy, Souter, Ginsburg, and Breyer. "We are not persuaded that the execution of mentally retarded criminals will measurably advance the deterrent or the retributive purpose of the death penalty," the Court said.

The majority cited a growing national consensus on the issue since the high court ruled in 1989 that such executions may be unacceptable. In the past 13 years, the number of states that do not allow the execution of mentally retarded death-row prisoners has grown from 2 to 18. "It is fair to say that a national consensus has developed against it," Justice Stevens wrote.

However, in a blistering dissent, Justice Scalia scoffed at what he called "the 47 percent consensus." He said the 18 states represent less than half of the 38 states that permit capital punishment in any case (though he neglected to mention that if you add the 12 states without capital punishment for anyone, the total is 30 out of 50). "If one is to say as the court does today that *all* executions of the mentally retarded are so morally repugnant as to violate our national standards of decency, surely the consensus it points to must be one that has set its righteous face against *all* such executions," Justice Scalia wrote. Chief Justice Rehnquist and Justice Thomas joined Justice Scalia in dissenting.

The most immediate effect of the ruling will be in the states that allowed execution of the retarded up to now. Already, inmates in those states are arguing that they are retarded and that their sentences should be converted to life in prison. Also, the Atkins decision has stimulated controversy in psychological circles (see Bersoff, 2002; but see Fulero, 2003).

Children and the Death Penalty

Considerations of the ability to understand and maturity of judgment also may be raised when children are sentenced to die. Those states that have the death penalty differ in their lower age limits of eligibility for execution, but 25 states have a minimum death penalty age of less than 18, and the Supreme Court (in *Stanford v. Kentucky,* 1989) upheld the death sentence given to a 16-year-old. Children as young as 15 have been put on death row. Oklahoma in 1999 executed a man who, 13 years earlier, had killed his parents when he was 16. In April 2003, Oklahoma executed another man who was 17 at the time he committed his crime. From 1985 to 1993, a total of nine people who were juveniles when they committed their crimes were executed. From 1998 to 2003, another 13 were executed, the last in 2003.

The case of the Tison brothers in Arizona questions whether the same assumptions about maturity and independence of judgment that apply to adult offenders apply to children and makes salient the special needs for psychological assessment of young people scheduled for execution. In the summer of 1978, the brothers' father, Gary Tison, was serving a life sentence in the Arizona State Prison in Florence, Arizona, for murdering a prison guard 11 years before. Along with another prisoner, he planned an escape and implicated his wife and their three sons (ages 18, 19, and 20) in the action. The sons put pistols and sawed-off shotguns in a cooler and smuggled them into the prison. In the process, two of the sons, Donny and Ricky, pointed guns at two of the prison staff. Gary Tison and the other prisoner, Randy Greenawalt, disarmed several guards and locked them in a storeroom. Then they walked out of the prison. Not a shot was fired.

The two escapees, along with the three Tison boys, drove their old car west, along an isolated desert road. Late at night, a tire blew out; one of the sons stopped a passing car, driven by John Lyons, a young U.S. Marine, accompanied by his wife, their 15-year-old niece, and their 2-year-old son. Once the Marine's car stopped, Gary Tison emerged from the shadows, drew his gun, and confiscated the car; then he and the others maneuvered both cars down a dusty road and ordered the Lyons family out of its car. Tison instructed his boys to get some water for the family out of the family car; when they were some distance away, he and Greenawalt used 16 shotgun blasts to execute the four members of the Lyons family. The three sons watched in stunned disbelief. Using the Lyons's car, the Tisons continued to evade the authorities. The boys remained passive and compliant to their father's demands. According to one observer, "It was their deference to authority, their desire to please, that kept them from making the independent judgments required to break from their father's powerful and destructive influence" (Clarke, 1988, p. 83).

Twelve days after the prison break, and after murdering another couple and driving through two police roadblocks, the so-called Tison gang was apprehended; the eldest son, Donny Tison, was shot and killed; Greenawalt and the other two brothers, Raymond and Ricky Tison, were captured. But Gary Tison fled into the night; he was found dead in the desert 11 days later. The brothers were convicted of various counts of armed robbery, kidnapping, and motor-vehicle theft as well as four counts of **felony murder** (that is, Arizona statutes said they could be charged with murder although they did not do the killing). Arizona is one of 23 states in which offenders can be convicted of capital murder even though they had no intent to kill or inflict serious bodily injury (Coyne & Entzeroth, 1994). Although several of the previously listed mitigating factors appeared to be present (their youth, the absence of any prior criminal record, and the duress upon them), the surviving Tison

boys were sentenced to death. Upon appeal, the Arizona Supreme Court upheld the sentences, noting that the boys provided their father with the shotguns, helped abduct the victims, did nothing to stop their killings, and stayed with their father after the murders. The U.S. Supreme Court, in considering the case (in *Tison v. Arizona,* 1987), ruled that the death sentences "were constitutionally permissible [even though] neither petitioner intended to kill the victims and neither inflicted fatal gunshot wounds" (quoted by Clarke, 1988, p. 291).

When a father orders his children to comply, even in the participation of an illegal act, is it appropriate to conduct a psychological analysis of the motivations and reasoning level of the children involved? Do people aged 16, 17, or 18 possess the common sense and maturity of judgment of adults? Currently, 70 people on death row were sentenced to death for crimes they committed as juveniles. All are males, and 37% are in Texas. The typical case is that of a 17-year-old African American or Hispanic male whose victim was a White adult.

Evaluating Defense Arguments

As noted earlier, defense attorneys have a challenging job when they begin the penalty phase of a capital murder case. The jury has already concluded that the defendant committed the crime. Furthermore, before the trial, the jurors went through the death-qualification process. Those opposed to the death penalty were dismissed from the panel; the remaining potential jurors, who would form the actual jury, did not hold such reservations. A number of studies by psychologists have concluded that these remaining jurors are conviction-prone; for a review of this research, see the articles by Allen, Mabry, and McKelton (1998) and by Craig Haney and his colleagues (Haney, Hurtado, & Vega, 1994; Haney, Sontag, & Costanzo, 1994; see also Wrightsman, Nietzel, & Fortune, 1998). Also, recall from chapter 2 of the current text that the

Supreme Court in the case of *Lockhart v. McCree* (1986) rejected the applicability of psychological research findings and upheld the use of the **death-qualified jury** procedure. But the problem remains; a survey by Dillehay and Sandys (1996) of 148 jurors in felony cases found that 28% of those who were death-qualified would *automatically* impose the death penalty if given the opportunity.

How do defense attorneys respond to the task of persuading a jury at the penalty phase? Box 15-4 described some of the types of closing arguments used by prosecutors and defense attorneys during the penalty phase in capital murder cases. One type of contribution by the forensic psychologist as a consultant to the defense attorney is an evaluation of various types of arguments. A study by Lawrence T. White (1987) initiated that process. In this laboratory study, college students serving as mock jurors were given one of four different responses by the defense during the penalty phase: (a) no defense witnesses and no defense argument, (b) testimony by witnesses and a closing argument that reflected opposition to the death penalty on the basis of moral principles, (c) testimony by acquaintances of the defendant and a closing argument emphasizing that the defendant's actions were a product of mental illness, or, finally, (d) testimony by the defendant's mother and by a clinical psychologist and a closing argument that provided a situational explanation (specifically, an inadequate family experience and adverse social conditions) for the defendant's criminal behavior. Results for three different crimes (each of which was a murder, but varying in aggravating factors) found that the defense based on a conceptual argument against the death penalty was most effective; White suggested that it may "provide some jurors with the justification they need to vote for life" (1987, p. 126). The mental-illness argument was the least effective; mock jurors expressed their opinions that mental illness was no excuse and that the defendant could have sought help for his or her problems.

The Problem of Jury Instructions

After hearing penalty phase evidence in the bifurcated trial procedure, the judge gives instructions to the jurors about what factors can be considered as aggravating or mitigating (see preceding; see also Luginbuhl & Middledorf, 1988). Unfortunately, a great deal of research now suggests that jurors have a disturbingly low understanding or comprehension of these instructions and often misunderstand what they are supposed to do (see Diamond, 1993; Diamond & Levi, 1996; Haney & Lynch, 1997; Luginbuhl, 1992; Wiener, Pritchard, & Weston, 1995; Wiener, Hurt, Thomas, Sadler, Bauer, & Sargent, 1998). Although some lower courts have been presented with these arguments by attorneys for capital defendants, no case has yet reached the United States Supreme Court.

The Generation of Other Research Findings

The forensic psychologist, in the role of evaluation researcher, can also assess claims made in support of the death penalty. Two of these claims—that the availability of the death penalty deters crime and that executions cost less than life imprisonment—are evaluated in this section. The forensic psychologist, by applying tools of statistics and experimental design, can also highlight some of the biases in the application of the death penalty.

Does the Presence of a Death Penalty Deter Crime?

A commonly held belief is that the availability of capital punishment deters crime; it assumes that if punishment deters, then harsh punishment should deter best (Costanzo, 1997). The vast majority of the extensive research (reviewed by Bowers, 1984, 1988, and by Costanzo, 1997, chap. 6) concludes the opposite. For example, Bailey and Peterson (1994) have noted that every study that compares homicide rates in adjoining states has found that the states with the death penalty had *higher* homicide rates than did neighboring states without the death penalty. Similarly, studies of the murders of police officers and prison guards found a similar trend (Bailey & Peterson, 1994). When a state reinstitutes the death penalty, its homicide rate does not decrease; it is more likely that the opposite occurs (Costanzo, 1997).

In fact, some researchers believe that the data are consistent enough to demonstrate that the presence of a death penalty in a state creates a **brutalization effect,** in that human life is held less sacred. Bowers expressed this viewpoint as follows:

> The lesson of an execution may be that those who have gravely offended us deserve to die and should therefore be killed. If a potential offender feels betrayed, dishonored, or disgraced by another person, the example executions provide may provoke him to kill the person who has grievously offended him. The fact that such killings are to be performed only by duly appointed officials upon duly convicted offenders may be obscured by the message that such offenders deserve to die. In effect, the fundamental message of the execution may be lethal vengeance rather than deterrence. (1988, pp. 53–54)

Additionally, executions may stimulate further homicides by a process of suggestion. The assassination of President John F. Kennedy and two highly publicized mass murders led to significantly increased rates of violent crime in subsequent months, leading Leonard Berkowitz and Jacqueline Macaulay to offer a theory of imitative violence in which the processes of generalization lead to violent ideas and images. They wrote,

> If inhibitions against aggression are not evoked by the witnessed violence or by the observers' anticipation of negative consequences of aggressive behavior, and if the observers are ready to act violently, the event can also evoke

open aggression. And again, these aggressive responses need not resemble the instigating violence too closely. (1971, p. 239)

William Bowers's examination of the data from nearly 70 different studies of murder rates concluded that executions do increase murder rates and that "this effect is slight in magnitude (though not in consequence), that it occurs within the first month or two of an execution, and that it dissipates thereafter" (1988, p. 71).

Even the long-time district attorney of Manhattan in New York City, Robert M. Morgenthau, wrote, "Prosecutors must reveal the dirty little secret they too often share only among themselves: The death penalty actually hinders the fight against crime" (1995, p. A11). Similarly, a survey conducted in 1995 of 386 police chiefs and sheriffs found that most did not believe that the death penalty significantly reduced the number of homicides: "Most people do not think about the death penalty before they commit a crime," the police chief of Los Angeles said (Murphy, 1995, p. 11A).

The issue of the future behavior of those sentenced to death is also relevant to the question of the deterrence value of this punishment. Two studies are especially of interest. Marquart and Sorenson (1989) used as their subjects more than 500 people whose death sentences were commuted as a result of the Supreme Court's *Furman v. Georgia* (1972) ruling. (Most of these had been convicted of murder, a few of rape.) What happened to these prisoners over the next 15 years? Of the 300 who were still in prison, 4 killed other prisoners and 2 killed guards or correction officers. Other than these acts, these prisoners committed few acts of violence. Of the 250 released to the community, one committed another murder during the next 15 years, and 12% were arrested for new felonies. Most of them (around 80%) had no other arrests.

A second study, by Sorensen and Wrinkle (1996), compared the behavior in prison of 93 prisoners sentenced to death, 232 sentenced to life with the possibility of parole, and 323 sentenced to life in prison without the possibility of parole. No significant differences occurred in the rates of violence among these types, and their base rate for the occurrence of violent acts was no higher than for inmates convicted of noncapital offenses.

Which Costs the Government More: Execution or Life in Prison?

As Costanzo (1997) observed, a purely economic analysis may seem insensitive or irrelevant to the discussion of a life-or-death issue, but it is the case that assertions regarding financial costs often emerge in arguments about the value of the death penalty. On first thought, it would seem that it would cost the government less money to execute a convicted murderer than it would cost to keep that murderer in prison for 20, 30, or 40 years. In fact, executions cost the state $2 million more than imprisoning the convict for life (Costanzo, 1997, chap. 4; Verhovek, 1995). Surprisingly, the bulk of the expense occurs at the trial level, partially because of the increased procedural safeguards in a capital case (Ross, 1998). Every portion of the guilt-determination phase takes longer, including jury selection. The number and complexity of motions are greater in a capital trial (Epstein, 1995).

Sources of Bias in the Application of the Death Sentence

One hundred years ago, lynchings of Blacks for the alleged rape or murder of Whites were so frequent in the Southern states that newspapers would report that "a Negro man was hanged for the usual crime" (Costanzo, 1997). More recently, evaluation research by social scientists and others has demonstrated a continuing racial bias in the sentence of death, as chapter 1 illustrated in discussing the *amicus* brief submitted to the Supreme Court in the case of *McCleskey v. Kemp* (1987). That case dealt with sentences in the state of Georgia, but equivalent examples of racial bias have been shown in several other states (Paternoster & Kazyaka, 1988).

But putting racial bias aside, the likelihood of a person convicted of homicide being sentenced to death depends upon the state in which the murder occurs. That state-by-state differences are present is easy to demonstrate. First, 12 states and the District of Columbia have no death penalty. Second, the number of sentences of death in recent years varies widely from state to state; Texas, with more than 160 executions since 1976, accounts for almost one third of the total, while Virginia and Florida, together, have executed another 100. In contrast, several of those states with the death penalty have executed no one. It follows from these differences that a much less severe crime can lead to a death sentence in Texas or Florida than in, say, New Jersey or Oregon. Even within a state, there are "hot zones," or counties notorious for their use of the death penalty. In Texas in 1995, of the 397 inmates on death row, 113 came from one county (Lewin, 1995).

SUMMARY

Those psychologists who are opposed to the death penalty may do so because of a belief that it violates basic values of justice and human worth. Or, their opposition may stem from awareness that a certain percentage of those who are executed are innocent. These psychologists may be sympathetic to the powerless, and, in this situation, they are aware of the power of the prosecutor and the police and the sometimes ineffective counsel provided to the defendant. But there is a danger in translating this value into an advocacy orientation; the task of the forensic psychologist is to provide an objective evaluation to the defense attorney or the court.

In cases involving the death penalty, forensic psychologists can play a significant role at several points. Prior to a trial, a judge may order a competency evaluation. If a trial is scheduled, the psychologist may conduct a change-of-venue survey if the defense attorney feels that the community is biased against the defendant. Psychologists can also assist in developing a theory of the case and in jury selection. Trials are bifurcated into the guilt-determination phase and the sentencing phase. For the latter phase, in which the jury (in most states) assigns the punishment, the psychologist can assist the defense attorney by preparing a mitigation assessment— that is, determining whether there are factors in the defendant's background or personality that would lead jurors to temper their sentences. If the defendant is sentenced to death and appeals the sentence, the psychologist can assist in the appeal by conducting a thorough psychological evaluation of competency to be executed.

Forensic psychologists—acting as research scientists—also have contributions to make. Beliefs about the death penalty, especially those that advocate it, often rest on its assumed deterrence value and its assumed lessened cost (compared to life in prison). Empirical research by psychologists and other social scientists questions these assumptions. Psychological research also can demonstrate the racial and gender bias in the application of the death penalty.

KEY TERMS

aggravating factors
bifurcated trial
brutalization effect
capital case
competency-for-execution evaluation
death-qualification procedure
death-qualified jury
exculpatory evidence
felony murder
fundamental attribution error
guilt-determination phase
habeas corpus
harmless error
mitigating factors
mitigation assessment
penalty phase
sentencing phase
theory of the case

INFOTRAC® COLLEGE EDITION

InfoTrac College Edition is a FREE, powerful, online learning resource, consisting of full-text articles from thousands of journals and periodicals. With each new copy of *Forensic Psychology*, Second Edition, you receive 4 months of free access to the InfoTrac College Edition database. By doing a simple keyword search (try using the Key Terms in the list above), you can quickly generate a list of relevant articles from thousands of possibilities and can select articles to read, explore, and print for reference or further study. InfoTrac College Edition's continuously updated collection of articles can be useful for doing reading and writing assignments that reach beyond the pages of this text!

SUGGESTED READINGS

Costanzo, M. (1997). *Just revenge: Costs and consequences of the death penalty.* New York: St. Martin's Press.

An impassioned, articulate assault on the death penalty by a research-oriented social psychologist. Contains chapter-length reviews of several issues, including the cost of the death penalty and its impact as a deterrent.

Haas, K. C., & Inciardi, J. A. (Eds.). *Challenging capital punishment: Legal and social science approaches.* Thousand Oaks, CA: Sage.

A collection of contributed chapters by social scientists that brings research findings to bear on the question of the appropriateness of the death penalty.

Huff, C. R., Rattner, A., & Sagarin, E. (1996). *Convicted but innocent: Wrongful conviction and public policy.* Thousand Oaks, CA: Sage.

The focus of this book extends beyond capital crimes, but it is useful in illustrating the magnitude of the problem and the sources of error when innocent people are found guilty.

Nelson, P. (1994). *Defending the devil: My story as Ted Bundy's last lawyer.* New York: William Morrow.

Polly Nelson was an associate at a Washington, D.C., law firm, fresh out of law school, when she was offered Ted Bundy's death penalty appeal as a pro bono project. For the next 3 years, until he was executed in January 1989, that's what she did. A remarkably candid, even self-critical, examination of a lawyer's feelings, as well as a thorough demonstration of the steps in the death-sentence appeal process.

Radelet, M. L., Bedau, H. A., & Putnam, C. E. (1992). *In spite of innocence: Erroneous convictions in capital cases.* Boston: Northeastern University Press.

An analysis of 400 cases in which a possibly innocent person was convicted of a capital crime; some were executed, while most of the others spent years in prison. Each case is briefly described.

Von Drehle, D. (1995). *Among the lowest of the dead: The culture of death row.* New York: Times Books/Random House.

A bitter indictment of the judges, prosecutors, defense attorneys, and wardens whose lives affect the inmates on Florida's death row. Also includes a description of how various states responded to the Supreme Court's decision in *Furman v. Georgia* (1972) that the death penalty could not be administered in an arbitrary or capricious manner.

16

Influencing Public Policy*

Application of Psychological Knowledge to Decisions by Legal-System Policy Makers

Ways of Influencing Legislatures

Testimony by Psychologists

Psychologists and the Courts

The Use of *Amicus* Briefs

History of the Relationship

Direct Attempts to Influence the Courts

Ballew v. Georgia (1978): Too Little and Too Late?

Involvement by the American Psychological Association

Ways of Classifying APA Briefs

What Are the APA's Goals in Submitting Science-Translation Briefs?

The Effectiveness of APA Briefs

How Do We Measure Effectiveness?

Is It Better to Be Ignored or Rejected?

The Relationship of the APA *Amicus* Brief to the Supreme Court's Decision

An Example of a Decision Consistent with the APA's Goals But Not Directly Reflecting the APA's Input: Ake v. Oklahoma (1985)

An Example of Rejection of the APA Brief: Lockhart v. McCree (1986)

What Can We Learn From Individual Cases?

The Potency of Deeply Held Values

Identifying and Representing Our Goals Accurately

Summary

Key Terms

Suggested Readings

*Much of the material in this chapter is based on chapters 6–10 of *Judicial Decision Making: Is Psychology Relevant?* by Lawrence Wrightsman, published in 1999 by Plenum Publishing Company.

APPLICATION OF PSYCHO-LOGICAL KNOWLEDGE TO DECISIONS BY LEGAL-SYSTEM POLICY MAKERS

Recall that this book began by defining forensic psychology as any application of psychological knowledge to the legal system. The focus of this chapter is the direct attempts by groups of psychologists to bring about legal reform and to influence specific decisions made in the legal system. Do such actions fall under the rubric of "forensic psychology"? Following the definition in chapter 1, the answer is clearly yes. Decisions made by legislatures and the courts affect a number of phenomena that are subject to psychological analysis; insanity, joint custody, hypnotically refreshed testimony, sexual harassment, and competency of a defendant to be executed are only a few of the examples described earlier in this book.

Who makes public policy decisions? Is psychological knowledge relevant to some of these decisions? Assuming that it is, how does the field of psychology influence those decisions? And what are the obstacles to its having an influence? Simply put, the executive branch may identify public policy needs, the legislative branch decides whether to make them law, and the judicial branch intervenes if executive actions or legislative decisions violate constitutional guidelines or conflict with other laws. In a broad sense, each branch of government plays a role in policy formulation and institutionalization; although many judges would deny that they "make public policy," a decision that, for example, segregation by race in the public schools is unconstitutional clearly is a statement of governmental policy, especially when it tells school systems that they must desegregate their schools "with all deliberate speed."

Ways of Influencing Legislatures

Three means by which the field of psychology may bring psychological knowledge to the attention of national or state legislative bodies are (a) lobbying, (b) placing psychologists on legislative staffs, and (c) providing expert testimony at legislative hearings. For example, representatives of the American Psychological Association may meet with members of the U. S. Congress to advocate a greater allocation of budget money for predoctoral and postdoctoral training in the social sciences, for further research funding, or for support of intervention programs that reflect sound psychological research. Lobbying may include issuing press releases on significant research findings or meeting with key congressional staff members. In the last 15 years, a number of scientific organizations, coordinated by the American Association for the Advancement of Science, have provided financial support for the placement of some of their members as congressional fellows; for example, a psychologist may serve on the staff of a specific member of Congress with a goal of advising the congressperson on the desirability of certain legislation. Some of these congressional fellows later become legislative staff members.

Testimony by Psychologists

As legislative committees consider the wisdom of proposed legislation, psychologists can testify about the relevance of their perspective. Two examples in which such testimony was effective are the following:

- John Monahan (1977), a psychologist on the faculty of the law school at the University of Virginia, testified effectively before the California legislature with regard to abolishing the use of indeterminate sentences.
- In the early 1980s, the U.S. Department of Labor proposed changes that would increase the number of hours that children

and adolescents could work when school was in session from 18 up to 24 hours per week. Also, it proposed that the curfew on school-night employment be set at 9 p.m. rather than 7 p.m. In doing so, the Department of Labor claimed that such changes would not "interfere with [the] health or well-being" of children (quoted by Greenberger, 1983, p. 104). The chair of the Subcommittee on Labor Standards of the U.S. House of Representatives, George Miller, asked Ellen Greenberger, a psychologist at the University of California, Irvine, to testify about her research that was contradictory to the Department of Labor's claim. Her highly publicized testimony that working longer hours had a detrimental effect on school performance and family life was apparently so effective that the Department of Labor withdrew its proposal while the hearings were still being held.

But seldom is the effect of testimony by psychologists so demonstrable; legislative votes reflect many influences, and more often, the relationship between research and policy is complex and even undecipherable (Takanishi & Melton, 1987). Furthermore, the use of psychologists as expert witnesses has been developed more at the national than at the state legislative level; state psychological associations may be actively involved in the legislative process, but such activity has usually been limited to issues involving psychology as a profession (Melton, 1985).

Psychologists and the Courts

Although the courts are often seen as that branch of government having the least impact, court decisions regulate our society, not just with regard to the definition of what is legal but also with respect to many quasi-legal relationships between individuals. We are beginning to understand a little more about the possible influence that the field of psychology can have on judicial decisions.

THE USE OF *AMICUS* BRIEFS

The major emphasis of this chapter is on decisions by appellate courts that are relevant to the application of psychology to legal issues. Several methods exist for the field of psychology to influence judicial decisions. As illustrated in several of the previous chapters, experts may testify at a hearing or a trial. Or, when the field of psychology seeks to bring about a particular judicial ruling, it may—as a plaintiff—file a lawsuit and seek redress through the courts. In certain so-called **guild issues,** or professional issues in which the organization seeks to safeguard the integrity of the profession, the American Psychological Association has done so—for example, when insurance companies denied coverage of insured clients' psychotherapy bills if the psychotherapist was a psychologist rather than a psychiatrist. But more often, psychologists have sought to educate or influence the courts through the submission of **amicus curiae briefs,** or arguments by a third party to the dispute that seek, as "a friend of the court," to inform the judges on matters relevant to the dispute. The focus of this chapter is on the use of *amicus* briefs to bring to the attention of appellate judges a relevant psychological perspective.

History of the Relationship

Typically, the case of *Muller v. Oregon,* which the Supreme Court resolved in 1908, is cited as the earliest U.S. Supreme Court case to benefit from a social-science perspective. And it certainly is a landmark, because it was the first to include a brief (prepared by Louis Brandeis, later to become a Supreme Court justice himself) reviewing empirical work on the issue at hand, which was the effects of long working hours on women. But does the social science perspective have an even earlier history in the Court's decision making? Tomkins and Oursland (1991) argued that it does, specifically that "social scientific perspectives have *consistently* been a part of legal decision making in cases that address social issues" (p. 103, italics in original). Even though those judicial opinions earlier than *Muller v. Oregon* did not cite social science facts or perspectives as the *authority,* the impact of such factors may be detected.

Tomkins and Oursland chose two 19th-century cases as examples of their claim; both were race-related—a fortuitous choice, as the determinants of judicial decisions about the proper role of race in our society reflect a continuing concern by the field of psychology, as well as the topic of several chapters of this book. The *Dred Scott* case (officially, *Dred Scott v. Sandford*) in 1857 brought focus to the question whether—given the legality of slavery in many states at that time—African Americans were citizens of the United States and hence had the right to bring suit in federal court. The case, which had begun more than a decade earlier, reflected the petitions filed by Mr. Scott and his wife, Harriet Scott, who sought freedom from their owner, Irene Emerson. The majority opinion, in a 7 to 2 vote, was delivered by Chief Justice Roger Taney, a Southerner. The 241-page opinion noted that "for more than a century [the black race has] been regarded as beings of an inferior order, and altogether unfit to associate with the white race, either in social or political relations" (*Dred Scott v. Sandford,* 1857, p. 407). More relevant to Tomkins and Oursland's conclusion was the Chief Justice's statement that the preceding view was the dominant "social scientific" position at that time or, as Taney expressed it, a belief "regarded as an axiom in morals as well as politics" (p. 407; see also Hovenkamp, 1985).

This predominant view did not change during the last half of the 19th century, even though the focus shifted from slavery to what was then called racial "mixing." The *Plessy v. Ferguson* decision in 1896 is singled out by social scientists interested in racial desegregation because it remained in effect until it was overturned in 1954 by the decision in *Brown v. Board of Education of Topeka.* Hence, it is instructive to examine the rationale used by the Court in its 7 to 1 decision. Homer Plessy, classified as a "colored" person in Louisiana because one of his great-grandparents was African American, questioned

the constitutionality of an 1890 Louisiana law that required "equal but separate accommodations for the white and colored races" in all passenger trains (*Plessy v. Ferguson,* 1896, p. 540). Not only did the Court uphold this law but it did so because the requirement was consistent with the "established usages, customs, and traditions of the people" (p. 550). Even while claiming that the law did not imply invidious distinctions between the races, Justice Henry Brown's majority opinion concluded that the Louisiana law "could not have been intended to abolish distinctions based upon color, or to enforce social, as distinguished from political equality, or a commingling of the two races upon terms unsatisfactory to either" (p. 544).

Hovenkamp (1985) concluded that the *Plessy* decision reflected the commonplace assumption 100 years ago: Racial mixing was harmful. Similarly, Tomkins and Oursland noted that a belief about the inferiority of African Americans "was basic to most white Americans (including scientists) and the prospect of miscegenation was particularly horrifying to many whites who feared that sexual intermingling with the black race would toll the death knell for the white race" (1991, p. 112). In fact, the *Plessy* decision apparently evoked little comment at the time, reflecting how congruent were its values with those of the scientific community (Lofgren, 1987).

Thus, it can be argued that, in the broadest sense, the courts have traditionally acted in ways consistent with the thinking of social scientists, but such a conclusion seems more fitting for earlier times than today. In retrospect, the values of the two approaches (the legal and the scientific) seemed to be in more agreement 100 years ago than now. Now, the Court chooses to agree with the empirical findings of psychology only when the latter are consistent with the preexisting values of the justices.

Direct Attempts to Influence the Courts

The influence of social science thinking in the preceding 19th-century decisions was a subtle one; it was not until the mid-20th century that social scientists actively sought to influence court decisions. Chapter 2 described the role of the research by Kenneth and Mamie Clark on African American children's reactions to differently colored dolls in arguments before the Court with regard to the *Brown v. Board of Education* case. Also, a concerned group of social scientists submitted an *amicus* brief in anticipation of the Court's consideration of the *Brown* decision (Allport et al., 1953). Whether the statement from the 35 prominent social scientists influenced the Court's decision remains controversial; it is most likely that the justices had made up their minds without it, but included a footnote about it in their decision, to combat anticipated public resistance to their conclusion. But this midcentury attempt was an isolated one; it was not until the last quarter of the 20th century that the submission of *amicus* briefs by psychologists became an organized activity. The case of *Ballew v. Georgia,* decided by the Court in 1978, became a precursor.

Ballew v. Georgia (1978): Too Little and Too Late?

In the mid-1970s, Claude Ballew was leading a seemingly uneventful life, managing an adult movie theater in Atlanta, when he was arrested, and later convicted by a five-person jury, for showing an obscene film (*Behind the Green Door*). Mr. Ballew decided to challenge the then-rather-new Georgia law that permitted this drastic reduction in jury size, claiming that it interfered with his constitutional right to due process. But the Georgia courts, to his displeasure, upheld the state law, and so Mr. Ballew's only choice was to seek redress at the U.S. Supreme Court.

An Offer of Services

When Elizabeth Decker Tanke and Tony J. Tanke (a social scientist and a lawyer, respectively) learned that the Supreme Court had agreed to rule on Mr. Ballew's appeal, they offered their assistance to each side. The Tankes

provided the appellee with excerpts from Michael Saks's (1977) book on jury size and decisions and from their own bibliography (Tanke & Tanke, 1977), which listed several studies of the effects of jury size.

Use of Social Science Information by One Side

The counsel for the state of Georgia cited these studies during the oral arguments before the Supreme Court, and later the Court's library obtained a copy of their bibliography from the Tankes. In fact, the availability of these sources doubtless contributed to their being cited in the Court's majority opinion in its *Ballew v. Georgia* (1978) decision.

Amicus Briefs as Attempts to Influence

Thus, awareness by the justices of the existence of social science research on the effects of jury size occurred only because of the Tankes' intervention. A more systematic way to bring attention to what are considered relevant issues is the use of the *amicus* brief. Historically, an *amicus curiae* may be defined as:

> a friend of the court . . . a bystander, who without having an interest in the case, of his [*sic*] own knowledge makes a suggestion on a point of law or of fact for the information of the presiding judge. (Tanke & Tanke, quoting *Abbott's Dictionary of Terms and Phrases,* 1979, p. 1137)

The procedure can be traced to an appearance by Henry Clay before the U.S. Supreme Court in 1821, although more than 100 years passed before the Supreme Court issued formal rules about the submission of such briefs (Krislov, 1963; Menez, 1984).

The American Psychological Association did not file an *amicus* brief in the *Ballew* case; the only one submitted was done by the Citizens for Decency Through Law, Inc., an organization that sought to uphold Mr. Ballew's obscenity conviction. It would have been to the Court's benefit to have had "a true *amicus* brief—a presentation by concerned social scientists who, without seeking to advance a special interest in the merits of the case, offered guidance to the Court in a discussion of their work" (Tanke & Tanke, 1979, p. 1137).

Justice Blackmun's Consideration of Empirical Research and Statistical Logic

Justice Harry Blackmun, who wrote the majority opinion in *Ballew*, had access to social science research; in contrast, those earlier decisions by the Court on matters of the jury's size and decisions were devoid of any awareness of the quality of recent empirical work. The issues had surfaced a decade before; in *Williams v. Florida* (1970), the Supreme Court had upheld Williams's robbery conviction by a Florida jury of 6 people, thereby rejecting the claim that he was constitutionally entitled to a 12-person jury under the Sixth and Fourteenth Amendments. In the case of *Colgrove v. Battin* (1973), the Court approved the use of 6-person juries in civil trials, stating that "four very recent studies have provided convincing empirical evidence" (p. 159).

In the *Williams* decision, the Court saw the issue of size as related to the jury's function; although it acknowledged that "the number [of jurors] be large enough to promote group deliberation, free from outside attempts at intimidation, and to provide a fair possibility for obtaining a representative cross-section of the community," it ruled that a jury of only six people fulfilled such requirements (*Williams v. Florida*, 1970, p. 100).

Do 6-person juries render verdicts different from those of the traditional 12-person ones? Is a smaller jury prejudicial to a criminal defendant? The absence of an *amicus* brief from a group of psychologists in the *Williams* case is most disturbing because the Court's opinion stated (in two footnotes) that the available research findings—using trials of civil cases—found "no discernible difference" in the decisions of 6-person and 12-person juries. But the Court had no appreciation for the quality of the research; the "jury experiments" cited by the

Court were mostly expressions of opinions based on "uncontrolled observations that might be likened to clinical case studies" (Saks, 1977, p. 9).

As Michael Saks's (1977) useful review noted, none of the studies cited in the *Williams* opinion was published in a refereed social science journal. One simply asserted its conclusion without any evidence; three were anecdotal observations; one simply reported that a smaller jury was used; and the remaining one focused on the financial savings from the use of fewer jurors. None of these qualified as well-designed empirical research. This conclusion can also be made for the studies underpinning the previously mentioned *Colgrove v. Battin* decision regarding civil-trial juries (Zeisel & Diamond, 1974). (Ironically, had these been offered by expert witnesses as the basis for their conclusions, a trial judge should have rejected them on the grounds that they lacked validity.)

Yet, they contributed to the Court's acceptance of six-person juries. In fairness, it must be noted that subsequent work by psychologists, carrying out controlled experiments, did not find large differences in the verdicts by juries of different sizes, but clear differences were present in the group *process*. Saks (1977) described these as follows:

> Large juries, compared to small juries, spend more time deliberating, engage in more communication per unit time, manifest better recall of testimony, induce less disparity between majority and minority factions in their rating of perceived jury performance and in sociometric ratings, and less disparity between convicting and acquitting juries in number of arguments generated, facilitate markedly better community representation, and though not achieving statistical significance, more consistent verdicts. (1977, p. 105)

Twenty years later, Saks, with his coauthor Mollie Marti (1997), examined the studies on this question done in the intervening two decades and found essentially the same results. Thus, based on the empirical work, we may question whether 6-person and 12-person juries function equivalently. But recall that Mr. Ballew's jury was composed of only *five* jurors.

In the *Ballew* case, in contrast to earlier ones, the majority opinion was written by a justice who was characteristically responsive to social science findings and relatively proficient in their use (Grofman & Scarrow, 1980). In many ways, Justice Blackmun's opinion was a model for the judicial use of empirical research; for example, it contained a 10-page, well-documented discussion of both the legal literature and the social science literature on the effects of the jury's size; Justice Blackmun had 71 citations to 19 different social science sources (Acker, 1990). Apparently for the first time, the description of social science research findings was elevated from a footnote to the main text of a Supreme Court opinion (Saks, 1977). Tanke and Tanke (1979) summarized Justice Blackmun's conclusions as follows:

1. The smaller juries are *less* likely to encourage dissent, overcome biases of individual jurors, or aid the jurors in recalling significant evidence.
2. A reduction in the size of the jury produces less consistent and reliable verdicts and increases the likelihood of a conviction.
3. When the jury is smaller, it is less likely to fail to reach a verdict.
4. Smaller juries, by that very fact, are less representative of minority viewpoints.

But Justice Blackmun chose to focus his distinction between juries of six people (which previously had been approved by the Supreme Court) and Mr. Ballew's five-person jury. His majority opinion concluded that although it could not "discern a clear line between six members and five," it had substantial doubt about "the reliability and appropriate representation of panels smaller than six" (*Ballew v. Georgia,* 1978, p. 239). Thus, the Court ruled that five was too small.

The fact is that no research was (or is) available comparing juries of five people with juries of six people. But the irony is that Justice Black-

mun used social science and statistical findings "to support his belief that juries of five are too small, but he was not willing to use the same body of research, almost all of which compared 6- and 12-person juries, to refute the Court's approval of the 6-person jury" (Tanke & Tanke, 1979, p. 1133). Judges are reluctant to overturn past decisions, and in this case, the research came too late.

A Diversity of Opinions

Other reasons exist for a conclusion that the *Ballew* case opinion was not a total victory for psychology and social science. Even though the Court unanimously voted to overturn Mr. Ballew's obscenity conviction, only one other justice (John Paul Stevens) endorsed the reasons given by Justice Blackmun. For example, Justice White voted against the acceptability of five jurors not on the basis of research findings but because "a jury of fewer than six would fail to represent the sense of community" (p. 245).

Most disturbing was the opinion of Justice Lewis Powell (with which Chief Justice Burger and Justice Rehnquist agreed). While noting that "a line must be drawn somewhere," Justice Powell added,

> I have reservations as to the wisdom—as well as the necessity—of Mr. Justice Blackmun's heavy reliance on numerology derived from statistical studies. Moreover, neither the validity nor the methodology employed by the studies cited was subjected to the traditional testing mechanisms of the adversary process. The studies relied on merely represent unexamined findings of persons interested in the jury system. (p. 246)

Conclusions

The decision in the *Ballew* case must be considered a bittersweet triumph for social science. As Tanke and Tanke (1979) observed, "For the first time, inferences drawn from such research became the central justification for the Court's decision rather than merely a pedagogically interesting sideshow" (p. 1133). But the opinions of other justices reflected the legal system's heavy reliance on the precedent of past rulings and the use of the adversary process (especially cross-examination) to evaluate the claims of science. Despite these reservations, the outcome reflected a new level of acknowledgment of psychology's advisory role.

INVOLVEMENT BY THE AMERICAN PSYCHOLOGICAL ASSOCIATION

The year that the *Ballew* case was decided, 1979, the American Psychological Association established an Office of Legal Counsel and a Committee on Legal Issues (COLI); one of their functions is to decide whether psychological data, conclusions, and recommendations are relevant to cases that are appealed to the United States Supreme Court and other appellate courts throughout the country. If judged to be, the APA then submits an *amicus curiae* brief. In the last 25 years, the APA has submitted over 150 such briefs, about half of which went to the Supreme Court (Foote, 1998).

Ways of Classifying APA Briefs

The *amicus* briefs that have been submitted by the American Psychological Association cover a variety of topics, from the sexual rights of homosexual people to the use of psychological tests in personnel selection. As noted earlier, submission of some briefs is motivated by the APA's goal of protecting its rights as a profession; for example, the first brief sponsored by the APA as an organization, submitted in 1962 for the case of *Jenkins v. United States,* dealt with the rights of psychologists as expert witnesses to state their professional opinions. Since then, a number of briefs have dealt with professional issues, such as client-therapist confidentiality (8 cases) and access to patients (10 cases). But our emphasis in this chapter is on those APA briefs in which psychological knowledge and expertise are applied to topics of

national concern—such as the death penalty, abortion, and children as court witnesses— in the hopes of influencing public policy.

The latter type—those concerned with public policy—may have varying goals. Roesch, Golding, Hans, and Reppucci (1991) suggested that *amicus* briefs can be organized along a continuum. At one end is a **science-translation brief,** intended to be an "objective summary of research" (p. 6); at the other end is an **advocacy brief,** which "takes a position on some legal or public policy issue" (p. 6).

Where do we draw the line between a science-translation brief and an advocacy brief? Saks (1993), commenting on the APA's briefs, observed that "in at least three cases I know of . . . , some members of the brief-writing group came away with the distinct impression that the brief was being written in order to advance the interests of one of the parties to the litigation, or to produce a particular outcome, rather than to share knowledge with the Court for the Court's benefit." (p. 243)

This comment reflects the inevitable result when a brief attempts to be sensitive to the diverse membership of the APA.

What Are the APA's Goals in Submitting Science-Translation Briefs?

Psychologists disagree as to how much advocacy is appropriate in APA briefs. These disagreements also influence the stated goals in science-translation briefs. One goal, as implied earlier, is to influence the court's decision. Perhaps the way to express this goal with the greatest chance of agreement among psychologists is to state that the APA has knowledge that the court doesn't have. Saks (1993), emphasizing the objective goal of such briefs, sees the APA as a knowledge broker, "a neutral, honest provider of information, unconcerned with which party is helped or harmed by the data and the brief" (p. 243). Implicit here is that the brief reports on any diversity in research findings and differences in psychologists' conclusions (Saks, 1993, p. 241).

A related goal is to point out to the court where the relevant research can be found; that is, to educate the court to be able to distinguish between good research and bad research. Such briefs "may reduce the likelihood that judicial use of spurious, unsubstantiated opinions about human behavior will establish precedent for future cases" (Grisso & Saks, 1991, p. 207). Previously, we described the use of nonempirical "studies" in the *Williams v. Florida* jury-size decision; in contrast, substantial empirical studies now exist that are relevant to this issue. But a general question remains: How much do we have to know in order to submit a brief? How much do psychologists have to agree? Are all studies "worth" the same? Saks (1993) noted that we have no agreed-upon standards to guide us.

Whether psychologists should submit an *amicus* brief reflects the same distinction made in an earlier chapter regarding whether to testify as an expert on eyewitness accuracy. Some psychologists would submit a brief when the knowledge at their disposal improves the quality of judicial decision making to any significant degree. Others would wait until the research findings are so consistent and so powerful that they reflect near-100% reliability. Regardless where we draw the dividing point on acceptability, in the words of Grisso and Saks (1991, p. 210), we should value our credibility. The American Psychological Association, in contrast to most professional organizations that submit briefs, has a reputation for providing data-oriented arguments that reflect a broader appreciation of the issues than do most briefs.

THE EFFECTIVENESS OF APA BRIEFS

The purposes of this book are to examine how psychological concepts, methods, and findings are applied to the legal system and to describe the various roles for psychologists in applying these findings. Central to this thrust is this question: How effective are we in these applications? Specifically, do the APA *amicus* briefs achieve their goals?

How Do We Measure Effectiveness?

In discussing effectiveness, we need to recognize the presence of diverse goals. For example, one purpose is to advance the policy agenda of organized psychology, to "get the message out" (Tremper, 1987). Similarly, the submission of briefs may raise the consciousness of the judiciary regarding the usefulness of psychology as a basis for governmental policy decisions, regardless whether the recommendations of the APA are followed in the case at hand. For example, in several cases involving the battered woman syndrome (*Hawthorne v. Florida,* 1985, and *New Jersey v. Kelly,* 1984), the APA submitted briefs to point out that the topic had a sufficiently well developed foundation, so that when trial judges excluded expert testimony on the topic, they exceeded their judicial discretion. The goal of achieving a court ruling consistent with the APA's goals and findings is, of course, one motivation.

The simplest way to measure impact on the judicial procedures would be to determine whether the Supreme Court's majority opinion was consistent with the thrust of the APA's brief. This assumes that the direction or recommendation of the APA brief can clearly be determined. Thus, a "hit rate" or success rate is determined, based on the outcome or disposition. But even if the two are congruent, it is difficult to infer an effect from the APA brief because so many causes are possible for each Supreme Court decision (Tremper, 1987).

Thus, a second suggestion for measuring impact is to determine if the specific *amicus* brief is cited or quoted in the Supreme Court's decision. Roesch et al. (1991) noted that "impact" studies rely primarily on citation counts for an indication of whether the courts have used such research in their opinions. But even if a psychological brief is cited, we don't know the reason for the Supreme Court's having done so; is it because of perceived relevance, or just post-hoc justification or window-dressing? Recall the controversy over Footnote 11 in the *Brown v. Board of Education* decision. Another procedure is to determine if the Supreme Court's opinion discussed the references cited in the *amicus* brief, but "even then an element of conjecture remains in attempting to isolate the *amicus* brief's unique influence" (Tremper, 1987, p. 498).

Is It Better to Be Ignored or Rejected?

What if the Supreme Court's decision is contrary to the APA's recommendation? Is it then better to be rejected or ignored? Several psychologists (including some of those who drafted most of the APA briefs) apparently consider it noteworthy when a brief receives attention from the justices or the media, even when the decision conflicts with the psychologists' goals. Chapter 1 described the Supreme Court's opinion in the *Lockhart v. McCree* (1986) case, in which Justice Rehnquist devoted several pages of his opinion to a critique of the relevant empirical research on bias in death-qualified jurors. About this case, Tremper (1987) wrote, "the majority regarded the research as sufficiently important to warrant devoting several pages of its opinion to critiquing the studies' methodologies" (p. 499). Regarding two cases (*McCleskey v. Kemp*, described in chapter 1, and *Bowers v. Hardwick*, to be discussed later in this chapter), Grisso and Saks (1991) concluded that the Court took psychological evidence seriously enough to discuss it. And with respect to the *Hardwick* case, Bersoff and Ogden (1991) wrote, "Although the [APA] brief did not persuade the majority to modify its pinched interpretation of the right to privacy, its position was prominently and positively represented in the media" (p. 953).

Sometimes the effect of the APA's having taken a position does not surface in a court decision until years later. In 1986, in the *Bowers v. Hardwick* decision, the Supreme Court upheld the state of Georgia's law that made homosexual sexual relations illegal. The American Psychological Association had submitted an *amicus* brief that reviewed extensive research concluding that

persons with a homosexual orientation did not differ in regard to their psychological adjustment from those with a heterosexual orientation. Furthermore, the brief noted the stigmatizing effect of laws banning sodomy. The majority opinion did not mention the APA's brief, although a dissent by Justice Blackmun did. After the *Bowers v. Hardwick* decision was announced, it received a great deal of publicity (and criticism); several years later, one of the justices who voted with the majority, Lewis Powell, revealed that he had probably made a mistake. In another case 17 years after *Hardwick,* the case of *Lawrence v. Texas* (2003)—also involving the rights of people with a homosexual orientation—the Court voted to support gay rights. Many possible reasons exist for this shift, but the APA's brief and the resulting publicity about the normality of people with a homosexual orientation may have had a gradual, eventual influence.

THE RELATIONSHIP OF THE APA *AMICUS* BRIEF TO THE SUPREME COURT'S DECISION

Few cases are chosen by the Supreme Court for review; Box 16-1 describes the often confusing steps from the initial trial to that level. When the Supreme Court does agree to consider a case, the justices (with the assistance of their law clerks) carefully review all the submitted briefs, including any *amicus curiae* briefs provided by other parties. Although one purpose of *amicus* briefs is to inform the Court, usually their main goal is to persuade the justices to render a decision that favors one of the contesting parties. Thus, when the American Psychological Association submits a brief, several outcomes may result:

1. The Court's decision may be consistent with the recommendations by the APA, and the rationale of the Court for its majority opinion may clearly reflect the APA's perspective and influence. In extreme examples of this

BOX 16-1

Steps in the Appellate Process

In every civil trial, each side has a right to appeal, and in criminal trials, those defendants who have been found guilty have the same right. The location of the appeal depends on the origin of the case—whether it was tried in a state court or a federal court. Appeals in state trials are transmitted to state appellate courts. A few states have only one level, usually titled the state supreme court; most states have two levels of appellate courts. (Just to make matters more complex, two states—Texas and Oklahoma—each have two courts of last resort—one for appeals in civil cases and one for appeals in criminal cases.) After appeals to all levels of the state courts have been extinguished, an appeal can be made to the federal courts.

An appeal in a federal trial, that is, in a U.S. district court, remains, of course, in the federal system. The various states, the District of Columbia, and U.S. territories are divided into 13 "circuits" (technically, circuit courts of appeal). An appeal of the outcome of a federal trial goes first to a panel of judges in that circuit (circuit courts have more judges than does the nine-judge Supreme Court). If the panel of three judges rules in favor of one side, the other may appeal to the full circuit court, requesting an **en banc** decision, or a decision from the full court.

Only after a decision has been rendered by lower level appellate courts can it be carried to the U.S. Supreme Court for review. The Supreme Court receives more than 7,000 appeals a year; it usually chooses to grant **certiorari,** or act on, only 70 to 80 of these. Those that are chosen often reflect what the Court considers constitutional issues; another reason for a

case to be granted "cert" is that two circuit courts have reached conflicting positions on the issue at hand.

When a case outcome is appealed, the terminology changes; instead of *plaintiff* and *defendant,* the two parties are called the **petitioner** and the **respondent** (or sometimes the **appellant** and the **appellee**). The petitioner is the party that initiates the appeal, the first-named party in the appeal; the respondent is the second party. But as the case works its way through different court levels, the petitioner may become the respondent and vice versa. For example, the case that eventually came before the Supreme Court as *Lockhart v. McCree* was initially listed, at trial, as *State* (of Arkansas) *v. McCree,* as the state brought charges against Mr. McCree as a criminal defendant. After he was found guilty, Mr. McCree appealed; at that point, he was the petitioner, and his name came first in the case listing. His appeal was denied by the state appeals court (in *McCree v. State,* 1979), and so he appealed to the federal courts. The federal district court agreed with him and overturned his conviction, and the U.S. Court of Appeals for the Eighth Circuit affirmed this reversal. Thus, the state of Arkansas appealed this reversal to the Supreme Court, so that when that Court agreed to take the case, it was titled *Lockhart v. McCree,* rather than the opposite. (Lockhart was the director of the Arkansas Department of Corrections; just to add further confusion, when states are parties in appeals, some states use their state names, such as *Miranda v. Arizona,* but others use the name of a state official, sometimes the governor, sometimes the attorney general, or a prison official.)

type, the majority opinion may use language drawn directly from the APA brief. This is exemplified in the case of *Maryland v. Craig* (1990), described in Box 16-2.

Likewise, the decision regarding the sexual harassment case of *Harris v. Forklift Systems, Inc.* (1993), described in detail in chapter 14, reflected a decision quite congruent with one of the positions advocated in the APA's brief. Not only was the Court's decision on the basic matter of dispute consistent with the APA's position—by a unanimous vote!—but on foundation issues the Court also ruled in the APA's direction.

The American Psychological Association was one of 12 organizations to file an *amicus* brief for the *Harris* case. Its brief took to task the requirement that "psychological injury" be present. One of its conclusions was that "scientific research suggests that a psychological injury requirement is not an adequate or even useful measure of what the courts of appeals use it to measure: sexual harassment sufficiently severe or persistent to alter conditions of employment" (American Psychological Association, 1993, p. 5). Having to prove psychological injuries places emphasis on the victim and his or her

BOX 16-2

The APA and the Case of *Maryland v. Craig*

A committee of the American Psychology-Law Society drafted an *amicus* brief on behalf of the American Psychological Association in the case of *Maryland v. Craig* (1990); the APA's Office of Legal Counsel then revised and transmitted this brief to the Supreme Court. This case dealt with the rights of sexually abused children when they are called upon to testify at trial. It asked if any special procedures, done to protect such children from the psychological harm of facing their alleged attacker, were constitutional, given the right of defendants to confront their accusers. At the trial of Sandra Ann Craig, the judge let four children, ages 4 to 7, testify over closed-circuit television. Each child witness, the prosecuting attorney, and the defense attorney were in an adjacent room, with a TV camera; the child could not see the defendant. The latter remained in the courtroom, as did the jury; they watched the direct and cross-examination of the child on a television monitor.

The psychologists' brief argued that some but not all children could be traumatized by the traditional trial procedures, and hence some limitation was warranted on the defendant's rights to confront such children. The Court, by a 5 to 4 vote, concluded that "the Confrontation Clause of the Constitution does not guarantee criminal defendants an *absolute* right to a face-to-face meeting with the witnesses against them at trial"

(1990, p. 3159, italics in the original). But the Court remanded the case to Maryland for a new trial, instructing the judge to determine beforehand whether the children serving as witnesses would suffer emotional distress when testifying.

The majority opinion, written by Justice Sandra Day O'Connor, referred to large sections of the APA's brief. For example, the APA's brief stated,

> Requiring child witnesses to undergo face-to-face confrontation, therefore, may in some cases actually disserve the truth-seeking rationale that underlies the confrontation clause. (quoted by Goodman, Levine, Melton, & Ogden, 1991, p. 14)

Compare the preceding to what Justice O'Connor wrote:

> Indeed, where face-to-face confrontation causes significant emotional distress in a child witness, there is evidence that such confrontation would in fact *disserve* the Confrontation Clause's truth-seeking goal. (p. 3169, italics in original)

The recognition by the Court of the possible trauma of testifying was congruent with the APA's goal in its brief, and hence the decision reflected a success for efforts by the field of psychology to influence court outcomes.

"ability to withstand harassment," instead of placing the onus on the conduct of the alleged harasser. For those reasons, the APA urged the Court to rule that "psychological injury" is *not* an element of a claim of a hostile work environment. Furthermore, it asked the Court to hold that harassing conduct is actionable "if it is severe and/or pervasive enough to provide different conditions and privileges of work to members of a protected class than to other employees" (APA, 1993, p. 6).

The APA brief also reviewed empirical studies on differences between women's and men's perceptions of sexual harassment. These consistently concluded that men are more tolerant of sexual harassment than are women, and women are more likely than men to label sexually aggressive behavior at

work as harassment. Other studies cited in the brief found that men are more likely to attribute the causes of harassing behavior to characteristics of victims, while women are more likely to attribute them to qualities of the perpetrator. These and other research findings were offered "as a factor the Court may find helpful in fashioning an objective test for determining whether a work environment is actionable under Title VII" (APA, 1993, p. 6). But the majority opinion, written by Justice O'Connor, did not refer to gender differences.

2. The Court's decision may be consistent with that preferred by the APA, but the written opinion may not reflect any detectable influence from the APA brief. In some cases, the APA rationale may be reviewed but rejected, even while the

Court's decision is congruent with the APA's values.

3. The Court's decision may be contrary to that recommended by the APA brief. Within this category, we may distinguish between decisions that reject the APA's brief and those that fail to mention it. An example of each type is presented here.

An Example of a Decision Consistent with the APA's Goals But Not Directly Reflecting the APA's Input: *Ake v. Oklahoma* (1985)

The Court's decision in *Ake v. Oklahoma* (1985) is an example of a ruling that was in line with the APA's recommendation but showed no direct influence of the APA brief. Perhaps the reason for the latter was the surprising rationale for the APA's arguments.

The Facts of the Case

Late in 1979, Glen Burton Ake was arrested and charged with the murder of a couple and the wounding of their two children. When he was arraigned, his behavior was so bizarre that the trial judge spontaneously decided to have him examined by a psychiatrist. He was diagnosed as probably having paranoid schizophrenia and was committed to an Oklahoma state hospital until he was competent to stand trial. After several months, during which Mr. Ake received tranquilizing drugs, the hospital's chief forensic psychiatrist informed the judge that Mr. Ake had become competent to stand trial. As the trial was to begin, his attorney announced that Mr. Ake intended to plead not guilty by reason of insanity, and he asked the judge to provide funds to pay a psychiatrist to examine the defendant. The attorney's rationale was that "to enable him to prepare and present such a defense adequately, . . . a psychiatrist would have to examine Ake with respect to his mental condition at the time of the offense" (*Ake v. Oklahoma,* 1985, p. 1090). The judge refused; Mr. Ake went on trial,

and the jury rejected his insanity defense and found him guilty on all counts. On appeal, Mr. Ake's argument that he should have been provided the services of a court-appointed psychiatrist was rejected by the Oklahoma Court of Criminal Appeals. The U.S. Supreme Court agreed to hear his appeal.

The APA's *Amicus* Brief

One purpose of the brief submitted by the APA (in conjunction with the Oklahoma Psychological Association) was to have the decision of the Oklahoma appeals court reversed and the case remanded for a new trial. Also, the APA and the OPA wished to inform the Court about the nature of psychological evaluations and the need for expert testimony in insanity defense proceedings. But, surprisingly, most of the arguments in the brief were of a constitutional nature. For example, in its "Summary of Argument" (p. 3), the APA brief of June 2, 1984, noted,

> The Court has long recognized the special nature of capital cases and has interpreted the Constitution to require adherence to the highest standards of procedural fairness to minimize the possibility in such cases of erroneous determinations of criminal responsibility and excessive punishments. In this case, there is no doubt that the defendant committed the heinous offenses with which he was charged. However, there is serious question whether the defendant had sufficient understanding of the wrongfulness of his offenses to be criminally responsible for them under the laws of Oklahoma. *Amici* submit that fundamental fairness requires the state to provide defendant Ake an adequate opportunity to establish his insanity defense (APA, 1984, pp. 3–4).

At a later point, the brief states,

> *Amici* believe that to deny defendant an adequate opportunity to support his plea of insanity, solely because of his indigence, was to arbitrarily and effectively deprive defen-

dant of the benefit of the insanity defense in violation of due process of law and other constitutional guarantees. (p. 5)

In addition to the constitutional argument based on procedural fairness, the APA's brief used a logical argument. It noted that in Oklahoma, the insanity defense is an **affirmative defense;** that is, the defendant is required to provide evidence that generates a reasonable doubt about his or her sanity at the time of the crime. In this case, the defendant was unable to do so without a psychological evaluation. This latter fact was especially important given that less than 6 months after the crime, Mr. Ake had been determined by psychiatric experts and the presiding judge to be mentally ill and incompetent to stand trial. The APA's brief argued that unless Mr. Ake was provided a psychological evaluation by the defense, an unacceptably high risk existed for an erroneous determination that he had been sane at the time of the crime.

In keeping with its second purpose, the APA brief proposed that "the detection and diagnosis of mental disorders and assessment of facts relevant to mental processes is recognized to be well beyond the competence of most lay people" (p. 4) and that psychological evaluations performed by qualified mental health professionals "to support [defendants'] only defense to the charges against them is a small price to pay to maintain the integrity of our criminal process" (p. 5). The brief noted that in other contexts, expert psychological assessments of mental conditions have been viewed by the courts as being of considerable probative value and—sometimes—as indispensable.

Only in its latter arguments did the APA brief rely upon psychological or empirical sources: The emphasis here was to question the ability to predict dangerousness in the future. The APA brief stated,

In the present case, the state relied on the testimony of two state psychiatrists that defendant is likely to be dangerous in the future to support its request for the death penalty. But the state denied defendant the means to effectively cross-examine or rebut such testimony. (p. 5)

The Supreme Court's Decision

The decision in the *Ake* case reflected an 8 to 1 vote; Justice Rehnquist dissented. The majority decision, written by Justice Thurgood Marshall, stated that Mr. Ake should have been allowed a psychiatric evaluation to determine his state of mind at the time the crimes were committed; thus, he was denied due process of law. Because his only defense was that he was insane at the time of the crime, he should have been granted court-appointed assistance. The majority decision did not cite the APA's brief directly, but almost all the issues brought to the Court by the APA brief were also mentioned in the majority opinion, including issues of fairness and the need for a professional evaluation.

The Aftermath

The Supreme Court remanded the case to the Oklahoma courts for retrial. At Mr. Ake's second trial, in 1986, a court-appointed psychiatrist testified that he had diagnosed the defendant with paranoid schizophrenia and that Mr. Ake had been hearing voices since 1973. He stated that Mr. Ake had gone to the victims' home in an attempt to find the source of the voices and to make them stop. Despite this testimony, the jury in the second trial also found the defendant guilty. However, instead of being sentenced to death, this time he was given a sentence of life in prison. (Whether the testimony by the defense psychiatrist led to the lesser sentence is a matter of conjecture. Mr. Ake's accomplice, Steven Hatch, was convicted, sentenced to death, and executed in 1997.)

The Impact of the APA's Brief

What conclusions can be drawn about the impact of the APA/OPA brief upon the majority opinion in the *Ake* case? The opinion did not cite, refer to, or quote from the psychologists' brief, although both cover the same general issues. The Court was already familiar with what psychiatry could provide when insanity is offered as a defense. And, certainly, matters of due process and procedural fairness, described in the APA's brief, were already salient for the Court. So, in one sense, the contents of the APA brief made no difference in the outcome. Yet, this was a case for which it was essential for the APA to express an opinion. If the professional organization of psychologists failed to justify their status in such a case, the Court might take note of the lack of confidence by psychologists in their procedures. The submission of a brief was a necessity, even if the likelihood of specific influence was small.

An Example of Rejection of the APA Brief: *Lockhart v. McCree* (1986)

The case of *Lockhart v. McCree* (1986) was described in chapter 1 as an illustration of the conflict between psychological research conclusions and the reasoning used in the legal profession. It is used here to illustrate the proposition that on some matters it is futile for the APA to hope to change the opinion of certain judges.

The Facts of the Case

When Ardia McCree was put on trial for capital murder in Arkansas, the judge excluded, for cause, eight prospective jurors who stated that they could not, under any circumstances, vote for the death penalty, were they to find Mr. McCree guilty of murder. The eventual jury did find Mr. McCree guilty of murder and sentenced him to life in prison without parole rather than death.

Mr. McCree appealed, objecting to the procedure of dismissing prospective jurors prior to the determination of guilt. He claimed the procedure violated his right under the Sixth and Fourteenth Amendments to have his guilt or innocence determined by a jury that was impartial and selected from a representative cross section of the community. Both the federal district court and the Eighth Circuit Court of Appeals,

after reviewing psychological research, sided with Mr. McCree and ordered a new trial for him. At that point, the state of Arkansas asked the Supreme Court to review the case.

The APA Brief

The APA could hardly decline the opportunity to provide an *amicus* brief to the Supreme Court in this case. As Donald Bersoff (1987) observed,

> In few, if any, other cases has the Court so explicitly sought guidance from psychologists and other social scientists as it did in *Witherspoon* [an earlier case in which the defendant claimed that the procedure of death-qualifying jurors was prejudicial]; in few, if any, other cases would the quality and force of social science research be so directly at issue as it was likely to be in Lockhart. (p. 54)

Furthermore, the state of Arkansas and 16 other states that submitted *amicus* briefs in support of Arkansas had made a wholesale attack on social science research. Lockhart's petition (for the state of Arkansas) argued that the earlier court decision had "relied on pseudo-scientific data as circumstantial 'proof' of 'facts' which may not be subject to proof under any methodology now available to social science researchers" (quoted by Bersoff, 1987, p. 54). Lockhart's brief spoke of the "folly" of relying on "such evidence" and argued that "compared to the 'hard' sciences, such as physics, the findings of 'soft' social sciences are ambiguous and subject to radical change with altered methodology. . . . Statistical significance as a measure of proof is better than nothing but not much" (quoted by Bersoff, 1987, p. 54).

The purpose of the APA brief was to present research findings that supported the argument that **death-qualified juries** were more conviction-prone and were more unrepresentative than the typical criminal juries. The brief noted that in the decision of *Witherspoon v. Illinois,* back in 1968, the Supreme Court had declined to rule that death-qualified juries were prejudicial and therefore unconstitutional because the research data available at that time were, in the Court's view, too tentative and fragmentary. (Only three studies were available in 1968.) The Court in its *Witherspoon* decision left open the possibility that it would rule differently if further research more clearly demonstrated death-qualified juries' nonneutrality.

Between 1968 and 1986, more than a dozen studies were done; they consistently concluded that "death-qualified juries are prosecution prone, unrepresentative of the community, and that death qualification impairs proper jury functioning" (APA, 1986, p. 3). Furthermore, as Thompson (1989b) noted, these more recent studies were "increasingly sophisticated studies designed to answer objections the courts had to earlier research. Because no single study could answer all these objections, they sought convergent validity through an array of studies looking at the difference between death qualified and excludable jurors in different ways" (p. 193).

The APA's brief also evaluated the data in light of the petitioner's eight major criticisms of the research and concluded that the objections were either mistaken or unrelated to the relevant research. The brief concluded that "the research clearly satisfies the criteria for evaluating the methodological soundness, reliability, and utility of empirical research" (APA, 1986, p. 3). Thus, the brief was heavily empirical in its orientation, with the empirical issues brought to bear on the question of the constitutional right to due process.

The Supreme Court's Decision

The majority decision of the Supreme Court, authored by Justice Rehnquist, rejected the APA brief, holding that "the Constitution does not prohibit the States from 'death-qualifying' juries in capital cases" (p. 1764); the relief given to Mr. McCree by lower courts was overturned. As noted in chapter 1, Justice Rehnquist provided a detailed critique of the empirical research. But this detailed annihilation of research findings was not enough; Justice Rehnquist added,

Having identified some of the more serious problems with McCree's studies, however, we

will assume for purposes of this opinion that the studies are both methodologically valid and adequate to establish that "death qualification" in fact produces juries somewhat more "conviction-prone" than "non-death-qualified" juries. We hold, nonetheless, that the Constitution does not prohibit the States from "death qualifying" juries in capital cases. (p. 1764)

Two reasons were offered by Justice Rehnquist for the decision:

1. With respect to the Sixth Amendment requirement of representativeness, the courts have interpreted this to mean a representative venire or jury pool, not that the actual jury drawn from that pool must be representative.
2. Mr. McCree presented no evidence that the specific jury that decided his guilt was biased. Justice Rehnquist wrote, "McCree does not claim that his conviction was tainted by any of the kinds of jury bias or partiality that we have previously recognized as violative of the Constitution" (p. 1767).

In contrast, a dissenting opinion written by Justice Thurgood Marshall (joined by Justices Brennan and Stevens) supported Mr. McCree's claims and based its conclusions on the results of the psychological research. For example, it noted that "the data strongly suggest that death qualification excludes a significantly large subset—at least 11% to 17%—of potential jurors" (p. 1772), including a disproportionate number of Blacks and women. The opinion also recognized the unanimity of results obtained by researchers using diverse types of subjects and methodologies, and it cited specific empirical articles; it concluded that the defendant "presented overwhelming evidence that death-qualified juries are substantially more likely to convict or to convict on more serious charges than are juries on which unalterable opponents of capital punishment are allowed to serve" (p. 1771).

Some psychologist-observers have commented on the effectiveness of the APA's brief, regardless of the outcome; Charles Tremper noted "the majority regarded the research as sufficiently important to warrant devoting several pages of its opinion to critiquing the studies' methodologies" (1987, p. 499). Donald Bersoff noted, "It is very clear that the dissent had carefully read the APA's brief, because much of its critique of the majority's view of the social science evidence relied on, and in some cases, closely paraphrased, that brief" (1987, p. 56). The minority opinion faulted the majority for its refusal to take social science evidence into consideration, stating,

> Faced with the near unanimity of authority supporting [the] claim that death qualification gives the prosecution particular advantage in the guilt phase of capital trials, the majority here makes but a weak effort to contest that proposition. Instead, it merely assumes . . . "that death-qualification in fact produces juries somewhat more conviction-prone than non-death-qualified juries" . . . and then holds that this result does not offend the Constitution. This disregard for the clear import of the evidence tragically misconstrues the settled constitutional principles that guarantee a defendant the right to a fair trial and an impartial jury whose composition is not biased toward the prosecution. (pp. 1774– 1775)

An Evaluation

Commenting on this and other cases in which the APA has submitted a brief, Bersoff (1986, 1987) concluded that in cases in which the Supreme Court disagrees with evidence from the social sciences, the fault sometimes rests upon the social scientists themselves. In the case of *Lockhart v. McCree,* however, it is his belief that "the Court itself is primarily responsible" (1987, p. 57). An even more critical view of the Court was expressed by William Thompson (1989b), who questioned whether concerns about the disposition of thousands of prisoners on death row were the major influences upon Justice Rehnquist's decision. Thompson noted

that tremendous political ramifications as well as practical ones would result from declaring death-qualification unconstitutional.

Regardless of the reason for the decision, it is clear that even the most methodologically impeccable empirical evidence would not have convinced Justice Rehnquist, a point made by Donald Bersoff. But Bersoff's view of the majority's treatment of the research is certainly a generous one; he wrote,

> The validity of social science evidence in general was not addressed by the majority, although it was urged to do so by the state and its supporting *amici*. And, even though the majority eventually concluded that the social science evidence was not germane to its decision, it did not ignore it either. It gave a respectful hearing and, it must be said, echoed the objective critique APA provided in its amicus brief. The Court's emphasis on the admitted lack of perfection in these studies was of far greater import to it, however, than it was to APA. Although I do not agree with the majority's analysis, the opinion does not appear to undermine the usefulness of social science evidence in judicial decision making. It does teach social scientists, however, that if they wish to contribute to constitutional adjudication, they must do so in the most methodologically rigorous and situation-specific way possible. (1987, p. 58)

Bersoff's comments cause us to reconsider: What is the goal of the APA's submission of briefs? He chose to emphasize the conclusion that the Court could not ignore or dismiss the usefulness of social science evidence; he wrote, "Unlike prior cases in which such evidence was criticized as 'numerology,' the majority (and, to a much greater extent, the dissent) was attentive to the import of the findings, even almost grudgingly accepting of them" (1987, p. 58). He concluded that the decision in this case could not be said to be a victory, but also it was not a defeat.

WHAT CAN WE LEARN FROM AN ANALYSIS OF INDIVIDUAL CASES?

What psychologists consider to be acceptable research methods and clear-cut research findings are not enough to guarantee their acceptance by the legal system. Psychologists are trained to believe "the data speak for themselves," but this credo does not carry over to a world in which another discipline has made the rules.

The Potency of Deeply Held Values

Judges' values differ from those of psychologists; Ewing concluded that judicial reasoning "is driven more by moral intuition and concern for public safety than by empirical fact" (1991, p. 159). What judges consider "common sense" often has more influence than a raft of results from empirical studies. For example, on the issue of predicting future dangerousness, Justice Byron White, in the *Barefoot v. Estelle* (1983) case, was more willing to place his trust in the jury's ability to detect dangerousness than to rely on cautions from the psychological evidence. Box 16-3 provides another example; psychological research on the maturity of adolescents' decision making about abortion had no impact when it ran counter to the justices' values about the rights of minors.

Identifying and Representing Our Goals Accurately

Given the obstacles to having influence, how should organized psychology proceed with the courts? Psychologists and other social scientists have offered several thoughtful suggestions. Shari Diamond (1989), in her presidential address to the American Psychology-Law Society, encouraged psychologists to focus on the **"trouble cases"**—those cases for which legal doctrine does not provide the court with clear guidance.

Courts are more likely to be receptive to social science research in such unsettled matters.

One procedure is for psychologists to go more than halfway in disseminating their findings. They can offer to speak to law-school classes, continuing education seminars for attorneys, and judicial conferences; they can seek to disseminate their findings in law reviews as well as psychological journals. When judges cite **secondary sources** (authorities other than a case, a statute, or a regulation) in their opinion, such sources are much more likely to be law review articles or legal reference books than social science journals (Hafemeister & Melton, 1987).

James R. Acker (1990) reviewed citations to social science research in 200 criminal cases decided by the U.S. Supreme Court between 1958 and 1983 and concluded that often these citations were made even though the studies had *not* been mentioned in the parties' briefs or in any *amicus* briefs; he wrote, "In the samples of cases considered here, the vast majority of social science authorities cited in the Court's decisions had been located through the justices' own efforts, rather than through prior discussion in the briefs or otherwise" (1990, p. 40). The last term in Acker's survey was the 1982–1983 term; since then, the APA has submitted the vast majority of its *amicus* briefs. But Acker's point should remind us that judges are not always averse to considering such information; the problem is that the sources they usually consult do not include the relevant social science information.

Also, psychology needs to be careful not to go beyond the topics of its own expertise. Psychology's unique contribution is not in constitutional analysis, but in the analysis of human behavior (Grisso & Saks, 1991). The justices do not need a group of psychologists to tell them how to interpret the U.S. Constitution. The following are some examples in which the APA's brief crossed the line beyond its expertise as a science:

- In its brief for *Price Waterhouse v. Hopkins* (1987), the APA concluded that gender stereotyping was present at Price Waterhouse

BOX 16-3
Parental Notification Requirements When Adolescents Seek Abortions

In 1985, the Ohio legislature passed a law making it a crime for a physician or other person to perform an abortion on an unmarried minor woman unless the physician provided timely notice (defined as 24 hours) to one of the minor's parents of his or her intention to perform an abortion. The law also provided certain ways that the adolescent could bypass this requirement of parental notification. The law was challenged by an abortion clinic, a physician, and others; when the case reached the U.S. Supreme Court, it was known as *Ohio v. Akron Center for Reproductive Health et al.* (1990); other states passed similar laws about the same time, leading to other court challenges. The American Psychological Association decided to respond to both the Ohio challenge and one in Minnesota, in the case of *Hodgson et al. v. Minnesota* (1990). The Minnesota legislation was even more restrictive, requiring that the minor notify *both* parents 48 hours before the scheduled abortion, regardless of whether the parents were living together.

The purpose of the brief submitted by the APA (in conjunction with the National Association of Social Workers and another organization) was to present empirical research on issues of parental notification; the brief argued that such adolescents typically have good reasons not to involve their parents in their abortion decisions. The APA brief also characterized the new laws as reflecting a view of minors as immature and unable to make competent choices concerning abortion. Two studies were given detailed coverage in the brief, because they compared abortion decision making by adolescents and adults at the time that they sought

out information at a clinic. In one (Lewis, 1980), 16 unmarried adolescents, aged 14–17, and 26 unmarried women, aged 18–25, were asked to consider their options when they learned they were pregnant. No difference was found between the two groups in the decisions they made or in the knowledge of pregnancy-related laws. The study concluded that minors "differed very little" from adults in the frequency with which they mentioned various considerations and consequences when asked to describe factors that could affect their choice of abortion or motherhood.

The second study, by Ambuel and Rappaport (1989), compared the decision making of 15 adolescents aged 14–15, 19 adolescents aged 16–17, and 40 adults aged 18–21, as they sought a pregnancy test at a woman's health clinic. Individual interviews assessed decision-making competence through measures of quality and clarity of reasoning, number and types of factors considered, the independence of the decision, and the consideration of risks and benefits, including immediate and future consequences. Those minors aged 14 to 17 who considered abortion as an option equaled adults on all four measures of competence.

Did the APA's argument that minors were mature decision makers have any impact on the Court? Not on the majority, which, in a 6 to 3 vote, upheld the laws as constitutional. The majority opinion ignored the argument of adolescent maturity, instead concluding that the laws did not violate adolescents' constitutional rights. Implicit in the Supreme Court's decision was a value that adolescents are not entitled to some of the rights given to adults.

and that it was "transformed into discriminatory behavior" (p. 11); the latter is a legal question, not for the APA to decide.

- In its brief for *Ohio v. Akron Center for Reproductive Health et al.* (1990a), the APA made a far-reaching claim, without documentation: "Parental notification statutes are actually destructive of the family role in child rearing" (p. 16).
- In a brief submitted for a case involving the possible execution of a mentally retarded defendant (*Penry v. Lynaugh*, 1989), the APA

claimed that "the execution of a person with mental retardation, such as John Paul Penry, cannot serve any valid penological purpose" (p. 4). The APA also submitted a brief in the *Atkins v. Virginia* (2002) case discussed in an earlier chapter arguing against the execution of the mentally retarded.

Psychology can best serve the courts by "being a reliable, credible informant regarding human behavior, addressing what is known and not known about it, how this is probative for the legal question, and what psychology's legal theories and data suggest will be the effects of various legal decisions on behavior" (Grisso & Saks, 1991, p. 210). This admonition by Grisso and Saks could well serve as a beacon for whatever the forensic psychologist chooses to do, whether the activity is testifying in court, advising the police, preparing a child custody evaluation, or preparing an *amicus* brief.

SUMMARY

One application of forensic psychology is the attempt to bring current psychological knowledge to bear on public-policy decisions. Organized psychology can lobby with legislatures, place psychologists on congressional staffs, and testify at legislative hearings. Although some examples of success can be demonstrated, the legislative decision is often a complicated one, reflecting the impact of experts, public opinion, and other political considerations.

Another application of psychology to the legal system is the systematic attempt to provide information to appellate judges as they make their decisions. The term *amicus curiae brief* refers to a statement, prepared by a third party and submitted to the court prior to its decision, with the goal of informing the court of relevant findings. Typically, a purpose of an *amicus* brief is to influence the court to decide in favor of one party; such briefs are called *advocacy briefs*. But the field of psychology also has the opportunity to provide the judicial system with summaries of research findings that bear on the issue at hand; such briefs are called *science-translation briefs*.

The first systematic effort by psychologists and other social scientists to provide an *amicus* brief to the Supreme Court came in conjunction with the *Brown v. Board of Education* decision in 1954; whether this brief had any impact on the Court's decision is still debated, although the justices clearly welcomed the brief as support for their then-controversial decision. The

American Psychological Association, in the last 20 years, has submitted almost 100 *amicus* briefs to the U.S. Supreme Court and to other federal and state appellate courts; these cover an extensive array of topics, from death-qualified jurors to sexual harassment, employment testing, and the rights of mental patients.

In some cases, the decision of the court has been congruent with the thrust of the APA brief; when this has occurred, in some instances, the effect of the APA brief can be clearly discerned in the court's published opinion. In other cases, the court may rule in keeping with the psychologists' position, but show no influence from the *amicus* brief. In some cases, the empirically based conclusions of psychological research conflict with the judges' values, leading to majority opinions opposite to the recommendations; this occurred in cases involving the use of death-qualified juries and the requirement of parental notification by adolescents seeking an abortion.

Regardless of the obstacles faced in cases in which the judges' values may conflict with research findings, it is essential that when psychology tries to influence the courts, it does so by being credible and informative.

KEY TERMS

advocacy brief
affirmative defense
amicus curiae **brief**
appellant
appellee
certiorari
death-qualified jury
en banc
guild issues
petitioner
respondent
science-translation brief
secondary sources
"trouble cases"

INFOTRAC®
COLLEGE EDITION

InfoTrac College Edition is a FREE, powerful, online learning resource, consisting of full-text articles from thousands of journals and periodicals. With each new copy of *Forensic Psychology,* Second Edition, you receive 4 months of free access to the InfoTrac College Edition database. By doing a simple keyword search (try using the Key Terms in the list above), you can quickly generate a list of relevant articles from thousands of possibilities and can select articles to read, explore, and print for reference or further study. InfoTrac College Edition's continuously updated collection of articles can be useful for doing reading and writing assignments that reach beyond the pages of this text!

SUGGESTED READINGS

Bersoff, D. N. (1986). Psychologists and the judicial system: Broader perspectives. *Law and Human Behavior, 10,* 151–165.

An article reviewing and analyzing the effect of psychology on change in the legal system, by the psychologist-lawyer who prepared many of the APA's *amicus* briefs to the U.S. Supreme Court.

Goodman, G. S., Levine, M., Melton, G. B., & Ogden, D. W. (1991). Child witnesses and the confrontation clause: American Psychological Association brief in *Maryland v. Craig. Law and Human Behavior, 15,* 13–29.

A description of the preparation of an influential brief by psychologists; a copy of the brief is part of the article.

Grisso, T., & Saks, M. J. (1991). Psychology's influence on constitutional interpretation: A comment on how to succeed. *Law and Human Behavior, 15,* 205–211.

A very sensible article about how forensic psychologists should proceed when preparing *amicus* briefs.

Melton, G. B. (1987). *Reforming the law: Impact of child development research.* New York: Guilford Press.

A collection of contributed chapters on the interaction between legal policy and social science. Chapters are devoted to such relevant topics as ways of introducing research to audiences of legal experts, the use of *amicus* briefs, and the ethical and practical dilemmas in disseminating psychological research.

Saks, M. J. (1993). Improving APA science translation *amicus* briefs. *Law and Human Behavior, 17,* 235–247.

A sensible analysis and set of recommendations to psychologists who try to influence the courts.

Thompson, W. C. (1989). Death qualification after *Wainwright v. Witt* and *Lockhart v. McCree. Law and Human Behavior, 13,* 185–215.

An elegant analysis by a psychologist-lawyer of the use of empirical research by the U.S. Supreme Court on one topic: death-qualified juries.

Wrightsman, L. S. (1999). *Judicial decision making: Is psychology relevant?* New York: Plenum.

Chapters 1–5 apply psychological concepts to explain appellate judicial decision making; chapters 6–10 present an expansion of topics described in this chapter.

References

Abidin, R. (1990). *Parenting Stress Index* (3rd ed.). Odessa, FL: Psychological Assessment Resources.

Abidin, R. R. (1998, August). *Parenting Stress Index: Its empirical validation.* Paper presented at the meeting of the American Psychological Association, San Francisco.

Abraham, L. (1995, August 13). Mumia Abu-Jamal, celebrity cop killer. *New York Times,* p. A15.

Abramson, L. (1997). *The defense is ready: Life in the trenches of criminal law.* New York: Simon and Schuster.

Acker, J. R. (1990). Social science in Supreme Court criminal cases and briefs: The actual and potential contribution of social scientists as *amicus curiae. Law and Human Behavior, 14,* 25–42.

Acker, J. R., & Toch, H. (1985). Battered women, straw men, and expert testimony: A comment on *State v. Kelly. Criminal Law Bulletin, 21,* 125–155.

Ackerman, M. J. (1994). *Clinician's guide to child custody evaluations.* New York: John Wiley.

Ackerman, M. J. (2001). *Clinician's guide to child custody evaluations* (2nd ed.). New York: John Wiley.

Ackerman, M. J., & Ackerman, M. (1997). Custody evaluation practices: A survey of experienced professionals (revisited). *Professional Psychology: Research and Practice, 28,* 137–145.

Ackerman, M. J., & Schoendorf, K. (1992). *Ackerman-Schoendorf Scales for Parent Evaluation of Custody (ASPECT): Manual.* Los Angeles: Western Psychological Services.

Adams, R. D. (with Hoffer, W., & Hoffer, M. M.). (1991). *Adams v. Texas.* New York: St. Martin's Press.

Adams, R. L., Parsons, O. A., & Culbertson, J. L. (1996). *Neuropsychology for clinical practice : Etiology, assessment, and treatment.* Washington, DC: American Psychological Association.

Adams, R. L. & Rankin, E. J. (1996). A practical guide to forensic neuropsychological evaluations and testimony. In R. L. Adams, O. A. Parsons, & J. L. Culbertson (Eds.), *Neuropsychology for clinical practice: Etiology, assessment, and treatment.* Washington, DC: American Psychological Association.

Adler, S. J. (1994). *The jury: Trial and error in the American courtroom.* New York: Times Books.

Adler, T. (1993, September). APA files *amicus* brief in grant application case. *APA Monitor,* 26.

Ainsworth, P. B. (1995). *Psychology and policing in a changing world.* Chichester, UK: Wiley.

Ake v. Oklahoma, 105 S. Ct. 1087 (1985).

Akehurst, L., Kohnken, G., Vrij, A., & Bull, R. (1996). Laypersons' and police officers' beliefs regarding deceptive behavior. *Applied Cognitive Psychology, 10,* 461–471.

Albiston, C. R., Maccoby, E. E., & Mnookin, R. H. (1990). Does joint legal custody matter? *Stanford Law and Policy Review, 2,* 167–179.

Allan, A., & Louw, D. A. (1997). The ultimate opinion rule and psychologists: A comparison of the expectations and experiences of South African lawyers. *Behavioral Sciences and the Law, 15,* 307–320.

Allen, M., Mabry, E., & McKelton, D. (1998). Impact of juror attitudes about the death penalty on juror evaluations of guilt and punishment: A meta-analysis. *Law and Human Behavior, 22,* 715–731.

Allen, S. W., Cutler, B. L., & Berman, G. L. (1993, August). Analyses comparing various hostage negotiation techniques. Paper presented at the meeting of the American Psychological Association, Toronto.

Allison, J. A., & Wrightsman, L. S. (1993). *Rape: The misunderstood crime.* Thousand Oaks, CA: Sage.

Allport, F. H., Allport, G., Bruner, J., Chein, I., Cook, S. W., Davis, A., et al. (1953). The effects of segregation and the consequences of desegregation: A social science statement. *Minnesota Law Review, 37,* 427–439.

Alm, R. (1994, February 5). Hostage wounded by police. *Kansas City Star,* pp. A1, A17.

Alphonso v. Charity Hospital of Louisiana at New Orleans, 413 So.2d 982 (La. App. 1982).

Ambuel, B., & Rappaport, J. (1987, August). *Developmental change in adolescents' legal competence to consent to abortion.* Paper presented at the meeting of the American Psychological Association, New Orleans.

American Bar Association Task Force on Fair Trial and Free Press. (1978). *Standards relating to the administration of criminal justice, fairness, and free press* (2nd ed.). Chicago: American Bar Association.

American Home Products Corp. v. Johnson & Johnson, 654 F. Supp. 568 (S.D.N.Y. 1987).

American Law Institute. (1962). *Model penal code.* Washington, DC: Author.

American Psychiatric Association. (1987). *Diagnostic and statistical manual of mental disorders–Revised* (3rd ed.). Washington, DC: Author.

American Psychiatric Association. (1994). *Diagnostic and statistical manual of mental disorders* (4th ed.). Washington, DC: Author.

American Psychological Association. (1984, March). Text of position on insanity defense. *APA Monitor,* p. 11.

American Psychological Association. (1984). *Amicus curiae brief, Ake v. Oklahoma.* Washington, DC: Author.

American Psychological Association. (1986). *Amicus curiae brief, Lockhart v. McCree.* Washington, DC: Author.

American Psychological Association. (1987). *Amicus curiae brief, Price Waterhouse v. Ann B. Hopkins.* Washington, DC: Author.

American Psychological Association. (1989). *Amicus curiae brief, Penry v. Lynaugh.* Washington, DC: Author.

American Psychological Association. (1990). *Amicus curiae brief, Ohio v. Akron Center for Reproductive Health et al.* Washington, DC: Author.

American Psychological Association. (1991). *In the Supreme Court of the United States:* Price Waterhouse v. Ann B. Hopkins, *Amicus curiae brief for the American Psychological Association. American Psychologist, 46,* 1061–1070.

American Psychological Association. (1992). *Ethical principles of psychologists and code of conduct.* Washington, DC: Author.

American Psychological Association. (1993). *Amicus curiae brief, Harris v. Forklift Systems, Inc.* Washington, DC: Author.

American Psychological Association. (1994). Guidelines for child custody evaluations in divorce proceedings. *American Psychologist, 49,* 677–680.

American Psychological Association. (1995). *Lesbian and gay parenting: A resource for psychologists.* Washington, DC: Author.

American Psychological Association. (2002). Ethical principles of psychologists and code of conduct. *American Psychologist, 57,* 1060–1073.

American Society of Trial Consultants. (1998, Spring). Proposed minimum standards for survey research in connection with motions to change venue. *Court Call,* 1–6.

Amnesty International. (1987). *United States of America: The death penalty.* New York: Author.

Anderson, C. A., Lepper, M. R., & Ross, L. (1980). Perseverance of social theories: The role of explanation in the persistence of discredited information. *Journal of Personality and Social Psychology, 39,* 1030–1049.

Andrews, D. A., & Bonta, J. (1998). *The psychology of criminal conduct* (2nd ed.). Cincinnati, OH: Anderson.

Andrews, D. A., Bonta, J., & Hoge, R. D. (1990). Classification for effective rehabilitation: Rediscovering psychology. *Criminal Justice and Behavior, 17,* 19.

Angier, N. (1993, June 30). Court ruling on scientific evidence: A just burden. *New York Times,* p. A8.

Annin, P. (1970, December 10). Unfriendly persuasion. *Newsweek,* p. 73.

Arditti, J. A. (1995). Review of the Ackerman-Schoendorf Scales for Parental Evaluation of Custody. In J. Conoley & J. C. Impara (Eds.), *Twelfth Mental Measurements Yearbook* (pp. 20–22). Lincoln: University of Nebraska Press.

Arizona v. Fulminante, 111 S. Ct. 1246 (1991).

Arnett, P. A., Hammeke, T. A., & Schwartz, L. (1993, August). *Quantitative and qualitative performance on Rey's 15-item test.* Paper presented at the meeting of the American Psychological Association, Toronto.

Arnold, S., & Gold, A. (1978–1979). The use of a public opinion poll on a change of venue application. *Criminal Law Quarterly, 21,* 445–464.

Aron, C. J. (1993, July 19). Women battered by life and law lose twice. *National Law Journal,* 13–14.

Aron, N. (1998, December 7). On death row, good defense hard to find. *USA Today*, p. 25A.

Aronson, E. (1990, November). *Subtle coercion during police interrogation: The Bradley Page murder trial*. Invited address, Williams College, Williamstown, MA.

Aronson, E. (1992). *The social animal* (6th ed.). New York: W. H. Freeman.

Aronson, E., & Bridgeman, D. (1992). Jigsaw groups and the desegregated classroom: In pursuit of common goals. In E. Aronson (Ed.), *Readings on the social animal* (pp. 430–440). New York: W. H. Freeman.

Aronson, E., Stephan, C., Sikes, J., Blaney, N., & Snapp, N. (1978). *The jigsaw classroom*. Thousand Oaks, CA: Sage.

Arvey, R. D., & Cavanaugh, M. A. (1995). Using surveys to assess the prevalence of sexual harassment: Some methodological problems. *Journal of Social Issues, 51*(1), 39–52.

Asch, S. E. (1956). Studies of independence and conformity: A minority of one against a unanimous majority. *Psychological Monographs, 70* (9, Whole No. 416).

Ashcraft v. Tennessee, 322 U.S. 143 (1944).

Associated Press. (1986, May 12). A crime that doesn't pay. *Kansas City Star*, p. 5A.

Associated Press. (1992, February 23). FBI says 25 serial killers are still at large. *Lawrence Journal-World*, p. 13C.

Associated Press. (1993, November 4). Tape of therapy allowed in trial of two brothers. *New York Times*, p. A7.

Associated Press. (1994, December 27). He stopped a suicide, but not his own. *Kansas City Star*, p. A-3.

Associated Press. (1995, September 10). Budget cuts threaten death row defenders. *Lawrence Journal-World*, p. 7F.

Associated Press. (1997, March 17). Psychologist report offers insight to O.J. guardianship. *Lawrence Journal-World*, p. 5A.

Associated Press. (1998, December 5). Shooting defendant called mentally ill. *Kansas City Star*, p. A47.

Atkins v. Virginia, 536 U.S. 304 (2002).

Aubry, A., & Caputo, R. (1965). *Criminal interrogation*. Springfield, IL: Charles C Thomas.

Aubry, A., & Caputo, R. (1980). *Criminal interrogation* (3rd ed.). Springfield, IL: Charles C Thomas.

B v. B, 242 S.E.2d 248 (W.Va. 1978).

Bagby, R. M., Nicholson, R. A., Rogers, R., & Nussbaum, D. (1992). Domains of competency to stand trial: A factor analytic study. *Law and Human Behavior, 16*, 491–508.

Bailey, W. C., & Peterson, R. D. (1994). Murder, capital punishment, and deterrence: A review of the evidence and an examination of police killings. *Journal of Social Issues, 50*(2), 53–74.

Baldus, D., Woodworth, G., & Pulaski, C. (1990). *Equal justice and the death penalty: A legal and empirical analysis.* Boston: Northeastern University Press.

Baldus, D. C., & Cole, J. W. (1980). *Statistical proof of discrimination.* New York: McGraw-Hill.

Baldus, D. C., Woodworth, G., & Pulaski, C. A., Jr. (1992). Law and statistics in conflict: Reflections on *McCleskey v. Kemp.* In D. K. Kagehiro & W. S. Laufer (Eds.), *Handbook of psychology and law* (pp. 251–271). New York: Springer-Verlag.

Ballew v. Georgia, 435 U.S. 223 (1978).

Barak, A. (1992). Combatting sexual harassment. *American Psychologist, 47*, 818–819.

Barber, T. X. & Wilson, S. C. (1978–1979). The Barber Suggestibility Scale and the Creative Imagination Scale: Experimental and clinical applications. *American Journal of Clinical Hypnosis, 21*, 84–96.

Bard, M., & Sangrey, D. (1979). *The crime victim's book.* New York: Basic Books.

Barefoot v. Estelle, 463 U.S. 880 (1983).

Barland, G. H. (1981). *A validity and reliability study of counterintelligence screening test.* Security Support Battalion, 902nd Military Intelligence Group, Fort Meade, MD. (Cited by Carroll, 1988).

Barland, G. H., & Raskin, D. C. (1975). An evaluation of field techniques in detection and deception. *Psychophysiology, 12*, 321–330.

Barnett, O. W., & LaViolette, A. D. (1993). *It could happen to anyone: Why battered women stay.* Thousand Oaks, CA: Sage.

Barovick, H. (1998, June 15). DWB: Driving while Black. *Time*, p. 35.

Barr, J. (1979). *Within a dark wood.* Garden City, NY: Doubleday.

Barrett, G. V., & Morris, S. B. (1993). The American Psychological Association's *amicus curiae* brief in *Price Waterhouse v. Hopkins:* The values of science versus the values of the law. *Law and Human Behavior, 17*, 201–215.

Barrett, J. D., Ruhnke, D. A., & Goldstein, A. M. (1999, January 23). *Role of the forensic psychologist in death penalty mitigation.* Workshop presented for the American Academy of Forensic Psychology, Palm Springs, CA.

Barrett, L. I. (1991, June 3). Cheating on the tests. *Time*, p. 57.

Bartol, C. R. (1991). Predictive validation of the MMPI for small-town police officers who fail. *Professional Psychology: Research and Practice, 22*, 127–132.

Bartol, C. R., & Bartol, A. M. (1999). History of forensic psychology. In A. K. Hess & I. B. Weiner (Eds.), *Handbook of forensic psychology* (2nd ed., pp. 3–23). New York: John Wiley.

Bartol, C. R., & Bartol, A. M. (2004). *Psychology and law: Theory, research, and application* (3rd ed.). Belmont, CA: Wadsworth/Thomson.

Basow, S. (1986). *Gender stereotypes.* Pacific Grove, CA: Brooks/Cole.

Bassuk, E. (1980). The crisis theory perspective on rape. In S. L. McCombie (Ed.), *The rape crisis intervention handbook* (pp. 121–129). New York: Plenum.

Bastian, L. D., Lancaster, A. R., & Reyst, H. E. (1996). *Department of Defense 1995 Sexual Harassment Survey* (DMDC Report 96-014). Washington, DC: Defense Manpower Data Center. (Cited by Foote & Goodman-Delahunty, 1999.)

Bauschard, L. (1986). *Voices set free: Battered women speak from prison.* St. Louis: Women's Self Help Center.

Bazelon, D. (1982). Veils, values, and social responsibility. *American Psychologist, 37,* 115–121.

Beaber, R., Marston, A., Michelli, J., & Mills, M. (1985). A brief test for measuring malingering in schizophrenic individuals. *American Journal of Psychiatry, 144,* 1478–1481.

Beck, A. T., Schuyler, D., & Herman, I. (1974). Development of Suicidal Intent Scales. In A. T. Beck, H. L. P. Resnik, & D. J. Letteri (Eds.), *The prevention of suicide* (pp. 45–56). Bowie, MD: Charles Press.

Beck, J. C., & Shumsky, R. (1997). A comparison of retained and appointed counsel in cases of capital murder. *Law and Human Behavior, 21*(5), 525–538.

Becker, J. V., & Murphy, W. D. (1998). What we know and do not know about assessing and treating sex offenders. *Psychology, Public Policy, and Law, 4,* 116–137.

Becker, J. V., Skinner, L. J., Abel, G. G., Axelrod, R., & Treacy, E. C. (1984). Depressive symptoms associated with sexual assault. *Journal of Sex and Marital Therapy, 10,* 185– 192.

Bedau, H. A., & Radelet, M. L. (1987). Miscarriages of justice in potentially capital cases. *Stanford Law Review, 40,* 21–179.

Begley, S. (1993, March 22). The meaning of junk. *Newsweek,* 62–64.

Behn, N. (1994). *Lindbergh: The crime.* New York: Penguin Books.

Behrman, B., & Davey, S. (2001). Eyewitness identification in actual criminal cases: An archival analysis. *Law and Human Behavior, 25,* 475–491.

Beisecker, T. (1992). *Graduate programs at KU for the legal consultant.* Unpublished manuscript, Department of Communication Studies, University of Kansas, Lawrence.

Bekerian, D. A., & Jackson, J. L. (1997). Critical issues in offender profiling. In J. L. Jackson & D. A. Bekerian (Eds.), *Offender profiling: Theory, research, and practice* (pp. 209–220). New York: John Wiley.

Belsky, J. (1980). Child maltreatment: An ecological integration. *American Psychologist, 35,* 320–335.

Belsky, J. (1993). Etiology of child maltreatment: A developmental-ecological analysis. *Psychological Bulletin, 114,* 413–434.

Benedetto, R. (1995, July 25). 3 of 4: Retain programs that combat bias. *USA Today,* p. 3A.

Benjamin, G. A. H., & Gollan, J. (2003). *Family evaluation in custody litigation: Reducing risks of ethical infractions and malpractice.* Washington, DC: American Psychological Association.

Bennett, C., & Hirshhorn, R. (1993). *Bennett's guide to jury selection and trial dynamics in civil and criminal litigation.* St. Paul, MN: West.

Bennett, W. L., & Feldman, M. S. (1981). *Reconstructing reality in the courtroom.* New Brunswick, NJ: Rutgers University Press.

Benokraitis, N. V., & Feagin, J. R. (1986). *Modern sexism: Blatant, subtle, and covert discrimination.* Englewood Cliffs, NJ: Prentice Hall.

Berg, A. S. (1998). *Lindbergh.* New York: Putnam Publishing Group.

Berger, V. (1997, June 16). Execution of mentally disabled killer shames our "civilized" society. *National Law Journal,* p. A22.

Berkowitz, L., & Macaulay, J. (1971). The contagion of criminal violence. *Sociometry, 34,* 238– 260.

Berlin, F. S. (1994). Jeffrey Dahmer: Was he ill? Was he impaired? Insanity revisited. *American Journal of Forensic Psychiatry, 15,* 5–29.

Berliner, L. (1998). The use of expert testimony in child sexual abuse cases. In S. J. Ceci & H. Hembrooke (Eds.), *Expert witnesses in child abuse cases* (pp. 11–27). Washington, DC: American Psychological Association.

Bermant, G. (1986). Two conjectures about the issue of expert testimony. *Law and Human Behavior, 10,* 97–100.

Bernard, L. C., & Fowler, W. (1990). Assessing the validity of memory complaints: Performance of brain-damaged and normal individuals on Rey's test to detect malingering. *Journal of Clinical Psychology, 46,* 432–436.

Bernstein, P. (1996). *Against the Gods.* New York: John Wiley.

Bersoff, D. N. (1981). Testing and the law. *American Psychologist, 36,* 1047–1056.

Bersoff, D. N. (1986). Psychologists and the judicial system: Broader perspectives. *Law and Human Behavior, 10,* 151–165.

Bersoff, D. N. (1987). Social science data and the Supreme Court: *Lockhart* as a case in point. *American Psychologist, 42*(1), 52–58.

Bersoff, D. N. (1993, August). *Daubert v. Merrell Dow: Issues and outcome.* Paper presented at the meeting of the American Psychological Association, Toronto.

Bersoff, D. N. (2002). Some contrarian concerns about law, psychology, and public policy. *Law and Human Behavior, 26,* 565–574.

Bersoff, D. N., & Ogden, D. W. (1991). APA *amicus* brief: Furthering lesbian and gay male civil rights. *American Psychologist, 46,* 950–956.

Beutler, L. E., Nussbaum, P. D., & Meredith, K. E. (1988). Changing personality patterns of police officers. *Professional Psychology: Research and Practice, 19,* 503–507.

Biddle, N. A. (1994, September 19). "He didn't commit suicide." *Newsweek,* p. 35.

Biernat, M., & Crandall, C. S. (1999). Racial attitudes. In J. P. Robinson, P. R. Shaver, & L. S. Wrightsman (Eds.), *Measures of political attitudes* (pp. 297–411). San Diego: Academic Press.

Birnbaum, S. L., & Crawford, G. E. (1993, May 17). Justices to review causation evidence. *National Law Journal,* pp. 18, 25–26.

Birnbaum, S. L., & Jackson, J. R. (1994, May 16). Almost a year after the *Daubert* ruling, courts start to recognize and apply the strict new standard on scientific expert testimony. *National Law Journal,* pp. B5, B7.

Bischoff, L. G. (1995). Review of Parent Awareness Skills Survey. In J. C. Conoley & J. C. Impara (Eds.), *Twelfth mental measurements yearbook* (pp. 735–736). Lincoln: University of Nebraska Press.

Blackman, J. (1986). Potential uses for expert testimony: Ideas toward the representation of battered women who kill. *Women's Rights Law Reporter, 9*(3 & 4), 227–238.

Blackman, J., & Brickman, E. (1984). The impact of expert testimony on trials of battered women who kill their husbands. *Behavioral Sciences and the Law, 2,* 413–422.

Blagrove, M. (1996). Effects of length of sleep deprivation on interrogative suggestibility. *Journal of Experimental Psychology: Applied, 2,* 48–59.

Blau, T. H. (1994). *Psychological services for law enforcement.* New York: John Wiley.

Blinkhorn, S. (1988). Lie detection as a psychometric procedure. In A. Gale (Ed.), *The polygraph test: Lies, truth and science* (pp. 29–38). London: Sage.

Block, A. P. (1990). Rape trauma syndrome as scientific expert testimony. *Archives of Sexual Behavior, 19,* 309–323.

Blumenthal, J. A. (1998). The reasonable woman standard: A meta-analytic review of gender differences in perceptions of sexual harassment. *Law and Human Behavior, 22,* 33–57.

Boat, B. W., & Everson, M. D. (1988). Use of anatomical dolls among professionals in sexual abuse evaluation. *Child Abuse and Neglect, 12,* 171–174.

Bochnak, E. (Ed.). (1981). *Women's self-defense cases: Theory and practice.* Charlottesville, VA: Michie.

Boehm, V. R. (1968). Mr. Prejudice, Miss Sympathy, and the authoritarian personality: An application of psychological measuring techniques to the problem of jury bias. *Wisconsin Law Review, 1968,* 734–750.

Boer, D. P., Hart, S. D., Kropp, P. R., & Webster, C. D. (1997). *The Sexual Violence Risk-20 guide (SVR-20).* Burnaby, British Columbia, Canada: The Mental Health, Law and Policy Institute, Simon Fraser University.

Boeschen, L. E., Sales, B. D., & Koss, M. P. (1998). Rape trauma experts in the courtroom. *Psychology, Public Policy, and Law, 4,* 414–432.

Boland, P. L., & Quirk, S. A. (1994). At issue: Should child abuse be prosecuted decades after an alleged incident occurred? *American Bar Association Journal, 80,* 42.

Bolton, B. (1985). Review of Inwald Personality Inventory. In J. V. Mitchell (Ed.), *The ninth mental measurements yearbook* (pp. 711–713). Lincoln: Buros Institute of Mental Measurements, University of Nebraska.

Bond, S. B., & Mosher, D. L. (1986). Guided imagery of rape: Fantasy, reality, and the willing victim myth. *Journal of Sex Research, 22,* 162–183.

Bongar, B., Berman, A., Maris, R., Silverman, M., Harris, E., & Packman, W. (1998). *Risk management with suicidal patients.* New York: Guilford.

Bonnie, R., & Slobogin, C. (1980). The role of mental health professionals in the criminal process: The case for informed speculation. *Virginia Law Review, 66,* 427–522.

Bonnie, R. J. (1990). Dilemmas in administering the death penalty: Conscientious abstention, professional ethics, and the needs of the legal system. *Law and Human Behavior, 14,* 67–90.

Borawick v. Shay, 68 F.3d 597 (1995).

Borchard, E. M. (1932). *Convicting the innocent: Sixty-five actual errors of criminal justice.* Garden City, NY: Doubleday.

Borgida, E., Frazier, P., & Swim, J. (1987). Prosecuting sexual assault: The use of expert testimony on rape trauma syndrome. In R. Hazelwood & A. Burgess (Eds.), *Practical aspects of rape investigation: A multidisciplinary approach* (pp. 347–360). New York: Elsevier.

Borgida, E., & Nisbett, R. (1977). The differential impact of abstract vs. concrete information on decisions. *Journal of Applied Social Psychology, 7,* 258–271.

Bornstein, B. (1999). The ecological validity of jury simulations: Is the jury still out? *Law and Human Behavior, 23,* 75–92.

Bornstein, B. H., Whisenhunt, B. L., Nemeth, R. J., & Dunaway, D. L. (2002). Pretrial publicity and civil cases: A two-way street? *Law and Human Behavior, 26,* 3–17.

Borum, R. (1988). A comparative study of negotiator effectiveness with "mentally-disturbed hostage-taker" scenarios. *Journal of Police and Criminal Psychology, 4,* 17–20.

Borum, R. (1996). Improving the clinical practice of violence risk assessment: Technology, guidelines, and training. *American Psychologist, 51,* 945–956.

Borum, R. (1998). Forensic assessment instruments. In G. P. Koocher, J. C. Norcross, & S. S. Hill, III (Eds.), *Psychologists' desk reference* (pp. 487–491). New York: Oxford University Press.

Borum, R., & Fulero, S. M. (1999). Empirical research on the insanity defense and attempted reforms: Evidence toward informed policy. *Law and Human Behavior, 23,* 117–135.

Bothwell, R. K., Deffenbacher, K. A., & Brigham, J. C. (1987). Correlation of eyewitness accuracy and confidence: Optimality hypothesis revisited. *Journal of Applied Psychology, 72,* 691–695.

Bottoms, B. L., & Davis, S. (1993, September). Scientific evidence no longer subject to "Frye test." *APA Monitor,* 14.

Bovard, J. (1994, November). Drug-courier profiles. *Playboy,* 46–48.

Bowen, W. G., & Bok, D. (1998). *The shape of the river: Long-term consequences of considering race in college and university admissions.* Princeton, NJ: Princeton University Press.

Bowers v. Hardwick, 478 U.S. 1039, 106 S. Ct. 2841 (1986).

Bowers, W. J. (1988). The effect of executions is brutalization, not deterrence. In K. C. Haas & J. A. Inciardi (Eds.), *Challenging capital punishment: Legal and social science approaches* (pp. 49–90). Thousand Oaks, CA: Sage.

Bowers, W. J. (with Pierce, G. L., & McDevitt, J. F.). (1984). *Legal homicide: Death as punishment in America, 1864–1982.* Boston: Northeastern University Press.

Bradfield, A. L., & Wells, G. L. (2000). The perceived validity of eyewitness identification testimony: A test of the five *Biggers* criteria. *Law and Human Behavior, 24,* 581–594.

Bradfield, A. L., Wells, G. L, & Olson, E. A. (2002). The damaging effect of confirming feedback on the relation between eyewitness certainty and identification accuracy. *Journal of Applied Psychology, 87,* 112–120.

Bragg, R. (1995, July 18). Sheriff says prayer and a lie led Susan Smith to confess. *New York Times,* pp. A1, A8.

Brandon, R., & Davies, C. (1973). *Wrongful imprisonment: Mistaken convictions and their consequences.* London: George Allen & Unwin.

Braswell, A. L. (1987). Resurrection of the ultimate issue rule: Federal Rule of Evidence 704(b) and the insanity defense. *Cornell Law Review, 72,* 620–640.

Brekke, N., & Borgida, E. (1988). Expert scientific testimony in rape trials: A social-cognitive analysis. *Journal of Personality and Social Psychology, 55,* 372–386.

Brenner, M. (1997, February). American nightmare: The ballad of Richard Jewell. *Vanity Fair,* 100–107, 150–165.

Bricklin, B. (1994). *The Bricklin Perceptual Scales: Child-perception-of-parents series.* Furlong, PA: Village.

Bricklin, B. (1995). *The custody evaluation handbook: Research-based solutions and applications.* New York: Brunner-Mazel.

Brigham, J. C. (1971). Ethnic stereotypes. *Psychological Bulletin, 76,* 15–38.

Brigham, J. C. (1992). A personal account of the research expert in court. *Contemporary Psychology, 37,* 529–531.

Brigham, J. C. (1999). What is forensic psychology, anyway? *Law and Human Behavior, 23,* 273–298.

Brigham, J. C., & Bothwell, R. K. (1983). The ability of prospective jurors to estimate the accuracy of eyewitness identifications. *Law and Human Behavior, 7,* 19–30.

Brigham, J. C., & Cairns, D. L. (1988). The effect of mugshot inspections on eyewitness identification accuracy. *Journal of Applied Social Psychology, 18,* 1394–1410.

Brigham, J. C., Maass, A., Snyder, L. D., & Spaulding, K. (1982). Accuracy of eyewitness identifications in a field setting. *Journal of Personality and Social Psychology, 42,* 673–681.

Brigham, J. C., & Wolfskeil, M. P. (1983). Opinions of attorneys and law enforcement personnel on the accuracy of eyewitness identifications. *Law and Human Behavior, 7,* 337–349.

Bright, S. B. (1994). Counsel for the poor: The death sentence not for the worst crime but for the worst lawyer. *Yale Law Journal, 103,* 1835–1883.

Bristow, A. R. (1984). *State v. Marks:* An analysis of expert testimony on rape trauma syndrome. *Victimology: An International Journal, 9,* 273–281.

British Psychological Society (1986). Report of the working group on the use of the polygraph in criminal investigations and personnel screening. *Bulletin of the British Psychological Society, 39,* 81–94.

Brodsky, S. L. (1973). *Psychologists in the criminal justice system.* Urbana: University of Illinois Press.

Brodsky, S. L. (1990). Professional ethics and professional morality in the assessment of competency for execution: A response to Bonnie. *Law and Human Behavior, 14,* 91–97.

Brodsky, S. L. (1998, March). *Change of venue assessments in civil litigation: Expanding the scope of evaluation.* Paper presented at the meeting of the American Psychology-Law Society, Redondo Beach, CA.

Brodsky, S. L. (1991). *Testifying in court: Guidelines and maxims for the expert witness.* Washington, DC: American Psychological Association.

Brody, J. E. (1998, August 28). Researchers unravel the motives of stalkers. *New York Times,* pp. B9, B13.

Brott, A. A. (1994, August 8–14). The facts take a battering. *Washington Post National Weekly Edition,* pp. 24–25.

Brown v. Board of Education of Topeka, 347 U.S. 483 (1954).

Brown v. Mississippi, 297 U.S. 278 (1936).

Brown, D., Scheflin, A. W., & Hammond, D. C. (1998). *Memory, trauma, treatment, and the law.* New York: Norton.

Brown, D. C. (1994). Subgroup norming: Legitimate testing practice or reverse discrimination? *American Psychologist, 49,* 927–928.

Brown, E., Deffenbacher, K., & Sturgill, W. (1977). Memory for faces and the circumstances of encounters. *Journal of Applied Psychology, 62,* 311–318.

Brown, L., & Willis, A. (1985). Authoritarianism in British recruits: Importation, socialization, or myth? *Journal of Occupational Psychology, 58,* 97–108.

Brown, N. (1996). *Can judges decide?* Unpublished manuscript, Department of Psychology, University of Kansas, Lawrence.

Browne, A. (1987). *When battered women kill.* New York: Free Press.

Browne, A., & Williams, K. (1989). Resource availability for women at risk and partner homicide. *Law and Society Review, 23,* 75.

Brownmiller, S. (1975). *Against our will: Men, women, and rape.* New York: Simon & Schuster.

Brownmiller, S., & Alexander, D. (1992, January/February). From Carmita Wood to Anita Hill. *Ms. Magazine,* 70–71.

Bruck, M. (1998). The trials and tribulations of a novice expert witness. In S. J. Ceci & H. Hembrooke (Eds.), *Expert witnesses in child abuse cases* (pp. 85–104). Washington, DC: American Psychological Association.

Bruck, M., & Ceci, S. J. (1993). *Amicus brief for the case of* State of New Jersey v. Michaels *presented by Committee of Concerned Social Scientists.* Supreme Court of New Jersey, Docket #36,333. (Reprinted in *Psychology, Public Policy, and Law, 1,* 272–322, 1995.)

Bruck, M., Ceci, S. J., Francouer, E., & Renick, A. (1995). Anatomically detailed dolls do not facilitate preschoolers' reports of pediatric examination involving genital touching. *Journal of Experimental Psychology: Applied, 1,* 95–109.

Bruck, M., Ceci, S. J., & Hembrooke, H. (1998). Reliability and credibility of young children's reports:

From research to policy and practice. *American Psychologist, 53,* 136–51.

Brussel, J. A. (1968). *Casebook of a crime psychiatrist.* New York: Bernard Geis Associates.

Buckhout, R. (1974). Eyewitness testimony. *Scientific American, 231,* 23–31.

Buckhout, R. (1983). Psychologist v. the judge: Expert testimony on identification. *Social Action and the Law, 9*(3), 67–76.

Buckhout, R., & Friere, V. (1975). *Suggestibility in lineups and photospreads: A casebook for lawyers* (Center for Responsive Psychology Monograph No. CR-5). New York: Brooklyn College.

Bulkley, J. A., & Horwitz, M. J. (1994). Adults sexually abused as children: Legal actions and issues. *Behavioral Sciences and the Law, 12,* 65–87.

Bull, R. (1988). What is the lie-detector test? In A. Gale (Ed.), *The polygraph test: Lies, truth, and science* (pp. 10–18). London: Sage.

Burge, S. K. (1988). Post-traumatic stress disorder in victims of rape. *Journal of Traumatic Stress, 1*(2), 193–209.

Burgess, A. W., & Holmstrom, L. L. (1974). Rape trauma syndrome. *American Journal of Psychiatry, 131,* 981–999.

Burgess, A. W., & Holmstrom, L. L. (1985). Rape trauma syndrome and post-traumatic stress response. In A. W. Burgess (Ed.), *Research handbook on rape and sexual assault* (pp. 46–61). New York: Garland.

Burtt, H. (1931). *Legal psychology.* Englewood Cliffs, NJ: Prentice-Hall.

Bussey, Jr. v. Commonwealth, Appellee Supreme Court, September 6, 697 S.W.2d 139 (Ky. 1985).

Butcher, J. N., Dahlstrom, W. G., Graham, J. R., Tellegen, A., & Kaemmer, B. (1989). *The Minnesota Multiphasic Personality Inventory-2 (MMPI-2): Manual for administration and scoring.* Minneapolis: University of Minnesota Press.

Buxton, A. (1999). Children of gay and lesbian parents. In R. Galatzer-Levy, L. Krauss, & B. Leventhal (Eds.), *The scientific basis for custody decisions in divorce* (pp. 319–356). New York: John Wiley.

Byczynski, L. (1987, December 29). Is joint custody better? *Kansas City Times,* pp. A1, A4.

Caddell, P. H., & Cooper, M. (1998, December 23). The death of liberal outrage. *Wall Street Journal,* p. A14.

California v. Greenwood, 108 S. Ct. 1625 (1988).

Callahan, L., Mayer, C., & Steadman, H. J. (1987). Insanity defense reform in the United States— Post-Hinckley. *Mental and Physical Disability Law Reporter, 11,* 54–59.

Campbell, J. C. (1995). *Assessing dangerousness: Violence by sexual offenders, batterers, and child abusers* (pp. 114–137). Thousand Oaks, CA: Sage.

Cannon, L. (1998). *Official negligence: How Rodney King and the riots changed Los Angeles and the LAPD.* New York: Times Books.

Caplan, L. (1984). *The insanity defense and the trial of John W. Hinckley, Jr.* New York: David R. Godine.

Carelli, R. (1995, October 20). As death rows grow, help dwindles. *Kansas City Star,* p. C-5.

Carelli, R. (1997, December 7). High court to rule in harassment case. *Kansas City Star,* pp. A-1, A-22.

Carlson, H. M., & Sutton, M. S. (1975). The effects of different police roles on attitudes and values. *Journal of Psychology, 91,* 57–64.

Carlson, R. A. (1995). Review of the Perception-of-Relationship Test. In J. C. Conoley & J. C. Impara (Eds.), *Twelfth mental measurements yearbook* (p. 746). Lincoln: University of Nebraska Press.

Carr, C. (1994). *The alienist.* New York: Random House.

Carr, C. (1997). *The angel of darkness.* New York: Ballantine.

Carroll, D. (1988). How accurate is polygraph lie detection? In A. Gale (Ed.), *The polygraph test: Lies, truth and science* (pp. 19–28). London: Sage.

Carroll, J. S. (1980). An appetizing look at law and psychology. *Contemporary Psychology, 25,* 362–363.

Carson, D. (1988). Risk: A four letter word for lawyers. In P. J. Hessing & G. Van den Heuvel (Eds.), *Lawyers on psychology and psychologists on law* (pp. 57–63). Amsterdam: Swets & Zeitlinger.

Cassell, P. G. (1996a). All benefits, no costs: The grand illusion of *Miranda's* defenders. *Northwestern University Law Review, 90,* 1084–1124.

Cassell, P. G. (1996b). *Miranda's* social costs: An empirical reassessment. *Northwestern University Law Review, 90,* 387–499.

Cassell, P. G. (1998). Protecting the innocent from false confessions and lost confessions—and from *Miranda. Journal of Criminal Law and Criminology, 78,* 497–556.

Cassell, P. G. (1999). The guilty and the "innocent": An examination of alleged cases of wrongful conviction from false confessions. *Harvard Journal of Law and Public Policy, 22,* 523–603.

Cassell, P. G., & Hayman, B. S. (1996). Police interrogation in the 1990s: An empirical study of the effects of *Miranda. UCLA Law Review, 43,* 839–931.

Cattell, J. McK. (Ed.). (1894). *Proceedings of the American Psychological Association.* New York: Macmillan.

Cattell, J. McK. (1895). Measurements of the accuracy of recollection. *Science, 2,* 761–766.

Cauffman, E. (1996). *Maturity of judgment in adolescence: Psychosocial factors in adolescent decision-making.* Unpublished doctoral dissertation, Temple University, Philadelphia, PA.

Ceci, S. J., & Bruck, M. (1993). Suggestibility of the child witness: A historical review and synthesis. *Psychological Bulletin, 113,* 403–439.

Ceci, S. J., & Bruck, M. (1995). *Jeopardy in the courtroom: A scientific analysis of children's testimony.* Washington, DC: American Psychological Association.

Ceci, S. J., & Hembrooke, H. (1998a). Introduction. In S. J. Ceci & H. Hembrooke (Eds.), *Expert witnesses in child abuse cases* (pp. 1–8). Washington, DC: American Psychological Association.

Ceci, S. J., & Hembrooke, H. (Eds.). (1998b). *Expert witnesses in child abuse cases.* Washington, DC: American Psychological Association.

Ceci, S. J., Ross, D. F., & Toglia, M. P. (1987). Suggestibility of children's memory: Psycholegal implications. *Journal of Experimental Psychology: General, 116,* 38–49.

Ceci, S. J., Toglia, M. P., & Ross, D. F. (Eds.). (1987). *Children's eyewitness memory.* New York: Springer-Verlag.

Chamallas, M. (1990). Listening to Dr. Fiske: The easy case of *Price Waterhouse v. Hopkins. Vermont Law Review, 15,* 89–124.

Chandler, J. (1990). *Modern police psychology.* Springfield, IL: Charles C Thomas.

Chang, W. C. (1996). Toward equal opportunities: Fairness, values, and affirmative action programs. *Journal of Social Issues, 52*(4), 93–97.

Chesebro, K. (1993). Galileo's retort: Peter Huber's junk scholarship. *American University Law Review, 42,* 1637–1726.

Christiaanson, S. A., & Hubinette, B. (1993). Hands up! A study of witnesses' emotional reactions and memories associated with bank robberies. *Applied Cognitive Psychology, 7,* 365–379.

Civil Rights Act of 1991, Pub. L. No. 102-166, 105 Stat. 1071 (1991).

Clark, K. B., & Clark, M. P. (1952). Racial identification and preference in Negro children. In G. E. Swanson, T. M. Newcomb, & E. L. Hartley (Eds.), *Readings in social psychology* (Rev. ed., pp. 551–560). New York: Holt.

Clark, M. (1997). *Without a doubt.* New York: Viking Penguin.

Clarke, J. W. (1988). *Last rampage: The escape of Gary Tison.* Boston: Houghton-Mifflin.

Clifford, B. R., & Scott, J. (1978). Individual and situational factors in eyewitness testimony. *Journal of Applied Psychology, 63,* 352–359.

Clingempeel, W. G., & Reppucci, N. D. (1982). Joint custody after divorce: Major issues and goals for research. *Psychological Bulletin, 91,* 102–127.

"Closed head injuries." (1994, January 17). Lawyer's Service Directory. *National Law Journal,* p. 36.

Cloud, J. (1998, March 23). Sex and the law. *Time,* 48–54.

Cohn, D. S. (1991). Anatomical doll play of preschoolers referred for sexual abuse and those not referred. *Child Abuse and Neglect, 15,* 567–573.

Cole, D. (1999). *No equal justice: Race and class in the American criminal justice system.* New York: New Press.

Colgrove v. Battin, 413 U.S. 149 (1973).

Collins v. Brierly, 492 F.2d 735 (3rd Cir. 1974).

Colorado v. Connelly, 497 U.S. 157 (1986).

Committee on Ethical Guidelines for Forensic Psychologists. (1991). Specialty guidelines for forensic psychologists. *Law and Human Behavior, 15,* 655–665.

Commonwealth v. Graham, 408 Pa. 155, 182 A.2d 727 (1962).

Commonwealth v. Abdul-Salaam, 544 Pa. 514, 524, 678 A.2d 342, 347 (1996).

Conger, J. (1995). Review of Perception-of-Relationships Test. In J. C. Conoley & J. C. Impara (Eds.), *Twelfth mental measurements yearbook* (pp. 747–748). Lincoln: University of Nebraska Press.

Connors, E., Lundregan, T., Miller, N., & McEwan, T. (1996). *Convicted by juries, exonerated by science: Case studies in the use of DNA evidence to establish innocence after trial.* Alexandria, VA: National Institute of Justice.

Conte, J. R., Sorenson, E., Fogarty, L., & Rosa, J. (1991). Evaluating children's reports of sexual abuse: Results from a survey of professionals. *American Journal of Orthopsychiatry, 61,* 428–437.

Cook, S. W. (1971). *The effect of unintended interracial contact upon racial interaction and attitude change.* (Final report, Project No. 5–1320). Washington, DC: U.S. Department of Health, Education, and Welfare, Office of Education.

Cook, S. W. (1975). Interpersonal and attitudinal outcomes in cooperating interracial groups. *Journal of Research and Development in Education, 12,* 97–113.

Cook, S. W. (1979). Social science and school desegregation: Did we mislead the Supreme Court? *Personality and Social Psychology Bulletin, 5,* 420–434.

Cook, S. W. (1984). The 1954 social science statement and school segregation: A reply to Gerard. *American Psychologist, 39,* 819–832.

Cooper, D. K., & Grisso, T. (1997). Five-year research update (1991–1995): Evaluations for competence to stand trial. *Behavioral Sciences and the Law, 15*(3), 347–364.

Cornwell, P. D. (1991). *Body of evidence.* New York: Charles Scribner's.

Costantini, E., & King, J. (1980–1981). The partial juror: Correlates and causes of prejudgment. *Law and Society Review, 15,* 9–40.

Costanzo, M. (1997). *Just revenge: Costs and consequences of the death penalty.* New York: St. Martin's Press.

Costanzo, M., & Costanzo, S. (1992). Jury decision-making in the capital penalty phase: Legal assumptions, empirical findings, and a research agenda. *Law and Human Behavior, 16,* 185–201.

Costanzo, M., & Peterson, J. (1994). Attorney persuasion in the capital penalty phase: A content analysis of closing arguments. *Journal of Social Issues, 50*(2), 125–147.

Court transcript: A lawyer without precedent. (1997, June). *Harper's Magazine,* 24–26.

Cowan, C. L., Thompson, W. C., & Ellsworth, P. C. (1984). The effects of death qualification on jurors' predispositions to convict and on the quality of deliberation. *Law and Human Behavior, 8,* 53–79.

Cox, G. D. (1991, October 28). Assumption of risks. *National Law Journal,* pp. 1, 24–25.

Cox, G. D. (1992, August 3). Tort tales lash back. *National Law Journal,* pp. 1, 36–37.

Cox, G. D. (1993, May 3). Consultant appointed in Denny case. *National Law Journal,* p. 38.

Coy v. Iowa, 487 U.S. 1012 (1988).

Coyle, M. (1993, July 12). Supreme Court eases admissibility of experts. *National Law Journal,* p. 12.

Coyle, M. (1995, September 18). Republicans take aim at death row lawyers. *National Law Journal,* A1, A25.

Coyle, M. (1998, December 21). Suit: Death defense is a sham. *National Law Journal,* pp. 1, 14–15.

Coyle, M., & Lavelle, M. (1993, February 8). Does innocence void death sentence? *National Law Journal,* pp. 5, 19.

Coyne, R., & Entzeroth, L. (1994). *Capital punishment and the judicial process.* Durham, NC: Carolina Academic Press.

Craig, K. M., & Waldo, C. R. (1996). "So, what's a hate crime anyway?" Young adults' perceptions of hate crimes, victims, and perpetrators. *Law and Human Behavior, 20,* 113–129.

Cramer, D. (1986). Gay parents and their children: A review of research and practical implications. *Journal of Counseling and Development, 64,* 504–507.

Crenshaw, M. (1986). The psychology of political terrorism. In M. G. Hermann (Ed.), *Political psychology* (pp. 379–413). San Francisco: Jossey-Bass.

Crichton, M. (1993). *Disclosure.* New York: Knopf.

Crocker, P. L. (1985). The meaning of equality for battered women who kill men in self-defense. *Harvard Women's Law Review, 8,* 121–153.

Crosby, F. (1994, September 8). *Affirmative action: Illusions and realities.* Ferne Forman Fisher Lecture, University of Kansas, Lawrence.

Cull, J., & Gill, W. (1982). *Suicide Probability Scale*. Los Angeles: Western Psychological Services.

Cull, J. G., & Gill, W. S. (1999). *Suicide Probability Scale, Revised Version*. Los Angeles: Western Psychological Services.

Culombe v. Connecticut, 367 U.S. 568 (1961).

Cutler, B. L., Berman, G. L., Penrod, S. D., & Fisher, R. P. (1994). Conceptual, practical, and empirical issues associated with eyewitness identification test media. In D. F. Ross, J. D. Read, & M. P. Toglia (Eds.), *Adult eyewitness testimony: Current trends and developments* (pp. 163–181). New York: Cambridge University Press.

Cutler, B. L., & Penrod, S. D. (1989). Forensically relevant moderators of the relation between eyewitness identification accuracy and confidence. *Journal of Applied Psychology, 74,* 650–652.

Cutler, B. L., & Penrod, S. D. (1995). *Mistaken identification: The eyewitness, psychology, and the law*. New York: Cambridge University Press.

Cutler, B. L., Penrod, S. D., & Martens, T. K. (1987). The reliability of eyewitness identification: The role of system and estimator variables. *Law and Human Behavior, 11,* 233–258.

Daily Journal Court Rules Service. (1994, October 21). *The O. J. Simpson juror questionnaire*. Los Angeles: Daily Journal Corporation.

Dane, F. C. (1985). In search of reasonable doubt: A systematic examination of selected quantification approaches. *Law and Human Behavior, 9,* 141–158.

Darley, J., Fulero, S., Haney, C., & Tyler, T. (2002). Psychological jurisprudence. In J. R. P. Ogloff (Ed.), *Taking psychology and law into the 21st century: Perspectives in law and psychology, Vol. 14*. New York: Plenum.

Daubert v. Merrell Dow Pharmaceuticals, Inc., 113 S. Ct. 2786 (1993).

Davey, M. (2003, July 17). Illinois will require taping of homicide interrogations. *New York Times*, p. A16.

Davis v. North Carolina, 384 U.S. 737 (1966).

Davis, J. H. (1989). Psychology and the law: The last 15 years. *Journal of Applied Social Psychology, 19,* 199–230.

Davis, J., & Gonzalez, R. (1996, February). *Relative and absolute judgments of eyewitness identification*. Paper presented at the meeting of the American Psychology-Law Society, Hilton Head, S.C.

Davis, R. W. (1986). Pretrial publicity, the timing of the trial, and mock jurors' decision processes. *Journal of Applied Social Psychology, 16,* 590–607.

Davis, S., & Beisecker, T. (1994). Discovering trial consultant work product: A new way to borrow an adversary's wits? *American Journal of Trial Advocacy, 17,* 581.

Dawes, R. M. (1988). *Rational choice in an uncertain world*. San Diego: Harcourt Brace Jovanovich.

Dawes, R. M. (1994). *House of cards: Psychology and psychotherapy built on myth*. New York: Free Press.

Dawes, R. M., Faust, D., & Meehl, P. E. (1989). Clinical versus actuarial judgment. *Science, 243,* 1668–1674.

Dawson, B., & Geddie, L. (1991, August). *Low income, minority preschoolers' behavior with sexually anatomically detailed dolls*. Paper presented at the meeting of the American Psychological Association, San Francisco, CA.

Dawson, B., Vaughan, A. R., & Wagner, W. G. (1992). Normal responses to sexually anatomically detailed dolls. *Journal of Family Violence, 7,* 135–152.

Dawson, J. (1980). Are statistics being fair to employment discrimination plaintiffs? *Jurimetrics Journal, 21,* 1–20.

Dear, G. (2003). Utility of the Suicide Intent Scale within a prison setting. *International Journal of Forensic Psychology, 1,* 133–137.

Deaux, K. (1995). How basic can you be? The evolution of research on gender stereotypes. *Journal of Social Issues, 51*(1), 11–20.

Decker, S. H., & Wagner, A. E. (1982). Race and citizen complaints against the police: An analysis of their interaction. In J. R. Greene (Ed.), *Managing police work: Issues and analysis* (pp. 107–122). Newbury Park, CA: Sage.

Dedman, B. (1998, August 9). Study of assassins concludes there is no common profile. *Kansas City Star*, p. A-15.

Deed, M. L. (1991). Court-ordered child custody evaluations: Helping or victimizing vulnerable families. *Psychotherapy, 28,* 76–84.

Deeley, P. (1971). *Beyond the breaking point*. London: Arthur Baker Ltd.

Deffenbacher, K. A., & Loftus, E. F. (1982). Do jurors share a common understanding concerning eyewitness behavior? *Law and Human Behavior, 6,* 15–30.

Deitchman, M. A., Kennedy, W. A., & Beckham, J. J. (1991). Self-selection factors in the participation of mental health professionals in competency for execution evaluations. *Law and Human Behavior, 15,* 287–303.

Delprino, R., & Bahn, C. (1988). National survey of the extent and nature of psychological services in police departments. *Professional Psychology, 19,* 421–425.

Denmark v. State, 95 Fla. 757, 116 So. 757 (1928).

Devenport, J. L., Penrod, S. D., & Cutler, B. L. (1997). Eyewitness identification evidence: Evaluating common sense evaluations. *Psychology, Public Policy, and Law, 3,* 338–361.

Dexter, H. R., Cutler, B. L., & Moran, G. L. (1992). A test of voir dire as a remedy for the prejudicial effects of pretrial publicity. *Journal of Applied Social Psychology, 22,* 819– 832.

Diamond, B. (1959). The fallacy of the impartial expert. *Archives of Criminal Psychodynamics, 3,* 221–236.

Diamond, S. S. (1989). Using psychology to control law: From deceptive advertising to criminal sentencing. *Law and Human Behavior, 13,* 239–252.

Diamond, S. S. (1990). Scientific jury selection: What social scientists know and don't know. *Judicature, 73*(4), 178–183.

Diamond, S. S. (1993). Instructing on death: Psychologists, jurors, and judges. *American Psychologist, 43,* 423–434.

Diamond, S. S., & Levi, J. N. (1996). Improving decisions on death by revising and testing jury instructions. *Judicature, 79,* 224–232.

Dietrich, J. F., & Smith, J. (1986). The nonmedical use of drugs including alcohol among police personnel: A critical literature review. *Journal of Police Science and Administration, 14,* 300–306.

Dietz, P. E. (1996). The quest for excellence in forensic psychiatry. *Bulletin of the American Academy of Psychiatry and the Law, 24*(2), 153–163.

Dillehay, R. C., & Sandys, M. R. (1996). Life under *Wainwright v. Witt:* Juror dispositions and death qualification. *Law and Human Behavior, 20,* 147–165.

Dillehay, R. D., & Nietzel, M. T. (1980). Constructing a science of jury behavior. In L. Wheeler (Ed.), *Review of personality and social psychology* (pp. 246–264). Newbury Park, CA: Sage.

DiVasto, P. V. (1985). Measuring the aftermath of rape. *Journal of Psychosocial Nursing and Mental Health Services, 23,* 33–35.

Doe v. Doe, 111 Va. 736, 284 S.E.2d 799 (1981).

Dolnick, L., Case, T., & Williams, K. D. (2003). Stealing thunder as a courtroom tactic revisited: Processes and boundaries. *Law and Human Behavior, 27,* 267–288.

Donohue, J. J., III. (1998). Did *Miranda* diminish police effectiveness? *Stanford Law Review, 50,* 1147–1172.

Douglas, J. E., & Munn, C. (1992, February). Violent crime scene analysis: Modus operandi, signature, and staging. *F.B.I. Law Enforcement Bulletin,* 1–10.

Douglas, J. E., & Olshaker, M. (1995). *Mindhunter: Inside the FBI's elite serial crime unit.* New York: Scribner.

Douglas, J. E., & Olshaker, M. (1996). *Unabomber: On the trail of America's most-wanted serial killer.* New York: Pocket Books.

Douglas, J. E., & Olshaker, M. (1997). *Journey into darkness.* New York: Pocket Star Books.

Douglas, J. E., & Olshaker, M. (1998). *Obsession.* New York: Scribner.

Douglas, J. E., Ressler, R. K., Burgess, A. W., & Hartman, C. R. (1986). Criminal profiling from crime scene analysis. *Behavioral Sciences and the Law, 4,* 401–421.

Douglas, K. S., & Webster, C. D. (1999). Assessing risk of violence in mentally and personality disordered individuals. In R. Roesch, S. Hart, & J. Ogloff (Eds.), *Psychology and law: The state of the discipline.* New York: Plenum.

Dovidio, J. F. (1995). *Bias in evaluative judgments and personnel selection: The role of ambiguity.* Unpublished manuscript, Department of Psychology, Colgate University, Hamilton, NY. (Cited by Dovidio & Gaertner, 1996.)

Dovidio, J. F., & Gaertner, S. L. (Eds.). (1986). *Prejudice, discrimination, and racism.* San Diego: Academic Press.

Dovidio, J. F., & Gaertner, S. L. (1996). Affirmative action, unintentional racial biases, and intergroup relations. *Journal of Social Issues, 52*(4), 51–75.

Doyle, A. C. (1892). A case of identity. In *The original illustrated Sherlock Holmes.* Secaucus, NJ: Castle.

Doyle, A. C. (1892). The man with the twisted lip. In *The original illustrated Sherlock Holmes.* Secaucus, NJ.: Castle.

Dred Scott v. Sandford, 60 U.S. (19 How.) 393 (1857).

Drinan, R. F. (1973). The rights of children in modern American family law. In A. E. Wilkerson (Ed.), *The rights of children: Emergent concepts in law and society* (pp. 37–46). Philadelphia: Temple University Press.

Drozd, L. M. (1998, August). *Domestic violence and custody.* Paper presented at the meeting of the American Psychological Association, San Francisco.

Dunnette, M. D., & Motowidlo, S. J. (1976, November). *Police selection and career assessment.* Washington, DC: Law Enforcement Assistance Association, United States Department of Justice.

Durham v. United States, 214 F.2d 862 (D.C. Cir. 1954).

Dusky v. United States, 362 U.S. 402 (1960).

Duthie, B., & McIvor, D. L. (1990). A new system for cluster-coding child molester MMPI profile types. *Criminal Justice and Behavior, 17,* 199–214.

Dutton, D. G. (1981). *The criminal justice system response to wife assault.* Ottawa: Solicitor General of Canada, Research Division.

Dutton, D. G. (1988). *The domestic assault of women: Psychological and criminal justice perspectives.* Boston: Allyn and Bacon.

Dutton, D. G. (1995). *The domestic assault of women: Psychological and criminal justice perspectives* (Rev. ed.). Vancouver, B.C., Canada: UBC Press.

Dutton, D. G., & Kropp, P. R. (2000). A review of domestic violence risk instruments. *Trauma, Violence and Abuse, 1,* 171 –181.

Dutton, D. G., & Levens, B. R. (1977). Domestic crisis intervention: Attitude survey of trained and untrained police officers. *Canadian Police College Journal, 1*(2), 75–92.

Dutton, M. A. (1992). *Empowering and healing the battered woman: A model for assessment and intervention*. New York: Springer.

Dutton, M. A. (1993). Understanding women's responses to domestic violence: A redefinition of battered woman syndrome. *Hofstra Law Review, 21,* 1191–1242.

Dutton-Douglas, M. A., Perrin, S., & Chrestman, K. (1990, August). *MMPI differences among battered women*. Paper presented at the meeting of the American Psychological Association, Boston.

Dyk, T. B., & Castanias, G. A. (1993, August 2). *Daubert doesn't end debate on experts. National Law Journal,* pp. 17–19.

Dywan, J., Kaplan, R. D., & Pirozzolo, F. J. (1991). Introduction. In J. Dywan, R. D. Kaplan, & F. J. Pirozzolo (Eds.), *Neuropsychology and the law* (pp. xi–xv). New York: Springer- Verlag.

Ebert, L. B. (1993). *Frye* after *Daubert:* The role of scientists in admissibility issues as seen through analysis of the DNA profiling cases. *University of Chicago Law School Roundtable, 1993,* 219–253.

Ebbinghaus, H. E. (1885). *Memory: A contribution to experimental psychology*. New York: Dover.

Egeth, H. E. (1993). What do we *not* know about eyewitness identification? *American Psychologist, 48,* 577–580.

Ekman, P. (1985). *Telling lies: Clues to deceit in the marketplace, politics, and marriage*. New York: Norton.

Ekman, P., & O'Sullivan. M. (1991). Who can catch a liar? *American Psychologist, 46,* 913–920.

Elliott, R. (1987). *Litigating intelligence: IQ tests, special education, and social science in the courtroom*. Dover, MA: Auburn House.

Elliott, R. (1991a). Response to Ellsworth. *Law and Human Behavior, 15,* 91–94.

Elliott, R. (1991b). Social science data and the APA: The *Lockhart* brief as a case in point. *Law and Human Behavior, 15,* 59–76.

Elliott, R. (1993). Expert testimony about eyewitness identification: A critique. *Law and Human Behavior, 17,* 423–437.

Ellis, H. D., Shepherd, J. W., & Davies, G. M. (1980). The deterioration of verbal descriptions of faces over different delay intervals. *Journal of Police Science and Administration, 8,* 101–106.

Ellison v. Brady, 924 F.2d 871 (9th Cir. 1991).

Ellison, K. W. (1985). Community involvement in police selection. *Social Action and the Law, 11*(3), 77–78.

Ellison, K. W., & Buckhout, R. (1981). *Psychology and criminal justice*. New York: Harper and Row.

Ellsworth, P. C. (1991). To tell what we know or wait for Godot? *Law and Human Behavior, 15,* 77–90.

Emery, R. (1994). *Renegotiating family relationships: Divorce, child custody, and mediation*. New York: Guilford.

Emery, R., & Wyer, M. (1987). Divorce mediation. *American Psychologist, 42,* 472–480.

Engelbrecht, S. B., & Wrightsman, L. S. (1994). Unpublished research, University of Kansas, Lawrence.

Epstein, J. G. (1995, January 16). Death penalty adds to our tax burdens. *National Law Journal,* A23-A24.

Epperson, D. L., Kaul, J. D., & Hesselton, D. (1998, October). Final report of the development of the Minnesota Sex Offender Screening Tool–Revised (MnSOST-R). Presentation at the 17th Annual Research and Treatment Conference of the Association for the Treatment of Sexual Abusers, Vancouver, B.C., Canada.

Erard, B. H., & Seltzer, M. K. (1994). Evolving standard of scientific acceptance under *Daubert. Michigan Bar Journal, 73*(2), 161–163.

Erickson, W. D., Luxenburg, M. G., Walbek, N. H., & Seely, R. K. (1987). Frequency of MMPI two-point code types among sex offenders. *Journal of Consulting and Clinical Psychology, 55,* 566–570.

Ernsdorff, G. N., & Loftus, E. F. (1993). Let sleeping memories lie? Words of caution about tolling the statute of limitations in cases of memory repression. *Journal of Criminal Law and Criminology, 84,* 129–174.

Everington, C. (1990). The Competence Assessment for Standing Trial for Defendants With Mental Retardation (CAST-MR): A validation study. *Criminal Justice and Behavior, 17,* 147–168.

Everington, C., & Dunn, C. (1995). A second validation study of the Competence Assessment for Standing Trial for Defendants With Mental Retardation (CAST-MR). *Criminal Justice and Behavior, 22,* 44–59.

Everington, C., & Luckasson, R. (1992). *Competence assessment for standing trial for defendants with mental retardation (CAST-MR)*. Worthington, OH: International Diagnostic Services.

Everson, M. D., & Boat, B. W. (1990). Sexualized doll play among young children: Implications for the use of anatomical dolls in sexual abuse evaluations. *Journal of the American Academy of Child and Adolescent Psychiatry, 29,* 736–742.

Everson, M. D., & Boat, B. W. (1994). Putting the anatomical doll controversy in perspective: An examination of the major uses and criticisms of the dolls in child sexual abuse evaluations. *Child Abuse and Neglect, 11,* 113–129.

Ewing, C. (1985). *Schall v. Martin:* Preventive detention and dangerousness through the looking glass. *Buffalo Law Review, 34,* 173–226.

Ewing, C. P. (1987). *Battered women who kill: Psychological self-defense as legal justification*. Lexington, MA: Lexington Books, D. C. Heath.

Ewing, C. P. (1990). Psychological self-defense: A proposed justification for battered women who kill. *Law and Human Behavior, 14,* 579–594.

Ewing, C. P. (1991). Preventive detention and execution: The constitutionality of punishing future crimes. *Law and Human Behavior, 15,* 139–163.

Ewing, C. P., Aubrey, M., & Jamieson, L. (1986, August). *The battered woman syndrome: Expert testimony and public attitudes.* Paper presented at the meeting of the American Psychological Association, Washington, DC.

Eyman, J. R., & Eyman, S. K. (1992). Psychological testing for potentially suicidal individuals. In B. Bongar (Ed.), *Suicide: Guidelines for assessment, management and treatment* (pp. 127–143). New York: Oxford University Press.

Faigman, D. (1986). The battered woman syndrome and self-defense: A legal and empirical dissent. *Virginia Law Review, 72,* 619–647.

Faigman, D. L. (1995). The evidentiary status of social science under *Daubert:* Is it "scientific," "technical," or "other" knowledge? *Psychology, Public Policy, and the Law, 1,* 960–979.

Faigman, D. L., Kaye, D. H., Saks, M. J., & Sanders, J. (1997). *Modern scientific evidence: The law and science of expert testimony.* St. Paul, MN: West.

Faigman, D. L., Porter, E., & Saks, M. J. (1994). Check your crystal ball at the courthouse door, please: Exploring the past, understanding the present, and worrying about the future of scientific evidence. *Cardozo Law Review, 15,* 1799–1835.

Faigman, D. L., & Wright, A. J. (1997). The battered woman syndrome in the age of science. *Arizona Law Review, 39,* 67–115.

Falk, P. J. (1989). Lesbian mothers: Psychosocial assumptions in family law. *American Psychologist, 44,* 941–947.

Faller, K. C. (1996). Interviewing children who may have been abused: A historical perspective and overview of controversies. *Child Maltreatment, 1,* 83–95.

Fargo, M. (1994, April). Using juror questionnaires to supplement voir dire. *Court Call,* 1–3.

Farley, L. (1978). *Sexual shakedown: The sexual harassment of women on the job.* New York: McGraw-Hill.

Farmer, J. (2003). Unpublished letter, available at *http://www.state.nj.us/lps/dcj/agguide/photoid.pdf.*

Faust, D., & Ziskin, J. (1988). The expert witness in psychology and psychiatry. *Science, 241,* 31–35.

Federal Judicial Center. (1994). *Reference manual on scientific evidence.* Washington, DC: Author.

Federal Rules of Evidence. (1984). St. Paul, MN: West.

Feigenson, N. (1995). The rhetoric of torts: How advocates help jurors think about causation, reasonableness, and responsibility. *Hastings Law Journal, 47,* 61–165.

Feigenson, N., Park, J., & Salovey, P. (1997). Effect of blameworthiness and outcome severity on attributions of responsibility and damage awards in comparative negligence cases. *Law and Human Behavior, 21,* 597–617.

Felchlia, M. (1992). Construct validity of the Competency Screening Test. *Dissertation Abstracts International, 53*(1-B), 604.

Feldman-Summers, S., Gordon, P. E., & Meagher, J. R. (1979). The impact of rape on sexual satisfaction. *Journal of Abnormal Psychology, 88,* 101–105.

Felner, R. D., Rowlison, R. T., Farber, S. S., & Primavera, J. (1987). Child custody resolution: A study of social science involvement and input. *Professional Psychology: Research and Practice, 18,* 468–474.

Felner, R. D., & Terre, L. (1987). Child custody dispositions and children's adaptation following divorce. In L. A. Weithorn (Ed.), *Psychology and child custody determinations: Knowledge, roles, and expertise* (pp. 106–153). Lincoln: University of Nebraska Press.

Feuer, A. (2004, January 6). New York settles lawsuit with Diallo family for $3 million. *New York Times,* p. A16.

Fields, G. (1993, December 16). Indictment: D.C. cops bragged about crimes. *USA Today,* p. 3A.

Fienberg, S. E. (Ed.). (1989). *The evolving role of statistical assessments as evidence in the courts.* New York: Springer-Verlag.

Finch, M., & Ferraro, M. (1986). The empirical challenge to death qualified juries: On further examination. *Nebraska Law Review, 65,* 21–74.

Finkel, N., & Fulero, S. (1992). Insanity: Making law in the absence of evidence. *International Journal of Medicine and Law, 11,* 383–404.

Finkel, N., Fulero, S., Haugaard, J., Levine, M., & Small, M. (2001). Everyday life and legal values: A concept paper. *Law and Human Behavior, 25,* 109–123.

Finkel, N. J., Meister, K. H., & Lightfoot, D. M. (1991). The self-defense defense and community sentiment. *Law and Human Behavior, 15,* 585–602.

Finn, P., & McNeil, T. (1987, October 7). *The response of the criminal justice system to bias crime: An exploratory review.* Contract Report submitted to the National Institute of Justice.

Finnegan, W. (1998, March 18). Defending the Unabomber. *New Yorker,* 52–63.

Fischhoff, B. (1994). What forecasts (seem to) mean. *International Journal of Forecasting, 10,* 387–403.

Fisher, C. B., & Whiting, K. A. (1998). How valid are child sexual abuse validations? In S. J. Ceci & H. Hembrooke (Eds.), *Expert witnesses in child abuse cases* (pp. 159–184). Washington, DC: American Psychological Association.

Fisher, R. P. (1995). Interviewing victims and witnesses of crime. *Psychology, Public Policy, and Law, 1,* 732–764.

Fisher, R. P., Geiselman, R. E., & Amador, M. (1989). Field test of the cognitive interview: Enhancing the recollection of actual victims and witnesses of crime. *Journal of Applied Psychology, 74,* 722–727.

Fisher, R. P., Geiselman, R. E., & Raymond, D. S. (1987). Critical analysis of police interview techniques. *Journal of Police Science and Administration, 15,* 177–185.

Fisk, M. C. (1994, April 4). Verdicts and settlements. *National Law Journal,* p. A16.

Fisk, M. C. (1998a, April 20). Judges slash worker awards. *National Law Journal,* pp. A1, A20.

Fisk, M. C. (1998b, November 23). Winning: Successful strategies from 10 of the nation's top trial lawyers. *National Law Journal,* pp. B5–B16.

Fiske, S. T., Bersoff, D. N., Borgida, E., Deaux, K., & Heilman, M. E. (1991). Social science research on trial: Use of sex stereotyping research in *Price Waterhouse v. Hopkins. American Psychologist, 46,* 1049–1060.

Fiske, S. T., Bersoff, D. N., Borgida, E., Deaux, K., & Heilman, M. E. (1993). What constitutes a scientific review? A majority retort to Barrett and Morris. *Law and Human Behavior, 17,* 217–233.

Fitzgerald, L. F., Drasgow, F., Hulin, C. L., Gelfand, M. J., & Magley, V. J. (1997). Antecedents and consequences of sexual harassment in organizations: A test of an integrated model. *Journal of Applied Psychology, 82,* 578–589.

Fitzgerald, L. F., & Hesson-McInnis, M. (1989). The dimensions of sexual harassment: A structural analysis. *Journal of Vocational Behavior, 35,* 309–326.

Fitzgerald, L. F., Shullman, S. L., Bailey, N., Richards, M., Swecker, J., Gold, Y., Ormerod, A. J.., & Weitzman, L. (1988). The incidence and dimensions of sexual harassment in academia and the workplace. *Journal of Vocational Behavior, 32,* 152–175.

Fitzgerald, L. F., Swan, S., & Fischer, K. (1995). Why didn't she just report him? The psychological and legal implications of women's responses to sexual harassment. *Journal of Social Issues, 51*(1), 117–138.

Fitzgerald, R., & Ellsworth, P. C. (1984). Due process vs. crime control: Death qualification and juror attitudes. *Law and Human Behavior, 8,* 31–51.

Foa, E. B., Olasov, B., & Steketee, G. (1987). *Treatment of rape victims.* Paper presented at the State-of-the-Art in Sexual Assault conference, Charleston, SC.

Foley, L. A. (1993). *A psychological view of the legal system.* Madison, WI: Brown & Benchmark.

Follingstad, D. R. (1994, March). *Rape trauma syndrome in the courtroom.* Workshop presented for the American Academy of Forensic Psychology, Santa Fe, NM.

Follingstad, D. R. (1994, March 10). *The use of battered woman syndrome in court.* Workshop presented for the American Academy of Forensic Psychology, Santa Fe, NM.

Follingstad, D. R., Polek, D. S., Hause, E. S., Deaton, L. H., Bulger, M. W., & Conway, Z. D. (1989). Factors predicting verdicts in cases where battered women kill their husbands. *Law and Human Behavior, 13,* 253–270.

Foote, W. E. (1998, August). *APA and the amicus process: COLI's perspective.* Symposium paper presented at the meeting of the American Psychological Association, San Francisco.

Foote, W. E., & Goodman-Delahunty, J. (1999). Same-sex harassment: Implications of the *Oncale* decision for forensic evaluation of plaintiffs. *Behavioral Sciences and the Law, 17,* 123–139.

Ford v. Wainwright, 474 U.S. 699, (1986).

Forman, B. (1980). Psychotherapy with rape victims. *Psychotherapy: Theory, Research and Practice, 17,* 304–311.

Foster, H. H. (1969). Confessions and the station house syndrome. *DePaul Law Review, 18,* 683–701.

Fowler, R. D. (1986, May). Howard Hughes: A psychological autopsy. *Psychology Today,* 22–33.

Fowler, R., De Vivo, P. P., & Fowler, D. J. (1985). Analyzing police hostage negotiations: The verbal interaction analysis technique. *Journal of Crisis Intervention, 2,* 16–28.

Fox, R. E. (1991). Proceedings of the American Psychological Association, Incorporated, for the year 1990. *American Psychologist, 46,* 689–726.

Frank, E., & Stewart, B. D. (1984). Depressive symptoms in rape victims: A revisit. *Journal of Affective Disorders, 7,* 77–85.

Frank, G. (1966). *The Boston Strangler.* New York: Signet.

Frank, J. (1957). *Not guilty.* New York: Doubleday.

Frank, M. G., & Ekman, P. (1997). The ability to detect deceit generalizes across different types of high-stake lies. *Journal of Personality and Social Psychology, 72,* 1429–1439.

Franklin, B. (1994, August 22). Gender myths still play a role in jury selection. *National Law Journal,* A1, A25.

Franklin, C. (1970). *The third degree.* London: Robert Hale.

Frazier v. Cupp, 394 U.S. 731 (1969).

Frazier, P. A. (1990). Victim attributions and post-rape trauma. *Journal of Personality and Social Psychology, 59,* 298–304.

Frazier, P. A. (1993, March). Should only peer-reviewed research be admissible in court? *APA Monitor,* p. 12.

Frazier, P. A., & Borgida, E. (1985). Rape trauma syndrome evidence in court. *American Psychologist, 40,* 984–993.

Frazier, P. A., & Borgida, E. (1988). Juror common understanding and the admissibility of rape trauma syndrome evidence in court. *Law and Human Behavior, 12,* 101–122.

Frazier, P. A., & Borgida, E. (1992). Rape trauma syndrome: A review of case law and psychological research. *Law and Human Behavior, 16,* 293–311.

Frazier, P. A., Cochran, C. C., & Olson, A. M. (1995). Social science research on lay definitions of sexual harassment. *Journal of Social Issues, 51*(1), 21–37.

Fredman, S. G. (1995, August). *Child custody evaluations from the bench: A judge's perspective.* Paper presented at the meeting of the American Psychological Association, New York City.

Frey, B. (1994). *Development of a structured preference scale and a deductive preference scale.* Unpublished doctoral dissertation, University of Kansas, Lawrence.

Frey, D. L., & Gaertner, S. L. (1986). Helping and the avoidance of inappropriate interracial behavior: A strategy that perpetuates a nonprejudicial self-image. *Journal of Personality and Social Psychology, 50,* 1083–1090.

Friedland, N., & Merari, A. (1985). The psychological impact of terrorism: A double-edged sword. *Political Psychology, 6,* 591–604.

Friedman, G. (1993). *A guide to divorce mediation.* New York: Workman.

Frye v. United States, 293 F. 1013, 34 A.L.R. 145 (D.C. Cir. 1923).

Fulero, S. M. (1987). The role of behavioral research in the free press/fair trial controversy. *Law and Human Behavior, 11,* 259–264.

Fulero, S. M. (1988). *Tarasoff:* Ten years later. *Professional Psychology: Research and Practice, 19,* 184–190.

Fulero, S. M. (1988, August). *Eyewitness expert testimony: An overview and annotated bibliography, 1931–1988.* Paper presented at the meeting of the American Psychological Association, Atlanta.

Fulero, S. M. (1995). Review of the Psychopathy Checklist–Revised (PCL-R). In J. Impara (Ed.), *Mental measurements yearbook* (12th ed., pp. 453–454). Lincoln: University of Nebraska Press.

Fulero, S. M. (1997). Babies, bathwater, and being "hoisted by own petard." *National Psychologist, 6*(3), 10–11.

Fulero, S. M. (1999). A history of Division 41 of the American Psychological Association (American Psychology-Law Society): A Rock and Roll Odyssey. In D. Dewsbury (Ed.), *Unification through division: Histories of divisions of the American Psychological Association, Vol. 4* (pp. 109–127). Washington, DC: American Psychological Association.

Fulero, S. M. (2002a). Foreword: Empirical and legal perspectives on the impact of pretrial publicity: Effects and remedies [Special issue; S. M. Fulero, Ed.]. *Law and Human Behavior, 26*(1), 1–2.

Fulero, S. M. (2002b). Afterword: The past, present, and future of applied pretrial publicity research [Special issue; S. M. Fulero, Ed.]. *Law and Human Behavior, 26*(1), 127–133.

Fulero, S. M. (2003, August). *APA amicus involvement and the* Atkins *case: A contrarian response to contrarian concerns.* Paper presented at the annual meeting of the American Psychological Association, Toronto, Ontario, Canada.

Fulero, S. M. (2004). Expert psychological testimony on the psychology of interrogations and confessions. In G. D. Lassiter (Ed.), *Interrogations, confessions, and entrapment* (pp. 247–263). New York: Kluwer Publishers.

Fulero, S. M., & Finkel, N. J. (1991). Barring ultimate issue testimony: An "insane" rule? *Law and Human Behavior, 15,* 495–507.

Fulero, S. M., & Mossman, D. (1998, March). *Legal psychology and legal scholarship: A review of the reviews.* Paper presented at the meeting of the American Psychology-Law Society, Redondo Beach, CA.

Fulero, S. M., & Penrod, S. (1990). The myths and realities of attorney jury selection folklore and scientific jury selection: What works? *Ohio Northern University Law Review, 17,* 229–253.

Furman v. Georgia, 408 U.S. 238 (1972).

Fuselier, G. D. (1988). Hostage negotiation consultant: Emerging role for the clinical psychologist. *Professional Psychology: Research and Practice, 19,* 175–179.

Gaertner, S. L., & Bickman, L. (1971). Effects of race on the elicitation of helping behavior: The wrong number technique. *Journal of Personality and Social Psychology, 20,* 218–222.

Gaertner, S. L., & Dovidio, J. F. (1977). The subtlety of white racism, arousal, and helping behavior. *Journal of Personality and Social Psychology, 35,* 691–702.

Gaertner, S. L., & Dovidio, J. F. (1986). The aversive form of racism. In J. F. Dovidio and S. L. Gaertner (Eds.), *Prejudice, discrimination, and racism* (pp. 61–89). San Diego, CA: Academic Press.

Gale, A. (1988). Introduction: The polygraph test, more than scientific investigation. In A. Gale (Ed.), *The polygraph test: Lies, truth and science* (pp. 1–9). London: Sage.

Gamson, W. A., & Modigliani, A. (1987). The changing culture of affirmative action. In R. D. Braungart (Ed.), *Research in political sociology* (Vol. 3). Greenwich, CT: JAI Press.

Garb, H. N. (1998). *Studying the clinician: Judgment research and psychological assessment.* Washington, DC: American Psychological Association

Garcia, A. (1998). Is *Miranda* dead, was it overruled, or is it irrelevant? *St. Thomas Law Review, 10,* 461–498.

Gardner, E. S. (1952). *Court of last resort.* New York: William Sloane Associates.

Garrison, E. G. (1991). Children's competence to participate in divorce custody decision making. *Journal of Clinical Child Psychology, 20,* 78–87.

Garven, S., Wood, J. M., Malpass, R. S., & Shaw, J. S., III. (1998). More than suggestion: The effect of interviewing techniques from the McMartin Preschool case. *Journal of Applied Psychology, 83*, 347–359.

Gatowski, S., Dobbin, S., Richardson, J., Ginsburg, G., Merlino, M., & Dahir, V. (2001). Asking the gatekeepers: A national survey of judges on judging expert evidence in a post-*Daubert* world. *Law and Human Behavior, 25*, 433–458.

Geberth, V. J. (1981, September). Psychological profiling. *Law and Order*, 46–49.

Geberth, V. J. (1990). *Practical homicide investigation: Tactics, procedures, and forensic techniques* (2nd ed.). New York: Elsevier.

Geiselman, R. E., Fisher, R. P., MacKinnon, D. P., & Holland, H. L. (1985). Eyewitness memory enhancement in the police interview: Cognitive retrieval mnemonics versus hypnosis. *Journal of Applied Psychology, 70*, 401–412.

Geiselman, R. E., & Machlovitz, H. (1987). Hypnosis memory recall: Implications for forensic use. *American Journal of Forensic Psychology, 1*, 37–47.

Geiselman, R. E., & Padilla, J. (1988). Interviewing child witnesses with the cognitive interview. *Journal of Police Science and Administration, 16*, 236–242.

Geller, W. A. (1993). *Videotaping interrogations and confessions.* Washington, DC: U.S. Department of Justice.

Gelles, R., & Tolman, R. (1998). *The Kingston Screening Instrument for Domestic Violence (K- SID).* Providence: University of Rhode Island.

General Electric Co. v. Joiner, 522 U.S. 136 (1997).

Genz, J. L., & Lester, D. (1976). Authoritarianism in policemen as a function of experience. *Journal of Police Science and Administration, 4*, 9–13.

George, R., & Clifford, B. R. (1992). Making the most of witnesses. *Policing, 8*, 185–198.

Gerard, A. B. (1994). *The Parent-Child Relationship Inventory: Reflections on form and function.* Paper presented at the meeting of the American Psychological Association, New York.

Gerard, H. (1983). School desegregation: The social science role. *American Psychologist, 38*, 869–872.

Germann, A. C. (1969). Community policing: An assessment. *Journal of Criminal Law, Criminology, and Police Science, 60*, 84–96.

Gettleman, J. (2002, October 25). The hunt for a sniper: The profiling—A frenzy of speculation was wide of the mark. *New York Times*, p. A23.

Gilbert v. California, 388 U.S. 263 (1967).

Gillespie, C. (1989). *Justifiable homicide.* Columbus: Ohio State University Press.

Gleick, E. (1995, June 19). Rich justice, poor justice. *Time*, 40–47.

Gless, A. G. (1995). Some post-*Daubert* trial tribulations of a simple country judge: Behavioral science evidence in trial courts. *Behavioral Sciences and the Law, 13*, 261–291.

Goddard, R. W. (1986). Post-employment: The changing current in discrimination charges. *Personnel Journal, 65*, 34–40.

Godfrey v. Georgia, 446 U.S. 420 (1980).

Godinez v. Moran, 113 S. Ct. 2680 (1993).

Gold, V. (1987). Covert advocacy: Reflections on the use of psychological persuasion techniques in the courtroom. *North Carolina Law Review, 65*, 481–508.

Goldberg, P. (1968). Are women prejudiced against women? *Transaction, 5*, 28–30.

Golding, S. L. (1990). Mental health professionals in the courts: The ethics of expertise. *International Journal of Law and Psychiatry, 13*, 281–307.

Golding, S. L. (1999, August). *The voir dire of forensic experts: Issues of qualification and training; Sheepskins for sale: Shortcut to slaughter?* Paper presented at the meeting of the American Psychological Association, Boston, MA.

Golding, S. L., & Roesch, R. (1987). The assessment of criminal responsibility: A historical approach to a current controversy. In I. B. Weiner & A. K. Hess (Eds.), *Handbook of forensic psychology* (pp. 395–436). New York: Wiley.

Golding, S. L., Roesch, R., & Schreiber, J. (1984). Assessment and conceptualization of competency to stand trial: Preliminary data on the Interdisciplinary Fitness Interview. *Law and Human Behavior, 8*, 321–334.

Goldstein, G., & Incagnoli, T. M. (Eds.). (1997). *Contemporary approaches to neuropsychological assessment.* New York: Plenum.

Goldstein, J., Freud, A., & Solnit, A. J. (1979). *Beyond the best interests of the child.* New York: Free Press.

Goldstein, R. L. (1989). The psychiatrist's guide to right and wrong: Part 4: The insanity defense and the ultimate issue rule. *Bulletin of the American Academy of Psychiatry and the Law, 17*, 269–281.

Gonzalez, R., Ellsworth, P. C., & Pembroke, M. (1993). Response biases in lineups and showups. *Journal of Personality and Social Behavior, 6*, 1–13.

Goodman, E. (1994, March 18). Film tells story of battering. *Lawrence Journal-World*, p. 9B.

Goodman, G. S. (1984). Children's testimony in historical perspective. *Journal of Social Issues, 40*(2), 9–31.

Goodman, G. S., Levine, M., Melton, G. B., & Ogden, D. W. (1991). Child witnesses and the confrontation clause: American Psychological Association brief in *Maryland v. Craig. Law and Human Behavior, 15*, 13–29.

Goodman, G. S., Quas, J. A., Batterman-Faunce, J. M., Riddlesberger, M. M., & Kuhn, J. (1997). Children's reaction to and memory for a stressful experience: Influences of age, knowledge, anatomical dolls, and parental attachment. *Applied Developmental Science, 1,* 54–75.

Goodman, G. S., Redlich, A. D., Qin, J., Ghetti, S., Tyda, K. S., Schaaf, J. M., & Hahn, A. (1999). Evaluating eyewitness testimony in adults and children. In A. K. Hess & I. B. Weiner (Eds.), *Handbook of forensic psychology* (2nd ed., pp. 218–272). New York: John Wiley.

Goodman, G. S., Tobey, A. E., Batterman-Faunce, J. M., Orcutt, H., Thomas, S., Shapiro, C., & Sachsenmaier, T. (1998). Face-to-face confrontation: Effects of closed-circuit technology on children's eyewitness testimony and jurors' decisions. *Law and Human Behavior, 22,* 165–203.

Goodman-Delahunty, J. (1999). Civil law: Employment and discrimination. In R. Roesch, S. D. Hart, & J. R. P. Ogloff (Eds.), *Psychology and the law: The state of the discipline* (pp. 277–337). New York: Kluwer Academic/Plenum.

Goodpaster, G. (1983). The trial for life: Effective assistance of counsel in death penalty cases. *New York University Law Review, 58,* 300–361.

Gordon, W. L., III. (1997). Reflections of a criminal defense lawyer on the Simpson trial. *Journal of Social Issues, 53,* 417–424.

Gorenstein, G. W., & Ellsworth, P. C. (1980). Effect of choosing an incorrect photograph on a later identification by an eyewitness. *Journal of Applied Psychology, 65,* 615–622.

Gottfredson, L. S. (1994). The science and politics of race-norming. *American Psychologist, 49,* 955–963.

Gough, H. G. (1975). *Manual for the California Psychological Inventory.* Palo Alto, CA: Consulting Psychologists Press.

Gould, J. (1998). *Conducting scientifically crafted child custody evaluations.* Thousand Oaks, CA: Sage.

Gould, K. (1995). A therapeutic analysis of competency evaluation requests: The defense attorney's dilemma. *International Journal of Law and Psychiatry, 18,* 83–100.

Graham, J. R. (1987). *The MMPI: A practical guide* (2nd ed.). New York: Oxford University Press.

Grano, J. D. (1993). *Confessions, truth, and the law.* Ann Arbor: University of Michigan Press.

Gratz v. Bollinger, 539 U.S. 244 (2003).

Gray, E. B. (1993). A day in the life of a multi-door courthouse. *Negotiation Journal, 9,* 215–222.

Green, M. D. (1992). Expert witnesses and sufficiency of evidence in toxic substance litigation: The legacy of *Agent Orange* and Bendectin litigation. *Northwestern University Law Review, 86,* 643–699.

Greenberg, S. A., & Shuman, D. W. (1997). Irreconcilable conflict between therapeutic and forensic roles. *Professional Psychology: Research and Practice, 28,* 505–557.

Greenberger, E. (1983). A researcher in the policy area: The case of child labor. *American Psychologist, 38,* 104–111.

Greene, E., Downey, C., & Goodman-Delahunty, J. (1999) Juror decisions about damages in employment discrimination cases. *Behavioral Sciences and the Law, 17,* 107–122.

Greenhouse, L. (1992, October 14). High court to decide admissibility of scientific evidence in U.S. Courts. *New York Times,* p. A9.

Greenhouse, L. (1995, January 5). Court denies execution stay for man conceded innocent. *New York Times,* p. A7.

Greenhouse, L. (1997, November 4). Justices grapple with merits of polygraphs at trial. *New York Times,* p. A14.

Greenstone, J. L. (1995a). Hostage negotiations team training for small police departments. In M. I. Kurke & E. M. Scrivner (Eds.), *Police psychology into the 21st century* (pp. 279–296). Hillsdale, NJ: Lawrence Erlbaum Associates.

Greenstone, J. L. (1995b). Tactics and negotiating techniques (TNT): The way of the past and the way of the future. In M. I. Kurke & E. M. Scrivner (Eds.), *Police psychology into the 21st century* (pp. 357–371). Hillsdale, NJ: Lawrence Erlbaum Associates.

Greenwald, J. P., Tomkins, A. J., Kenning, M., & Zavodny, D. (1990). Psychological self-defense jury instructions: Influence on verdicts for battered women defendants. *Behavioral Sciences and the Law, 8,* 171–180.

Greenwood, P. W., & Petersilia, J. (1976). *The criminal investigation process.* Washington, DC: Law Enforcement Assistance Association.

Gregg v. Georgia, 428 U.S. 153 (1976).

Greif, G. L., & Hegar, R. L. (1993). *When parents kidnap.* New York: Free Press.

Griggs v. Duke Power, 401 U.S. 424 (1971).

Grisham, J. (1996). *The runaway jury.* New York: Dell.

Grisso, T. (1984, June). *Forensic assessment in juvenile and family cases: The state of the art.* Keynote address, Summer Institute on Mental Health Law, University of Nebraska, Lincoln.

Grisso, T. (1986). *Evaluating competencies: Forensic assessments and instruments.* New York: Plenum.

Grisso, T. (1997). The competence of adolescents as trial defendants. *Psychology, Public Policy, and Law, 3,* 3–32.

Grisso, T. (1998). *Forensic evaluation of juveniles.* Sarasota, FL: Professional Resource Press.

Grisso, T., Miller, M., & Sales, B. (1987). Competency to stand trial in juvenile court. *International Journal of Law and Psychiatry, 10,* 1–20.

Grisso, T., & Saks, M. J. (1991). Psychology's influence on constitutional interpretation: A comment on how to succeed. *Law and Human Behavior, 15,* 205–211.

Grofman, B., & Scarrow, H. (1980). Mathematics, social science, and the law. In M. J. Saks & C. H. Baron (Eds.), *The use/nonuse/misuse of applied social research in the courts* (pp. 117–127). Cambridge, MA: Abt Books.

Groscup, J., Penrod, S., Studebaker, C., Huss, M., & O'Neil, K. (2002). The effects of *Daubert v. Merrell Dow* Pharmaceuticals on the admissibility of expert testimony in state and federal criminal cases. *Psychology, Public Policy, and Law, 8,* 339–372.

Gross, S. (1997, August). *High stakes mistakes: Why judicial errors are common in capital cases.* Symposium paper presented at the meeting of the American Psychological Association, Chicago.

Gross, S. R. (1980, September). *Social science and the law: Educating the judiciary and the limits of prescience.* Paper presented at the meeting of the American Psychological Association, Montreal.

Groth-Marnat, G. (1990). *The handbook of psychological assessment* (2nd ed.). New York: John Wiley.

Grove, W. M., & Meehl, P. E. (1996). Comparative efficiency of informal (subjective, impressionistic) and formal (mechanical, algorithmic) prediction procedures: The clinical-statistical controversy. *Psychology, Public Policy, and Law, 2,* 297–323.

Gruber, J. E. (1992). A typology of personal and environmental sexual harassment: Research and policy implications for the 1990s. *Sex Roles, 26,* 447–464.

Grubin, D. (1988). *Sex offending against children: Understanding the risk.* London: Home Office.

Grutter v. Bollinger, 539 U.S. 306 (2003).

Grych, J. H., & Fincham, F. D. (1992). Interventions for children of divorce: Toward greater integration of research and action. *Psychological Bulletin, 111,* 434–454.

Gudjonsson, G. H. (1984). A new scale of interrogative suggestibility. *Personality and Individual Differences, 5,* 303–314.

Gudjonsson, G. H. (1988). How to defeat the polygraph tests. In A. Gale (Ed.), *The polygraph test: Lies, truth and science* (pp. 126–136). London: Sage.

Gudjonsson, G. H. (1989). Compliance in an interrogation situation: A new scale. *Personality and Individual Differences, 10,* 535–540.

Gudjonsson, G. H. (1991). Suggestibility and compliance among alleged false confessors and resisters in criminal trials. *Medicine, Science, and the Law, 31,* 147–151.

Gudjonsson, G. H. (1992). *The psychology of interrogations, confessions and testimony.* New York and Chichester: John Wiley.

Gudjonsson, G. H. (1997). *The Gudjonsson Suggestibility Scales Manual.* East Sussex, UK: Psychology Press.

Gudjonsson, G. H. (2003). *The psychology of interrogations and confessions: A handbook.* New York and Chichester: John Wiley.

Gudjonsson, G. H., & Copson, G. (1997). The role of the expert in criminal investigation. In J. L. Jackson & D. A. Bekerian (Eds.), *Offender profiling: Theory, research and practice* (pp. 62–76). New York: John Wiley.

Gudjonsson, G. H., & Lebegue, B. (1989). Psychological and psychiatric aspects of a coerced-internalized false confession. *Journal of the Forensic Science Society, 29*(4), 261–269.

Guidubaldi, J., & Cleminshaw, H. (1998, August). *The Parenting Satisfaction Scale: Development, validity, and applications.* Paper presented at the meeting of the American Psychological Association, San Francisco.

Gutek, B. A. (1985). *Sex and the workplace: The impact of sexual behavior and harassment on women, men, and organizations.* San Francisco: Jossey-Bass.

Gutek, B. A., & O'Connor, M. (1995). The empirical basis for the reasonable woman standard. *Journal of Social Issues, 51*(1), 151–166.

Gwynne, S. C. (1995, January 16). Guilty, innocent, guilty. *Time,* p. 38.

Hafemeister, T. L., & Melton, G. B. (1987). The impact of social science research on the judiciary. In G. B. Melton (Ed.), *Reforming the law: Impact of child development research* (pp. 29–59). New York: Guilford.

Hageman, M. J. (1979). Who joins the force for what reason: An argument for "the new breed." *Journal of Police Science and Administration, 15,* 110–117.

Hagen, M. (1997). *Whores of the court: The fraud of psychiatric testimony and the rape of American justice.* New York: HarperCollins.

Hale, M., Jr. (1980). *Human science and social order: Hugo Münsterberg and the origins of applied psychology.* Philadelphia: Temple University Press.

Hall, G. C. N. (1989). WAIS-R and MMPI profiles of men who have assaulted children: Evidence of limited utility. *Journal of Personality Assessment, 53,* 404–412.

Hall, G. C. N., Maiuro, R. D., Vitaliano, P. P., & Proctor, W. D. (1986). The utility of the MMPI with men who have sexually assaulted children. *Journal of Clinical and Consulting Psychology, 54,* 493–496.

Hamdi, E., Amin, Y., & Mattar, T. (1991). Clinical correlates of intent in attempted suicide. *Acta Psychiatrica Scandinavica, 83,* 406–411.

Haney, C. (1980). Psychology and legal change: On the limits of a factual jurisprudence. *Law and Human Behavior, 4,* 147–199.

Haney, C., Hurtado, A., & Vega, L. (1994). "Modern" death qualification: New data on its biasing effects. *Law and Human Behavior, 18,* 619–633.

Haney, C., & Lynch, M. (1994). Comprehending life and death matters: A preliminary study of California's capital penalty instructions. *Law and Human Behavior, 18,* 411–436.

Haney, C., & Lynch, M. (1997). Clarifying life and death matters: An analysis of instructional comprehension and penalty phase closing arguments. *Law and Human Behavior, 21*(6), 575–595.

Haney, C., Sontag, L., & Costanzo, S. (1994). Deciding to take a life: Capital juries, sentencing instructions, and the jurisprudence of death. *Journal of Social Issues, 50*(2), 149–176.

Hans, V. (1988). Death by jury. In K. C. Haas & J. A. Inciardi (Eds.), *Challenging capital punishment: Legal and social science approaches* (pp. 149–175). Thousand Oaks, CA: Sage.

Hanson, R. K. (1997). *The development of a brief Actuarial Risk Scale for Sexual Offense Recidivism (User Report 97-04).* Ottawa: Department of the Solicitor General of Canada.

Hanson, R. K. & Bussiere, M. T. (1998). Predicting relapse: A meta-analysis of sexual offender recidivism studies. *Journal of Consulting and Clinical Psychology, 66,* 348–362.

Hanson, R. K., & Thornton, D. (1999). *Static-99: Improving actuarial risk assessments for sex offenders (User Report 99-02).* Ottawa: Department of the Solicitor General of Canada.

Hanson, R. K., & Thornton, D. (2000). Improving risk assessments for sex offenders: A comparison of three actuarial scales. *Law and Human Behavior, 24,* 119–136.

Hare, R. (1991). *The Hare Psychopathy Checklist–Revised Manual (PCL-R).* North Tonawanda, NY: Multi-Health Systems, Inc.

Hare, R. (1996). Psychopathy: A clinical construct whose time has come. *Criminal Justice and Behavior, 23,* 25–54.

Hargrave, G. E., & Hiatt, D. (1987). Law enforcement selection with the interview, MMPI, and CPI: A study of reliability and validity. *Journal of Police Science and Administration, 15,* 110–117.

Hargrave, G. E., & Hiatt, D. (1989). Use of the California Psychological Inventory in law enforcement officer selection. *Journal of Personality Assessment, 53,* 267–277.

Hargrave, G. E., Hiatt, D., Ogard, E., & Karr, C. (1993). Comparison of the MMPI and the MMPI-2 for a sample of police officers. Unpublished manuscript cited by Blau, 1994.

Harris v. Forklift Systems, Inc., 114 S. Ct. 367 (1993).

Harris, G. T., Rice, M. E., & Quinsey, V. L. (1993). Violent recidivism of mentally disordered offenders: The development of a statistical prediction instrument. *Criminal Justice and Behavior, 20,* 315–335.

Harris, P. (1997). *Black rage confronts the law.* New York: New York University Press.

Harris, T. (1981). *The red dragon.* New York: Putnam.

Hart, S. D. (1998a). The role of psychopathy in assessing risk for violence: Conceptual and methodological issues. *Legal and Criminological Psychology, 3,* 123–140.

Hart, S. D. (1998b). Psychopathy and risk for violence. In D. J. Cooke, A. E. Forth, & R. D. Hare (Eds.), *Psychopathy: Theory, research, and implications for society* (pp. 355–373). Dordrecht, The Netherlands: Kluwer.

Hart, S. D., Cox, D. N., & Hare, R. D. (1995). *The Hare Psychopathy Checklist: Screening Version (PCL: SV).* North Tonawanda, NY: Multi-Health Systems, Inc.

Hart, S. D., & Dempster, R. J. (1997). Impulsivity and psychopathy. In C. D. Webster & M. A. Jackson (Eds.), *Impulsivity: Theory, assessment, and treatment* (pp. 212–232). New York: Guilford.

Hart, S. D., Forth, A. E., & Hare, R. D. (1990). Performance of criminal psychopaths on selected neuropsychological tests. *Journal of Abnormal Psychology, 99,* 374–379.

Hart, S. D., & Hare, R. D. (1997). Psychopathy: Assessment and association with criminal conduct. In D. Stoff, J. Breiling, & J. Maser (Eds.), *Handbook of Antisocial Behavior* (pp. 22–35). New York: Wiley.

Hassel, C. (1975). The hostage situation: Exploring motivation and cause. *The Police Chief, 42*(9), 55–58.

Hathaway, S. R., & McKinley, J. C. (1983). *The Minnesota Multiphasic Personality Inventory: Manual.* New York: Psychological Corporation.

Hawthorne v. Florida, 470 So.2d 770 (Fla. Dist. Ct. App. 1985).

Hayakawa, H., Fischbeck, P., & Fischhoff, B. (2000a). The Japanese automobile insurance industry: Regulation, market structure, and possible impacts of deregulation. *Journal of Insurance Regulation, 18,* 385–403.

Hayakawa, H., Fischbeck, P., & Fischhoff, B. (2000b). Mental models of auto risks and insurance: Japanese and American motorists. *Journal of Risk Research, 3,* 51–67.

Hayakawa, H., Fischbeck, P., & Fischhoff, B. (2000c). Traffic accident statistics and risk perceptions in Japan and the United States. *Accident Analysis and Prevention, 32,* 827–835.

Haynes, R. B. (1985). The predictive value of the clinical assessment for the diagnosis, prognosis, and treatment response of patients. In C. D. Webster, M. Ben-Aron, & S. Hucker (Eds.), *Dangerousness: Probability and prediction, psychiatry and public policy.* Cambridge: Cambridge University Press.

Hays, G. (1992). *Policewoman One: My twenty years on the LAPD.* New York: Berkley Books.

Hazelwood, R. R., & Douglas, J. E. (1980). The lust murderer. *FBI Law Enforcement Bulletin, 50*(7), 10–15.

Heider, F. (1958). *The psychology of interpersonal relations.* New York: Wiley.

Heilbrun, A. B. (1990). Differentiation of death-row murderers and life-sentence murderers by antisociality and intelligence measures. *Journal of Personality Assessment, 54,* 617–627.

Heilbrun, K. (1987). The assessment of competency for execution: An overview. *Behavioral Sciences and the Law, 5,* 383–396.

Heilbrun, K. (1998, Spring). Forensic psychology as a specialization: What role for AP-LS? *American Psychology-Law Society News,* 36–41.

Heilbrun, K., Nezu, C. M., Keeney, M., Chung, S., & Wasserman, A. (1998). Sexual offending: Linking assessment, intervention, and decision-making. *Psychology, Public Policy, and Law, 4,* 138–174.

Heilbrun, K. S., & McClaren, H. A. (1988). Assessment of competency for execution: A guide for mental health professionals. *Bulletin of the American Academy of Psychiatry and Law, 16,* 205–216.

Henkel, J., Sheehan, E. P., & Reichel, P. (1997). Relation of police misconduct to authoritarianism. *Journal of Social Behavior and Personality, 12,* 551–555.

Herbert, B. (1997, January 6). The hanging tree. *New York Times,* p. A13.

Herrera v. Collins, 113 S. Ct. 853 (1993).

Hess, A. K., & Weiner, I. B. (Eds.). (1999). *Handbook of forensic psychology* (2nd ed.). New York: John Wiley.

Hiatt, D., & Hargrave, G. E. (1988a). MMPI profiles of problem police officers. *Journal of Personality Assessment, 52,* 722–731.

Hiatt, D., & Hargrave, G. E. (1988b). Predicting job performance with psychological screening. *Journal of Police Science and Administration, 16,* 122–125.

Hibler, N. S. (1995). Hypnosis for investigative purposes. In M. I. Kurke and E. M. Scrivner (Eds.), *Police psychology into the 21st century* (pp. 319–336). Hillsdale, NJ: Lawrence Erlbaum Associates.

Hibler, N. S., & Kurke, M. I. (1995). Ensuring personal reliability through selection and training. In M. I. Kurke and E. M. Scrivner (Eds.), *Police psychology into the 21st century* (pp. 57–91). Hillsdale, NJ: Lawrence Erlbaum Associates.

Hilgard, E. R., & Hilgard, J. R. (1975). *Hypnosis in the relief of pain.* Los Altos, CA: Kaufmann.

Hinz, T., & Pezdek, K. (2001). The effect of exposure to multiple lineups on face identification accuracy. *Law and Human Behavior, 25,* 185–198.

Hodgson et al. v. Minnesota, 110 S. Ct. 2926 (1990).

Hogan, R. (1971). Personality characteristics of highly rated policemen. *Personnel Psychology, 24,* 679–686.

Hoge, S., Bonnie, R., Poythress, N., & Monahan, J. (1992). Attorney-client decision-making in criminal cases: Client competence and participation as perceived by their attorneys. *Behavioral Sciences and the Law, 10,* 385–394.

Hoge, S. K., Poythress, N., Bonnie, R. J., Monahan, J., Eisenberg, M., & Feucht-Haviar, T. (1997). The MacArthur adjudicative competence study: Diagnosis, psychopathology, and competence-related abilities. *Behavioral Sciences and the Law, 15,* 329–345.

Holbrook v. Flynn, 475 U.S. 560 (1986).

Holbrook, S. H. (1987). *Dreamers of the American dream.* Garden City, NY: Doubleday.

Holmes, R. M., & Holmes, S. T. (1996). *Profiling violent crimes.* Thousand Oaks, CA: Sage.

Honts, C. R., & Hodes, R. L. (1982a). The effect of simple physical countermeasures on the detection of deception. *Psychophysiology, 19,* 564.

Honts, C. R., & Hodes, R. L. (1982b). The effects of multiple physical countermeasures on the detection of deception. *Psychophysiology, 19,* 564–565.

Honts, C. R., Raskin, D. C., & Kircher, J. C. (1983). Detection of deception: Effectiveness of physical countermeasures under high motivation conditions. *Psychophysiology, 20,* 446–447.

Honts, C. R., Raskin, D. C., & Kircher, J. C. (1984). Effects of spontaneous countermeasures on the detection of deception. *Psychophysiology, 21,* 583.

Hopkins v. Price Waterhouse, 618 F. Supp. 1109 (D.D.C. 1985).

Hopwood v. State of Texas, 78 F.3d 932 (5th Cir. 1996).

Horowitz, I. A., & Willging, T. E. (1984). *The psychology of law: Integrations and applications.* Boston: Little, Brown.

Horvath, F. S. (1977). The effect of selected variables on interpretation of polygraph records. *Journal of Applied Psychology, 62,* 127–136.

Hotaling, G., & Sugarman, D. (1986). An analysis of risk markers in husband to wife violence: The current state of knowledge. *Violence and Victims, 1,* 101–124.

Hovey v. Superior Court, 28 Cal.3d 1, 168 Cal. Rptr. 128, 616 P.2d 1301 (1980).

Hubbert, J. B. (1992, October). "Keep it confidential": Our duty to research respondents. Paper presented at the meeting of the American Society of Trial Consultants, Kansas City, MO.

Huber, P. (1991). *Galileo's revenge: Junk science in the courtroom.* New York: Basic Books.

Hudson, J. R. (1970). Police encounters that lead to citizen complaints. *Social Problems, 18,* 179–193.

Huff, C. R., Rattner, A., & Sagarin, E. (1996). *Convicted but innocent: Wrongful conviction and public policy.* Thousand Oaks, CA: Sage.

Humm, D. G., & Humm, K. A. (1950). Humm-Wadsworth Temperament Scale appraisals compared with criteria of job success in the Los Angeles Police Department. *Journal of Psychology, 30,* 63–75.

Hutchins, R. M., & Slesinger, D. (1928a). Some observations on the law of evidence— Spontaneous exclamations. *Columbia Law Review, 28,* 432–440.

Hutchins, R. M., & Slesinger, D. (1928b). Some observations on the law of evidence—Memory. *Harvard Law Review, 41,* 860–873.

Hutchins, R. M., & Slesinger, D. (1928c). Some observations on the law of evidence—The competency of witnesses. *Yale Law Journal, 37,* 1017–1028.

Iacono, W. G., & Lykken, D. T. (1997). The validity of the lie detector: Two surveys of scientific opinion. *Journal of Applied Psychology, 82,* 426–433.

Iacono, W. G., & Patrick, C. J. (1987). What psychologists should know about lie detection. In I. B. Weiner & A. K. Hess (Eds.), *Handbook of forensic psychology* (pp. 460–489). New York: John Wiley.

Iacono, W. G., & Patrick, C. J. (1999). Polygraph ("lie detector") testing: The state of the art. In A. K. Hess & I. B. Weiner (Eds.), *The handbook of forensic psychology* (2nd ed., pp. 440–473). New York: John Wiley.

Ibn-Tamas v. United States, 407 A.2d 626 (1979).

Ilfeld, F. W., Ilfeld, H. Z., & Alexander, J. R. (1982). Does joint custody work? A first look at outcome data of relitigation. *American Journal of Psychiatry, 139,* 62–66.

Imbler v. Craven, 298 F. Supp. 795 (1969).

Imbler v. Pachtman, 424 U.S. 409 (1976).

Imwinkelreid, E. J. (1992). Attempts to limit the scope of the *Frye* standard for the admission of scientific evidence: Confronting the real cost of the general acceptance test. *Behavioral Sciences and the Law, 10,* 441–454.

Inbau, F. (1976). Legally permissible criminal interrogation tactics and techniques. *Journal of Police Science and Administration, 4*(2), 249–251.

Inbau, F. E., & Reid, J. E. (1962). *Criminal interrogation and confessions.* Baltimore, MD: Williams and Wilkins.

Inbau, F. E., Reid, J. F., & Buckley, J. P. (1986). *Criminal interrogation and confessions* (3rd ed.). Baltimore, MD: Williams and Wilkins.

Inbau, F. E., Reid, J. F., Buckley, J. P., & Jayne, B. (2001). *Criminal interrogation and confessions* (4th ed.). Baltimore, MD: Williams and Wilkins.

In re *Amber B.,* 236 Cal. Rpt. 623, 191 Cal. 3d 682 (1987).

In re *Imbler,* 387 P.2d 6 (1963).

In re *Marriage of Rosson,* 224 Cal. Rpt. 250, 178 Cal. App. 3d 1094 (1986).

International Brotherhood of Teamsters v. United States, 431 U.S. 324 (1977).

Inwald, R. (1990). *Fitness-for-duty evaluation guidelines: A survey for police/public safety administrators and mental health professionals.* Paper presented at the meeting of the American Psychological Association, Boston, MA.

Inwald, R. E. (1992). *Inwald Personality Inventory Technical Manual* (Rev. ed.). Kew Gardens, NY: Hilson Research Inc.

Inwald, R., Knatz, H., & Shusman, E. (1983). *Inwald Personality Inventory Manual.* Kew Gardens, NY: Hilson Research Inc.

Inwald, R., & Shusman, E. (1984). The IPI and MMPI as predictors of academy performance for police recruits. *Journal of Police Science and Administration, 12,* 1–11.

Irvin v. Dowd, 366 U.S. 717 (1961).

Irving, B. L., & Hilgendorf, E. L. (1980). *Police interrogation: The psychological approach* (Research Study No. 2). London: Royal Commission on Criminal Procedure.

Isikoff, M. (1994, March 21–27). The Foster case: Grist for the Whitewater rumor mill. *Washington Post National Weekly Edition,* p. 8.

Iverson, G. L., Franzen, M. D., & Hammond, J. A. (1993, August). *Examination of inmates' ability to malinger on the MMPI-2.* Paper presented at the meeting of the American Psychological Association, Toronto.

Jackman, M. R. (1978). General and applied tolerance: Does education increase commitment to racial integration? *American Journal of Political Science, 22,* 302–324.

Jackson v. State, 553 So.2d 719 (Fla. 4th DCA, 1989)

Jackson, J. L., & Bekerian, D. A. (1997a). Does offender profiling have a role to play? In J. L. Jackson & D. A. Bekerian (Eds.), *Offender profiling: Theory, research and practice* (pp. 1–7). New York: John Wiley.

Jackson, J. L., & Bekerian, D. A. (Eds.). (1997b). *Offender profiling: Theory, research and practice.* New York: John Wiley.

Jackson, J. L., van den Eshof, P., & de Kleuver, E. E. (1997). A research approach to offender profiling. In J. L. Jackson & D. A. Bekerian (Eds.), *Offender profiling: Theory, research and practice* (pp. 107–132). New York: John Wiley.

Jaffe, P. G., Hastings, E., Reitzel, D., & Austin, G. W. (1993). The impact of police laying charges. In N. Z. Hilton (Ed.), *Legal responses to wife assault* (pp. 62–95). Newbury Park, CA: Sage.

James, G. (1994, January 17). Off-duty officer shoots himself. *New York Times,* p. B12.

Janik, J. (1993, August). *Pre-employment interviews of law enforcement officer candidates.* Paper presented at the meeting of the American Psychological Association, Toronto.

Janoff-Bulman, R. (1979). Characterological versus behavioral self-blame: Inquiries into depression and rape. *Journal of Personality and Social Psychology, 37,* 1798–1809.

Janofsky, M. (1998, June 5). Maryland troopers stop drivers by race, suit says. *New York Times,* p. A10.

Janofsky, J. S., Spears, S., & Neubauer, D. N. (1988). Psychiatrists' accuracy in predicting violent behavior on an inpatient unit. *Hospital and Community Psychiatry, 39,* 1090–1094.

Janus, E. S., & Meehl, P. (1997). Assessing the legal standard for predictions of dangerousness in sex offender commitment proceedings. *Psychology, Public Policy, and Law, 3,* 33–64.

Jeffers, H. P. (1991). *Who killed Precious?* New York: Pharos Books.

Jenkins v. United States, 307 F.2d 637 (1962).

Jenkins, P., & Davidson, B. (1990). Battered women in the criminal justice system: An analysis of gender stereotypes. *Behavioral Sciences and the Law, 8,* 161–170.

Jobes, D. A., Berman, A. L., & Josselson, A. R. (1986a). The impact of psychological autopsies on medical examiners' determination of manner of death. *Journal of Forensic Sciences, 31,* 177–189.

Jobes, D. A., Berman, A. L., & Josselson, A. R. (1986b). Improving the validity and reliability of medico-legal certifications of "suicide." *Suicide and Life-Threatening Behavior, 17,* 310–325.

Jobes, D. A., Casey, J. O., Berman, A. L., & Wright, M. D. (1991). Empirical criteria for the determination of suicide manner of death. *Journal of Forensic Sciences, 36,* 244–256.

Johnson v. Zerbst, 304 U.S. 458 (1938).

Johnson, J. (1994, May 16). Witness for the prosecution. *New Yorker,* 42–51.

Johnson, K. (1998, April 16). New breed of bad cop sells badge, public trust. *USA Today,* p. 8A.

Johnson, K. (1999, May 19). ACLU campaign yields race bias suit. *USA Today,* p. 4A.

Johnson, M. K., & Foley, M. A. (1984). Differentiating fact from fantasy: The reliability of children's memory. *Journal of Social Issues, 40*(2), 33–50.

Johnson, W. G., & Mullett, N. (1987). Georgia Court Competency Test-R. In M. Hersen & A. S. Bellack (Eds.), *Dictionary of behavioral assessment techniques.* New York: Pergamon.

Jones v. Tri-County Electric Cooperative, 512 F.2d 13 (5th Cir. 1975).

Jones, A. (1981). *Women who kill.* New York: Holt, Rinehart.

Jones, A. (1994a, March 10). Crimes against women. *USA Today,* p. 9A.

Jones, A. (1994b). *Next time, she'll be dead: Battering and how to stop it.* Boston: Beacon Press.

Jones, E. E. (1990). *Interpersonal perception.* San Francisco: Freeman.

Jones, E. E., & Davis, K. E. (1965). A theory of correspondent inferences: From acts to dispositions. In L. Berkowitz (Ed.), *Advances in experimental social psychology* (Vol. 2, pp. 219–266). San Diego: Academic Press.

Jones, E. E., & Harris, V. A. (1967). The attribution of attitudes. *Journal of Experimental Social Psychology, 3,* 1–24.

Jones, J. W. (1995). Counseling issues and police diversity. In M. I. Kurke & E. M. Scrivner (Eds.), *Police psychology into the 21st century* (pp. 207–254). Hillsdale, NJ: Lawrence Erlbaum Associates.

Jones, S., & Israel, P. (1998). *Others unknown: The Oklahoma City bombing case and conspiracy.* New York: Public Affairs.

Judges, D. P. (2000). Two cheers for the Department of Justice's eyewitness evidence: A guide for law enforcement. *Arkansas Law Review, 53,* 231–297.

Juni, S. (1992). Review of Inwald Personality Inventory. In J. J. Kramer & J. C. Conoley (Eds.), *Eleventh mental measurements yearbook* (pp. 415–418). Lincoln: Buros Institute of Mental Measurements, University of Nebraska.

Jurow, G. L. (1971). New data on the effect of a "death qualified" jury on the guilt determination process. *Harvard Law Review, 84,* 567–611.

Kagehiro, D. K., & Stanton, W. C. (1985). Legal vs. quantified definitions of standards of proof. *Law and Human Behavior, 9,* 159–178.

Kahneman, D., Slovic, P., & Tversky, A. (Eds.). (1982). *Judgments under uncertainty: Heuristics and biases.* Cambridge, England: Cambridge University Press.

Kahneman, D., & Tversky, A. (1973). On the psychology of prediction. *Psychological Review, 80,* 237–251.

Kalven, H., & Zeisel, H. (1966). *The American jury.* Boston: Little, Brown.

Kaminker, L. (1992, November 16). An angry cry for mute voices. *Newsweek,* p. 16.

Kamisar, Y., LaFave, W., & Israel, J. (1994). *Modern criminal procedure* (8th ed.). St. Paul, MN: West.

Kandel, E., & Freed, D. (1989). Frontal-lobe dysfunction and antisocial behavior: A review. *Journal of Clinical Psychology, 45,* 404–413.

Kansas v. Hendricks, 117 S. Ct. 2106 (1997).

Kantrowitz, B. (1992). Sexual harassment in America: An overview. In C. Wekesser, K. L. Swisher, & C. Pierce (Eds.), *Sexual harassment* (pp. 16–23). San Diego: Greenhaven Press.

Kaplan, D. A. (1991, December 16). The finest or the fattest? *Newsweek,* p. 58.

Kargon, R. (1986). Expert testimony in historical perspective. *Law and Human Behavior, 10,* 15–27.

Kasian, M., Spanos, N. P., Terrance, C. A., & Peebles, S. (1993). Battered women who kill: Jury simulation and legal defenses. *Law and Human Behavior, 17,* 289–312.

Kassin, S. M. (1997). The psychology of confession evidence. *American Psychologist, 52,* 221–233.

Kassin, S. M. (1998a). Clinical psychology in court: House of junk science? *Contemporary Psychology, 43,* 321–324.

Kassin, S. M. (1998b). Eyewitness identification procedures: The fifth rule. *Law and Human Behavior, 22,* 649–653.

Kassin, S. M. (2002, November 11). False confessions and the jogger case. *New York Times,* p. A15.

Kassin, S. M., & Barndollar, K. A. (1992). The psychology of eyewitness testimony: A comparison of experts and prospective jurors. *Journal of Applied Social Psychology, 22,* 1241–1249.

Kassin, S. M., Ellsworth, P. C., & Smith, V. L. (1989). The "general acceptance" of psychological research on eyewitness testimony: A survey of the experts. *American Psychologist, 44,* 1089–1098.

Kassin, S. M., Ellsworth, P. C., & Smith, V. L. (1994). Deja vu all over again: Elliott's critique of eyewitness experts. *Law and Human Behavior, 18,* 203–210.

Kassin, S. M. & Fong, C. T. (1999). "I'm innocent!": Effects of training on judgments of truth and deception in the interrogation room. *Law and Human Behavior, 23,* 499–516.

Kassin, S. M., & Kiechel, K. L. (1996). The social psychology of false confessions: Compliance, internalization, and confabulation. *Psychological Science, 7,* 125–128.

Kassin, S. M., & McNall, K. (1991). Police interrogation and confessions: Communicating promises and threats by pragmatic implication. *Law and Human Behavior, 15,* 233–251.

Kassin, S. M., & Neumann, K. (1997). On the power of confession evidence: An experimental test of the "fundamental difference" hypothesis. *Law and Human Behavior, 21,* 469–484.

Kassin, S. M., & Norwick, R. J. (2004). Why people waive their *Miranda* rights: The power of innocence. *Law and Human Behavior, 28,* 211–222.

Kassin, S. M., & Sukel, H. (1997). Coerced confessions and the jury: An experimental test of the "harmless error" rule. *Law and Human Behavior, 21,* 27–46.

Kassin, S. M., Tubb, V. A., Hosch, H. M., & Memon, A. (2001). On the "general acceptance" of eyewitness testimony research: A new survey of the experts. *American Psychologist, 56,* 405–416.

Kassin, S. M., & Wrightsman, L. S. (1980). Prior confessions and mock juror verdicts. *Journal of Applied Social Psychology, 10,* 133–146.

Kassin, S. M., & Wrightsman, L. S. (1981). Coerced confessions, judicial instruction, and mock juror verdicts. *Journal of Applied Social Psychology, 11,* 489–506.

Kassin, S. M., & Wrightsman, L. S. (1983). The construction and validation of a Juror Bias Scale. *Journal of Research in Personality, 17,* 423–442.

Kassin, S. M., & Wrightsman, L. S. (1985). Confession evidence. In S. M. Kassin & L. S. Wrightsman (Eds.), *The psychology of evidence and trial procedure* (pp. 67–94). Thousand Oaks, CA: Sage.

Katel, P. (1998, May 4). Kidnapping within the family. *USA Today,* p. 3A.

Katsh, M. E. (Ed.). (1998). *Taking sides: Clashing views on controversial legal issues* (8th ed.). Guilford, CT: Dushkin/McGraw-Hill.

Katz, I., & Hass, R. G. (1988). Racial ambivalence and American value conflict: Correlational and priming studies of dual cognitive structures. *Journal of Personality and Social Psychology, 55,* 893–905.

Katz, I., Wackenhut, J., & Hass, R. G. (1986). Racial ambivalence, value duality, and behavior. In J. Dovidio & S. L. Gaertner (Eds.), *Prejudice, discrimination, and racism* (pp. 35–59). San Diego, CA: Academic Press.

Kaye, D. H. (1982a). The numbers game: Statistical inference in discrimination cases. *Michigan Law Review, 80,* 833–856.

Kaye, D. H. (1982b). Statistical evidence of discrimination. *Journal of American Statistical Association, 77,* 773–783.

Kaye, D. H., & Aicklin, M. (Eds.). (1986). *Statistical methods in discrimination litigation.* New York: Marcel Dekker.

Kaye, D. H., & Koehler, J. J. (1991). Can jurors understand probabilistic evidence? *Journal of the Royal Statistical Society 154* (Series A, Pt. 1), 75–81.

Kebbell, M. R. (2000). The law concerning the conduct of identification parades in England and Wales: How well does it satisfy the recommendations of the American Psychology-Law Society? *Law and Human Behavior, 24,* 309–315.

Kebbell, M. R., & Wagstaff, G. F. (1997). Why do the police interview eyewitnesses? Interview objectives and the evaluation of eyewitness performance. *Journal of Psychology, 131,* 595–601.

Keilin, W. G., & Bloom, L. J. (1986). Child custody evaluation practices: A survey of experienced professionals. *Professional Psychology: Research and Practice, 17,* 338–346.

Kelly v. United States, 250 F. 947 (9th Cir. 1918).

Kelman, H. (1958). Compliance, identification, and internalization: Three processes of opinion change. *Journal of Conflict Resolution, 2,* 51–60.

Kendall-Tackett, K. A., Williams, L. M., & Finkelhor, D. (1993). Impact of sexual abuse on children: A review and synthesis of recent empirical studies. *Psychological Bulletin, 113,* 164–180.

Kennedy, L. (1985). *The airman and the carpenter: The Lindbergh kidnapping and the framing of Richard Hauptmann.* New York: Viking.

Kerr, N. L., Kramer, G. P., Carroll, J. S., & Alfini, J. J. (1991). On the effectiveness of voir dire in criminal cases with prejudicial pretrial publicity: An empirical study. *American University Law Review, 40,* 665–701.

Kidder, L. H., Lafleur, R. A., & Wells, C. V. (1995). Recalling harassment, reconstructing experience. *Journal of Social Issues, 51*(1), 53–67.

Kilpatrick, D. G. (1983, Summer). Rape victims: Detection, assessment and treatment. *Clinical Psychologist,* 92–95.

Kilpatrick, D. G., & Amick, A. E. (1985). Rape trauma. In M. Hersen & C. G. Last (Eds.), *Behavior therapy casebook* (pp. 86–103). New York: Springer.

Kilpatrick, D. G., Best, C. L., Veronen, L. J., Amick, A. E., Villeponteaux, L. A., & Ruff, G. A. (1985). Mental health correlates of criminal victimization: A random community survey. *Journal of Consulting and Clinical Psychology, 53,* 866–873.

Kilpatrick, D. G., Resick, P., & Veronen, L. (1981). Effects of a rape experience: A longitudinal study. *Journal of Social Issues, 37*(4), 105–112.

Kilpatrick, D. G., & Veronen, L. J. (1984). *Treatment of fear and anxiety in victims of rape* (Final report, NIMH Grant No. HMH29602). Rockville, MD: National Institute of Mental Health.

Kilpatrick, D. G., Veronen, L. J., & Best, C. L. (1985). Factors predicting psychological distress among rape victims. In C. R. Figley (Ed.), *Trauma and its wake* (pp. 113–141). New York: Brunner/Mazel.

Kissel, S., & Freeling, N. W. (1990). *Evaluating children for courts using psychological tests.* Springfield, IL: Charles C Thomas.

Kitzmann, K. M., & Emery, R. E. (1993). Procedural justice and parents' satisfaction in a field study of child custody dispute resolution. *Law and Human Behavior, 17,* 553–568.

Klassen, D., & O'Connor, W. (1989). Assessing the risk of violence in released mental patients: A cross-validation study. *Psychological Assessment, 1,* 75–81.

Kleinmuntz, B., & Szucko, J. (1984). A field study of the fallibility of polygraph lie detection. *Nature, 308,* 449–450.

Kline, M., Tschann, J. M., Johnston, J. R., & Wallerstein, J. S. (1989). Children's adjustment in joint and sole physical custody families. *Developmental Psychology, 25,* 430–438.

Klonoff, R. H., & Colby, P. L. (1990). *Sponsorship strategy: Evidentiary tactics for winning jury trials.* Charlottesville, VA: Michie Press.

Kluger, R. (1976). *Simple justice.* New York: Knopf.

Knapp, S. J., & Vandecreek, L. (1985). Psychotherapy and privileged communications in child custody cases. *Professional Psychology: Research and Practice, 16,* 398–407.

Koch, M. A., & Lowery, C. R. (1984). Visitation and the noncustodial father. *Journal of Divorce, 8,* 47–65.

Koehler, J. J. (1992). Probabilities in the courtroom: An evaluation of the objections and policies. In D. K. Kagehiro & W. S. Laufer (Eds.), *Handbook of psychology and law* (pp. 167–184). New York: Springer-Verlag.

Koehler, J. J. (2001). The psychology of numbers in the courtroom: How to make DNA match statistics seem impressive or insufficient. *Southern California Law Review, 74,* 1275–1306.

Kohlmann, R. H. (1996). The presumption of innocence: Patching the tattered cloak after *Maryland v. Craig. St. Mary's Law Journal, 27,* 389–421.

Kolasa, B. J. (1972). Psychology and law. *American Psychologist, 27,* 499–503.

Kolata, G., & Peterson, I. (2001, July 21). New way to insure eyewitnesses can ID the right bad guy. *New York Times,* p. A1.

Kolb, B., & Whishaw, I. A. (1990). *Fundamentals of human neuropsychology* (3rd ed.). New York: W. H. Freeman.

Konecni, V., & Ebbesen, E. (1981). A critique of the theory and method in social psychological approaches to legal issues. In B. D. Sales (Ed.), *The trial process* (pp. 481–498). New York: Plenum.

Konecni, V. J., & Ebbesen, E. B. (1986). Courtroom testimony by psychologists on eyewitness identification issues: Critical notes and reflections. *Law and Human Behavior, 10,* 117–126.

Koocher, G. P., Goodman, G. S., White, C. S., Friedrich, W. N., Sivan, A. B., & Reynolds, C. R. (1995). Psychological science and the use of anatomically detailed dolls in child sexual-abuse assessments. *Psychological Bulletin, 118,* 199–222.

Koss, M. P. (1988). Hidden rape: Incidence, prevalence, and descriptive characteristics of sexual aggression and victimization in a national sample of college students. In A. W. Burgess (Ed.), *Sexual assault* (Vol. 2, pp. 3–25). New York: Garland.

Koss, M. P., & Harvey, M. R. (1991). *The rape victim: Clinical and community interventions* (2nd ed.). Thousand Oaks, CA: Sage.

Kotlowitz, A. (1999, February 8). The unprotected. *New Yorker,* 42–53.

Kovera, M. B., & Borgida, E. (1998). Expert scientific testimony on child witnesses in the age of *Daubert.* In S. J. Ceci & H. Hembrooke (Eds.), *Expert witnesses in child abuse cases* (pp. 185–215). Washington, DC: American Psychological Association.

Kramer, G. P., Kerr, N. L., & Carroll, J. S. (1990). Pretrial publicity, judicial remedies, and jury bias. *Law and Human Behavior, 14,* 409–438.

Kramer, M. (1997, December 15). How cops go bad. *Time,* 78–83.

Kraske, S. (1986, November 25). Victim of abduction, rapes recounts ordeal of terror. *Kansas City Star,* pp. 1A, 8A.

Krauss, E., & Bonora, B. (1983). *Jurywork: Systematic techniques* (2nd ed.). St. Paul, MN: West.

Krauss, D. A. & Sales, B. D. (1999). The problem of "helpfulness" in applying Daubert to expert testimony: Child custody determinations in family law as an exemplar. *Psychology, Public Policy, and Law, 5,* 78–99.

Krauss, D. A., & Sales, B. D. (2000). Legal standards, expertise, and experts in child custody decision-making. *Psychology, Public Policy, and Law, 6,* 843–879.

Krauss, D. A., & Sales, B. D. (2001). The child custody standard: What do twenty years of research teach us? In S. White (Ed.), *Handbook of youth and justice* (pp. 411–435). New York: Kluwer Academic/Plenum.

Kravitz, D. A. (1995). Attitudes toward affirmative action plans directed at blacks: Effects of plan and individual differences. *Journal of Applied Social Psychology, 25,* 2192–2220.

Kravitz, D. A., Cutler, B. L., & Brock, P. (1993). Reliability and validity of the original and revised Legal Attitudes Questionnaire. *Law and Human Behavior, 17,* 661–677.

Kressel, N. J., & Kressel, D. F. (2002). *Stack and sway: The new science of jury consulting.* Boulder, CO: Westview Press.

Krislov, S. (1963). The *amicus curiae* brief: From friendship to advocacy. *Yale Law Journal, 72,* 694–721.

Kroes, W., Margolis, B., & Hurrell, J. (1974). Job stress in policemen. *Journal of Police Science and Administration, 2*(2), 145–155.

Kropp, P. R., & Hart, S. D. (1997). Assessing risk of violence in wife assaulters: The Spousal Assault Risk Assessment Guide. In C. D. Webster & M. A. Jackson (Eds.), *Impulsivity: Theory, assessment, and treatment.* New York: Guilford.

Kropp, P. R., & Hart, S. D. (2000). The Spousal Assault Risk Assessment (SARA) Guide: Reliability and validity in adult male offenders. *Law and Human Behavior, 24,* 101–118.

Kropp, P. R., Hart, S. D., Webster, C. D., & Eaves, D. (1995). *Spouse Assault Risk Assessment guide (SARA).* Toronto: Multi-Health Systems Inc.

Kropp, P. R., Hart, S. D., Webster, C. D., & Eaves, D. (1998). *Manual for the Spousal Assault Risk Assessment Guide* (3rd ed.). Toronto: Multi-Health Systems.

Kuehnle, K. (1996). *Assessing allegations of child sexual abuse.* Sarasota, FL: Professional Resource Press.

Kumho Tire Co. Ltd. v. Carmichael, 526 U.S. 137 (1999).

Kumho Tire Co. Ltd. v. Carmichael, United States Supreme Court No. 97-1709 (2000), *amicus brief, Law and Human Behavior, 24,* 387–400.

Kurke, M. I., & Scrivner, E. M. (Eds.). (1995). *Police psychology into the 21st century.* Hillsdale, NJ: Lawrence Erlbaum Associates.

Laboratory of Community Psychiatry. (1974). *Competency to stand trial and mental illness.* Northvale, NJ: Jason Aronson.

Lacayo, R. (1991, April 8). Confessions that were taboo are now just a technicality. *Time,* 26–27.

LaFortune, K. A., & Carpenter, B. N. (1998). Custody evaluations: A survey of mental health professionals. *Behavioral Sciences and the Law, 16,* 207–224.

Landau, J. (1997, May 5). Out of order. *New Republic,* 9–10.

Landers, S. (1988, June). Use of "detailed dolls" questioned. *APA Monitor,* 24–25.

Landon, J. (1992, August). Expert: Dunn may be devious. *Topeka Capital-Journal,* p. C-1.

Landsman, S. (1995). Of witches, madmen, and products liability: A historical survey of the use of expert testimony. *Behavioral Sciences and the Law, 13,* 131–157.

Langer, W. C. (1972). *The mind of Adolf Hitler.* New York: Basic Books.

Langevin, R., Paitich, D., Freeman, R., Mann, K., & Handy, L. (1978). Personality characteristics and sexual anomalies in males. *Canadian Journal of Behavioural Science, 10,* 222–238.

Larry P. et al. v. Riles et al., 343 F. Supp. 306 (1972); 495 F. Supp. 929 (1979).

Lassiter, G. D., & Irvine, A. A. (1986). Videotaped confession: The impact of camera point of view on judgments of coercion. *Journal of Applied Social Psychology, 16,* 268–276.

Lasso, R. (1998, September 11). *Affirmative action: One step in the struggle for civil rights.* Invited address, University of Kansas, Lawrence.

Lathan v. Deegan, 450 F.2d 181 (2d Cir. 1971).

Laufer, W. S., & Walt, S. D. (1992). The law and psychology of precedent. In D. K. Kagehiro & W. S. Laufer (Eds.), *Handbook of psychology and law* (pp. 39–55). New York: Springer-Verlag.

Lavin, M., & Sales, B. D. (1998). Moral justifications for limits on expert testimony. In S. J. Ceci & H. Hembrooke (Eds.), *Expert witnesses in child abuse cases* (pp. 59–81). Washington, DC: American Psychological Association.

Lavrakas, P. J., & Bickman, L. (1975, August). *What makes a good witness?* Paper presented at the annual meeting of the American Psychological Association, Chicago, IL.

Lawlor, R. J. (1998). The expert witness in child sexual abuse cases: A clinician's view. In S. J. Ceci & H. Hembrooke (Eds.), *Expert witnesses in child abuse cases* (pp. 105–122). Washington, DC: American Psychological Association.

Lawrence, R. (1984). Checking the allure of increased conviction rates: The admissibility of expert testimony on rape trauma syndrome in criminal proceedings. *University of Virginia Law Review, 79,* 1657–1704.

Lawson, S. (1994, March 28). Jury is still out on trial consultants, but many small firms find them valuable. *Lawyers Weekly USA,* p. B14.

Lee, A., Boone, K. B., Lesser, I., Wohl, M., Wilkins, S., & Parks, C. (2000). Performance of older depressed patients on two cognitive malingering tests: False positive rates for the Rey 15-item memorization and dot counting tests. *Clinical Neuropsychologist, 14,* 303–308.

Lee, G. P., Loring, D. W., & Martin, R. C. (1992). Rey's 15-item visual memory test for the detection of malingering: Normative observations on patients with neurological disorders. *Psychological Assessment, 1,* 43–46.

Lego v. Twomey, 404 U.S. 477 (1972).

Leippe, M. R. (1995). The case for expert testimony about eyewitness memory. *Psychology, Public Policy, and Law, 1,* 909–959.

Leippe, M. R., Wells, G. L., & Ostrom, T. M. (1978). Crime seriousness as a determinant of accuracy in eyewitness identification. *Journal of Applied Psychology, 63,* 345–351.

Lemmon, J. A. (1985). *Family mediation practice.* New York: Collier.

Leo, J. (1993, November 29). An empty ruling on harassment. *U.S. News and World Report,* p. 20.

Leo, R. A. (1992). From coercion to deception: The changing nature of police interrogation in America. *Crime, Law, and Social Change, 18,* 35–39.

Leo, R. A. (1996a). The impact of *Miranda* revisited. *Journal of Criminal Law and Criminology, 86,* 621–692.

Leo, R. A. (1996b). Inside the interrogation room. *Journal of Criminal Law and Criminology, 86,* 266–303.

Leo, R. A. (1996c). *Miranda's* revenge: Police interrogation as a confidence game. *Law and Society Review, 30,* 259–288.

Leo, R. A., & Ofshe, R. J. (1998). Criminal law: Using the innocent to scapegoat *Miranda:* Another reply to Paul Cassell. *Journal of Criminal Law and Criminology, 88,* 557–577.

Levens, B. R., & Dutton, D. G. (1980). *The social service role of the police: Domestic crisis intervention.* Ottawa: Solicitor General of Canada.

Lewin, T. (1995, February 23). Who decides who will die? Even within states, it varies. *New York Times,* pp. A1, A13.

Lewis, A. (1980). A comparison of minors' and adults' pregnancy decisions. *American Journal of Orthopsychiatry, 50,* 446–453.

Lewis, A. (1991, August 5). Defining the issue. *New York Times,* p. A13.

Lewis, A. (1993, April 23). After the buck stops. *New York Times,* p. A19.

Lewis, N. A. (1992, October 8). Supreme Court hears case of a Texan on death row. *New York Times,* p. A15.

Leyra v. Denno, 347 U.S. 556 (1954).

Lezak, M. D. (1995). *Neuropsychological assessment* (3rd ed.). New York: Oxford University Press.

Liggins, D. L. (1999). Note: Urban survival syndrome: Novel concept or recognized defense? *American Journal of Trial Advocacy, 23,* 215–230.

Lind, E. A., & Tyler, T. R. (1988). *The social psychology of procedural justice.* New York: Plenum.

Lindsay, D. S., & Read, J. D. (1995). "Memory work" and recovered memories of childhood sexual abuse: Scientific evidence and public, professional, and personal issues. *Psychology, Public Policy, and Law, 1,* 846–908.

Lindsay, R. C. L. (1994). Biased lineups: Where do they come from? In D. Ross, J. Read, & M. Toglia (Eds.), *Adult eyewitness testimony: Current trends and developments* (pp. 182– 200). New York: Cambridge University Press.

Lindsay, R. C. L., Lea, J. A., & Fulford, J. A. (1991). Sequential lineup presentation: Technique matters. *Journal of Applied Psychology, 76,* 741–745.

Lindsay, R. C. L., Pozzulo, J. D., Craig, W., Lee, K., & Corber, S. (1997). Simultaneous lineups, sequential lineups, and showups: Eyewitness identification decisions of adults and children. *Law and Human Behavior, 21,* 391–404.

Lindsay, R. C. L., Wallbridge, H., & Drennan, D. (1987). Do the clothes make the man? An exploration of the effect of lineup attire on eyewitness identification accuracy. *Canadian Journal of Behavioural Science, 19,* 463–478.

Lindsay, R. C. L., & Wells, G. L. (1980). What price justice? Exploring the relationship of lineup fairness to identification accuracy. *Law and Human Behavior, 4,* 303–314.

Lindsay, R. C. L., Wells, G. L., & Rumpel, C. (1981). Can people detect eyewitness identification accuracy within and across situations? *Journal of Applied Psychology, 66,* 79–89.

Linedecker, C., & Burt, W. (1990). *Nurses who kill.* New York: Windsor.

Link, B., & Stueve, A. (1994). Psychotic symptoms and the violent/illegal behavior of mental patients compared to community controls. In J. Monahan & H. Steadman (Eds.), *Violence and mental disorder: Developments in risk assessment* (pp. 137–159). Chicago: University of Chicago Press.

Lipsitt, P. D., Lelos, D., & McGarry, A. L. (1971). Competency for trial: A screening instrument. *American Journal of Psychiatry, 128,* 105–109.

Lipton, J. P. (1977). On the psychology of eyewitness testimony. *Journal of Applied Psychology, 62,* 90–93.

Liss, M. B., & McKinley-Pace, M. J. (1999). Best interests of the child: New twists on an old theme. In R. Roesch, S. D. Hart, & J. R. P. Ogloff (Eds.), *Psychology and law: The state of the discipline* (pp. 339–372). New York: Kluwer Academic/Plenum Publishers.

Litigation Sciences (1988). *Litigation Sciences: The leader in jury research.* Rolling Hills Estates, CA: Litigation Sciences.

Litwack, T. (2001). Actuarial versus clinical assessments of dangerousness. *Psychology, Public Policy, and Law, 7,* 409–443.

Litwack, T., & Schlesinger, L. (1999). Dangerousness risk assessments: Research, legal, and clinical considerations. In A. Hess & I. Weiner (Eds.), *Handbook of forensic psychology* (2nd ed., pp. 171–217). New York: Wiley.

Lloyd-Bostock, S. (1989). *Law in practice.* Chicago: Lyceum.

Lockhart v. McCree, 476 U.S. 162, 106 S. Ct. 1758 (1986).

Lockett v. Ohio, 438 U.S. 586 (1978).

Lofgren, C. (1987). *The Plessy case: A legal-historical interpretation.* New York: Oxford University Press.

Loftus, E. F. (1975). Leading questions and the eyewitness report. *Cognitive Psychology, 7,* 560–572.

Loftus, E. F. (1979). *Eyewitness testimony.* Cambridge, MA: Harvard University Press.

Loftus, E. F. (1983). Silence is not golden. *American Psychologist, 65,* 9–15.

Loftus, E. F. (1993a). The reality of repressed memories. *American Psychologist, 48,* 518–537.

Loftus, E. F. (1993b). Psychologists in the eyewitness world. *American Psychologist, 48,* 550–552.

Loftus, E. F., & Hoffman, H. G. (1989). Misinformation and memory: The creation of new memories. *Journal of Experimental Psychology: General, 118,* 100–104.

Loftus, E. F., & Ketcham, K. (1991). *Witness for the defense: The accused, the eyewitness, and the expert who puts memory on trial.* New York: St. Martin's Press.

Loftus, E. F., & Ketcham, K. (1994). *The myth of repressed memory: False memories and allegations of sexual abuse.* New York: St. Martin's Griffin.

Loftus, E. F., & Rosenwald, L. A. (1995). Recovered memories: Unearthing the past in court. *Journal of Psychiatry and Law, 23,* 349–361.

Loh, W. D. (1981). Perspectives on psychology and law. *Journal of Applied Social Psychology, 11,* 314–355.

Lopez, S. (1998, May 11). Hide and seek. *Time,* 56–60.

Los Angeles Times (1993, April 23). President defends Reno, calls for investigation. *Kansas City Star,* p. A-1.

Lott, B., Reilly, M. E., & Howard, D. (1982). Sexual assault and harassment: A campus community case study. *Signs, 8,* 296–319.

Louisell, D. W. (1955). The psychologist in today's legal world. *Minnesota Law Review, 39,* 235–260.

Louisell, D. W. (1957). The psychologist in today's legal world: Part II. *Minnesota Law Review, 41,* 731–750.

Low, P. W., Jeffries, J. C., & Bonnie, R. J. (1986). *The trial of John W. Hinckley, Jr.: A case study in the insanity defense.* Mineola, NY: Foundation Press.

Lowery, C. R. (1981). Child custody in divorce proceedings: A survey of judges. *Professional Psychology, 12,* 492–498.

Lowery, C. R. (1984). The wisdom of Solomon: Criteria for child custody from the legal and clinical points of view. *Law and Human Behavior, 8,* 371–380.

Lowery, C. R. (1986). Maternal and joint custody: Differences in the decision process. *Law and Human Behavior, 10,* 303–315.

Luepnitz, D. A. (1982). *Child custody: A study of families after divorce.* Lexington, MA: Heath.

Luepnitz, D. A. (1986). A comparison of maternal, paternal, and joint custody: Understanding the varieties of post-divorce family life. *Journal of Divorce, 9,* 1–12.

Luginbuhl, J. (1992). Comprehension of judges' instructions in the penalty phase of a capital trial: Focus on mitigating circumstances. *Law and Human Behavior, 16,* 203–218.

Luginbuhl, J., & Middledorf, K. (1988). Death penalty beliefs and jurors' responses to aggravating and mitigating circumstances in capital trials. *Law and Human Behavior, 12,* 263–281.

Lukas, J. A. (1997). *Big trouble.* New York: Simon & Schuster.

Lunde, D. T., & Morgan, J. (1980). *The die song: A journey into the mind of a mass murderer.* New York: W. W. Norton.

Lupfer, M., Cohen, R., Bernard, J. L., Smalley, D., & Schippmann, J. (1985). An attributional analysis of jurors' judgments in civil cases. *Journal of Social Psychology, 125,* 743–751.

Luus, C. A. E. (1991). *Eyewitness confidence: Social influence and belief perseverance.* Unpublished doctoral dissertation, Iowa State University.

Luus, C. A. E., & Wells, G. L. (1994). The malleability of eyewitness confidence: Co-witness and perseverance effects. *Journal of Applied Psychology, 79,* 714–723.

Lykken, D. T. (1981, June). The lie detector and the law. *Criminal Defense, 8(3),* 19–27.

Lykken, D. T. (1985). The probity of the polygraph. In S. M. Kassin & L. S. Wrightsman (Eds.), *The psychology of evidence and trial procedure* (pp. 95–123). Newbury Park, CA: Sage.

Lykken, D. T. (1988). The case against polygraph testing. In A. Gale (Ed.), *The polygraph test: Lies, truth and science* (pp. 111–125). London: Sage.

Lykken, D. T. (1998). *A tremor in the blood: Uses and abuse of the lie detector.* New York: Plenum.

Lyons v. Oklahoma, 322 U.S. 596 (1944).

Lyons, A., & Truzzi, M. (1991). *The blue sense: Psychic detectives and crime.* New York: Mysterious Press.

Maccoby, E. E., & Mnookin, R. H. (1992). *Dividing the child: Social and legal dilemmas of custody.* Cambridge, MA: Harvard University Press.

Magley, V. J., Waldo, C. R., Drasgow, F., & Fitzgerald, L. F. (1998). *The impact of sexual harassment on military personnel: Is it the same for men and women?* Unpublished manuscript, University of Illinois at Urbana-Champaign. (Cited by Foote & Goodman-Delahunty, 1999.)

Maher, G. (1977). *Hostage: A police approach to a contemporary crisis.* Springfield, IL: Charles C Thomas.

Malamuth, N. (1981). Rape proclivity among males. *Journal of Social Issues, 37*(4), 138–154.

Malpass, R. S., & Devine, P. G. (1980). Realism and eyewitness identification research. *Law and Human Behavior, 4,* 347–358.

Malpass, R. S., & Devine, P. G. (1981). Eyewitness identification: Lineup instructions and the absence of the offender. *Journal of Applied Psychology, 66,* 482–489.

Malpass, R. S., & Devine, P. G. (1983). Measuring the fairness of eyewitness identification lineups. In S. M. A. Lloyd-Bostock & B. R. Clifford (Eds.), *Evaluating witness evidence* (pp. 81–102). New York: Wiley.

Mandelbaum, R. (1989, November). Jury consultants: What can they do, and is it worth it? *Inside Litigation, 3*(11), 1, 13–19.

Manning, A. (1998, February 23). Operating with sexism. *USA Today,* pp. 1D–2D.

Manshel, L. (1990). *Nap time.* New York: William Morrow.

Manson v. Braithwaite, 432 U.S. 98 (1977).

Marafiote, R. A. (1985). *The custody of children: A behavioral assessment model.* New York: Plenum.

Marquart, J. W., & Sorensen, J. R. (1989). A national study of the *Furman*-commuted inmates: Assessing the threat to society from capital offenders. *Loyola of Los Angeles Law Review, 23,* 5–28.

Marston, W. (1924). Studies in testimony. *Journal of Criminal Law and Criminology, 15,* 8–11.

Marxsen, D., Yuille, J. C., & Nisbet, M. (1995). The complexities of eliciting and assessing children's statements. *Psychology, Public Policy, and Law, 1,* 450–460.

Maryland v. Craig, 110 S. Ct. 3157 (1990).

Mason, M. A. (1991). The McMartin case revisited: The conflict between social work and criminal justice. *Social Work, 36,* 391–395.

Mason, M. A. (1998). Expert testimony regarding the characteristics of sexually abused children: A controversy on both sides of the bench. In S. J. Ceci & H. Hembrooke (Eds.), *Expert witnesses in child abuse cases* (pp. 217–234). Washington, DC: American Psychological Association.

Matlon, R. J. (1991, October). *Opening statements and closing arguments: A research review.* Paper presented at the meeting of the American Society of Trial Consultants, San Francisco.

Mauet, T. A. (1992). *Fundamentals of trial techniques* (3rd ed.). Boston: Little, Brown.

Mauro, T. (1993, November 10). Court clears air on sexual harassment. *USA Today,* pp. 1A–2A.

Mauro, T. (1998, April 30). Death penalty case brings high court rebuke. *USA Today,* p. 1A.

Mayer, J., & Abramson, J. (1994). *Strange justice: The selling of Clarence Thomas.* Boston: Houghton Mifflin.

McAlary, M. (1987). *Buddy boys: When good cops turn bad.* New York: G. P. Putnam's Sons.

McAlary, M. (1994). *Good cop, bad cop.* New York: Pocket Books.

McAllister, B. (1995, November 20–26). The problem that won't go away. *Washington Post National Weekly Edition,* p. 33.

McAuliff, B. D., & Kovera, M. B. (1998, August). *Are laypersons' beliefs about suggestibility consistent with expert opinion?* Paper presented at the meeting of the American Psychological Association, San Francisco.

McCandless, S. R., & Sullivan, L. P. (1991, May 6). Two courts adopt new standard to determine sexual harassment. *National Law Journal,* pp. 18–20.

McCarty, D. G. (1929). *Psychology for the lawyer.* New York: Prentice Hall.

McCleskey v. Kemp, 481 U.S. 279, 107 S. Ct. 1756 (1987).

McCloskey, M., & Egeth, H. E. (1983). Eyewitness identification: What can a psychologist tell a jury? *American Psychologist, 38,* 550–563.

McCloskey, M., Egeth, H., & McKenna, J. (1986). The experimental psychologist in court: The ethics of expert testimony. *Law and Human Behavior, 10,* 1–13.

McConahay, J. B. (1983). Modern racism and modern discrimination: The effects of race, racial attitudes, and context on simulated hiring decisions. *Personality and Social Psychology Bulletin, 9,* 551–558.

McConahay, J. B. (1986). Modern racism, ambivalence, and the Modern Racism Scale. In J. F. Dovidio & S. L. Gaertner (Eds.), *Prejudice, discrimination, and racism* (pp. 91–125). San Diego, CA: Academic Press.

McConahay, J. B., & Hough, J. C. (1976). Symbolic racism. *Journal of Social Issues, 32*(2), 23–45.

McCord, D. (1985). The admissibility of expert testimony regarding rape trauma syndrome in rape precautions. *Boston College Law Review, 26,* 1143–1213.

McCormick, J. (1998, November 9). The wrongly condemned. *Newsweek,* 64–66.

McCree v. State, 266 Ark. 465, 585 S.W.2d 938 (1979).

McCullough, G. W. (1994, March). *Juror decisions as a function of linguistic structure of the opening statement and closing argument.* Paper presented at the meeting of the American Psychology-Law Society, Santa Fe.

McCurdy, K., & Daro, D. (1993). *Current trends in child abuse reporting and fatalities: The results of the 1992 annual fifty state survey* (Working paper number 808). Chicago: National Center on Child Abuse Prevention Research.

McGough, L. (1998). A legal commentary: The impact of *Daubert* on 21st century child sexual abuse prosecutions. In S. J. Ceci & H. Hembrooke (Eds.), *Expert witnesses in child abuse cases* (pp. 265–281).

Washington, DC: American Psychological Association.

McGuire, W. (1964). Inducing resistance to persuasion: Some contemporary approaches. In L. Berkowitz (Ed.), *Advances in experimental social psychology* (Vol. 1, pp. 191–229). Orlando: Academic Press.

McIver, W., Wakefield, H., & Underwager, R. (1989). Behavior of abused and non-abused children in interviews with anatomically correct dolls. *Issues in Child Abuse Accusations, 1,* 39–48.

McKinzey, R. K. (1995). Neuropsychological assessment in capital cases. *CACJ Forum, 22,* 50– 55.

McMains, M. (1988). Psychologists' roles in hostage negotiations. In J. Reese & J. Horn (Eds.), *Police psychology: Operational assistance* (pp. 281–317). Washington, DC: U.S. Government Printing Office.

McNamara, J. (1967). Uncertainties in police work: The relevance of police recruits' backgrounds and training. In D. Bordua (Ed.), *The police: Six sociological essays* (pp. 163–252). New York: John Wiley.

McNiel, D. (1998). Empirically based clinical evaluation and management of the potentially violent patient (pp. 95–116). In P. K. Kleespies (Ed.), *Emergencies in mental health practice: Evaluation and management.* New York: Guilford.

McNiel, D., Borum, R., Douglas, K., Hart, S., Lyon, D., Sullivan, L., & Hemphill, J. (2002). Risk assessment. In J. R. P. Ogloff (Ed.), *Taking psychology and law into the 21st century: Perspectives in law and psychology* (pp. 182–202). Vol. 14. New York: Plenum Publishing.

McPoyle, T. J. (1981). The investigative technique of criminal profiling. *Your Virginia State Trooper, 3*(1), 87.

McQuiston, J. T. (1994, May 6). Rifkin depicted as delusional. *New York Times,* p. B16.

Meadows, R. J. (1987). Beliefs of law enforcement administrators and criminal justice educators toward the needed skill competencies in entry-level police training curriculum. *Journal of Police Science and Administration, 15,* 1–9.

Meehl, P. E. (1954). *Clinical versus statistical prediction: A theoretical analysis and a review of the evidence.* Minneapolis: University of Minnesota Press.

Meloy, J. R. (Ed.). (1998). *The psychology of stalking: Clinical and forensic perspectives.* San Diego, CA: Academic Press.

Melton, G. B. (1985). Organized psychology and legal policy making: Involvement in the post-Hinckley debate. *Professional Psychology: Research and Practice, 16,* 810–822.

Melton, G. B. (Ed.). (1987). *Reforming the law: Impact of child development research.* New York: Guilford Press.

Melton, G. B. (1993, August). *Are opinions by experts expert opinions?* Invited address presented at the meeting of the American Psychological Association, Toronto.

Melton, G. B. (1995). Review of the Ackerman-Schoendorf Scales for Parental Evaluation of Custody. In J. Conoley & J. C. Impara (Eds.), *Twelfth mental measurements yearbook* (p. 22). Lincoln: University of Nebraska Press.

Melton, G. B., Huss, M. T., & Tomkins, A. J. (1999). Training in forensic psychology and the law. In A. K. Hess & I. B. Weiner (Eds.), *Handbook of forensic psychology* (2nd ed., pp. 700–720). New York: John Wiley.

Melton, G. B., & Limber, S. (1989). Psychologists' involvement in cases of child maltreatment: Limits of role and expertise. *American Psychologist, 44,* 1225–1233.

Melton, G. B., Petrila, J., Poythress, N. G., & Slobogin, C. (1987). *Psychological evaluations for the courts.* New York: Guilford Press.

Melton, G. B., Petrila, J., Poythress, N. G., & Slobogin, C. (1997). *Psychological evaluations for the courts* (2nd ed.). New York: Guilford Press.

Melton, G. B., & Saks, M. J. (1990). AP-LS's pro bono *amicus* brief project. *American Psychology-Law Society News, 10,* 5.

Melton, G. B., Weithorn, L. A., & Slobogin, C. (1985). *Community mental health centers and the courts: An evaluation of community-based forensic services.* Lincoln: University of Nebraska Press.

Menez, J. F. (1984). *Decision making in the Supreme Court of the United States: A political and behavioral view.* Lanham, MD: University Press of America.

Meritor Savings Bank v. Vinson, 106 S. Ct. 2399 (1986).

Merrell Dow Pharmaceuticals, Inc. v. Havner, WL 86436 (Tex. Ct. App. Mar. 21, 1994).

Meyer, C., & Taylor, S. (1986). Adjustment to rape. *Journal of Personality and Social Psychology, 50,* 1226–1234.

Michaud, S. G., & Aynesworth, H. (1991). *Ted Bundy: Conversations with a killer.* New York: New American Library.

Michaud, S. G. (with Hazelwood, R.). (1998). *The evil that men do: FBI profiler Roy Hazelwood's journey into the minds of sexual predators.* New York: St. Martin's Press.

Milano, C. (1989, August). Re-evaluating recruitment to better target top minority talent. *Management Review,* 29–32.

Miller, J. S., & Allen, R. J. (1998). The expert as educator. In S. J. Ceci & H. Hembrooke (Eds.), *Expert witnesses in child abuse cases* (pp. 137–155). Washington, DC: American Psychological Association.

Miller, K. S., & Radelet, M. L. (1993). *Executing the mentally ill: The criminal justice system and the case of Alvin Ford.* Thousand Oaks, CA: Sage.

Milner, J. (1995). Physical child abuse assessment. In J. C. Campbell (Ed). *Assessing dangerousness: Violence by sexual offenders, batterers, and child abusers* (pp. 41–67). Thousand Oaks, CA: Sage.

Mills, R. B., McDevitt, R. J., & Tonkin, S. (1966). Situational tests in metropolitan police recruit selection. *Journal of Criminal Law, Criminology, and Police Science, 57,* 99–104.

Miner v. Miner, 11 Ill. 43 (1849).

Monahan, J. (1977). Community psychology and public policy: The premise and the pitfalls. In B. D. Sales (Ed.), *Psychology in the legal process* (pp. 197–213). New York: Spectrum.

Monahan, J. (1981). *Predicting violent behavior: an assessment of the clinical techniques.* Thousand Oaks, CA: Sage.

Monahan, J. (1992). Mental disorder and violent behavior: Perceptions and evidence. *American Psychologist, 47,* 511–521.

Monahan, J., & Steadman, H. J. (1983). *Mentally disordered offenders: Perspectives from law and social science.* New York: Plenum Press.

Monahan, J., & Steadman, H. (1994). Toward the rejuvenation of risk research. In J. Monahan & H. Steadman (Eds.), *Violence and mental disorder: Developments in risk assessment* (pp. 1–17). Chicago: University of Chicago Press.

Monahan, J., Steadman, H. J., Silver, E., Appelbaum, P. S., Robbins, P. C., Mulvey, E. P., Roth, L. H., Grisso, T., & Banks, S. (2001). *Rethinking risk assessment: The MacArthur study of mental disorder and violence.* Oxford: Oxford University Press.

Monahan, J., & Walker, L. (1986). Social authority: Obtaining, evaluating, and establishing social science in law. *University of Pennsylvania Law Review, 134,* 477–517.

Monahan, J., & Walker, L. (1988). Social science research in law: A new paradigm. *American Psychologist, 43,* 465–472.

Monahan, J., & Walker, L. (1990). *Social sciences in law: Cases and materials* (2nd ed.). Westbury, NY: Foundation Press.

Monahan, J., & Walker, L. (1991). Judicial use of social science research. *Law and Human Behavior, 15,* 571–584.

Moran, G., & Cutler, B. L. (1991). The prejudicial impact of pretrial publicity. *Journal of Applied Social Psychology, 21,* 345–367.

Moran, G., & Cutler, B. L. (1997). Bogus publicity items and the contingency between awareness and media-induced pretrial prejudice. *Law and Human Behavior, 21,* 339–344.

Moran, G., Cutler, B. L., & DeLisa, A. (1994). Attitudes toward tort reform, scientific jury selection, and juror bias: Verdict inclination in criminal and civil trials. *Law and Psychology Review, 18,* 309–328.

Morgenthau, R. M. (1995, February 7). What prosecutors won't tell you. *New York Times,* p. A11.

Morison, S., & Greene, E. (1992). Juror and expert knowledge of child sexual abuse. *Child Abuse and Neglect, 16,* 595–613.

Morris, N., & Miller, M. (1985). Predictions of dangerousness. In M. Tonry and N. Morris (Eds.), *Crime and justice: An annual review of research* (Vol. 6). Chicago: University of Chicago Press.

Morris, R. J. (1995, August). *Ethical issues in the conduct of child custody evaluations.* Paper presented at the meeting of the American Psychological Association, New York.

Morse, S. J. (1978). Law and mental health professionals: The limits of expertise. *Professional Psychology, 9,* 389–399.

Morse, S. J. (1990). The misbegotten marriage of soft psychology and bad law: Psychological self-defense as a justification for homicide. *Law and Human Behavior, 14,* 595–618.

Moskowitz, M. J. (1977). Hugo Munsterberg: A study in the history of applied psychology. *American Psychologist, 32,* 824–842.

Mossman, D. (1992). The psychiatrist and execution competency: Fording murky ethical waters. *Case Western Reserve Law Review, 43,* 19–21.

Mossman, D. (1994). Assessing predictions of violence: Being accurate about accuracy. *Journal of Consulting and Clinical Psychology, 62,* 783–792.

Mossman, K. (1973, May). Jury selection: An expert's view. *Psychology Today,* 78–79.

Muller v. Oregon, 208 U.S. 412 (1908).

Münsterberg, H. (1908). *On the witness stand.* Garden City, NY: Doubleday.

Murphy, W. D., & Peters, J. M. (1992). Profiling child sexual abusers: Psychological considerations. *Criminal Justice and Behavior, 19*(1), 24–37.

Murphy, P. V. (1995, February 23). Death penalty useless. *USA Today,* p. 11A.

Murray v. Giarratano, 492 U.S. 1 (1989).

Murray, B. (1998, September). Helping the Secret Service assess dangerous minds. *APA Monitor, 1,* 37.

Murray, D. M., & Wells, G. L. (1982). Does knowledge that a crime was staged affect eyewitness performance? *Journal of Applied Social Psychology, 12,* 42–53.

Myers, J. E. B. (1992). *Legal issues in child abuse and neglect.* Thousand Oaks, CA: Sage.

Myers, J. E. B., Bays, J., Becker, J., Berliner, L., Corwin, D. L., & Saywitz, K. J. (1989). Expert testimony in child sexual abuse litigation. *Nebraska Law Review, 68,* 1–145.

Nacoste, R. W. (1985). Selection procedure and responses to affirmative action: The case of favorable treatment. *Law and Human Behavior, 9,* 225–242.

Nacoste, R. W. (1987). Social psychology and affirmative action: The importance of process in policy analysis. *Journal of Social Issues, 43*(1), 127–132.

Nacoste, R. W. (1994). If empowerment is the goal . . .: Affirmative action and social interaction. *Basic and Applied Social Psychology, 15,* 87–112.

Nacoste, R. W. (1996). How affirmative action can pass constitutional and social psychological muster. *Journal of Social Issues, 52*(4), 133–144.

Nagel, T. W. (1983, October). *Tensions between law and psychology: Fact, myth, or ideology?* Paper presented at the meeting of the American Psychology-Law Society, Chicago.

Narby, D. J., Cutler, B. L., & Moran, G. (1993). A meta-analysis of the association between authoritarianism and jurors' perceptions of defendant culpability. *Journal of Applied Psychology, 78,* 34–42.

Nathan, D. (1987). The making of a modern witch trial. *Village Voice, 33,* 19–32.

National Advisory Commission on Criminal Justice Standards and Goals. (1973). *Report on police.* Washington, DC: U.S. Government Printing Office.

Neiderland, W. G. (1982). The survivor syndrome: Further observations and dimensions. *Journal of the American Psychoanalytic Association, 30,* 413–425.

Neil v. Biggers, 409 U.S. 188 (1972).

Nelson, P. (1994). *Defending the devil: My story as Ted Bundy's last lawyer.* New York: William Morrow.

New Jersey v. Kelly, 97 N.J. 178, 478 A.2d 364 (1984).

Newman, S. A. (1994). Assessing the quality of testimony in cases involving children. *Journal of Psychiatry and Law, 22,* 181–234.

Nicholson, R. (1999). Forensic assessment. In R. Roesch, S. D. Hart, & J. R. P. Ogloff (Eds.), *Psychology and law: The state of the discipline* (pp. 121–173). New York: Kluwer Academic/Plenum Publishers.

Nicholson, R. A., Briggs, S. R., & Robertson, H. C. (1988). Instruments for assessing competency to stand trial: How do they work? *Professional Psychology: Research and Practice, 19,* 383–394.

Nicholson, R. A., & Johnson, W. G. (1991). Prediction of competency to stand trial: Contribution of demographics, type of offense, clinical characteristics, and psychological ability. *International Journal of Law and Psychiatry, 14,* 287–297.

Niederhoffer, A. (1967). *Behind the shield: The police in urban society.* Garden City, NY: Doubleday.

Nietzel, M. T., & Dillehay, R. C. (1982). The effects of variations in voir dire procedures in capital murder trials. *Law and Human Behavior, 6,* 1–13.

Nietzel, M. T., & Dillehay, R. C. (1983). Psychologists as consultants for changes of venue: The use of public opinion surveys. *Law and Human Behavior, 7,* 309–335.

Nietzel, M. T., & Dillehay, R. C. (1986). *Psychological consultation in the courtroom.* New York: Pergamon Press.

Nims, J. (1998, August). *NIMS Observation Checklist.* Paper presented at the meeting of the American Psychological Association, San Francisco.

Nisbett, R., Borgida, E., Crandall, C., & Reed, H. (1982). Popular induction: Information is not necessarily informative. In D. Kahneman, P. Slovic, & A. Tversky (Eds.), *Judgment under uncertainty: Heuristics and biases* (pp. 101–116). New York: Cambridge University Press.

Norris, F. H. (1992). Epidemiology of trauma: Frequency and impact of different potentially traumatic events of different demographic groups. *Journal of Consulting and Clinical Psychology, 60,* 409–418.

Norris, J. (1992). *Jeffrey Dahmer.* New York: Pinnacle Books.

Note. (1953). Voluntary false confessions: A neglected area in criminal investigation. *Indiana Law Journal, 28,* 374–392.

O'Barr, W. M. (1982). *Linguistic evidence: Language, power, and strategy in the courtroom.* San Diego, CA: Academic Press.

O'Brien, D. (1985). *Two of a kind: The hillside stranglers.* New York: New American Library.

Office of Technology Assessment. (1983). *Scientific validity of polygraph testing: A research review and evaluation.* Washington, DC: U.S. Congress.

Ofshe, R. (1992). Inadvertent hypnosis during interrogation: False confessions due to dissociative state, misidentified multiple personality, and the satanic cult hypothesis. *International Journal of Clinical and Experimental Hypnosis, 40,* 125–156.

Ofshe, R. J., & Leo, R. A. (1997). The social psychology of police interrogation: The theory and classification of true and false confessions. *Studies in Law, Politics, and Society, 16,* 189–215.

Ofshe, R., & Watters, E. (1994). *Making monsters: False memories, psychotherapy, and sexual hysteria.* New York: Scribner's.

Ogletree, C. J. (1987). Are confessions really good for the soul? A proposal to Mirandize *Miranda. Harvard Law Review, 100,* 1826–1845.

Ogloff, J. R. P. (1995). The legal basis of forensic applications of the MMPI-2. In Y. S. Ben-Porath, J. R. Graham, G. C. N. Hall, R. D. Hirschman, & M. S. Zaragoza (Eds.), *Forensic applications of the MMPI-2* (pp. 18–47). Thousand Oaks, CA: Sage.

Ogloff, J. R. P. (2000). Two steps forward and one step backward: The law and psychology movement(s) in the 20th century. *Law and Human Behavior, 24,* 457–483.

Ogloff, J. R. P., & Otto, R. K. (1993). Psychological autopsy: Clinical and legal perspectives. *Saint Louis University Law Journal, 37,* 607–646.

Ogloff, J. R. P., Roberts, C. F., & Roesch, R. (1993). The insanity defense: Legal standards and clinical assessment. *Applied and Preventive Psychology, 2,* 163–178.

Ogloff, J. R. P., Wallace, D. H., & Otto, R. K. (1992). Competencies in the criminal process. In D. K. Kagehiro & W. S. Laufer (Eds.), *Handbook of psychology and law* (pp. 343–360). New York: Springer-Verlag.

O'Hara, C. E., & O'Hara, G. L. (1956). *Fundamentals of criminal investigation.* Springfield, IL: Charles C Thomas.

O'Hara, C. E., & O'Hara, G. L. (1980). *Fundamentals of criminal investigation* (5th ed.). Springfield, IL: Charles C Thomas.

Ohio v. Akron Center for Reproductive Health et al., 110 S. Ct. 2972 (1990).

Okpaku, S. R. (1976). Psychology: Impediment or aid in child custody cases? *Rutgers Law Review, 29,* 1117–1153.

Olsen, J. (1991). *Predator: Rape, madness, and injustice in Seattle.* New York: Dell.

Olsen-Fulero, L., & Fulero, S. (1997). An empathy-complexity theory of rape story making. *Psychology, Public Policy, and Law, 3,* 402–427.

Olson, W. K. (1991). *The litigation explosion: What happened when America unleashed the lawsuit.* New York: Dutton.

Oncale v. Sundowner Offshore Services, 118 S. Ct. 998 (1998).

Opotow, S. (1996). Affirmative action, fairness, and the scope of justice. *Journal of Social Issues, 52*(4), 19–24.

Orlando, J. A., & Koss, M. P. (1983). The effect of sexual victimization on sexual satisfaction: A study of the negative association hypothesis. *Journal of Abnormal Psychology, 92,* 104–106.

Orne, M. T. (1979). The use and misuse of hypnosis in court. *International Journal of Clinical and Experimental Hypnosis, 27,* 311–341.

Orne, M. T., Axelrad, A. D., Diamond, B. L., Gravitz, M. A., Heller, A., Mutter, C. B., Spiegel, D., Spiegel, H., & Smith, R. J. (1985). Scientific status of refreshing recollection by the use of hypnosis. *Journal of the American Medical Association, 253,* 1918–1923.

Orne, M. T., Soskis, D. A., Dinges, D. F., & Orne, E. C. (1984). Hypnotically induced testimony. In G. L. Wells & E. F. Loftus (Eds.), *Eyewitness testimony: Psychological perspectives* (pp. 171–213). New York: Cambridge University Press.

Orth, M. (1999). *Vulgar favors: Andrew Cunanan, Gianni Versace, and the largest failed manhunt in U.S. history.* New York: Delacorte.

Ostrov, E. (1985, August). *Validation of police officer recruit candidates' self-reported drug use on the Inwald Personality Inventory.* Paper presented at the meeting of the American Psychological Association, Los Angeles.

Ostrov, E. (1986). Police/law enforcement and psychology. *Behavioral Sciences and the Law, 4,* 353–370.

Otto, A. L., Penrod, S. D., & Dexter, H. R. (1994). The biasing impact of pretrial publicity on juror judgments. *Law and Human Behavior, 18,* 453–469.

Otto, R. (1992). Prediction of dangerous behavior: A review and analysis of "second generation" research. *Forensic Reports, 5,* 103–133.

Otto, R. (1996, August). *Outline on custody evaluations.* Tampa, FL: Florida Mental Health Institute.

Otto, R. K., Buffington-Vollum, J., & Edens, J. F. (2003). Child custody evaluations: Research and practice. In A. Goldstein (Ed.), *Handbook of psychology: Vol. 11. Forensic psychology* (pp. 179–208). New York: Wiley.

Otto, R. K., & Collins, R. P. (1995). Use of MMPI-2/MMPI-A in child custody evaluations. In Y. S. Ben-Porath, J. R. Graham, G. C. N. Hall, R. D. Hirschman, & M. S. Zaragoza (Eds.), *Forensic applications of the MMPI-2* (pp. 222–252). Thousand Oaks, CA: Sage.

Otto, R., Edens, J., & Barcus, E. (2000). The use of psychological testing in child custody evaluations. *Family and Conciliation Courts Review, 38,* 312–340.

Otto, R. K., Edens, J. F., Poythress, N. G., & Nicholson, R. A. (1998, March). *Psychometric properties of the MacArthur Competence Assessment Tool-Criminal Adjudication (MacCAT-CA).* Paper presented at the meeting of the American Psychology-Law Society, Redondo Beach, CA.

Otto, R. K., & Heilbrun, K. (2002). The practice of forensic psychology: A look toward the future in light of the past. *American Psychologist, 57,* 5–18.

Otto, R. K., Poythress, N., Starr, L., & Darkes, J. (1993). An empirical study of the reports of APA's peer review panel in the congressional review of the USS *Iowa* incident. *Journal of Personality Assessment, 61,* 425–442.

Padawer-Singer, A., & Barton, A. H. (1975). The impact of pretrial publicity on jurors' verdicts. In R. J. Simon (Ed.), *The jury system in America: A critical overview* (pp. 123–139). Thousand Oaks, CA: Sage.

Page, C. (2002, October 27). The bearing of arms in America: Sniper suspect exposes the profiling myth. *Chicago Tribune,* p. B-9.

Painter v. Bannister, 140 N.W.2d 152 (Iowa 1966).

Palmore v. Sidoti, 466 U.S. 429 (1984).

Palmer, S. (1960). *A study of murder.* New York: Thomas Crowell.

Parker, L. (1998, April 24–26). The "great pretender." *USA Today,* pp. 1A–2A.

Paris, M. L. (1996). Trust, lies, and interrogation. *Virginia Journal of Social Policy and Law, 3,* 15–44.

PASE v. Hannon, 506 F. Supp. 831 (1980).

Paternoster, R., & Kazyaka, A. (1988). Racial considerations in capital punishment: The failure of evenhanded justice. In K. C. Haas & J. A. Inciardi (Eds.), *Challenging capital punishment: Legal and social science approaches* (pp. 113–148). Thousand Oaks, CA: Sage.

Paterson, E. J. (1979). How the legal system responds to battered women. In D. M. Moore (Ed.), *Battered women* (pp. 79–99). Newbury Park, CA: Sage.

Patterson, C. J. (1992). Children of lesbian and gay parents. *Child Development, 63,* 1025–1042.

Peak, K. J., & Glensor, R. W. (1996). *Community policing and problem solving: Strategies and practices.* Upper Saddle River, NJ: Prentice Hall.

Pekkanen, J. (1976). *Victims: An account of a rape.* New York: Popular Library.

Pence, E., & Paymor, M. (1985). *Power and control: Tactics of men who batter: An educational curriculum.* Duluth, MN: Minnesota Program Development, Inc.

Pennington, N., & Hastie, R. (1981). Juror decision making models: The generalization gap. *Psychological Bulletin, 89,* 246–287.

Pennington, N., & Hastie, R. (1986). Evidence evaluation in complex decision making. *Journal of Personality and Social Psychology, 51,* 242–258.

Pennington, N., & Hastie, R. (1993). The story model for juror decision making. In R. Hastie (Ed.), *Inside the juror: The psychology of juror decision making* (pp. 192–221). New York: Cambridge University Press.

Penrod, S. D., & Cutler, B. L. (1987). Assessing the competence of juries. In I. B. Weiner & A. K. Hess (Eds.), *Handbook of forensic psychology.* New York: John Wiley.

Penrod, S., & Cutler, B. L. (1995). Witness confidence and witness accuracy: Assessing their forensic relation. *Psychology, Public Policy, and Law, 1,* 817–845.

Penrod, S. D., Fulero, S. M., & Cutler, B. L. (1995). Expert psychological testimony on eyewitness reliability before and after Daubert: The state of the law and the science. *Behavioral Sciences and the Law, 13,* 229–259.

Penry v. Lynaugh, 492 U.S. 302 (1989).

People v. Bledsoe, 203 Cal. Rep. 450 (1984).

People v. Diaz, No. 2714 (Sup. Ct. Bronx Co., N.Y. 1983).

People v. LeGrand, 196 N.Y. Misc. 2d 179 (Sup. Ct. N.Y. County 2002)

People v. Lopez, 60 Cal. 2d 223, 384 P.2d 16 (1963).

People v. Mathews, 91 Cal. App. 3d 1018 (1979).

People v. McRae, 23 Crim. L. Rep. (BNA) 2507 (N.Y. Sup. Ct. July 17, 1978).

People v. Raymond Buckey et al., Los Angeles Sup. Ct. No. A750900 (1990).

People v. Smith, 743 N.Y.S.2d 246 (2002).

People v. Stadwick, 207 Cal. App. 2d 767 (1962).

People v. Torres, 128 Misc. 2d 129, 488 N.Y.2d 358 (Sup. Ct. 1985).

Perkins, D. D. (1988). The use of social science in public interest litigation: A role for community psycholo-

gists. *American Journal of Community Psychology, 16,* 465–485.

Perlin, M. L. (1996). The insanity defense: Deconstructing the myths and reconstructing the jurisprudence. In B. D. Sales & D. W. Shuman (1996), *Law, mental health, and mental disorder* (pp. 341–359). Pacific Grove, CA: Brooks/Cole.

Perot, A. R., Brooks, L., & Gersh, T. L. (1992, August). *Development of the Beliefs About Sexual Harassment Scale.* Paper presented at the meeting of the American Psychological Association, Washington, DC.

Perry, N. W., & Wrightsman, L. S. (1991). *The child witness: Legal issues and dilemmas.* Thousand Oaks, CA: Sage.

Pettigrew, T. F., & Meertens, R. W. (1995). Subtle and blatant prejudice in Western Europe. *European Journal of Social Psychology, 25,* 57–75.

Petty, R. E., & Cacioppo, J. T. (1977). Forewarning, cognitive responding, and resistance to persuasion. *Journal of Personality and Social Psychology, 35,* 645–655.

Pezdek, K., & Banks, W. P. (Eds.). (1996). *The recovered memory/false memory debate.* San Diego, CA: Academic Press.

Pierce, D. (1981). Predictive validity of a suicidal intent scale: A five year follow up. *British Journal of Psychiatry, 139,* 391–396.

Pierce, D. (1984). Suicidal intent and repeated self-harm. *Psychological Medicine, 14,* 655–659.

Pigott, M. A., Foley, L. A., Covati, C. J., & Wasserman, A. (1998, March). *Mock jurors' perceptions of a male plaintiff in sexual harassment litigation.* Paper presented at the meeting of the American Psychology-Law Society, Redondo Beach, CA.

Pinizzotto, A. J. (1984). Forensic psychology: Criminal personality profiling. *Journal of Police Science and Administration, 12,* 32–40.

Pinizzotto, A. J., & Finkel, N. J. (1990). Criminal personality profiling: An outcome and process study. *Law and Human Behavior, 14,* 215–233.

Pirozzolo, F. J., Funk, J., & Dywan, J. (1991). Neuropsychology and its applications to the legal forum. In J. Dywan, R. D. Kaplan, & F. J. Pirozzolo (Eds.), *Neuropsychology and the law* (pp. 1–23). New York: Springer-Verlag.

Pitera, M. J. (1995, April). *Jury selection: Two perspectives.* Unpublished manuscript, Department of Psychology, University of Kansas, Lawrence.

Plass, P. S., Finkelhor, D., & Hotaling, G. T. (1997). Risk factors for family abduction: Demographic and family interaction characteristics. *Journal of Family Violence, 12,* 313–332.

Platania, J., Moran, G., & Cutler, B. (1994, July). Prosecution misconduct. *The Champion,* 19–22.

Plessy v. Ferguson, 163 U.S. 537 (1896).

Plevan, B. P. (1993, December 6). *Harris* won't end harassment questions. *National Law Journal,* pp. 19–20.

Plous, S. (1996). Ten myths about affirmative action. *Journal of Social Issues, 52*(4), 25–31.

Podlesny, J. A., & Raskin, D. C. (1977). Physiological measures and the detection of deception. *Psychological Bulletin, 84,* 782–799.

Podrygula, S. (1997). *Psychological tests used in child custody assessment: The current state of the art.* Workshop co-sponsored by the American Bar Association and the American Psychological Association: Children, Divorce, and Custody: Lawyers and Psychologists Working Together. Los Angeles, CA.

Pogrebin, M. R., Poole, E. D., & Regoli, R. M. (1986). Stealing money: An assessment of bank embezzlers. *Behavioral Sciences and the Law, 4,* 481–490.

Pokorny, A. D. (1983). Prediction of suicide in psychiatric patients: Report of a prospective study. *Archives of General Psychiatry, 40,* 249–257.

Pollock, A. (1977). The use of public opinion polls to obtain changes of venue and continuance in criminal trials. *Criminal Justice Journal, 1,* 269–288.

Poole, D. A., & White, L. T. (1991). Effect of question repetition on the eyewitness testimony of children and adults. *Developmental Psychology, 27,* 975–986.

Pope, K., Butcher, J., & Seelen, J. (1993). *The MMPI, MMPI-2, and MMPI in court: A practical guide for expert witnesses and attorneys.* Washington, DC: American Psychological Association.

Posey, A. J. & Dahl, L. M. (2002). Beyond pretrial publicity: Legal and ethical issues associated with change of venue surveys. *Law and Human Behavior, 26,* 107–126.

Post, J. M. (1991). Saddam Hussein of Iraq: A political psychology profile. *Political Psychology, 12,* 279–289.

Powitsky, R. J. (1979). The use and misuse of psychologists in a hostage situation. *The Police Chief, 46,* 30–33.

Poythress, N. G. (1980). Assessment and prediction in the hostage situation: Optimizing the use of psychological data. *The Police Chief, 47,* 34–38.

Poythress, N. G. (1992). Expert testimony on violence and dangerousness: Roles for mental health professionals. *Forensic Reports, 5,* 135–150.

Poythress, N., Bonnie, R., Hoge, S., Monahan, J., & Oberlander, L. (1994). Client abilities to assist counsel and make decisions in criminal cases: Findings from three studies. *Law and Human Behavior, 18,* 437–452.

Poythress, N., Otto, R. K., Darkes, J., & Starr, L. (1993). APA's expert panel in the congressional review of the USS *Iowa* incident. *American Psychologist, 48,* 8–15.

Pratkanis, A. R., & Turner, M. E. (1996). The proactive removal of discriminatory barriers: Affirmative action as effective help. *Journal of Social Issues, 52*(4), 111–132.

President's Commission on Law Enforcement and the Administration of Justice. (1967). *Task force report: The police.* Washington, DC: Superintendent of Documents.

Press, A. (1983, January 10). Divorce American style. *Newsweek,* 42–48.

Price Waterhouse v. Hopkins, 109 S. Ct. 1775 (1989).

Price Waterhouse v. Hopkins, 825 F.2d 458 (D.C. Cir. 1987).

Pruett, M. K., & Santangelo, C. (1999). Joint custody and empirical knowledge: The estranged bedfellow of divorce. In R. M. Galatzer-Levy & L. Kraus (Eds.), *The scientific basis of custody decisions.* New York: John Wiley.

Pryor, J. B. (1987). Sexual harassment proclivities in men. *Sex Roles, 17,* 269–290.

Pryor, J. B., Giedd, J. L., & Williams, K. B. (1995). A social psychological model for predicting sexual harassment. *Journal of Social Issues, 51*(1), 69–84.

Pryor, J. B., LaVite, C., & Stoller, L. (1993). A social psychological analysis of sexual harassment: The person/situation interaction. *Journal of Vocational Behavior, 42,* 68–83.

Pryor, J. B., & Whalen, N. J. (1997). A typology of sexual harassment: Characteristics of harassers and the social circumstances under which harassment occurs. In W. O'Donohue (Ed.), *Sexual harassment: Theory, research, and treatment* (pp. 129–151). New York: Allyn & Bacon.

Pulaski, C. (1980). Criminal trials: "A search for truth" or something else? *Criminal Law Bulletin, 16,* 41, 44–45.

Pyszczynski, T., Greenberg, J., Mack, D., & Wrightsman, L. S. (1981). Opening statements in a jury trial: The effect of promising more than the evidence can show. *Journal of Applied Social Psychology, 11,* 434–444.

Pyszczynski, T., & Wrightsman, L. S. (1981). The effects of opening statements on mock jurors' verdicts in a simulated criminal trial. *Journal of Applied Social Psychology, 11,* 301–313.

Quayle, D. (1992). Civil justice reform. *American University Law Review, 41,* 559–569.

Quindlen, A. (1994, March 16). Victim and valkyrie. *New York Times,* p. A15.

Quinsey, V. L., Harris, G. T., Rice, M. E., & Cormier, C. A. (1998). *Violent offenders: Appraising and managing risk.* Washington, DC: American Psychological Association.

Quinsey, V. L., Lalumiere, M. L., Rice, M. E., & Harris, G. T. (1995). Predicting sexual offenses. In J. C. Campbell (Ed.), *Assessing dangerousness: Violence by sexual offenders, batterers, and child abusers* (pp. 114–137). Thousand Oaks, CA: Sage.

Rabinowitz, D. (1990, May). From the mouths of babes to a jail cell: Child abuse and the abuse of justice. *Harper's Magazine,* 52–63.

Rachlin, H. (1991). *The making of a cop.* New York: Pocket Books.

Rachlin, H. (1995). *The making of a detective.* New York: W. W. Norton.

Radelet, M. L., & Bedau, H. A. (1988). Fallibility and finality: Type II errors and capital punishment. In K. C. Haas & J. A. Inciardi (Eds.), *Challenging capital punishment: Legal and social science approaches* (pp. 91–112). Thousand Oaks, CA: Sage.

Radelet, M. L., Bedau, H. A., & Putnam, C. E. (1992). *In spite of justice: Erroneous convictions in capital cases.* Boston: Northeastern University Press.

Radin, E. D. (1964). *The innocents.* New York: William Morrow.

Rand Corporation. (1975). *The criminal investigation process* (Vols. 1–3; Rand Corporation Technical Report R-1777-DOJ). Santa Monica, CA: Author.

Rappeport, M. (1993, October 11). Statistics fine-tune simple courtroom evidence. *National Law Journal,* 15–16.

Raskin, D. C. (1989). Polygraph techniques for the detection of deception. In D. C. Raskin (Ed.), *Psychological methods in criminal investigation and evidence* (pp. 247–296). New York: Springer.

Raskin, D. C., & Esplin, P. W. (1991). Statement validity assessment: Interview procedures and content analysis of children's statements of sexual abuse. *Behavioral Assessment, 13,* 265–291.

Raskin, D. C., & Hare, R. (1978). Psychopathy and detection of deception in a prison population. *Psychophysiology, 15,* 126–136.

Rattner, A. (1988). Convicted but innocent: Wrongful conviction and the criminal justice system. *Law and Human Behavior, 12,* 283–293.

Realmuto, G. M., Jensen, J. B., & Wescoe, S. (1990). Specificity and sensitivity of sexually anatomically correct dolls in substantiating abuse: A pilot study. *Journal of the American Academy of Child and Adolescent Psychiatry, 29,* 743–746.

Rebello, J. (1993, March 31). High court hears "junk science" case involving Marion. *Kansas City Star,* pp. A-1, A-9.

Rees, L., Boulay, L., & Tombaugh, T. (2001). Depression and the Test of Memory Malingering (TOMM). *Archives of Clinical Neuropsychology, 16,* 501–506.

Reese, J. T. (1995). A history of police psychological services. In M. I. Kurke & E. M. Scrivner (Eds.), *Police psychology into the 21st century* (pp. 31–44). Hillsdale, NJ: Lawrence Erlbaum Associates.

Reese, J., Horn, J., & Dunning, C. (Eds.). (1991). *Critical incidents in policing.* Washington, DC: U.S. Government Printing Office.

Regents of the University of California v. Bakke, 438 U.S. 265 (1978).

Regina v. Norman, 87 C.C.C.3d, 153 (1993).

Reich, J., & Tookey, L. (1986). Disagreements between court and psychiatrist on competency to stand trial. *Journal of Clinical Psychiatry, 47,* 616–623.

Reid, J. E. (1945). Stimulated blood pressure responses in lie detection tests and a method for their detection. *Journal of Criminal Law, Criminology and Police Science, 36,* 201–204.

Reinhold, R. (1990, September 7). Case of two brothers accused of killing parents may test secrecy limit in patient-therapist tie. *New York Times,* p. B9.

Reiser, M. (1972). *The police department psychologist.* Springfield, IL: Charles C Thomas.

Reiser, M. (1974). Some organizational stressors on policemen. *Journal of Police Science and Administration, 2,* 156–159.

Reiser, M. (1980). *Handbook of investigative hypnosis.* Los Angeles: LEHI Publishing Company.

Reiser, M. (1982a). Crime specific psychological consultation. *The Police Chief, 49*(3), 53–56.

Reiser, M. (1982b). *Police psychology: Collected papers.* Los Angeles: LEHI Publishing Company.

Reiser, M. (1982c). Selection and promotion of policemen. In M. Reiser (Ed.), *Police psychology: Collected papers* (pp. 84–92). Los Angeles: LEHI Publishing Company.

Reiser, M. (1985). Investigative hypnosis: Scientism, memory tricks, and power plays. In J. K. Zeig (Ed.), *Ericksonian psychotherapy: Vol. I. Structures.* New York: Brunner/Mazel. (Cited by Steblay and Bothwell, 1994).

Reiser, M. (1989). Investigative hypnosis. In D. C. Raskin (Ed.), *Psychological methods in criminal investigation and evidence* (pp. 151–190). New York: Springer.

Ressler, R., Burgess, A., & Douglas, J. (1988). *Sexual homicide.* Lexington, MA: Lexington Books.

Ressler, R. K., Burgess, A. W., Douglas, J. E., Hartman, C. R., & D'Agostino, R. B. (1986). Sexual killers and their victims: Identifying patterns through crime scene analysis. *Journal of Interpersonal Violence, 1,* 288–308.

Ressler, R. K., Burgess, A. W., Hartman, C. R., Douglas, J. E., & McCormack, A. (1986). Murderers who rape and mutilate. *Journal of Interpersonal Violence, 1,* 273–287.

Ressler, R. K., & Shachtman, T. (1992). *Whoever fights monsters.* New York: St. Martin's Press.

Rice, M., & Harris, G. (1995). Violent recidivism: Assessing predictive validity. *Journal of Consulting and Clinical Psychology, 63,* 737–748.

Rice, M., & Harris, G. (1997). The treatment of mentally disordered offenders. *Psychology, Public Policy, and Law, 3,* 126–183.

Rideau v. Louisiana, 373 U.S. 723 (1963).

Rieke, R. D., & Stutman, R. K. (1990). *Communication in legal advocacy.* Columbia: University of South Carolina Press.

Riger, S. (1991). Gender dilemmas in sexual harassment policies and procedures. *American Psychologist, 46,* 497–505.

Riley, J. A. (1998, March). *The Revision of the Competency Assessment Instrument.* Paper presented at the meeting of the American Psychology-Law Society, Redondo Beach, CA.

Ring, K. (1971). *Let's get started: An appeal to what's left in psychology.* Unpublished manuscript, University of Connecticut, Storrs.

Risinger, D. M., & Saks, M. J. (1996). Science and non-science in the courts: *Daubert* meets handwriting identification expertise. *Iowa Law Review, 82,* 21–55.

Robinette, P. R. (1999). *Differential treatment of corporate defendants as a form of actor identity and evaluator expectations.* Unpublished doctoral dissertation, University of Kansas, Lawrence.

Robinson, E. (1935). *Law and the lawyers.* New York: Macmillan.

Rock v. Arkansas, 107 S. Ct. 2704 (1987).

Rodham, H. (1974). Children under the law. *Harvard Educational Review, 43,* 487–514.

Rodriguez, J. H., LeWinn, L. M., & Perlin, M. L. (1983). The insanity defense under siege: Legislative assaults and legal rejoinders. *Rutgers Law Journal, 14,* 397–430.

Roehl, J., & Guertin, K. (1998). *Current use of dangerousness assessments in sentencing domestic violence offenders: Final report.* Pacific Grove, CA: Justice Research Center.

Roehl, J., & Guertin, K. (2000). Intimate partner violence: The current use of risk assessments in sentencing offenders. *Justice System Journal, 21,* 171–197.

Roesch, R., & Golding, S. L. (1980). *Competency to stand trial.* Urbana: University of Illinois Press.

Roesch, R., & Golding, S. L. (1987). Defining and assessing competence to stand trial. In I. Weiner & A. Hess (Eds.), *Handbook of forensic psychology* (pp. 378–394). New York: John Wiley.

Roesch, R., Golding, S. L., Hans, V. P., & Reppucci, N. D. (1991). Social science and the courts: The role of *amicus curiae* briefs. *Law and Human Behavior, 15,* 1–11.

Roesch, R., Webster, C., & Eaves, D. (1994). *The Fitness Interview Test-Revised: A method for examining fitness to stand trial.* Burnaby, B.C., Canada: Department of Psychology, Simon Fraser University.

Roesch, R., Zapf, P. A., Eaves, D., & Webster, C. D. (1998). *The Fitness Interview Test-Revised.* Burnaby, B.C., Canada: Mental Health, Law, and Policy Institute, Simon Fraser University.

Rogers v. Richmond, 365 U.S. 534 (1960).

Rogers, R. (1984). *Rogers Criminal Responsibility Assessment Scales (R-CRAS) and test manual.* Odessa, FL: Psychological Assessment Resources.

Rogers, R. (1986). *Conducting insanity evaluations.* New York: Van Nostrand Reinhold.

Rogers, R. (1987). APA's position on the insanity defense: Empiricism versus emotionalism. *American Psychologist, 42,* 840–848.

Rogers, R. (1988). Structured interviews and dissimulation. In R. Rogers (Ed.), *Clinical assessment of malingering and deception* (pp. 250–268). New York: Guilford Press.

Rogers, R. (1990). Models of feigned mental illness. *Professional Psychology: Research and Practice, 21,* 182–188.

Rogers, R., & Cavanaugh, J. L. (1981). The Rogers Criminal Responsibility Assessment scales. *Illinois Medical Journal, 160,* 164–169.

Rogers, R., Cavanaugh, J. L., Seman, W., & Harris, M. (1984). Legal outcome and clinical findings: A study of insanity evaluations. *Bulletin of the American Academy of Psychiatry and the Law, 12,* 75–83.

Rogers, R., Dolmetsch, R., Wasyliw, O. E., & Cavanaugh, J. L. (1982). Scientific inquiry in forensic psychology. *International Journal of Law and Psychiatry, 5,* 187–203.

Rogers, R., & Ewing, C. P. (1989). Ultimate opinion proscriptions: A cosmetic fix and plea for empiricism. *Law and Human Behavior, 13,* 357–374.

Rogers, R., & Ewing, C. P. (1992). The measurement of insanity: Debating the merits of the R-CRAS and its alternatives. *International Journal of Law and Psychiatry, 15,* 113–123.

Rogers, R., Gillis, J. R., Bagby, R. M., & Monteiro, E. (1991). Detection of malingering on the Structured Interview of Reported Symptoms (SIRS): A study of coached and uncoached simulators. *Psychological Assessment: A Journal of Consulting and Clinical Psychology, 3,* 673–677.

Rogers, R., & McKee, G. R. (1995). Use of the MMPI-2 in the assessment of criminal responsibility. In Y. S. Ben-Porath, J. R. Graham, G. C. N. Hall, R. D. Hirschman, & M. S. Zaragoza (Eds.), *Forensic applications of the MMPI-2* (pp. 103–126). Thousand Oaks, CA: Sage.

Rogers, R., Sewell, K. W., & Goldstein, A. M. (1994). Explanatory models of malingering: A prototypical analysis. *Law and Human Behavior, 18,* 543–552.

Rogers, R., & Shuman, D. W. (2000). *Conducting insanity evaluations* (2nd ed.). New York: Guilford Publications.

Rogers, R., Wasyliw, O. E., & Cavanaugh, J. L. (1984). Evaluating insanity: A study of construct validity. *Law and Human Behavior, 8,* 293–303.

Rohman, L. W., Sales, B. D., & Lou, M. (1990). The best interests standard in child custody decisions.

In D. Weisstub (Ed.), *Law and mental health: International perspectives* (Vol. 5, pp. 40–90). Elmsford, NJ: Pergamon.

Romer v. Evans, 64 U.S.L.W. 4353 (1996).

Rosen, J. (1993a, November 1). Reasonable women. *New Republic,* 12–13.

Rosen, J. (1993b, November 16). Fast-food justice. *New York Times,* p. A15.

Rosen, P. (1972). *The Supreme Court and social science.* Urbana: University of Illinois Press.

Rosenbaum, R. (1993, April). The F.B.I.'s agent provocateur. *Vanity Fair,* 122–136.

Rosenberg, C. E. (1968). *The trial of the assassin Guiteau: Psychiatry and the law in the Gilded Age.* Chicago: University of Chicago Press.

Rosenberg, T. (1995, July 16). The deadliest D.A. *New York Times Magazine,* p. 20.

Rosenhan, D. L. (1973). On being sane in insane places. *Science, 179,* 250–258.

Rosenthal, R. (1995). *State of New Jersey v. Margaret Kelly Michaels:* An overview. *Psychology, Public Policy, and Law, 1,* 246–271.

Ross, L., & Nisbett, R. E. (1991). *The person and the situation.* New York: McGraw-Hill.

Ross, M. B. (1998, November 23). Capital punishment simply costs too much. *National Law Journal,* p. A22.

Rossi, D. (1982, January). Crime scene behavioral analysis: Another tool for the law enforcement investigator. *The Police Chief,* 152–155.

Roth, S., & Lebowitz, L. (1988). The experience of sexual trauma. *Journal of Traumatic Stress, 1*(1), 79–107.

Rothberg, J. M., & Geer-Williams, C. (1992). A comparison and review of suicide prediction scales. In R. W. Maris, A. L. Berman, J. T. Maltsberger, & R. I. Yufit (Eds.), *Assessment and prediction of suicide* (pp. 202–217). New York: Guilford.

Royal, R. F., & Schutt, S. R. (1976). *The gentle art of interviewing and interrogation: A professional manual and guide.* Englewood Cliffs, NJ: Prentice Hall.

Ruby, C. L., & Brigham, J. C. (1997). The usefulness of the criteria-based content analysis technique in distinguishing between truthful and fabricated allegations: A critical review. *Psychology, Public Policy, and Law, 3,* 705–737.

Ruch, L. O., Gartrell, J. W., Amedeo, S. R., & Coyne, B. J. (1991). The Sexual Assault Symptoms Scale: Measuring self-reported sexual assault trauma in the emergency room. *Psychological Assessment, 3,* 3–8.

Ruch, L. O., Gartrell, J. W., Ramelli, A., & Coyne, B. J. (1991). The Clinical Trauma Assessment: Evaluating sexual assault victims in the emergency room. *Psychological Assessment, 3,* 405–411.

Ruddy, C. (1997). *The strange death of Vincent Foster.* New York: Free Press.

Rule, A. (1989). *The stranger beside me.* New York: Signet.

Rutledge, P. B. (1996). The standard of review for the voluntariness of a confession on direct appeal in federal court. *University of Chicago Law Review, 63,* 1311–1345.

Ryan, J., & Butler, J. M. (1996, December 23). Without Supreme Court precedent, federal courts struggle with the issue of whether Title VII lawsuits may be brought for same-sex sexual harassment. *National Law Journal,* p. B8.

Sackett, P. R., & Wilk, S. L. (1994). Within-group norming and other forms of score adjustment in preemployment testing. *American Psychologist, 49,* 929–954.

Saks, M. J. (1976). The limits of scientific jury selection. *Jurimetrics Journal, 17,* 3–22.

Saks, M. J. (1977). *Jury verdicts: The role of group size and social decision rule.* Lexington, MA: D. C. Heath.

Saks, M. J. (1987). Social scientists can't rig juries. In L. S. Wrightsman, S. M. Kassin, & C. E. Willis (Eds.), *In the jury box: Controversies in the courtroom* (pp. 48–61). Thousand Oaks, CA: Sage.

Saks, M. J. (1992). Normative and empirical issues about the role of expert witnesses. In D. K. Kagehiro & W. S. Laufer (Eds.), *Handbook of psychology and law* (pp. 185–203). New York: Springer-Verlag.

Saks, M. J. (1993). Improving APA science translation *amicus* briefs. *Law and Human Behavior, 17,* 235–247.

Saks, M. J. (1998). Merlin and Solomon: Lessons from the law's formative encounters with forensic identification science. *Hastings Law Journal, 49,* 1069–1149.

Saks, M. J., & Marti, M. W. (1997). A meta-analysis of the effects of jury size. *Law and Human Behavior, 21,* 451–467.

Saks, M. J., & Van Duizend, R. (1983). *The use of scientific evidence in litigation.* Williamsburg, VA: National Center for State Courts.

Sales, B., Manber, R., & Rohman, L. (1992). Social science research and child-custody decision making. *Applied and Preventive Psychology, 1,* 23–40.

Sales, B. D., & Shuman, D. W. (Eds.). (1996). *Law, mental health, and mental disorder.* Pacific Grove, CA: Brooks/Cole.

Sanders, G. S., & Stanley, S. C. (1994, February 28). Courts contemplate harassment claims after *Harris* decision. *National Law Journal,* pp. S10–S12.

Sanders, J. (1992). The Bendectin litigations: A case study in the life cycle of mass torts. *Hastings Law Journal, 43,* 301–413.

Sanders, J. (1993). From science to evidence: The testimony on causation in the Bendectin cases. *Stanford Law Review, 46,* 1–86.

Sanders, J. (1994). Scientific validity, admissibility, and mass torts after *Daubert. Minnesota Law Review, 78,* 1387–1441.

Sanders, L. (1981). *The third deadly sin*. New York: Berkeley.

Sanders, R. (1989, August). Self-defense: Battered woman syndrome. *The Advocate*, 37–45.

Sasaki, D. W. (1988). Guarding the guardians: Police trickery and confessions. *Stanford Law Review, 40*, 1593–1616.

Sattler, J. M. (1991). How good are federal judges in detecting differences in item difficulty on intelligence tests for ethnic groups? *Psychological Assessment, 3*, 125–129.

Saunders, D. (1992). A typology of men who batter women: Three types derived from cluster analysis. *American Journal of Orthopsychiatry, 62*, 264–275.

Saunders, D. (1994). Child custody decisions in families experiencing woman abuse. *Social Work, 39*, 51–59.

Saunders, D. (1995). Prediction of wife assault. In J. C. Campbell (Ed.), *Assessing dangerousness: Violence by sexual offenders, batterers, and child abusers* (pp. 68–95). Thousand Oaks, CA: Sage.

Saxton v. American Telephone and Telegraph Co., No. 92-1545, 1993 U.S. App. LEXIS 31599 (7th Cir. Dec. 3, 1993).

Saywitz, K., Geiselman, R. E., & Bornstein, G. (1992). Effects of cognitive interviewing and practice on children's recall performance. *Journal of Applied Psychology, 77*, 744–756.

Saywitz, K., & Snyder, L. (1996). Narrative elaboration: Test of a new procedure for interviewing children. *Journal of Consulting and Clinical Psychology, 64*, 1347–1357.

Saywitz, K. J., & Dorado, J. S. (1998). Interviewing children when sexual abuse is suspected. In G. P. Koocher, J. C. Norcross, & S. S. Hill, III (Eds.), *Psychologists' desk reference* (pp. 503–509). New York: Oxford University Press.

Saywitz, K. J., Goodman, G. S., Nicholas, E., & Moan, S. F. (1991). Children's memories of a physical examination involving genital touch: Implications for reports of child sexual abuse. *Journal of Consulting and Clinical Psychology, 59*, 682–691.

Scaduto, A. (1976). *Scapegoat: The lonesome death of Bruno Richard Hauptmann*. New York: G. P. Putnam.

Schall v. Martin, 467 U.S. 253 (1984).

Scheflin, A. W., & Shapiro, J. L. (1989). *Trance on trial*. New York: Guilford Press.

Scheflin, A. W., Spiegel, H., & Spiegel, D. (1999). Forensic uses of hypnosis. In A. K. Hess & I. B. Weiner (Eds.), *The handbook of forensic psychology* (2nd ed., pp. 474–498). New York: John Wiley.

Scheid, T. L. (1999). Employment of individuals with mental disabilities: Business' response to the ADA's challenge. *Behavioral Sciences and the Law, 17*, 73–91.

Schmalleger, F. (1995). *Criminal justice today* (3rd ed.). Englewood, Cliffs, NJ: Prentice Hall.

Schneider, B. E. (1987). Graduate women, sexual harassment, and university policy. *Journal of Higher Education, 58*(1), 46–65.

Schneider, E. M. (1986). Describing and changing: Women's self-defense work and the problem of expert testimony on battering. *Women's Rights Law Reporter, 9*(3-4), 195–222.

Schretlen, D. (1986). *Malingering: Use of a psychological test battery to detect two kinds of simulation*. Ann Arbor, MI: University Microfilms International.

Schulhofer, S. J. (1996). *Miranda*'s practical effect: Substantial benefits and vanishingly small social costs. *Northwestern University Law School, 90*, 500–564.

Schulhofer, S. J. (1999, March 1). "Miranda" now on endangered species list. *National Law Journal*, p. A22.

Schuller, R. A. (1992). The impact of battered woman syndrome evidence on jury decision processes. *Law and Human Behavior, 16*, 597–620.

Schuller, R. A. (1994). Applications of battered woman syndrome evidence in the courtroom. In M. Costanzo & S. Oskamp (Eds.), *Violence and the law* (pp. 113–134). Thousand Oaks, CA: Sage.

Schuller, R. A., & Vidmar, N. (1992). Battered woman syndrome evidence in the courtroom: A review of the literature. *Law and Human Behavior, 16*, 273–291.

Schuller, R. A., Smith, V. L., & Olson, J. M. (1994). Jurors' decisions in trials of battered women who kill: The role of prior beliefs and expert testimony. *Journal of Applied Social Psychology, 24*, 316–337.

Schulman, J., Shaver, P., Colman, R., Emrich, B., & Christie, R. (1973, May). Recipe for a jury. *Psychology Today*, 37–44, 77–84.

Schulman, M. (1979). *A survey of spousal violence against women in Kentucky*. Washington, DC: Law Enforcement.

Schutz, B. M., Dixon, E. B., Lindenberger, J. C., & Ruther, N. J. (1989). *Solomon's sword: A practical guide to conducting child custody evaluations*. San Francisco: Jossey-Bass.

Schwartz, B. (1988). *Behind Bakke: Affirmative action and the Supreme Court*. New York: New York University Press.

Scogin, F., Schumacher, J., Howland, K., & McGee, J. (1989, August). *The predictive validity of psychological testing and peer evaluations in law enforcement settings*. Paper presented at the meeting of the American Psychological Association, New Orleans.

Scott, E. (1992). Judgment and reasoning in adolescent decision making. *Villanova Law Review, 37*, 1607–1699.

Scott, E., & Derdeyn, A. P. (1984). Rethinking joint custody. *Ohio State Law Journal, 45*, 455–498.

Scott, E., Reppucci, N., & Woolard, J. (1995). Evaluating adolescent decision making in legal contexts. *Law and Human Behavior, 19*, 221–244.

Sears v. Rutishauser, 466 N.E.2d 210, Ill. (1984).

Sears, D. O. (1988). Symbolic racism. In P. A. Katz & D. A. Taylor (Eds.), *Eliminating racism: Profiles in controversy* (pp. 53–84). New York: Plenum.

Seelye, K. Q. (1994, May 12). Senate rejects race-based death row challenges. *New York Times,* p. A10.

Seligman, M. E. P. (1975). *Helplessness: On depression, development, and death.* San Francisco: W. H. Freeman.

Seligman, M. E. P., & Maier, S. F. (1967). Failure to escape traumatic shock. *Journal of Experimental Psychology, 74,* 1–9.

Selkin, J. (1987). *The psychological autopsy in the courtroom: Contributions of the social sciences to resolving issues surrounding equivocal deaths.* Denver, CO: Author.

Selkin, J., & Loya, J. (1979, February). Issues in the psychological autopsy of a controversial public figure. *Professional Psychology,* 87–93.

Selzer, M. L. (1971). The Michigan Alcoholism Screening Test: The quest for a new diagnostic instrument. *American Journal of Psychiatry, 127,* 1653–1658.

Semler, C., Brewer, N., & Wells, G. L. (in press). Effects of postidentification feedback on eyewitness identification and nonidentification. *Journal of Applied Psychology.*

Seppa, N. (1997, May). Sexual harassment in the military lingers on. *APA Monitor,* 40–41.

Serrill, M. S. (1984, September 17). Breaking the spell of hypnosis. *Time,* 62.

Shaffer, M. B. (1992). Review of the Bricklin Perceptual Scales. In J. J. Kramer & J. C. Conoley (Eds.), *Eleventh mental measurements yearbook* (pp. 118–119). Lincoln: University of Nebraska Press.

Shaw, J. S., III. (1996). Increases in eyewitness confidence resulting from postevent questioning. *Journal of Experimental Psychology: Applied, 2,* 126–146.

Shaw, J. S., Garven, S., & Wood, J. M. (1997). Co-witness information can alter witnesses' immediate memory reports. *Law and Human Behavior, 21,* 503–523.

Shaw, J. S., III, & McClure, K. A. (1996). Repeated postevent questioning can lead to elevated levels of eyewitness confidence. *Law and Human Behavior, 20,* 629–653.

Sheppard v. Maxwell, 384 U.S. 333 (1966).

Sherman, R. (1993, October 4). "Junk science" rule used broadly. *National Law Journal,* pp. 3, 28.

Shiller, V. M. (1986a). Joint versus maternal custody for families with latency age boys: Parent characteristics and child adjustment. *American Journal of Orthopsychiatry, 56,* 486–489.

Shiller, V. M. (1986b). Loyalty conflicts and family relationships in latency age boys: A comparison of joint and maternal custody. *Journal of Divorce, 9,* 17–38.

Shneidman, E. S. (1981). The psychological autopsy. *Suicide and Life-Threatening Behavior, 11,* 325–340.

Shneidman, E. S., & Farberow, N. L. (1961). Sample investigations of equivocal deaths. In N. L. Farberow & E. S. Shneidman (Eds.), *The cry for help* (pp. 118–129). New York: McGraw-Hill.

Shusman, E. J., & Inwald, R. E. (1991a). A longitudinal validation study of correctional officer job performance as predicted by the IPI and the MMPI. *Journal of Criminal Justice, 19*(4), 173–180.

Shusman, E. J., & Inwald, R. E. (1991b). Predictive validity of the Inwald Personality Inventory. *Criminal Justice and Behavior, 18,* 419–426.

Shusman, E. J., Inwald, R. E., & Knatz, H. F. (1987). A cross-validation study of police recruit performance as predicted by the IPI and MMPI. *Journal of Police Science and Administration, 15,* 162–169.

Shusman, E. J., Inwald, R., & Landa, B. (1984). A validation study of correction officer job performance as predicted by the IPI and MMPI. *Criminal Justice and Behavior, 11,* 309–329.

Shuy, R. W. (1998). *The language of confession, interrogation, and deception.* Thousand Oaks, CA: Sage.

Siegal, M., Waters, L. J., & Dinwiddy, L. S. (1988). Misleading children: Causal attributions for inconsistency under repeated questioning. *Journal of Experimental Child Psychology, 45,* 438–456.

Silver, E., Cirincione, C., & Steadman, H. J. (1994). Demythologizing inaccurate perceptions of the insanity defense. *Law and Human Behavior, 18,* 63–70.

Silver, E., Mulvey, E. P., & Monahan, J. (1999). Assessing violence risk among discharged psychiatric patients: Toward an ecological approach. *Law and Human Behavior, 23,* 235–253.

Silverstein, J. M. (1985). The psychologist as panel member. *Social Action and the Law, 11*(3), 72–74.

Silverton, L., & Gruber, C. (1998). *Malingering Probability Scale (MPS) Manual.* Los Angeles: Western Psychological Services.

Silverton, L., Gruber, C. P., & Bindman, S. (1993, August). *The Malingering Probability Scale for Mental Disorders (MPS-MD): A scale to detect malingering.* Paper presented at the meeting of the American Psychological Association, Toronto.

Simmons v. United States, 390 U.S. 385 (1968).

Simon, D. (1991). *Homicide: A year on the killing streets.* New York: Ivy Books.

Simpson, B., Jensen, E., & Owen, J. (1988, October). Police employee assistance program. *The Police Chief,* 83–85.

Sinclair v. United States, 279 U.S. 749 (1929).

Singleton, G. W., & Teahan, J. (1978). Effects of job related stress on the physical and psychological adjustment of police officers. *Journal of Police Science and Administration, 6,* 355–361.

Sjostedt, G., & Langstrom, N. (2001). Actuarial assessment of sex offender recidivism risk: A cross-validation of the RRASOR and the Static-99 in Sweden. *Law and Human Behavior, 25,* 629–645.

Skafte, D. (1985). *Child custody evaluations: A practical guide.* Thousand Oaks, CA: Sage.

Skedsvold, P. R., & Mann, T. L. (1996a). Affirmative action: Linking research, policy, and implementation. *Journal of Social Issues, 52*(4), 3–18.

Skedsvold, P. R., & Mann, T. L. (Eds.). (1996b). The affirmative action debate: What's fair in policy and programs? *Journal of Social Issues, 52*(4), 1–160.

Skeem, J. L., Golding, S. L., Cohn, N. B., & Berge, G. (1998). Logic and reliability of evaluations of competence to stand trial. *Law and Human Behavior, 22,* 519–547.

Skinner, L. J., & Berry, K. K. (1993). Anatomically detailed dolls and the evaluation of child sexual abuse allegations. *Law and Human Behavior, 17,* 399–421.

Skolnick, J. H. (1966). *Justice without trial: Law enforcement in a democratic society.* New York: John Wiley.

Skolnick, J. H., & Bayley, D. H. (1986). *The new blue line: Police innovation in six American cities.* New York: Free Press.

Skolnick, J. H., & Leo, R. A. (1992). The ethics of deceptive interrogation. In J. W. Bizzack (Ed.), *Issues in policing: New perspectives* (pp. 75–95). Lexington, KY: Auburn House.

Slade, M. (1994, February 25). Law firms begin reining in sex-harassing partners. *New York Times,* p. B12.

Slind-Flor, V. (1994, March 14). Helping judges to judge science. *National Law Journal,* pp. A5, A12.

Slobogin, C. (1985). The guilty but mentally ill verdict: An idea whose time should not have come. *George Washington Law Review, 53,* 494–527.

Slobogin, C. (1996). Dangerousness as a criterion in the criminal process. In B. D. Sales & D. W. Shuman (Eds.), *Law, mental health, and mental disorder* (pp. 360–383). Pacific Grove, CA: Brooks/Cole.

Slobogin, C. (1997). Deceit, pretext, and trickery: Investigate laws by the police. *Oregon Law Review, 76,* 775–816.

Slobogin, C., Melton, G. B., & Showalter, C. R. (1984). The feasibility of a brief evaluation of mental state at the time of the offense. *Law and Human Behavior, 8,* 305–321.

Small, M. A. (1988). Performing competency to be executed evaluations: A psycholegal analysis for preventing the execution of the insane. *Nebraska Law Review, 67,* 718–734.

Smith, D. H., & Stotland, E. (1973). A new look at police officer selection. In J. R. Snibbe & H. M. Snibbe (Eds.), *The urban policeman in transition* (pp. 5–24). Springfield, IL: Charles C Thomas.

Smith, G. P., & Burger, G. (1993, August). *Detection of malingering: A validation test of the SLAM Test.* Paper presented at the meeting of the American Psychological Association, Toronto.

Smith, M. C. (1983). Hypnotic memory enhancement of witnesses: Does it work? *Psychological Bulletin, 94,* 387–407.

Sorensen, J., & Wrinkle, R. D. (1996). No hope for parole: Disciplinary infractions among death- sentenced and life-without-parole inmates. *Criminal Justice and Behavior, 23,* 542–552.

Soskis, D. A. (1983). Behavioral sciences and law enforcement personnel: Working together on the problem of terrorism. *Behavioral Sciences and the Law, 1,* 47–58.

Spano v. New York, 360 U.S. 315 (1959).

Sparrow, M. K., Moore, M. H., & Kennedy, D. M. (1990). *Beyond 911: A new era of policing.* New York: Basic Books.

Spence, G. (1995). *How to argue and win every time.* New York: St. Martin's Press.

Spencer, J. R. (1998). The role of experts in the common law and the civil law: A comparison. In S. J. Ceci & H. Hembrooke (Eds.), *Expert witnesses in child abuse cases* (pp. 29–58). Washington, DC: American Psychological Association.

Spencer, J. R., & Flin, R. (1990). *The evidence of children.* London: Blackstone.

Spiecker, S. C. (1998). *The influence of opening statement/closing argument organizational strategy on juror decision making.* Unpublished doctoral dissertation, University of Kansas, Lawrence.

Spiecker, S. C., & Worthington, D. L. (2003). The influence of opening statement/closing argument strategy on juror verdict and damage awards. *Law and Human Behavior, 27,* 437–456.

Spiegel, D., & Spiegel, H. (1987). Forensic uses of hypnosis. In I. B. Weiner and A. K. Hess (Eds.), *Handbook of forensic psychology* (pp. 490–507). New York: John Wiley.

Spiegel, H., & Spiegel, D. (1978). *Trance and treatment: Clinical uses of hypnosis.* New York: Basic Books.

Spielberger, C. D. (Ed.). (1979). *Police selection and evaluation: Issues and problems.* Washington, DC: Hemisphere.

Sporer, S. L. (1981). *Toward a comprehensive history of legal psychology.* Unpublished manuscript, University of Erlagen-Nürnberg. (Cited by Wells and Loftus, 1984).

Sporer, S. L. (1993). Eyewitness identification accuracy, confidence, and decision times in simultaneous and sequential lineups. *Journal of Applied Psychology, 78,* 22–33.

Stahl, P. M. (1994). *Conducting child custody evaluations: A comprehensive guide.* Thousand Oaks, CA: Sage.

Stahl, P. M. (1999a). *Complex issues in child custody evaluations.* Thousand Oaks, CA: Sage.

Stahl, P. M. (1999b, Fall). Starting a child custody evaluation practice. *Academy of Family Psychology Newsletter, 2(2),* 6–7.

Stanford v. Kentucky, 492 U.S. 361 (1989).

Starr, V. H., & Kauffman, K. (1993, July). Ethical issues: You make the call. *Court Call,* p. 5.

State v. Alberico, 116 N.M. 156, 861 P.2d 192 (1993).

State v. Cressey, 628 A.2d 696 (N.H. 1993).

State v. Echols, 128 Ohio App.3d 677 (1998).

State v. Horne, 710 S.W.2d 310 (Mo. Ct. App. 1986).

State v. Hurd, 86 N.J. 525, 432 A.2d 86 (1981).

State v. Jackson, 308 N.C. 549 (1983).

State v. Kelly, 478 A.2d 364 (1984).

State v. Lewis, 848 P.2d 394 (Idaho, 1993).

State v. Lowe, 599 N.E.2d 783 (Ohio, 1991).

State v. Marks, 231 Kan. 647 P.2d 1292 (1982).

State v. McCoy, 179 W.Va. 223, 386 S.E.2d 731 (1988).

State v. McQuillen, 236 Kan. 689 P.2d 822 (1984).

State v. Michaels, 625 A.2d 489 (N.J. Sup. Ct. App. Div. 1993).

State v. Milbradt, 756 P.2d 620 (Ore. 1988).

State v. Rimmasch, 775 P.2d 388 (Utah 1989).

State v. Rossell, 113 Mont. 457, 127 P.2d 379 (1942).

State v. Saldana, Minn. 324 N.W.2d 227 (1982).

State v. Willis, 256 Kan. 837, 888 P.2d 192 (1993).

Steadman, H. (1993). *Reforming the insanity defense: An evaluation of pre- and post-Hinckley reforms.* New York: Guilford.

Steadman, H. J., & Cocozza, J. J. (1974). *Careers of the criminally insane: Excessive social control of deviance.* Lexington, MA: Lexington Books.

Steadman, H. J., & Hartshorne, E. (1983). Defendants incompetent to stand trial. In J. Monahan & H. J. Steadman (Eds.), *Mentally disordered offenders: Perspectives from law and social science* (pp. 39–64). New York: Plenum.

Steadman, H. J., Robbins, P. C., Monahan, J., Appelbaum, P., Grisso, T., Mulvey, E. P., & Roth, L. (1996). The MacArthur Violence Risk Assessment Study. *American Psychology-Law Society News, 16(3),* 1–4.

Steblay, N., Besirevic, J., Fulero, S., & Jimenez-Lorente, B. (1999). The effects of pretrial publicity on juror verdicts: A meta-analytic review. *Law and Human Behavior, 23,* 219–235.

Steblay, N. M. (1997). Social influence in eyewitness recall: A meta-analytic review of lineup instruction effects. *Law and Human Behavior, 21,* 283–298.

Steblay, N. M., & Bothwell, R. K. (1994). Evidence for hypnotically refreshed testimony: The view from the laboratory. *Law and Human Behavior, 18,* 635–651.

Steblay, N., Dysart, J., Fulero, S., & Lindsay, R. C. L. (2003). A meta-analytic comparison of showup and lineup identification accuracy. *Law and Human Behavior, 27,* 523–540.

Steinberg, L., & Cauffman, E. (1996). Maturity of judgment in adolescence: Psychosocial factors in adolescent decision making. *Law and Human Behavior, 20,* 249–272.

Steinman, S. (1981). The experience of children in a joint-custody arrangement: A report of a study. *American Journal of Orthopsychiatry, 51,* 403–414.

Steinman, S. B., Zemmelman, S. E., & Knoblauch, T. M. (1985). A study of parents who sought joint custody following divorce: Who reaches agreement and sustains joint custody and who returns to court. *Journal of the American Academy of Child Psychiatry, 24,* 554–562.

Steketee, G., & Foa, E. B. (1987). Rape victims: Posttraumatic stress responses and their treatment. *Journal of Anxiety Disorders, 1,* 69–86.

Steller, M., & Koehnken, G. (1989). Criteria-based statement analysis. In D. C. Raskin (Ed.), *Psychological methods in criminal investigation and evidence* (pp. 217–245). New York: Springer.

Stern, L. W. (1903). *Beiträge zur Psychologie der Aussage* [Contributions to the Psychology of Testimony]. Leipzig: Verlag Barth.

Stern, W. (1939). The psychology of testimony. *Journal of Abnormal and Social Psychology, 34,* 3–20.

Stevens, J. A. (1997). Standard investigatory tools and offender profiling. In J. L. Jackson & D. A. Bekerian (Eds.), *Offender profiling: Theory, research and practice* (pp. 76–91). New York: John Wiley.

Stewart, J. B. (1998, March 30). The bench: A pocket primer for the president, in case he's deposed again. *New Yorker,* p. 43.

Stinson, V., Devenport, J. L., Cutler, B. L., & Kravitz, D. A. (1996). How effective is the presence-of-counsel safeguard? Attorney perceptions of suggestiveness, fairness, and correctability of biased lineup procedures. *Journal of Applied Psychology, 81,* 64–75.

Stovall v. Denno, 388 U.S. 293 (1967).

Stratton, J. (1978). The police department psychologist: Is there any value? *The Police Chief, 44(5),* 70–74.

Stratton, J. A. (1980). Psychological services for police. *Journal of Police Science and Administration, 8,* 31–39.

Straus, M. A. (1979). Measuring family conflict and violence: The conflict tactics scale. *Journal of Marriage and the Family, 41,* 75–88.

Straus, M. A., & Gelles, R. J. (1986). Societal change in family violence from 1975 to 1985 as revealed by two national surveys. *Journal of Marriage and the Family, 48,* 465–479.

Straus, M. A., & Gelles, R. J. (1988). How violent are American families? Estimates from the National Family Violence Resurvey and other studies. In G. T. Hotaling, D. Finkelhor, J. T. Kirkpatrick, & M. A.

Straus (Eds.), *Family abuse and its consequences* (pp. 14–36). Newbury Park, CA: Sage.

Straus, M. A., Gelles, R. J., & Steinmetz, S. (1980). *Behind closed doors: Violence in the American family.* Garden City, NY: Doubleday Anchor.

Strawbridge, P., & Strawbridge, D. (1990). *A networking guide to recruitment, selection, and probationary training of police officers in major police departments in the United States of America.* New York: John Jay College of Criminal Justice.

Strickland v. Washington, 466 U.S. 668 (1984).

Strier, F. (1998, March). *The future of trial consulting: Issues and projections.* Paper presented at the meeting of the American Psychology-Law Society, Redondo Beach, CA.

Strier, F. (1999). Whither trial consulting: Issues and projections. *Law and Human Behavior, 23,* 93–115.

Studebaker, C. A., & Penrod, S. D. (1997). Pretrial publicity: The media, the law, and common sense. *Psychology, Public Policy, and Law, 3,* 428–460.

Studebaker, C. A., Robbennolt, J. K., Pathak-Sharma, M. K., & Penrod, S. D. (2000). Assessing pretrial publicity effects: Integrating content analytic results. *Law and Human Behavior, 24,* 317–336.

Studebaker, C. A., Robbennolt, J. K., Penrod, S. D., Pathak-Sharma, M. K., Groscup, J. L., & Devenport, J. L. (2002). Studying pretrial publicity effects: New methods for testing and improving external validity. *Law and Human Behavior, 26,* 19–41.

Stuntz, W. J. (1989). Waiving rights in criminal procedure. *Virginia Law Review, 75,* 761–824.

Sue, S., Smith, R. E., & Pedroza, G. (1975). Authoritarianism, pretrial publicity and awareness of bias in simulated jurors. *Psychological Reports, 37,* 1299–1302.

Sullivan, K., & Sevilla, G. (1993, August 30–September 5). A look inside a rapist's mind. *Washington Post National Weekly Edition,* p. 32.

Summit, R. (1983). The child sexual abuse accommodation syndrome. *Child Abuse and Neglect,* 7(2), 177–192.

Summit, R. (1992). Abuse of the child sexual abuse accommodation syndrome. *Journal of Child Sexual Abuse, 1*(4), 153–161.

Swartz, J. D. (1985). Review of Inwald Personality Inventory. In J. V. Mitchell (Ed.), *Ninth mental measurements yearbook* (pp. 713–714). Lincoln: Buros Institute of Mental Measurements, University of Nebraska.

Swartz, M. (1997, November 17). Family secret. *New Yorker,* 90–107.

Swenson, W. M., & Grimes, P. B. (1969). Characteristics of sex offenders admitted to a Minnesota state hospital for pre-sentence psychiatric investigation. *Psychiatric Quarterly Supplement, 34,* 110–123.

Swisher, K. (1994, February 14–20). Corporations are seeing the light on harassment. *Washington Post National Weekly Edition,* p. 21.

Symposium. (1994). Scientific evidence after the death of Frye. *Cardozo Law Review, 15,* 1745– 2294.

Tagatz v. Marquette University, 861 F.2d 1040 (1988).

Takanishi, R., & Melton, G. B. (1987). Child development research and the legislative process. In G. B. Melton (Ed.), *Reforming the law: Impact of child development research* (pp. 86– 101). New York: Guilford.

Tanford, J. A. (1990). The limits of a scientific jurisprudence: The Supreme Court and psychology. *Indiana Law Journal, 66,* 137–173.

Tanford, J. A., & Tanford, S. (1988). Better trials through science: A defense of psychologist-lawyer collaboration. *North Carolina Law Review, 66,* 741–780.

Tanke, E. D., & Tanke, T. J. (1977). The psychology of the jury: An annotated bibliography. *JSAS Catalog of Selected Documents in Psychology, 7,* 108. (Ms No. 1591).

Tanke, E. D., & Tanke, T. J. (1979). Getting off a slippery slope: Social science in the judicial process. *American Psychologist, 34,* 1130–1138.

Tapp, J. L. (1976). Psychology and the law: An overture. *Annual Review of Psychology, 27,* 359–404.

Tapp, J. L. (1977). Psychology and the law: A look at the interface. In B. D. Sales (Ed.), *Psychology in the legal process* (pp. 1–15). New York: Spectrum.

Tasker, F., & Golombok, S. (1995). Adults raised as children in lesbian families. *American Journal of Orthopsychiatry, 65,* 203–215.

Taylor, R. (1990). The *Larry P.* decision a decade later: Problems and future directions. *Mental Retardation, 28*(1), 3–6.

Taylor, S. (1982, September). Too much justice. *Harpers Magazine,* 56–66.

Technical Working Group on Eyewitness Evidence (1999). *Eyewitness evidence: A guide for law enforcement* (Document No. NCJ 178240). Washington, DC: United States Department of Justice, National Institute of Justice. Available at *http://www.oip.usdoj.gov.*

Technical Working Group on Eyewitness Evidence (2003). *Eyewitness evidence: A trainer's manual for law enforcement* (Document No. NCJ 188678). Washington, DC: United States Department of Justice, National Institute of Justice.

Terman, L. M. (1917). A trial of mental and pedagogical tests in a civil service examination for policemen and firemen. *Journal of Applied Psychology, 1,* 17–29.

Terpstra, D. E., & Baker, D. D. (1987). A hierarchy of sexual harassment. *Journal of Psychology, 121,* 599–605.

Terpstra, D. E., & Baker, D. D. (1988). Outcomes of sexual harassment charges. *Academy of Management Journal, 31,* 185–194.

Terpstra, D. E., & Baker, D. D. (1992). Outcomes of federal court decisions on sexual harassment. *Academy of Management Journal, 35,* 181–190.

Terry, D. (1995, August 8). Black journalist granted stay of execution by judge who sentenced him. *New York Times,* p. A6.

Terry, D. (1998, November 16). Survivors make the case against death row. *New York Times,* p. A12.

Thibaut, J., & Walker, L. (1975). *Procedural justice: A psychological analysis.* Hillsdale, NJ: Lawrence Erlbaum Associates.

Thibaut, J., & Walker, L. (1978). A theory of procedure. *California Law Review, 66,* 541–566.

Thomann, D. A., & Wiener, R. L. (1987). Physical and psychological causality as determinants of culpability in sexual harassment cases. *Sex Roles, 17,* 573–591.

Thomas, J. G. (1979). Police use of trickery as an interrogation technique. *Vanderbilt Law Review, 32,* 1167–1213.

Thompson, R. A. (1983). The father's case in child custody disputes: The contributions of psychological research. In M. E. Lamb & A. Sagi (Eds.), *Fatherhood and family policy.* Hillsdale, NJ: Erlbaum.

Thompson, W. C. (1989a). Are juries competent to evaluate statistical evidence? *Law and Contemporary Problems, 52,* 9–41.

Thompson, W. C. (1989b). Death qualification after *Wainwright v. Witt* and *Lockhart v. McCree. Law and Human Behavior, 13,* 185–215.

Thornberry, T. P., & Jacoby, J. E. (1979). *The criminally insane: A community follow-up of mentally ill offenders.* Chicago: University of Chicago Press.

Tison v. Arizona, 481 U.S. 137 (1987).

Toch, H. (1961). *Legal and criminal psychology.* New York: Holt, Rinehart & Winston.

Tolman, R. M., & Bennett, L. W. (1990). A review of research on men who batter. *Journal of Interpersonal Violence, 5,* 87–118.

Tomkins, A. J. (1995). Introduction to behavioral science evidence in the wake of *Daubert. Behavioral Sciences and the Law, 13,* 127–130.

Tomkins, A. J., & Cecil, J. S. (1987, August). *The use of social science in constitutional decision making.* Paper presented at the meeting of the American Psychological Association, New York.

Tomkins, A. J., & Oursland, K. (1991). Social and social science perspectives in judicial interpretations of the Constitution: A historical view and an overview. *Law and Human Behavior, 15,* 101–120.

Tomkins, A. J., & Pfeifer, J. E. (1992). Modern social scientific theories and data concerning discrimination: Implications for using social science evidence in the courts. In D. K. Kagehiro & W. S. Laufer (Eds.), *Handbook of psychology and law* (pp. 385–407). New York: Springer-Verlag.

Toobin, J. (1994, October 31). Juries on trial. *New Yorker,* 42–47.

Toufexis, A. (1989, February 6). The lasting worlds of divorce. *Time,* 61.

Toufexis, A. (1991, May 6). Mind games with monsters. *Time,* 68–69.

Tremper, C. (1987). Organized psychology's efforts to influence judicial policy-making. *American Psychologist, 42,* 496–501.

Trone, J. (1999). *Calculating intimate danger: Mosaic and the emerging practice of risk assessment.* New York: Vera Institute of Justice.

Tversky, A., & Kahneman, D. (1973). Availability: A heuristic for judging frequency and probability. *Cognitive Psychology, 5,* 207–232.

Tversky, A., & Kahneman, D. (1974). Judgment under uncertainty: Heuristics and biases. *Science, 185,* 1124–1131.

Tversky, A., & Kahneman, D. (1983). Extensional versus intuitive reasoning: The conjunction fallacy in probability judgment. *Psychological Bulletin, 90,* 293–315.

Tyler, T. R., & Folger, R. (1980). Distributional and procedural aspects of satisfaction with citizen-police encounters. *Basic and Applied Social Psychology, 1,* 281–292.

U.S. Equal Employment Opportunity Commission. Final amendment to guidelines on discrimination because of sex under Title VII of the Civil Rights Act of 1964, as amended. 29 C.F.R., pt. 1604. 45 Fed. Reg. 74,675–74,677 (Nov. 10, 1980).

Ulrich, D., & Trumbo, D. (1965). The selection interview since 1949. *Psychological Bulletin, 63,* 100–116.

Underwager, R., & Wakefield, H. (1992). Poor psychology produces poor law. *Law and Human Behavior, 16,* 233–243.

Undeutsch, U. (1982). Statement reality analysis. In A. Trankell (Ed.), *Reconstructing the past: The role of psychologists in criminal trials* (pp. 27–56). Stockholm: Norstedt & Somers.

Undeutsch, U. (1984). Courtroom evaluations of eyewitness testimony. *International Review of Applied Psychology, 33,* 51–67.

Undeutsch, U. (1989). The development of statement reality analysis. In J. C. Yuille (Ed.), *Credibility assessment* (pp. 101–120). Dordrecht, The Netherlands: Kluwer.

Uniform Marriage and Divorce Act. (1979). Uniform Laws Annotated, 9A.

United States v. Ash, 413 U.S. 300 (1973).

United States v. Brawner, 471 F.2d 969 (D.C. Cir. 1972).

United States v. Castaneda-Castaneda, 729 F.2d 1360 (11th Cir. 1984).

United States v. Crumby, 895 F. Supp. 1354 (D. Ariz. 1995).

United States v. Dickerson, No. 97-4750 (1999).

United States v. Gillespie, 852 F.2d 475 (1988).

United States v. Hall, 93 F.3d 1337 (7th Cir. 1996).

United States v. Lech, 895 F. Supp. 582 (S.D.N.Y. 1995).

United States v. Norwood, 939 F. Supp. 1132 (Dist. Ct. N.J. 1996).

United States v. Scheffer, 118 S. Ct. 1261 (1998).

United States v. Smithers, 212 F.3d 306 (2000).

United States v. Wade, 388 U.S. 218 (1967).

United States National Commission on Law Observance and Enforcement. (1931). *Report on lawlessness in law enforcement.* Washington, DC: U.S. Government Printing Office.

Ustad, K. L., Rogers, R., Sewell, K. W., & Guarnaccia, C. A. (1996). Restoration of competency to stand trial: Assessment with the Georgia Court Competency Test and the Competency Screening Test. *Law and Human Behavior, 20,* 131–146.

Van den Haag, E. (1960). Social science testimony in the desegregation cases: A reply to Professor Kenneth Clark. *Villanova Law Review, 6,* 69–79.

Van den Haag, E. (1975). *Punishing criminals.* New York: Basic Books.

Verhovek, S. H. (1993, May 5). Investigators puzzle over last minutes of Koresh. *New York Times,* p. A10.

Verhovek, S. H. (1995, February 22). Across the U.S., executions are neither swift nor cheap. *New York Times,* pp. A1, A12.

Vermunt, R., Blaauw, E., & Lind, E. A. (1998). Fairness evaluations of encounters with police officers and correctional officers. *Journal of Applied Social Psychology, 28,* 1107–1124.

Veronen, L. J., Kilpatrick, D. G., & Resick, P. A. (1979). Treatment of fear and anxiety in rape victims: Implications for the criminal justice system. In W. H. Parsonage (Ed.), *Perspectives on victimology* (pp. 148–159). Thousand Oaks, CA: Sage.

Vick, D. W. (1995). Poorhouse justice: Underfunded indigent defense services and arbitrary death sentences. *Buffalo Law Review, 43,* 329–460.

Vidmar, N. (1995). *Medical malpractice and the American jury.* Ann Arbor: University of Michigan Press.

Vidmar, N. (2002). Case studies of pre- and midtrial prejudice in criminal and civil litigation. *Law and Human Behavior, 26,* 73–106.

Vidmar, N., Lempert, R. O., Diamond, S. S., Hans, V. P., Landsman, S., MacCoun, R., et al., (1998). *In the Supreme Court of the United States. Kumho Tire Company, Ltd., et al., v. Patrick Carmichael, et al.* (*Amicus* brief)

Visher, G. (1987). Juror decision making: The importance of evidence. *Law and Human Behavior, 11,* 1–14.

Volgy, S. S., & Everett, C. A. (1985). Joint custody reconsidered: Systemic criteria for mediation. *Journal of Divorce, 8,* 131–150.

Volokh, E. (1992). Freedom of speech and workplace harassment. *U.C.L.A. Law Review, 39,*1791–1872.

Von Drehle, D. (1995). *Among the lowest of the dead: The culture of death row.* New York: Times Books/Random House.

Vorpagel, R. E. (1982, January). Painting psychological profiles: Charlatanism, charisma, or a new science? *The Police Chief,* 156–159.

Vuyanich v. Republic National Bank, 723 F.2d 1195 (1984).

Wagenaar, W. A. (1988). *Identifying Ivan.* Cambridge, MA: Harvard University Press.

Waid, W. M., Orne, E. C., & Orne, M. T. (1981). Selective memory for social information, alertness, and physiological arousal in the detection of deception. *Journal of Applied Psychology, 66,* 224–232.

Wainwright v. Witt, 469 U.S. 412 (1985).

Wakefield, H., & Underwager, R. (1998). Coerced or nonvoluntary confessions. *Behavioral Sciences and the Law, 16,* 423–440.

Wald, M., Ayres, R., Hess, D. W., Schantz, M., & Whitebread, C. H. (1967). Interrogations in New Haven: The impact of *Miranda. Yale Law Journal, 76,* 1519–1648.

Waldo, C. R., Berdahl, J. L., & Fitzgerald, L. F. (1998). Are men sexually harassed? If so, by whom? *Law and Human Behavior, 22,* 59–79.

Walker, L., & Monahan, J. (1987). Social frameworks: A new use of social science in law. *Virginia Law Review, 73,* 559–612.

Walker, L. E. (1998, August). *Forensic psychology: Psychologists, Solomon, and child custody decisions.* Symposium introduction presented at the meeting of the American Psychological Association, San Francisco.

Walker, L. E. A. (1979). *The battered woman.* New York: Harper and Row.

Walker, L. E. A.(1984a). Battered women, psychology, and public policy. *American Psychologist, 39,* 1178–1182.

Walker, L. E. A. (1984b). *The battered woman syndrome.* New York: Springer.

Walker, L. E. A. (1992). Battered woman syndrome and self-defense. *Notre Dame Journal of Law, Ethics, and Public Policy, 6,* 321–334.

Walker L. E. A. (1993). Battered women as defendants. In N. Z. Hilton (Ed.), *Legal responses to wife assault: Current trends and evaluation* (pp. 233–257). Thousand Oaks, CA: Sage.

Walker, N. E., Brooks, C. M., & Wrightsman, L. S. (1998). *Children's rights in the United States: In search of a national policy.* Thousand Oaks, CA: Sage.

Walker, N. G. (1992). Review of Inwald Personality Inventory. In J. J. Kramer & J. C. Conoley (Eds.), *Eleventh mental measurements yearbook* (pp. 418–419). Lincoln: Buros Institute of Mental Measurements, University of Nebraska.

Walkley, J. (1987). *Police interrogation: Handbook for investigators.* London: Police Review Publications.

Wallerstein, J. S., & Blakeslee, S. (1989). *Second chances: Men, women, and children a decade after divorce.* New York: Ticknor and Fields.

Wallerstein, J., & Kelly, J. B. (1980). *Surviving the breakup: How children and parents cope with divorce.* New York: Basic Books.

Wallston, B. S., & O'Leary, V. E. (1981). Sex and gender make a difference: The differential perceptions of men and women. In L. Wheeler (Ed.), *Review of personality and social psychology* (Vol. 2, pp. 9–41). Thousand Oaks, CA: Sage.

Walters, G. D. (2003). Predicting institutional adjustment and recidivism with the Psychopathy Checklist factor scores: A meta-analytic review. *Law and Human Behavior, 27,* 541–558.

Warshaw, R. (1988). *I never called it rape.* New York: Harper & Row.

Watkins, J. G. (1989). Hypnotic hypernesia and forensic hypnosis: A cross-examination. *American Journal of Clinical Hypnosis, 32*(2), 71–83.

Webb, C. C., & Chapian, M. (1985). *Forgive me.* Old Tappan, NJ: Fleming H. Revell.

Webster, C., Douglas, K., Eaves, D., & Hart, S. (1997). *HCR-20: Assessing risk for violence (Version 2).* Burnaby, B.C.: Simon Fraser University, Mental Health, Law, and Policy Institute.

Wegner, D. M. (1989). *White bears and other unwanted thoughts: Suppression, obsession, and the psychology of mental control.* New York: Viking.

Wegner, D. M. (1994). Ironic processes of mental control. *Psychological Review, 101,* 34–52.

Wekesser, C., Swisher, K. L., & Pierce, C. (Eds.). (1992). *Sexual harassment.* San Diego, CA: Greenhaven Press.

Weisman, J. (1980). *Evidence.* New York: Viking.

Weiss, D. S., & Lalonde, R. N. (1998, August). *Responses of female undergraduates to sexual harassment by male instructors.* Paper presented at the meeting of the American Psychological Association, San Francisco.

Weithorn, L. A. (Ed.). (1987). *Psychology and child custody determinations: Knowledge, roles, and expertise.* Lincoln: University of Nebraska Press.

Weithorn, L. A., & Grisso, T. (1987). Psychological evaluations in divorce custody: Problems, principles, and procedures. In L. A. Weithorn (Ed.), *Psychology and child custody determinations: Knowledge, roles, and expertise* (pp. 157–180). Lincoln: University of Nebraska Press.

Weitzman, L. J. (1985). *The divorce revolution: The unexpected social and economic consequences for women and children in America.* New York: Free Press.

Weitzenhoffer, A. M., & Hilgard, E. R. (1959). *Stanford Hypnotic Susceptibility Scale: Forms A and B.* Palo Alto, CA: Consulting Psychologists Press.

Weld, H., & Danzig, A. (1940). A study of the way in which a verdict is reached by a jury. *American Journal of Psychology, 53,* 518–536.

Wells, G. L. (1978). Applied eyewitness testimony research: System variables and estimator variables. *Journal of Personality and Social Psychology, 36,* 1546–1557.

Wells, G. L. (1984a). How adequate is human intuition for judging eyewitness testimony? In G. L. Wells & E. F. Loftus (Eds.), *Eyewitness testimony: Psychological perspectives* (pp. 256–272). New York: Cambridge University Press.

Wells, G. L. (1984b). The psychology of lineup identifications. *Journal of Applied Social Psychology, 14,* 89–103.

Wells, G. L. (1986). Expert psychological testimony: Empirical and conceptual analysis of effects. *Law and Human Behavior, 10,* 83–95.

Wells, G. L. (1988). *Eyewitness identification: A system handbook.* Toronto, Ontario, Canada: Carswell.

Wells, G. L. (1993). What do we know about eyewitness identification? *American Psychologist, 48,* 553–571.

Wells, G. L. (1995). Scientific study of witness memory: Implications for public and legal policy. *Psychology, Public Policy, and Law, 1,* 726–731.

Wells, G. L., & Bradfield, A. L. (1998). "Good, you identified the suspect": Feedback to eyewitnesses distorts their reports of the witnessing experience. *Journal of Applied Psychology, 83,* 360–376.

Wells, G. L., & Bradfield, A. L. (1999). Distortions in eyewitnesses' recollections: Can the postidentification feedback effect be moderated? *Psychological Science, 10,* 138–144.

Wells, G., Fisher, R., Lindsay, R., Turtle, J., Malpass, R., & Fulero, S. (2000). From the lab to the police station: A successful application of eyewitness research. *American Psychologist, 55,* 581–598.

Wells, G. L., & Leippe, M. R. (1981). How do triers of fact infer the accuracy of eyewitness identification? Using memory for peripheral detail can be misleading. *Journal of Applied Psychology, 66,* 682–687.

Wells, G. L., Leippe, M. R., & Ostrom, T. M. (1979). Guidelines for empirically assessing the fairness of a lineup. *Law and Human Behavior, 3,* 285–293.

Wells, G. L., Lindsay, R. C. L., & Ferguson, T. (1979). Accuracy, confidence, and juror perceptions in eyewitness identification. *Journal of Applied Psychology, 64,* 440–448.

Wells, G. L., & Loftus, E. F. (1984). Eyewitness research: Then and now. In G. L. Wells & E. F. Loftus (Eds.), *Eyewitness testimony: Psychological perspectives* (pp. 1–11). Cambridge: Cambridge University Press.

Wells, G. L., & Loftus, E. F. (2002). Eyewitness memory for people and events. In A. Goldstein (Ed.),

Handbook of psychology: Vol. 11. Forensic psychology (pp. 149–160). New York: John Wiley & Sons.

Wells, G. L., Miene, P. K., & Wrightsman, L. S. (1985). The timing of the defense opening statement: Don't wait until the evidence is in. *Journal of Applied Social Psychology, 15,* 758–772.

Wells, G. L., & Murray, D. M. (1984). Eyewitness confidence. In G. L. Wells & E. F. Loftus (Eds.), *Eyewitness testimony: Psychological perspectives* (pp. 155–170). Cambridge: Cambridge University Press.

Wells, G. L., Olson, E., & Charman, S. (2003). Distorted retrospective eyewitness reports as functions of feedback and delay. *Journal of Experimental Psychology: Applied, 9,* 42–52.

Wells, G. L., Rydell, S. M., & Seelau, E. P. (1993). On the selection of distractors for eyewitness lineups. *Journal of Applied Psychology, 78,* 835–844.

Wells, G. L., & Seelau, E. (1995). Eyewitness identification: Psychological research and legal policy on lineups. *Psychology, Public Policy, and Law, 1,* 765–791.

Wells, G. L., Seelau, E., Rydell, S., & Luus, C. A. E. (1994). Recommendations for properly conducted lineup identification tasks. In D. F. Ross, J. D. Read, & M. P. Toglia (Eds.), *Adult eyewitness testimony: Current trends and developments* (pp. 223–244). New York: Cambridge University Press.

Wells, G. L., Small, M., Penrod, S., Malpass, R. S., Fulero, S. M., & Brimacombe, C. A. E. (1998). Eyewitness identification procedures: Recommendations for lineups and photospreads. *Law and Human Behavior, 22,* 603–647.

Wells, W. P., & Cutler, B. L. (1990). The right to counsel at videotaped lineups: An emerging dilemma. *Connecticut Law Review, 22,* 373–395.

Whipple, G. M. (1909). The observer as reporter: A survey of the "psychology of testimony." *Psychological Bulletin, 6,* 153–170.

Whipple, G. M. (1910). Recent literature on the psychology of testimony. *Psychological Bulletin, 7,* 365–368.

Whipple, G. M. (1911). The psychology of testimony. *Psychological Bulletin, 8,* 307–309.

Whipple, G. M. (1912). The psychology of testimony and report. *Psychological Bulletin, 9,* 264–269.

White, E. K., & Honig, A. L. (1995). The role of the police psychologist in training. In M. I. Kurke & E. M. Scrivner (Eds.), *Police psychology into the 21st century* (pp. 257–277). Hillsdale, NJ: Lawrence Erlbaum Associates.

White, L. T. (1987). Juror decision making in the capital murder trial: An analysis of crimes and defense strategies. *Law and Human Behavior, 11,* 113–130.

White, S. (1988). Should investigatory use of anatomical dolls be defined by the courts? *Journal of Interpersonal Violence, 3,* 471–475.

White, S., & Santilli, G. (1988). A review of clinical practices and research data on anatomical dolls. *Journal of Interpersonal Violence, 3,* 430–442.

White, S., Strom, G., Santilli, G., & Halpin, B. (1986). Interviewing young sexual abuse victims with anatomically correct dolls. *Child Abuse and Neglect, 10,* 519–529.

Wiehl, L. (1995, August 11). Program for death-row appeals facing its own demise. *New York Times,* p. A13.

Wiener, R., Hurt, L., Thomas, S., Sadler, M., Bauer, C., & Sargent, T. (1998). The role of declarative and procedural knowledge in capital murder cases. *Journal of Applied Social Psychology, 28,* 124–144.

Wiener, R., Pritchard, C., & Weston, M. (1995). Comprehensibility of approved jury instructions in capital cases. *Journal of Applied Psychology, 80,* 455–467.

Wiener, R. L. (1995). Social analytic jurisprudence in sexual harassment litigation: The role of social framework and social fact. *Journal of Social Issues, 51*(1), 167–180.

Wiggins, E. C., & Brandt, J. (1988). The detection of simulated amnesia. *Law and Human Behavior, 12,* 57–78.

Wigmore, J. H. (1909). Professor Münsterberg and the psychology of testimony: Being a report of the case of *Cokestone v. Munsterberg. Illinois Law Review, 3,* 399–455.

Wildman, R. W., II, Batchelor, E. S., Thompson, L., Nelson, F. R., Moore, J. T., Patterson, M. E., & DeLaosa, M. (1978). *The Georgia Court Competency Test: An attempt to develop a rapid, quantitative measure of fitness for trial.* Unpublished manuscript, Forensic Services Division, Central State Hospital, Milledgeville, GA.

Williams v. Florida, 399 U.S. 78 (1970).

Williams, A. L. (1999, March 26). Did doctors' biases speed mother's death? *USA Today,* p. 15A.

Williams, K. D., Bourgeois, M. J., & Croyle, R. T. (1993). The effects of stealing thunder in criminal and civil trials. *Law and Human Behavior, 17,* 597–609.

Williams, K. D., & Dolnick, L. (2001). Revealing the worst first: Stealing thunder as a social influence strategy. In J. Forgas, K. D. Williams, & L. Wheeler (Eds.), *The social mind: Cognitive and motivational aspects of interpersonal behavior* (pp. 213–231). New York: The Psychology Press.

Williams, K. R., & Houghton, A. B. (in press). Assessing the risk of domestic violence re-offending: A validation study. *Law and Human Behavior.*

Williams, W., & Miller, K. (1981). The processing and disposition of incompetent mentally ill offenders. *Law and Human Behavior, 5,* 245–261.

Wilson, J. P., & Keane, T. M. (Eds.). (1997). *Assessing psychological trauma and PTSD.* New York: Guilford Press.

Winick, B. J., & LaFond, J. Q. (Eds.). (1998). Sex offenders: Scientific, legal, and policy perspectives [Special issue]. *Psychology, Public Policy, and Law, 4,* 1–570.

Witherspoon v. Illinois, 391 U.S. 510 (1968).

Wolfner, G., Faust, D., & Dawes, R. M. (1993). The use of anatomically detailed dolls in sexual abuse evaluations: The state of the science. *Applied & Preventive Psychology, 2,* 1–11.

Wood, J. M., Schreiber, N., Martinez, Y., McLaurin, K., Strok, R., Velarde, L., et al. (1997). *Interviewing techniques in the McMartin Preschool and Kelly Michaels cases: A quantitative analysis.* Unpublished paper, University of Texas at El Paso.

Wood, J. M., Nezworski, M. T., Lilienfeld, S. O., & Garb, H. N. (2003). *What's wrong with the Rorschach? Science confronts the controversial inkblot test.* San Francisco: Jossey-Bass.

Woody, R. H. (1977). Psychologists in child custody. In B. D. Sales (Ed.), *Psychology and the legal process* (pp. 249–267). New York: Plenum.

Wortz, C. (1999, Winter). 1998 membership survey report. *Court Call,* p. 15.

Woychuk, D. (1996). *Attorney for the damned: A lawyer's life with the criminally insane.* New York: Free Press.

Wright, L. (1994). *Remembering Satan.* New York: Knopf.

Wrightsman, L. S. (1972). *Social psychology in the seventies.* Pacific Grove, CA: Brooks/Cole.

Wrightsman, L. S. (1999). *Judicial decision making: Is psychology relevant?* New York: Plenum.

Wrightsman, L. S., Batson, A. L., & Edkins, V. A. (2004). *Measures of legal attitudes.* Belmont, CA: Wadsworth.

Wrightsman, L. S., Greene, E., Nietzel, M. T., & Fortune, W. H. (2002). *Psychology and the legal system* (5th ed.). Pacific Grove, CA: Brooks/Cole.

Wrightsman, L. S., & Heili, A. (1992, September). *Measuring bias in civil trials.* Unpublished manuscript, University of Kansas, Lawrence.

Wrightsman, L. S., & Kassin, S. M. (1993). *Confessions in the courtroom.* Thousand Oaks, CA: Sage.

Wrightsman, L. S., Nietzel, M. T., & Fortune, W. H. (1998). *Psychology and the legal system* (4th ed.). Pacific Grove, CA: Brooks/Cole.

Wyer, M. M., Gaylord, S. J., & Grove, E. T. (1987). The legal context of child custody evaluations. In L. A. Weithorn (Ed.), *Psychology and child custody evaluations* (pp. 3– 22). Lincoln: University of Nebraska Press.

Yakir, D. (1991, February 24). "I had to realize how angry I was." *Parade Magazine,* 4–5.

Yant, M. (1991). *Presumed guilty: When innocent people are wrongly convicted.* Buffalo, NY: Prometheus.

Yarmey, A. D. (1979). *The psychology of eyewitness testimony.* New York: Free Press.

Yarmey, A. D. (1984). Age as a factor in eyewitness memory. In G. L. Wells & E. F. Loftus (Eds.), *Eyewitness testimony: Psychological perspectives* (pp. 142–154). Cambridge: Cambridge University Press.

Yarmey, A. D. (1986). Ethical responsibilities governing the statements experimental psychologists make in expert testimony. *Law and Human Behavior, 12,* 101–116.

Yarmey, A. D., & Jones, H. P. T. (1983). Is the psychology of eyewitness identification a matter of common sense? In S. M. A. Lloyd-Bostock & B. R. Clifford (Eds.), *Evaluating witness evidence: Recent psychological research and new perspectives* (pp. 13–40). Chichester, UK: Wiley.

Yarmey, A. D., Yarmey, M. J., & Yarmey, A. L. (1996). Accuracy of eyewitness identifications in showups and lineups. *Law and Human Behavior, 20,* 459–477.

Yonah, A., & Gleason, J. M. (Eds.). (1981). *Behavioral and quantitative perspectives on terrorism.* New York: Pergamon.

Yong v. United States, 107 F.2d 490 (5th Cir. 1939).

Young, D. (1996). Unnecessary evil: Police lying in interrogations. *Connecticut Law Review, 28,* 425–477.

Youngstrom, N. (1991, October). Spotting serial killer difficult, experts note. *APA Monitor,* p. 32.

Zapf, P. (1998, March). *An examination of the construct of competence in a civil and criminal context: A comparison of the MacCAT-T, the MacCAT-CA, and the FIT-R.* Paper presented at the meeting of the American Psychology-Law Society, Redondo Beach, CA.

Zapf, P., & Roesch, R. (1997). Assessing fitness to stand trial: A comparison of institution-based evaluations and a brief screening interview. *Canadian Journal of Community Mental Health, 16,* 53–66.

Zeisel, H., & Diamond, S. S. (1974). Convincing empirical evidence on the six-member jury. *University of Chicago Law Review, 41,* 281–295.

Zimbardo, P. G. (1967, June). The psychology of police confessions. *Psychology Today, 1,* 17–20, 25–27.

Zippo Manufacturing Co. v. Rogers Imports, 216 F. Supp. 670 (1963).

Ziskin, J. (1995). *Coping with psychiatric and psychological testimony* (5th ed., Vols. 1–3). Los Angeles: Law and Psychology Press.

Ziskin, J., & Faust, D. (1988). *Coping with psychiatric and psychological testimony* (4th ed., Vols. 1–3). Los Angeles: Law and Psychology Press.

Zizzo, F. (1985). Psychological intervention and specialized law enforcement groups. *Emotional First Aid: A Journal of Crisis Intervention, 2*(1), 25–27.

Zuckerman, M., DePaulo, B. M., & Rosenthal, R. (1981). Verbal and nonverbal communication of deception. *Advances in Experimental Social Psychology, 14,* 1–59.

Name Index

Abel, G. G., 160
Abidin, R., 205
Abraham, L., 327
Abramson, J., 324
Abramson, L., 268
Acker, J. R., 40, 358, 369
Ackerman, M., 200, 205
Ackerman, M. J., 200, 203, 204, 205, 206, 210
Adams, A. M., 295
Adams, R. D., 335, 336, 339
Adams, R. L., 26
Adler, S. J., 289
Aicklin, M., 296
Ainsworth, P. B., 55
Akehurst, L., 255
Akers, R. L., 328, 329
Albison, C. R., 209
Alexander, D., 312
Alexander, J. R., 209
Alfini, J. J., 264
Allan, A., 115
Allen, M., 346
Allen, R. J., 48
Allen, S. W., 68
Allison, J. A., 157, 159, 219
Allport, F. H., 356
Alm, R., 66
Alvarez, W., 160, 162
Amador, M., 219, 220

Ambuel, B., 370
Amedeo, S. R., 161
American Bar Association Task Force on Fair Trial and Free Press, 264
American Law Institute, 107
American Psychiatric Association, 122, 160
American Psychological Association, 11, 35, 36, 46, 198, 200, 206, 273, 284, 364–364, 366, 367, 369–370
American Society of Trial Consultants, 28, 266
Amick, A. E., 157, 162
Amin, Y., 136
Amnesty International, 341
Anderson, C. A., 266
Anderson, E. R., 207
Andrews, D. A., 130
Angier, N., 39
Annin, P., 239
Appelbaum, P., 129
Arditti, J. A., 205
Arnett, P. A., 122
Arnold, S., 262
Aron, C. J., 146
Aron, N., 337
Aronson, E., 306
Arvey, R. D., 313
Asch, S. E., 238
Associated Press, 30, 52, 76, 116, 190, 341
Aubrey, M. R., 152
Aubry, A., 245, 253

Subject Index

TO THE OWNER OF THIS BOOK:

We hope that you have found *Forensic Psychology,* 2e useful. So that this book can be improved in a future edition, would you take the time to complete this sheet and return it? Thank you.

School and address:_____

Department:_____

Instructor's name:_____

1. What I like most about this book is:_____

_____

_____

2. What I like least about this book is:

_____

_____

3. My general reaction to this book is:

_____

_____

4. The name of the course in which I used this book is:

_____

5. Were all of the chapters of the book assigned for you to read?_____

   If not, which ones weren't?_____

6. In the space below, or on a separate sheet of paper, please write specific suggestions for improving this book and anything else you'd care to share about your experience in using this book.

_____

_____

FOLD HERE

BUSINESS REPLY MAIL
FIRST-CLASS MAIL   PERMIT NO. 34   BELMONT CA

POSTAGE WILL BE PAID BY ADDRESSEE

Attn: Michele Sordi, Psychology Editor

Wadsworth/Thomson Learning
10 Davis Drive
Belmont, CA   94002-9801

NO POSTAGE NECESSARY IF MAILED IN THE UNITED STATES

FOLD HERE

OPTIONAL:

Your name: _____ Date: _____

May we quote you, either in promotion for *Forensic Psychology,* 2e, or in future publishing ventures?

Yes: _____ No: _____

Sincerely yours,

Larry Wrightsman and Sol Fulero